Rail Guide

2011

Colin J. Marsden

Ian Allan PUBLISHING

First published 2010
Reprinted 2010
This Second Edition first published 2011

ISBN 978 0 7110 3458 7

Published by Ian Allan Publishing.

An imprint of Ian Allan Publishing Ltd, Hersham, Surrey KT12 4RG.
Printed in England by Ian Allan Printing Ltd, Hersham, Surrey KT12 4RG.

Visit the Ian Allan Publishing website at www.ianallanpublishing.com

Distributed in the United States of America and Canada by BookMasters Distribution Services.

Front Cover Top: *DB Schenker-liveried Class 67 No. 67018* Keith Heller *departs from Dawlish Warren on 24 May 2010
powering First Great Western's 08.00 Cardiff to Paignton service.* **CJM**

Front Cover Bottom: *London Overground Class 378 stock has now taken over from Class 313s on London area electrified
services. Three-car set No. 378007 is seen at Clapham Junction on 22 April 2010 with a service from Willesden Junction. This
set has now been augmented to a four-car set and renumbered 378207.* **CJM**

Back Cover Top: *Plasser & Theurer 09-3X-D-RT Tamper/Liner No. DR73111* Reading Panel 1965 - 2005 *is seen at Bristol
Temple Meads on 4 May 2010.* **CJM**

Back Cover Bottom: *Painted in Arriva Trains Wales turquoise livery, Cargo-D owned Mk3 RFM No. 10249 is illustrated at
Newport formed in the daily Holyhead to Cardiff service on 4 May 2010.* **CJM**

Acknowledgement – The Author would like to record his thanks to the many railway staff who have provided
invaluable information for the production of this book. Also to the many photographers, especially
Nathan Williamson, Tony Christie, Stacey Thew, John Binch and Brian Morrison for providing many of the
images. I would also like to express my thanks to Jean Marsden for reading the updated manuscript. **CJM**

The return of the Ian Allan *ABC Rail Guide* last year, bringing together a complete numeric listing of all locomotives, multiple unit stock and departmental vehicles to be found in the UK, together with light rail vehicles was a huge success, with many encouraging comments received from readers, several offering suggestions of future issues in terms of content and layout.

The largest mail bag came from those readers who wanted to see the inclusion of 'on track plant', such as tamping machines, track re-layers and the like. We took all this onboard and this year for the first time in an Ian Allan publication we provide a spotters listing of all vehicles, these are listed under the Network Rail section, even though many are owned and operated by the private engineering operators.

Another request we had was the inclusion of a space to mark off locos and vehicles seen, this has been achieved by placing an open square on the left side of each entry in the numeric cross reference list towards the back.

2010 saw many changes to the UK rail scene, the Class 172 and 378s were delivered to London Overground, the first of the new Class 379s was completed for National Express East Anglia, more Class 70s were delivered to Freightliner and the first of the second tranche of Class 390 'Pendolino' sets was delivered to Edge Hill.

Few new train orders were placed through the year, except for confirmation of the Thameslink upgrade programme which will see new trains ordered for delivery 2018, this will displace Class 319s to First Great Western and the new electrified route to Blackpool. Confirmation has also been received of a new train order for Crossrail.

Information on a replacement for the present HST fleet is expected by Government in spring 2011, but they have already announced that no further life extension of the present HST fleet will be undertaken.

Some changes took place to operators, Fastline ceased to exist with the assets of Fastline/Jarvis sold off, while Hanson Traction, one of the smaller main line operators was swallowed up by British American Railways.

The 2011 edition of *Rail Guide* encompasses all these changes, with revised tables, a complete new set of illustrations and details of new formations, shed and operator changes.

To complement *Rail Guide 2011*, a new edition of the Ian Alan *ABC Traction Recognition* will be published this summer, providing full technical details and illustrations of all classes and sub-classes of current rolling stock.

Colin J. Marsden
Dawlish, January 2011

Information in *Rail Guide 2011* is correct to 11 January 2011.

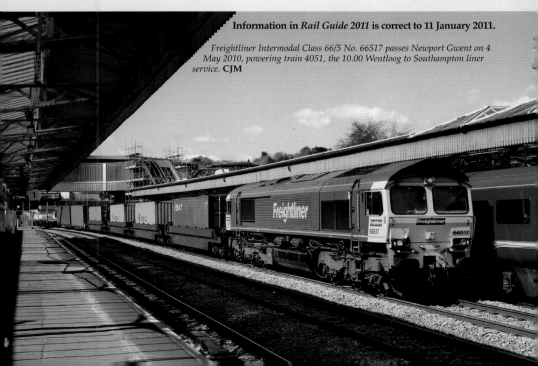

Freightliner Intermodal Class 66/5 No. 66517 passes Newport Gwent on 4 May 2010, powering train 4051, the 10.00 Wentloog to Southampton liner service. **CJM**

Train Operators, The Association of Train Operating Companies, and Network Rail welcome rail enthusiasts and photographers, but in today's safety led railway and with the continued concerns about possible transport terrorism, guidelines are very important and we encourage all to follow these published guidelines as much as possible. They are available to view and download from the National Rail and ATOC websites, but are reproduced in full below to assist you with this information. ■

The Official Railway Enthusiasts Guidelines

■ Network Rail welcomes rail enthusiasts to our stations.

■ The following guidelines are designed to help you to have a safe and enjoyable experience. Please keep them with you when you are at Network Rail managed stations.

■ You may also wish to take a copy of the Railway Bye-laws which are available from the Office of Public Sector Information website.

Before you enter the platform

■ When you arrive at a station, please let the staff at the Network Rail Reception Desk know that you are on the station. This will help keep station staff informed so that they can go about their duties without concern as to your reasons for being there.

■ You may require a platform ticket to allow access to platforms.

While you are on the platform

■ You need to act safely & sensibly at all times.
  ● Stay clear of the platform edge and stay behind the yellow lines where they are provided.
  ● Be aware of your surroundings.

Please DO NOT:
  ● Trespass on to the tracks or any other part of the railway that is not available to passengers.
  ● Use flash photography because it can distract train drivers and train despatch staff and so is potentially very dangerous.
  ● Climb on any structure or interfere with platform equipment.
  ● Obstruct any signalling equipment or signs which are vital to the safe running of the railway.
  ● Wear anything which is similar in colour to safety clothing, such as high-visibility jackets, as this could cause confusion to drivers and other railway employees.
  ● Gather together in groups at busy areas of the platform (e.g. customer information points, departure screens, waiting areas, seating etc.) or where this may interfere with the duties of station staff.

■ If possible, please try to avoid peak hours which are Monday – Friday 6:00am (06.00) – 10:30am (10.30) and 3:30pm (15.30) – 7:30pm (19.30).

Extra Eyes and Ears

■ If you see anything suspicious or notice any unusual behaviour or activities, please tell a member of staff immediately.

■ For emergencies and serious incidents, either call:
  The British Transport Police on 0800 40 50 40.
  The Police on 999.

■ Your presence at a station can be very helpful to us as extra "eyes and ears" and can have a positive security benefit.

Photography

■ You can take photographs at stations provided you do not sell them. However, you are not allowed to take photographs of security related equipment, such as CCTV cameras.

■ Flash photography on platforms is not allowed at any time. It can distract train drivers and train despatch staff and so is potentially very dangerous.

■ Tripod legs must be kept away from platform edges and behind the yellow lines. On busy stations, you may not be allowed to use a tripod because it could be a dangerous obstruction to passengers.

Railway Bye-laws

For safety & ease of travel on the railway system (which includes passengers, staff, property and equipment), the Bye-laws must be observed by everyone. A copy of the Bye-laws can be obtained at stations or downloaded from the Office of Public Sector Information website.

General

Train operators must put the safety of their passengers and staff first. You may very occasionally be asked by station staff to move to another part of the station or to leave the station altogether. Station staff should be happy to explain why this is necessary. If you are travelling by train, they may ask you to remain in the normal waiting areas with other passengers. If this occurs, please follow their instructions with goodwill as staff have many things to consider, including the safety & security of all passengers, and are authorised to use judgement in this regard.

Below: *To mark the 175th anniversary of the Great Western Railway, First Great Western repainted Class 57/6 No. 57604 Pendennis Castle in mock Great Western lined green livery. The loco is usually deployed on the overnight sleeper services between London Paddington and Penzance, but on 4 September 2010 it was used to power the final summer Saturday 09.09 Bristol to Weymouth and return service. The loco is seen arriving at Bristol Temple Meads to form the outward working.* **Tony Christie**

Contents

Arriva Wales: 8, c2c: 14, Chiltern: 17, CrossCountry: 21, East Midlands: 26, Eurostar: 32, FCC: 36, FGW: 43, FSR: 56, FTP: 65, Grand Central: 68, Heathrow: 70, Hull Trains: 72, IOW: 73, LM: 74, London Overground: 82, Merseyrail: 85, East Anglia: 88, East Coast: 99, Northern: 106, SWT: 114, SET: 125, Southern: 135, Virgin: 144, W&S: 150.

Colas: 152, DB Schenker (EWS): 154, Euro Cargo Rail: 169, Direct Rail Services: 170, Royal Mail: 174, Europorte GBRF: 175, Freightliner: 178, Mendip Rail: 184, SNCF: 185.

Eurotunnel: 186

Network Rail: 188, Royal Train: 191, Track Machines: 194, Balfour Beatty: 209.

Alstom: 210, Bombardier: 210, Brush-Barclay: 211, Knights Rail Services: 211, Railcare Ltd: 212, Rail Vehicle Engineering: 213, Siemens Transportation: 214, Wabtec: 214, Pullman Group: 215.

Europhoenix Ltd: 216, Porterbrook: 216.

Alstom: 217, Bombardier: 217, Brush Traction: 217, Electro-Motive: 218, General Electric: 218, Hitachi Europe Ltd: 218, Siemens Transportation: 219.

Angel Trains: 220, British American: 220, Cargo-D: 222, Electric Traction Ltd: 223, Eversholt: 223, HNRC: 224, Nemesis Rail: 226, Porterbrook: 227, Transmart Trains: 227.

Bo'ness: 228, Flying Scotsman: 228, GSWR: 228, Hoskins: 228, Mid-Hants: 228, NYMR: 228, Railfilms: 229, Ridings: 229, Riviera: 230, SRPS: 233, Stratford 47: 233, VSOE: 233, Vintage: 235, West Coast Railway: 235. Loco Support: 240.

Loco, DMU, EMU: 241, Coaching Stock: 242.

Locomotives: 243, Diesel Units: 247, Electric Units: 249.

Class 03 - Class 66: 250, Class 86 - Class 87: 251.

Diesel & Electric: 252, Steam: 253.

Standard: 254, Drop Head: 254, Dellner: 254-255, BSI: 254, Tightlock: 254.

London Underground: 258, Docklands Light Railway: 260, Croydon Tramlink: 261, Manchester Metrolink: 261, Nottingham Express Transit: 263, Midland Metro: 263, Sheffield Super Tram: 264, Tyne & Wear: 264, Glasgow: 265.

Livery Codes: 266, Pool Codes: 268, Preserved Site Codes: 269, Depot Codes: 270, Operator Codes: 272, Owner Codes: 273, Station Codes: 274, DMU & EMU Vehicle Codes: 282, Number Cross Link: 283.

Arriva Trains Wales

Passenger Train Operating Companies - Arriva Trains Wales

Address: ✉ St Mary's House, 47 Penarth Road, Cardiff, CF10 5DJ
✆ customer.relations@arrivatrainswales.co.uk
✆ 0845 6061 660
ⓘ www.arrivatrainswales.co.uk

Managing Director: Tim Bell
Franchise Dates: 7 December 2003 - 6 December 2018
Principal Routes: Cardiff to Swansea and West Wales
Cardiff Valleys
Cardiff - Hereford - Shrewsbury - Crewe - Manchester Piccadilly
Cardiff - Hereford - Shrewsbury - Chester - Bangor - Holyhead
Manchester - Crewe - Bangor - Holyhead
Shrewsbury - Pwllheli/Aberystwyth
Swansea - Shrewsbury
Depots: Cardiff Canton (CF), Chester (CH), Holyhead* (HD)
Machynlleth (MN), Shrewsbury* (SX) * Stabling point
Parent Company: Deutsche Bahn AG (DB Regio)

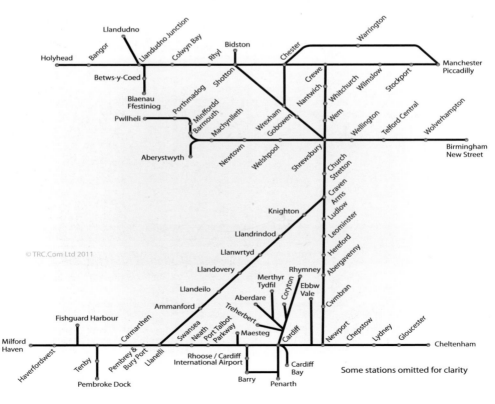

Some stations omitted for clarity

© TRC.Com Ltd 2011

Class 57/3

Vehicle Length: 63ft 6in (19.38m)
Height: 12ft 10½in (3.91m)
Width: 9ft 2in (2.79m)

Engine: EMD 645-12F3B
Horsepower: 2,750hp (2,051kW)
Electrical Equipment: Brush

Number	Depot	Pool	Livery	Owner	Operator
57313 (47371)	MA	ATTB	BLU	PTR	ATW/VWC
57314 (47372)	MA	ATTB	ATE	PTR	ATW
57315 (47234)	MA	ATTB	ATE	PTR	ATW
57316 (47290)	MA	ATTB	BLU	PTR	ATW/VWC

Right: *Painted in the unbranded mid-blue livery, one of the standby Arriva Trains Wales hire locos No. 57316 is seen at Newport powering the daily Holyhead to Cardiff service on 4 May 2010.* **CJM**

■ Class 57/3 locos owned by Porterbrook and on lease to Virgin Trains, sub-leased to Arriva Trains Wales

Class 121

Length: 64ft 6in (19.66m)
Height: 12ft 8½in (3.87m)
Width: 9ft 3in (2.81m)

Engine: 2 x Leyland 150hp
Horsepower: 300hp (224kW)
Seats (total/car): 65S

Number	Formation DMBS	Depot	Livery	Owner	Operator	Note
121032	55032	CF	ATW	ATW	ATW	Previously Departmental No. 977842

Right: *Arriva Trains Wales operates just one 'Heritage' Class 121 set, deployed exclusively on the 'shuttle' service between Cardiff Queen Street and Cardiff Bay. The vehicle No. 55032 is seen at Cardiff Queen Street.* **CJM**

Class 142

Vehicle Length: 51ft 0½in (15.55m)
Height: 12ft 8in (3.86m)
Width: 9ft 2½in (2.80m)

Engine: 1 x Cummins LTA10-R per vehicle
Horsepower: 460hp (343kW)
Seats (total/car): 90S, 46S/44S

Number	Formation DMS+DMSL	Depot	Livery	Owner	Operator		Number	Formation	Depot	Livery	Owner	Operator
142002	55543+55593	CF	ATW	ANG	ATW		142076	55726+55772	CF	ATW	ANG	ATW
142006	55547+55597	CF	ATW	ANG	ATW		142077	55727+55773	CF	ATW	ANG	ATW
142010	55551+55601	CF	ATW	ANG	ATW		142080	55730+55776	CF	ATW	ANG	ATW
142069	55719+55765	CF	ATW	ANG	ATW		142081	55731+55777	CF	ATW	ANG	ATW
142072	55722+55768	CF	ATW	ANG	ATW		142082	55732+55778	CF	ATW	ANG	ATW
142073	55723+55769	CF	ATW	ANG	ATW		142083	55733+55779	CF	ATW	ANG	ATW
142074	55724+55770	CF	ATW	ANG	ATW		142085	55735+55781	CF	ATW	ANG	ATW
142075	55725+55771	CF	ATW	ANG	ATW							

Name applied
142072 **Myfanwy**

Arriva Trains Wales

Left: *A total of 15 Class 142 BRE-Leyland 'Railbus' units operate for Arriva Trains Wales on Cardiff area branch line duties. The sets operate either singularly, in pairs or in multiple with Class 143s. Set No. 142006 is seen at Radyr coupled to a Class 143.* **CJM**

Class 143

Vehicle Length: 51ft 0½in (15.55m)
Height: 12ft 2½in (3.73m)
Width: 8ft 10½in (2.70m)

Engine: 1 x Cummins LTA10-R per vehicle
Horsepower: 460hp (343kW)
Seats (total/car): 92S, 48S/44S

Number	Formation DMS+DMSL	Depot	Livery	Owner	Operator
143601	55642+55667	CF	ATW	BCC	ATW
143602	55651+55668	CF	ATW	PTR	ATW
143604	55645+55670	CF	ATW	PTR	ATW
143605	55646+55671	CF	ATW	PTR	ATW
143606	55647+55672	CF	ATW	PTR	ATW
143607	55648+55673	CF	ATW	PTR	ATW
143608	55649+55674	CF	ATW	PTR	ATW
143609	55650+55675	CF	ATW	CCC	ATW
143610	55643+55676	CF	ATW	BCC	ATW
143614	55655+55680	CF	ATW	BCC	ATW
143615	55657+55682	CF	ATW	PTR	ATW
143622	55663+55688	CF	ATW	PTR	ATW
143623	55664+55689	CF	ATW	PTR	ATW
143624	55665+55690	CF	ATW	PTR	ATW
143625	55666+55691	CF	ATW	PTR	ATW

Name applied
143609   Sir Tom Jones

Left: *ATW Class 143 No. 143606 arrives at Radyr with a Cardiff bound service formed with its DMS car No. 55647 leading.* **CJM**

Class 150/2

Vehicle Length: 64ft 9¾in (19.74m)
Height: 12ft 4½in (3.77m)
Width: 9ft 3⅛in (2.82m)

Engine: 1 x NT855R5 of 285hp per vehicle
Horsepower: 570hp (425kW)
Seats (total/car): 128S, 60S/68S

Number	Formation DMSL+DMS	Depot	Livery	Owner	Operator
150208	52208+57208	CF	ATW	PTR	ATW
150236	52236+57236	CF	ATW	PTR	ATW
150240	52240+57240	CF	ATW	PTR	ATW
150241	52241+57241	CF	ATW	PTR	ATW
150242	52242+57242	CF	ATW	PTR	ATW
150245	52245+57245	CF	ATW	PTR	ATW
150250	52250+57250	CF	ATW	PTR	ATW
150251	52251+57251	CF	ATW	PTR	ATW
150252	52252+57252	CF	ATW	PTR	ATW
150253	52253+57253	CF	ATW	PTR	ATW
150254	52254+57254	CF	ATW	PTR	ATW
150256	52256+57256	CF	ATW	PTR	ATW
150258	52258+57258	CF	ATW	PTR	ATW
150259	52259+57259	CF	ATW	PTR	ATW
150260	52260+57260	CF	ATW	PTR	ATW
150262	52262+57262	CF	ATW	PTR	ATW
150264	52264+57264	CF	ATW	PTR	ATW
150267	52267+57267	CF	ATW	PTR	ATW
150278	52278+57278	CF	ATW	PTR	ATW
150279	52279+57279	CF	ATW	PTR	ATW
150280	52280+57280	CF	ATW	PTR	ATW
150281	52281+57281	CF	ATW	PTR	ATW
150282	52282+57282	CF	ATW	PTR	ATW
150283	52283+57283	CF	ATW	PTR	ATW
150284	52284+57284	CF	ATW	PTR	ATW
150285	52285+57285	CF	ATW	PTR	ATW

Above: *Twenty-six Porterbrook-owned Class 150/2s operate for ATW; set No. 150242 is illustrated at Radyr.* **CJM**

Class 153

Vehicle Length: 76ft 5in (23.29m)
Height: 12ft 3⅛in (3.75m)
Width: 8ft 10in (2.70m)

Engine: 1 x NT855R5 of 285hp
Horsepower: 285hp (213kW)
Seats (total/car): 72S

Number	Formation DMSL	Depot	Livery	Owner	Operator						
						153323	52323	CF	ATW	PTR	ATW
						153327	52327	CF	ATW	ANG	ATW
153303	52303	CF	ATW	ANG	ATW	153353	57353	CF	ATW	ANG	ATW
153312	52312	CF	ATW	ANG	ATW	153362	57362	CF	ATW	ANG	ATW
153320	52320	CF	ATW	PTR	ATW	153367	57367	CF	ATW	PTR	ATW

Right: *Cardiff Canton has an allocation of eight single car Class 153s, modified from two-car Class 155 sets, for use on longer distance services mainly in West Wales. However a vehicle is sometimes used as cover for the 'Bubble' car used on the Cardiff Bay 'shuttle' service, as was the case when No. 153367 was captured at Cardiff Queen Street in October 2009.*
Stacey Thew

Class 158

Vehicle Length: 76ft 1¾in (23.21m)
Height: 12ft 6in (3.81m)
Width: 9ft 3¼in (2.82m)

Engine: 1 x Perkins 2006-TWH of 350hp per vehicle
Horsepower: 700hp (522kW)
Seats (total/car): 134S, 66S/68S

Number	Formation DMSL+DMSL	Depot	Livery	Owner	Operator						
						158829	52829+57829	MN	ATW	ANG	ATW
						158830	52830+57830	MN	ATW	ANG	ATW
158818	52818+57818	MN	ATW	ANG	ATW	158831	52831+57831	MN	WAL	ANG	ATW
158819	52819+57819	MN	WAL	ANG	ATW	158832	52832+57832	MN	WAL	ANG	ATW
158820	52820+57820	MN	ATW	ANG	ATW	158833	52833+57833	MN	WAL	ANG	ATW
158821	52821+57821	MN	ATW	ANG	ATW	158834	52834+57834	MN	WAL	ANG	ATW
158822	52822+57822	MN	ATW	ANG	ATW	158835	52835+57835	MN	WAL	ANG	ATW
158823	52823+57823	MN	ATW	ANG	ATW	158836	52836+57836	MN	WAL	ANG	ATW
158824	52824+57824	MN	ATW	ANG	ATW	158837	52837+57837	CF	ATW	ANG	ATW
158825	52825+57825	MN	WAL	ANG	ATW	158838	52838+57838	CF	ATW	ANG	ATW
158826	52826+57826	MN	WAL	ANG	ATW	158839	52839+57839	CF	WAL	ANG	ATW
158827	52827+57827	MN	WAL	ANG	ATW	158840	52840+57840	CF	ATW	ANG	ATW
158828	52828+57828	MN	ATW	ANG	ATW	158841	52841+57841	CF	WAL	ANG	ATW

All sets are fitted with operational European Rail Traffic Management System (ERTMS) equipment for operation on the Cambrian Line.

Right: *The ATW Class 158 long-distance passenger fleet is allocated to Machynlleth and Cardiff Canton depots; in late 2010 some sets were still painted in the previous 'Alphaline' silver livery. ATW-liveried set No. 158824 is shown at Newport heading for Cardiff.* **CJM**

Arriva Trains Wales

Class 175/0
Coradia 1000

	Vehicle Length: 75ft 7in (23.06m)	Engine: 1 x Cummins N14 of 450hp per vehicle
	Height: 12ft 4in (3.75m)	Horsepower: 900hp (671kW)
	Width: 9ft 2in (2.80m)	Seats (total/car): 118S, 54S/64S

Number	Formation DMSL+DMSL	Depot	Livery	Owner	Operator
175001	50701+79701	CH	ATW	ANG	ATW
175002	50702+79702	CH	ATW	ANG	ATW
175003	50703+79703	CH	ATW	ANG	ATW
175004	50704+79704	CH	ATW	ANG	ATW
175005	50705+79705	CH	ATW	ANG	ATW
175006	50706+79706	CH	ATW	ANG	ATW
175007	50707+79707	CH	ATW	ANG	ATW
175008	50708+79708	CH	ATW	ANG	ATW
175009	50709+79709	CH	ATW	ANG	ATW
175010	50710+79710	CH	ATW	ANG	ATW
175011	50711+79711	CH	ATW	ANG	ATW

Left: *Chester depot is responsible for the entire allocation of main line Class 175 two and three car sets, used on ATW longer distance services including the Holyhead to Cardiff duty. Painted in full ATW livery, two-car set No. 175004 is seen at Cardiff. These Class 175 sets built by Alstom are technically the same as the Class 180s but with different front end and internal layouts.* **Tony Christie**

Class 175/1
Coradia 1000

	Vehicle Length: 75ft 7in (23.06m)	Engine: 1 x Cummins N14 of 450hp per vehicle
	Height: 12ft 4in (3.75m)	Horsepower: 1,350hp (1,007kW)
	Width: 9ft 2in (2.80m)	Seats (total/car): 186S, 54S/68S/64S

Number	Formation DMSL+MSL+DMSL	Depot	Livery	Owner	Opt'r
175101	50751+56751+79751	CH	ATW	ANG	ATW
175102	50752+56752+79752	CH	ATW	ANG	ATW
175103	50753+56753+79753	CH	ATW	ANG	ATW
175104	50754+56754+79754	CH	ATW	ANG	ATW
175105	50755+56755+79755	CH	ATW	ANG	ATW
175106	50756+56756+79756	CH	ATW	ANG	ATW
175107	50757+56757+79757	CH	ATW	ANG	ATW
175108	50758+56758+79758	CH	ATW	ANG	ATW
175109	50759+56759+79759	CH	ATW	ANG	ATW
175110	50760+56760+79760	CH	ATW	ANG	ATW
175111	50761+56761+79761	CH	ATW	ANG	ATW
175112	50762+56762+79762	CH	ATW	ANG	ATW
175113	50763+56763+79763	CH	ATW	ANG	ATW
175114	50764+56764+79764	CH	ATW	ANG	ATW
175115	50765+56765+79765	CH	ATW	ANG	ATW
175116	50766+56766+79766	CH	ATW	ANG	ATW

Below: *Three-car 'Coradia 1000' set No. 175116 poses at Cardiff with a Chester and Holyhead bound service in May 2010. All sets are maintained at Chester depot under a contract maintenance deal, and all are painted in the latest Arriva Trains Wales livery.* **CJM**

Arriva Trains Wales

Class AC2E / TSO

Vehicle Length: 66ft 0in (20.11m)
Height: 12ft 9½in (3.89m)
Width: 9ft 3in (2.81m)
Seats (total/car): 62S

Number	Type	Depot	Livery	Owner	Operator	Number	Type	Depot	Livery	Owner	Operator
5853	TSO	CF	ATW	ATW	ATW	5869(S)	TSO	LM		ATW	ATW	-

Class AC2F / TSO

Vehicle Length: 66ft 0in (20.11m)
Height: 12ft 9½in (3.89m)
Width: 9ft 3in (2.81m)
Seats (total/car): 60S

Number	Type	Depot	Livery	Owner	Operator	Number	Type	Depot	Livery	Owner	Operator
5913(S)	TSO	CF	ATW	ATW	-	6119	TSO	CF	ATW	ATW	ATW
5965	TSO	CF	ATW	ATW	ATW	6137	TSO	CF	ATW	ATW	ATW
5976	TSO	CF	ATW	ATW	ATW	6162(S)	TSO	LM	ATW	ATW	-
6013(S)	TSO	LM	ATW	ATW	-	6170(S)	TSO	LM	ATW	ATW	-
6035(S)	TSO	LM	ATW	ATW	-	6183	TSO	CF	ATW	ATW	ATW

Class AE2E / BSO

Vehicle Length: 66ft 0in (20.11m)
Height: 12ft 9½in (3.89m)
Width: 9ft 3in (2.81m)
Seats (total/car): 60S

Number	Type	Depot	Livery	Owner	Operator	Number	Type	Depot	Livery	Owner	Operator
9503	BSO	CF	ATW	ATW	ATW	9509	BSO	CF	ATW	ATW	ATW

Class AE2F / BSO

Vehicle Length: 66ft 0in (20.11m)
Height: 12ft 9½in (3.89m)
Width: 9ft 3in (2.81m)
Seats (total/car): 60S

Number	Type	Depot	Livery	Owner	Operator	Number	Type	Depot	Livery	Owner	Operator
9521	BSO	CF	ATW	ATW	ATW	9524(S)	BSO	LM	ATW	ATW	-
						9539	BSO	CF	ATW	ATW	ATW

Class AJ1G / RFM

Vehicle Length: 75ft 0in (22.86m)
Height: 12ft 9in (3.88m)
Width: 8ft 11in (2.71m)
Bogie Type: BT10

Number	Type	Depot	Livery	Owner	Operator	Number	Type	Depot	Livery	Owner	Operator
10249 (10012)	RFM	CF	ATW	DBR	ATW	10259 (10025)	RFM	CF	ATW	ATW	ATW

Right & Below: *The Arriva Trains loco hauled service between Holyhead and Cardiff uses a small batch of Mk2 stock with two Mk3 RFMs. The stock is allocated to Cardiff Canton and the operational fleet is painted in full ATW branded livery. A number of spare vehicles are stored at Long Marston. On the right, Mk2f BSO No. 9539 is illustrated from its brake end, while below is ATW Mk3, RFM No. 10249, viewed from the first class seating end. Both:* **CJM**

c2c

Address:	✉ 10th Floor, 207 Old Street, London, EC1V 9NR
	🖅 c2c.customerrelations@nationalexpress.com
	✆ 0845 6014873
	ⓘ www.c2c-online.co.uk
Managing Director:	Julian Drury
Franchise Dates:	26 May 1996 - 26 May 2013
Principal Routes:	London Fenchurch Street - Shoeburyness
	Barking - Pitsea via Purfleet
	Ockendon branch
	London Liverpool Street - Barking (limited service)
Depots:	East Ham (EM), Shoeburyness*
	* Stabling point
Parent Company:	National Express

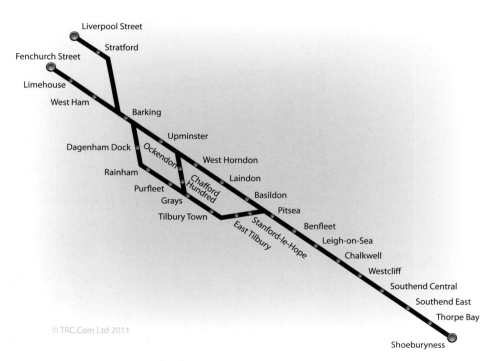

Right: *The UK's most reliable fleet of trains are the Class 357s from the Bombardier Electrostar family. The entire fleet is allocated to East Ham depot with the sets deployed on the c2c network radiating from London Fenchurch Street. Painted in white National Express c2c livery Class 357/0 No. 357023, owned by Porterbrook, is seen at Barking.* **CJM**

Class 357/0
Electrostar

Vehicle Length: (Driving) 68ft 1in (20.75m) Width: 9ft 2½in (2.80m)
(Inter) 65ft 11½in (20.10m) Horsepower: 2,011hp (1,500kW)
Height: 12ft 4½in (3.78m) Seats (total/car): 282S, 71S/78S/62S/71S

Number	Formation DMSO(A)+MSO+PTSO+DMSO(B)	Depot	Livery	Owner	Opt'	Name
357001	67651+74151+74051+67751	EM	NE2	PTR	C2C	Barry Flaxman
357002	67652+74152+74052+67752	EM	NE2	PTR	C2C	Arthur Lewis Stride 1841-1922
357003	67653+74153+74053+67753	EM	NE2	PTR	C2C	Jason Leonard
357004	67654+74154+74054+67754	EM	NE2	PTR	C2C	Tony Amos
357005	67655+74155+74055+67755	EM	NE2	PTR	C2C	
357006	67656+74156+74056+67756	EM	NE2	PTR	C2C	
357007	67657+74157+74057+67757	EM	NE2	PTR	C2C	
357008	67658+74158+74058+67758	EM	NE2	PTR	C2C	
357009	67659+74159+74059+67759	EM	NE2	PTR	C2C	
357010	67660+74160+74060+67760	EM	SPL	PTR	C2C	
357011	67661+74161+74061+67761	EM	NE2	PTR	C2C	John Lowing
357012	67662+74162+74062+67762	EM	NE2	PTR	C2C	
357013	67663+74163+74063+67763	EM	NE2	PTR	C2C	
357014	67664+74164+74064+67764	EM	NE2	PTR	C2C	
357015	67665+74165+74065+67765	EM	NE2	PTR	C2C	
357016	67666+74166+74066+67766	EM	NE2	PTR	C2C	
357017	67667+74167+74067+67767	EM	NE2	PTR	C2C	
357018	67668+74168+74068+67768	EM	NE2	PTR	C2C	
357019	67669+74169+74069+67769	EM	NE2	PTR	C2C	
357020	67670+74170+74070+67770	EM	NE2	PTR	C2C	
357021	67621+74171+74071+67771	EM	NE2	PTR	C2C	
357022	67672+74172+74072+67772	EM	NE2	PTR	C2C	
357023	67673+74173+74073+67773	EM	NE2	PTR	C2C	
357024	67674+74174+74074+67774	EM	NE2	PTR	C2C	
357025	67675+74175+74075+67775	EM	NE2	PTR	C2C	
357026	67676+74176+74076+67776	EM	NE2	PTR	C2C	
357027	67677+74177+74077+67777	EM	NE2	PTR	C2C	
357028	67678+74178+74078+67778	EM	NE2	PTR	C2C	London, Tilbury & Southend Railway 1854-2004
357029	67679+74179+74079+67779	EM	C2C	PTR	C2C	Thomas Whitelegg 1840-1922
357030	67680+74180+74080+67780	EM	NE2	PTR	C2C	Robert Harben Whitelegg 1871-1957
357031	67681+74181+74081+67781	EM	NE2	PTR	C2C	
357032	67682+74182+74082+67782	EM	C2C	PTR	C2C	
357033	67683+74183+74083+67783	EM	NE2	PTR	C2C	
357034	67684+74184+74084+67784	EM	NE2	PTR	C2C	
357035	67685+74185+74085+67785	EM	NE2	PTR	C2C	
357036	67686+74186+74086+67786	EM	C2C	PTR	C2C	
357037	67687+74187+74087+67787	EM	NE2	PTR	C2C	
357038	67688+74188+74088+67788	EM	NE2	PTR	C2C	
357039	67689+74189+74089+67789	EM	NE2	PTR	C2C	
357040	67690+74190+74090+67790	EM	NE2	PTR	C2C	
357041	67691+74191+74091+67791	EM	NE2	PTR	C2C	
357042	67692+74192+74092+67792	EM	C2C	PTR	C2C	
357043	67693+74193+74093+67793	EM	NE2	PTR	C2C	
357044	67694+74194+74094+67794	EM	NE2	PTR	C2C	
357045	67695+74195+74095+67795	EM	NE2	PTR	C2C	
357046	67696+74196+74096+67796	EM	C2C	PTR	C2C	

Passenger Train Operating Companies - c2c

c2c

Class 357/2
Electrostar

Vehicle Length: (Driving) 68ft 1in (20.75m)	Width: 9ft 2½in (2.80m)	
(Inter) 65ft 11½in (20.10m)	Horsepower: 2,011hp (1,500kW)	
Height: 12ft 4½in (3.78m)	Seats (total/car): 282S, 71S/78S/62S/71S	

Number	Formation DMSO(A)+MSO+PTSO+DMSO(B)	Depot	Livery	Owner	Operator	Name
357201	68601+74701+74601+68701	EM	NE2	ANG	C2C	Ken Bird
357202	68602+74702+74602+68702	EM	NE2	ANG	C2C	Kenny Mitchell
357203	68603+74703+74603+68703	EM	NE2	ANG	C2C	Henry Pumfrett
357204	68604+74704+74604+68704	EM	NE2	ANG	C2C	Derek Flowers
357205	68605+74705+74605+68705	EM	NE2	ANG	C2C	John D'Silva
357206	68606+74706+74606+68706	EM	NE2	ANG	C2C	Martin Aungier
357207	68607+74707+74607+68707	EM	NE2	ANG	C2C	John Page
357208	68608+74708+74608+68708	EM	NE2	ANG	C2C	Dave Davis
357209	68609+74709+74609+68709	EM	NE2	ANG	C2C	James Snelling
357210	68610+74710+74610+68710	EM	C2C	ANG	C2C	
357211	68611+74711+74611+68711	EM	NE2	ANG	C2C	
357212	68612+74712+74612+68712	EM	NE2	ANG	C2C	
357213	68613+74713+74613+68713	EM	NE2	ANG	C2C	Upminster IECC
357214	68614+74714+74614+68714	EM	NE2	ANG	C2C	
357215	68615+74715+74615+68715	EM	NE2	ANG	C2C	
357216	68616+74716+74616+68716	EM	NE2	ANG	C2C	
357217	68617+74717+74617+68717	EM	NE2	ANG	C2C	Allan Burnell
357218	68618+74218+74618+68718	EM	NE2	ANG	C2C	
357219	68619+74719+74619+68719	EM	NE2	ANG	C2C	
357220	68620+74720+74620+68720	EM	NE2	ANG	C2C	
357221	68621+74721+74621+68721	EM	NE2	ANG	C2C	
357222	68622+74722+74622+68722	EM	C2C	ANG	C2C	
357223	68623+74723+74623+68723	EM	C2C	ANG	C2C	
357224	68624+74724+74624+68724	EM	C2C	ANG	C2C	
357225	68625+74725+74625+68725	EM	C2C	ANG	C2C	
357226	68626+74726+74626+68726	EM	C2C	ANG	C2C	
357227	68627+74727+74627+68727	EM	C2C	ANG	C2C	
357228	68628+74728+74628+68728	EM	C2C	ANG	C2C	

Below: *The Angel Trains batch of Class 357s are classified as Class 357/2 and share duties with the Porterbrook fleet. Set No. 357203* Henry Pumfrett *displays the latest National Express c2c branded white livery at Southend Central.* **Brian Morrison**

Chiltern Railways

Address: ✉ 2nd floor, Western House, Rickfords Hill, Aylesbury, Buckinghamshire, HP20 2RX
🖰 Via website (www.chilternrailways.co.uk)
✆ 08456 005165
ⓘ www.chilternrailways.co.uk

Managing Director: Adrian Shooter CBE
Franchise Dates: 21 July 1996 - 1 March 2022
Principal Routes: London Marylebone - Birmingham Snow Hill
London Marylebone - Aylesbury
Hatton - Stratford-upon-Avon
Depots: Aylesbury (AL), Wembley*
* Stabling point
Parent Company: Deutsche Bahn AG (DB Regio)

© TRC.Com Ltd 2011

Chiltern Railways

Passenger Train Operating Companies - Chiltern Railways

Class 121

Length: 64ft 6in (19.66m)	Engine: 2 x Leyland 150hp
Height: 12ft 8½in (3.87m)	Horsepower: 300hp (224kW)
Width: 9ft 3in (2.81m)	Seats (total/car): 65S

Number	Formation DMBS	Depot	Livery	Owner	Operator
121020	55020	AY	BLU	CRW	CRW
121034	55034	AY	GRN	CRW	CRW

Left: *Chiltern Railways operates a Class 121 'Heritage' DMMU on its Aylesbury to Princes Risborough route. Two vehicles are now available, one (121020) painted in blue and No. 121034 in green. No. 121020 is illustrated.* **Kim Fullbrook**

Class 165/0 (2-car)
Networker Turbo

Vehicle Length: (driving) 75ft 2½in (22.91m), (inter) 74ft 6½in (22.72m)	
Height: 12ft 5¼in (3.79m)	Engine: 1 x Perkins 2006 TWH of 350hp per vehicle
Width: 9ft 2½in (2.81m)	Horsepower: 700hp (522kW)
Seats (total/car): 183S, 89S/94S	

Number	Formation DMSL+DMS	Depot	Livery	Owner	Operator	Number	Formation	Depot	Livery	Owner	Operator
165001	58801+58834	AL	CRW	ANG	CRW	165014	58814+58847	AL	CRW	ANG	CRW
165002	58802+58835	AL	CRW	ANG	CRW	165015	58815+58848	AL	CRW	ANG	CRW
165003	58803+58836	AL	CRW	ANG	CRW	165016	58816+58849	AL	CRW	ANG	CRW
165004	58804+58837	AL	CRW	ANG	CRW	165017	58817+58850	AL	CRW	ANG	CRW
165005	58805+58838	AL	CRW	ANG	CRW	165018	58818+58851	AL	CRW	ANG	CRW
165006	58806+58839	AL	CRW	ANG	CRW	165019	58819+58852	AL	CRW	ANG	CRW
165007	58807+58840	AL	CRW	ANG	CRW	165020	58820+58853	AL	CRW	ANG	CRW
165008	58808+58841	AL	CRW	ANG	CRW	165021	58821+58854	AL	CRW	ANG	CRW
165009	58809+58842	AL	CRW	ANG	CRW	165022	58822+58855	AL	CRW	ANG	CRW
165010	58810+58843	AL	CRW	ANG	CRW	165023	58873+58867	AL	CRW	ANG	CRW
165011	58811+58844	AL	CRW	ANG	CRW	165024	58874+58868	AL	CRW	ANG	CRW
165012	58812+58845	AL	CRW	ANG	CRW	165025	58874+58869	AL	CRW	ANG	CRW
165013	58813+58846	AL	CRW	ANG	CRW	165026	58876+58870	AL	CRW	ANG	CRW
						165027	58877+58871	AL	CRW	ANG	CRW
						165028	58878+58872	AL	CRW	ANG	CRW

Left: *Introduced by Network SouthEast as modernisation for the Chiltern routes from London Marylebone, the Class 165 fleet are another highly successful and reliable train design. Painted in standard Chiltern livery, two-car set No. 165004 departs from Marylebone. On the right is one of the later 'Turbostar' sets No. 168113.* **Tony Christie**

Class 165/0 (3-car)
Networker Turbo

Vehicle Length: (driving) 75ft 2½in (22.91m), (inter) 74ft 6½in (22.72m)	
Height: 12ft 5¼in (3.79m)	Engine: 1 x Perkins 2006 TWH of 350hp per vehicle
Width: 9ft 2½in (2.81m)	Horsepower: 1,050hp (783kW)
Seats (total/car): 289S, 89S/106S/94S	

Number	Formation DMSL+MS+DMS	Depot	Livery	Owner	Operator	Number	Formation	Depot	Livery	Owner	Operator
165029	58823+55404+58856	AL	CRW	ANG	CRW	165034	58828+55409+58861	AL	CRW	ANG	CRW
165030	58824+55405+58857	AL	CRW	ANG	CRW	165035	58829+55410+58862	AL	CRW	ANG	CRW
165031	58825+55406+58858	AL	CRW	ANG	CRW	165036	58830+55411+58863	AL	CRW	ANG	CRW
165032	58826+55407+58859	AL	CRW	ANG	CRW	165037	58831+55412+58864	AL	CRW	ANG	CRW
165033	58827+55408+58860	AL	CRW	ANG	CRW	165038	58832+55413+58865	AL	CRW	ANG	CRW
						165039	58833+55414+58866	AL	CRW	ANG	CRW

Class 168/0
Turbostar

		Vehicle Length: 77ft 6in (23.62m)		Engine: 1 x MTU 6R 183TD13H 422hp per vehicle		
		Height: 12ft 4½in (3.77m)		Horsepower: 1,688hp (1,259kW)		
		Width: 8ft 10in (2.69m)		Seats (total/car): 278S, 60S/73S/77S/68S		

Number	Formation DMSL(A)+MSL+MS+DMSL(B)	Depot	Livery	Owner	Operator
168001	58151+58651+58451+58251	AL	CRW	PTR	CRW
168002	58152+58652+58452+58252	AL	CRW	PTR	CRW
168003	58153+58653+58453+58253	AL	CRW	PTR	CRW
168004	58154+58654+58454+58254	AL	CRW	PTR	CRW
168005	58155+58655+58455+58255	AL	CRW	PTR	CRW

Right: *The original five Class 168 'Turbostar' sets sport a slightly different cab end design, before this was refined into the production style. Four car set No. 168001 is viewed at Haddenham & Thame Parkway on 23 October 2008, forming the 14.08 London Marylebone to Birmingham Snow Hill service.* **Brian Morrison**

Class 168/1
Turbostar

	Vehicle Length: 77ft 6in (23.62m)	Engine: 1 x MTU 6R 183TD13H of 422hp per vehicle		
	Height: 12ft 4½in (3.77m)	Horsepower: 3/4-Car 1,266hp (944kW)/1,688hp (1,259kW)		
	Width: 8ft 10in (2.69m)	Seats (total/car): 3-car - 208S, 59S/73S/76S, 4-car - 284S, 59S/73S/76S/76S		

Number	Formation DMSL(A)+MS+MS+DMSL(B)	Depot	Livery	Owner	Operator	Notes
168106	58156+58756§+58456+58256	AL	CRW	PTR	CRW	§ is a MSL vehicle
168107	58157+58457+58757§+58257	AL	CRW	PTR	CRW	§ is a MSL vehicle
168108	58158+58458+58258	AL	CRW	PTR	CRW	
168109	58159+58459+58259	AL	CRW	PTR	CRW	
168110	58160+58460+58260	AL	CRW	PTR	CRW	
168111	58161+58461+58261	AL	CRW	HSB	CRW	58461 was originally 58661
168112	58162+58462+58262	AL	CRW	HSB	CRW	58462 was originally 58662
168113	58163+58463+58263	AL	CRW	HSB	CRW	58463 was originally 58663

Class 168/2
Turbostar

	Vehicle Length: 77ft 6in (23.62m)	Engine: 1 x MTU 6R 183TD13H of 422hp per vehicle		
	Height: 12ft 4½in (3.77m)	Horsepower: 3/4-Car 1,266hp (944kW)/1,688hp (1,259kW)		
	Width: 8ft 10in (2.69m)	Seats (total/car): 3-car - 204S, 59S/76S/69S, 4-car - 277S, 59S/73S/76S/69S		

Number	Formation DMSL(A)+MS+MS+DMSL(B)	Depot	Livery	Owner	Operator
168214	58164+58464+58264	AL	CRW	PTR	CRW
168215	58165+58465+58365+58265	AL	CRW	PTR	CRW
168216	58166+58466+58366+58266	AL	CRW	PTR	CRW
168217	58167+58467+58367+58267	AL	CRW	PTR	CRW
168218	58168+58468+58268	AL	CRW	PTR	CRW
168219	58169+58469+58269	AL	CRW	PTR	CRW

Right: *When the production Class 168/1s and 168/2s were introduced the new standard cab front end design was installed, giving a more pleasing appearance to the train. Three-car Class 168/1 No. 168111 heads south at Banbury with a Birmingham to London Marylebone service.*
Tony Christie

Passenger Train Operating Companies - Chiltern Railways

Chiltern Railways

Class 172/1

Vehicle Length: 73ft 4in (22.37m)		Engine: MTU 6H1800 of 360kW		
Height: 12ft 4½in (3.77m)		Horsepower: 965hp (720kW)		
Width: 8ft 8in (2.69m)		Seats (total/car): 121S, 53S/68S		

Number	Formation DMS+DMS	Depot	Livery	Owner	Operator
172101	59111+59211	AL	CRW	ANG	CRW
172102	59112+59212	AL	CRW	ANG	CRW
172103	59113+59213	AL	CRW	ANG	CRW
172104	59114+59214	AL	CRW	ANG	CRW

Sets on order, scheduled for delivery in spring 2011

Class 960 - Service Units

Class 121 and 122		Class 117	
Length: 64ft 6in (19.66m)	Engine: 2 x Leyland 150hp	Length: 64ft 0in (19.50m)	Engine: 2 x Leyland 150hp
Height: 12ft 8½in (3.87m)	Horsepower: 300hp (224kW)	Height: 12ft 8½in (3.87m)	Horsepower: 300hp (224kW)
Width: 9ft 3in (2.81m)	Seats (total/car): -	Width: 9ft 3in (2.81m)	Seats (total/car): -

Number	Formation	Depot	Livery	Owner	Operator	Notes
960010	977858 ●	AL	MAR	NRL	CRW	Ex Class 121 55024, Sandite
960013	977866 ●	AL	NSE	NRL	CRW	Ex Class 121 55030, Sandite
960014	977873	AL	BLG	CRW	CRW	Ex Class 121 55022, route learning/Sandite
960015	975042 ●	AL	YEL	NRL	CRW	Ex Class 122 55019, Sandite
960021	977723 ●	AL	RTK	NRL	CRW	Ex Class 121 55021, Sandite
960301	977987+977992+977988	AL	GRN	CRW	CRW	Ex Class 117, 51371/51375/51413 - used for water jetting

● Sold for disposal via Chiltern Railways November 2010

Left: Eight Heritage DMMU vehicles in Departmental use are still allocated to Aylesbury depot, which are mainly used for autumn rail adhesion improvement. During the non leaf-fall season the vehicles can usually be found stabled around Aylesbury station or depot. Here No. 960014 (former Class 121 No. 55022) carrying blue/grey livery with Wrexham & Shropshire branding sits with maroon liveried No. 960010 (the original No. 55024) adjacent to Aylesbury station. **Brian Morrison**

Class 01.5 (0-6-0)

Number		Depot	Pool	Livery	Owner	Operator	Name
01509 (433) RH468043		AL	MBDL	BLU	CRW	CRW	*Lesley*

Left: To shunt the Chiltern fleet of stock, especially the DMMU fleet, Aylesbury depot has one 0-6-0 diesel shunting loco, Ruston & Hornsby No. 468043, which is now classified under TOPS as a Class 01.5 and numbered 01509 and named Lesley. The loco operates within the confines of Aylesbury depot and has restricted access to the mainline at Aylesbury station. **Brian Morrison**

Cross Country Trains

Passenger Train Operating Companies - Cross Country Trains

Address: ✉ Cannon House, 18 The Priory, Queensway, Birmingham, B4 6BS
🖰 info@crosscountrytrains.co.uk
✆ 0870 0100084
ⓘ www.crosscountrytrains.co.uk

Managing Director: Andy Cooper
Franchise Dates: 11 November 2007 - 1 May 2016
Principal Routes: Penzance/Paignton -
Manchester/Edinburgh/Aberdeen
Bournemouth - Manchester/
Edinburgh/Aberdeen
Birmingham - Stansted
Nottingham - Cardiff
Depots: Central Rivers (CZ),
Tyseley (TS),
Craigentinny (EC)
Parent Company: Deutsche Bahn AG
(DB Regio)

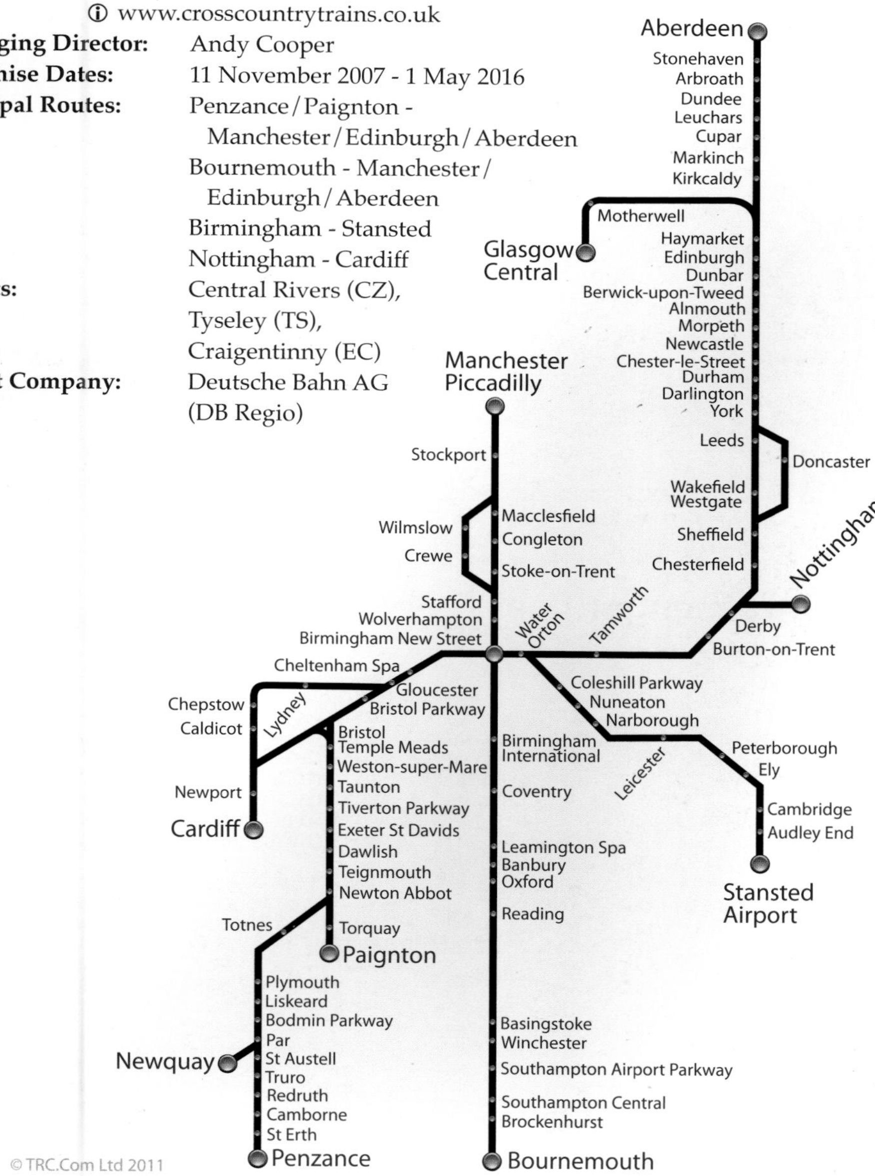

Aberdeen
Stonehaven
Arbroath
Dundee
Leuchars
Cupar
Markinch
Kirkcaldy

Motherwell
Glasgow Central
Haymarket
Edinburgh
Dunbar
Berwick-upon-Tweed
Alnmouth
Morpeth
Newcastle
Manchester Piccadilly
Chester-le-Street
Durham
Darlington
York

Stockport
Leeds
Doncaster

Wakefield Westgate
Macclesfield
Wilmslow
Congleton
Sheffield
Crewe
Chesterfield
Stoke-on-Trent
Nottingham

Stafford
Wolverhampton
Birmingham New Street
Water Orton
Tamworth
Derby
Burton-on-Trent

Cheltenham Spa
Chepstow
Gloucester
Bristol Parkway
Coleshill Parkway
Nuneaton
Narborough
Caldicot
Lydney
Bristol Temple Meads
Weston-super-Mare
Birmingham International
Peterborough
Ely
Newport
Taunton
Coventry
Leicester
Cardiff
Tiverton Parkway
Exeter St Davids
Dawlish
Leamington Spa
Cambridge
Audley End
Teignmouth
Banbury
Oxford
Newton Abbot
Stansted Airport
Totnes
Torquay
Reading
Paignton

Plymouth
Liskeard
Bodmin Parkway
Par
Basingstoke
Winchester
Newquay
St Austell
Truro
Southampton Airport Parkway
Redruth
Camborne
Southampton Central
St Erth
Brockenhurst
Penzance
Bournemouth

Passenger Train Operating Companies - Cross Country Trains

Cross Country Trains

Class 43 – HST

Vehicle Length: 58ft 5in (18.80m)
Height: 12ft 10in (3.90m)
Width: 8ft 11in (2.73m)
Engine: MTU 16V4000 R41R
Horsepower: 2,250hp (1,680kW)
Electrical Equipment: Brush

Number	Depot	Pool	Livery	Owner	Operator							
43207 (43007)	EC	EHPC	AXC	ANG	AXC	43321 (43121)	EC	EHPC	AXC	PTR	AXC
43285 (43085)	EC	EHPC	AXC	PTR	AXC	43357 (43157)	EC	EHPC	AXC	PTR	AXC
43301 (43101)	EC	EHPC	AXC	PTR	AXC	43366 (43166)	EC	EHPC	AXC	ANG	AXC
43303 (43103)	EC	EHPC	AXC	PTR	AXC	43378 (43178)	EC	EHPC	AXC	ANG	AXC
43304 (43104)	EC	EHPC	AXC	ANG	AXC	43384 (43184)	EC	EHPC	AXC	ANG	AXC

Above: *To supplement the Cross Country 'Voyager' fleet, Cross Country operates a fleet of up to five HST formations with a batch of 10 Class 43 power cars; all are allocated to Edinburgh Craigentinny and carry Cross Country livery. Led by car No. 43207 (the original No. 43007) a westbound train passes Langstone Rock, Devon.* **CJM**

HST passenger fleet

Vehicle Length: 75ft 0in (22.86m)
Height: 12ft 9in (3.88m)
Width: 8ft 11in (2.71m)
Bogie Type: BT10

GH1G - TF *Seating 40F*

Number	Depot	Livery	Owner
41026	EC	AXC	ANG
41035	EC	AXC	ANG
41193 (11060)	EC	AXC	PTR
41194 (11016)	EC	AXC	PTR
41195¤ (11020)	EC	AXC	PTR ¤ = TFD

GH2G - TS *Seating 82S*

Number	Depot	Livery	Owner
42036	EC	AXC	ANG
42037	EC	AXC	ANG
42038	EC	AXC	ANG
42051	EC	AXC	ANG
42052	EC	AXC	ANG
42053	EC	AXC	ANG
42097	EC	AXC	ANG
42234	EC	AXC	PTR
42290	EC	AXC	PTR
42342 (44082)	EC	AXC	ANG
42366 (12007)	EC	AXC	PTR
42367 (12025)	EC	AXC	PTR
42368 (12028)	EC	AXC	PTR
42369 (12050)	EC	AXC	PTR
42370 (12086)	EC	AXC	PTR
42371 (12052)	EC	AXC	PTR

Number	Depot	Livery	Owner	
42372 (12055)	EC	AXC	PTR	
42373 (12071)	EC	AXC	PTR	
42374 (12075)	EC	AXC	PTR	
42375 (12113)	EC	AXC	PTR	
42376 (12085)	EC	AXC	PTR	
42377 (12102)	EC	AXC	PTR	
42378 (12123)	EC	AXC	PTR	
42379* (41036)	EC	AXC	ANG	*=TSD
42380* (41025)	EC	AXC	ANG	*=TSD

GJ2G - TGS *Seating 67S*

Number	Depot	Livery	Owner
44012	EC	AXC	ANG
44017	EC	AXC	ANG
44021	EC	AXC	ANG
44052	EC	AXC	PTR
44072	EC	AXC	PTR

GH3G - TCC *Seating 30F/10S*

Number	Depot	Livery	Owner
45001 (12004)	EC	AXC	PTR
45002 (12106)	EC	AXC	PTR
45003 (12076)	EC	AXC	PTR
45004 (12077)	EC	AXC	PTR
45005 (12080)	EC	AXC	PTR

Class 170/1
Turbostar

Vehicle Length: 77ft 6in (23.62m)
Height: 12ft 4½in (3.77m)
Width: 8ft 10in (2.69m)

Engine: 1 x MTU 6R 183TD13H 422hp per vehicle
Horsepower: 1,266hp (944kW)
Seats (total/car): 9F/191S 52S/80S/9F-59S

Number	Formation DMS+MS+DMCL	Depot	Livery	Owner	Operator
170101	50101+55101+79101	TS	AXC	PTR	AXC
170102	50102+55102+79102	TS	AXC	PTR	AXC
170103	50103+55103+79103	TS	AXC	PTR	AXC
170104	50104+55104+79104	TS	AXC	PTR	AXC
170105	50105+55105+79105	TS	AXC	PTR	AXC
170106	50106+55106+79106	TS	AXC	PTR	AXC
170107	50107+55107+79107	TS	AXC	PTR	AXC
170108*	50108+55108+79108	TS	AXC	PTR	AXC
170109*	50109+55109+79109	TS	AXC	PTR	AXC
170110	50110+55110+79110	TS	AXC	PTR	AXC

Vehicle Length: 77ft 6in (23.62m)
Height: 12ft 4½in (3.77m)
Width: 8ft 10in (2.69m)

Engine: 1 x MTU 6R 183TD13H 422hp per vehicle
Horsepower: 844hp (629kW)
Seats (total/car): 9F-111S 59S/9F-52S

Number	Formation DMS+DMCL	Depot	Livery	Owner	Operator	Number	Formation	Depot	Livery	Owner	Operator
						170114	50114+79114	TS	AXC	PTR	AXC
						170115	50115+79115	TS	AXC	PTR	AXC
170111*	50111+79111	TS	AXC	PTR	AXC	170116	50116+79116	TS	AXC	PTR	AXC
170112	50112+79112	TS	AXC	PTR	AXC	170117	50117+79117	TS	AXC	PTR	AXC
170113	50113+79113	TS	AXC	PTR	AXC						

* Fitted with passenger counters

Class 170/3
Turbostar

Vehicle Length: 77ft 6in (23.62m)
Height: 12ft 4½in (3.77m)
Width: 8ft 10in (2.69m)

Engine: 1 x MTU 6R 183TD13H 422hp per vehicle
Horsepower: 1,266hp (944kW)
Seats (total/car): 9F-191S 59S/80S/9F-52S

Number	Formation DMSL+MS+DMCL	Depot	Livery	Owner	Operator
170397	50397+56397+79397	TS	AXC	PTR	AXC
170398	50398+56398+79398	TS	AXC	PTR	AXC

Class 170/5
Turbostar

Vehicle Length: 77ft 6in (23.62m)
Height: 12ft 4½in (3.77m)
Width: 8ft 10in (2.69m)

Engine: 1 x MTU 6R 183TD13H 422hp per vehicle
Horsepower: 844hp (629kW)
Seats (total/car): 9F-111S 59S/9F-52S

Number	Formation DMSL+DMCL	Depot	Livery	Owner	Operator	Number	Formation	Depot	Livery	Owner	Operator
						170520	50520+79520	TS	AXC	PTR	AXC
						170521	50521+79521	TS	AXC	PTR	AXC
170518	50518+79518	TS	AXC	PTR	AXC	170522	50522+79522	TS	AXC	PTR	AXC
170519	50519+79519	TS	AXC	PTR	AXC	170523	50523+79523	TS	AXC	PTR	AXC

Class 170/6
Turbostar

Vehicle Length: 77ft 6in (23.62m)
Height: 12ft 4½in (3.77m)
Width: 8ft 10in (2.69m)

Engine: 1 x MTU 6R 183TD13H 422hp per vehicle
Horsepower: 1,266hp (944kW)
Seats (total/car): 9F-191S 59S/80S/9F-52S

Number	Formation DMSL+MS+DMCL	Depot	Livery	Owner	Operator
170636	50636+56636+79636	TS	AXC	PTR	AXC
170637	50637+56637+79637	TS	AXC	PTR	AXC
170638	50638+56638+79638	TS	AXC	PTR	AXC
170639	50639+56639+79639	TS	AXC	PTR	AXC

Right: *The four different sub-classes of Class 170 operated by Cross Country are all allocated to Tyseley depot in Birmingham and all operate universal duties. All are painted in Cross Country maroon and silver livery and some now sport advertising branding. Three-car set No. 170107 is seen at Derby, viewed from its DMCL vehicle.*
CJM

Cross Country Trains

Class 220
Voyager

Vehicle Length: 77ft 6in (23.62m)	*Engine: 1 x Cummins 750hp per vehicle*
Height: 12ft 4in (3.75m)	*Horsepower: 3,000hp (2,237kW)*
Width: 8ft 11in (2.73m)	*Seats (total/car): 26F/174S 42S/66S/66S/26F*

Number	Formation DMS+MS+MS+DMF	Depot	Livery	Owner	Operator
220001	60301+60701+60201+60401	CZ	AXC	HBS	AXC
220002	60302+60702+60202+60402	CZ	AXC	HBS	AXC
220003	60303+60703+60203+60403	CZ	AXC	HBS	AXC
220004	60304+60704+60204+60404	CZ	AXC	HBS	AXC
220005	60305+60705+60205+60405	CZ	AXC	HBS	AXC
220006	60306+60706+60206+60406	CZ	AXC	HBS	AXC
220007	60307+60707+60207+60407	CZ	AXC	HBS	AXC
220008	60308+60708+60208+60408	CZ	AXC	HBS	AXC
220009	60309+60709+60209+60409	CZ	AXC	HBS	AXC
220010	60310+60710+60210+60410	CZ	AXC	HBS	AXC
220011	60311+60711+60211+60411	CZ	AXC	HBS	AXC
220012	60312+60712+60212+60412	CZ	AXC	HBS	AXC
220013	60313+60713+60213+60413	CZ	AXC	HBS	AXC
220014	60314+60714+60214+60414	CZ	AXC	HBS	AXC
220015	60315+60715+60215+60415	CZ	AXC	HBS	AXC
220016	60316+60716+60216+60416	CZ	AXC	HBS	AXC
220017	60317+60717+60217+60417	CZ	AXC	HBS	AXC
220018	60318+60718+60218+60418	CZ	AXC	HBS	AXC
220019	60319+60719+60219+60419	CZ	AXC	HBS	AXC
220020	60320+60720+60220+60420	CZ	AXC	HBS	AXC
220021	60321+60721+60221+60421	CZ	AXC	HBS	AXC
220022	60322+60722+60222+60422	CZ	AXC	HBS	AXC
220023	60323+60723+60223+60423	CZ	AXC	HBS	AXC
220024	60324+60724+60224+60424	CZ	AXC	HBS	AXC
220025	60325+60725+60225+60425	CZ	AXC	HBS	AXC
220026	60326+60726+60226+60426	CZ	AXC	HBS	AXC
220027	60327+60727+60227+60427	CZ	AXC	HBS	AXC
220028	60328+60728+60228+60428	CZ	AXC	HBS	AXC
220029	60329+60729+60229+60429	CZ	AXC	HBS	AXC
220030	60330+60730+60230+60430	CZ	AXC	HBS	AXC
220031	60331+60731+60231+60431	CZ	AXC	HBS	AXC
220032	60332+60732+60232+60432	CZ	AXC	HBS	AXC
220033	60333+60733+60233+60433	CZ	AXC	HBS	AXC
220034	60334+60734+60234+60434	CZ	AXC	HBS	AXC

Below: *The core Cross Country fleet consists of 34 Class 220 and 23 Class 221 Voyager units, all allocated to Central Rivers depot near Burton. Carrying a yellow and blue band to its coupling cover, indicating the first class end (yellow) and a refurbished set with revised catering (blue), set No. 220004 passes Powderham en route for Plymouth.* **CJM**

Class 221
Super Voyager

Vehicle Length: 77ft 6in (23.62m)	Engine: 1 x Cummins 750hp per vehicle
Height: 12ft 4in (3.75m)	Horsepower: 3,750hp (2,796kW)
Width: 8ft 11in (2.73m)	Seats (total/car): 26F/236S 42S/66S/66S/62S/26F

Originally fitted with tilt system to allow higher speeds over curves. Equipment now isolated

Number	Formation DMS+MS+MS+MS+DMF	Depot	Livery	Owner	Operator	
221119	60369+60769+60969+60869+60469	CZ	AXC	HBS	AXC	
221120	60370+60770+60970+60870+60470	CZ	AXC	HBS	AXC	
221121	60371+60771+60971+60871+60471	CZ	AXC	HBS	AXC	
221122	60372+60772+60972+60872+60472	CZ	AXC	HBS	AXC	
221123	60373+60773+60973+60873+60473	CZ	AXC	HBS	AXC	
221124	60374+60774+60974+60874+60474	CZ	AXC	HBS	AXC	
221125	60375+60775+60975+60875+60475	CZ	AXC	HBS	AXC	
221126	60376+60776+60976+60876+60476	CZ	AXC	HBS	AXC	
221127	60377+60777+60977+60877+60477	CZ	AXC	HBS	AXC	
221128	60378+60778+60978+60878+60478	CZ	AXC	HBS	AXC	
221129	60379+60779+60979+60879+60479	CZ	AXC	HBS	AXC	
221130	60380+60780+60980+60880+60480	CZ	AXC	HBS	AXC	
221131	60381+60781+60981+60881+60481	CZ	AXC	HBS	AXC	
221132	60382+60782+60982+60882+60482	CZ	AXC	HBS	AXC	
221133	60383+60783+60983+60883+60483	CZ	AXC	HBS	AXC	
221134	60384+60784+60984+60884+60484	CZ	AXC	HBS	AXC	
221135	60385+60785+60985+60885+60485	CZ	AXC	HBS	AXC	
221136	60386+60786+60986+60886+60486	CZ	AXC	HBS	AXC	
221137	60387+60787+60987+60887+60487	CZ	AXC	HBS	AXC	
221138	60388+60788+60988+60888+60488	CZ	AXC	HBS	AXC	
221139	60389+60789+60989+60889+60489	CZ	AXC	HBS	AXC	
221140	60390+60790+60990+60890+60490	CZ	AXC	HBS	AXC	
221141	60391+60791+60991+60491	CZ	AXC	HBS	AXC	*(Four-car set)*

● A proposal exists for all Class 220-222 sets to receive an additional intermediate pantograph coach, allowing dual diesel-electric operation. The project calls for the building of 123 new pantograph carriages and the rebuilding of 21 existing intermediate vehicles to accommodate a pantograph pick up. No agreement for this project has yet been reached. If the project was to go ahead, vehicle construction would be undertaken by Bombardier at Derby.

Below: *In the split up of assets between Virgin Trains and Cross Country, following the transfer of the Cross Country franchise to Arriva, Cross Country became the operator of just one four-car Class 221 'Super Voyager' set No. 221141. Originally the Class 221 sets incorporated tilting suspension, but in recent years this equipment has been isolated. Set No. 221141 is viewed from its DMF end at Derby forming a Cross Country service to Plymouth.* **CJM**

East Midlands Trains

Address: ✉ 1 Prospect Place, Millennium Way, Pride Park, Derby, DE24 8HG
🖳 getintouch@eastmidlandstrains.co.uk
☎ 08457 125678
ⓘ www.eastmidlandstrains.co.uk

Managing Director: Tim Shoveller
Franchise Dates: 11 November 2007 - 31 March 2015
Principal Routes: St Pancras-Sheffield/York/Leeds/Nottingham
Norwich/Skegness/Cleethorpes - Nottingham/Crewe/
Liverpool and Matlock
Depots: Derby (DY), Nottingham (NM), Neville Hill (NL)
Parent Company: Stagecoach

Class 08

Vehicle Length: 29ft 3in (8.91m)
Height: 12ft 8⅝in (3.87m)
Width: 8ft 6in (2.59m)
Engine: English Electric 6K
Horsepower: 400hp (298kW)
Electrical Equipment: English Electric

Number	Depot	Pool	Livery	Owner	Operator						
08525	NL	EMSL	SCE	EMT	EMT	08899	DY	EMSL	BLU	EMT	EMT
08690	NL	EMSL	SCE	EMT	EMT	08908	DY	EMSL	SCE	EMT	EMT
						08950	NL	EMSL	SCE	EMT	EMT

Left: *To assist with shunting operations at the sizeable maintenance complex at Etches Park, Derby and Neville Hill depot in Leeds, six Class 08s are on the books of East Midlands Trains. Special adaptor couplers are fitted to enable connection to Class 222 stock which are fitted with Dellner couplers. Blue-liveried No. 08899 is seen attached to a Class 222 at Etches Park. Note the headlight required for main line operation.* **EMT**

Class 43 – HST

Vehicle Length: 58ft 5in (18.80m)
Height: 12ft 10in (3.90m)
Width: 8ft 11in (2.73m)
Engine: Paxman VP185
Horsepower: 2,100hp (1,565kW)
Electrical Equipment: Brush

Number	Depot	Pool	Livery	Owner	Operator						
43043	NL	EMPC	MML	PTR	EMT	43066	NL	EMPC	SCE	PTR	EMT
43044	NL	EMPC	SCE	PTR	EMT	43072	NL	EMPC	SCE	PTR	EMT
43045	NL	EMPC	SCE	PTR	EMT	43073	NL	EMPC	MML	PTR	EMT
43046	NL	EMPC	SCE	PTR	EMT	43074	NL	EMPC	MML	PTR	EMT
43047	NL	EMPC	SCE	PTR	EMT	43075	NL	EMPC	MML	PTR	EMT
43048	NL	EMPC	SCE	PTR	EMT	43076	NL	EMPC	SCE	PTR	EMT
43049	NL	EMPC	SCE	PTR	EMT	43081	NL	EMPC	SCE	PTR	EMT
43050	NL	EMPC	SCE	PTR	EMT	43082	NL	EMPC	SCE	PTR	EMT
43052	NL	EMPC	SCE	PTR	EMT	43083	NL	EMPC	SCE	PTR	EMT
43054	NL	EMPC	SCE	PTR	EMT	43089	NL	EMPC	SCE	PTR	EMT
43055	NL	EMPC	SCE	PTR	EMT						
43058	NL	EMPC	SCE	PTR	EMT						
43059	NL	EMPC	MML	PTR	EMT						
43060	NL	EMPC	MML	PTR	EMT						
43061	NL	EMPC	SCE	PTR	EMT						
43064	NL	EMPC	SCE	PTR	EMT						

Names applied

43048	*T. C. B Miller MBE*
43049	*Neville Hill*
43076	*In Support of Help for Heroes*
43082	*Railway Children The Voice for Street Children Worldwide*

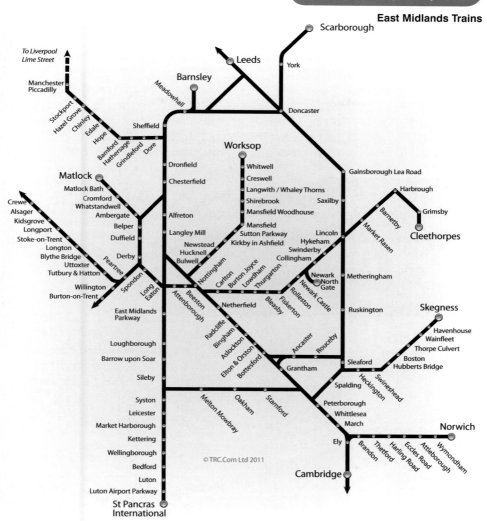

To Liverpool Lime Street

Manchester Piccadilly

Scarborough

Leeds

York

Barnsley

Meadowhall

Doncaster

Stockport
Hazel Grove
Chinley
Edale
Hope
Bamford
Hathersage
Grindleford
Dore

Sheffield

Worksop

Dronfield
Whitwell
Gainsborough Lea Road

Matlock

Chesterfield
Creswell
Langwith / Whaley Thorns
Shirebrook
Saxilby

Harbrough

Matlock Bath
Cromford
Whatstandwell
Ambergate

Mansfield Woodhouse

Barnetby

Grimsby

Crewe
Alsager
Kidsgrove
Longport
Stoke-on-Trent
Longton
Blythe Bridge
Uttoxter
Tutbury & Hatton

Alfreton

Belper

Langley Mill

Mansfield
Sutton Parkway

Lincoln

Market Rasen

Cleethorpes

Duffield

Kirkby in Ashfield
Hykeham
Swinderby

Newstead
Hucknall
Bulwell

Collingham

Derby

Nottingham
Carlton
Burton Joyce
Lowdham
Thurgarton

Newark North Gate

Metheringham

Willington
Burton-on-Trent

Peartree
Spondon
Long Eaton

Attenborough

Beeston

Netherfield
Bleasby
Fiskerton
Rolleston

Newark Castle

Ruskington

Skegness

East Midlands Parkway

Radcliffe
Bingham
Aslockton
Elton & Orston
Bottesford

Ancaster
Rauceby

Sleaford

Havenhouse
Wainfleet
Thorpe Culvert
Boston
Hubberts Bridge

Loughborough

Barrow upon Soar

Grantham

Swineshead
Heckington

Sileby

Spalding

Syston
Leicester
Market Harborough
Kettering
Wellingborough
Bedford
Luton
Luton Airport Parkway

Melton Mowbray
Oakham
Stamford

Peterborough
Whittlesea
March

Norwich

Wymondham
Attleborough
Eccles Road
Harling Road
Thetford
Brandon

Ely

St Pancras International

© TRC.Com Ltd 2011

Cambridge

Right: *The East Midlands Trains main line operation, based on services between Leeds, Sheffield, Derby, Nottingham and London St Pancras is a mix of HSTs and Class 222 sets. In this view at Derby, Class 222 set No. 222006 can be seen on the left, while an East Midlands Trains-liveried HST power car No. 43052 awaits departure on the right with a semi-fast service to London. On the far right an East Midlands Trains, former Central Trains-liveried green Class 153 can be seen.* **CJM**

East Midlands Trains

Class 153

Vehicle Length: 76ft 5in (23.29m)	Engine: 1 x NT855R5 of 285hp
Height: 12ft 3⅛in (3.75m)	Horsepower: 285hp (213kW)
Width: 8ft 10in (2.70m)	Seats (total/car): 66S

Number	Formation DMSL	Depot	Livery	Owner	Operator
153302	52302	NM	EMT	ANG	EMT
153308	52308	NM	EMT	ANG	EMT
153310	52310	NM	EMT	PTR	EMT
153311	52311	NM	EMT	PTR	EMT
153313	52313	NM	EMT	PTR	EMT
153319	52319	NM	EMT	ANG	EMT
153321	52321	NM	EMT	PTR	EMT
153326	52326	NM	EMT	PTR	EMT
153355	57355	NM	EMT	ANG	EMT
153357	57357	NM	EMT	ANG	EMT
153374	57374	NM	EMT	ANG	EMT
153376	57376	NM	EMT	PTR	EMT
153379	57379	NM	EMT	PTR	EMT
153381	57381	NM	EMT	PTR	EMT
153383	57383	NM	EMT	PTR	EMT
153384	57384	NM	EMT	PTR	EMT
153385	57385	NM	EMT	PTR	EMT

Left: The East Midlands Trains domestic DMU fleet is allocated to Nottingham Eastcroft depot, with Class 153 and 156 sets now sporting the latest Stagecoach outer suburban mid-blue livery with end of vehicle orange/red swirls. A pair of EMT Class 153s, with set No. 153308 nearest the camera, stands at Derby with a Matlock bound service. **CJM**

Class 156

Vehicle Length: 75ft 6in (23.03m)	Engine: 1 x Cummins NT855R5 of 285hp
Height: 12ft 6in (3.81m)	Horsepower: 570hp (425kW)
Width: 8ft 11in (2.73m)	Seats (total/car): 148 or 150S, 70 or 72S/78S

Number	Formation DMSL+DMS	Depot	Livery	Owner	Operator
156401	52401+57401	NM	EMT	PTR	EMT
156403	52403+57403	NM	EMT	PTR	EMT
156404	52404+57404	NM	EMT	PTR	EMT
156405	52405+57405	NM	EMT	PTR	EMT
156406	52406+57406	NM	EMT	PTR	EMT
156408	52408+57408	NM	EMT	PTR	EMT
156410	52410+57410	NM	EMT	PTR	EMT
156411	52411+57411	NM	EMT	PTR	EMT
156413	52413+57413	NM	EMT	PTR	EMT
156414	52414+57414	NM	EMT	PTR	EMT
156415	52415+57415	NM	EMT	PTR	EMT

■ Four additional Class 156s Nos. 156470/473/497/498 are due to be transferred from Northern Rail to EMT in July 2011.

Left: Longer distance local services operated by East Midlands Trains are formed of Class 156 stock. In 2010 eleven sets were allocated to Nottingham, but a further four sets are due to be added to the roster in 2011. Set No. 156414 is illustrated. **CJM**

Class 158

Vehicle Length: 76ft 1¾in (23.21m)	Engine: 158770-813 - 1 x Cummins NT855R5 of 350hp
Height: 12ft 6in (3.81m)	Horsepower: 700hp (522kW)
Width: 9ft 3¼in (2.82m)	Engine: 158846-862 - 1 x Perkins 2006TWH of 350hp
	Horsepower: 700hp (522kW)
	Engine: 158863-865 - 1 x Cummins NT855R5 of 400hp
	Horsepower: 800hp (597kW)
	Seats (total/car): 146S - 74S, 72S

Number	Formation DMSL+DMSL	Depot	Livery	Owner	Operator
158770	52770+57770	NM	SCE	PTR	EMT
158773	52773+57773	NM	SCE	PTR	EMT
158774	52774+57774	NM	SCE	PTR	EMT
158777	52777+57777	NM	SCE	PTR	EMT

158780	52780+57780	NM	SCE	ANG	EMT	158852	52852+57852	NM	SCE	ANG	EMT
158783	52783+57783	NM	SCE	ANG	EMT	158854	52854+57854	NM	SCE	ANG	EMT
158785	52785+57785	NM	SCE	ANG	EMT	158856	52856+57856	NM	SCE	ANG	EMT
158788	52788+57788	NM	SCE	ANG	EMT	158857	52857+57857	NM	SCE	ANG	EMT
158799	52799+57799	NM	SCE	PTR	EMT	158858	52858+57858	NM	SCE	ANG	EMT
158806	52806+57806	NM	SCE	PTR	EMT	158862	52862+57862	NM	SCE	ANG	EMT
158810	52810+57810	NM	SCE	PTR	EMT	158863	52863+57863	NM	SCE	ANG	EMT
158812	52812+57812	NM	SCE	PTR	EMT	158864	52864+57864	NM	SCE	ANG	EMT
158813	52813+57813	NM	SCE	PTR	EMT	158865	52865+57865	NM	SCE	ANG	EMT
158846	52846+57846	NM	SCE	ANG	EMT	158866	52866+57866	NM	SCE	ANG	EMT
158847	52847+57847	NM	SCE	ANG	EMT						

Right: *A total of 25 two-car Class 158s are operated by East Midlands Trains, allocated to Nottingham Eastcroft and used on longer distance services. All have recently been fully refurbished by Delta Rail of Derby and are painted in the Stagecoach main line while colour scheme. Set No. 158810 is illustrated. Note the slight livery difference between the East Midlands Trains and South West Trains Class 158s.*
Cliff Beeton

Class 222

Vehicle Length: 77ft 6in (23.62m)	Horsepower: 5,250hp (3,914kW)
Height: 12ft 4in (3.75m)	Seats (total/car): 106F/236S
Width: 8ft 11in (2.73m)	38S/68S/68S/62S/42F/42F/22F
Engine: 1 x Cummins QSK9R of 750hp per vehicle	

Number	Formation	Depot	Livery	Owner	Operator
	DMS+MS+MS+MSRMB+MF+MF+DMRFO				
222001	60161+60551+60561+60621+60341+60445+60241	DY	SCE	HSB	EMT
222002	60162+60544+60562+60622+60342+60346+60242	DY	SCE	HSB	EMT
222003	60163+60553+60563+60623+60343+60446+60243	DY	SCE	HSB	EMT
222004	60164+60554+60564+60624+60344+60345+60244	DY	SCE	HSB	EMT
222005	60165+60555+60565+60625+60443+60347+60245	DY	SCE	HSB	EMT
222006	60166+60556+60566+60626+60441+60447+60246	DY	SCE	HSB	EMT

Name applied
222003 (60163) *Tornado*

Vehicle Length: 77ft 6in (23.62m)	Horsepower: 3,750hp (2,796kW)
Height: 12ft 4in (3.75m)	Seats (total/car): 50F/190S
Width: 8ft 11in (2.73m)	38S/68S/62S/28F-22S/22F
Engine: 1 x Cummins QSK9R of 750hp per vehicle	

Number	Formation	Depot	Livery	Owner	Operator
	DMS+MS+MSRMB+MC+DMRFO				
222007	60167+60567+60627+60442+60247	DY	SCE	HSB	EMT
222008	60168+60545+60628+60918+60248	DY	SCE	HSB	EMT
222009	60169+60557+60629+60919+60249	DY	SCE	HSB	EMT
222010	60170+60546+60630+60920+60250	DY	SCE	HSB	EMT
222011	60171+60531+60631+60921+60251	DY	SCE	HSB	EMT
222012	60172+60532+60632+60922+60252	DY	SCE	HSB	EMT
222013	60173+60536+60633+60923+60253	DY	SCE	HSB	EMT
222014	60174+60534+60634+60924+60254	DY	SCE	HSB	EMT
222015	60175+60535+60635+60925+60255	DY	SCE	HSB	EMT
222016	60176+60533+60636+60926+60256	DY	SCE	HSB	EMT
222017	60177+60537+60637+60927+60257	DY	SCE	HSB	EMT
222018	60178+60444+60638+60928+60258	DY	SCE	HSB	EMT
222019	60179+60547+60639+60929+60259	DY	SCE	HSB	EMT
222020	60180+60543+60640+60930+60260	DY	SCE	HSB	EMT
222021	60181+60552+60641+60931+60261	DY	SCE	HSB	EMT
222022	60182+60542+60642+60932+60262	DY	SCE	HSB	EMT
222023	60183+60541+60643+60933+60263	DY	SCE	HSB	EMT

East Midlands Trains

Left: *Three different configurations of Class 222 operate for East Midlands Trains, formed into either seven, five or four car formations. Refurbishment due in 2011 will see all interiors the same throughout the sub-classes. Seven-car set No. 222004 is seen at Derby after arrival with a service from London St Pancras. All sets are allocated to Derby Etches Park depot.* **CJM**

Class 222/1

Vehicle Length: 77ft 6in (23.62m)	Horsepower: 3,000hp (2,237kW)
Height: 12ft 4in (3.75m)	Seats (total/car): 33F/148S
Width: 8ft 11in (2.73m)	22F/11F-46S/62S/40S
Engine: 1 x Cummins OSK9R of 750hp per vehicle	

Number	Formation DMF+MC+MSRMB+DMS	Depot	Livery	Owner	Operator
222101	60271+60571+60681+60191	DY	SCE	HSB	EMT
222102	60272+60572+60682+60192	DY	SCE	HSB	EMT
222103	60273+60573+60683+60193	DY	SCE	HSB	EMT
222104	60274+60574+60684+60194	DY	SCE	HSB	EMT

Left: *Four Class 222 four-car sets were originally built for use by First Hull Trains, but after these were displaced by five car Class 180s, the Class 222s were transferred to East Midlands Trains to supplement their fleet. The sets were quickly repainted into standard East Midlands Trains livery and in 2011 will be included in a fleet refurbishment project.* **CJM**

● A proposal exists for all Class 220-222 sets to receive an additional intermediate pantograph coach, allowing dual diesel-electric operation. The project calls for the building of 123 new pantograph carriages and the rebuilding of 21 existing intermediate vehicles to accommodate a pantograph pick up. No agreement for this project has yet been reached. If the project was to go ahead, vehicle construction would be undertaken by Bombardier at Derby.

HST Passenger Fleet

Vehicle Length: 75ft 0in (22.86m)	Width: 8ft 11in (2.71m)
Height: 12ft 9in (3.88m)	Bogie Type: BT10

GK1G - TRFB *Seating 17F*

Number	Depot	Livery	Owner
40700	NL	SCE	PTR
40728	NL	SCE	PTR
40730	NL	SCE	PTR
40732	NL	SCE	PTR
40741	NL	SCE	PTR
40746	NL	SCE	PTR
40749	NL	SCE	PTR
40751	NL	SCE	PTR
40753	NL	SCE	PTR
40754	NL	SCE	PTR
40756	NL	SCE	PTR

GH1G - TF *Seating 46F*

Number	Depot	Livery	Owner
41041	NL	SCE	PTR
41046	NL	SCE	PTR
41057	NL	SCE	PTR
41061	NL	SCE	PTR
41062	NL	SCE	PTR
41063	NL	SCE	PTR
41064	NL	SCE	PTR
41067	NL	SCE	PTR
41068	NL	SCE	PTR
41069	NL	SCE	PTR
41070	NL	SCE	PTR

Number	Depot	Livery	Owner
41071	NL	SCE	PTR
41072	NL	SCE	PTR
41075	NL	SCE	PTR
41076	NL	SCE	PTR
41077	NL	SCE	PTR
41079	NL	SCE	PTR
41084	NL	SCE	PTR
41111	NL	SCE	PTR
41112	NL	SCE	PTR
41113	NL	SCE	PTR
41117	NL	SCE	PTR
41154	NL	SCE	PTR
41156	NL	SCE	PTR

GH2G - TS *Seating 74S*

Number	Depot	Livery	Owner
42100	NL	SCE	PTR
42111	NL	SCE	PTR
42112	NL	SCE	PTR
42113	NL	SCE	PTR
42119	NL	SCE	PTR
42120	NL	SCE	PTR
42121	NL	SCE	PTR
42123	NL	SCE	PTR
42124	NL	SCE	PTR
42125	NL	SCE	PTR
42131	NL	SCE	PTR
42132	NL	SCE	PTR
42133	NL	SCE	PTR
42135	NL	SCE	PTR
42136	NL	SCE	PTR
42137	NL	SCE	PTR
42139	NL	SCE	PTR
42140	NL	SCE	PTR
42141	NL	SCE	PTR
42148	NL	SCE	PTR
42149	NL	SCE	PTR
42151	NL	SCE	PTR
42152	NL	SCE	PTR
42153	NL	SCE	PTR
42155	NL	SCE	PTR
42156	NL	SCE	PTR
42157	NL	SCE	PTR
42164	NL	SCE	PTR
42165	NL	SCE	PTR
42194	NL	SCE	PTR
42205	NL	SCE	PTR
42210	NL	SCE	PTR
42220	NL	SCE	PTR
42225	NL	SCE	PTR
42227	NL	SCE	PTR
42229	NL	SCE	PTR
42230	NL	SCE	PTR
42327	NL	SCE	PTR
42328	NL	SCE	PTR
42329	NL	SCE	PTR
42331	NL	SCE	PTR
42335	NL	SCE	PTR
42337	NL	SCE	PTR
42339	NL	SCE	PTR
42341	NL	SCE	PTR
42384¤	NL	SCE	PTR

¤ **Modified from 41078**

GJ2G - TGS *Seating 63S*

Number	Depot	Livery	Owner
44027	NL	SCE	PTR
44041	NL	SCE	PTR
44044	NL	SCE	PTR
44046	NL	SCE	PTR
44047	NL	SCE	PTR
44048	NL	SCE	PTR
44051	NL	SCE	PTR
44054	NL	SCE	PTR
44070	NL	SCE	PTR
44071	NL	SCE	PTR
44073	NL	SCE	PTR
44085	NL	SCE	PTR

Right: *Since taking over the East Midlands franchise at the end of 2007, Stagecoach have made a huge investment in refurbishing rolling stock and improving the passenger journey experience. By 2011 all passenger HST stock had been refurbished and repainted in the East Midlands livery based on the Stagecoach theme. Mk3 FO No. 41068 is illustrated. First class vehicles can be identified by a row of red dots above the passenger side windows.*
Tony Christie

Service Stock

HST Barrier Vehicles

Number	Depot	Livery	Owner	Former Identity
6392	NL	PTR	PTR	BG - 81588/92183
6395	NL	PTR	EMT	BG - 81506/92148
6397	NL	PTR	PTR	BG - 81600/92190
6398	NL	MAI	EMT	BG - 81471/92126
6399	NL	MAI	EMT	BG - 81367/92994

Right: *An amazing acquisition into the East Midlands Trains fleet were two ex-Southern Region 4SUB driving cars. These were at Derby E Shed at the time of privatisation and taken over by Midland MainLine as stores and office accommodation, remaining at Derby Etches Park and taken over by East Midlands Trains. One of the vehicles is shown in mid 2010 on its own length of isolated track. The vehicles have subsequently been purchased for use in the 5BEL restoration project.* **CJM**

Class 930 Service Unit

Number	Depot	Livery	Owner	Formation
930010	DY	BLU	EMT	975600 (10988) + 975601 (10843) Former Class 405 SUB vehicles

Eurostar

Passenger Train Operating Companies - Eurostar

Address: ✉ Eurostar, Times House, Bravingtons Walk, Regent Quarter,
London, N1 9AW

✆ new.comments@eurostar.com

✆ 08701 606 600

ⓘ www.eurostar.com

Managing Director: Nicolas Petrovic / Richard Brown

Principal Routes: St Pancras International - Brussels and Paris also serving
Disneyland Paris, Avignon and winter sport service
to Bourg St Maurice

Owned Stations: St Pancras International, Stratford International, Ebbsfleet

Depots: Temple Mills [UK] (TI), Forest [Belgium] (FF), Le Landy [France] (LY)

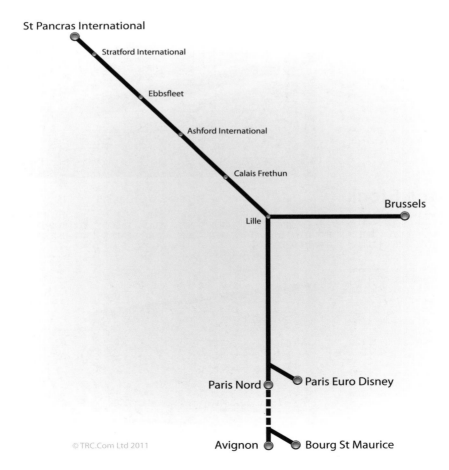

Class 373

Vehicle Length: (DM) 72ft 8in (22.15m), (MS) 71ft 8in (21.84)
(TS, TBK, TE, TBF) 61ft 4in (18.70m)
Height: 12ft 4½in (3.77m)
Width: 9ft 3in (2.81m)
Horsepower: 16,400hp (12,249kW)
Seats (total/car): 103F/272S, 0/48S/56S/56S/56S/56S/56SI0/39F/39F/24F

Formation: DM+MSO+TSO+TSO+TSO+RB+TFO+TFO+TBFO

Number	Formation	Depot	Livery	Owner	Operator	Name
UK sets						
373001	3730010+3730011+3730012+3730013+3730014+3730015+3730016+3730017+3730018+3730019	TI	EUS	EUS	EUS	Tread Lightly
373002	3730020+3730021+3730022+3730023+3730024+3730025+3730026+3730027+3730028+3730029	TI	EUS	EUS	EUS	Voyage Vert
373003	3730030+3730031+3730032+3730033+3730034+3730035+3730036+3730037+3730038+3730039	TI	EUS*	EUS	EUS	Tri City Athlon 2010
373004	3730040+3730041+3730042+3730043+3730044+3730045+3730046+3730047+3730048+3730049	TI	EUS*	EUS	EUS	Tri City Athlon 2010
373005	3730050+3730051+3730052+3730053+3730054+3730055+3730056+3730057+3730058+3730059	TI	EUS	EUS	EUS	
373006	3730060+3730061+3730062+3730063+3730064+3730065+3730066+3730067+3730068+3730069	TI	EUS	EUS	EUS	
373007	3730070+3730071+3730072+3730073+3730074+3730075+3730076+3730077+3730078+3730079	TI	EUS	EUS	EUS	Waterloo Sunset
373008	3730080+3730081+3730082+3730083+3730084+3730085+3730086+3730087+3730088+3730089	TI	EUS	EUS	EUS	Waterloo Sunset
373009	3730090+3730091+3730092+3730093+3730094+3730095+3730096+3730097+3730098+3730099	TI	EUS	EUS	EUS	Remembering Fromelles
373010	3730100+3730101+3730102+3730103+3730104+3730105+3730106+3730107+3730108+3730109	TI	EUS	EUS	EUS	Remembering Fromelles
373011	3730110+3730111+3730112+3730113+3730114+3730115+3730116+3730117+3730118+3730119	TI	EUS	EUS	EUS	
373012	3730120+3730121+3730122+3730123+3730124+3730125+3730126+3730127+3730128+3730129	TI	EUS	EUS	EUS	
373013	3730130+3730131+3730132+3730133+3730134+3730135+3730136+3730137+3730138+3730139	TI	EUS	EUS	EUS	
373014	3730140+3730141+3730142+3730143+3730144+3730145+3730146+3730147+3730148+3730149	TI	EUS	EUS	EUS	
373015	3730150+3730151+3730152+3730153+3730154+3730155+3730156+3730157+3730158+3730159	TI	EUS	EUS	EUS	
373016	3730160+3730161+3730162+3730163+3730164+3730165+3730166+3730167+3730168+3730169	TI	EUS	EUS	EUS	
373017	3730170+3730171+3730172+3730173+3730174+3730175+3730176+3730177+3730178+3730179	TI	EUS	EUS	EUS	
373018	3730180+3730181+3730182+3730183+3730184+3730185+3730186+3730187+3730188+3730189	TI	EUS‡	EUS	EUS	
373019	3730190+3730191+3730192+3730193+3730194+3730195+3730196+3730197+3730198+3730199	TI	EUS	EUS	EUS	
373020	3730200+3730201+3730202+3730203+3730204+3730205+3730206+3730207+3730208+3730209	TI	EUS	EUS	EUS	
373021	3730210+3730211+3730212+3730213+3730214+3730215+3730216+3730217+3730218+3730219	TI	EUS	EUS	EUS	
373022	3730220+3730221+3730222+3730223+3730224+3730225+3730226+3730227+3730228+3730229	TI	EUS	EUS	EUS	
Belgian sets						
373101	3731010+3731011+3731012+3731013+3731014+3731015+3731016+3731017+3731018+3731019	FF[S]	EUS	SNB	EUS	
373102	3731020+3731021+3731022+3731023+3731024+3731025+3731026+3731027+3731028+3731029	FF[S]	EUS	SNB	EUS	
373103	3731030+3731031+3731032+3731033+3731034+3731035+3731036+3731037+3731038+3731039	FF	EUS	SNB	EUS	
373104	3731040+3731041+3731042+3731043+3731044+3731045+3731046+3731047+3731048+3731049	FF	EUS	SNB	EUS	
373105	3731050+3731051+3731052+3731053+3731054+3731055+3731056+3731057+3731058+3731059	FF	EUS	SNB	EUS	
373106	3731060+3731061+3731062+3731063+3731064+3731065+3731066+3731067+3731068+3731069	FF	EUS	SNB	EUS	
373107	3731070+3731071+3731072+3731073+3731074+3731075+3731076+3731077+3731078+3731079	FF	EUS	SNB	EUS	
373108	3731080+3731081+3731082+3731083+3731084+3731085+3731086+3731087+3731088+3731089	FF	EUS	SNB	EUS	
French sets						
373201	3732010+3732011+3732012+3732013+3732014+3732015+3732016+3732017+3732018+3732019	LY	EUS	SNF	EUS	
373202	3732020+3732021+3732022+3732023+3732024+3732025+3732026+3732027+3732028+3732029	LY	EUS	SNF	EUS	
373203¤	3732030+3732031+3732032+3732033+3732034+3732035+3732036+3732037+3732038+3732039	LY	SNT	SNF	EUS	
373204¤	3732040+3732041+3732042+3732043+3732044+3732045+3732046+3732047+3732048+3732049	LY	SNT	SNF	EUS	
373205	3732050+3732051+3732052+3732053+3732054+3732055+3732056+3732057+3732058+3732059	LY	EUS	SNF	EUS	London 2012
373206	3732060+3732061+3732062+3732063+3732064+3732065+3732066+3732067+3732068+3732069	LY	EUS	SNF	EUS	London 2012

Passenger Train Operating Companies - Eurostar

Train Operating Companies

Eurostar

Number	Formation	Depot	Livery	Owner	Operator	Name
373207	3732070+3732071+3732072+3732073+3732074+3732075+3732076+3732077+3732078+3732079	LY	EUS		SNF	Michel Hollard
373208	3732080+3732081+3732082+3732083+3732084+3732085+3732086+3732087+3732088+3732089	LY	EUS		SNF	Michel Hollard
373209	3732090+3732091+3732092+3732093+3732094+3732095+3732096+3732097+3732098+3732099	LY	EUS		SNF	The Da Vinci Code
373210	3732100+3732101+3732102+3732103+3732104+3732105+3732106+3732107+3732108+3732109	LY	EUS		SNF	The Da Vinci Code
373211	3732110+3732111+3732112+3732113+3732114+3732115+3732116+3732117+3732118+3732119	LY	EUS		SNF	
373212	3732120+3732121+3732122+3732123+3732124+3732125+3732126+3732127+3732128+3732129	LY	EUS		SNF	
373213	3732130+3732131+3732132+3732133+3732134+3732135+3732136+3732137+3732138+3732139	LY	EUS		SNF	
373214	3732140+3732141+3732142+3732143+3732144+3732145+3732146+3732147+3732148+3732149	LY	EUS		SNF	
373215	3732150+3732151+3732152+3732153+3732154+3732155+3732156+3732157+3732158+3732159	LY	EUS		SNF	
373216	3732160+3732161+3732162+3732163+3732164+3732165+3732166+3732167+3732168+3732169	LY	EUS		SNF	
373217	3732170+3732171+3732172+3732173+3732174+3732175+3732176+3732177+3732178+3732179	LY	EUS		SNF	
373218	3732180+3732181+3732182+3732183+3732184+3732185+3732186+3732187+3732188+3732189	LY	EUS		SNF	
373219	3732190+3732191+3732192+3732193+3732194+3732195+3732196+3732197+3732198+3732199	LY	EUS		SNF	
373220	3732200+3732201+3732202+3732203+3732204+3732205+3732206+3732207+3732208+3732209	LY	EUS		SNF	
373221	3732210+3732211+3732212+3732213+3732214+3732215+3732216+3732217+3732218+3732219	LY	EUS		SNF	
373222	3732220+3732221+3732222+3732223+3732224+3732225+3732226+3732227+3732228+3732229	LY	EUS		SNF	
373223	3732230+3732231+3732232+3732233+3732234+3732235+3732236+3732237+3732238+3732239	LY	EUS		SNF	
373224	3732240+3732241+3732242+3732243+3732244+3732245+3732246+3732247+3732248+3732249	LY	EUS		SNF	
373225 ¤	3732250+3732251+3732252+3732253+3732254+3732255+3732256+3732257+3732258+3732259	LY			SNT	
373226 ¤	3732260+3732261+3732262+3732263+3732264+3732265+3732266+3732267+3732268+3732269	LY			SNT	
373227 ¤	3732270+3732271+3732272+3732273+3732274+3732275+3732276+3732277+3732278+3732279	LY			SNT	
373228 ¤	3732280+3732281+3732282+3732283+3732284+3732285+3732286+3732287+3732288+3732289	LY			SNT	
373229	3732290+3732291+3732292+3732293+3732294+3732295+3732296+3732297+3732298+3732299	LY	EUS		SNF	
373230	3732300+3732301+3732302+3732303+3732304+3732305+3732306+3732307+3732308+3732309	LY	EUS		SNF	
373231	3732310+3732311+3732312+3732313+3732314+3732315+3732316+3732317+3732318+3732319	LY	EUS		SNF	
373232	3732320+3732321+3732322+3732323+3732324+3732325+3732326+3732327+3732328+3732329	LY	EUS		SNF	

Vehicle Length: (DM) 72ft 8in (22.15m), (MS) 71ft 8in (21.84) (TS, TBK, TF, TBF) 61ft 4in (18.70m)
Height: 12ft 4¼in (3.77m)
Width: 9ft 3in (2.81m)
Horsepower: 16,400hp (12,249kW)
Seats (total/car): 103F/272S, 0/48S/56S/56S/56S/56S/0/39F/39F/24F

■ These 14 short half-sets are loaned to SNCF for domestic duties until 2013.

* Advertising livery - London Virgins. ‡ de Gaulle 70th branding ¤ Operated in France on domestic services.

Number Formation   Depot Livery Owner Operator

DM+MSO+TSO+TSO+TSO+RB+TFO+TBFO

Regional sets

Number	Formation	Depot	Livery	Owner	Operator
373301	3733010+3733011+3733012+3733013+3733015+3733016+3733017+3733019	LY	EUS	EUS	SNF
373302	3733020+3733021+3733022+3733023+3733025+3733026+3733027+3733029	LY	EUS	EUS	SNF
373303	3733030+3733031+3733032+3733033+3733035+3733036+3733037+3733039	LY	EUS	EUS	SNF
373304	3733040+3733041+3733042+3733043+3733045+3733046+3733047+3733049	LY	EUS	EUS	SNF
373305	3733050+3733051+3733052+3733053+3733055+3733056+3733057+3733059	LY	EUS	EUS	SNF
373306	3733060+3733061+3733062+3733063+3733065+3733066+3733067+3733069	LY	EUS	EUS	SNF
373307	3733070+3733071+3733072+3733073+3733075+3733076+3733077+3733079	LY	EUS	EUS	SNF
373308	3733080+3733081+3733082+3733083+3733085+3733086+3733087+3733089	LY	EUS	EUS	SNF
373309	3733090+3733091+3733092+3733093+3733095+3733096+3733097+3733099	LY	EUS	EUS	SNF
373310	3733100+3733101+3733102+3733103+3733105+3733106+3733107+3733109	LY	EUS	EUS	SNF
373311	3733110+3733111+3733112+3733113+3733115+3733116+3733117+3733119	LY	EUS	EUS	SNF
373312	3733120+3733121+3733122+3733123+3733125+3733126+3733127+3733129	LY	EUS	EUS	SNF
373313	3733130+3733131+3733132+3733133+3733135+3733136+3733137+3733139	LY	EUS	EUS	SNF
373314	3733140+3733141+3733142+3733143+3733145+3733146+3733147+3733149	LY	EUS	EUS	SNF

Above: *St Pancras International is the London base for the Eurostar operation, with sets from all three countries' allocation operating as one pool. Three sets are seen under the wonderful Barlow roof, with French-owned set No. (37)3231 nearest the camera.* **CJM**

Spare DM

Number		Depot	Livery	Owner	Operator
3999	(Spare vehicle used as required to cover for maintenance)	TI	EUS	EUS	EUS

Right: *When the Eurostar fleet was built by Alstom, one extra driving car was produced, which could operate as required without modification in any Eurostar set, either a Three Capitals or North of London unit. The vehicle was allocated the number 373999 and was originally allocated to North Pole, being transferred to Temple Mills, when London operations moved from Waterloo to St Pancras. No. 3999 is seen leading a southbound international train at Ashford. Note the 'Olympic 2012' branding just to the front of the driver's cabside window.* **Tony Christie**

● Ten new Eurostar e320 16-car sets have been ordered from Siemens; these will have a 200mph (320km/h) capacity and seat 900. The sets, scheduled for delivery in 2014, will have the ability to operate throughout Europe. Length: 400m, Power: 16,00kW from 25kV ac and 1.5/3kV dc. Driving cars = 25.7m, Intermediate cars = 14.2m, 32 2-axle bogies per train.

Class 08

Vehicle Length: 29ft 3in (8.91m)
Height: 12ft 8⅝in (3.87m)
Width: 8ft 6in (2.59m)
Engine: English Electric 6K
Horsepower: 400hp (298kW)
Electrical Equipment: English Electric

Number	Depot	Pool	Livery	Owner	Opt'r
08948	TI	GPSS	TTG	EUS	EUS

Right: *Eurostar power cars or half sets which need to be shunted within the depot at Temple Mills frequently require to be hauled by a diesel locomotive. For this purpose, Eurostar own one Class 08 No. 08948. This is a heavily modified loco with drop head Scharfenberg couplers and an extended buffer beam. The loco is painted in two-tone grey livery with wasp warning ends.* **CJM**

First Capital Connect

Passenger Train Operating Companies – First Capital Connect

Address: ✉ Hertford House, 1 Cranwood Street, London, EC1V 9QS
✎ customer.relations.fcc@firstgroup.com
☎ 0845 026 4700
ⓘ www.firstcapitalconnect.co.uk

Managing Director: Neil Lawson
Franchise Dates: 1 April 2006 - 31 March 2015
Principal Routes: London King's Cross-King's Lynn, Peterborough/Cambridge
Moorgate-Hertford Loop and Letchworth
Bedford-Brighton (Thameslink)
Luton-Wimbledon/
Sutton (Thameslink)
Depots: Bedford Cauldwell Walk (BF),
Hornsey (HE),
Brighton (BI)*
* Stabling point
Parent Company: First Group PLC

King's Lynn
Watlington
Downham Market
Littleport
Ely
Waterbeach
Cambridge
Peterborough
Foxton
Huntingdon
Shepreth
St Neots
Meldreth
Sandy
Royston
Bedford
Biggleswade
Ashwell & Morden
Flitwick
Arlesey
Baldock
Harlington
Letchworth
Leagrave
Garden City
Luton
Hitchin
Luton Airport Parkway
Stevenage
Watton-at-Stone
Harpenden
Hertford North
Knebworth
St Albans
Welwyn North
Bayford
Radlett
Welwyn Garden City
Cuffley
Elstree & Borehamwood
Hatfield
Crews Hill
Welham Green
Gordon Hill
Mill Hill Broadway
Brookmans Park
Enfield Chase
Potters Bar
Grange Park
Hendon
Hadley Wood
New Barnet
Winchmore Hill
Cricklewood
Oakleigh Park
Palmers Green
New Southgate
West Hampstead Thameslink
Bowes Park
Kentish Town
Alexandra Palace
Hornsey
Harringay
Drayton Park
Finsbury Park
Highbury & Islington
London King's Cross
Essex Road
Farringdon
Moorgate
Old Street
City Thameslink
London Blackfriars
© TRC.Com Ltd 2011
Elephant & Castle
Loughborough Junction
Herne Hill
London Bridge
Tulse Hill
Streatham
Haydons
East Croydon
Road
Tooting
Wimbledon
Redhill
Mitcham Eastfields
Gatwick Airport
Wimbledon Chase
Three Bridges
Mitcham Junction
Balcombe
South Merton
Hackbridge
Haywards Heath
Carshalton
Morden South
Wivelsfield
Sutton
St Helier
Burgess Hill
Sutton
West
Hassocks
Common
Sutton
Preston Park
Brighton

Class 313/0 & 313/1

Vehicle Length: (Driving) 64ft 11½in (20.75m)		Width: 9ft 3in (2.82m)		
(Inter) 65ft 4¼in (19.92m)		Horsepower: 880hp (656kW)		
Height: 11ft 9in (3.58m)		Seats (total/car): 231S, 74S/83S/74S		

Number	Formation DMSO+PTSO+BDMSO	Depot	Livery	Owner	Operator	Name
313018	62546+71230+62160	HE	FCC	HSB	FCC	
313024	62552+71236+62616	HE	FCC	HSB	FCC	
313025	62553+71237+62617	HE	FCC	HSB	FCC	
313026	62554+71238+62618	HE	FCC	HSB	FCC	
313027	62555+71239+62619	HE	FCC	HSB	FCC	
313028	62556+71240+62620	HE	FCC	HSB	FCC	
313029	62557+71241+62621	HE	FCC	HSB	FCC	
313030	62558+71242+62622	HE	FCC	HSB	FCC	
313031	62559+71243+62623	HE	FCC	HSB	FCC	
313032	62560+71244+62643	HE	FCC	HSB	FCC	
313033	62561+71245+62625	HE	FCC	HSB	FCC	
313035	62563+71247+62627	HE	FCC	HSB	FCC	
313036	62564+71248+62628	HE	FCC	HSB	FCC	
313037	62565+71249+62629	HE	FCC	HSB	FCC	
313038	62566+71250+62630	HE	FCC	HSB	FCC	
313039	62567+71251+62631	HE	FCC	HSB	FCC	
313040	62568+71252+62632	HE	FCC	HSB	FCC	
313041	62569+71253+62633	HE	FCC	HSB	FCC	
313042	62570+71254+62634	HE	FCC	HSB	FCC	
313043	62571+71255+62635	HE	FCC	HSB	FCC	
313044	62572+71256+62636	HE	FCC	HSB	FCC	
313045	62573+71257+62637	HE	FCC	HSB	FCC	
313046	62574+71258+62638	HE	FCC	HSB	FCC	
313047	62575+71259+62639	HE	FCC	HSB	FCC	
313048	62576+71260+62640	HE	FCC	HSB	FCC	
313049	62577+71261+62641	HE	FCC	HSB	FCC	
313050	62578+71262+62649	HE	FCC	HSB	FCC	
313051	62579+71263+62624	HE	FCC	HSB	FCC	
313052	62580+71264+62644	HE	FCC	HSB	FCC	
313053	62581+71265+62645	HE	FCC	HSB	FCC	
313054	62582+71266+62646	HE	FCC	HSB	FCC	*Captain William Leefe Robinson VC*
313055	62583+71267+62647	HE	FCC	HSB	FCC	
313056	62584+71268+62648	HE	FCC	HSB	FCC	
313057	62585+71269+62642	HE	FCC	HSB	FCC	
313058	62586+71270+62650	HE	FCC	HSB	FCC	
313059	62587+71271+62651	HE	FCC	HSB	FCC	
313060	62588+71272+62652	HE	FCC	HSB	FCC	
313061	62589+71273+62653	HE	FCC	HSB	FCC	
313062	62590+71274+62654	HE	FCC	HSB	FCC	
313063	62591+71275+62655	HE	FCC	HSB	FCC	
313064	62592+71276+62656	HE	FCC	HSB	FCC	
313122	62550+71234+61614	HE	FCC	HSB	FCC	
313123	62551+71235+61615	HE	FCC	HSB	FCC	
313134	62562+71246+61626	HE	FCC	HSB	FCC	*City of London*

Right: *The original dual power 1972-design EMUs for the Moorgate electrification of the Great Northern route are still in service, now working for First Capital Connect. All sets are now painted in FCC livery and allocated to Hornsey depot. Set No. 313024 is seen on the underground section of the network at Moorgate.*
CJM

First Capital Connect

Class 317/3

Vehicle Length: (Driving) 65ft 0¾in (19.83m) Width: 9ft 3in (2.82m)
(Inter) 65ft 4¼in (19.92m) Horsepower: 1,000hp (746kW)
Height: 12ft 1½in (3.58m) Seats (total/car): 22F/269S, 74S/79S/22F-46S/70S

Number	Formation DTSO+MSO+TCO+DTSO	Depot	Livery	Owner	Operator	Name
317337	77036+62671+71613+77084	HE	FCC	ANG	FCC	
317338	77037+62698+71614+77085	HE	FCC	ANG	FCC	
317339	77038+62699+71615+77086	HE	FCC	ANG	FCC	
317340	77039+62700+71616+77087	HE	FCC	ANG	FCC	
317341	77040+62701+71617+77088	HE	FCC	ANG	FCC	
317342	77041+62702+71618+77089	HE	FCC	ANG	FCC	
317343	77042+62703+71619+77090	HE	FCC	ANG	FCC	
317344	77029+62690+71620+77091	HE	FCC	ANG	FCC	
317345	77044+62705+71621+77092	HE	FCC	ANG	FCC	*Driver John Webb*
317346	77045+62706+71622+77093	HE	FCC	ANG	FCC	
317347	77046+62707+71623+77094	HE	FCC	ANG	FCC	
317348	77047+62708+71624+77095	HE	FCC	ANG	FCC	*Richard A. Jenner*

Left: *The First Capital Connect 'Urban Lights' livery is applied to most trains operated by FCC, which looks very smart when clean. Class 317/3 No. 317341 is illustrated. These Class 317s were originally built for the 'Bed-Pan' electrification between Bedford and London St Pancras, but were later displaced, by the introduction of Class 319s.* **Brian Morrison**

Class 319/0

Vehicle Length: (Driving) 65ft 0¾in (19.83m) Width: 9ft 3in (2.82m)
(Inter) 65ft 4¼in (19.92m) Horsepower: 1,326hp (990kW)
Height: 11ft 9in (3.58m) Seats (total/car): 319S, 82S/82S/77S/78S

Number	Formation DTSO(A)+MSO+TSO+DTSO(B)	Depot	Livery	Owner	Operator	Name
319001	77291+62891+71772+77290	SU	FCC	PTR	FCC	
319002	77293+62892+71773+77292	SU	FCC	PTR	FCC	
319003	77295+62893+71774+77294	SU	FCC	PTR	FCC	
319004	77297+62894+71775+77296	SU	FCC	PTR	FCC	
319005	77299+62895+71776+77298	SU	FCC	PTR	FCC	
319006	77301+62896+71777+77300	SU	FCC	PTR	FCC	
319007	77303+62897+71778+77302	SU	FCC	PTR	FCC	
319008	77305+62898+71779+77304	SU	SOU	PTR	FCC	
319009	77307+62899+71780+77306	SU	SOU	PTR	FCC	
319010	77309+62900+71781+77308	SU	FCC	PTR	FCC	
319011	77311+62901+71782+77310	SU	SOU	PTR	FCC	*John Ruskin College*
319012	77313+62902+71783+77312	SU	SOU	PTR	FCC	
319013	77315+62903+71784+77314	SU	SOU	PTR	FCC	*The Surrey Hills*

Class 319/2

Vehicle Length: (Driving) 65ft 0¾in (19.83m) Width: 9ft 3in (2.82m)
(Inter) 65ft 4¼in (19.92m) Horsepower: 1,326hp (990kW)
Height: 11ft 9in (3.58m) Seats (total/car): 18F/212S, 64S/60S/52S/18F-36S

Number	Formation DTSO+MSO+TSO+DTCO	Depot	Livery	Owner	Operator	Name/Notes
319214	77317+62904+71785+77316	SU	SOU	PTR	FCC	
319215	77319+62905+71786+77318	SU	ADV	PTR	FCC	*(Visit Switzerland livery)*
319216	77321+62906+71787+77320	SU	SOU	PTR	FCC	
319217	77323+62907+71788+77322	BF	SOU	PTR	FCC	*Brighton*
319218	77325+62908+71789+77324	BF	SOU	PTR	FCC	*Croydon*
319219	77327+62909+71790+77326	BF	SOU	PTR	FCC	
319220	77329+62910+71791+77328	BF	SOU	PTR	FCC	

Class 319/3

Vehicle Length: (Driving) 65ft 0¾in (19.83m) Width: 9ft 3in (2.82m)
(Inter) 65ft 4¼in (19.92m) Horsepower: 1,326hp (990kW)
Height: 11ft 9in (3.58m) Seats (total/car): 300S, 70S/78S/74S/78S

Number	Formation DTSO(A)+MSO+TSO+DTSO(B)	Depot	Livery	Owner	Operator	Name
319361	77459+63043+71929+77458	BF	FCC	PTR	FCC	
319362	77461+63044+71930+77460	BF	FCC	PTR	FCC	
319363	77463+63045+71931+77462	BF	FCC	PTR	FCC	
319364	77465+63046+71932+77464	BF	TLP	PTR	FCC	*Transforming Blackfriars*
319365	77467+63047+71933+77466	BF	TLP	PTR	FCC	*Transforming Farringdon*
319366	77469+63048+71934+77468	BF	FCC	PTR	FCC	
319367	77471+63049+71935+77470	BF	FCC	PTR	FCC	
319368	77473+63050+71936+77472	BF	FCC	PTR	FCC	
319369	77475+63051+71937+77474	BF	FCC	PTR	FCC	
317370	77477+63052+71938+77476	BF	FCC	PTR	FCC	
319371	77479+63053+71939+77478	BF	FCC	PTR	FCC	
319372	77481+63054+71940+77480	BF	FCC	PTR	FCC	
319373	77483+63055+71941+77482	BF	FCC	PTR	FCC	
319374	77485+63056+71942+77484	BF	FCC	PTR	FCC	*Bedford Cauldwell Walk TMD*
319375	77487+63057+71943+77486	BF	FCC	PTR	FCC	
319376	77489+63058+71944+77488	BF	FCC	PTR	FCC	
319377	77491+63059+71945+77490	BF	FCC	PTR	FCC	
319378	77493+63060+71946+77492	BF	FCC	PTR	FCC	
319379	77495+63061+71947+77494	BF	FCC	PTR	FCC	
319380	77497+63082+71948+77496	BF	FCC	PTR	FCC	
319381	77973+63093+71978+77974	BF	FCC	PTR	FCC	
319382	77975+63094+71980+77976	BF	FCC	PTR	FCC	
319383	77977+63096+71981+77978	BF	FCC	PTR	FCC	
319384	77979+63096+71982+77980	BF	FCC	PTR	FCC	
319385	77981+63097+71983+77982	BF	FCC	PTR	FCC	
319386	77983+63098+71984+77984	BF	FCC	PTR	FCC	

Class 319/4

Vehicle Length: (Driving) 65ft 0¾in (19.83m) Width: 9ft 3in (2.82m)
(Inter) 65ft 4¼in (19.92m) Horsepower: 1,326hp (990kW)
Height: 11ft 9in (3.58m) Seats (total/car): 12F/277S, 12F-54S/77S/72S/74S

Number	Formation DTCO+MSO+TSO+DTSO	Depot	Livery	Owner	Operator	Name
319421	77331+62911+71792+77330	BF	FCC	PTR	FCC	
319422	77333+62912+71793+77332	BF	FCC	PTR	FCC	
319423	77335+62913+71794+77334	BF	FCC	PTR	FCC	
319424	77337+62914+71795+77336	BF	FCC	PTR	FCC	
319425	77339+62915+71796+77338	BF	FCC	PTR	FCC	*Transforming Travel*
319426	77341+62916+71797+77340	BF	FCC	PTR	FCC	
319427	77343+62917+71798+77342	BF	FCC	PTR	FCC	
319428	77345+62918+71799+77344	BF	FCC	PTR	FCC	
319429	77347+62919+71800+77346	BF	FCC	PTR	FCC	
319430	77349+62920+71801+77348	BF	FCC	PTR	FCC	
319431	77351+62921+71802+77350	BF	FCC	PTR	FCC	
319432	77353+62922+71803+77352	BF	FCC	PTR	FCC	
319433	77355+62923+71804+77354	BF	FCC	PTR	FCC	
319434	77357+62924+71805+77356	BF	FCC	PTR	FCC	
319435	77359+62925+71806+77358	BF	FCC	PTR	FCC	*Adrian Jackson-Robbins Chairman 1987-2007 Association of Public Transport Users*
319436	77361+62926+71807+77360	BF	FCC	PTR	FCC	
319437	77363+62927+71808+77362	BF	FCC	PTR	FCC	
319438	77365+62928+71809+77364	BF	FCC	PTR	FCC	
319439	77367+62929+71810+77366	BF	FCC	PTR	FCC	
319440	77369+62930+71811+77368	BF	FCC	PTR	FCC	
319441	77371+62931+71812+77370	BF	FCC	PTR	FCC	
319442	77373+62932+71813+77372	BF	FCC	PTR	FCC	
319443	77375+62933+71814+77374	BF	FCC	PTR	FCC	
319444	77377+62934+71815+77376	BF	FCC	PTR	FCC	
319445	77379+62935+71816+77378	BF	FCC	PTR	FCC	

First Capital Connect

319446	77381+62936+71817+77380	BF	FCC	PTR	FCC	*St Pancras International*
319447	77431+62961+71866+77430	BF	FCC	PTR	FCC	
319448	77433+62962+71867+77432	BF	FCC	PTR	FCC	
319449	77435+62963+71868+77434	BF	FCC	PTR	FCC	*King's Cross Thameslink*
319450	77437+62964+71869+77436	BF	FCC	PTR	FCC	
319451	77439+62965+71870+77438	BF	FCC	PTR	FCC	
319452	77441+62966+71871+77440	BF	FCC	PTR	FCC	
319453	77443+62967+71872+77442	BF	FCC	PTR	FCC	
319454	77445+62968+71873+77444	BF	FCC	PTR	FCC	
319455	77447+62969+71874+77446	BF	FCC	PTR	FCC	
319456	77449+62970+71875+77448	BF	FCC	PTR	FCC	
319457	77451+62971+71876+77450	BF	FCC	PTR	FCC	
319458	77453+62972+71877+77452	BF	FCC	PTR	FCC	
319459	77455+62973+71878+77454	BF	FCC	PTR	FCC	
319460	77457+62974+71879+77456	BF	FCC	PTR	FCC	

Left: *The Thameslink route services operated by First Capital Connect are formed of Class 319 stock, based at Bedford and Selhurst. Most units are painted in First Group 'Urban Lights' corporate colours, as shown on set No. 319429.* **John Wills**

Class 321/4

Vehicle Length: (Driving) 65ft 0¾in (19.83m)
(Inter) 65ft 4¼in (19.92m)
Height: 12ft 4¾in (3.78m)
Width: 9ft 3in (2.82m)
Horsepower: 1,328hp (996kW)
Seats (total/car): 28F/271S, 28F-40S/79S/74S/78S

Number	Formation DMCO+MSO+TSO+DMSO	Depot	Livery	Owner	Operator	Name
321401	78095+63063+71949+77943	HE	FCC	HSB	FCC	
321402	78096+63064+71950+77944	HE	FCC	HSB	FCC	
321403	78097+63065+71951+77945	HE	FCC	HSB	FCC	*Stewart Fleming Signalman King's Cross*
321404	78098+63066+71952+77946	HE	FCC	HSB	FCC	
321405	78099+63067+71953+77947	HE	FCC	HSB	FCC	
321406	78100+63068+71954+77948	HE	FCC	HSB	FCC	
321407	78101+63069+71955+77949	HE	FCC	HSB	FCC	
321408	78102+63070+71956+77959	HE	FCC	HSB	FCC	
321409	78103+63071+71957+77960	HE	FCC	HSB	FCC	
321410	78104+63072+71958+77961	HE	FCC	HSB	FCC	
321418	78112+63080+71968+77962	HE	FCC	HSB	FCC	
321419	78113+63081+71969+77963	HE	FCC	HSB	FCC	
321420	78114+63082+71970+77964	HE	FCC	HSB	FCC	

Left: *To increase capacity on the FCC Great Northern route from London King's Cross, a batch of 10 Class 321/4 sets are allocated to Hornsey and are refreshed to FCC standards and carry First 'Urban Lights' livery. The sets were transferred to FCC following displacement from Silverlink (London Overground) services at Bletchley. Set No. 321406 in FCC colours and 321405 in Silverlink livery pass Alexandra Palace in mid-2010.* **Brian Morrison**

Class 365
Networker Express

Vehicle Length: (Driving) 68ft 6½in (20.89m)	Width: 9ft 2½in (2.81m)
(Inter) 65ft 9¾in (20.89m)	Horsepower: 1,684hp (1,256kW)
Height: 12ft 4½in (3.77m)	Seats (total/car): 24F/239S, 12F-56S/59S/68S/12F-56S

Number	Formation DMCO(A)+TSO+PTSO+DMCO(B)	Depot	Livery	Owner	Operator	Name
365501	65894+72241+72240+65935	HE	FCC	HSB	FCC	
365502	65895+72243+72242+65936	HE	FCC	HSB	FCC	
365503	65896+72245+72244+65937	HE	FCC	HSB	FCC	
365504	65897+72247+72246+65938	HE	FCC	HSB	FCC	
365505	65898+72249+72248+65939	HE	FCC	HSB	FCC	
365506	65899+72251+72250+65940	HE	FCC	HSB	FCC	
365507	65900+72253+72252+65941	HE	FCC	HSB	FCC	
365508	65901+72255+72254+65942	HE	FCC	HSB	FCC	
365509	65902+72257+72256+65943	HE	FCC	HSB	FCC	
365510	65903+72259+72258+65944	HE	FCC	HSB	FCC	
365511	65904+72261+72260+65945	HE	FCC	HSB	FCC	
365512	65905+72263+72262+65946	HE	FCC	HSB	FCC	
365513	65906+72265+72264+65947	HE	FCC	HSB	FCC	Hornsey Depot
365514	65907+72267+72266+65948	HE	FCC	HSB	FCC	Captain George Vancouver
365515	65908+72269+72268+65949	HE	FCC	HSB	FCC	
365516	65909+72271+72270+65950	HE	FCC	HSB	FCC	
365517	65910+72273+72272+65951	HE	FCC	HSB	FCC	
365518	65911+72275+72274+65952	HE	FCC	HSB	FCC	The Fenman
365519	65912+72277+72276+65953	HE	FCC	HSB	FCC	
365520	65913+72279+72278+65954	HE	FCC	HSB	FCC	
365521	65914+72281+72280+65955	HE	FCC	HSB	FCC	
365522	65915+72283+72282+65956	HE	FCC	HSB	FCC	
365523	65916+72285+72284+65957	HE	FCC	HSB	FCC	
365524	65917+72287+72286+65958	HE	FCC	HSB	FCC	
365525	65918+72289+72288+65959	HE	FCC	HSB	FCC	
365526(S)	65919+72291+72290+65960	HE	NSE	HSB	¤	
365527	65920+72293+72292+65961	HE	FCC	HSB	FCC	
365528	65921+72296+72294+65962	HE	FCC	HSB	FCC	Robert Stripe Passengers' Champion
365529	65922+72297+72296+65963	HE	FCC	HSB	FCC	
365530	65923+72299+72298+65964	HE	FCC	HSB	FCC	The Interlink Partnership Promoting Integrated Transport Since 1999
365531	65924+72301+72300+65965	HE	FCC	HSB	FCC	
365532	65925+72303+72302+65966	HE	FCC	HSB	FCC	
365533	65926+72305+72304+65967	HE	FCC	HSB	FCC	
365534	65927+72307+72306+65968	HE	FCC	HSB	FCC	
365535	65928+72309+72308+65969	HE	FCC	HSB	FCC	
365536	65929+72311+72310+65970	HE	FCC	HSB	FCC	
365537	65930+72313+72312+65971	HE	FCC	HSB	FCC	
365538	65931+72315+72314+65972	HE	FCC	HSB	FCC	
365539	65932+72317+72316+65973	HE	FCC	HSB	FCC	
365540	65933+72319+72318+65974	HE	FCC	HSB	FCC	
365541	65934+72321+72320+65975	HE	FCC	HSB	FCC	

¤ Set No. 365526 is stored at Bombardier Crewe with extensive collision damage sustained in the Potters Bar derailment.

Right: *Hornsey depot in North London is the home for the Great Northern allocation of FCC stock, with sizeable heavy maintenance, cleaning and stabling sidings. Three Class 365 'Networker Express' units are seen inside the repair shed. From left to right these are sets Nos. 365514, 365532 and 365534.* **CJM**

First Capital Connect

Class 377/5
Electrostar

Vehicle Length: (Driving) 66ft 9in (20.40m)
(Inter) 65ft 6in (19.99m)
Height: 12ft 4in (3.77m)

Width: 9ft 2in (2.80m)
Horsepower: 2,012hp (1,500kW) (ac), dual voltage sets
Seats (total/car): 20F-221S, 10F-48/69S/56S/10F-48S

Number	Formation	Depot	Livery	Owner	Operator
	DMCO(A)+MSO+PTSO+DMCO(B)				
377501	73501+75901+74901+73601	BF	FCC	PTR	FCC *(Sub-lease from Southern)*
377502	73502+75902+74902+73602	BF	FCC	PTR	FCC *(Sub-lease from Southern)*
377503	73503+75903+74903+73603	BF	FCC	PTR	FCC *(Sub-lease from Southern)*
377504	73504+75904+74904+73604	BF	FCC	PTR	FCC *(Sub-lease from Southern)*
377505	73505+75905+74905+73605	BF	FCC	PTR	FCC *(Sub-lease from Southern)*
377506	73506+75906+74906+73606	BF	FCC	PTR	FCC *(Sub-lease from Southern)*
377507	73507+75907+74907+73607	BF	FCC	PTR	FCC *(Sub-lease from Southern)*
377508	73508+75908+74908+73608	BF	FCC	PTR	FCC *(Sub-lease from Southern)*
377509	73509+75909+74909+73609	BF	FCC	PTR	FCC *(Sub-lease from Southern)*
377510	73510+75910+74910+73610	BF	FCC	PTR	FCC *(Sub-lease from Southern)*
377511	73511+75911+74911+73611	BF	FCC	PTR	FCC *(Sub-lease from Southern)*
377512	73512+75912+74912+73612	BF	FCC	PTR	FCC *(Sub-lease from Southern)*
377513	73513+75913+74913+73613	BF	FCC	PTR	FCC *(Sub-lease from Southern)*
377514	73514+75914+74914+73614	BF	FCC	PTR	FCC *(Sub-lease from Southern)*
377515	73515+75915+74915+73615	BF	FCC	PTR	FCC *(Sub-lease from Southern)*
377516	73516+75916+74916+73616	BF	FCC	PTR	FCC *(Sub-lease from Southern)*
377517	73517+75917+74917+73617	BF	FCC	PTR	FCC *(Sub-lease from Southern)*
377518	73518+75918+74918+73618	BF	FCC	PTR	FCC *(Sub-lease from Southern)*
377519	73519+75919+74919+73619	BF	FCC	PTR	FCC *(Sub-lease from Southern)*
377520	73520+75920+74920+73620	BF	FCC	PTR	FCC *(Sub-lease from Southern)*
377521	73521+75921+74921+73621	BF	FCC	PTR	FCC *(Sub-lease from Southern)*
377522	73522+75922+74922+73622	BF	FCC	PTR	FCC *(Sub-lease from Southern)*
377523	73523+75923+74923+73623	BF	FCC	PTR	FCC *(Sub-lease from Southern)*

Below: *First Capital Connect operates 23 Class 377/5 Bombardier Electrostar sets on its Bedford-Brighton core route. The sets were originally ordered for use by Southern, but transferred to FCC due to stock shortages. The sets carry the First Capital Connect 'Urban Lights' colours and are allocated to Bedford Cauldwell Walk depot. Set No. 377517 departs from East Croydon on 2 September 2010 forming a Bedford to Brighton service.* **CJM**

Passenger Train Operating Companies - First Capital Connect

First Great Western

Address:	✉ Milford House, 1 Milford Street, Swindon, SN1 1HL
	⌕ fgwfeedback@firstgroup.com
	✆ 08457 000125
	ⓘ www.firstgreatwestern.co.uk
Managing Director:	Mark Hopwood
Franchise Dates:	1 April 2006 - 31 March 2016
Principal Routes:	Paddington-Penzance/Paignton, Bristol, Swansea
	Thames Valley local lines
	Local lines in Bristol, Exeter, Plymouth and Cornwall
	Bristol-Weymouth, Portsmouth/Brighton
Depots:	Exeter (EX), Old Oak Common (OO), Laira (LA), Landore (LE),
	St Philip's Marsh (PM), Penzance (PZ), Reading (RG)
Parent Company:	First Group PLC

Class 08

Vehicle Length: 29ft 3in (8.91m)	Engine: English Electric 6K
Height: 12ft 8⅝in (3.87m)	Horsepower: 400hp (298kW)
Width: 8ft 6in (2.59m)	Electrical Equipment: English Electric

Number	Depot	Pool	Livery	Owner	Operator
08410	PZ	EFSH	GWG	FGP	FGW
08483	OO	EFSH	GWG	FGP	FGW
08641	LA	EFSH	FGB	FGP	FGW
08644	LA	EFSH	GWG	FGP	FGW
08645	LA	EFSH	GWG	FGP	FGW
08663(S)	PM	EFSH	GWG	FGP	FGW

Number	Depot	Pool	Livery	Owner	Operator
08795	LE	EFSH	GWG	FGP	FGW
08822	LE	EFSH	GWG	FGP	FGW
08836	OC	EFSH	GWG	FGP	FGW

Names applied

08483	*Dusty - Driver David Miller*
08645	*Mike Baggott*

Above: *First Great Western operating by far the largest fleet of HST stock has a constant need to shunt vehicles at depots on a daily basis. The operator therefore has a fleet of Class 08s on its books. All are fitted with either swing or easily fitted buck-eye couplers allowing attachment of a standard hook coupler to a buck-eye coupling on HST stock. The locos are allocated to the five depots which deal with HST stock: Plymouth Laira, Penzance, Old Oak Common, Bristol St Philip's Marsh and Swansea Landore. No. 08836 in part FGW and part BR blue is shown at Old Oak Common* **Nathan Williamson**

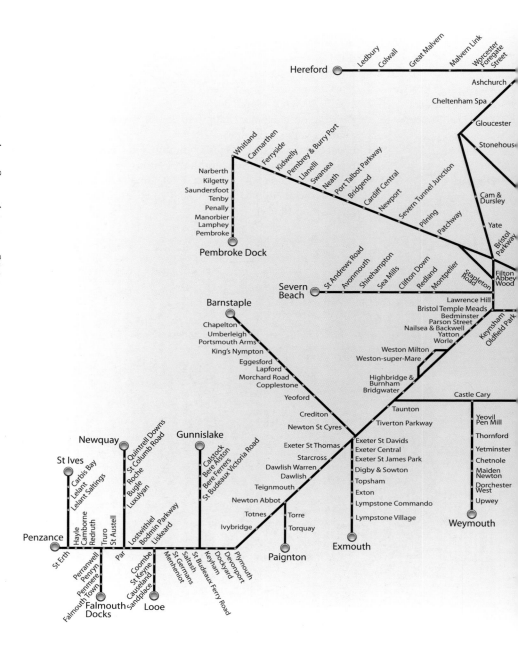

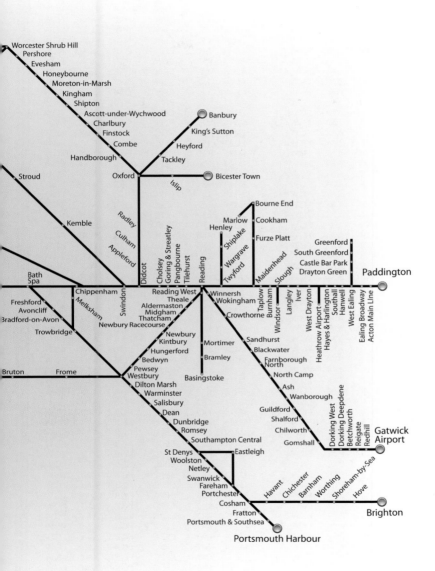

© TRC.Com Ltd 2011

First Great Western

Class 43 – HST

Vehicle Length: 58ft 5in (18.80m)
Height: 12ft 10in (3.90m)
Width: 8ft 11in (2.73m)
Engine: MTU 16V4000 R41R
Horsepower: 2,250hp (1,680kW)
Electrical Equipment: Brush

Number	Depot	Pool	Livery	Owner	Operator
43002	LA	EFPC	FGB	ANG	FGW
43003	LA	EFPC	FGB	ANG	FGW
43004	LA	EFPC	FGB	ANG	FGW
43005	LA	EFPC	FGB	ANG	FGW
43009	LA	EFPC	FGB	ANG	FGW
43010	LA	EFPC	FGB	ANG	FGW
43012	LA	EFPC	FGB	ANG	FGW
43015	LA	EFPC	FGB	ANG	FGW
43016	LA	EFPC	FGB	ANG	FGW
43017	LA	EFPC	FGB	ANG	FGW
43018	LA	EFPC	FGB	ANG	FGW
43020	LA	EFPC	FGB	ANG	FGW
43021	LA	EFPC	FGB	ANG	FGW
43022	LA	EFPC	FGB	ANG	FGW
43023	LA	EFPC	FGB	ANG	FGW
43024	LA	EFPC	FGB	ANG	FGW
43025	LA	EFPC	FGB	ANG	FGW
43026	LA	EFPC	FGB	ANG	FGW
43027	LA	EFPC	FGB	ANG	FGW
43028	LA	EFPC	FGB	ANG	FGW
43029	LA	EFPC	FGB	ANG	FGW
43030	LA	EFPC	FGB	ANG	FGW
43031	LA	EFPC	FGB	ANG	FGW
43032	LA	EFPC	FGB	ANG	FGW
43033	LA	EFPC	FGB	ANG	FGW
43034	LA	EFPC	FGB	ANG	FGW
43035	LA	EFPC	FGB	ANG	FGW
43036	LA	EFPC	FGB	ANG	FGW
43037	LA	EFPC	FGB	ANG	FGW
43040	LA	EFPC	FGB	ANG	FGW
43041	OO	EFPC	FGB	ANG	FGW
43042	OO	EFPC	FGB	ANG	FGW
43053	LE	EFPC	FGB	PTR	FGW
43056	LE	EFPC	FGB	PTR	FGW
43063	OO	EFPC	FGB	PTR	FGW
43069	OO	EFPC	FGB	PTR	FGW
43070	OO	EFPC	FGB	PTR	FGW
43071	OO	EFPC	FGB	PTR	FGW
43078	OO	EFPC	FGB	PTR	FGW
43079	OO	EFPC	FGB	PTR	FGW
43086	OO	EFPC	FGB	PTR	FGW
43087	OO	EFPC	FGB	PTR	FGW
43088	OO	EFPC	FGB	PTR	FGW
43091	OO	EFPC	FGB	PTR	FGW
43092	OO	EFPC	FGB	PTR	FGW
43093	OO	EFPC	FGB	PTR	FGW
43094	OO	EFPC	FGB	PTR	FGW
43097	OO	EFPC	FGB	PTR	FGW
43098	OO	EFPC	FGB	PTR	FGW
43122	OO	EFPC	FGB	FGP	FGW
43124	LE	EFPC	FGB	ANG	FGW
43125	LE	EFPC	FGB	ANG	FGW
43126	LE	EFPC	FGB	ANG	FGW
43127	LE	EFPC	FGB	ANG	FGW
43128	LE	EFPC	FGB	ANG	FGW
43129	LE	EFPC	FGB	ANG	FGW
43130	LE	EFPC	FGB	ANG	FGW
43131	LE	EFPC	FGB	ANG	FGW
43132	LE	EFPC	FGB	ANG	FGW
43133	LE	EFPC	FGB	ANG	FGW
43134	LE	EFPC	FGB	ANG	FGW
43135	LE	EFPC	FGB	ANG	FGW
43136	LE	EFPC	FGB	ANG	FGW
43137	LE	EFPC	FGB	ANG	FGW
43138	LE	EFPC	FGB	ANG	FGW
43139	LE	EFPC	FGB	ANG	FGW
43140	LE	EFPC	FGB	ANG	FGW
43141	LE	EFPC	FGB	ANG	FGW
43142	LE	EFPC	FGB	ANG	FGW
43143	LE	EFPC	FGB	ANG	FGW
43144	LE	EFPC	FGB	ANG	FGW
43145	LE	EFPC	FGB	ANG	FGW
43146	LE	EFPC	FGB	ANG	FGW
43147	LE	EFPC	FGB	ANG	FGW
43148	LE	EFPC	FGB	ANG	FGW
43149	LE	EFPC	FGB	ANG	FGW
43150	LE	EFPC	FGB	ANG	FGW
43151	LE	EFPC	FGB	ANG	FGW
43152	LE	EFPC	FGB	ANG	FGW
43153	OO	EFPC	FGB	FGP	FGW
43154	OO	EFPC	FGB	FGP	FGW
43155	OO	EFPC	FGB	FGP	FGW
43156	OO	EFPC	FGB	PTR	FGW
43158	OO	EFPC	FGB	FGP	FGW
43159	OO	EFPC	FGB	PTR	FGW
43160	OO	EFPC	FGB	PTR	FGW
43161	OO	EFPC	FGB	PTR	FGW
43162	OO	EFPC	FGB	ANG	FGW
43163	OO	EFPC	FGB	ANG	FGW
43164	OO	EFPC	FGB	ANG	FGW
43165	OO	EFPC	FGB	ANG	FGW
43168	OO	EFPC	FGB	ANG	FGW
43169	OO	EFPC	FGB	ANG	FGW
43170	OO	EFPC	FGB	ANG	FGW
43171	OO	EFPC	FGB	ANG	FGW
43172	OO	EFPC	FGB	ANG	FGW
43174	OO	EFPC	FGB	ANG	FGW
43175	OO	EFPC	FGB	ANG	FGW
43176	OO	EFPC	FGB	ANG	FGW
43177	OO	EFPC	FGB	ANG	FGW
43179	OO	EFPC	FGB	ANG	FGW
43180	OO	EFPC	FGB	PTR	FGW
43181	OO	EFPC	FGB	ANG	FGW
43182	OO	EFPC	FGB	ANG	FGW
43183	OO	EFPC	FGB	ANG	FGW
43185	OO	EFPC	FGB	ANG	FGW
43186	OO	EFPC	FGB	ANG	FGW
43187	OO	EFPC	FGB	ANG	FGW
43188	OO	EFPC	FGB	ANG	FGW
43189	OO	EFPC	FGB	ANG	FGW
43190	OO	EFPC	FGB	ANG	FGW
43191	OO	EFPC	FGB	ANG	FGW
43192	OO	EFPC	FGB	ANG	FGW
43193	OO	EFPC	FGB	PTR	FGW
43194	OO	EFPC	FGB	FGP	FGW
43195	OO	EFPC	FGB	PTR	FGW
43196	OO	EFPC	FGB	PTR	FGW
43197	OO	EFPC	FGB	PTR	FGW
43198	OO	EFPC	FGB	FGP	FGW

Names applied

43003	*Isambard Kingdom Brunel*
43004	*First for the Future / First ar gyfer y dyfodoi*
43009	*First Transforming Travel*
43021	*David Austin – Cartoonist*
43025	*The Institution of Railway Operators*
43027	*Glorious Devon*
43030	*Christian Lewis Trust*
43033	*Driver Brian Cooper 15 June 1947 – 5 October 1989*
43037	*Penydarren*
43040	*Bristol St Philip's Marsh*
43053	*University of Worcester*
43056	*Royal British Legion*
43070	*The Corps of Royal Electrical and Mechanical Engineers*
43087	*11 Explosive Ordnance Disposal Regiment Royal Logistic Corps*
43097	*Environment Agency*
43127	*Sir Peter Parker 1924-2002 – Cotswold Line 150*
43132	*We Save the Children - Will You?*
43137	*Newton Abbot 150*
43139	*Driver Stan Martin 25 June 1960 – 6 November 2004*
43143	*Stroud 700*
43156	*Dartington International Summer School*
43163	*Exeter Panel Signal Box 21st Anniversary 2009*
43165	*Prince Michael of Kent*
43169	*The National Trust*
43175	*GWR 175th Anniversary*
43179	*Pride of Laira*
43185	*Great Western*
43189	*Railway Heritage Trust*
43198	*Oxfordshire 2007*

Below: *FGW's HST fleet has all been refurbished in the last five years, with power cars re-engined to include an MTU power unit. Performance is good with few on line failures. All power cars and passenger vehicles are painted in First Great Western livery. A full HST set led by power car No. 43137 arrives at Newport with a Swansea service.* **CJM**

Class 57/6

Vehicle Length: 63ft 6in (19.38m)	Engine: EMD 645-12E3
Height: 12ft 10½sin (3.91m)	Horsepower: 2,500hp (1,860kW)
Width: 9ft 2in (2.79m)	Electrical Equipment: Brush

Number	Depot	Pool	Livery	Owner	Operator	Name
57602 (47337)	OO	EFOO	FGB	PTR	FGW	*Restormel Castle*
57603 (47349)	OO	EFOO	GWG	PTR	FGW	*Tintagel Castle*
57604 (47209)	OO	EFOO	GWR	PTR	FGW	*Pendennis Castle*
57605 (47206)	OO	EFOO	FGB	PTR	FGW	*Totnes Castle*

Right: *FGW operate four Porterbrook-owned Class 57/6 locos dedicated to the overnight sleeper services between London and Penzance. All are allocated to Old Oak Common. In 2010 to mark the 175th anniversary of the Great Western Railway, No. 57604 was repainted into mock Great Western green livery and is illustrated at Exeter St Davids.* **Tony Christie**

First Great Western

HST Passenger Fleet

Vehicle Length: 75ft 0in (22.86m) Width: 8ft 11in (2.71m)
Height: 12ft 9in (3.88m) Bogie Type: BT10

Passenger Train Operating Companies - First Great Western

GN2G - TSRMB *Seating 70S*

Number		Depot	Livery	Owner
40101	(42170)	LA	FGW	PTR
40102	(42223)	LA	FGW	PTR
40103	(42316)	LA	FGW	PTR
40104	(42254)	LA	FGW	PTR
40105	(42084)	LA	FGW	PTR
40106	(42162)	LA	FGW	PTR
40107	(42334)	LA	FGW	PTR
40108	(42314)	LA	FGW	PTR
40109	(42262)	LA	FGW	PTR
40110	(42187)	LA	FGW	PTR
40111	(42248)	LA	FGW	PTR
40112	(42336)	LA	FGW	PTR
40113	(42309)	LA	FGW	PTR
40114	(42086)	LA	FGW	PTR
40115	(42320)	LA	FGW	PTR
40116	(42147)	LA	FGW	PTR
40117	(42249)	LA	FGW	PTR
40118	(42338)	LA	FGW	PTR
40119	(42090)	LA	FGW	PTR

GN1G - TRFB *Seating 23F*

Number	Depot	Livery	Owner
40204	LA	FGW	ANG
40205	LA	FGW	ANG
40207	LA	FGW	ANG
40210	LA	FGW	ANG
40221	LA	FGW	ANG
40231	LA	FGW	ANG

GK1G - TRFB *Seating 17F*

Number	Depot	Livery	Owner
40703	LA	FGW	ANG
40707	LA	FGW	ANG
40710	LA	FGW	ANG
40713	LA	FGW	ANG
40715	LA	FGW	ANG
40716	LA	FGW	ANG
40718	OO	FGW	ANG
40721	LA	FGW	ANG
40722	LA	FGW	ANG
40724¤	LA	FGW	ANG
40725¤	LA	FGW	ANG
40726¤	LA	FGW	ANG
40727	LA	FGW	ANG
40733	LA	FGW	ANG
40734	LA	FGW	ANG
40736¤	OO	FGW	ANG
40738¤	LA	FGW	ANG
40739	LA	FGW	ANG
40743	LA	FGW	ANG
40744¤	LA	FGW	ANG
40745¤	LA	FGW	ANG
40752	LA	FGW	ANG
40755	LA	FGW	ANG
40757	LA	FGW	ANG

GL1G - TRFB *Seating 17F*

Number	Depot	Livery	Owner
40801	OO	FGW	PTR
40802	OO	FGW	PTR
40803	OO	FGW	PTR
40806	OO	FGW	PTR
40807	OO	FGW	PTR
40808	OO	FGW	PTR
40809	OO	FGW	PTR
40810	OO	FGW	PTR
40811	OO	FGW	PTR

GN1G - TRB *Seating 23F*

Number	Depot	Livery	Owner
40900	LA	FGW	FGP
40901	LA	FGW	FGP
40902	LA	FGW	FGP
40903	LA	FGW	FGP
40904	LA	FGW	FGP

GH1G - TF *Seating 48F*

Number	Depot	Livery	Owner
41003	LA	FGW	ANG
41004	OO	FGW	ANG
41005	OO	FGW	ANG
41006	OO	FGW	ANG
41007	OO	FGW	ANG
41008	OO	FGW	ANG
41009	LA	FGW	ANG
41010	LA	FGW	ANG
41011	LA	FGW	ANG
41012	LA	FGW	ANG
41015	LA	FGW	ANG
41016	LA	FGW	ANG
41017	OO	FGW	ANG
41018	OO	FGW	ANG
41019	LA	FGW	ANG
41020	LA	FGW	ANG
41021	LA	FGW	ANG
41022	LA	FGW	ANG
41023	LA	FGW	ANG
41024	LA	FGW	ANG
41027	OO	FGW	ANG
41028	OO	FGW	ANG
41029	OO	FGW	ANG
41030	OO	FGW	ANG
41031	LA	FGW	ANG
41032	LA	FGW	ANG
41033	OO	FGW	ANG
41034	OO	FGW	ANG
41037	LA	FGW	ANG
41038	LA	FGW	ANG
41045	LA	FGW	FGP
41051	LA	FGW	ANG
41052	LA	FGW	ANG
41055	OO	FGW	ANG
41056	OO	FGW	ANG
41059	LA	FGW	FGP
41065	OO	FGW	ANG
41081	OO	FGW	PTR
41085	LA	FGW	FGP
41086	LA	FGW	FGP
41089	OO	FGW	ANG
41093	LA	FGW	ANG
41094	LA	FGW	ANG
41096	LA	FGW	PTR
41101	OO	FGW	ANG
41102	OO	FGW	ANG
41103	LA	FGW	ANG
41104	LA	FGW	ANG
41105	LA	FGW	ANG
41106	OO	FGW	ANG
41108	OO	FGW	PTR
41109	OO	FGW	PTR
41110	OO	FGW	ANG
41114	LA	FGW	FGP
41116	LA	FGW	ANG
41119	OO	FGW	PTR
41121	LA	FGW	ANG
41122	LA	FGW	ANG
41123	LA	FGW	ANG
41124	LA	FGW	ANG
41125	OO	FGW	ANG
41126	OO	FGW	ANG
41127	OO	FGW	ANG
41128	OO	FGW	ANG
41129	LA	FGW	ANG
41130	LA	FGW	ANG
41131	OO	FGW	ANG
41132	OO	FGW	ANG
41133	OO	FGW	ANG
41134	LA	FGW	ANG
41135	LA	FGW	ANG
41136	OO	FGW	ANG
41137	OO	FGW	ANG
41138	OO	FGW	ANG
41139	OO	FGW	ANG
41140	LA	FGW	ANG
41141	LA	FGW	ANG
41142	LA	FGW	ANG
41143	LA	FGW	ANG
41144	LA	FGW	ANG
41145	LA	FGW	ANG
41146	LA	FGW	ANG
41147	OO	FGW	PTR
41148	OO	FGW	PTR
41149	OO	FGW	PTR
41153	OO	FGW	PTR
41155	OO	FGW	PTR
41157	LA	FGW	ANG
41158	LA	FGW	ANG
41160	LA	FGW	FGP
41161	OO	FGW	PTR
41162	LA	FGW	FGP
41163	LA	FGW	FGP
41166	LA	FGW	FGP
41167	LA	FGW	FGP
41168	OO	FGW	PTR
41169	OO	FGW	PTR
41176	OO	FGW	PTR
41179	OO	FGW	ANG
41180	OO	FGW	ANG
41181	OO	FGW	PTR
41182	OO	FGW	PTR
41183	OO	FGW	PTR
41184	OO	FGW	PTR
41186	OO	FGW	PTR
41187	OO	FGW	PTR
41189	OO	FGW	PTR
41191	OO	FGW	PTR
41192	OO	FGW	PTR

GH2G - TS *Seating 68-84S*

Number	Depot	Livery	Owner
42003	OO	FGW	ANG
42004	LA	FGW	ANG
42005 ●	LA	FGW	ANG
42006	LA	FGW	ANG
42007	LA	FGW	ANG
42008	OO	FGW	ANG
42009	LA	FGW	ANG
42010 ●	LA	FGW	ANG
42012	LA	FGW	ANG
42013	LA	FGW	ANG
42014	LA	FGW	ANG

42015	LA	FGW	ANG
42016	LA	FGW	ANG
42019 •	LA	FGW	ANG
42021	LA	FGW	ANG
42023	LA	FGW	ANG
42024	OO	FGW	ANG
42025	OO	FGW	ANG
42026	OO	FGW	ANG
42027	OO	FGW	ANG
42028	LA	FGW	ANG
42029	LA	FGW	ANG
42030	LA	FGW	ANG
42031	LA	FGW	ANG
42032	LA	FGW	ANG
42033 •	LA	FGW	ANG
42034	LA	FGW	ANG
42035	LA	FGW	ANG
42039 •	OO	FGW	ANG
42040	OO	FGW	ANG
42041	OO	FGW	ANG
42042 •	OO	FGW	ANG
42043	OO	FGW	ANG
42044	OO	FGW	ANG
42045	LA	FGW	ANG
42046	LA	FGW	ANG
42047	LA	FGW	ANG
42048 •	OO	FGW	ANG
42049	OO	FGW	ANG
42050	OO	FGW	ANG
42054	LA	FGW	ANG
42055	LA	FGW	ANG
42056	LA	FGW	ANG
42060	OO	FGW	ANG
42061	OO	FGW	ANG
42062	OO	FGW	ANG
42066	OO	FGW	ANG
42067	OO	FGW	ANG
42068	OO	FGW	ANG
42069	OO	FGW	ANG
42070 •	OO	FGW	ANG
42071	OO	FGW	ANG
42072	LA	FGW	ANG
42073	OO	FGW	ANG
42074 •	OO	FGW	ANG
42075	LA	FGW	ANG
42076	LA	FGW	ANG
42077	LA	FGW	ANG
42078	LA	FGW	ANG
42079	OO	FGW	ANG
42080	OO	FGW	ANG
42081	OO	FGW	ANG
42083	OO	FGW	ANG
42085 •	OO	FGW	ANG
42087	OO	FGW	ANG
42089	OO	FGW	ANG
42092	LA	FGW	FGP
42093	LA	FGW	FGP
42094	LA	FGW	FGP
42095	LA	FGW	FGP
42096 •	LA	FGW	ANG
42098 •	OO	FGW	ANG
42099	OO	FGW	ANG
42101	OO	FGW	PTR
42102	OO	FGW	PTR
42103	LA	FGW	FGP
42105	LA	FGW	FGP
42107	LA	FGW	ANG
42108	LA	FGW	FGP
42115 •	OO	FGW	PTR
42118	OO	FGW	ANG
42126	OO	FGW	ANG
42129 •	LA	FGW	ANG
42138	OO	FGW	ANG
42143	LA	FGW	ANG
42144	LA	FGW	ANG
42145	LA	FGW	ANG
42166	OO	FGW	PTR
42167	LA	FGW	FGP
42168 •	LA	FGW	FGP
42169	LA	FGW	FGP
42173	OO	FGW	PTR
42174	OO	FGW	PTR
42175	LA	FGW	FGP
42176 •	LA	FGW	FGP
42177	LA	FGW	FGP
42178 •	OO	FGW	PTR
42183	LA	FGW	ANG
42184	LA	FGW	ANG
42185	LA	FGW	ANG
42195	OO	FGW	PTR
42196	OO	FGW	ANG
42197 •	OO	FGW	ANG
42200	LA	FGW	ANG
42201	OO	FGW	ANG
42202	OO	FGW	ANG
42203	OO	FGW	ANG
42204	OO	FGW	ANG
42206	LA	FGW	ANG
42207	LA	FGW	ANG
42208	LA	FGW	ANG
42209	LA	FGW	ANG
42211	OO	FGW	ANG
42212 •	OO	FGW	ANG
42213	OO	FGW	ANG
42214	OO	FGW	ANG
42216	OO	FGW	ANG
42217	OO	FGW	PTR
42218	OO	FGW	PTR
42221 •	OO	FGW	ANG
42222	OO	FGW	PTR
42224	OO	FGW	PTR
42231	LA	FGW	FGP
42232 •	LA	FGW	FGP
42233	LA	FGW	FGP
42236 •	OO	FGW	ANG
42245	LA	FGW	ANG
42247 •	OO	FGW	PTR
42250	LA	FGW	ANG
42251	OO	FGW	ANG
42252	LA	FGW	ANG
42253	LA	FGW	ANG
42255	LA	FGW	ANG
42256	LA	FGW	ANG
42257	LA	FGW	ANG
42258 •	OO	FGW	PTR
42259	LA	FGW	ANG
42260	OO	FGW	ANG
42261	OO	FGW	ANG
42263 •	LA	FGW	ANG
42264	OO	FGW	ANG
42265 •	LA	FGW	ANG
42266	OO	FGW	PTR
42267	LA	FGW	ANG
42268	LA	FGW	ANG
42269	LA	FGW	ANG
42271	OO	FGW	ANG
42272	OO	FGW	ANG
42273	OO	FGW	ANG
42275	LA	FGW	ANG
42276	LA	FGW	ANG
42277	LA	FGW	ANG
42279	LA	FGW	ANG
42280	LA	FGW	ANG
42281	LA	FGW	ANG
42283	OO	FGW	ANG
42284	OO	FGW	ANG
42285	OO	FGW	ANG
42287	OO	FGW	ANG
42288	OO	FGW	ANG
42289	OO	FGW	ANG
42291	LA	FGW	ANG
42292	LA	FGW	ANG
42293	LA	FGW	ANG
42294	OO	FGW	PTR
42295	LA	FGW	ANG
42296	LA	FGW	ANG
42297	LA	FGW	ANG
42299	LA	FGW	ANG
42300	LA	FGW	ANG
42301	LA	FGW	ANG
42302	LA	FGW	FGP
42303 •	LA	FGW	FGP
42304	LA	FGW	FGP
42305	LA	FGW	FGP
42308 •	OO	FGW	PTR
42310	OO	FGW	PTR
42315	OO	FGW	PTR
42317	OO	FGW	PTR
42319 •	OO	FGW	PTR
42321	OO	FGW	PTR
42325	LA	FGW	ANG
42332 •	LA	FGW	ANG
42333	LA	FGW	ANG
42343	LA	FGW	ANG
42344	OO	FGW	ANG
42345	LA	FGW	ANG
42346	OO	FGW	ANG
42347	OO	FGW	ANG
42348	OO	FGW	ANG
42349 •	OO	FGW	ANG
42350	LA	FGW	ANG
42351 •	LA	FGW	ANG
42353	LA	FGW	FGP
42356	OO	FGW	ANG
42360 •	LA	FGW	ANG
42361	LA	FGW	ANG
42362	OO	FGW	ANG
42364	OO	FGW	PTR
42365	OO	FGW	PTR
42381 (41058)	OO	FGW	PTR
42382 (12128)	OO	FGW	PTR
42383 (12172)	OO	FGW	PTR

• Volo Television fitted

GJ2G - TGS *Seating 67-71S*

Number	*Depot*	*Livery*	*Owner*
44000	OO	FGW	PTR
44001	LA	FGW	ANG
44002	OO	FGW	ANG
44003	OO	FGW	ANG
44004	LA	FGW	ANG
44005	LA	FGW	ANG
44007	LA	FGW	ANG
44008	OO	FGW	ANG
44009	LA	FGW	ANG
44010	LA	FGW	ANG
44011	LA	FGW	ANG
44013	OO	FGW	ANG
44014	OO	FGW	ANG
44015	LA	FGW	ANG

First Great Western

44016	OO	FGW	ANG		44037	OO	FGW	ANG		44076	LA	FGW	FGP
44018	LA	FGW	ANG		44038	LA	FGW	ANG		44078	OO	FGW	PTR
44020	OO	FGW	ANG		44039	LA	FGW	ANG		44079	OO	FGW	PTR
44022	OO	FGW	ANG		44040	LA	FGW	ANG		44081	LA	FGW	FGP
44023	OO	FGW	ANG		44042	OO	FGW	PTR		44083	OO	FGW	PTR
44024	OO	FGW	ANG		44043	OO	FGW	ANG		44086	LA	FGW	ANG
44025	LA	FGW	ANG		44049	LA	FGW	ANG		44090	OO	FGW	PTR
44026	OO	FGW	ANG		44055	LA	FGW	FGP		44091	OO	FGW	PTR
44028	LA	FGW	ANG		44059	LA	FGW	ANG		44093	OO	FGW	ANG
44029	LA	FGW	ANG		44060	OO	FGW	PTR		44097	OO	FGW	PTR
44030	OO	FGW	ANG		44064	OO	FGW	ANG		44100	LA	FGW	FGP
44032	LA	FGW	ANG		44066	LA	FGW	ANG		44101	OO	FGW	PTR
44033	OO	FGW	ANG		44067	OO	FGW	ANG					
44034	LA	FGW	ANG		44068	LA	FGW	FGP		¤ Due off lease			
44035	LA	FGW	ANG		44069	OO	FGW	PTR					
44036	OO	FGW	ANG		44074	LA	FGW	FGP					

Left: *To conform with the Disability Discrimination Act, the doors of all trains must be a contrasting colour to the majority of the bodywork. In terms of First Great Western pink is used for the doors. One of the 2009 converted TSRMB vehicles No. 40117 is shown. These vehicles incorrectly show a first class yellow band over one door and the vestibule, where in fact it should be red to indicate the location of the micro buffet counter.* **CJM**

Class 142

Vehicle Length: 51ft 0½in (15.55m)	Engine: 1 x Cummins LTA10-R per vehicle
Height: 12ft 8in (3.86m)	Horsepower: 460hp (343kW)
Width: 9ft 2¼in (2.80m)	Seats (total/car): 97S, 53S/44S

Number	Formation DMS+DMSL	Depot	Livery	Owner	Operator
142001	55542+55592	EX	FGN	ANG	FGW
142009	55550+55600	EX	NOU	ANG	FGW
142029	55570+55620	EX	FGN	ANG	FGW
142030	55571+55621	EX	FGN	ANG	FGW
142063	55713+55759	EX	FGN	ANG	FGW
142064	55714+55760	EX	FGN	ANG	FGW
142068	55718+55764	EX	FGN	ANG	FGW

● The seven FGW Class 142s are scheduled to be transferred to Northern Rail in May 2011.

Class 143

Vehicle Length: 51ft 0½in (15.55m)	Engine: 1 x Cummins LTA10-R per vehicle
Height: 12ft 2¼in (3.73m)	Horsepower: 460hp (343kW)
Width: 8ft 10½in (2.70m)	Seats (total/car): 92S, 48S/44S

Number	Formation DMS+DMSL	Depot	Livery	Owner	Operator
143603	55658+55689	EX	FGL	PTR	FGW
143611	55652+55677	EX	FGL	PTR	FGW
143612	55653+55678	EX	FGL	PTR	FGW
143617	55644+55683	EX	FGL	PTR	FGW
143618	55659+55684	EX	FGL	PTR	FGW
143619	55660+55685	EX	FGL	PTR	FGW
143620	55661+55686	EX	FGL	PTR	FGW
143621	55662+55687	EX	FGL	PTR	FGW

Left: *Exeter depot has an allocation of eight Class 143 'Pacer' units, deployed on Exeter-Exmouth, Paignton and Barnstaple services. The sets all have 2+2 seating and are facelifted in terms of passenger accommodation. The outsides of sets are finished in FGW 'Dynamic Local Lines' colours with location branding. Set No. 143612 is seen arriving at Paignton with a service from Exmouth.* **CJM**

Class 150/1

Vehicle Length: 64ft 9¾in (19.74m)
Height: 12ft 4½in (3.77m)
Width: 9ft 3⅛in (2.82m)

Engine: 1 x NT855R5 of 285hp per vehicle
Horsepower: 570hp (425kW)
Seats (total/car): 141S, 71S/70S

Number	Formation DMSL+DMS	Depot	Livery	Owner	Operator
150101	52101+57101	EX	CTL	PTR	FGW
150102	52102+57102	EX	CTL	PTR	FGW
150106	52106+57106	EX	CTL	PTR	FGW
150108	52108+57108	EX	CTL	PTR	FGW
150120	**52120+57120**	**EX**	**SLF**	**PTR**	**FGW**
150121	**52121+57121**	**EX**	**SLF**	**PTR**	**FGW**
150122	52122+57122	EX	CTL	PTR	FGW
150123	**52123+57123**	**EX**	**SLF**	**PTR**	**FGW**
150124	52124+57124	EX	CTL	PTR	FGW
150125	52125+57125	EX	CTL	PTR	FGW
150126	52126+57126	EX	WMD	PTR	FGW
150127	**52127+57127**	**EX**	**FGB**	**PTR**	**FGW**
150128	**52128+57128**	**EX**	**SLF**	**PTR**	**FGW**
150129	**52129+57129**	**EX**	**SLF**	**PTR**	**FGW**
150130	**52130+57130**	**EX**	**SLF**	**PTR**	**FGW**
150131	**52130+57130**	**EX**	**SLF**	**PTR**	**FGW**
150132	52132+57132	EX	WMD	PTR	FGW

● Units shown in light type are scheduled to transfer to FGW from London Midland in early 2011.

Right: *At the end of 2010 FGW operated eight Class 150/1 sets, but further units are due to transfer in from London Midland. All sets are then expected to be facelifted and receive standard FGW livery. The first set to sport the new colours, No. 150127 is seen at Severn Tunnel Junction on 15 December 2010 after repaint by Pullman Rail at Cardiff.*
Alex Brown

Class 150/2

Vehicle Length: 64ft 9¾in (19.74m)
Height: 12ft 4½in (3.77m)
Width: 9ft 3⅛in (2.82m)

Engine: 1 x NT855R5 of 285hp per vehicle
Horsepower: 570hp (425kW)
Seats (total/car): 116S, 60S/56S

Number	Formation DMSL+DMS	Depot	Livery	Owner	Operator
150219	52219+57219	EX	FGL	PTR	FGW
150221	52221+57221	EX	FGL	PTR	FGW
150232	52232+57232	EX	FGL	PTR	FGW
150233	52233+57233	EX	FGL	PTR	FGW
150234	52234+57234	EX	FGL	PTR	FGW
150238	52238+57238	EX	FGL	PTR	FGW
150239	52239+57239	EX	FGL	PTR	FGW
150243	52243+57243	EX	FGL	PTR	FGW
150244	52244+57244	EX	FGL	PTR	FGW
150246	52246+57246	EX	FGL	PTR	FGW
150247	52247+57247	EX	FGL	PTR	FGW
150248	52248+57248	EX	FGL	PTR	FGW
150249	52249+57249	EX	FGL	PTR	FGW
150261	52261+57261	EX	FGL	PTR	FGW
150263	52263+57263	EX	FGL	PTR	FGW
150265	52265+57265	EX	FGL	PTR	FGW
150266	52266+57266	EX	FGL	PTR	FGW

Below: *The backbone of FGW local services in the West Country is based on a fleet of 17 Class 150/2, allocated to Exeter. All are refurbished with 2+2 seating. Set No. 150261 is seen stabled outside Exeter depot. In 2011 this depot will have revised fuelling equipment to allow three vehicle length trains to be fuelled; the present limit is two.* **CJM**

First Great Western

Class 153

Vehicle Length: 76ft 5in (23.29m)	Engine: 1 x NT855R5 of 285hp
Height: 12ft 3⅜in (3.75m)	Horsepower: 285hp (213kW)
Width: 8ft 10in (2.70m)	Seats (total/car): 72S

Number	Formation DMSL	Depot	Livery	Owner	Operator
153305	52305	EX	FGL	ANG	FGW
153318	52318	EX	FGL	ANG	FGW
153329	52329	EX	FGL	ANG	FGW
153361	57361	EX	FGL	ANG	FGW
153368	57368	EX	FGL	ANG	FGW
153369	57369	EX	FGL	ANG	FGW
153370	57370	EX	FGL	ANG	FGW
153372	57372	EX	FGL	ANG	FGW
153373	57373	EX	FGL	ANG	FGW
153377	57377	EX	FGL	ANG	FGW
153380	57380	EX	FGL	ANG	FGW
153382	57382	EX	FGL	ANG	FGW

Left: *Officially on FGW's books based at Exeter for branch line use, the 12 Class 153 single 'Bubble' cars can be found on most routes served by Exeter depot every day, frequently strengthening two-car sets for peak hour and school loadings. All sets are in full FGW 'Local Lines' colours. Set No. 153368 is seen coupled to a Class 142 approaching Dawlish Warren with a summer service from Paignton to Exmouth. The near end is the small cab end, formed during the conversion from two-car Class 155s.* **CJM**

Class 158/0 (2-car)

Vehicle Length: 76ft 1¾in (23.21m)	Engine: 1 x Cummins NTA855R of 350hp per vehicle
Height: 12ft 6in (3.81m)	Horsepower: 700hp (522kW)
Width: 9ft 3¼in (2.82m)	Seats (total/car): 134S, 66S/68S

Number	Formation DMSL+DMSL	Depot	Livery	Owner	Operator
158749	52749+57749	PM	FGL	PTR	FGW
158763	52763+57763	PM	FGL	PTR	FGW
158766	52766+57766	PM	FGL	PTR	FGW
158767	52767+57767	PM	FGL	PTR	FGW
158769	52769+57769	PM	FGL	PTR	FGW

● The five two-car Class 158s are to be reformed as three-car sets in 2011.

Left: *First Great Western's longer distance 'Local Lines' services, such as Cardiff to Portsmouth are formed of Class 158 stock, in either two or three car sets. Five two car sets are operated, based at Bristol St Philip's Marsh. Set No. 158748 is viewed at Gloucester on a Great Malvern service.* **CJM**

Class 158/0 (3-car)

158798

Vehicle Length: 76ft 1¾in (23.21m)	Engine: 1 x Cummins NTA855R of 350hp per vehicle
Height: 12ft 6in (3.81m)	Horsepower: 1,050hp (783kW)
Width: 9ft 3¼in (2.82m)	Seats (total/car): 200S, 66S/66S/68S

158950 - 158959

Vehicle Length: 76ft 1¾in (23.21m)	Engine: 1 x Cummins NTA855R of 350hp per vehicle
Height: 12ft 6in (3.81m)	Horsepower: 1,050hp (783kW)
Width: 9ft 3¼in (2.82m)	Seats (total/car): 204S, 66S/70S/68S

Number	Formation DMSL+MSL+DMSL		Depot	Livery	Owner	Operator
158798	52798+58715+57798		PM	FGL	PTR	FGW

Number	Formation DMSL+DMSL+DMSL		Depot	Livery	Owner	Operator
158950	(158751/761)	57751+52761+57761	PM	FGL	PTR	FGW

158951	(158751/764)	52751+52764+57764	PM	FGL	PTR	FGW
158952	(158745/762)	57745+52762+57762	PM	FGL	PTR	FGW
158953	(158745/750)	52745+52750+57750	PM	FGL	PTR	FGW
158954	(158747/760)	57747+52760+57760	PM	FGL	PTR	FGW
158955	(158747/765)	52747+52765+57765	PM	FGL	PTR	FGW
158956	(158748/768)	57748+52768+57768	PM	FGL	PTR	FGW
158957	(158748/771)	52748+52771+57771	PM	FGL	PTR	FGW
158958	(158746/776)	57746+52776+57776	PM	FGL	PTR	FGW
158959	(158746/778)	52746+52778+57778	PM	FGL	PTR	FGW

Right: *FGW's three-car Class 158 fleet is made up of one original three-car (as built) set with a MS vehicle in the centre and 10 sets formed of three driving cars, formed up by the reformation of five sets giving one driving car to 10 two car sets. The middle cab is retained to enable fleet flexibility. Three-car set No. 158959 departs from Newport with a service for Cardiff. The leading car of this set came from two-car unit No. 158746.* **CJM**

Class 165/1 (3-car)
Networker Turbo

Vehicle Length: (driving) 75ft 2½in (22.91m), (inter) 74ft 6½in (22.72m)
Height: 12ft 5¼in (3.79m)
Width: 9ft 5½in (2.81m)
Engine: 1 x Perkins 2006TWH of 350hp
Horsepower: 1,050hp (783kW)
Seats (total/car): 16F/270S, 16F-66S/106S/98S

Number	Formation DMCL+MS+DMS	Depot	Livery	Owner	Operator
165101	58953+55415+58916	RG	FGT	ANG	FGW
165102	58954+55416+58917	RG	FGT	ANG	FGW
165103	58955+55417+58918	RG	FGT	ANG	FGW
165104	58956+55418+58919	RG	FGT	ANG	FGW
165105	58957+55419+58920	RG	FGT	ANG	FGW
165106	58958+55420+58921	RG	FGT	ANG	FGW
165107	58959+55421+58922	RG	FGT	ANG	FGW
165108	58960+55422+58923	RG	FGT	ANG	FGW
165109	58961+55423+58924	RG	FGT	ANG	FGW
165110	58962+55424+58925	RG	FGT	ANG	FGW
165111	58963+55425+58926	RG	FGT	ANG	FGW
165112	58964+55426+58927	RG	FGT	ANG	FGW
165113	58965+55427+58928	RG	FGT	ANG	FGW
165114	58966+55428+58929	RG	FGT	ANG	FGW
165116	58968+55430+58931	RG	FGT	ANG	FGW
165117	58969+55431+58932	RG	FGT	ANG	FGW

Right: *The FGW Thames area local services are operated by either Class 165 or 166 sets. The Class 165s are formed in either two or three-car formations. In this view is three-car set No. 165106 at Reading awaiting departure with a stopping service to London Paddington. The set's DMCL vehicle is leading.* **CJM**

Passenger Train Operating Companies - First Great Western

First Great Western

Class 165/1 (2-car)
Networker Turbo

Vehicle Length: 75ft 2½in (22.91m)
Height: 12ft 5¼in (3.79m)
Width: 9ft 5½in (2.81m)
Engine: 1 x Perkins 2006TWH of 350hp per car
Horsepower: 700hp (522kW)
Seats (total/car): 16F/170S, 16F-72S/98S

Number	Formation DMCL+DMS	Depot	Livery	Owner	Operator
165118	58879+58933	RG	FGT	ANG	FGW
165119	58880+58934	RG	FGT	ANG	FGW
165120	58881+58935	RG	FGT	ANG	FGW
165121	58882+58936	RG	FGT	ANG	FGW
165122	58883+58937	RG	FGT	ANG	FGW
165123	58884+58938	RG	FGT	ANG	FGW
165124	58885+58939	RG	FGT	ANG	FGW
165125	58886+58940	RG	FGT	ANG	FGW
165126	58887+58941	RG	FGT	ANG	FGW
165127	58888+58942	RG	FGT	ANG	FGW
165128	58889+58943	RG	FGT	ANG	FGW
165129	58890+58944	RG	FGT	ANG	FGW
165130	58891+58945	RG	FGT	ANG	FGW
165131	58892+58946	RG	FGT	ANG	FGW
165132	58893+58947	RG	FGT	ANG	FGW
165133	58894+58948	RG	FGT	ANG	FGW
165134	58895+58949	RG	FGT	ANG	FGW
165135	58896+58950	RG	FGT	ANG	FGW
165136	58897+58951	RG	FGT	ANG	FGW
165137	58898+58952	RG	FGT	ANG	FGW

Left: A total of 20 two-car Class 165/1 sets are allocated to Reading for Thames line use; these sets usually operate on the Reading-Basingstoke and London area branch lines as well as on the Reading-Gatwick route. All sets sport full First Great Western 'Dynamic Lines' livery. Set No. 165122 is seen at Reading awaiting a move onto the Wokingham line. The set's DMS vehicle is nearest the camera. **CJM**

Class 166
Networker Turbo Express

Vehicle Length: (driving) 75ft 2½in (22.91m), (inter) 74ft 6½in (22.72m)
Height: 12ft 5¼in (3.79m)
Width: 9ft 5½in (2.81m)
Engine: 1 x Perkins 2006TWH of 350hp per car
Horsepower: 1,050hp (783kW)
Seats (total/car): 32F/243S, 16F-75S/96S/16F-72S

Number	Formation DMCL(A)+MS+DMCL(B)	Depot	Livery	Owner	Operator
166201	58101+58601+58122	RG	FGT	ANG	FGW
166202	58102+58602+58123	RG	FGT	ANG	FGW
166203	58103+58603+58124	RG	FGT	ANG	FGW
166204	58104+58604+58125	RG	FGT	ANG	FGW
166205	58105+58605+58126	RG	FGT	ANG	FGW
166206	58106+58606+58127	RG	FGT	ANG	FGW
166207	58107+58607+58128	RG	FGT	ANG	FGW
166208	58108+58608+58129	RG	FGT	ANG	FGW
166209	58109+58609+58130	RG	FGT	ANG	FGW
166210	58110+58610+58131	RG	FGT	ANG	FGW
166211	58111+58611+58132	RG	FGT	ANG	FGW
166212	58112+58612+58133	RG	FGT	ANG	FGW
166213	58113+58613+58134	RG	FGT	ANG	FGW
166214	58114+58614+58135	RG	FGT	ANG	FGW
166215	58115+58615+58136	RG	FGT	ANG	FGW
166216	58116+58616+58137	RG	FGT	ANG	FGW
166217	58117+58617+58138	RG	FGT	ANG	FGW
166218	58118+58618+58139	RG	FGT	ANG	FGW
166219	58119+58619+58140	RG	FGT	ANG	FGW
166220	58120+58620+58141	RG	FGT	ANG	FGW
166221	58121+58621+58142	RG	FGT	ANG	FGW

Further Reading

For full technical information and class details of all traction classes covered in the *Ian Allan ABC Rail Guide 2011*, see our companion volume *Traction Recognition*. A new edition will be published summer 2011 – visit www.ianallanpublishing.com for details.

Right: *When Network SouthEast ordered 'Networker' stock to modernise the Thames routes, 21 'Express' sets were authorised, based on the Class 165 but incorporating air conditioning and a revised interior. All sets are allocated to Reading and should be rostered to work on the longer distance services. Set No. 166213 is illustrated at Reading.* **Stacey Thew**

Mk3 Hauled Stock

Vehicle Length: 75ft 0in (22.86m)			Width: 8ft 11in (2.71m)	
Height: 12ft 9in (3.88m)			Bogie Type: BT10	

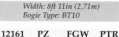

AJ1G - RFB *Seating 18F*

Number	Depot	Livery	Owner
10219	PZ	FGW	PTR
10225	PZ	FGW	PTR
10232	PZ	FGW	PTR

AU4G - SLEP *Comps 12*

Number	Depot	Livery	Owner
10532	PZ	FGW	PTR
10534	PZ	FGW	PTR
10563	PZ	FGW	PTR

Number	Depot	Livery	Owner
10584	PZ	FGW	PTR
10589	PZ	FGW	PTR
10590	PZ	FGW	PTR
10594	PZ	FGW	PTR
10601	PZ	FGW	PTR
10612	PZ	FGW	PTR
10616	PZ	FGW	PTR

AC2G - TSO *Seating 70S*

Number	Depot	Livery	Owner
12100	PZ	FGW	PTR

12161	PZ	FGW	PTR

AE1H - BFO *Seating 36F*

Number	Depot	Livery	Owner
17173	PZ	FGW	PTR
17174	PZ	FGW	PTR
17175	PZ	FGW	PTR

Right: *The First Great Western Mk3 stock which is operated on the Paddington to Penzance overnight sleeper services have all been refurbished. The seating saloons have 2+1 seating and use the original style HST seating and tables as used in the FO vehicles, providing a very comfortable travelling environment for overnight non-sleeping passengers. The interior of a TSO vehicle is shown.* **CJM**

Service Stock

HST Barrier Vehicles

Number	Depot	Livery	Owner	Former Identity
6330	LA	FGB	ANG	BFK - 14084
6336	LA	FGB	ANG	BG - 81591/92185
6338	LA	FGB	ANG	BG - 81581/92180
6348	LA	FGB	ANG	BG - 81233/92963

Right: *To provide the ability to couple conventional rolling stock and locomotives to buck-eye fitted HST trailer vehicles a small fleet of coupling barrier coaches are maintained by FGW and owned by Angel Trains. The vehicles are allocated to Laira and converted from a BFK and BG stock. Painted in unbranded FGW blue, former BFK No. 6330 is illustrated; this vehicle was previously passenger coach No. 14084. Today all its passenger windows are plated over.* **CJM**

First Scotrail

Address:	✉ Atrium Court, 50 Waterloo Street, Glasgow, G2 6HQ
	✍ scotrail.enquiries@firstgroup.com
	✆ 08700 005151
	ⓘ www.firstscotrail.com

Managing Director:	Steve Montgomery
Franchise Dates:	17 October 2004 - 30 November 2014
Principal Routes:	All Scottish services, plus Scotrail sleeper services
Depots:	Corkerhill (CK), Glasgow Shields Road (GW), Haymarket (HA), Inverness (IS)
Parent Company:	First Group PLC

Class 156

Vehicle Length: 75ft 6in (23.03m)
Height: 12ft 6in (3.81m)
Width: 8ft 11in (2.73m)

Engine: 1 x Cummins NT855R5 of 285hp
Horsepower: 570hp (425kW)
Seats (total/car): 142S, 70 or 72S

Number	Formation DMSL+DMS	Depot	Livery	Owner	Operator
156430	52430+57430	CK	FSS	ANG	FSR
156431	52431+57431	CK	FSS	ANG	FSR
156432	52432+57432	CK	FSS	ANG	FSR
156433	52433+57433	CK	FSS	ANG	FSR
156434	52434+57434	CK	FSS	ANG	FSR
156435	52435+57435	CK	FSS	ANG	FSR
156436	52436+57436	CK	FSS	ANG	FSR
156437	52437+57437	CK	FSS	ANG	FSR
156439	52439+57439	CK	FSS	ANG	FSR
156442	52442+57442	CK	FSS	ANG	FSR
156445	52445+57445	CK	FSS	ANG	FSR
156446	52446+57446	CK	FSR	ANG	FSR
156447	52447+57447	CK	FSR	ANG	FSR
156449	52449+57449	CK	FSR	ANG	FSR
156450	52450+57450	CK	FSR	ANG	FSR
156453	52453+57453	CK	FSR	ANG	FSR
156456	52456+57456	CK	FSR	ANG	FSR
156457	52457+57457	CK	FSR	ANG	FSR
156458	52458+57458	CK	FSR	ANG	FSR
156462	52462+57462	CK	FSR	ANG	FSR
156465	52465+57465	CK	FSR	ANG	FSR
156467	52467+57467	CK	FSR	ANG	FSR
156474	52474+57474	CK	FSR	ANG	FSR
156476	52476+57476	CK	FSR	ANG	FSR
156477	52477+57477	CK	FSR	ANG	FSR
156478	52478+57478	CK	FSR	ANG	FSR
156485	52485+57485	CK	FSR	ANG	FSR
156492	52492+57492	CK	FSR	ANG	FSR
156493	52493+57493	CK	FSR	ANG	FSR
156494	52494+57494	CK	FSS	ANG	FSR
156495	52495+57495	CK	FSS	ANG	FSR
156496	52496+57496	CK	FSR	ANG	FSR
156499	52499+57499	CK	FSR	ANG	FSR
156500	52500+57500	CK	FSS	ANG	FSR
156501	52501+57501	CK	FSS	ANG	FSR
156502	52502+57502	CK	FSS	ANG	FSR
156503	52503+57503	CK	FSS	ANG	FSR
156504	52504+57504	CK	FSS	ANG	FSR
156505	52505+57505	CK	FSS	ANG	FSR
156506	52506+57506	CK	FSS	ANG	FSR
156507	52507+57507	CK	FSS	ANG	FSR
156508	52508+57508	CK	FSS	ANG	FSR
156509	52509+57509	CK	FSS	ANG	FSR
156510	52510+57510	CK	FSS	ANG	FSR
156511	52511+57511	CK	FSS	ANG	FSR
156512	52512+57512	CK	FSS	ANG	FSR
156513	52513+57513	CK	FSS	ANG	FSR
156514	52514+57514	CK	FSS	ANG	FSR

Left: *In new First Scotrail Saltire livery, Class 156 No. 156434 climbs to Pinmore summit, south of Girvan, on 10 April 2010, forming the 12.29 Ayr to Stranraer. During 2011 the entire Scotrail Class 156 fleet will sport this very distinctive livery.* **Brian Morrison**

Passenger Train Operating Companies - First Scotrail

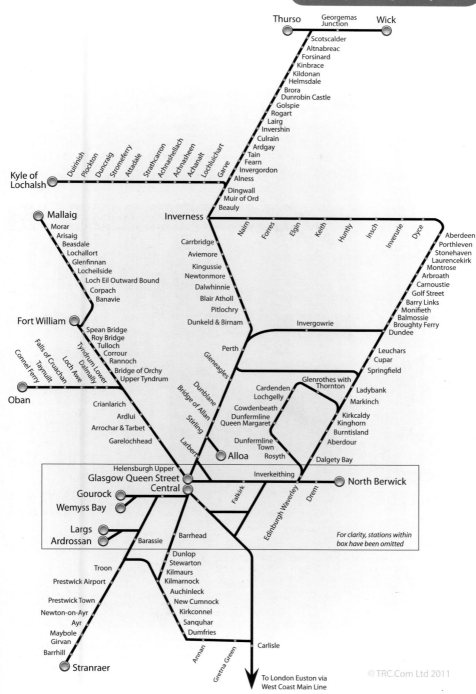

Thurso — Georgemas Junction — Wick

Scotscalder
Altnabreac
Forsinard
Kinbrace
Kildonan
Helmsdale
Brora
Dunrobin Castle
Golspie
Rogart
Lairg
Invershin
Culrain
Ardgay
Tain
Fearn
Invergordon
Alness

Dingwall
Muir of Ord
Beauly

Kyle of Lochalsh

Duirinish
Plockton
Duncraig
Stromeferry
Attadale
Strathcarron
Achnashellach
Achnasheen
Achanalt
Lochluichart
Garve

Inverness

Nairn
Forres
Elgin
Keith
Huntly
Insch
Inverurie
Dyce

Aberdeen
Porthleven
Stonehaven
Laurencekirk
Montrose
Arbroath
Carnoustie
Golf Street
Barry Links
Monifieth
Balmossie
Broughty Ferry
Dundee

Mallaig
Morar
Arisaig
Beasdale
Lochailort
Glenfinnan
Locheilside
Loch Eil Outward Bound
Corpach
Banavie

Carrbridge
Aviemore
Kingussie
Newtonmore
Dalwhinnie
Blair Atholl
Pitlochry
Dunkeld & Birnam

Invergowrie

Fort William

Spean Bridge
Roy Bridge
Tulloch
Corrour
Rannoch
Bridge of Orchy
Upper Tyndrum

Tyndrum Lower

Perth

Gleneagles

Leuchars
Cupar
Springfield

Falls of Cruachan
Taynuilt
Connel Ferry

Loch Awe
Dalmally

Dunblane
Bridge of Allan

Glenrothes with Thornton

Ladybank
Markinch

Oban

Crianlarich
Ardlui
Arrochar & Tarbet
Garelochhead

Stirling

Cardenden
Lochgelly
Cowdenbeath
Dunfermline Queen Margaret

Kirkcaldy
Kinghorn
Burntisland
Aberdour

Larbert

Dunfermline Town
Rosyth

Dalgety Bay

Alloa

Helensburgh Upper
Glasgow Queen Street
Central

Inverkeithing

North Berwick

Gourock
Wemyss Bay

Falkirk

Drem

Edinburgh Waverley

Largs
Ardrossan

Barassie

Barrhead

Barrhead

For clarity, stations within box have been omitted

Dunlop
Stewarton
Kilmaurs
Kilmarnock
Auchinleck
New Cumnock
Kirkconnel
Sanquhar
Dumfries

Troon
Prestwick Airport
Prestwick Town
Newton-on-Ayr
Ayr
Maybole
Girvan
Barrhill

Carlisle

Annan
Gretna Green

Stranraer

To London Euston via West Coast Main Line

© TRC.Com Ltd 2011

Passenger Train Operating Companies - First Scotrail

First Scotrail

Class 158

Vehicle Length: 76ft 1¾in (23.21m)
Height: 12ft 6in (3.81m)
Width: 9ft 3¼in (2.82m)

Engine: 1 x Cummins NTA855R of 350hp per vehicle
Horsepower: 700hp (522kW)
Seats (total/car): 14F/116S, 14F-46S/70S
* 138S, 68S/70S

Number	Formation DMCL/DMSL*+DMS	Depot	Livery	Owner	Operator
158701	52701+57701	IS	FSR	PTR	FSR
158702	52702+57702	IS	FSR	PTR	FSR
158703	52703+57703	IS	FSR	PTR	FSR
158704	52704+57704	IS	FSR	PTR	FSR
158705	52705+57705	IS	FSR	PTR	FSR
158706	52706+57706	IS	FSR	PTR	FSR
158707	52707+57707	IS	FSR	PTR	FSR
158708	52708+57708	IS	FSR	PTR	FSR
158709	52709+57709	IS	FSR	PTR	FSR
158710	52710+57710	IS	FSR	PTR	FSR
158711	52711+57711	IS	FSR	PTR	FSR
158712	52712+57712	IS	FSR	PTR	FSR
158713	52713+57713	IS	FSR	PTR	FSR
158714	52714+57714	IS	FSR	PTR	FSR
158715	52715+57715	IS	FSR	PTR	FSR
158716	52716+57716	IS	FSR	PTR	FSR
158717	52717+57717	IS	FSR	PTR	FSR
158718	52718+57718	IS	FSR	PTR	FSR
158719	52719+57719	IS	FSR	PTR	FSR
158720	52720+57720	IS	FSR	PTR	FSR
158721	52721+57721	IS	FSR	PTR	FSR
158722	52722+57722	IS	FSR	PTR	FSR
158723	52723+57723	IS	FSR	PTR	FSR
158724	52724+57724	IS	FSR	PTR	FSR
158725	52725+57725	IS	FSR	PTR	FSR
158726	52726+57726	HA	FSR	PTR	FSR
158727	52727+57727	IS	FSR	PTR	FSR
158728	52728+57728	IS	FSR	PTR	FSR
158729	52729+57729	HA	FSR	PTR	FSR
158730	52730+57730	HA	FSR	PTR	FSR
158731	52731+57731	HA	FSR	PTR	FSR
158732	52732+57732	HA	FSR	PTR	FSR
158733	52733+57733	HA	FSR	PTR	FSR
158734	52734+57734	HA	FSR	PTR	FSR
158735	52735+57735	HA	FSR	PTR	FSR
158736	52736+57736	HA	FSR	PTR	FSR
158737	52737+57737	HA	FSR	PTR	FSR
158738	52738+57738	HA	FSR	PTR	FSR
158739	52739+57739	HA	FSR	PTR	FSR
158740	52740+57740	HA	FSR	PTR	FSR
158741	52741+57741	HA	FSR	PTR	FSR
158782	52782*+57782	HA	FSS	ANG	FSR
158786	52786*+57786	HA	FSS	ANG	FSR
158789	52789*+57789	HA	FSS	ANG	FSR
158867	52867*+57867	HA	FSS	ANG	FSR
158868	52868*+57868	HA	FSS	ANG	FSR
158869	52869*+57869	HA	FSS	ANG	FSR
158870	52870*+57870	HA	FSS	ANG	FSR
158871	52871*+57871	HA	FSS	ANG	FSR

Name applied
158707 - Far North Line

Left: *The First Scotrail fleet of Class 158s operate on the longer distance services, together with the operator's Class 170 fleet. In September 2010 a start was made on applying the latest First Scotrail Saltire livery. Set No. 155581, the first in the revised livery, is seen posed outside Railcare Glasgow Works.* **Bill Wilson**

Class 170/3
Turbostar

Vehicle Length: 77ft 6in (23.62m)
Height: 12ft 4½in (3.77m)
Width: 8ft 10in (2.69m)

Engine: 1 x MTU 6R 183TD13H 422hp per vehicle
Horsepower: 1,266hp (944kW)
Seats (total/car): 24F/140S, 12F-45S/43S/12F-52S

Number	Formation DMCL+MS+DMSL	Depot	Livery	Owner	Operator
170393	50393+55393+79393	HA	FSR	PTR	FSR
170394	50394+55394+79394	HA	FSR	PTR	FSR
170395	50395+55395+79395	HA	FSR	PTR	FSR
170396	50396+55396+79396	HA	FSR	PTR	FSR

Class 170/4
Turbostar

Vehicle Length: 77ft 6in (23.62m)
Height: 12ft 4½in (3.77m)
Width: 8ft 10in (2.69m)

Engine: 1 x MTU 6R 183TD13H 422hp per vehicle
Horsepower: 1,266hp (944kW)
(170431/432 have 3 x 483hp engines giving 1,449hp)
Seats (total/car): 18F/168S 9F-43S/76S/9F-49S

Number	Formation DMCL+MS+DMCL	Depot	Livery	Owner	Operator	Name
170401	50401+55401+79401	HA	FSR	PTR	FSR	
170402	50402+55402+79402	HA	FSR	PTR	FSR	
170403	50403+55403+79403	HA	FSR	PTR	FSR	
170404	50404+55404+79404	HA	FSR	PTR	FSR	

170405	50405+55405+79405	HA	FSR	PTR	FSR	
170406	50406+55406+79406	HA	FSR	PTR	FSR	
170407	50407+55407+79407	HA	FSR	PTR	FSR	*University of Aberdeen*
170408	50408+55408+79408	HA	FSR	PTR	FSR	
170409	50409+55409+79409	HA	FSR	PTR	FSR	
170410	50410+55410+79410	HA	FSR	PTR	FSR	
170411	50411+55411+79411	HA	FSR	PTR	FSR	
170412	50412+55412+79412	HA	FSR	PTR	FSR	
170413	50413+55413+79413	HA	FSR	PTR	FSR	
170414	50414+55414+79414	HA	FSR	PTR	FSR	
170415	50415+55415+79415	HA	FSR	PTR	FSR	
170416	50416+55416+79416	HA	FSR	HSB	FSR	
170417	50417+55417+79417	HA	FSR	HSB	FSR	
170418	50418+55418+79418	HA	FSR	HSB	FSR	
170419	50419+55419+79419	HA	FSR	HSB	FSR	
170420	50420+55420+79420	HA	FSR	HSB	FSR	
170421	50421+55421+79421	HA	FSR	HSB	FSR	
170422	50422+55422+79422	HA	FSR	HSB	FSR	
170423	50423+55423+79423	HA	FSR	HSB	FSR	
170424	50424+55424+79424	HA	FSR	HSB	FSR	
170425	50425+55425+79425	HA	FSR	PTR	FSR	
170426	50426+55426+79426	HA	FSR	PTR	FSR	
170427	50427+55427+79427	HA	FSR	PTR	FSR	
170428	50428+55428+79428	HA	FSR	PTR	FSR	
170429	50429+55429+79429	HA	FSR	PTR	FSR	
170430	50430+55430+79430	HA	FSR	PTR	FSR	
170431	50431+55431+79431	HA	FSR	PTR	FSR	
170432	50432+55432+79432	HA	FSR	PTR	FSR	
170433	50433+55433+79433	HA	FSR	PTR	FSR	*Investor in People*
170434	50434+55434+79434	HA	FSS	PTR	FSR	

Class 170/4
Turbostar

Vehicle Length: 77ft 6in (23.62m)
Height: 12ft 4½in (3.77m)
Width: 8ft 10in (2.69m)

Engine: 1 x MTU 6R 183TD13H 422hp per vehicle
Horsepower: 1,266hp (944kW)
Seats: 170450-170471 (total/car) 198S, 55S/76S/67S
170472-170478 (total/car) 200S, 57S/76S/67S

Number	Formation	Depot	Livery	Owner	Opt'r
	DMSL+MS+DMSL				
170450	50450+55450+79450	HA	FSR	PTR	FSR
170451	50451+55451+79451	HA	FSR	PTR	FSR
170452	50452+55452+79452	HA	FSR	PTR	FSR
170453	50453+55453+79453	HA	FSR	PTR	FSR
170454	50454+55454+79454	HA	FSR	PTR	FSR
170455	50455+55455+79455	HA	FSR	PTR	FSR
170456	50456+55456+79456	HA	FSR	PTR	FSR
170457	50457+55457+79457	HA	FSR	PTR	FSR
170458	50458+55458+79458	HA	FSR	PTR	FSR
170459	50459+55459+79459	HA	FSR	PTR	FSR
170460	50460+55460+79460	HA	FSR	PTR	FSR
170461	50461+55461+79461	HA	FSR	PTR	FSR
170470	50470+55470+79470	HA	FSR	PTR	FSR
170471	50471+55471+79471	HA	FSP	PTR	FSR
170472	50472+55472+79472	HA	FSP	PTR	FSR
170473	50473+55473+79473	HA	FSP	PTR	FSR
170474	50474+55474+79474	HA	FSP	PTR	FSR
170475	50475+55475+79475	HA	FSP	PTR	FSR
170476	50476+55476+79476	HA	FSP	PTR	FSR
170477	50477+55477+79477	HA	FSP	PTR	FSR
170478	50478+55478+79478	HA	FSP	PTR	FSR

Right: *A sizeable number of Class 170 'Turbostar' DMUs operate for First Scotrail, owned by Porterbrook and HSBC Rail. The sets are all three-car variants and are allocated to Edinburgh Haymarket depot. Set No. 170456, an all standard class accommodation unit, is illustrated.*
John Wills

First Scotrail

Class 314

	Vehicle Length: (Driving) 64ft 11½in (19.80m)	Width: 9ft 3in (2.82m)
	(Inter) 65ft 4¼in (19.92m)	Horsepower: 880hp (656kW)
Height: 11ft 6½in (3.58m)		Seats (total/car): 212S, 68S/76S/68S

Number	Formation	Depot	Livery	Owner	Operator	Name
	DMSO(A)+PTSO+DMSO(B)					
314201	64583+71450+64584	GW	FSP	ANG	FSR	
314202	64585+71451+64586	GW	FSP	ANG	FSR	
314203	64587+71452+64588*	GW	FSP	ANG	FSR	
314204	64589+71453+64590	GW	FSP	ANG	FSR	European Union
314205	64591+71454+64592	GW	FSP	ANG	FSR	
314206	64593+71455+64594	GW	FSP	ANG	FSR	
314207	64595+71456+64596	GW	FSP	ANG	FSR	
314208	64597+71457+64598	GW	FSP	ANG	FSR	
314209	64599+71458+64600	GW	FSP	ANG	FSR	
314210	64601+71459+64602	GW	FSP	ANG	FSR	
314211	64603+71460+64604	GW	FSP	ANG	FSR	
314212	64604+71461+64606	GW	FSP	ANG	FSR	
314213	64607+71462+64608	GW	FSP	ANG	FSR	
314214	64609+71463+64610	GW	FSP	ANG	FSR	
314215	64611+71464+64612	GW	FSP	ANG	FSR	
314216	64613+71465+64614	GW	FSP	ANG	FSR	

* 64588 rebuilt from Class 507 car No. 64426 and seats 74S

Left: *Most members of Class 314 operate on the Cathcart Circle Lines with a small number on Inverclyde duties. These are the oldest of the Scotrail EMUs currently in service. A six car formation of sets Nos. 314203 and 314206 approaches Mount Florida on 20 June 2010 forming the 17.23 Glasgow Central to Neilston.*
Robin Ralston

Class 318

	Vehicle Length: (Driving) 65ft 0¾in (19.83m)	Width: 9ft 3in (2.82m)
	(Inter) 65ft 4¼in (19.92m)	Horsepower: 1,328hp (996kW)
Height: 12ft 1½in (3.70m)		Seats (total/car): 216S, 66S/79S/71S

Number	Formation	Depot	Livery	Owner	Operator	Name
	DTSO(A)+MSO+DTSO(B)					
318250	77240+62866+77260	GW	FSP	HSB	FSR	
318251	77241+62867+77261	GW	FSP	HSB	FSR	
318252	77242+62868+77262	GW	FSP	HSB	FSR	
318253	77243+62869+77263	GW	FSP	HSB	FSR	
318254	77244+62870+77264	GW	FSP	HSB	FSR	
318255	77245+62871+77265	GW	FSP	HSB	FSR	
318256	77246+62872+77266	GW	FSP	HSB	FSR	
318257	77247+62873+77267	GW	FSP	HSB	FSR	
318258	77248+62874+77268	GW	FSP	HSB	FSR	
318259	77249+62875+77269	GW	FSP	HSB	FSR	Citizens' Network
318260	77250+62876+77270	GW	FSP	HSB	FSR	
318261	77251+62877+77271	GW	FSP	HSB	FSR	
318262	77252+62878+77272	GW	FSP	HSB	FSR	
318263	77253+62879+77273	GW	FSP	HSB	FSR	
318264	77254+62880+77274	GW	FSP	HSB	FSR	
318265	77255+62881+77275	GW	FSP	HSB	FSR	
318266	77256+62882+77276	GW	FSP	HSB	FSR	Strathclyder
318267	77257+62883+77277	GW	FSP	HSB	FSR	
318268	77258+62884+77278	GW	FSP	HSB	FSR	
318269	77259+62885+77279	GW	FSP	HSB	FSR	
318270	77288+62890+77289	GW	FSP	HSB	FSR	

Right: *In 2010 the 21 members of Class 318 were used on the Ayrshire Coast Line, Inverclyde Line and Argyle Line, but following introduction of new Class 380s, the sets are destined for transfer totally to the Argyle Line. Originally these sets were built with front end gangways, but following refurbishment these were removed. Set No. 318265 passes Glengarnock on 16 June 2010 forming the 18.45 Glasgow Central to Largs.* **Robin Ralston**

Class 320

Vehicle Length: (Driving) 65ft 0¾in (19.83m)
(Inter) 65ft 4¼in (19.92m)
Height: 12ft 4¾in (3.78m)
Width: 9ft 3in (2.82m)
Horsepower: 1,328hp (996kW)
Seats (total/car): 227S, 76S/76S/75S

Number	Formation DTSO(A)+MSO+DTSO(B)	Depot	Livery	Owner	Operator	Name
320301	77899+63021+77921	GW	FSP	HSB	FSR	
320302	77900+63022+77922	GW	FSP	HSB	FSR	
320303	77901+63023+77923	GW	FSP	HSB	FSR	
320304	77902+63024+77924	GW	FSP	HSB	FSR	
320305	77903+63025+77925	GW	FSP	HSB	FSR	Glasgow School of Art 1845 – 150 – 1995
320306	77904+63026+77926	GW	FSP	HSB	FSR	Model Rail Scotland
320307	77905+63027+77927	GW	FSP	HSB	FSR	
320308	77906+63028+77928	GW	FSP	HSB	FSR	High Road 20th Anniversary 2000
320309	77907+63029+77929	GW	FSP	HSB	FSR	Radio Clyde 25th Anniversary
320310	77908+63030+77930	GW	FSP	HSB	FSR	
320311	77909+63031+77931	GW	FSP	HSB	FSR	Royal College of Physicians and Surgeons of Glasgow
320312	77910+63032+77932	GW	FSP	HSB	FSR	Sir William A Smith Founder of the Boys' Brigade
320313	77911+63033+77933	GW	FSP	HSB	FSR	
320314	77912+63034+77934	GW	FSP	HSB	FSR	
320315	77913+63035+77935	GW	FSP	HSB	FSR	
320316	77914+63036+77936	GW	FSP	HSB	FSR	
320317	77915+63037+77937	GW	FSP	HSB	FSR	
320318	77916+63038+77938	GW	FSP	HSB	FSR	
320319	77917+63039+77939	GW	FSP	HSB	FSR	
320320	77918+63040+77940	GW	FSP	HSB	FSR	
320321	77919+63041+77941	GW	FSP	HSB	FSR	The Rt. Hon. John Smith, QC, MP
320322	77920+63042+77942	GW	FSP	HSB	FSR	Festival Glasgow Orchid

Right: *The 22 strong Class 320 fleet are allocated to Glasgow Shields Depot and are currently deployed on the North Clyde Line. However, following introduction of new Class 380 stock in 2011, the sets are to be transferred to other routes including the Argyle Line. In 2011 these sets are due for refurbishment by Wabtec, Doncaster which will include installation of a toilet in each set, fitting yaw dampers to permit 90mph running and repaint into the latest Scotrail Saltire livery. Set No. 320311 is seen at Lanark Junction.* **Robin Ralston**

Passenger Train Operating Companies - First Scotrail

First Scotrail

Class 322

Vehicle Length: (Driving) 65ft 0¾in (19.83m)	Width: 9ft 3in (2.82m)
(Inter) 65ft 4¼in (19.92m)	Horsepower: 1,328hp (996kW)
Height: 12ft 4¾in (3.78m)	Seats (total/car): 291S, 74S/83S/76S/58S

Number	Formation	Depot	Livery	Owner	Operator	Name
	DTSO(A)+MSO+TSO+DTSO(B)					
322481	78163+62137+72023+77985	GW	FSR	HSB	FSR	*North Berwick Flyer 1850-2000*
322482	78164+62138+72024+77986	GW	FSR	HSB	FSR	
322483	78165+62139+72025+77987	GW	FSR	HSB	FSR	
322484	78166+63140+72026+77988	GW	FSR	HSB	FSR	
322485	78167+63141+72027+77898	GW	FSR	HSB	FSR	

■ *Scheduled to come off-lease following delivery of Class 380 'Desiro' stock and transfer to National Express East Anglia.*

Left: *The five Class 322 units are currently allocated to Glasgow Shields and operated on the North Berwick Line. These sets are due to finish their operation in Scotland in summer 2011. Set No. 322481 is illustrated at its home depot painted in First Scotrail colours.* **Bill Wilson**

Class 334
Juniper

Vehicle Length: (Driving) 69ft 0¾in (21.04m)	Width: 9ft 2¾in (2.80m)
(Inter) 65ft 4½in (19.93m)	Horsepower: 1,448hp (1,080kW)
Height: 12ft 3in (3.77m)	Seats (total/car): 183S, 64S/55S/64S

Number	Formation	Depot	Livery	Owner	Operator	Name
	DMSO(A)+PTSO+DMSO(B)					
334001	64101+74301+65101	GW	FSP	HSB	FSR	*Donald Dewar*
334002	64102+74302+65102	GW	FSP	HSB	FSR	
334003	64103+74303+65103	GW	FSP	HSB	FSR	
334004	64104+74304+65104	GW	FSP	HSB	FSR	
334005	64105+74305+65105	GW	FSP	HSB	FSR	
334006	64106+74306+65106	GW	FSS	HSB	FSR	
334007	64107+74307+65107	GW	FSP	HSB	FSR	
334008	64108+74308+65108	GW	FSP	HSB	FSR	
334009	64109+74309+65109	GW	FSP	HSB	FSR	
334010	64110+74310+65110	GW	FSP	HSB	FSR	
334011	64111+74311+65111	GW	FSP	HSB	FSR	
334012	64112+74312+65112	GW	FSS	HSB	FSR	
334013	64113+74313+65113	GW	FSP	HSB	FSR	
334014	64114+74314+65114	GW	FSP	HSB	FSR	
334015	64115+74315+65115	GW	FSP	HSB	FSR	
334016	64116+74316+65116	GW	FSP	HSB	FSR	
334017	64117+74317+65117	GW	FSP	HSB	FSR	
334018	64118+74318+65118	GW	FSP	HSB	FSR	
334019	64119+74319+65119	GW	FSP	HSB	FSR	
334020	64120+74320+65120	GW	FSP	HSB	FSR	
334021	64121+74321+65121	GW	FSP	HSB	FSR	*Larkhill*
334022	64122+74322+65122	GW	FSP	HSB	FSR	
334023	64123+74323+65123	GW	FSP	HSB	FSR	
334024	64124+74324+65124	GW	FSP	HSB	FSR	
334025	64125+74325+65125	GW	FSP	HSB	FSR	
334026	64126+74326+65126	GW	FSP	HSB	FSR	
334027	64127+74327+65127	GW	FSP	HSB	FSR	
334028	64128+74328+65128	GW	FSP	HSB	FSR	
334029	64129+74329+65129	GW	FSP	HSB	FSR	

334030	64130+74330+65130	GW	FSP	HSB	FSR
334031	64131+74331+65131	GW	FSP	HSB	FSR
334032	64132+74332+65132	GW	FSP	HSB	FSR
334033	64133+74333+65133	GW	FSP	HSB	FSR
334034	64134+74334+65134	GW	FSP	HSB	FSR
334035	64135+74335+65135	GW	FSP	HSB	FSR
334036	64136+74336+65136	GW	FSP	HSB	FSR
334037	64137+74337+65137	GW	FSP	HSB	FSR
334038	64138+74338+65138	GW	FSP	HSB	FSR
334039	64139+74339+65139	GW	FSP	HSB	FSR
334040	64140+74340+65140	GW	FSP	HSB	FSR

Right: *The Alstom-built Class 334 'Juniper' units are currently used on the Ayrshire Coast Line, but from mid 2011 will transfer to the new Airdrie to Bathgate line and North Clyde services. At present all sets are painted in Strathclyde carmine and cream, but the latest Scotrail colours are due to appear in early 2011. Set No. 334020 is illustrated.* **Brian Morrison**

Class 380
Desiro

Vehicle Length: 77ft 3in (23.57m)
Height: 12ft 1½in (3.7m)
Width: 9ft 2in (2.7m)
Horsepower: 2,682hp (2,000kW)
Seats: 3-car 208S. 4-car 282S

Number	Formation DMSO(A)+PTSO+DMSO(B)	Depot	Livery	Owner	Operator
380001	38501+38601+38701	GW	FSS	HSB	FSR
380002	38502+38602+38702	GW	FSS	HSB	FSR
380003	38503+38603+38703	GW	FSS	HSB	FSR
380004	38504+38604+38704	GW	FSS	HSB	FSR
380005	38505+38605+38705	GW	FSS	HSB	FSR
380006	38506+38606+38706	GW	FSS	HSB	FSR
380007	38507+38607+38707	GW	FSS	HSB	FSR
380008	38508+38608+38708	GW	FSS	HSB	FSR
380009	38509+38609+38709	GW	FSS	HSB	FSR
380010	38510+38610+38710	GW	FSS	HSB	FSR
380011	38511+38611+38711	GW	FSS	HSB	FSR
380012	38512+38612+38712	GW	FSS	HSB	FSR
380013	38513+38613+38713	GW	FSS	HSB	FSR
380014	38514+38614+38714	GW	FSS	HSB	FSR
380015	38515+38615+38715	GW	FSS	HSB	FSR
380016	38516+38616+38716	GW	FSS	HSB	FSR
380017	38517+38617+38717	GW	FSS	HSB	FSR
380018	38518+38618+38718	GW	FSS	HSB	FSR
380019	38519+38619+38719	GW	FSS	HSB	FSR
380020	38520+38620+38720	GW	FSS	HSB	FSR
380021	38521+38621+38721	GW	FSS	HSB	FSR
380022	38522+38622+38722	GW	FSS	HSB	FSR

Number	Formation DMSO(A)+PTSO+DMSO(B)	Depot	Livery	Owner	Operator
380101	38551+38651+38851+38751	GW	FSS	HSB	FSR
380102	38552+38652+38852+38752	GW	FSS	HSB	FSR
380103	38553+38653+38853+38753	GW	FSS	HSB	FSR
380104	38554+38654+38854+38754	GW	FSS	HSB	FSR
380105	38555+38655+38855+38755	GW	FSS	HSB	FSR
380106	38556+38656+38856+38756	GW	FSS	HSB	FSR
380107	38557+38657+38857+38757	GW	FSS	HSB	FSR
380108	38558+38658+38858+38758	GW	FSS	HSB	FSR
380109	38559+38659+38859+38759	GW	FSS	HSB	FSR
380110	38560+38660+38860+38760	GW	FSS	HSB	FSR
380111	38561+38661+38861+38761	GW	FSS	HSB	FSR
380112	38562+38662+38862+38762	GW	FSS	HSB	FSR

First Scotrail

380113	38563+38663+38863+38763	GW	FSS	HSB	FSR
380114	38564+38664+38864+38764	GW	FSS	HSB	FSR
380115	38565+38665+38865+38765	GW	FSS	HSB	FSR
380116	38566+38666+38866+38766	GW	FSS	HSB	FSR

Left: From late 2010 the first 'Desiro' Class 380 sets entered service with First Scotrail. Both three and four car derivatives will be introduced in 2011 for use on the Ayrshire Coast Line, Inverclyde services and between Edinburgh and North Berwick. Four-car set No. 380107 is seen during its pre-delivery test period at Wildenrath, Germany. **CJM**

Mk2 & Mk3 Hauled Stock

Mk2
Vehicle Length: 66ft 0in (20.11m) Width: 9ft 3in (2.81m)
Height: 12ft 9½in (3.89m) Seats (total/car): 60S

Mk3
Vehicle Length: 75ft 0in (22.86m) Width: 8ft 11in (2.71m)
Height: 12ft 9in (3.88m) Bogie Type: BT10

AN1F (Mk2) - RLO *Seating 28-30F*

Number	Depot	Livery	Owner
6700 (3347)	IS	FSS	HSB
6701 (3346)	IS	FSR	HSB
6702 (3421)	IS	FSR	HSB
6703 (3308)	IS	FSR	HSB
6704 (3341)	IS	FSR	HSB
6705 (3310)	IS	FSR	HSB
6706 (3283)	IS	FSR	HSB
6707 (3276)	IS	FSR	HSB
6708 (3370)	IS	FSR	HSB

AN1F (Mk2) - BUO *Seating 31U*

Number	Depot	Livery	Owner
9800 (5751)	IS	FSR	HSB
9801 (5760)	IS	FSR	HSB
9802 (5772)	IS	FSR	HSB
9803 (5799)	IS	FSR	HSB
9804 (5826)	IS	FSR	HSB
9805 (5833)	IS	FSR	HSB
9806 (5840)	IS	FSR	HSB
9807 (5851)	IS	FSR	HSB
9808 (5871)	IS	FSS	HSB
9809 (5890)	IS	FSR	HSB
9810 (5892)	IS	FSR	HSB

AU4G (Mk3) - SLEP *Comps 12*

Number	Depot	Livery	Owner
10501	IS	FSR	PTR

Mk3

10502	IS	FSR	PTR
10504	IS	FSR	PTR
10506	IS	FSR	PTR
10507	IS	FSR	PTR
10508	IS	FSR	PTR
10513	IS	FSR	PTR
10516	IS	FSS	PTR
10519	IS	FSR	PTR
10520	IS	FSR	PTR
10522	IS	FSR	PTR
10523	IS	FSR	PTR
10526	IS	FSR	PTR
10527	IS	FSR	PTR
10529	IS	FSR	PTR
10531	IS	FSR	PTR
10542	IS	FSR	PTR
10543	IS	FSR	PTR
10544	IS	FSR	PTR
10548	IS	FSR	PTR
10551	IS	FSR	PTR
10553	IS	FSR	PTR
10561	IS	FSR	PTR
10562	IS	FSS	PTR
10565	IS	FSR	PTR
10580	IS	FSR	PTR
10597	IS	FSR	PTR
10598	IS	FSR	PTR
10600	IS	FSR	PTR
10605	IS	FSR	PTR
10607	IS	FSR	PTR
10610	IS	FSR	PTR
10613	IS	FSR	PTR
10614	IS	FSR	PTR
10617	IS	FSR	PTR

AS4G (MK3) - SLE *Comps 13*

Number	Depot	Livery	Owner
10675	IS	FSR	PTR
10683	IS	FSR	PTR
10688	IS	FSR	PTR
10690	IS	FSR	PTR
10693	IS	FSR	PTR
10703	IS	FSR	PTR

AQ4G (Mk3) - SLED *Comps 11*

Number	Depot	Livery	Owner
10648	IS	FSR	PTR
10650	IS	FSR	PTR
10666	IS	FSR	PTR
10680	IS	FSR	PTR
10689	IS	FSR	PTR
10699	IS	FSR	PTR
10706	IS	FSR	PTR
10714	IS	FSR	PTR
10718	IS	FSR	PTR
10719	IS	FSR	PTR
10722	IS	FSR	PTR
10723	IS	FSR	PTR

Left: First Scotrail are responsible for the Anglo-Scottish overnight sleeper services linking London Euston with Glasgow, Edinburgh, Inverness, Aberdeen and Fort William. For this service a sizeable fleet of Mk2 and Mk3 vehicles are maintained by Inverness depot. Mk2f Brake Unclassified Open (BUO) No. 9805 is illustrated. **Tony Christie**

Passenger Train Operating Companies - First Scotrail

First TransPennine Express

Address: ✉ Floor 7, Bridgewater House, 60 Whitworth Street, Manchester, M1 6LT
🖷 tpecustomer.relations@firstgroup.com
✆ 0845 600 1671
ⓘ www.tpexpress.co.uk

Managing Director: Vernon Baker
Franchise Dates: 1 February 2004 - 31 January 2017
Principal Routes: Newcastle, Middlesbrough, Scarborough, Hull, Cleethorpes to Manchester, Liverpool, Barrow, Carlisle, Edinburgh and Glasgow
Depots: Ardwick (AK) - Siemens operated, York (YK), Crofton (XW)
Parent Company: First Group, Keolis

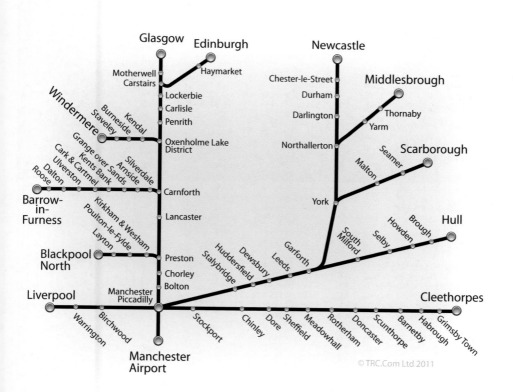

© TRC.Com Ltd 2011

First TransPennine Express

Class 170/3
Turbostar

Vehicle Length: 77ft 6in (23.62m)	Engine: 1 x MTU 6R 183TD13H 422hp per vehicle		
Height: 12ft 4½in (3.77m)	Horsepower: 844hp (629kW)		
Width: 8ft 10in (2.69m)	Seats (total/car): 8F/108S 8F-43S/65S		

Number	Formation DMCL+DMS	Depot	Livery	Owner	Operator
170301	50301+79301	XW	FTP	PTR	FTP
170302	50302+79302	XW	FTP	PTR	FTP
170303	50303+79303	XW	FTP	PTR	FTP
170304	50304+79304	XW	FTP	PTR	FTP
170305	50305+79305	XW	FTP	PTR	FTP
170306	50306+79306	XW	FTP	PTR	FTP
170307	50307+79307	XW	FTP	PTR	FTP
170308	50308+79308	XW	FTP	PTR	FTP
170309	50399+79399	XW	FTP	PTR	FTP

Below: *Delivered new to South West Trains and transferred to First TransPennine Express when extra Class 159s were introduced, these nine two-car sets operate on the Manchester-East Coast corridor. All are fully refurbished and painted in First TransPennine livery. Set No. 170309 is illustrated.* **Chris Perkins**

Class 185
Desiro

Vehicle Length: (driving) 77ft 11in (23.76m), (inter) 77ft 10½in (23.75m)			
Height: 12ft 4in (3.75m)	Engine: 1 x Cummins OSK19 of 750hp per car		
Width: 9ft 3in (2.81m)	Horsepower: 2,250hp (1,680kW)		
	Seats (total/car): 15F/154S, 15F-18S/72S/64S		

Number	Formation DMCL+MSL+DMS	Depot	Livery	Owner	Operator
185101	51101+53101+54101	AK	FTP	HSB	FTP
185102	51102+53102+54102	AK	FTP	HSB	FTP
185103	51103+53103+54103	AK	FTP	HSB	FTP
185104	51104+53104+54104	AK	FTP	HSB	FTP
185105	51105+53105+54105	AK	FTP	HSB	FTP
185106	51106+53106+54106	AK	FTP	HSB	FTP
185107	51107+53107+54107	AK	FTP	HSB	FTP
185108	51108+53108+54108	AK	FTP	HSB	FTP
185109	51109+53109+54109	AK	FTP	HSB	FTP
185110	51110+53110+54110	AK	FTP	HSB	FTP
185111	51111+53111+54111	AK	FTP	HSB	FTP
185112	51112+53112+54112	AK	FTP	HSB	FTP
185113	51113+53113+54113	AK	FTP	HSB	FTP
185114	51114+53114+54114	AK	FTP	HSB	FTP
185115	51115+53115+54115	AK	FTP	HSB	FTP
185116	51116+53116+54116	AK	FTP	HSB	FTP
185117	51117+53117+54117	AK	FTP	HSB	FTP

185118	51118+53118+54118	AK	FTP	HSB	FTP
185119	51119+53119+54119	AK	FTP	HSB	FTP
185120	51120+53120+54120	AK	FTP	HSB	FTP
185121	51121+53121+54121	AK	FTP	HSB	FTP
185122	51122+53122+54122	AK	FTP	HSB	FTP
185123	51123+53123+54123	AK	FTP	HSB	FTP
185124	51124+53124+54124	AK	FTP	HSB	FTP
185125	51125+53125+54125	AK	FTP	HSB	FTP
185126	51126+53126+54126	AK	FTP	HSB	FTP
185127	51127+53127+54127	AK	FTP	HSB	FTP
185128	51128+53128+54128	AK	FTP	HSB	FTP
185129	51129+53129+54129	AK	FTP	HSB	FTP
185130	51130+53130+54130	AK	FTP	HSB	FTP
185131	51131+53131+54131	AK	FTP	HSB	FTP
185132	51132+53132+54132	AK	FTP	HSB	FTP
185133	51133+53133+54133	AK	FTP	HSB	FTP
185134	51134+53134+54134	AK	FTP	HSB	FTP
185135	51135+53135+54135	AK	FTP	HSB	FTP
185136	51136+53136+54136	AK	FTP	HSB	FTP
185137	51137+53137+54137	AK	FTP	HSB	FTP
185138	51138+53138+54138	AK	FTP	HSB	FTP
185139	51139+53139+54139	AK	FTP	HSB	FTP
185140	51140+53140+54140	AK	FTP	HSB	FTP
185141	51141+53141+54141	AK	FTP	HSB	FTP
185142	51142+53142+54142	AK	FTP	HSB	FTP
185143	51143+53143+54143	AK	FTP	HSB	FTP
185144	51144+53144+54144	AK	FTP	HSB	FTP
185145	51145+53145+54145	AK	FTP	HSB	FTP
185146	51146+53146+54146	AK	FTP	HSB	FTP
185147	51147+53147+54147	AK	FTP	HSB	FTP
185148	51148+53148+54148	AK	FTP	HSB	FTP
185149	51149+53149+54149	AK	FTP	HSB	FTP
185150	51150+53150+54150	AK	FTP	HSB	FTP
185151	51151+53151+54151	AK	FTP	HSB	FTP

Above: *Fifty one three-car Class 185 'Desiro' DMUs are operated by First TransPennine Express and are allocated to Ardwick depot in Manchester. These high-quality sets form the backbone of FTPE services and are some of the most reliable DMUs in the UK. Set No. 185134 passes Gorton on 20 April 2010 bound for Middlesbrough.* **John Binch**

Grand Central

Address:	✉ River House, 17 Museum Street, York, YO1 7DJ
	✍ info@grandcentral.com
	✆ 0845 603 4852
	ⓘ www.grandcentral.co.uk
Managing Director:	Tom Clift
Franchise Dates:	Private Open Access Operator
Principal Routes:	London King's Cross-Sunderland/Bradford
Depots:	Heaton (HT)
Parent Company:	Equisshare Partners

Sunderland
Hartlepool
Eaglescliffe
Northallerton
Thirsk
York
Doncaster
London King's Cross

Bradford Interchange
Halifax
Brighouse
Wakefield Kirkgate
Pontefract Monkhill

© TRC.Com Ltd 2011

Below: Private Open Access Operator Grand Central operates a fleet of three HSTs on its core Sunderland to King's Cross route. In 2010-11 all power cars were refurbished with the latest MTU power units. A northbound GC service passes Doncaster led by unrefurbished Class 43/0 No. 43123. **Tony Christie**

Class 43 – HST

Vehicle Length: 58ft 5in (18.80m)
Height: 12ft 10in (3.90m)
Width: 8ft 11in (2.73m)
Engine: MTU 16V4000 R41R
Horsepower: 2,250hp (1,680kW)
Electrical Equipment: Brush

Number	Depot	Pool	Livery	Owner	Operator
43465 (43065)	HT	GCHP	GTL	ANG	GTL
43467 (43067)	HT	GCHP	GTL	ANG	GTL
43468 (43068)	HT	GCHP	GTO	ANG	GTL
43480 (43080)	HT	GCHP	GTO	ANG	GTL
43484 (43084)	HT	GCHP	GTL	ANG	GTL
43523 (43123)	HT	GCHP	GTL	ANG	GTL

Name applied
43123 (43523) - *'Valenta' 1972 - 2010*

Class 180
Zephyrs

Vehicle Length: (driving) 75ft 7in (23.71m), (inter) 75ft 5in (23.03m)
Height: 12ft 4in (3.75m)
Width: 9ft 2in (2.80m)
Engine: 1 x Cummins OSK19 of 750hp per car
Horsepower: 3,750hp (2,796kW)
Seats (total/car): 42F/226S, 46S/42F/68S/56S/56S

Number	Formation DMSL(A)+MFL+MSL+MSLRB+DMSL(B)	Depot	Livery	Owner	Operator	Name
180101	50901+54901+55901+56901+59901	HT	GTL	ANG	GTL	
180105	50905+54905+55905+56905+59905	HT	GTL	ANG	GTL	
180107	50907+54907+55907+56907+59907	HT	GTL	ANG	GTL	*Hart of the North*
180112	50912+54912+55912+56912+59912	HT	GTL	ANG	GTL	*James Herriot*
180114	50914+54914+55914+56914+59914	HT	GTL	ANG	GTL	

Above: *The Grand Central Railway leased Class 180 five-car sets from Angel Trains are refurbished and sport the operator's black and orange livery which looks very smart. With a plastic cover over its coupler, set No. 180114 is seen at York with a London King's Cross to Sunderland service.* **Chris Perkins**

Mk3 HST stock

Vehicle Length: 75ft 0in (22.86m)	Width: 8ft 11in (2.71m)
Height: 12ft 9in (3.88m)	Bogie Type: BT10

GK2G - TRSB *Seating 33S*

Number		Depot	Livery	Owner
40424	(40024)	HT	GTO	ANG
40426	(40026)	HT	GTL	ANG
40433	(40033)	HT	GTL	ANG

GH1G - TF *Seating 48F*

Number		Depot	Livery	Owner
41201	(11045)	HT	GTO	ANG
41202	(11017)	HT	GTL	ANG
41203	(11038)	HT	GTL	ANG
41204	(11023)	HT	GTL	ANG
41205	(11036)	HT	GTL	ANG
41206	(11055)	HT	GTL	ANG

GH2G - TS *Seating 64S *TSD Seating 60S*

Number		Depot	Livery	Owner
42401	(12149)	HT	GTO	ANG

42402	(12155)	HT	GTO	ANG
42403*	(12033)	HT	GTO	ANG
42404	(12152)	HT	GTL	ANG
42405	(12136)	HT	GTL	ANG
42406*	(12112)	HT	GTL	ANG
42407	(12044)	HT	GTL	ANG
42408	(12121)	HT	GTL	ANG
42409*	(12088)	HT	GTL	ANG

GJ2G - TGS *Seating 67S*

Number	Depot	Livery	Owner
44065 (S)	HT/LM	GTL	GTL
44088 (S)	HT/LM	GTL	GTL
44089 (S)	HT/LM	GTL	GTL

■ *Mk3 loco-hauled coaches 12058, 12104, 12165 owned by Grand Central stored at Long Marston.*

Grand Central also operate Mk2D BSO 9488 as a barrier vehicle.

Right: *Apart from the three TRSB vehicles and the stored TGS carriages, all the Grand Central HST passenger fleet has been rebuilt from loco-hauled Mk3 stock. The conversion work was undertaken by Axiom Rail at Stoke Marcroft. TS No. 42408 is shown at York. This vehicle was rebuilt from Mk3 TS No. 12121.*
Nathan Williamson

Heathrow Express / Heathrow Connect

Address: ✉ 6th Floor, 50 Eastbourne Terrace, Paddington, London, W2 6LX
✈ queries@heathrowexpress.com or queries@heathrowconnect.com
✆ 020 8750 6600
ⓘ www.heathrowexpress.com or www.heathrowconnect.com

Managing Director: Richard Robinson
Franchise Dates: Private Open Access Operator
Principal Routes: London Paddington - Heathrow Airport
Owned Stations: Heathrow Central, Heathrow Terminal 4, Heathrow Terminal 5
Depots: Old Oak Common HEX (OH)
Parent Company: Heathrow Express - British Airports Authority
    Heathrow Connect - British Airports Authority / First Group

Heathrow Express

© TRC.Com Ltd 2011

Heathrow Airport Terminal 5   Heathrow Airport Terminals 1-3   London Paddington

Heathrow Connect

Heathrow Airport Terminal 4   Heathrow Airport Terminals 1-3   Hayes   Southall   Hanwell   West Ealing   Ealing Broadway   London Paddington

Shuttle

Left: *Changes in 2010 saw a new 'shuttle' service introduced between Heathrow Terminals 1-3 and Terminal 4, formed of a dedicated Class 360 No. 360205 which has a revised interior and is painted in Heathrow Express colours. Reliveried and branded 'Heathrow Express', former Heathrow Connect Class 360/2 'Desiro' No. 360205 waits at Heathrow Terminal 4 on 29 June 2010, forming one of the four-an-hour shuttle services between there and Terminals 1-3.*
Brian Morrison

Class 332

Vehicle Length: (Driving) 77ft 10¾in (23.74m)		Width: 9ft 1in (2.75m)		
(Inter) 75ft 11in (23.143m)		Horsepower: 1,876hp (1,400kW)		
Height: 12ft 1½in (3.70m)		Seats 4-car (total/car): 26F-148S, 26F/56S/44S/48S		
		5-Car (total/car): 26F-204S, 26F/56S/44S/56S/48S		

Number	Formation	Depot	Livery	Owner	Operator
	DMFO+TSO+PTSO+(TSO)+DMSO				
332001	78400+72412+63400+ - +78401	OH	HEX	BAA	HEX
332002	78402+72409+63401+ - +78403	OH	HEX	BAA	HEX
332003	78404+72407+63402+ - +78405	OH	HEX	BAA	HEX
332004	78406+72406+63403+ - +78407	OH	HEX	BAA	HEX
332005	78408+72411+63404+72417+78409	OH	HEX	BAA	HEX
332006	78410+72410+63405+72415+78411	OH	HEX	BAA	HEX
332007	78412+72401+63406+72414+78413	OH	HEX	BAA	HEX

Vehicle Length: (Driving) 77ft 10¾in (23.74m)		Width: 9ft 1in (2.75m)		
(Inter) 75ft 11in (23.143m)		Horsepower: 1,876hp (1,400kW)		
Height: 12ft 1½in (3.70m)		Seats 4-car (total/car): 14F-148S, 48S/56S/44S/14F		
		5-Car (total/car): 14F-204S, 48S/56S/44S/56S/14F		

Number	Formation	Depot	Livery	Owner	Operator
	DMSO+TSO+PTSO+(TSO)+DMFLO				
332008	78414+72413+63407+72418+78415	OH	HEX	BAA	HEX
332009	78416+72400+63408+72416+78417	OH	HEX	BAA	HEX
332010	78418+72402+63409+ - +78419	OH	HEX	BAA	HEX
332011	78420+72403+63410+ - +78421	OH	HEX	BAA	HEX
332012	78422+72404+63411+ - +78423	OH	HEX	BAA	HEX
332013	78424+72408+63412+ - +78425	OH	HEX	BAA	HEX
332014	78426+72406+63413+ - +78427	OH	HEX	BAA	HEX

Class 360/2
Desiro

Vehicle Length: 66ft 9in (20.4m)		Horsepower: 1,341hp (1,000kW)	
Height: 12ft 1½in (3.7m)		Seats (total/car): 264S, 63S/66S/74S/74S/63S	
Width: 9ft 2in (2.79m)		(360205 - 280S using 2+2 seats)	

Number	Formation	Depot	Livery	Owner	Operator	
	DMSO(A)+PTSO+TSO+TSO+DMSO(B)					**Below:** Heathrow Express
360201	78431+63421+72431+72421+78441	OH	HEC	BAA	HEC	Class 332 No. 332013 overtakes
360202	78432+63422+72432+72422+78442	OH	HEC	BAA	HEC	Heathrow Connect Class 360 No.
360203	78433+63423+72433+72423+78443	OH	HEC	BAA	HEC	360202 at Southall. Both Class
360204	78434+63424+72434+72424+78444	OH	HEC	BAA	HEC	332 and 360 stock are maintained
360205	78435+63425+72435+72425+78445	OH	HEL	BAA	HEC	at Old Oak Common HEX depot.
						Brian Morrison

Hull Trains

Address: ✉ Europa House, 184 Ferensway, Kingston-upon-Hull, HU1 3UT
✎ customer.services@hulltrains.co.uk
✆ 0845 676 9905
ⓘ www.hulltrains.co.uk

General Manager:	James Adeshiyan
Franchise Dates:	Private Open Access Operator, agreement to 2016
Principal Route:	London King's Cross - Hull
Depots:	Old Oak Common (OO) [Operated by FGW], Crofton (XW)
Parent Company:	First Group PLC

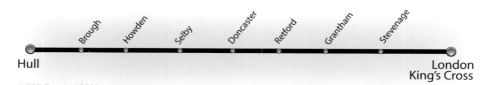

Hull — Brough — Howden — Selby — Doncaster — Retford — Grantham — Stevenage — London King's Cross

© TRC.Com Ltd 2011

Class 180
Adelante

Vehicle Length: (driving) 75ft 7in (23.71m), (inter) 75ft 5in (23.03m)
Height: 12ft 4in (3.75m)
Width: 9ft 2in (2.80m)
Engine: 1 x Cummins OSK19 of 750hp per car
Horsepower: 3,750hp (2,796kW)
Seats (total/car): 42F/226S, 46S/42F/68S/56S/56S

Number	Formation DMSL(A)+MFL+MSF+MSLRB+DMSL(B)	Depot	Livery	Owner	Operator
180109	50909+54909+55909+56909+59909	OO/XW	FHT	ANG	FHT
180110	50910+54910+55910+56910+59910	OO/XW	FHT	ANG	FHT
180111	50911+54911+55911+56911+59911	OO/XW	FHT	ANG	FHT
180113	50913+54913+55913+56913+59913	OO/XW	FHT	ANG	FHT

Below: *Following use on First Great Western, four of the Alstom-built Class 180s have found work with First Hull Trains, operating an infrequent semi-fast service between King's Cross and Hull. The trains carry First Hull Trains livery. Set No. 180110 is seen at London King's Cross.* **Nathan Williamson**

Island Line

Passenger Train Operating Companies - Island Line

Address: ✉ Ryde St Johns Road Station, Ryde, Isle of Wight, PO33 2BA
🖳 info@island-line.co.uk
✆ 01983 812591
ⓘ www.island-line.co.uk

Managing Director: Andy Pitt (South West Trains), **General Manager:** Andy Naylor
Franchise Dates: Part of SWT franchise 2 February 2007 - 28 February 2017
Principal Route: Ryde Pier Head - Shanklin
Owned Stations: All
Depots: Ryde St Johns (RY)
Parent Company: Stagecoach

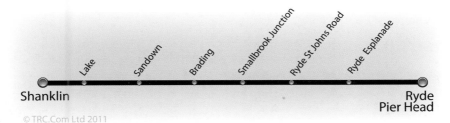

© TRC.Com Ltd 2011

Class 483

Vehicle Length: 52ft 4in (15.95m)	Horsepower: 670hp (500kW)	
Height: 9ft 5½in (2.88m)	Seats (total/car): 82S, 40S/42S	
Width: 8ft 8½in (2.65m)		

Number	Formation DMSO+DMSO	Depot	Livery	Owner	Operator
483002	122+224	RY	LUL	SWT	SIL
483004	124+224	RY	LUL	SWT	SIL
483006	126+226	RY	LUL	SWT	SIL
483007	127+227	RY	LUL	SWT	SIL
483008	128+228	RY	LUL	SWT	SIL
483009	129+229	RY	LUL	SWT	SIL

Below: *The six remaining Class 483 units operating rail services on the Isle of Wight are the oldest stock working on the national rail system in the UK. The sets are maintained at Ryde Works and all are now painted in mock London Underground red livery. Set No. 004 is seen at Ryde Pier Head.* **CJM**

London Midland

Address:	✉ 102 New Street, Birmingham, B2 4JB
	✍ comments@londonmidland.com
	✆ 0844 811 0133
	ⓘ www.londonmidland.com
Managing Director:	Mike Hodson
Franchise Dates:	11 November 2007 - 19 September 2015
Principal Routes:	London Euston - Liverpool Lime Street, West Midlands routes to Stratford, Worcester, Hereford, Shrewsbury, plus Bedford and St Albans Abbey branches
Depots:	Northampton (NN)*, Soho (SI), Tyseley (TS), Stourbridge Junction (SJ) * Operated by Siemens
Parent Company:	Govia

Class 08

Vehicle Length: 29ft 3in (8.91m)	Engine: English Electric 6K
Height: 12ft 8⅝in (3.87m)	Horsepower: 400hp (298kW)
Width: 8ft 6in (2.59m)	Electrical Equipment: English Electric

Number	Depot	Pool	Livery	Owner	Operator
08616 (3785)	TS	EJLO	LMI	LMI	LMI
08805	SI	EJLO	BLU	LMI	LMI

Names applied
08616	*Tyseley 100*	08805	*Concorde*

Left: *Two Class 08s are on the books of London Midland, used for depot shunting at Tyseley and Soho. The loco based at Tyseley No. 08616, which carries its original 1957 number 3785 on a cast Great Western style plate is painted in London Midland livery. The loco used at Soho, No. 08805 carried BR rail blue, but is devoid of the double arrow logo. No. 08805 is illustrated at Soho in September 2010.* **John Stretton**

Class 139

Vehicle Length: 28ft 6in (8.7m)	Engine: 1 x MVH420 2.0ltr LPG, flywheel hybrid
Width: 7ft 8in (2.4m)	Seats (total/car): 18S

Number	Formation DMS	Depot	Livery	Owner	Operator		Number	Formation	Depot	Livery	Owner	Operator
139001	39001	SJ	LMI	LMI	LMI		139002	39002	SJ	LMI	LMI	LMI

Left: *After a rocky start to operations, the two Class 139 Parry People Mover railcars are now successfully operating the Stourbridge Town to Stourbridge Junction shuttle service. The two vehicles are painted in full London Midland livery with Stourbridge Shuttle branding. The vehicles are restricted to just this line and receive maintenance in a specially built depot at Stourbridge Junction. Car No. 139002 departs from Stourbridge Town.* **Stacey Thew**

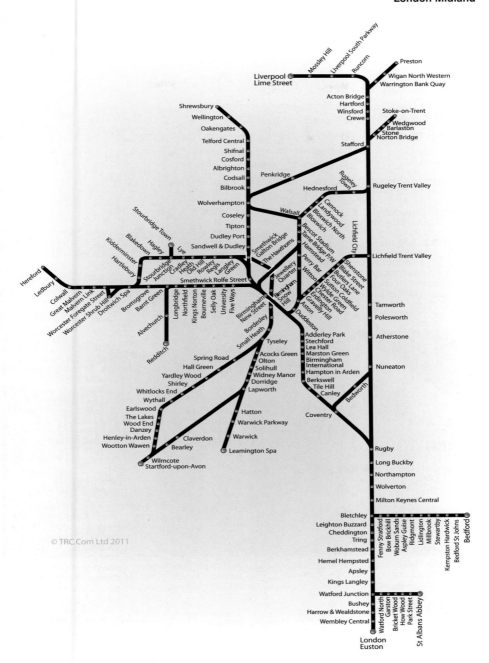

© TRC.Com Ltd 2011

London Midland

Class 150/0

Vehicle Length: (driving) 65ft 9¾in (20.05m), (inter) 66ft 2½in (20.18m)				
Height: 12ft 4½in (3.77m)		Engine: 1 x Cummins NT855R4 of 285hp per car		
Width: 9ft 3⅛in (2.82m)		Horsepower: 855hp (638kW)		
		Seats (total/car): 240S, 72S/92S/76S		

Number	Formation	Depot	Livery	Owner	Operator
	DMSL+MS+DMS				
150001	55200+55400+55300	TS	CTL	ANG	LMI
150002	55201+55401+55301	TS	CTL	ANG	LMI

Class 150/0

Vehicle Length: 64ft 9¾in (19.74m)		Engine: 1 x NT855R5 of 285hp per vehicle
Height: 12ft 4½in (3.77m)		Horsepower: 855hp (638kW)
Width: 9ft 3⅛in (2.82m)		Seats (total/car): 224S, 76S/76S/72S
		*220S, 72S/72S/76S

Number	Formation	Depot	Livery	Owner	Operator
	DMSL+DMSL+DMS or				
	DMSL+DMS+DMS*				
150003	52103+52210+57106	TS	WMD	ANG	LMI
150005	52105+52210+57105	TS	CTL	ANG	LMI
150007	52107+52202+57107	TS	CTL	ANG	LMI
150009	52109+57202+57109*	TS	CTL	ANG	LMI
150010	52110+57226+57210*	TS	WMD	ANG	LMI
150011	52111+52204+57111	TS	CTL	ANG	LMI
150012	52112+57206+58112*	TS	CTL	ANG	LMI
150013	52113+52226+57113	TS	CTL	ANG	LMI
150014	52114+57204+57114*	TS	CTL	ANG	LMI
150015	52115+52206+57115	TS	CTL	ANG	LMI
150016	52116+57212+57116*	TS	CTL	ANG	LMI
150017	52117+57209+57117*	TS	CTL	ANG	LMI
150018	52118+52220+57118	TS	WMD	ANG	LMI
150019	52119+57220+57119*	TS	CTL	ANG	LMI

Above: *Painted in a London Midland version of the former Central Trains green and blue livery, Class 150/1 No. 150106 is seen from its DMS end at Worcester Shrub Hill. This is one of the sets due to transfer to First Great Western in 2011 after London Midland receives its allocation of Class 172s currently under construction at Bombardier Derby.* **CJM**

Class 150/1

Vehicle Length: 64ft 9¾in (19.74m)		Engine: 1 x NT855R5 of 285hp per vehicle
Height: 12ft 4½in (3.77m)		Horsepower: 570hp (425kW)
Width: 9ft 3⅛in (2.82m)		Seats (total/car): 141S, 71S/70S

Number	Formation	Depot	Livery	Owner	Operator		Number	Formation	Depot	Livery	Owner	Operator
	DMSL+DMS						150104	52104+57104	TS	CTL	ANG	LMI
							150106	52106+57106	TS	CTL	ANG	LMI
150101	52101+57101	TS	CTL	ANG	LMI		150108	52108+57108	TS	CTL	ANG	LMI
150102	52102+57102	TS	CTL	ANG	LMI		150122	52122+57122	TS	CTL	ANG	LMI

150124	52124+57124	TS	CTL	ANG	LMI	150126	52126+57126	TS	WMD	ANG	LMI
150125	52125+57125	TS	CTL	ANG	LMI	150132	52132+57132	TS	WMD	ANG	LMI

● London Midland Class 150/1 sets due for transfer to First Great Western in 2011 after Class 172s delivered.

Class 150/2

Vehicle Length: 64ft 9¾in (19.74m)
Height: 12ft 4½in (3.77m)
Width: 9ft 3⅛in (2.82m)
Engine: 1 x NT855R5 of 285hp per vehicle
Horsepower: 570hp (425kW)
Seats (total/car): 141S, 71S/70S

Number	Formation	Depot	Livery	Owner	Operator						
	DMSL+DMS					150216	52216+57216	TS	CTL	ANG	LMI
150214	52214+57214	TS	CTL	ANG	LMI						

Class 153

Vehicle Length: 76ft 5in (23.29m)
Height: 12ft 3½in (3.75m)
Width: 8ft 10in (2.70m)
Engine: 1 x NT855R5 of 285hp
Horsepower: 285hp (213kW)
Seats (total/car): 72S

Number	Formation	Depot	Livery	Owner	Operator						
	DMSL					153356	57356	TS	LMI	PTR	LMI
						153364¤	57364	TS	LMI	PTR	LMI
153325	52325	TS	LMI	PTR	LMI	153365	57365	TS	LMI	PTR	LMI
153333	52333	TS	LMI	PTR	LMI	153366	57366	TS	LMI	PTR	LMI
153334	52334	TS	LMI	PTR	LMI	153371	57371	TS	LMI	PTR	LMI
153354¤	57354	TS	LMI	PTR	LMI	153375	57375	TS	LMI	PTR	LMI

¤ On loan to National Express East Anglia at Norwich Crown Point.

Right: *London Midland operate a fleet of 10 Class 153 single car or 'Bubble' units, all allocated to Tyseley and used on lightly patronised routes. All sets are now painted in London Midland corporate colours. Set No. 153364 is seen at Nuneaton on 2 August 2010.*
John Binch

Class 170/5
Turbostar

Vehicle Length: 77ft 6in (23.62m)
Height: 12ft 4½in (3.77m)
Width: 8ft 10in (2.69m)
Engine: 1 x MTU 6R 183TD13H 422hp per vehicle
Horsepower: 844hp (629kW)
Seats (total/car): 122S 55S/67S

Number	Formation	Depot	Livery	Owner	Operator						
	DMSL+DMSL					170509	50509+79509	TS	LMI	PTR	LMI
						170510	50510+79510	TS	LMI	PTR	LMI
170501	50501+79501	TS	LMI	PTR	LMI	170511	50511+79511	TS	LMI	PTR	LMI
170502	50502+79502	TS	LMI	PTR	LMI	170512	50512+79512	TS	LMI	PTR	LMI
170503	50503+79503	TS	LMI	PTR	LMI	170513	50513+79513	TS	LMI	PTR	LMI
170504	50504+79504	TS	LMI	PTR	LMI	170514	50514+79514	TS	LMI	PTR	LMI
170505	50505+79505	TS	LMI	PTR	LMI	170515	50515+79515	TS	LMI	PTR	LMI
170506	50506+79506	TS	LMI	PTR	LMI	170516	50516+79516	TS	LMI	PTR	LMI
170507	50507+79507	TS	LMI	PTR	LMI	170517	50517+79517	TS	LMI	PTR	LMI
170508	50508+79508	TS	LMI	PTR	LMI						

Class 170/6
Turbostar

Vehicle Length: 77ft 6in (23.62m)
Height: 12ft 4½in (3.77m)
Width: 8ft 10in (2.69m)
Engine: 1 x MTU 6R 183TD13H 422hp per vehicle
Horsepower: 1,266hp (944kW)
Seats (total/car): 196S 55S/74S/67S

Number	Formation	Depot	Livery	Owner	Operator
	DMSL+MS+DMSL				
170630	50630+56630+79630	TS	LMI	PTR	LMI
170631	50631+56631+79631	TS	LMI	PTR	LMI
170632	50632+56632+79632	TS	LMI	PTR	LMI
170633	50633+56633+79633	TS	LMI	PTR	LMI
170634	50634+56634+79634	TS	LMI	PTR	LMI
170635	50635+56635+79635	TS	LMI	PTR	LMI

London Midland

Longer distance London Midland operated services are formed of Class 170
'Turbostar' sets, in either two or three car consists. All are allocated to Tyseley
depot and carry full London Midland livery. All sets are refurbished internally.
Two car set No. 170506 is illustrated at Gloucester.
CJM

Class 172/2
Turbostar

Vehicle Length: 73ft 4in (22.37m)
Height: 12ft 4½in (3.77m)
Width: 8ft 8in (2.69m)

Engine: MTU 6H1800 of 360kW
Horsepower: 965hp (720kW)
Seats (total/car): 121S, 53S/68S

Number	Formation DMS+DMS	Depot	Livery	Owner	Operator
172211	50211+79211	TS	LMI	PTR	LMI
172212	50212+79212	TS	LMI	PTR	LMI
172213	50213+79213	TS	LMI	PTR	LMI
172214	50214+79214	TS	LMI	PTR	LMI
172215	50215+79215	TS	LMI	PTR	LMI
172216	50216+79216	TS	LMI	PTR	LMI
172217	50217+79217	TS	LMI	PTR	LMI
172218	50218+79218	TS	LMI	PTR	LMI
172219	50219+59219	TS	LMI	PTR	LMI
172220	50220+79220	TS	LMI	PTR	LMI
170221	50221+79221	TS	LMI	PTR	LMI
170222	50222+79222	TS	LMI	PTR	LMI

Class 172/3
Turbostar

Vehicle Length: (Driving) 73ft 4in (22.37m)
(Inter): (76ft 7in 23.36m)
Height: 12ft 4½in (3.77m)
Width: 8ft 8in (2.69m)

Engine: MTU 6H1800 of 360kW
Horsepower: 1449hp (1080kW)
Seats (total/car): 193S, 53S/72S/68S

Number	Formation DMSO+MS+DMSO	Depot	Livery	Owner	Opt'r
172331	50331+56331+79331	TS	LMI	PTR	LMI
172332	50332+56332+79332	TS	LMI	PTR	LMI
172333	50333+56333+79333	TS	LMI	PTR	LMI
172334	50334+56334+79334	TS	LMI	PTR	LMI
172335	50335+56335+79335	TS	LMI	PTR	LMI
172336	50336+56336+79336	TS	LMI	PTR	LMI
172337	50337+56337+79337	TS	LMI	PTR	LMI
172338	50338+56338+79338	TS	LMI	PTR	LMI
172339	50339+56339+79339	TS	LMI	PTR	LMI
172340	50340+56340+79340	TS	LMI	PTR	LMI
172341	50341+56341+79341	TS	LMI	PTR	LMI
172342	50342+56342+79342	TS	LMI	PTR	LMI
172343	50343+56343+79343	TS	LMI	PTR	LMI
172344	50344+56344+79344	TS	LMI	PTR	LMI
172345	50345+56345+79345	TS	LMI	PTR	LMI

Above: The first of 15 three-car gangway-fitted Class
172/3s for London Midland emerged in January 2011.
Un-branded set No. 172331 is illustrated during main
line testing. **Carl Westwood**

Class 321/4

Vehicle Length: (Driving) 65ft 0¾in (19.83m)
(Inter) 65ft 4¼in (19.92m)
Height: 12ft 4¾in (3.78m)

Width: 9ft 3in (2.82m)
Horsepower: 1,328kW (996kW)
Seats (total/car): 28F/271S, 28F-40S/79S/74S/78S

Number	Formation DMCO+MSO+TSO+DMSO	Depot	Livery	Owner	Operator
321411	78105+63073+71959+77953	NN	LMI	HSB	LMI
321412	78106+63074+71960+77954	NN	LMI	HSB	LMI
321413	78107+63075+71961+77955	NN	LMI	HSB	LMI
321414	78108+63076+71962+77956	NN	LMI	HSB	LMI
321415	78109+63077+71963+77957	NN	LMI	HSB	LMI
321416	78110+63078+71964+77958	NN	LMI	HSB	LMI
321417	78111+63079+71965+77959	NN	LMI	HSB	LMI

London Midland

Right: *To assist with main line services on the Birmingham to Euston corridor, especially at peak times, a fleet of seven Class 321/4 units have remained operational on the West Coast route with London Midland. All sets have been refurbished and are allocated to Northampton depot, alongside the core Class 350 'Desiro' fleet. Set No. 321411 is seen near Old Linslade with a Euston to Milton Keynes working.* **Michael J. Collins**

Class 323

Vehicle Length: (Driving) 76ft 8¼in (23.37m)			Width: 9ft 2¼in (2.80m)		
(Inter) 76ft 10¾in (23.44m)			Horsepower: 1,565hp (1,168kW)		
Height: 12ft 4¾in (3.78m)			Seats (total/car): 284S, 98S/88S/98S		

Number	Formation DMSO(A)+PTSO+DMSO(B)	Depot	Livery	Owner	Operator
323201	64001+72201+65001	SI	LMI	PTR	LMI
323202	64002+72202+65002	SI	LMI	PTR	LMI
323203	64003+72203+65003	SI	LMI	PTR	LMI
323204	64004+72204+65004	SI	LMI	PTR	LMI
323205	64005+72205+65005	SI	LMI	PTR	LMI
323206	64006+72206+65006	SI	LMI	PTR	LMI
323207	64007+72207+65007	SI	LMI	PTR	LMI
323208	64008+72208+65008	SI	LMI	PTR	LMI
323209	64009+72209+65009	SI	LMI	PTR	LMI
323210	64010+72210+65010	SI	LMI	PTR	LMI
323211	64011+72211+65011	SI	LMI	PTR	LMI
323212	64012+72212+65012	SI	LMI	PTR	LMI
323213	64013+72213+65013	SI	LMI	PTR	LMI
323214	64014+72214+65014	SI	LMI	PTR	LMI
323215	64015+72215+65015	SI	LMI	PTR	LMI
323216	64016+72216+65016	SI	LMI	PTR	LMI
323217	64017+72217+65017	SI	LMI	PTR	LMI
323218	64018+72218+65018	SI	LMI	PTR	LMI
323219	64019+72219+65019	SI	LMI	PTR	LMI
323220	64020+72220+65020	SI	LMI	PTR	LMI
323221	64021+72221+65021	SI	LMI	PTR	LMI
323222	64022+72222+65022	SI	LMI	PTR	LMI
323240	64040+72340+65040	SI	LMI	PTR	LMI
323241	64041+72341+65041	SI	LMI	PTR	LMI
323242	64042+72342+65042	SI	LMI	PTR	LMI
323243	64043+72343+65043	SI	LMI	PTR	LMI

Right: *A fleet of 26 Class 323 three-car electric sets operate on the Birmingham Cross-City route. All sets are based at Soho depot and since the franchise changes in 2007 all now sport London Midland City livery and have facelifted passenger interiors. Set No. 323215 is illustrated.* **Tony Christie**

Passenger Train Operating Companies - London Midland

Passenger Train Operating Companies - London Midland

London Midland

Class 350/1
Desiro

Vehicle Length: 66ft 9in (20.4m)		*Horsepower: 1,341hp (1,000kW)*	
Height: 12ft 1½in (3.78m)		*Seats (total/car): 24F-209S, 60S/24F-32S/57S/60S*	
Width: 9ft 2in (2.7m)			

Number	Formation	Depot	Livery	Owner	Operator
	DMSO(A)+TCO+PTSO+DMSO(B)				
350101	63761+66811+66861+63711	NN	LMI	ANG	LMI
350102	63762+66812+66862+63712	NN	LMI	ANG	LMI
350103	63765+66813+66863+63713	NN	LMI	ANG	LMI
350104	63764+66814+66864+63714	NN	LMI	ANG	LMI
350105	63763+66815+66868+63715	NN	LMI	ANG	LMI
350106	63766+66816+66866+63716	NN	LMI	ANG	LMI
350107	63767+66817+66867+63717	NN	LMI	ANG	LMI
350108	63768+66818+66865+63718	NN	LMI	ANG	LMI
350109	63769+66819+66869+63719	NN	LMI	ANG	LMI
350110	63770+66820+66870+63720	NN	LMI	ANG	LMI
350111	63771+66821+66871+63721	NN	LMI	ANG	LMI
350112	63772+66822+66872+63722	NN	LMI	ANG	LMI
350113	63773+66823+66873+63723	NN	LMI	ANG	LMI
350114	63774+66824+66874+63724	NN	LMI	ANG	LMI
350115	63775+66825+66875+63725	NN	LMI	ANG	LMI
350116	63776+66826+66876+63726	NN	LMI	ANG	LMI
350117	63777+66827+66877+63727	NN	LMI	ANG	LMI
350118	63778+66828+66878+63728	NN	LMI	ANG	LMI
350119	63779+66829+66879+63729	NN	LMI	ANG	LMI
350120	63780+66830+66880+63730	NN	LMI	ANG	LMI
350121	63781+66831+66881+63731	NN	LMI	ANG	LMI
350122	63782+66832+66882+63732	NN	LMI	ANG	LMI
350123	63783+66833+66883+63733	NN	LMI	ANG	LMI
350124	63784+66834+66884+63734	NN	LMI	ANG	LMI
350125	63785+66835+66885+63735	NN	LMI	ANG	LMI
350126	63786+66836+66886+63736	NN	LMI	ANG	LMI
350127	63787+66837+66887+63737	NN	LMI	ANG	LMI
350128	63788+66838+66888+63738	NN	LMI	ANG	LMI
350129	63789+66839+66889+63739	NN	LMI	ANG	LMI
350130	63790+66840+66890+63740	NN	LMI	ANG	LMI

Above: *Main line London Midland services are operated by two batches of Siemens 'Desiro' EMUs of Class 350. Sets are allocated to the large Siemens maintenance facility at Northampton. With a full height yellow painted front communicating door, Class 350/1 Angel Trains-owned No. 350119 hurries past South Kenton on 7 May 2010 with a Euston to Birmingham semi-fast service.* **CJM**

Class 350/2
Desiro

Vehicle Length: 66ft 9in (20.4m)	Horsepower: 1,341hp (1,000kW)	
Height: 12ft 1½in (3.78m)	Seats (total/car): 24F-243S, 70S/24F-42S/61S/70S	
Width: 9ft 2in (2.7m)		

Number	Formation DMSO(A)+TCO+PTSO+DMSO(B)	Depot	Livery	Owner	Operator
350231	61431+65231+67531+61531	NN	LMI	PTR	LMI
350232	61432+65232+67532+61532	NN	LMI	PTR	LMI
350233	61433+65233+67533+61533	NN	LMI	PTR	LMI
350234	61434+65234+67534+61534	NN	LMI	PTR	LMI
350235	61435+65235+67535+61535	NN	LMI	PTR	LMI
350236	61436+65236+67536+61536	NN	LMI	PTR	LMI
350237	61437+65237+67537+61537	NN	LMI	PTR	LMI
350238	61438+65238+67538+61538	NN	LMI	PTR	LMI
350239	61439+65239+67539+61539	NN	LMI	PTR	LMI
350240	61440+65240+67540+61540	NN	LMI	PTR	LMI
350241	61441+65241+67541+61541	NN	LMI	PTR	LMI
350242	61442+65242+67542+61542	NN	LMI	PTR	LMI
350243	61443+65243+67543+61543	NN	LMI	PTR	LMI
350244	61444+65244+67544+61544	NN	LMI	PTR	LMI
350245	61445+65245+67545+61545	NN	LMI	PTR	LMI
350246	61446+65246+67546+61546	NN	LMI	PTR	LMI
350247	61447+65247+67547+61547	NN	LMI	PTR	LMI
350248	61448+65248+67548+61548	NN	LMI	PTR	LMI
350249	61449+65249+67549+61549	NN	LMI	PTR	LMI
350250	61450+65250+67550+61550	NN	LMI	PTR	LMI
350251	61451+65251+67551+61551	NN	LMI	PTR	LMI
350252	61452+65252+67552+61552	NN	LMI	PTR	LMI
350253	61453+65253+67553+61553	NN	LMI	PTR	LMI
350254	61454+65254+67554+61554	NN	LMI	PTR	LMI
350255	61455+65255+67555+61555	NN	LMI	PTR	LMI
350256	61456+65256+67556+61556	NN	LMI	PTR	LMI
350257	61457+65257+67557+61557	NN	LMI	PTR	LMI
350258	61458+65258+67558+61558	NN	LMI	PTR	LMI
350259	61459+65259+67559+61559	NN	LMI	PTR	LMI
350260	61460+65260+67560+61560	NN	LMI	PTR	LMI
350261	61461+65261+67561+61561	NN	LMI	PTR	LMI
350262	61462+65262+67562+61562	NN	LMI	PTR	LMI
350263	61463+65263+67563+61563	NN	LMI	PTR	LMI
350264	61464+65264+67564+61564	NN	LMI	PTR	LMI
350265	61465+65265+67565+61565	NN	LMI	PTR	LMI
350266	61466+65266+67566+61566	NN	LMI	PTR	LMI
350267	61467+65267+67567+61567	NN	LMI	PTR	LMI

Right: *Following the successful introduction of 30 Class 350/1 sets, London Midland sought funding to obtain a further 37 sets, financed by Porterbrook and classified as Class 350/2. A number of interior changes are incorporated in these sets with a more cramped standard class layout with fewer tables. With a half yellow and half black front gangway door, Class 350/2 No. 350255 heads towards South Kenton with a semi-fast service bound for London Euston. The set's DMSO(A) vehicle is leading.* **CJM**

London Overground

Address:	✉ 125 Finchley Road, London, NW3 6HY
	⌨ overgroundinfo@tfl.gov.uk
	✆ 0845 601 4867
	ⓘ www.tfl.gov.uk/overground
Managing Director:	Steve Murphy
Principal Routes:	Clapham Junction - Willesden, Richmond - Stratford
	Gospel Oak - Barking, Euston - Watford
	East London Line – Dalston - West Croydon
Depots:	Willesden (WN) New Cross Gate (NX)
Parent Company:	Transport for London

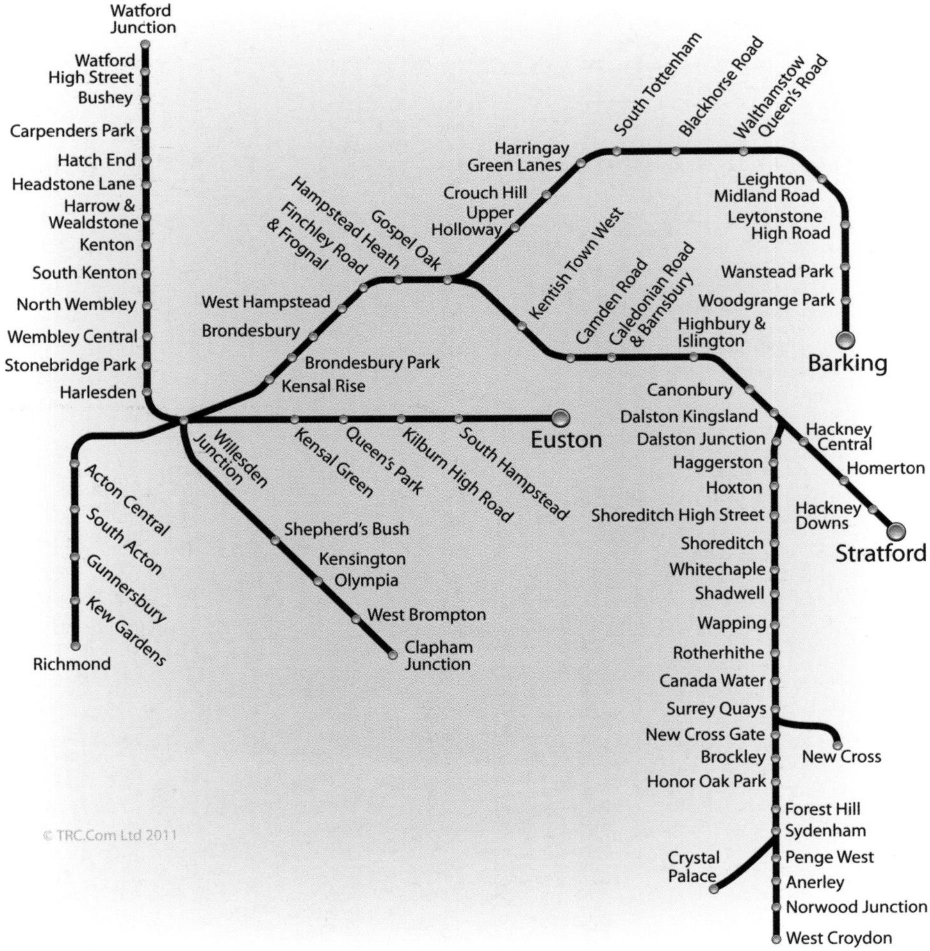

Watford Junction
Watford High Street
Bushey
Carpenders Park
Hatch End
Headstone Lane
Harrow & Wealdstone
Kenton
South Kenton
North Wembley
Wembley Central
Stonebridge Park
Harlesden

Hampstead Heath
Finchley Road & Frognal
Gospel Oak
West Hampstead
Brondesbury
Brondesbury Park
Kensal Rise

Harringay Green Lanes
Crouch Hill
Upper Holloway

South Tottenham
Blackhorse Road
Walthamstow Queens Road
Leighton Midland Road
Leytonstone High Road
Wanstead Park
Woodgrange Park
Highbury & Islington

Kentish Town West
Camden Road
Caledonian Road & Barnsbury

Barking

Willesden Junction
Kensal Green
Queen's Park
Kilburn High Road
South Hampstead

Euston

Canonbury
Dalston Kingsland
Dalston Junction
Haggerston
Hoxton
Shoreditch High Street
Shoreditch
Whitechaple
Shadwell
Wapping
Rotherhithe
Canada Water
Surrey Quays
New Cross Gate
Brockley
Honor Oak Park

Hackney Central
Homerton
Hackney Downs

Stratford

Acton Central
South Acton
Gunnersbury
Kew Gardens
Richmond

Shepherd's Bush
Kensington Olympia
West Brompton
Clapham Junction

New Cross

Forest Hill
Sydenham
Penge West
Anerley
Norwood Junction
West Croydon

Crystal Palace

Class 09/0

Vehicle Length: 29ft 3in (8.91m)			Engine: English Electric 6K		
Height: 12ft 8⅝in (3.87m)			Horsepower: 400hp (298kW)		
Width: 8ft 6in (2.59m)			Electrical Equipment: English Electric		

Number	Depot	Pool	Livery	Owner	Operator
09007	WN	-	LOG	LOL	LOL

Class 172/0
Turbostar

Vehicle Length: 73ft 4in (22.37m)			Engine: MTU 6H1800R83 of 360kW (483hp)		
Height: 12ft 4½in (3.77m)			Horsepower: 965hp (720kW)		
Width: 8ft 8in (2.69m)			Seats (total/car): 124S, 60S/64S		

Number	Formation DMS+DMS	Depot	Livery	Owner	Operator
172001	59311+59411	WN	LOG	ANG	LOG
172002	59312+59412	WN	LOG	ANG	LOG
172003	59313+59413	WN	LOG	ANG	LOG
172004	59314+59414	WN	LOG	ANG	LOG
172005	59315+59415	WN	LOG	ANG	LOG
172006	59316+59416	WN	LOG	ANG	LOG
172007	59317+59417	WN	LOG	ANG	LOG
172008	59318+59418	WN	LOG	ANG	LOG

Right: *Eight two-car Bombardier-built 'Turbostar' sets were introduced at the end of 2010 for use on the Gospel Oak to Barking route. The sets are the latest development of the 'Turbostar' family and incorporate a diesel-mechanical transmission. A number of serious problems delayed their introduction, including faults with the exhaust system. Set No. 172006 is seen arriving at Gospel Oak on 8 December 2010 with a service from Barking.* **CJM**

Class 378/1
Capitalstar

Vehicle Length: (Driving) (20.46m), (Inter) (20.14m)			Width: 9ft 2in (2.80m)		
Height: 11ft 9in (3.58m)			Horsepower: 4-car (1,500kW)		
750V dc sets			Seats (total/car): 146S, 36S/40S/34S/36S		

Number	Formation DMSO+MSO+TSO+DMSO	Depot	Livery	Owner	Operator
378135	38035+38235+38335+38135	NX	LOG	QWR	LOG
378136	38036+38236+38336+38136	NX	LOG	QWR	LOG
378137	38037+38237+38337+38137	NX	LOG	QWR	LOG
378138	38038+38238+38338+38138	NX	LOG	QWR	LOG
378139	38039+38239+38339+38139	NX	LOG	QWR	LOG
378140	38040+38240+38340+38140	NX	LOG	QWR	LOG
378141	38041+38241+38341+38141	NX	LOG	QWR	LOG
378142	38042+38242+38342+38142	NX	LOG	QWR	LOG
378143	38043+38243+38343+38143	NX	LOG	QWR	LOG
378144	38044+38244+38344+38144	NX	LOG	QWR	LOG
378145	38045+38245+38345+38145	NX	LOG	QWR	LOG
378146	38046+38246+38346+38146	NX	LOG	QWR	LOG
378147	38047+38247+38347+38147	NX	LOG	QWR	LOG
378148	38048+38248+38348+38148	NX	LOG	QWR	LOG
378149	38049+38249+38349+38149	NX	LOG	QWR	LOG
378150	38050+38250+38350+38150	NX	LOG	QWR	LOG
378151	38051+38251+38351+38151	NX	LOG	QWR	LOG
378152	38052+38252+38352+38152	NX	LOG	QWR	LOG
378153	38053+38253+38353+38153	NX	LOG	QWR	LOG
378154	38054+38254+38354+38154	NX	LOG	QWR	LOG

London Overground

Class 378/2
Capitalstar

Vehicle Length: (Driving) (20.46m), (Inter) (20.14m) Width: 9ft 2in (2.80m)
Height: 11ft 9in (3.58m)   Horsepower: 4-car (1,500kW)
Dual voltage - 750V dc third rail and 25kV ac overhead Seats (total/car): 146S, 36S/40S/34S/36S

Sets built as 3-car units as Class 378/0, MSO added and reclassified as 378/2

Number	Formation DMSO+MSO+PTSO+DMSO	Depot	Livery	Owner	Operator
378201 (378001)	38001+38201+38301+38101	WN	LOG	QWR	LOG
378202 (378002)	38002+38202+38302+38102	WN	LOG	QWR	LOG
378203 (378003)	38003+38203+38303+38103	WN	LOG	QWR	LOG
378204 (378004)	38004+38204+38304+38104	WN	LOG	QWR	LOG
378205 (378005)	38005+38205+38305+38105	WN	LOG	QWR	LOG
378206 (378006)	38006+38206+38306+38106	WN	LOG	QWR	LOG
378207 (378007)	38007+38207+38307+38107	WN	LOG	QWR	LOG
378208 (378008)	38008+38208+38308+38108	WN	LOG	QWR	LOG
378209 (378009)	38009+38209+38309+38109	WN	LOG	QWR	LOG
378210 (378010)	38010+38210+38310+38110	WN	LOG	QWR	LOG
378211 (378011)	38011+38211+38311+38111	WN	LOG	QWR	LOG
378212 (378012)	38012+38212+38312+38112	WN	LOG	QWR	LOG
378213 (378013)	38013+38213+38313+38113	WN	LOG	QWR	LOG
378214 (378014)	38014+38214+38314+38114	WN	LOG	QWR	LOG
378215 (378015)	38015+38215+38315+38115	WN	LOG	QWR	LOG
378216 (378016)	38016+38216+38316+38116	WN	LOG	QWR	LOG
378217 (378017)	38017+38217+38317+38117	WN	LOG	QWR	LOG
378218 (378018)	38018+38218+38318+38118	WN	LOG	QWR	LOG
378219 (378019)	38019+38219+38319+38119	WN	LOG	QWR	LOG
378220 (378020)	38020+38220+38320+38120	WN	LOG	QWR	LOG
378221 (378021)	38021+38221+38321+38121	WN	LOG	QWR	LOG
378222 (378022)	38022+38222+38322+38122	WN	LOG	QWR	LOG
378223 (378023)	38023+38223+38323+38123	WN	LOG	QWR	LOG
378224 (378024)	38024+38224+38324+38124	WN	LOG	QWR	LOG

Number	Formation DMSO+MSO+TSO+DMSO	Depot	Livery	Owner	Operator
378225	38025+38225+38325+38125	NX	LOG	QWR	LOG
378226	38026+38226+38326+38126	NX	LOG	QWR	LOG
378227	38027+38227+38327+38127	NX	LOG	QWR	LOG
378228	38028+38228+38328+38128	NX	LOG	QWR	LOG
378229	38029+38229+38329+38129	NX	LOG	QWR	LOG
378230	38030+38230+38330+38130	NX	LOG	QWR	LOG
378231	38031+38231+38331+38131	NX	LOG	QWR	LOG
378232	38032+38232+38332+38132	NX	LOG	QWR	LOG
378233	38033+38233+38333+38133	NX	LOG	QWR	LOG
378234	38034+38234+38334+38134	NX	LOG	QWR	LOG
378255ø	38035+38235+38335+38135	NX	LOG	QWR	LOG
378256ø	38036+38236+38336+38136	NX	LOG	QWR	LOG
378257ø	38037+38237+38337+38137	NX	LOG	QWR	LOG

ø Under construction Dec 2010

Left: The Class 378 sets built by Bombardier for London Overground operate core services on the Euston-Watford, Richmond to Stratford and Dalston to New Cross, Croydon and Crystal Palace routes. Class 378/1s are designed for dc third rail only operation, while the Class 378/2s are dual voltage ac/dc sets. Third rail set No. 378151 is seen at West Croydon with a service from Dalston Junction. CJM

Merseyrail

Address: ✉ Rail House, Lord Nelson Street, Liverpool, L1 1JF
✍ comment@merseyrail.org
☎ 0151 702 2534
ⓘ www.merseyrail.org

Managing Director: Bart Schmeink
Franchise Dates: 20 July 2003 - 31 July 2028
Principal Routes: All non main line services in Liverpool area
Depots: Birkenhead North (BD)
Parent Company: Serco / NedRailways

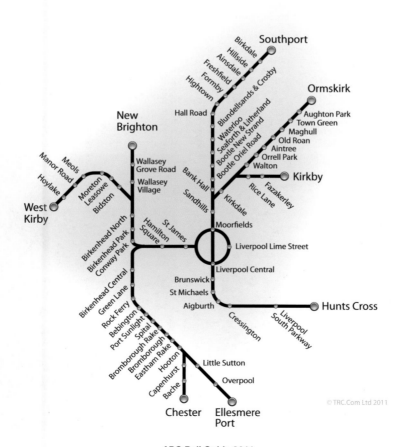

© TRC.Com Ltd 2011

Merseyrail

Class 507

Passenger Train Operating Companies - Merseyrail

Vehicle Length: (Driving) 64ft 11½in (19.80m)	*Width:* 9ft 3in (2.82m)
(Inter) 65ft 4¼in (19.92m)	*Horsepower:* 880hp (656kW)
Height: 11ft 6½in (3.58m)	*Seats (total/car):* 186S, 56S/74S/56S

Number	Formation DMSO+TSO+DMSO	Depot	Livery	Owner	Operator	Name
507001	64367+71342+64405	BD	MER	ANG	MER	
507002	64368+71343+64406	BD	MER	ANG	MER	
507003	64369+71344+64407	BD	MER	ANG	MER	
507004	64388+71345+64408	BD	MER	ANG	MER	Bob Paisley
507005	64371+71346+64409	BD	MER	ANG	MER	
507006	64372+71347+64410	BD	MER	ANG	MER	
507007	64373+71348+64411	BD	MER	ANG	MER	
507008	64374+71349+64412	BD	MER	ANG	MER	
507009	64375+71350+64413	BD	MER	ANG	MER	Dixie Dean
507010	64376+71351+64414	BD	MER	ANG	MER	
507011	64377+71352+64415	BD	MER	ANG	MER	
507012	64378+71353+64416	BD	MER	ANG	MER	
507013	64379+71354+64417	BD	MER	ANG	MER	
507014	64380+71355+64418	BD	MER	ANG	MER	
507015	64381+71356+64419	BD	MER	ANG	MER	
507016	64382+71357+64420	BD	MER	ANG	MER	
507017	64383+71358+64421	BD	MER	ANG	MER	
507018	64384+71359+64422	BD	MER	ANG	MER	
507019	64385+71360+64423	BD	MER	ANG	MER	
507020	64386+71361+64424	BD	MER	ANG	MER	John Peel
507021	64387+71362+64425	BD	MER	ANG	MER	Red Rum
507023	64389+71364+64427	BD	MER	ANG	MER	
507024	64390+71365+64428	BD	MER	ANG	MER	
507025	64391+71366+64429	BD	MER	ANG	MER	
507026	64392+71367+64430	BD	MER	ANG	MER	
507027	64393+71368+64431	BD	MER	ANG	MER	
507028	64394+71369+64432	BD	MER	ANG	MER	
507029	64395+71370+64433	BD	MER	ANG	MER	
507030	64396+71371+64434	BD	MER	ANG	MER	
507031	64397+71372+64435	BD	MER	ANG	MER	
507032	64398+71373+64436	BD	MER	ANG	MER	
507033	64399+71374+64437	BD	MER	ANG	MER	Cllr George Howard

The Merseyrail network operates a fleet of 32 Class 507 three-car third rail dc electric units. All sets are refurbished and are allocated to Birkenhead depot. Set No. 507033 is seen at New Brighton. John Binch

Class 508/1

Vehicle Length: (Driving) 64ft 11½in (19.80m)			Width: 9ft 3in (2.82m)		
(Inter) 65ft 4¼in (19.92m)			Horsepower: 880hp (656kW)		
Height: 11ft 6½in (3.58m)			Seats (total/car): 186S, 56S/74S/56S		

Number	Formation DMSO+TSO+DMSO	Depot	Livery	Owner	Operator
508103	64651+71485+64694	BD	MER	ANG	MER
508104	64652+71486+64964	BD	MER	ANG	MER
508108	64656+71490+64699	BD	MER	ANG	MER
508110	64658+71492+64701	BD	MER	ANG	MER
508111	64659+71493+64702	BD	MER	ANG	MER
508112	64660+71494+64703	BD	MER	ANG	MER
508114	64662+71496+64705	BD	MER	ANG	MER
508115	64663+71497+64708	BD	MER	ANG	MER
508117	64665+71499+64908	BD	MER	ANG	MER
508120	64668+71502+64711	BD	MER	ANG	MER
508122	64670+71504+64713	BD	MER	ANG	MER
508123	64671+71505+64714	BD	MER	ANG	MER
508124	64672+71506+64715	BD	MER	ANG	MER
508125	64673+71507+64716	BD	MER	ANG	MER
508126	64674+71508+64717	BD	MER	ANG	MER
508127	64675+71509+64718	BD	MER	ANG	MER
508128	64676+71510+64719	BD	MER	ANG	MER
508130	64678+71512+64721	BD	MER	ANG	MER
508131	64679+71513+64722	BD	MER	ANG	MER
508134	64682+71516+64725	BD	MER	ANG	MER
508136	64684+71518+64727	BD	MER	ANG	MER
508137	64685+71519+64728	BD	MER	ANG	MER
508138	64686+71520+64729	BD	MER	ANG	MER
508139	64687+71521+64730	BD	MER	ANG	MER
508140	64688+71522+64731	BD	MER	ANG	MER
508141	64689+71523+64732	BD	MER	ANG	MER
508143	64691+71525+64734	BD	MER	ANG	MER

Above: *Working alongside the Merseyrail Class 507 fleet are 27 Class 508 three-car sets, which were originally used on the Southern Region on services out of Waterloo. Now fully refurbished, the sets are painted in silver and yellow livery and sport a modernised front end with triangulation lighting and LED marker/tail lights. Set No. 508124 is seen at Southport.*
Nathan Williamson

National Express East Anglia

Address:	✉ Floor One, Oliver's Yard, 55 City Road, London, EC1V 1HQ
	🖅 nxea.customerrelations@nationalexpress.com
	☎ 0845 600 7245
	ⓘ www.nationalexpresseastanglia.com
Managing Director:	Andrew Chivers
Franchise Dates:	1 April 2004 - 13 October 2011
Principal Routes:	London Liverpool Street to Norwich, Cambridge, Enfield Town, Hertford East, Upminster, Southend Victoria, Southminster, Braintree, Sudbury, Clacton, Walton, Harwich Town, Felixstowe, Lowestoft, Great Yarmouth, Sheringham, Stansted Airport and Peterborough
Depots:	Ilford (IL), Norwich (NC), Clacton (CC)
Parent Company:	National Express

Class 90/0

Vehicle Length: 61ft 6in (18.74m)
Height: 13ft 0¼in (3.96m)
Width: 9ft 0in (2.74m)
Power Collection: 25kV ac overhead
Horsepower: 7,860hp (5,860kW)
Electrical Equipment: GEC

Number	Depot	Pool	Livery	Owner	Operator	Name
90001	NC	IANA	ORN	PTR	NXA	
90002	NC	IANA	ORN	PTR	NXA	
90003	NC	IANA	NXA	PTR	NXA	Raedwald of East Anglia
90004	NC	IANA	ORN	PTR	NXA	Eastern Daily Press 1870-2010 Serving Norfolk for 140 years
90005	NC	IANA	ORN	PTR	NXA	Vice-Admiral Lord Nelson
90006	NC	IANA	ORN	PTR	NXA	Roger Ford / Modern Railways
90007	NC	IANA	ORN	PTR	NXA	Sir John Betjeman
90008	NC	IANA	NXA	PTR	NXA	The East Anglian
90009	NC	IANA	ORN	PTR	NXA	
90010	NC	IANA	ORN	PTR	NXA	
90011	NC	IANA	ORN	PTR	NXA	Let's Go - East of England
90012	NC	IANA	ORN	PTR	NXA	Royal Anglian Regiment
90013	NC	IANA	ORN	PTR	NXA	The Evening Star
90014	NC	IANA	ORN	PTR	NXA	Norfolk and Norwich Festival
90015	NC	IANA	NXA	PTR	NXA	Colchester Castle

Left: *Following displacement from West Coast operations, 15 Class 90s were allocated to the East Anglia franchise to operate on the London Liverpool Street to Norwich route. In late 2010 three are painted in National Express silver/white livery and the balance are in light blue with National Express branding. National Express-liveried No. 90003* Raedwald of East Anglia *is seen approaching Colchester with a Norwich-Liverpool Street express. The Class 90s on East Anglia operate in push-pull mode with a Mk3 DVT at the remote end of the train. The Class 90s are formed at the London end of sets.* **Tony Christie**

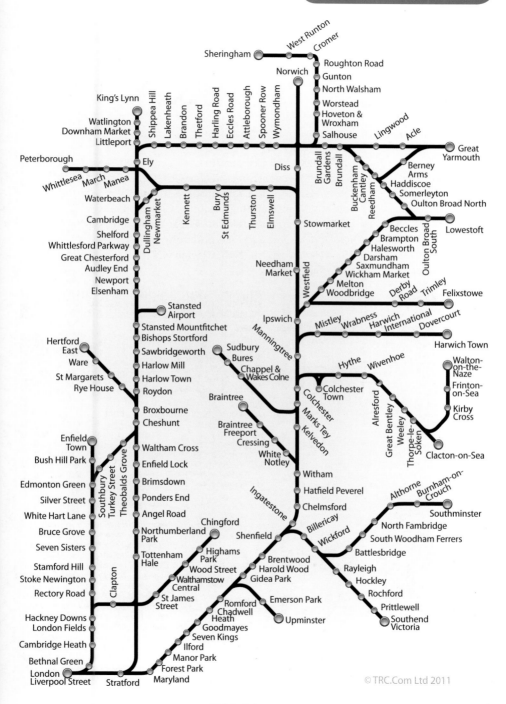

© TRC.Com Ltd 2011

National Express East Anglia

Mk 3 Hauled Stock

Vehicle Length: 75ft 0in (22.86m) Width: 8ft 11in (2.71m)
Height: 12ft 9in (3.88m) Bogie Type: BT10

Passenger Train Operating Companies - National Express East Anglia

AJ1G - RFM *Seating 24F*

Number	Depot	Livery	Owner
10200 (40519)	NC	ORN	PTR
10203 (40506)	NC	NXA	PTR
10206 (40507)	NC	ORN	PTR
10214 (11034)	NC	ORN	PTR
10216 (11041)	NC	ORN	PTR
10223 (11043)	NC	ORN	PTR
10228 (11035)	NC	NXA	PTR
10229 (11059)	NC	ORN	PTR
10241 (10009)	NC	NXA	PTR
10247 (10011)	NC	ORN	PTR

AN2G - TSOB *Seating 52S*

10401 (12168)	NC	NXA	PTR
10402 (12010)	NC	ORN	PTR
10403 (12135)	NC	ORN	PTR
10404 (12068)	NC	ORN	PTR
10405 (12137)	NC	ORN	PTR
10406 (12020)	NC	ORN	PTR

AD1G - FO, *FOD *Seating 48F/34F**

11021 (S)	NC	VTS	PTR
11066	NC	ORN	PTR
11067	NC	ORN	PTR
11068	NC	NXA	PTR
11069	NC	ORN	PTR
11070	NC	ORN	PTR
11072*	NC	ORN	PTR
11073*	NC	NXA	PTR
11074 (S)	NC	VTS	PTR
11075	NC	ORN	PTR
11076	NC	ORN	PTR
11077	NC	ORN	PTR
11078*	NC	ORN	PTR
11080	NC	ORN	PTR
11081	NC	ORN	PTR
11082	NC	NXA	PTR
11085*	NC	ORN	PTR
11087*	NC	NXA	PTR
11088*	NC	NXA	PTR
11090*	NC	ORN	PTR
11091*	NC	NXA	PTR
11092	NC	ORN	PTR
11093*	NC	ORN	PTR
11094*	NC	ORN	PTR
11095*	NC	ORN	PTR
11096*	NC	ORN	PTR

11098*	NC	ORN	PTR
11099*	NC	ORN	PTR
11100*	NC	NXA	PTR
11101*	NC	ORN	PTR

AC2G - TSO *Seating 80S*

12005	NC	ORN	PTR
12009	NC	ORN	PTR
12012	NC	ORN	PTR
12013	NC	ORN	PTR
12015	NC	ORN	PTR
12016	NC	ORN	PTR
12019	NC	ORN	PTR
12021	NC	NXA	PTR
12024	NC	ORN	PTR
12026	NC	ORN	PTR
12027	NC	NXA	PTR
12030	NC	ORN	PTR
12031	NC	ORN	PTR
12032	NC	ORN	PTR
12034	NC	ORN	PTR
12035	NC	NXA	PTR
12037	NC	ORN	PTR
12040	NC	ORN	PTR
12041	NC	ORN	PTR
12042	NC	ORN	PTR
12046	NC	ORN	PTR
12049	NC	ORN	PTR
12051	NC	NXA	PTR
12056	NC	ORN	PTR
12057	NC	ORN	PTR
12060	NC	ORN	PTR
12061	NC	ORN	PTR
12062	NC	ORN	PTR
12064	NC	ORN	PTR
12066	NC	ORN	PTR
12067	NC	ORN	PTR
12073	NC	ORN	PTR
12079	NC	ORN	PTR
12081	NC	ORN	PTR
12082	NC	ORN	PTR
12084	NC	NXA	PTR
12089	NC	ORN	PTR
12090	NC	ORN	PTR
12091	NC	ORN	PTR
12093	NC	ORN	PTR
12097	NC	NXA	PTR
12098	NC	ORN	PTR

12099	NC	ORN	PTR
12103	NC	ORN	PTR
12105	NC	ORN	PTR
12107	NC	ORN	PTR
12108	NC	NXA	PTR
12109	NC	ORN	PTR
12110	NC	ORN	PTR
12111	NC	NXA	PTR
12114	NC	NXA	PTR
12115	NC	ORN	PTR
12116	NC	ORN	PTR
12118	NC	NXA	PTR
12120	NC	ORN	PTR
12125	NC	ORN	PTR
12126	NC	ORN	PTR
12129	NC	NXA	PTR
12130	NC	ORN	PTR
12132	NC	NXA	PTR
12137	NC	ORN	PTR
12141	NC	ORN	PTR
12143	NC	ORN	PTR
12146	NC	NXA	PTR
12147	NC	ORN	PTR
12148	NC	ORN	PTR
12150	NC	ORN	PTR
12151	NC	ORN	PTR
12153	NC	NXA	PTR
12154	NC	ORN	PTR
12159	NC	ORN	PTR
12164	NC	ORN	PTR
12166	NC	ORN	PTR
12167	NC	ORN	PTR
12170	NC	ORN	PTR
12171	NC	ORN	PTR

NZAH - DVT

82102	NC	ORN	PTR
82103	NC	ORN	PTR
82104	NC	ORN	PTR
82105	NC	ORN	PTR
82107	NC	NXA	PTR
82112	NC	ORN	PTR
82114	NC	ORN	PTR
82118	NC	NXA	PTR
82121	NC	ORN	PTR
82127	NC	ORN	PTR
82132	NC	ORN	PTR
82133	NC	ORN	PTR
82136	NC	ORN	PTR
82139	NC	ORN	PTR
82143	NC	NXA	PTR
82152	NC	ORN	PTR

Left: *The East Anglia main line loco hauled services on the Liverpool Street to Norwich route use Mk3 stock; again this was displaced from West Coast services. All stock is allocated to Norwich Crown Point with vehicles in a mix of National Express white and turquoise liveries. RFM No. 10229 is illustrated in light blue livery.*
CJM

Class 153

	Vehicle Length: 76ft 5in (23.29m)	Engine: 1 x NT855R5 of 285hp
	Height: 12ft 3⅜in (3.75m)	Horsepower: 285hp (213kW)
	Width: 8ft 10in (2.70m)	Seats (total/car): 72S

Number	Formation DMSL	Depot	Livery	Owner	Operator	Name
153306	52306	NC	ORN	PTR	NXA	
153309	52309	NC	NXA	PTR	NXA	Gerard Fiennes
153314	52314	NC	ORN	PTR	NXA	
153322	52322	NC	ORN	PTR	NXA	Benjamin Britten
153335	52335	NC	NXA	PTR	NXA	Michael Palin

Right: *For East Anglia rural branch line services, five Class 153s are allocated to Norwich Crown Point. Light blue liveried with National Express branding No. 153306 is illustrated. This view shows the Class 153 from its original large cab end.* **Jamie Squibbs**

Class 156

	Vehicle Length: 75ft 6in (23.03m)	Engine: 1 x Cummins NT855R5 of 285hp
	Height: 12ft 6in (3.81m)	Horsepower: 570hp (425kW)
	Width: 8ft 11in (2.73m)	Seats (total/car): 146S, 70/76S

Number	Formation DMSL+DMS	Depot	Livery	Owner	Operator
156402	52402+57402	NC	ORN	PTR	NXA
156407	52407+57407	NC	ORN	PTR	NXA
156409	52409+57409	NC	ORN	PTR	NXA
156412	52412+57412	NC	ORN	PTR	NXA

Number	Formation	Depot	Livery	Owner	Operator
156416	52416+57416	NC	ORN	PTR	NXA
156417¤	52417+57417	NC	ORN	PTR	NXA
156418	52418+57418	NC	ORN	PTR	NXA
156419	52419+57419	NC	NXA	PTR	NXA
156422	52422+57422	NC	ORN	PTR	NXA

¤ Stored due to collision damage

Above: *Longer distance rural services radiating from Norwich use a fleet of nine Class 156 units, allocated to Norwich Crown Point and providing a good quality travelling experience, with passenger doors opening into vestibules at vehicle ends rather than direct into passenger saloons. Set No. 156419 is illustrated, showing the latest National Express livery.* **Brian Morrison**

Passenger Train Operating Companies - National Express East Anglia

National Express East Anglia

Class 170/2
Turbostar

Vehicle Length: 77ft 6in (23.62m)		Engine: 1 x MTU 6R 183TD13H 422hp per vehicle	
Height: 12ft 4½in (3.77m)		Horsepower: 1,266hp (944kW)	
Width: 8ft 10in (2.69m)		Seats (total/car): 7F-173S 7F-39S/68S/66S	

Number	Formation	Depot	Livery	Owner	Operator
	DMCL+MSL+DMSL				
170201	50201+56201+79201	NC	ORN	PTR	NXA
170202	50202+56202+79202	NC	ORN	PTR	NXA
170203	50203+56203+79203	NC	ORN	PTR	NXA
170204	50204+56204+79204	NC	ORN	PTR	NXA
170205	50205+56205+79205	NC	ORN	PTR	NXA
170206	50206+56206+79206	NC	ORN	PTR	NXA
170207	50207+56207+79207	NC	ORN	PTR	NXA
170208	50208+56208+79208	NC	ORN	PTR	NXA

Vehicle Length: 77ft 6in (23.62m)		Engine: 1 x MTU 6R 183TD13H 422hp per vehicle	
Height: 12ft 4½in (3.77m)		Horsepower: 844hp (629kW)	
Width: 8ft 10in (2.69m)		Seats (total/car): 9F-110S 57S/9F-53S	

Number	Formation	Depot	Livery	Owner	Operator		Number	Formation	Depot	Livery	Owner	Operator
	DMSL+DMCL						170271	50271+79271	NC	ORN	PTR	NXA
							170272	50272+79272	NC	ORN	PTR	NXA
170270	50270+79270	NC	ORN	PTR	NXA		170273	50273+79273	NC	ORN	PTR	NXA

Left: *Both two and three-car versions of 'Turbostar' DMUs operate for the East Anglian franchise. All are allocated to Norwich Crown Point and operate the longer distance diesel routes, as well as branch line duties around Norwich. Three-car set No. 170204 is seen at Stratford painted in National Express light blue livery. The set's DMCL vehicle is nearest the camera.* **CJM**

Class 315

Vehicle Length: (Driving) 64ft 11½in (19.80m)		Width: 9ft 3in (2.82m)	
(Inter) 65ft 4¼in (19.92m)		Horsepower: 880hp (656kW)	
Height: 11ft 6½in (3.58m)		Seats (total/car): 318S, 74S/86S/84S/74S	

Number	Formation	Depot	Livery	Owner	Operator	Name
	DMSO(A)+TSO+PTSO+DMSO(B)					
315801	64461+71281+71389+64462	IL	ORN	HSB	NXA	
315802	64463+71282+71390+64464	IL	ORN	HSB	NXA	
315803	64465+71283+71391+64466	IL	ORN	HSB	NXA	
315804	64467+71284+71392+64468	IL	ORN	HSB	NXA	
315805	64469+71285+71393+64470	IL	ORN	HSB	NXA	
315806	64471+71286+71394+64472	IL	ORN	HSB	NXA	
315807	64473+71287+71395+64474	IL	ORN	HSB	NXA	
315808	64475+71288+71396+64476	IL	ORN	HSB	NXA	
315809	64477+71289+71397+64478	IL	ORN	HSB	NXA	
315810	64479+71290+71398+64480	IL	ORN	HSB	NXA	
315811	64481+71291+71399+64482	IL	ORN	HSB	NXA	
315812	64483+71292+71400+64484	IL	ORN	HSB	NXA	*London Borough of Newham Host Borough 2012 Olympics Bid*
315813	64485+71293+71401+64486	IL	ORN	HSB	NXA	
315814	64487+71294+71402+64488	IL	ORN	HSB	NXA	
315815	64489+71295+71403+64490	IL	ORN	HSB	NXA	
315816	64491+71296+71404+64492	IL	ORN	HSB	NXA	
315817	64493+71297+71405+64494	IL	ORN	HSB	NXA	*Transport for London*
315818	64495+71298+71406+64496	IL	ORN	HSB	NXA	

315819	64497+71299+71407+64498	IL	ORN	HSB	NXA	
315820	64499+71300+71408+64500	IL	ORN	HSB	NXA	
315821	64501+71301+71409+64502	IL	ORN	HSB	NXA	
315822	64503+71302+71410+64504	IL	ORN	HSB	NXA	
315823	64505+71303+71411+64506	IL	ORN	HSB	NXA	
315824	64507+71304+71412+64508	IL	ORN	HSB	NXA	
315825	64509+71305+71413+64510	IL	ORN	HSB	NXA	
315826	64511+71306+71414+64512	IL	ORN	HSB	NXA	
315827	64513+71307+71415+64514	IL	ORN	HSB	NXA	
315828	64515+71308+71416+64516	IL	ORN	HSB	NXA	
315829	64517+71309+71417+64518	IL	ORN	HSB	NXA	*London Borough of Havering Celebrating 40 years*
315830	64519+71310+71418+64520	IL	ORN	HSB	NXA	
315831	64521+71311+71419+64522	IL	ORN	HSB	NXA	
315832	64523+71312+71420+64524	IL	ORN	HSB	NXA	
315833	64525+71313+71421+64526	IL	ORN	HSB	NXA	
315834	64527+71314+71422+64528	IL	ORN	HSB	NXA	
315835	64529+71315+71423+64530	IL	ORN	HSB	NXA	
315836	64531+71316+71424+64532	IL	ORN	HSB	NXA	
315837	64533+71317+71425+64534	IL	ORN	HSB	NXA	
315838	64535+71318+71426+64536	IL	ORN	HSB	NXA	
315839	64537+71319+71427+64538	IL	ORN	HSB	NXA	
315840	64539+71320+71428+64540	IL	ORN	HSB	NXA	
315841	64541+71321+71429+64542	IL	ORN	HSB	NXA	
315842	64543+71322+71430+64544	IL	ORN	HSB	NXA	
315843	64545+71323+71431+64546	IL	ORN	HSB	NXA	
315844	64547+71324+71432+64548	IL	ORN	HSB	NXA	
315845	64549+71325+71433+64550	IL	ORN	HSB	NXA	*Herbie Woodward*
315846	64551+71326+71434+64552	IL	ORN	HSB	NXA	
315847	64553+71327+71435+64554	IL	ORN	HSB	NXA	
315848	64555+71328+71436+64556	IL	ORN	HSB	NXA	
315849	64557+71329+71437+64558	IL	ORN	HSB	NXA	
315850	64559+71330+71438+64560	IL	ORN	HSB	NXA	
315851	64561+71331+71439+64562	IL	ORN	HSB	NXA	
315852	64563+71332+71440+64564	IL	ORN	HSB	NXA	
315853	64565+71333+71441+64566	IL	ORN	HSB	NXA	
315854	64567+71334+71442+64568	IL	ORN	HSB	NXA	
315855	64569+71335+71443+64570	IL	ORN	HSB	NXA	
315856	64571+71336+71444+64572	IL	ORN	HSB	NXA	
315857	64573+71337+71445+64574	IL	ORN	HSB	NXA	
315858	64575+71338+71446+64576	IL	ORN	HSB	NXA	
315859	64577+71339+71447+64578	IL	ORN	HSB	NXA	
315860	64579+71340+71448+64580	IL	ORN	HSB	NXA	
315861	64581+71341+71449+64582	IL	ORN	HSB	NXA	

Below: *A fleet of 61 four-car Class 315 suburban units operate local services from Liverpool Street; these are a derivative of the 1972 stock design. All sets are allocated to Ilford EMU depot. Sets are painted in light blue livery with a mid-height white band and National Express branding. Set No. 315857 is illustrated approaching Stratford.* **CJM**

Passenger Train Operating Companies - National Express East Anglia

National Express East Anglia

Class 317/5

	Vehicle Length: (Driving) 65ft 0¾in (19.83m)	Width: 9ft 3in (2.82m)
	(Inter) 65ft 4¼in (19.92m)	Horsepower: 1,000hp (746kW)
	Height: 12ft 1½in (3.58m)	Seats (total/car): 291S, 74S/79S/68S/70S

Number	Former Number	Formation DTSO(A)+MSO+TCO+DTSO(B)	Depot	Livery	Owner	Operator	Name
317501	(317301)	77024+62661+71577+77048	IL	NXA	ANG	NXA	
317502	(317302)	77001+62662+71578+77049	IL	NXA	ANG	NXA	
317503	(317303)	77002+62663+71579+77050	IL	NXA	ANG	NXA	
317504	(317304)	77003+62664+71580+77051	IL	NXA	ANG	NXA	
317505	(317305)	77004+62665+71581+77052	IL	NXA	ANG	NXA	
317506	(317306)	77005+62666+71582+77053	IL	NXA	ANG	NXA	
317507	(317307)	77006+62667+71583+77054	IL	NXA	ANG	NXA	*University of Cambridge 800 years 1209-2009*
317508	(317311)	77010+62697+71587+77058	IL	NXA	ANG	NXA	
317509	(317312)	77011+62672+71588+77059	IL	NXA	ANG	NXA	
317510	(317313)	77012+62673+71589+77060	IL	NXA	ANG	NXA	
317511	(317315)	77014+62675+71591+77062	IL	ORN	ANG	NXA	
317512	(317316)	77015+62676+71592+77063	IL	NXU	ANG	NXA	
317513	(317317)	77016+62677+71593+77064	IL	NXA	ANG	NXA	
317514	(317318)	77017+62678+71594+77065	IL	NXA	ANG	NXA	
317515	(317320)	77019+62680+71596+77067	IL	NXA	ANG	NXA	

Left: *The Class 317 fleets allocated to Ilford depot are mainly operated on the West Anglia routes. Many have been repainted in the latest National Express white and grey livery, while others retain the previous light blue scheme and some have recently been painted in plain white for an impending franchise change. Set No. 317501, (the original No. 317301 - the first of the design) is seen at Harlow Town, sporting full National Express livery.*
Brian Morrison

Class 317/6

	Vehicle Length: (Driving) 65ft 0¾in (19.83m)	Width: 9ft 3in (2.82m)
	(Inter) 65ft 4¼in (19.92m)	Horsepower: 1,000hp (746kW)
	Height: 12ft 1½in (3.58m)	Seats (total/car): 24F/200S, 64S/70S/62S/24F-48S

Number	Former Number	Formation DTSO+MSO+TSO+DTCO	Depot	Livery	Owner	Operator	Name
317649	(317349)	77200+62846+71734+77220	IL	NXU	ANG	NXA	
317650	(317350)	77201+62847+71735+77221	IL	ORN	ANG	NXA	
317651	(317351)	77202+62848+71736+77222	IL	NXU	ANG	NXA	
317652	(317352)	77203+62849+71739+77223	IL	ORN	ANG	NXA	
317653	(317353)	77204+62850+71738+77224	IL	ORN	ANG	NXA	
317654	(317354)	77205+62851+71737+77225	IL	ORN	ANG	NXA	*Richard Wells*
317655	(317355)	77206+62852+71740+77226	IL	ORN	ANG	NXA	
317656	(317356)	77207+62853+71742+77227	IL	ORN	ANG	NXA	
317657	(317357)	77208+62854+71741+77228	IL	ORN	ANG	NXA	
317658	(317358)	77209+62855+71743+77229	IL	ORN	ANG	NXA	
317659	(317359)	77210+62856+71744+77230	IL	ORN	ANG	NXA	
317660	(317360)	77211+62857+71745+77231	IL	ORN	ANG	NXA	
317661	(317361)	77212+62858+71746+77232	IL	ORN	ANG	NXA	
317662	(317362)	77213+62859+71747+77233	IL	ORN	ANG	NXA	
317663	(317363)	77214+62860+71748+77234	IL	ORN	ANG	NXA	
317664	(317364)	77215+62861+71749+77235	IL	ORN	ANG	NXA	
317665	(317365)	77216+62862+71750+77236	IL	ORN	ANG	NXA	
317666	(317366)	77217+62863+71752+77237	IL	ORN	ANG	NXA	
317667	(317367)	77218+62864+71751+77238	IL	ORN	ANG	NXA	
317668	(317368)	77219+62865+71753+77239	IL	ORN	ANG	NXA	
317669	(317369)	77280+62886+71762+77248	IL	ORN	ANG	NXA	
317670	(317370)	77281+62887+71763+77285	IL	ORN	ANG	NXA	
317671	(317371)	77282+62888+71764+77286	IL	ORN	ANG	NXA	
317672	(317372)	77283+62889+71765+77287	IL	ORN	ANG	NXA	

Class 317/7

Vehicle Length: (Driving) 65ft 0¾in (19.83m) Width: 9ft 3in (2.82m)
(Inter) 65ft 4¼in (19.92m) Horsepower: 1,000hp (746kW)
Height: 12ft 1½in (3.58m) Seats (total/car): 22F/172S, 52S/62S/42S/22F-16S

Number	Former Number	Formation DTSO+MSO+TSO+DTCO	Depot	Livery	Owner	Operator	Name
317708	(317308)	77007+62668+71584+77055	IL	NXA	ANG	NXA	
317709	(317309)	77008+62669+71585+77056	IL	NXA	ANG	NXA	*Len Camp*
317710	(317310)	77009+62670+71586+77057	IL	NXA	ANG	NXA	
317714	(317314)	77013+62674+71590+77061	IL	NXA	ANG	NXA	
317719	(317319)	77018+62679+71595+77066	IL	NXA	ANG	NXA	
317722	(317322/392)	77021+62682+71598+77069	IL	NXA	ANG	NXA	
317723	(317323/393)	77022+62683+71599+77070	IL	NXA	ANG	NXA	*The Tottenham Flyer*
317729	(317329)	77028+62689+71605+77076	IL	NXA	ANG	NXA	
317732	(317332)	77031+62692+71608+77079	IL	NXA	ANG	NXA	

Right: *Nine Class 317/7s are based at Ilford, dedicated to Stansted Airport services and have 'Stansted Express' bodyside branding in place of the National Express name. The sets have revised interiors to cope with large amounts of luggage transported. Several years ago these nine sets were given revised front ends, a roof level headlight and angled lamp clusters on the nose end. Set No. 317729 is seen at Ilford depot.* **CJM**

Class 317/8

Vehicle Length: (Driving) 65ft 0¾in (19.83m) Width: 9ft 3in (2.82m)
(Inter) 65ft 4¼in (19.92m) Horsepower: 1,000hp (746kW)
Height: 12ft 1½in (3.58m) Seats (total/car): 20F/265S, 74S/79S/20F-42S/70S

Number	Former Number	Formation DTSO(A)+MSO+TCO+DTSO(B)	Depot	Livery	Owner	Operator	Name
317881	(317321)	77020+62681+71597+77068	IL	NXA	ANG	NXA	
317882	(317324)	77023+62684+71600+77071	IL	NXU	ANG	NXA	
317883	(317325)	77000+62685+71601+77072	IL	NXU	ANG	NXA	
317884	(317326)	77025+62686+71602+77073	IL	NXU	ANG	NXA	
317885	(317327)	77026+62687+71603+77074	IL	NXU	ANG	NXA	
317886	(317328)	77027+62688+71604+77075	IL	NXU	ANG	NXA	
317887	(317330)	77043+62704+71606+77077	IL	NXU	ANG	NXA	
317888	(317331)	77030+62691+71607+77078	IL	NXA	ANG	NXA	
317889	(317333)	77032+62693+71609+77080	IL	NXA	ANG	NXA	
317890	(317334)	77033+62694+71610+77081	IL	NXA	ANG	NXA	
317891	(317335)	77034+62695+71611+77082	IL	NXA	ANG	NXA	
317892	(317336)	77035+62696+71612+77083	IL	NXA	ANG	NXA	*Ilford Depot*

Class 321/3

Vehicle Length: (Driving) 65ft 0¾in (19.83m) Width: 9ft 3in (2.82m)
(Inter) 65ft 4¼in (19.92m) Horsepower: 1,328hp (996kW)
Height: 12ft 4¾in (3.78m) Seats (total/car): 16F/292S, 16F-57S/82S/75S/78S

Number	Formation DTCO+MSO+TSO+DTSO	Depot	Livery	Owner	Operator	Name
321301	78049+62975+71880+77853	IL	NXA	HSB	NXA	
321302	78050+62976+71881+77854	IL	NXA	HSB	NXA	
321303	78051+62977+71882+77855	IL	NXA	HSB	NXA	
321304	78052+62978+71883+77856	IL	NXA	HSB	NXA	
321305	78053+62979+71884+77857	IL	NXA	HSB	NXA	
321306	78054+62980+71885+77858	IL	NXA	HSB	NXA	
321307	78055+62981+71886+77859	IL	NXA	HSB	NXA	
321308	78056+62982+71887+77860	IL	NXA	HSB	NXA	
321309	78057+62983+71888+77861	IL	NXA	HSB	NXA	
321310	78058+62984+71889+77862	IL	NGE	HSB	NXA	

National Express East Anglia

Number	Formation	Depot	Livery	Owner	Operator	Name
321311	78059+62985+71890+77863	IL	NXA	HSB	NXA	
321312	78060+62986+71891+77864	IL	NXA	HSB	NXA	*Southend-on-Sea*
321313	78061+62987+71892+77865	IL	NXA	HSB	NXA	*University of Essex*
321314	78062+62988+71893+77866	IL	NGE	HSB	NXA	
321315	78063+62989+71894+77867	IL	NXA	HSB	NXA	
321316	78064+62990+71895+77868	IL	NXA	HSB	NXA	
321317	78065+62991+71896+77869	IL	NXA	HSB	NXA	
321318	78066+62992+71897+77870	IL	NXA	HSB	NXA	
321319	78067+62993+71898+77871	IL	NXA	HSB	NXA	
321320	78068+62994+71899+77872	IL	NXA	HSB	NXA	
321321	78069+62995+71900+77873	IL	NXA	HSB	NXA	*NSPCC Essex Full Stop*
321322	78070+62996+71901+77874	IL	NXA	HSB	NXA	
321323	78071+62997+71902+77875	IL	NXA	HSB	NXA	
321324	78072+62998+71903+77876	IL	NXA	HSB	NXA	
321325	78073+62999+71904+77877	IL	NXA	HSB	NXA	
321326	78074+63000+71905+77878	IL	NXA	HSB	NXA	
321327	78075+63001+71906+77879	IL	NXU	HSB	NXA	
321328	78076+63002+71907+77880	IL	NXA	HSB	NXA	
321329	78077+63003+71908+77881	IL	NXA	HSB	NXA	
321330	78078+63004+71909+77882	IL	NXU	HSB	NXA	
321331	78079+63005+71910+77883	IL	NXU	HSB	NXA	
321332	78080+63006+71911+77884	IL	NXU	HSB	NXA	
321333	78081+63007+71912+77885	IL	NXU	HSB	NXA	*Amsterdam*
321334	78082+63008+71913+77886	IL	NXU	HSB	NXA	
321335	78083+63009+71914+77887	IL	NXU	HSB	NXA	*Geoffrey Freeman Allen*
321336	78084+63010+71915+77888	IL	NXU	HSB	NXA	
321337	78085+63011+71916+77889	IL	NXU	HSB	NXA	
321338	78086+63012+71917+77890	IL	NXU	HSB	NXA	
321339	78087+63013+71918+77891	IL	NXU	HSB	NXA	
321340	78088+63014+71919+77892	IL	NXU	HSB	NXA	
321341	78089+63015+71920+77893	IL	NGE	HSB	NXA	
321342	78090+63016+71921+77894	IL	NXU	HSB	NXA	*RSA Railway Study Association*
321343	78091+63017+71922+77895	IL	NGE	HSB	NXA	
321344	78092+63018+71923+77896	IL	NGE	HSB	NXA	
321345	78093+63019+71924+77897	IL	NGE	HSB	NXA	
321346	78094+63020+71925+77898	IL	NGE	HSB	NXA	
321347	78131+63105+71991+78280	IL	NGE	HSB	NXA	
321348	78132+63106+71992+78281	IL	NGE	HSB	NXA	
321349	78133+63107+71993+78282	IL	NGE	HSB	NXA	
321350	78134+63108+71994+78283	IL	NGE	HSB	NXA	*Gurkha*
321351	78135+63109+71995+78284	IL	NGE	HSB	NXA	
321352	78136+63110+71996+78285	IL	NGE	HSB	NXA	
321353	78137+63111+71997+78286	IL	NGE	HSB	NXA	
321354	78138+63112+71998+78287	IL	NGE	HSB	NXA	
321355	78139+63113+71999+78288	IL	NGE	HSB	NXA	
321356	78140+63114+72000+78289	IL	NGE	HSB	NXA	
321357	78141+63115+72001+78290	IL	NGE	HSB	NXA	
321358	78142+63116+72002+78291	IL	NGE	HSB	NXA	
321359	78143+63117+72003+78292	IL	NGE	HSB	NXA	
321360	78144+63118+72004+78293	IL	NGE	HSB	NXA	*Phoenix*
321361	78145+63119+72005+78294	IL	NGE	HSB	NXA	
321362	78146+63120+72006+78295	IL	NGE	HSB	NXA	
321363	78147+63121+72007+78296	IL	NGE	HSB	NXA	
321364	78148+63122+72008+78297	IL	NGE	HSB	NXA	
321365	78149+63123+72009+78298	IL	NGE	HSB	NXA	
321366	78150+63124+72010+78299	IL	NGE	HSB	NXA	

Class 321/4

Vehicle Length: (Driving) 65ft 0¾in (19.83m) Width: 9ft 3in (2.82m)
(Inter) 65ft 4¼in (19.92m) Horsepower: 1,328hp (996kW)
Height: 12ft 4¾in (3.78m) Seats (total/car): 16F/283S, 16F-52S/79S/74S/78S

Number	Formation	Depot	Livery	Owner	Operator	Name
	DTCO+MSO+TSO+DTSO					
321421	78115+63083+71969+77963	IL	NXA	HSB	NXA	
321422	78116+63084+71970+77964	IL	NXA	HSB	NXA	
321423	78117+63085+71971+77965	IL	NXU	HSB	NXA	

321424	78118+63086+71972+77966	IL	NXA	HSB	NXA	
321425	78119+63087+71973+77967	IL	NXA	HSB	NXA	
321426	78120+63088+71974+77968	IL	NXA	HSB	NXA	
321427	78121+63089+71975+77969	IL	NXA	HSB	NXA	
321428	78122+63090+71976+77970	IL	NXA	HSB	NXA	*The Essex Commuter*
321429	78123+69031+71977+77971	IL	NXA	HSB	NXA	
321430	78124+63092+71978+77972	IL	NXA	HSB	NXA	
321431	78151+63125+72011+78300	IL	NXA	HSB	NXA	
321432	78152+63126+72012+78301	IL	NXU	HSB	NXA	
321433	78153+63127+72013+78302	IL	NXU	HSB	NXA	
321434	78154+63128+72014+78303	IL	NXU	HSB	NXA	
321435	78155+63129+72015+78304	IL	NXS	HSB	NXA	
321436	78156+63130+72016+78305	IL	NXU	HSB	NXA	
321437	78157+63131+72017+78306	IL	NXU	HSB	NXA	
321438	78158+63132+72018+78307	IL	NGE	HSB	NXA	
321439	78159+63133+72019+78308	IL	NGE	HSB	NXA	
321440	78160+63134+72020+78309	IL	NGE	HSB	NXA	
321441	78161+63135+72021+78310	IL	NGE	HSB	NXA	
321442	78162+63136+72022+78311	IL	NGE	HSB	NXA	
321443	78125+63099+71985+78274	IL	NGE	HSB	NXA	
321444	78126+63100+71986+78275	IL	NGE	HSB	NXA	*Essex Lifeboats*
321445	78127+63101+71987+78276	IL	NGE	HSB	NXA	
321446	78128+63102+71988+78277	IL	NGE	HSB	NXA	*George Mullings*
321447	78129+63103+71989+78278	IL	NGE	HSB	NXA	
321448	78130+63104+71990+78279	IL	NGE	HSB	NXA	

Right: *The backbone of National Express Great Eastern outer-suburban duties is the Class 321 fleet, with members of the 321/3 and 321/4 sub-class in operation. In recent years the fleet has been increased with the transfer in of many extra Class 321/4 units from Silverlink. Carrying full National Express East Anglia livery, Class 321/3 No. 321315 pulls away from Stratford bound for London Liverpool Street.* **CJM**

Class 360/1
Desiro

Vehicle Length: 66ft 9in (20.4m)		Horsepower: 1,341hp (1,000kW)	
Height: 12ft 1½in (3.7m)		Seats (total/car): 16F/265S, 8F-59S/69S/78S/8F-59S	
Width: 9ft 2in (2.79m)			

Number	Formation DMCO(A)+PTSO+TSO+DMCO(B)	Depot	Livery	Owner	Operator
360101	65551+72551+74551+68551	IL	FNA	ANG	NXA
360102	65552+72552+74552+68552	IL	FNA	ANG	NXA
360103	65553+72553+74553+68553	IL	FNA	ANG	NXA
360104	65554+72554+74554+68554	IL	FNA	ANG	NXA
360105	65555+72555+74555+68555	IL	FNA	ANG	NXA
360106	65556+72556+74556+68556	IL	FNA	ANG	NXA
360107	65557+72557+74557+68557	IL	FNA	ANG	NXA
360108	65558+72558+74558+68558	IL	FNA	ANG	NXA
360109	65559+72559+74559+68559	IL	FNA	ANG	NXA
360110	65560+72560+74560+68560	IL	FNA	ANG	NXA
360111	65561+72561+74561+68561	IL	FNA	ANG	NXA
360112	65562+72562+74562+68562	IL	FNA	ANG	NXA
360113	65563+72563+74563+68563	IL	FNA	ANG	NXA
360114	65564+72564+74564+68564	IL	FNA	ANG	NXA
360115	65565+72565+74565+68565	IL	FNA	ANG	NXA
360116	65566+72566+74566+68566	IL	FNA	ANG	NXA
360117	65567+72567+74567+68567	IL	FNA	ANG	NXA
360118	65568+72568+74568+68568	IL	FNA	ANG	NXA
360119	65569+72569+74569+68569	IL	FNA	ANG	NXA

Below: *A batch of 21 Siemens 'Desiro' units are allocated to Ilford for outer-suburban use. These 100mph units were built in Germany and are well accepted by the public and very comfortable. One set No. 360115 is painted in National Express white and silver livery.* **CJM**

Train Operating Companies

National Express East Anglia

360120	65570+72570+74570+68570	IL	FNA	ANG	NXA
360121	65571+72571+74571+68571	IL	FNA	ANG	NXA

Class 379
Electrostar

Vehicle Length: (Driving) 66ft 9in (20.40m)
(Inter) 65ft 6in (19.99m)
Height: 12ft 4in (3.77m)

Width: 9ft 2in (2.80m)
Horsepower: 2,010hp (1,500kW)
Seats (total/car): 24F/189S, 60S/62S/43S/20F-24S

● On delivery early 2011.

Number	Formation	Depot	Livery	Owner	Operator
	DTSO+MSO+PTSO+DTCO				
379001	61201+61701+61901+62101	IL	NXU	LTS	NXA
379002	61202+61702+61902+62102	IL	NXU	LTS	NXA
379003	61203+61703+61903+62103	IL	NXU	LTS	NXA
379004	61204+61704+61904+62104	IL	NXU	LTS	NXA
379005	61205+61705+61905+62105	IL	NXU	LTS	NXA
379006	61206+61706+61906+62106	IL	NXU	LTS	NXA
379007	61207+61707+61907+62107	IL	NXU	LTS	NXA
379008	61208+61708+61908+62108	IL	NXU	LTS	NXA
379009	61209+61709+61909+62109	IL	NXU	LTS	NXA
379010	61210+61710+61910+62110	IL	NXU	LTS	NXA
379011	61211+61711+61911+62111	IL	NXU	LTS	NXA
379012	61212+61712+61912+62112	IL	NXU	LTS	NXA
379013	61213+61713+61913+62113	IL	NXU	LTS	NXA
379014	61214+61714+61914+62114	IL	NXU	LTS	NXA
379015	61215+61715+61915+62115	IL	NXU	LTS	NXA
379016	61216+61716+61916+62116	IL	NXU	LTS	NXA
379017	61217+61717+61917+62117	IL	NXU	LTS	NXA
379018	61218+61718+61918+62118	IL	NXU	LTS	NXA
379019	61219+61719+61919+62119	IL	NXU	LTS	NXA
379020	61220+61720+61920+62120	IL	NXU	LTS	NXA
379021	61221+61721+61921+62121	IL	NXU	LTS	NXA
379022	61222+61722+61922+62122	IL	NXU	LTS	NXA
379023	61223+61723+61923+62123	IL	NXU	LTS	NXA
379024	61224+61724+61924+62124	IL	NXU	LTS	NXA
379025	61225+61725+61925+62125	IL	NXU	LTS	NXA
379026	61226+61726+61926+62126	IL	NXU	LTS	NXA
379027	61227+61727+61927+62127	IL	NXU	LTS	NXA
379028	61228+61728+61928+62128	IL	NXU	LTS	NXA
379029	61229+61729+61929+62129	IL	NXU	LTS	NXA
379030	61230+61730+61930+62130	IL	NXU	LTS	NXA

Below: *Class 379 No. 379001 ran its first mileage accumulation run in the UK on 8 January 2011 from Ilford TMD to Norwich, then from Norwich to Harwich and back to Ilford. Here the future Stansted Express motive power passes Manningtree on the return run. No. 379001 had previously undertaken type test approval in the Czech Republic working on the Velim test track, returning to the UK at the end of 2010. When Rail Guide 2011 went to press two '379s' were operating test runs from Ilford.* **Bill Turvill**

East Coast

Address: ✉ East Coast House, 25 Skeldergate, York, YO1 6DH
✆ customers@eastcoast.co.uk
☎ 08457 225225
ⓘ www.eastcoast.co.uk

Managing Director: Karen Boswell
Operation Started: 13 November 2009*
Principal Routes: London King's Cross - Aberdeen/ Inverness, Edinburgh, Glasgow Hull, Leeds, Bradford, Skipton and Harrogate
Depots: Bounds Green (BN), Craigentinny (EC)
Parent Company: DfT (Directly Operated Railways Ltd)

* The Government took over operation from 13 November 2009 and will continue to operate the franchise as a 'stop-gap' measure using the in-place operational staff. A new franchise bid process is likely to be launched in 2011.

Inverness
Carrbridge
Aviemore
Kingussie
Newtonmore
Blair Atholl
Pitlochry
Dunkeld
Perth
Gleneagles
Dunblane
Stirling
Falkirk Grahamston
Motherwell
Glasgow Central

Aberdeen
Stonehaven
Montrose
Arbroath
Dundee
Leuchars
Kirkcaldy
Inverkeithing
Haymarket
Edinburgh
Dunbar
Berwick-upon-Tweed
Alnmouth
Morpeth
Newcastle
Durham
Darlington
Northallerton
York
Selby
Hull
Doncaster
Retford
Newark North Gate
Grantham
Peterborough
Stevenage
London King's Cross

Harrogate
Skipton
Keighley
Bradford Forster Square
Leeds

© TRC.Com Ltd 2011

East Coast

Class 43 – HST

				Vehicle Length: 58ft 5in (18.80m)		Engine: MTU 16V4000 R41R	
				Height: 12ft 10in (3.90m)		Horsepower: 2,250hp (1,680kW)	
				Width: 8ft 11in (2.73m)		Electrical Equipment: Brush	

Number		Depot	Pool	Livery	Owner	Operator	Name
43206	(43006)	EC	IECP	ECT	ANG	ICE	*Kingdom of Fife*
43208	(43008)	EC	IECP	NXE	ANG	ICE	
43238	(43038)	EC	IECP	NXE	ANG	ICE	
43239	(43039)	EC	IECP	NXE	ANG	ICE	
43251	(43051)	EC	IECP	ECT	PBR	ICE	
43257	(43057)	EC	IECP	NXE	PBR	ICE	
43277	(43077)	EC	IECP	ECT	PBR	ICE	
43290	(43090)	EC	IECP	NXE	PBR	ICE	*MTU Fascination of Power*
43295	(43095)	EC	IECP	NXE	ANG	ICE	
43296	(43096)	EC	IECP	ECT	PBR	ICE	
43299	(43099)	EC	IECP	NXE	PBR	ICE	
43300	(43100)	EC	IECP	NXE	PBR	ICE	*Craigentinny*
43302	(43102)	EC	IECP	NXE	PBR	ICE	
43305	(43105)	EC	IECP	NXE	ANG	ICE	
43306	(43106)	EC	IECP	NXE	ANG	ICE	
43307	(43107)	EC	IECP	NXE	ANG	ICE	
43308	(43108)	EC	IECP	ECT	ANG	ICE	
43309	(43109)	EC	IECP	NXE	ANG	ICE	
43310	(43110)	EC	IECP	ECT	ANG	ICE	
43311	(43111)	EC	IECP	ECT	ANG	ICE	
43312	(43112)	EC	IECP	ECT	ANG	ICE	
43313	(43113)	EC	IECP	ECT	ANG	ICE	
43314	(43114)	EC	IECP	ECT	ANG	ICE	
43315	(43115)	EC	IECP	NXE	ANG	ICE	
43316	(43116)	EC	IECP	NXE	ANG	ICE	
43317	(43117)	EC	IECP	NXE	ANG	ICE	
43318	(43118)	EC	IECP	ECT	ANG	ICE	
43319	(43119)	EC	IECP	NXE	ANG	ICE	
43320	(43120)	EC	IECP	NXE	ANG	ICE	
43367	(43167)	EC	IECP	NXE	ANG	ICE	*Deltic 50 1955 - 2005 v*

Above: *East Coast main line services which operate away from the overhead power network are formed of a fleet of HSTs, allocated to Edinburgh Craigentinny, with 30 Class 43 power cars on the East Coast books. All are in former National Express white and grey livery, off-set with East Coast branding. Power car No. 43320 is seen at Carlisle on the West Coast route, with a diverted East Coast service due to snow blocking the line at Berwick upon Tweed on 31 March 2010.*
Tony Christie

Passenger Train Operating Companies - East Coast

Class 91

Vehicle Length: 63ft 8in (19.40m)				Power Collection: 25kV ac overhead		
Height: 12ft 4in (3.75m)				Horsepower: 6,300hp (4,700kW)		
Width: 9ft 0in (2.74m)				Electrical Equipment: GEC		

Number		Depot	Pool	Livery	Owner	Operator
91101	(91001)	BN	IECA	ECS	HSB	ICE
91102	(91002)	BN	IECA	NXG	HSB	ICE
91103	(91003)	BN	IECA	NXG	HSB	ICE
91104	(91004)	BN	IECA	NXG	HSB	ICE
91105	(91005)	BN	IECA	NXG	HSB	ICE
91106	(91006)	BN	IECA	NXG	HSB	ICE
91107	(91007)	BN	IECA	ECS	HSB	ICE
91108	(91008)	BN	IECA	NXG	HSB	ICE
91109	(91009)	BN	IECA	NXG	HSB	ICE
91110	(91010)	BN	IECA	ECS	HSB	ICE
91111	(91011)	BN	IECA	NXE	HSB	ICE
91112	(91012)	BN	IECA	NXG	HSB	ICE
91113	(91013)	BN	IECA	NXG	HSB	ICE
91114	(91014)	BN	IECA	NXG	HSB	ICE
91115	(91015)	BN	IECA	NXG	HSB	ICE
91116	(91016)	BN	IECA	NXG	HSB	ICE
91117	(91017)	BN	IECA	NXG	HSB	ICE
91118	(91018)	BN	IECA	NXG	HSB	ICE
91119	(91019)	BN	IECA	NXG	HSB	ICE
91120	(91020)	BN	IECA	NXG	HSB	ICE
91121	(91021)	BN	IECA	NXG	HSB	ICE
91122	(91022)	BN	IECA	ECS	HSB	ICE
91124	(91024)	BN	IECA	NXG	HSB	ICE
91125	(91025)	BN	IECA	NXG	HSB	ICE
91126	(91026)	BN	IECA	NXG	HSB	ICE
91127	(91027)	BN	IECA	ECS	HSB	ICE
91128	(91028)	BN	IECA	NXG	HSB	ICE
91129	(91029)	BN	IECA	NXG	HSB	ICE
91130	(91030)	BN	IECA	NXG	HSB	ICE
91131	(91031)	BN	IECA	NXG	HSB	ICE
91132	(91023)	BN	IECA	NXG	HSB	ICE

Above: *During 2010 a start was made to re-livery the East Coast fleet, using a base silver colour, with East Coast branding. The re-livery of the first Mk4 set complete with Class 91 No. 91107 was done by Wabtec, Doncaster. The first re-liveried set is seen passing north through Doncaster station.* **David Carr**

Class 180

Vehicle Length: (driving) 75ft 7in (23.71m), (inter) 75ft 5in (23.03m)		
Height: 12ft 4in (3.75m)	Engine: 1 x Cummins OSK19 of 750hp per car	
Width: 9ft 2in (2.80m)	Horsepower: 3,750hp (2,796kW)	
	Seats (total/car): 42F/226S, 46S/42F/68S/56S/56S	

Number	Formation	Depot	Livery	Owner	Operator
	DMSL(A)+MFL+MSL+MSLRB+DMSL(B)				
180102	50902+54902+55902+56902+59902	OO	FST	ANG	- Scheduled for East Coast now stored
180103	50903+54903+55903+56903+59903	OO	FST	ANG	- Scheduled for East Coast now stored
180104	50904+54904+55904+56904+59904	OO	FST	ANG	- Scheduled for East Coast now stored
180106	50906+54906+55906+56906+59906	OO	FST	ANG	- Scheduled for East Coast now stored
180108	50908+54908+55908+56908+59908	OO	FST	ANG	- Scheduled for East Coast now stored

Mk3 HST Stock

Vehicle Length: 75ft 0in (22.86m)	Width: 8ft 11in (2.71m)	
Height: 12ft 9in (3.88m)	Bogie Type: BT10	

GK1G - TRFB *Seating 17F*

Number	Depot	Livery	Owner
40701	EC	NXE	PTR
40702	EC	NXE	PTR
40704	EC	NXE	ANG
40705	EC	NXE	ANG
40706	EC	NXE	ANG
40708	EC	ECT	PTR
40711	EC	NXE	ANG
40720	EC	NXE	ANG
40735	EC	NXE	ANG
40737	EC	NXE	ANG
40740	EC	NXE	ANG
40742	EC	NXE	ANG
40748	EC	NXE	ANG
40750	EC	NXE	ANG
40805	EC	NXG	ANG

GH1G - TF *Seating 48F*

Number	Depot	Livery	Owner
41039	EC	NXE	ANG
41040	EC	NXE	ANG
41043	EC	ECS	ANG
41044	EC	NXE	ANG

East Coast

Number	Depot	Livery	Owner	Number	Depot	Livery	Owner	Number	Depot	Livery	Owner
41058	EC	NXE	PTR	42110	EC	NXE	PTR	42238*	EC	NXE	ANG
41066	EC	NXE	ANG	42116*	EC	NXE	ANG	42239*	EC	NXE	ANG
41083	EC	NXE	PTR	42117	EC	NXE	PTR	42240	EC	NXE	ANG
41087	EC	NXE	ANG	42127*	EC	NXE	ANG	42241	EC	NXE	ANG
41088	EC	NXE	ANG	42128*	EC	NXE	ANG	42242	EC	NXE	ANG
41090	EC	NXE	ANG	42130	EC	NXE	PTR	42243	EC	NXE	ANG
41091	EC	NXE	ANG	42134	EC	NXE	ANG	42244	EC	NXE	ANG
41092	EC	NXE	ANG	42146	EC	ECT	ANG	42286	EC	ECT	PTR
41095	EC	NXE	ANG	42147	EC	NXE	PTR	42306	EC	NXE	PTR
41097	EC	NXE	ANG	42150	EC	ECT	ANG	42307	EC	NXE	PTR
41098	EC	NXE	ANG	42154	EC	ECT	ANG	42322	EC	ECT	PTR
41099	EC	NXE	ANG	42158	EC	NXE	ANG	42323	EC	NXE	ANG
41100	EC	NXE	ANG	42159*	EC	NXE	PTR	42326	EC	NXE	PTR
41115	EC	NXE	PTR	42160	EC	NXE	PTR	42330	EC	NXE	PTR
41118	EC	NXE	ANG	42161*	EC	NXE	PTR	42340	EC	NXE	ANG
41120	EC	ECT	ANG	42163	EC	NXE	PTR	42352(41176)	EC	NXE	PTR
41150	EC	ECT	ANG	42171	EC	NXE	ANG	42354(41175)	EC	ECT	ANG
41151	EC	NXE	ANG	42172	EC	NXE	ANG	42355(41172)	EC	NXE	ANG
41152	EC	NXE	ANG	42179	EC	NXE	ANG	42357(41174)	EC	NXE	ANG
41159	EC	NXE	PTR	42180	EC	NXE	ANG	42363(41082)	EC	NXE	ANG
41164	EC	NXE	ANG	42181	EC	NXE	ANG				
41165	EC	NXE	PTR	42182	EC	NXE	ANG				
41170(41001)	EC	NXE	ANG	42186	EC	ECT	ANG				
41185(42313)	EC	NXE	PTR	42188*	EC	NXE	ANG				
41190(42088)	EC	NXG	PTR	42189*	EC	NXE	ANG				

GJ2G - TGS *Seating 65S*

Number	Depot	Livery	Owner
44019	EC	NXE	ANG
44031	EC	NXE	ANG
44045	EC	NXE	ANG
44050	EC	ECT	PTR
44056	EC	NXE	ANG
44057	EC	NXE	PTR
44058	EC	NXE	ANG
44061	EC	NXE	ANG
44063	EC	NXE	ANG
44075	EC	NXE	PTR
44077	EC	NXE	ANG
44080	EC	NXE	ANG
44094	EC	ECT	ANG
44098	EC	NXE	ANG

GH2G - TS (*TSD) *Seating 76/62*S*

Number	Depot	Livery	Owner
42057	EC	NXE	ANG
42058	EC	NXE	ANG
42059	EC	NXE	ANG
42063	EC	NXE	ANG
42064	EC	NXE	ANG
42065	EC	NXE	ANG
42091*	EC	ECT	ANG
42106	EC	NXE	ANG
42109	EC	NXE	PTR

42190	EC	NXE	ANG
42191	EC	NXE	ANG
42192	EC	NXE	ANG
42193	EC	NXE	ANG
42198	EC	NXE	ANG
42199	EC	NXE	ANG
42215	EC	ECT	ANG
42219	EC	NXE	ANG
42226	EC	NXE	ANG
42228	EC	ECT	PTR
42235	EC	NXE	ANG
42237	EC	NXE	PTR

Left: Immediately following the surrender of the East Coast franchise by National Express, the National Express branding was removed, with the new East Coast trading title and website address applied to the base white and silver livery. Mk3 TF No. 41152 is illustrated.
Michael J. Collins

Mk4 Stock

Vehicle Length: 75ft 5in (23m) Width: 8ft 11in (2.73m)
Height: 12ft 5in (3.79m) Bogie Type: BT41

AJ2J - RSB *Seating 30S*

Number	Depot	Livery	Owner	Number	Depot	Livery	Owner	Number	Depot	Livery	Owner
10300	BN	NXG	HSB	10306	BN	NXG	HSB	10314	BN	NXG	HSB
10301	BN	NXG	HSB	10307	BN	ECS	HSB	10317	BN	NXG	HSB
10302	BN	ECS	HSB	10308	BN	NXG	HSB	10318	BN	NXG	HSB
10303	BN	NXG	HSB	10309	BN	NXG	HSB	10319	BN	NXG	HSB
10304	BN	NXG	HSB	10310	BN	NXG	HSB	10320	BN	NXG	HSB
10305	BN	NXG	HSB	10311	BN	NXG	HSB	10321	BN	NXG	HSB
				10312	BN	NXG	HSB	10323	BN	NXG	HSB
				10313	BN	NXG	HSB	10324	BN	NXG	HSB

Number	Depot	Livery	Owner
10325	BN	NXG	HSB
10326	BN	ECS	HSB
10328	BN	NXG	HSB
10329	BN	NXG	HSB
10330	BN	NXG	HSB
10331	BN	NXG	HSB
10332	BN	NXG	HSB
10333	BN	NXG	HSB

AD1J - FO *Seating 46F*

Number	Depot	Livery	Owner
11201	BN	NXG	HSB
11219	BN	ECS	HSB
11229	BN	NXG	HSB
11237	BN	NXG	HSB
11241	BN	NXG	HSB
11244	BN	NXG	HSB
11273	BN	NXG	HSB
11277(12408)	BN	NXG	HSB
11278(12479)	BN	NXG	HSB
11279(12521)	BN	NXG	HSB
11280(12523)	BN	NXG	HSB
11281(12418)	BN	NXG	HSB
11282(12524)	BN	NXG	HSB
11283(12435)	BN	NXG	HSB
11284(12487)	BN	NXG	HSB
11285(12537)	BN	NXG	HSB
11286(12482)	BN	NXG	HSB
11287(12527)	BN	NXG	HSB
11288(12517)	BN	NXG	HSB
11289(12528)	BN	NXG	HSB
11290(12530)	BN	NXG	HSB
11291(12535)	BN	NXG	HSB
11292(12451)	BN	NXG	HSB
11293(12536)	BN	NXG	HSB
11294(12529)	BN	NXG	HSB
11295(12475)	BN	NXG	HSB
11298(12416)	BN	ECS	HSB
11299(12532)	BN	ECS	HSB

AL1J - FOD *Seating 42F*

Number	Depot	Livery	Owner
11301(11215)	BN	ECS	HSB
11302(11203)	BN	ECS	HSB
11303(11211)	BN	NXG	HSB
11304(11257)	BN	NXG	HSB
11305(11261)	BN	ECS	HSB
11306(11276)	BN	NXG	HSB
11307(11217)	BN	NXG	HSB
11308(11263)	BN	NXG	HSB
11309(11262)	BN	NXG	HSB
11310(11272)	BN	NXG	HSB
11311(11221)	BN	NXG	HSB
11312(11225)	BN	NXG	HSB
11313(11210)	BN	NXG	HSB
11314(11207)	BN	NXG	HSB
11315(11238)	BN	NXG	HSB
11316(11227)	BN	NXG	HSB
11317(11223)	BN	NXG	HSB
11318(11251)	BN	NXG	HSB
11319(11247)	BN	NXG	HSB
11320(11255)	BN	NXG	HSB
11321(11245)	BN	NXG	HSB
11322(11228)	BN	NXG	HSB
11323(11235)	BN	NXG	HSB
11324(11253)	BN	NXG	HSB
11325(11231)	BN	NXG	HSB
11326(11206)	BN	NXG	HSB
11327(11236)	BN	NXG	HSB
11328(11274)	BN	NXG	HSB
11329(11243)	BN	NXG	HSB
11330(11249)	BN	NXG	HSB

AD1J - FO *Seating 46F*

Number	Depot	Livery	Owner
11401(11214)	BN	ECS	HSB
11402(11216)	BN	ECS	HSB
11403(11258)	BN	NXG	HSB
11404(11202)	BN	NXG	HSB
11405(11204)	BN	ECS	HSB
11406(11205)	BN	NXG	HSB
11407(11256)	BN	NXG	HSB
11408(11218)	BN	NXG	HSB
11409(11259)	BN	NXG	HSB
11410(11260)	BN	NXG	HSB
11411(11240)	BN	NXG	HSB
11412(11209)	BN	NXG	HSB
11413(11212)	BN	NXG	HSB
11414(11246)	BN	NXG	HSB
11415(11208)	BN	NXG	HSB
11416(11254)	BN	NXG	HSB
11417(11226)	BN	NXG	HSB
11418(11222)	BN	NXG	HSB
11419(11250)	BN	NXG	HSB
11420(11242)	BN	NXG	HSB
11421(11220)	BN	NXG	HSB
11422(11232)	BN	NXG	HSB
11423(11230)	BN	NXG	HSB
11424(11239)	BN	NXG	HSB
11425(11234)	BN	NXG	HSB
11426(11252)	BN	NXG	HSB
11427(11200)	BN	NXG	HSB
11428(11233)	BN	NXG	HSB
11429(11275)	BN	NXG	HSB
11430(11248)	BN	NXG	HSB
11998(10314)	BN	NXG	HSB
11999(10316)	BN	NXG	HSB

AI2J - TSOE *Seating 76S*

Number	Depot	Livery	Owner
12200	BN	NXG	HSB
12201	BN	NXG	HSB
12202	BN	NXG	HSB
12203	BN	NXG	HSB
12204	BN	NXG	HSB
12205	BN	NXG	HSB
12207	BN	ECS	HSB
12208	BN	NXG	HSB
12209	BN	ECS	HSB
12210	BN	NXG	HSB
12211	BN	NXG	HSB
12212	BN	NXG	HSB
12213	BN	NXG	HSB
12214	BN	NXG	HSB
12215	BN	NXG	HSB
12216	BN	NXG	HSB
12217	BN	NXG	HSB
12218	BN	NXG	HSB
12219	BN	NXG	HSB
12220	BN	NXG	HSB
12222	BN	NXG	HSB
12223	BN	NXG	HSB
12224	BN	NXG	HSB
12225	BN	NXG	HSB
12226	BN	NXG	HSB
12227	BN	NXG	HSB
12228	BN	NXG	HSB
12229	BN	NXG	HSB
12230	BN	NXG	HSB
12231	BN	NXG	HSB
12232	BN	ECS	HSB

AL2J - TSOD *Seating 68S*

Number	Depot	Livery	Owner
12300	BN	ECS	HSB
12301	BN	NXG	HSB
12302	BN	ECS	HSB
12303	BN	NXG	HSB
12304	BN	NXG	HSB
12305	BN	NXG	HSB
12307	BN	ECS	HSB
12308	BN	NXG	HSB
12309	BN	NXG	HSB
12310	BN	NXG	HSB
12311	BN	NXG	HSB
12312	BN	NXG	HSB
12313	BN	NXG	HSB
12315	BN	NXG	HSB
12316	BN	NXG	HSB
12317	BN	NXG	HSB
12318	BN	NXG	HSB
12319	BN	NXG	HSB
12320	BN	NXG	HSB
12321	BN	NXG	HSB
12322	BN	NXG	HSB
12323	BN	NXG	HSB
12324	BN	NXG	HSB
12325	BN	NXG	HSB
12326	BN	NXG	HSB
12327	BN	NXG	HSB
12328	BN	NXG	HSB
12329	BN	NXG	HSB
12330	BN	NXG	HSB
12331(12531)	BN	NXG	HSB

AC2J - TSO *Seating 76S*

Number	Depot	Livery	Owner
12400	BN	NXG	HSB
12401	BN	NXG	HSB
12402	BN	ECS	HSB
12403	BN	NXG	HSB
12404	BN	NXG	HSB
12405	BN	NXG	HSB
12406	BN	NXG	HSB
12407	BN	NXG	HSB
12409	BN	NXG	HSB
12410	BN	NXG	HSB
12411	BN	NXG	HSB
12414	BN	ECS	HSB
12415	BN	ECS	HSB
12417	BN	ECS	HSB
12419	BN	NXG	HSB

East Coast

12420	BN	NXG	HSB		12459	BN	NXG	HSB		12534	BN	NXG	HSB
12421	BN	NXG	HSB		12460	BN	NXG	HSB		12538	BN	NXG	HSB
12422	BN	NXG	HSB		12461	BN	NXG	HSB					
12423	BN	NXG	HSB		12462	BN	NXG	HSB		**NZAJ - DVT**			
12424	BN	NXG	HSB		12463	BN	NXG	HSB		*Number*	*Depot*	*Livery*	*Owner*
12425	BN	NXG	HSB		12464	BN	NXG	HSB		82200	BN	NXG	HSB
12426	BN	NXG	HSB		12465	BN	NXG	HSB		82201	BN	NXG	HSB
12427	BN	NXG	HSB		12466	BN	NXG	HSB		82202	BN	ECS	HSB
12428	BN	NXG	HSB		12467	BN	NXG	HSB		82203	BN	NXG	HSB
12429	BN	NXG	HSB		12468	BN	NXG	HSB		82204	BN	NXG	HSB
12430	BN	NXG	HSB		12469	BN	NXG	HSB		82205	BN	NXG	HSB
12431	BN	NXG	HSB		12470	BN	NXG	HSB		82206	BN	NXG	HSB
12432	BN	NXG	HSB		12471	BN	NXG	HSB		82207	BN	ECS	HSB
12433	BN	NXG	HSB		12472	BN	NXG	HSB		82208	BN	NXG	HSB
12434	BN	NXG	HSB		12473	BN	NXG	HSB		82209	BN	NXG	HSB
12436	BN	NXG	HSB		12474	BN	NXG	HSB		82210	BN	ECS	HSB
12437	BN	NXG	HSB		12476	BN	NXG	HSB		82211	BN	NXG	HSB
12438	BN	NXG	HSB		12477	BN	NXG	HSB		82212	BN	NXG	HSB
12439	BN	NXG	HSB		12478	BN	NXG	HSB		82213	BN	NXG	HSB
12440	BN	NXG	HSB		12480	BN	NXG	HSB		82214	BN	NXG	HSB
12441	BN	NXG	HSB		12481	BN	NXG	HSB		82215	BN	NXG	HSB
12442	BN	NXG	HSB		12483	BN	NXG	HSB		82216	BN	NXG	HSB
12443	BN	NXG	HSB		12484	BN	NXG	HSB		82217	BN	NXG	HSB
12444	BN	NXG	HSB		12485	BN	NXG	HSB		82218	BN	NXG	HSB
12445	BN	NXG	HSB		12486	BN	ECS	HSB		82219	BN	NXG	HSB
12446	BN	NXG	HSB		12488	BN	NXG	HSB		82220	BN	NXG	HSB
12447	BN	NXG	HSB		12489	BN	NXG	HSB		82222	BN	NXG	HSB
12448	BN	ECS	HSB		12513	BN	NXG	HSB		82223	BN	NXG	HSB
12449	BN	NXG	HSB		12514	BN	NXG	HSB		82224	BN	NXG	HSB
12450	BN	ECS	HSB		12515	BN	NXG	HSB		82225	BN	NXG	HSB
12452	BN	NXG	HSB		12518	BN	NXG	HSB		82226	BN	NXG	HSB
12453	BN	NXG	HSB		12519	BN	NXG	HSB		82227	BN	NXG	HSB
12454	BN	NXG	HSB		12520	BN	ECS	HSB		82228	BN	NXG	HSB
12456	BN	NXG	HSB		12522	BN	ECS	HSB		82229	BN	NXG	HSB
12457	BN	NXG	HSB		12526	BN	NXG	HSB		82230	BN	NXG	HSB
12458	BN	NXG	HSB		12533	BN	NXG	HSB		82231	BN	NXG	HSB

Below: *The Mk4 passenger fleet form the core East Coast electric passenger fleet, operating services between London King's Cross and Leeds/Edinburgh with Class 91s coupled at the north end of trains and DVTs on the south end. Painted in former GNER blue but with East Coast branding, DVT No. 82218 trails a northbound train out of York.* **Chris Perkins**

Service Stock

HST and Mk4 Barrier Vehicles

Number	Depot	Livery	Owner	Former Identity
6340	EC	NEG	ANG	BCK - 21251
6344	EC	NEG	ANG	BG - 92080
6346	EC	NEG	ANG	BSO - 9422
6352	BN	NEG	ANG	SK - 19465
6353	BN	NEG	ANG	SK - 19478
6354	BN	NEG	ANG	BSO - 9459
6355	BN	NEG	ANG	BSO - 9477
6358	BN	NEG	HSB	BSO - 9432
6359	BN	NEG	HSB	BSO - 9429
9393	EC	PTR	PTR	BG - 92196
9394	EC	PTR	PTR	BG - 92906

Right: *As with any operator of semi-fixed formation trains fitted with buck-eye couplers, a need for coupling adapter vans exists. On the East Coast eleven such coaches are on the books, some dedicated to Mk3 and others Mk4 stock. Painted in all-over blue livery, barrier coach No. 6344 is seen at Doncaster; this was rebuilt from BG No. 92080.* **Nathan Williamson**

Mk4 Set Formations

The East Coast Mk4 formations are booked to operate in fixed formations, but frequent changes are reported. This listing should be treated as a guide only.

Set No.	Loco	TSOE	TSO	TSO	TSO	TSOD	RSB	FO	FOD	FO	DVT
BN01	911xx	12207	12417	12415	12414	12307	10307	11298	11301	11401	82207
BN02	911xx	12232	12402	12450	12448	12302	10302	11299	11302	11402	82202
BN03	911xx	12201	12401	12459	12478	12301	10320	11277	11303	11403	82219
BN04	911xx	12202	12480	12421	12518	12327	10303	11278	11304	11404	82209
BN05	911xx	12209	12486	12520	12522	12300	10326	11219	11305	11405	82210
BN06	911xx	12208	12406	12420	12422	12313	10309	11279	11306	11406	82208
BN07	911xx	12231	12411	12405	12489	12329	10323	11280	11307	11407	82204
BN08	911xx	12205	12481	12485	12407	12328	10300	11229	11308	11408	82211
BN09	911xx	12230	12513	12483	12514	12308	10331	11281	11309	11409	82215
BN10	911xx	12214	12419	12488	12443	12305	10304	11282	11310	11410	82205
BN11	911xx	12203	12437	12436	12484	12315	10308	11283	11311	11411	82218
BN12	911xx	12212	12431	12404	12426	12330	10333	11284	11312	11412	82212
BN13	911xx	12228	12469	12430	12424	12311	10313	11285	11313	11413	82213
BN14	911xx	12229	12410	12526	12423	12312	10332	11201	11314	11414	82206
BN15	911xx	12226	12442	12409	12515	12309	10306	11286	11315	11415	82214
BN16	911xx	12213	12428	12445	12433	12304	10315	11287	11316	11416	82225
BN17	911xx	12223	12444	12427	12432	12303	10324	11288	11317	11417	82222
BN18	911xx	12215	12453	12468	12467	12324	10305	11289	11318	11418	82220
BN19	911xx	12211	12434	12400	12470	12310	10318	11290	11319	11419	82201
BN20	911xx	12224	12477	12439	12440	12326	10321	11241	11320	11420	82200
BN21	911xx	12222	12461	12441	12476	12323	10330	11244	11321	11421	82227
BN22	911xx	12210	12452	12460	12473	12316	10301	11291	11322	11422	82230
BN23	911xx	12225	12454	12456	12455	12318	10325	11292	11323	11423	82226
BN24	911xx	12219	12447	12425	12403	12319	10328	11293	11324	11424	82229
BN25	911xx	12217	12446	12519	12464	12322	10312	11294	11325	11425	82216
BN26	911xx	12220	12474	12465	12429	12325	10311	11295	11326	11426	82223
BN27	911xx	12216	12449	12466	12538	12317	10319	11237	11327	11427	82228
BN28	911xx	12218	12458	12463	12533	12320	10310	11273	11328	11428	82217
BN29	911xx	12204	12462	12457	12438	12321	10317	11998	11329	11429	82231
BN30	911xx	12227	12471	12534	12472	12331	10329	11999	11330	11430	82203
Spare cars		12200									82224

Northern Rail

Address:	✉ Northern House, 9 Rougier Street, York, YO1 6HZ
	✍ customer.relations@northernrail.org
	✆ 0845 000125
	ⓘ www.northernrail.org
Managing Director:	Ian Bevan
Franchise Dates:	12 December 2004 - 15 September 2013
Principal Routes:	Regional services in Merseyside, Greater Manchester, South/ North Yorkshire, Lancashire, Cumbria and the North East
Depots:	Newton Heath (NH), Heaton (HT), Longsight (LG), Neville Hill (NL)
Parent Company:	Serco/NedRailways

Class 142

Vehicle Length: 51ft 0½in (15.55m)
Height: 12ft 8in (3.86m)
Width: 9ft 2¼in (2.80m)
Engine: 1 x Cummins LTA10-R per vehicle
Horsepower: 460hp (343kW)
Seats (total/car): 106S, 56S/50S

Number	Formation DMS+DMSL	Depot	Livery	Owner	Operator
142003	55544+55594	NH	NOR	ANG	NOR
142004	55545+55595	NH	NOR	ANG	NOR
142005	55546+55596	NH	NOR	ANG	NOR
142007	55548+55598	NH	NOR	ANG	NOR
142011	55552+55602	NH	NOR	ANG	NOR
142012	55553+55603	NH	NOR	ANG	NOR
142013	55554+55604	NH	NOR	ANG	NOR
142014	55555+55605	NH	NOR	ANG	NOR
142015	55556+55606	HT	NOR	ANG	NOR
142016	55557+55607	HT	NOR	ANG	NOR
142017	55558+55608	HT	NOR	ANG	NOR
142018	55559+55609	HT	NOR	ANG	NOR
142019	55560+55610	HT	NOR	ANG	NOR
142020	55561+55611	HT	NOR	ANG	NOR
142021	55562+55612	HT	NOR	ANG	NOR
142022	55563+55613	HT	NOR	ANG	NOR
142023	55564+55614	NH	NOR	ANG	NOR
142024	55565+55615	HT	NOR	ANG	NOR
142025	55566+55616	HT	NOR	ANG	NOR
142026	55567+55617	HT	NOR	ANG	NOR
142027	55568+55618	NH	NOR	ANG	NOR
142028	55569+55619	NH	NOR	ANG	NOR
142031	55572+55622	NH	NOR	ANG	NOR
142032	55573+55623	NH	NOR	ANG	NOR
142033	55574+55624	NH	NOR	ANG	NOR
142034	55575+55625	HT	NOR	ANG	NOR
142035	55576+55626	NH	NOR	ANG	NOR
142036	55577+55627	NH	NOR	ANG	NOR
142037	55578+55628	NH	NOR	ANG	NOR
142038	55579+55629	NH	NOR	ANG	NOR
142039	55580+55630	NH	NOR	ANG	NOR
142040	55581+55631	NH	NOR	ANG	NOR
142041	55582+55632	NH	NOR	ANG	NOR
142042(S)	55583+55633	NH	NOR	ANG	NOR
142043	55584+55634	NH	NOR	ANG	NOR
142044	55585+55635	NH	NOR	ANG	NOR
142045	55586+55636	NH	NOR	ANG	NOR
142046	55587+55637	NH	NOR	ANG	NOR
142047	55588+55638	NH	NOR	ANG	NOR
142048	55589+55639	NH	NOR	ANG	NOR
142049	55590+55640	NH	NOR	ANG	NOR
142050	55591+55641	HT	NOR	ANG	NOR
142051	55701+55747	NH	NOR	ANG	NOR
142052	55702+55748	NH	NOR	ANG	NOR
142053	55703+55749	NH	NOR	ANG	NOR
142054	55704+55750	NH	NOR	ANG	NOR
142055	55705+55751	NH	NOR	ANG	NOR
142056	55706+55752	NH	NOR	ANG	NOR
142057	55707+55753	NH	NOR	ANG	NOR
142058	55708+55754	NH	NOR	ANG	NOR
142060	55710+55756	NH	NOR	ANG	NOR
142061	55711+55757	NH	NOR	ANG	NOR
142062	55712+55758	NH	NOR	ANG	NOR
142065	55715+55761	HT	NOR	ANG	NOR
142066	55716+55762	HT	NOR	ANG	NOR
142067	55717+55763	NH	NOR	ANG	NOR
142070	55720+55766	HT	NOR	ANG	NOR
142071	55721+55767	HT	NOR	ANG	NOR
142078	55728+55768	HT	NOR	ANG	NOR
142079	55729+55769	HT	NOR	ANG	NOR
142084	55764+55780	HT	NOR	ANG	NOR
142086	55736+55782	HT	NOR	ANG	NOR
142087	55737+55783	HT	NOR	ANG	NOR
142088	55738+55784	HT	NOR	ANG	NOR
142089	55739+55785	HT	NOR	ANG	NOR
142090	55740+55786	HT	NOR	ANG	NOR
142091	55741+55787	HT	NOR	ANG	NOR
142092	55742+55788	HT	NOR	ANG	NOR
142093	55743+55789	HT	NOR	ANG	NOR
142094	55744+55790	HT	NOR	ANG	NOR
142095	55745+55791	HT	NOR	ANG	NOR
142096	55746+55792	HT	NOR	ANG	NOR

■ The seven Class 142s working for First Great Western are scheduled to move to Northern Rail from May 2011.

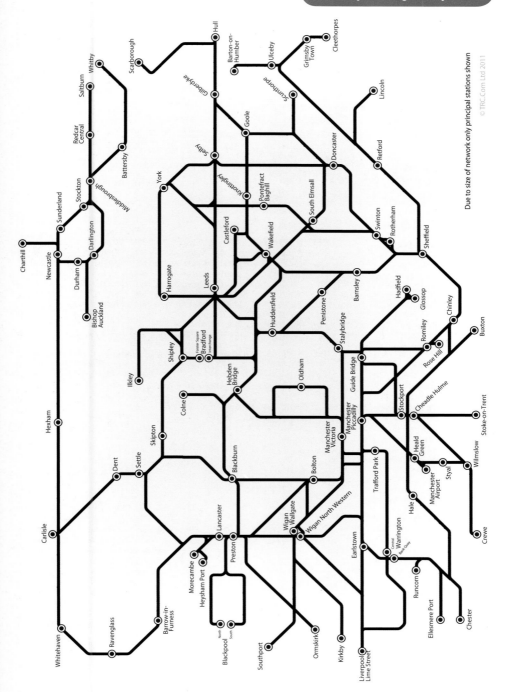

Due to size of network only principal stations shown

© TRC.Com Ltd 2011

Passenger Train Operating Companies - Northern Rail

Northern Rail

Left: *The largest fleet of Class 142s are operated by Northern Rail, with class members allocated to Heaton (Newcastle) and Newton Heath (Manchester). All sets now sport the distinctive Northern livery of blue, mauve and grey, with passenger doors offset in grey. Set No. 142045 is departing south from Preston.* **CJM**

Class 144

Vehicle Length: 50ft 2in (15.25m)	Height: 12ft 2½in (3.73m)	Width: 8ft 10½in (2.70m)	Engine: 1 x Cummins LTA10-R per vehicle	Horsepower: 460hp (343kW)
				Seats (total/car): 87S, 45S/42S

Number	Formation DMS+DMSL	Depot	Livery	Owner	Operator
144001	55801+55824	NL	NOR	PTR	NOR
144002	55802+55825	NL	NOR	PTR	NOR
144003	55803+55826	NL	NOR	PTR	NOR
144004	55804+55827	NL	NOR	PTR	NOR
144005	55805+55828	NL	NOR	PTR	NOR
144006	55806+55829	NL	NOR	PTR	NOR
144007	55807+55830	NL	NOR	PTR	NOR
144008	55808+55831	NL	NOR	PTR	NOR
144009	55809+55832	NL	NOR	PTR	NOR
144010	55810+55833	NL	NOR	PTR	NOR
144011	55811+55834	NL	NOR	PTR	NOR
144012	55812+55835	NL	NOR	PTR	NOR
144013	55813+55836	NL	NOR	PTR	NOR

Name applied
144001 *The Penistone Line Partnership*

Vehicle Length: 50ft 2in (15.25m)	Height: 12ft 2½in (3.73m)	Width: 8ft 10½in (2.70m)	Engine: 1 x Cummins LTA10-R per vehicle	Horsepower: 690hp (515kW)
				Seats (total/car): 145S, 45S/58S/42S

Number	Formation DMS+MS+DMSL	Depot	Livery	Owner	Operator
144014	55814+55850+55837	NL	NOR	PTR	NOR
144015	55815+55851+55838	NL	NOR	PTR	NOR
144016	55816+55852+55839	NL	NOR	PTR	NOR
144017	55817+55853+55840	NL	NOR	PTR	NOR
144018	55818+55854+55841	NL	NOR	PTR	NOR
144019	55819+55855+55842	NL	NOR	PTR	NOR
144020	55820+55856+55843	NL	NOR	PTR	NOR
144021	55821+55857+55844	NL	NOR	PTR	NOR
144022	55822+55858+55845	NL	NOR	PTR	NOR
144023	55823+55859+55846	NL	NOR	PTR	NOR

Left: *The Class 144 'Pacer' comes in both two and three car variants; all are allocated to Leeds Neville Hill depot and operate secondary line services. In recent times all have been facelifted and now sport the latest Northern livery. Three-car set No. 144014 stands at Morecambe attached to a Northern Class 153, while in the background we see Northern Rail Class 156 No. 156471.* **Tony Christie**

Class 150/1

Vehicle Length: 64ft 9¾in (19.74m)
Height: 12ft 4½in (3.77m)
Width: 9ft 3⅛in (2.82m)

Engine: 1 x NT855R5 of 285hp per vehicle
Horsepower: 570hp (425kW)
Seats (total/car): 124S, 59S/65S

Number	Formation DMSL+DMS	Depot	Livery	Owner	Operator	Number	Formation	Depot	Livery	Owner	Operator
						150141	52141+57141	NH	NOR	ANG	NOR
						150142	52142+57142	NH	NOR	ANG	NOR
150133	52133+57133	NH	NOR	ANG	NOR	150143	52143+57143	NH	NOR	ANG	NOR
150134	52134+57134	NH	NOR	ANG	NOR	150144	52144+57144	NH	NOR	ANG	NOR
150135	52135+57135	NH	NOR	ANG	NOR	150145	52145+57145	NH	NOR	ANG	NOR
150136	52136+57136	NH	NOR	ANG	NOR	150146	52146+57146	NH	NOR	ANG	NOR
150137	52137+57137	NH	NOR	ANG	NOR	150147	52147+57147	NH	NOR	ANG	NOR
150138	52138+57138	NH	NOR	ANG	NOR	150148	52148+57148	NH	NOR	ANG	NOR
150139	52139+57139	NH	NOR	ANG	NOR	150149	52149+57149	NH	NOR	ANG	NOR
150140	52140+57140	NH	NOR	ANG	NOR	150150	52150+57150	NH	NOR	ANG	NOR

Right: *Manchester Newton Heath depot has an allocation of 18 two-car Class 150/1 units, these non end gangway fitted sets operate on branch lines in the Manchester area and some Trans Pennine services. Set No. 150142 in full Northern Rail livery is seen at Sheffield.* **Nathan Williamson**

● Eight Class 150s are due to transfer from London Midland to Northern in early 2011.

Class 150/2

Vehicle Length: 64ft 9¾in (19.74m)
Height: 12ft 4½in (3.77m)
Width: 9ft 3⅛in (2.82m)

Engine: 1 x NT855R5 of 285hp per vehicle
Horsepower: 570hp (425kW)
Seats (total/car): 132S, 62S/70S

Number	Formation DMSL+DMS	Depot	Livery	Owner	Operator	Number	Formation	Depot	Livery		Owner	Operator
						150270	52270+57270	NH	NOR ¤	PTR		NOR
						150271	52271+57271	NH	NOR ¤	PTR		NOR
150201	52201+57201	NH	NOR	ANG	NOR	150272	52272+57272	NH	NOR ¤	PTR		NOR
150203	52203+57203	NH	NOR	ANG	NOR	150273	52273+57273	NH	NOR ¤	PTR		NOR
150205	52205+57205	NH	NOR	ANG	NOR	150274	52274+57274	NH	NOR ¤	PTR		NOR
150207	52207+57207	NH	NOR	ANG	NOR	150275	52275+57275	NH	NOR ¤	PTR		NOR
150211	52211+57211	NH	NOR	ANG	NOR	150276	52276+57276	NH	NOR ¤	PTR		NOR
150215	52215+57215	NH	NOR	ANG	NOR	150277	52277+57277	NH	NOR ¤	PTR		NOR
150218	52218+57218	NH	NOR	ANG	NOR							
150222	52222+57222	NH	NOR	ANG	NOR							
150223	52223+57223	NH	NOR	ANG	NOR							
150224	52224+57224	NH	NOR	ANG	NOR							
150225	52225+57225	NH	NOR	ANG	NOR							
150228	52228+57228	NH	NOR ¤	PTR	NOR							
150268	52268+57268	NH	NOR ¤	PTR	NOR							
150269	52269+57269	NH	NOR ¤	PTR	NOR							

¤ Advertising liveries
150228 - Outdoors
150269 - Family
150270 - City Life
150276 - Sport
150268 - Heritage

150271 - Arts
150272 - Colne Festival
150273 - Yorkshire
150274 - Events
150275 - Yorkshire
150277 - Yorkshire

Right: *Northern Rail has adorned several of its units in vinyls promoting the areas in which they operate. One example is Class 150/2 No. 150228 which advertises 'Visit Yorkshire.' On 7 August 2010, the unit is off the beaten track at Whaley Bridge with the 12.30 Buxton to Manchester Piccadilly service. All members of the Class 150/2 sub class are allocated to Newton Heath depot in Manchester.* **John Binch**

Northern Rail

Class 153

Vehicle Length: 76ft 5in (23.29m)			Engine: 1 x NT855R5 of 285hp		
Height: 12ft 3⅛in (3.75m)			Horsepower: 285hp (213kW)		
Width: 8ft 10in (2.70m)			Seats (total/car): 70S		

Number	Formation DMSL	Depot	Livery	Owner	Operator
153301	52301	NL	NOR	ANG	NOR
153304	52304	NL	NOR	ANG	NOR
153307	52307	NL	NOR	ANG	NOR
153315	52315	NL	NOR	ANG	NOR
153316	52316	NL	NOR	PTR	NOR
153317	52317	NL	NOR	ANG	NOR
153324	52324	NL	NOR	PTR	NOR
153328	52328	NL	NOR	ANG	NOR
153330	52330	NL	NOR	PTR	NOR
153331	52331	NL	NOR	ANG	NOR
153332	52332	NL	NOR	ANG	NOR
153351	57351	NL	NOR	ANG	NOR
153352	57352	NL	NOR	ANG	NOR
153358	57358	NL	NOR	PTR	NOR
153359	57359	NL	NOR	PTR	NOR
153360	57360	NL	NOR	PTR	NOR
153363	57363	NL	NOR	PTR	NOR
153378	57378	NL	NOR	ANG	NOR

Left: *18 single car Class 153s are operated by Northern Rail, allocated to Leeds Neville Hill depot and used on secondary lines or to strengthen two-car formations. With its small cab leading, set No. 153304 is seen stabled between duties at Preston.* **CJM**

Class 155

Vehicle Length: 76ft 5in (23.29m)			Engine: 1 x NT855R5 of 285hp		
Height: 12ft 3⅛in (3.75m)			Horsepower: 570hp (425kW)		
Width: 8ft 10in (2.70m)			Seats (total/car): 156S, 76S/80S		

Number	Formation DMSL+DMS	Depot	Livery	Owner	Operator
155341	52341+57341	NL	NOR	WYP*	NOR
155342	52342+57342	NL	NOR	WYP*	NOR
155343	52343+57343	NL	NOR	WYP*	NOR
155344	52344+57344	NL	NOR	WYP*	NOR
155345	52345+57345	NL	NOR	WYP*	NOR
155346	52346+57346	NL	NOR	WYP*	NOR
155347	52347+57347	NL	NOR	WYP*	NOR

* Managed by Porterbrook Leasing

Left: *The only remaining 2-car Class 155 Leyland built sets are seven owned by West Yorkshire PTE and managed by Porterbrook operating outer-suburban services in Yorkshire. All carry pictogram advertising livery, based on the Northern Rail livery scheme, and are very pleasing to the eye. Set No. 155342 is seen at Leeds while working a service to Manchester Victoria.* **John Binch**

Class 156

Vehicle Length: 75ft 6in (23.03m)			Engine: 1 x Cummins NT855R5 of 285hp		
Height: 12ft 6in (3.81m)			Horsepower: 570hp (425kW)		
Width: 8ft 11in (2.73m)			Seats (total/car): 146S, 70/76S		

Number	Formation DMSL+DMS	Depot	Livery	Owner	Operator
156420	52420+57420	NH	NOR	PTR	NOR
156421	52421+57421	NH	NOR	PTR	NOR
156423	52423+57423	NH	NOR	PTR	NOR
156424	52424+57424	NH	NOR	PTR	NOR
156425	52425+57425	NH	NOR	PTR	NOR
156426	52426+57426	NH	NOR	PTR	NOR
156427	52427+57427	NH	NOR	PTR	NOR
156428	52428+57428	NH	NOR	PTR	NOR
156429	52429+57429	NH	NOR	PTR	NOR
156438	52438+57438	HT	NOR	ANG	NOR

156440	52440+57440	NH	NOR	PTR	NOR
156441	52441+57441	NH	NOR	PTR	NOR
156443	52443+57443	HT	NOR	ANG	NOR
156444	52444+57444	HT	NOR	ANG	NOR
156448	52448+57448	HT	NOR	ANG	NOR
156451	52451+57451	HT	NOR	ANG	NOR
156452	52452+57452	NH	NOR	PTR	NOR
156454	52454+57454	HT	NOR	ANG	NOR
156455	52455+57455	NH	NOR	PTR	NOR
156459	52459+57459	NH	NOR	PTR	NOR
156460	52460+57460	NH	NOR	PTR	NOR
156461	52461+57461	NH	NOR	PTR	NOR
156463	52463+57463	HT	NOR	ANG	NOR
156464	52464+57464	NH	NOR	PTR	NOR
156466	52466+57466	NH	NOR	PTR	NOR
156468	52468+57468	NH	NOR	ANG	NOR
156469	52469+57469	HT	NOR	ANG	NOR
156470	52470+57470	NH	NOR	ANG	NOR
156471	52471+57471	NH	NOR	ANG	NOR
156472	52472+57472	NH	NOR	ANG	NOR
156473	52473+57473	NH	NOR	ANG	NOR
156475	52475+57475	HT	NOR	ANG	NOR
156479	52479+57479	NH	NOR	ANG	NOR
156480	52480+57480	HT	NOR	ANG	NOR
156481	52481+57481	NH	NOR	ANG	NOR
156482	52482+57482	NH	NOR	ANG	NOR
156483	52483+57483	NH	NOR	ANG	NOR
156484	52484+57484	HT	NOR	ANG	NOR
156486	52486+57486	NH	NOR	ANG	NOR
156487	52487+57487	NH	NOR	ANG	NOR
156488	52488+57488	NH	NOR	ANG	NOR
156489	52489+57489	NH	NOR	ANG	NOR
156490	52490+57490	HT	NOR	ANG	NOR
156491	52491+57491	NH	NOR	ANG	NOR
156497	52497+57497	NH	NOR	ANG	NOR
156498	52498+57498	NH	NOR	ANG	NOR

Names applied
156441 *William Huskisson MP*
156444 *Councillor Bill Cameron*
156459 *Benny Rothman -*
The Manchester Rambler
156460 *Driver John Axon GC*
156466 *Gracie Fields*
156464 *Lancashire DalesRail*

Right: *A fleet of 46 two-car Class 156s are operated by Northern Rail, allocated to Newton Heath and Heaton depot. These are used on longer distance services. Set No. 156471 is illustrated.* **Tony Christie**

Class 158

Vehicle Length: 76ft 1¾in (23.21m)	Engine: 1 x Cummins NTA855R of 350hp per vehicle
Height: 12ft 6in (3.81m)	Horsepower: 1,050hp (783kW)
Width: 9ft 3¼in (2.82m)	Seats (total/car): 208S, 68S/70S/70S

Number	Formation DMSL+MSL+DMSL	Depot	Livery	Owner	Operator
158752	52752+58716+57752	NL	NOR	PTR	NOR
158753	52753+58710+57753	NL	NOR	PTR	NOR
158754	52754+58708+57754	NL	NOR	PTR	NOR
158755	52755+58702+57755	NL	NOR	PTR	NOR
158756	52756+58712+57756	NL	NOR	PTR	NOR
158757	52757+58706+57757	NL	NOR	PTR	NOR
158758	52758+58714+57758	NL	NOR	PTR	NOR
158759	52759+58713+57759	NL	NOR	PTR	NOR

Vehicle Length: 76ft 1¾in (23.21m)	Engine: 1 x Cummins NTA855R of 350hp per vehicle
Height: 12ft 6in (3.81m)	Horsepower: 700hp (522kW)
Width: 9ft 3¼in (2.82m)	Seats (total/car): 138S, 68S/70S

Number	Formation DMSL+DMSL	Depot	Livery	Owner	Operator
158784	52784+57784	NH	NOR	ANG	NOR
158787	52787+57787	NH	NOR	ANG	NOR
158790	52790+57790	NH	NOR	ANG	NOR
158791	52791+57791	NH	NOR	ANG	NOR
159792	52792+57792	NH	NOR	ANG	NOR
158793	52793+57793	NH	NOR	ANG	NOR
158794	52794+57794	NH	NOR	ANG	NOR
158795	52795+57795	NH	NOR	ANG	NOR
158796	52796+57796	NH	NOR	ANG	NOR
158797	52797+57797	NH	NOR	ANG	NOR
158815	52815+57815	NL	NOR	ANG	NOR
158816	52816+57816	NL	NOR	ANG	NOR
158817	52817+57817	NL	NOR	ANG	NOR
158843	52843+57843	NL	NOR	ANG	NOR
158844	52844+57844	NL	NOR	ANG	NOR
158845	52845+57845	NL	NOR	ANG	NOR
158848	52848+57848	NL	NOR	ANG	NOR
158849	52849+57849	NL	NOR	ANG	NOR
158850	52850+57850	NL	NOR	ANG	NOR
158851	52851+57851	NL	NOR	ANG	NOR
158853	52853+57853	NL	NOR	ANG	NOR
158855	52855+57855	NL	NOR	ANG	NOR

Passenger Train Operating Companies - Northern Rail

Northern Rail

158859	52859+57859	NL	NOR	ANG	NOR	158861	52861+57861	NL	SPL§	ANG	NOR
158860	52860+57860	NL	NOR	ANG	NOR	158872	52872+57872	NL	NOR	ANG	NOR

Vehicle Length: 76ft 1¾in (23.21m) *Engine: 1 x Cummins NTA855R of 350hp per vehicle*
Height: 12ft 6in (3.81m) *Horsepower: 700hp (522kW)*
Width: 9ft 3¼in (2.82m) *Seats (total/car): 142S, 70S/72S*

Number	Formation	Depot	Livery	Owner	Operator						
	DMSL+DMS					158905	52905+57905	NL	NOR	HSB	NOR
158901	52901+57901	NL	NOR	HSB	NOR	158906	52906+57906	NL	NOR	HSB	NOR
158902	52902+57902	NL	NOR	HSB	NOR	158907	52907+57907	NL	NOR	HSB	NOR
158903	52903+57903	NL	NOR	HSB	NOR	158908	52908+57908	NL	NOR	HSB	NOR
158904	52904+57904	NL	NOR	HSB	NOR	158909	52909+57909	NL	NOR	HSB	NOR
						158910	52910+57910	NL	NOR	HSB	NOR

Names applied
158784 Barbara Castle
158791 County of Nottinghamshire
158796 Fred Trueman - Cricketing Legend
158860 Ian Dewhirst
158910 William Wilberforce

§ Carries Welcome to Yorkshire livery

Left: *Two and three-car formation Class 158s are operated by Northern Rail. Three-car set No. 158757 is seen under the overall roof at Preston. Sets in the 1589xx series are designated for standard class only use.* **CJM**

Class 321/9

Vehicle Length: (Driving) 65ft 0¾in (19.83m) *Width: 9ft 3in (2.82m)*
(Inter) 65ft 4¼in (19.92m) *Horsepower: 1,328hp (996kW)*
Height: 12ft 4¾in (3.78m) *Seats (total/car): 293S, 70S/79S/74S/70S*

Number	Formation	Depot	Livery	Owner	Operator
	DTCO+MSO+TSO+DTSO				
321901	77990+63153+72128+77993	NL	NOM	HSB	NOR
321902	77991+63154+72129+77994	NL	NOM	HSB	NOR
321903	77992+63155+72130+77995	NL	NOM	HSB	NOR

Left: *For use on the Leeds to Doncaster WYPTE route, three 4-car Class 321/9s sets are allocated to Leeds Neville Hill. The sets are very rarely seen on Wharfedale and Airedale routes. All are painted in a revised version of Northern Rail livery incorporating Metro branding and lettering with red bodies and blue markings on driving cars. Set No. 321901 is seen at Doncaster.* **Brian Morrison**

Class 323

Vehicle Length: (Driving) 76ft 8¼in (23.37m) *Width: 9ft 2¼in (2.80m)*
(Inter) 76ft 10¾in (23.44m) *Horsepower: 1,565hp (1,168kW)*
Height: 12ft 4¾in (3.78m) *Seats (total/car) 323223-225: 244S, 82S/80S/82S*
323226-239: 284S, 98S/88S/98S

Number	Formation	Depot	Livery	Owner	Operator
	DMSO(A)+PTSO+DMSO(B)				
323223	64023+72223+65023	LG	NOR	PTR	NOR
323224	64024+72224+65024	LG	NOR	PTR	NOR
323225	64025+72225+65025	LG	FSN	PTR	NOR
323226	64026+72226+65026	LG	FSN	PTR	NOR
323227	64027+72227+65027	LG	FSN	PTR	NOR
323228	64028+72228+65028	LG	NOR	PTR	NOR

323229	64029+72229+65029	LG	NOR	PTR	NOR
323230	64030+72230+65030	LG	FSN	PTR	NOR
323231	64031+72231+65031	LG	NOR	PTR	NOR
323232	64032+72232+65032	LG	NOR	PTR	NOR
323233	64033+72233+65033	LG	NOR	PTR	NOR
323234	64034+72234+65034	LG	NOR	PTR	NOR
323235	64035+72235+65035	LG	NOR	PTR	NOR
323236	64036+72236+65036	LG	NOR	PTR	NOR
323237	64037+72237+65037	LG	NOR	PTR	NOR
323238	64038+72238+65038	LG	FSN	PTR	NOR
323239	64039+72239+65039	LG	FSN	PTR	NOR

Right: *Northern Rail operates a fleet of 17 three-car Class 323 units in the Manchester area. Two varieties exist; those with high-density seating for normal use and those with low density seating and extra luggage space for working Manchester City Centre to Manchester Airport services. Most sets are painted in Northern Rail colours and all are allocated to Longsight depot. Set No. 323229 is seen at Flowery Field.* **John Binch**

Class 333

Vehicle Length: (Driving) 77ft 10¾in (23.74m)		Width: 9ft 0¼in (2.75m)
(Inter) 75ft 11in (23.14m)		Horsepower: 1,877hp (1,400kW)
Height: 12ft 1½in (3.79m)		Seats (total/car): 360S, 90S/73S/100S/90S

Number	Formation DMSO(A)+PTSO+TSO+DMSO(B)	Depot	Livery	Owner	Operator	Name
333001	78451+74461+74477+78452	NL	NOM	ANG	NOR	
333002	78453+74462+74478+78454	NL	NOM	ANG	NOR	
333003	78455+74463+74479+78456	NL	NOM	ANG	NOR	
333004	78457+74464+74480+78458	NL	NOM	ANG	NOR	
333005	78459+74465+74481+78460	NL	NOM	ANG	NOR	
333006	78461+74466+74482+78462	NL	NOM	ANG	NOR	
333007	78463+74467+74483+78464	NL	NOM	ANG	NOR	*Alderman J Arthur Godwin -*
						First Lord Mayor of Bradford 1907
333008	78465+74468+74484+78466	NL	NOM	ANG	NOR	
333009	78467+74469+74485+78468	NL	NOM	ANG	NOR	
333010	78469+74470+74486+78470	NL	NOM	ANG	NOR	
333011	78471+74471+74487+78472	NL	NOM	ANG	NOR	
333012	78473+74472+74488+78474	NL	NOM	ANG	NOR	
333013	78475+74473+74489+78476	NL	NOM	ANG	NOR	
333014	78477+74474+74490+78478	NL	NOM	ANG	NOR	
333015	78479+74475+74491+78480	NL	NOM	ANG	NOR	
333016	78481+74476+74492+78482	NL	NOM	ANG	NOR	

Right: *The 16 members of the four-car formation Class 333 are allocated to Leeds Neville Hill and deployed on Wharfedale and Airedale electrified routes. The sets are very similar to the Class 332s operated by Heathrow Express. The Class 333s are owned by Angel Trains and operated by Northern Rail on behalf of West Yorkshire Metro. The sets carry the Northern Rail Metro red and blue livery. Set No. 333001 is viewed at Saltaire.* **John Binch**

South West Trains

Address: ✉ Friars Bridge Court, 41-45 Blackfriars Road, London, SE1 8NZ
📧 customerrelations@swtrains.co.uk
✆ 08700 00 5151
ⓘ www.southwesttrains.co.uk

Managing Director: Andy Pitt
Franchise Dates: 4 December 1996 - February 2017
Principal Routes: London Waterloo-Weymouth, Exeter, Portsmouth and suburban services in Surrey, Berkshire, Hampshire
Depots: Wimbledon Park (WD), Bournemouth (BM), Clapham Junction (CJ)*, Salisbury (SA) * No stock allocated Northam (Siemens Transportation) (NT)
Parent Company: Stagecoach

Class 158

Vehicle Length: 76ft 1¾in (23.21m) *Engine: 1 x Cummins NTA855R of 350hp per vehicle*
Height: 12ft 6in (3.81m) *Horsepower: 700hp (522kW)*
Width: 9ft 3¼in (2.82m) *Seats (total/car): 13F-114S, 13F-44S/70S*

Number	Formation DMSL+DMSL	Depot	Livery	Owner	Operator
158880 (158737)	52737+57737	SA	SWM	PTR	SWT
158881 (158742)	52742+57742	SA	SWM	PTR	SWT
158882 (158743)	52743+57743	SA	SWM	PTR	SWT
158883 (158744)	52744+57744	SA	SWM	PTR	SWT
158884 (158772)	52772+57772	SA	SWM	PTR	SWT
158885 (158775)	52775+57775	SA	SWM	PTR	SWT
158886 (158779)	52779+57779	SA	SWM	PTR	SWT
158887 (158781)	52781+57781	SA	SWM	PTR	SWT
158888 (158802)	52802+57802	SA	SWM	PTR	SWT
158889 (158808)	52808+57808	SA	SWM	PTR	SWT
158890 (158814)	52814+57814	SA	SWM	PTR	SWT

Below: *For South West Trains diesel services radiating from Salisbury and not covered by Class 159s on the Waterloo-Exeter route, a batch of eleven Class 158s are used. These have been fully refurbished to SWT standards and are all standard class. Sets are allocated to Salisbury. No. 158885 is illustrated.* **Stacey Thew**

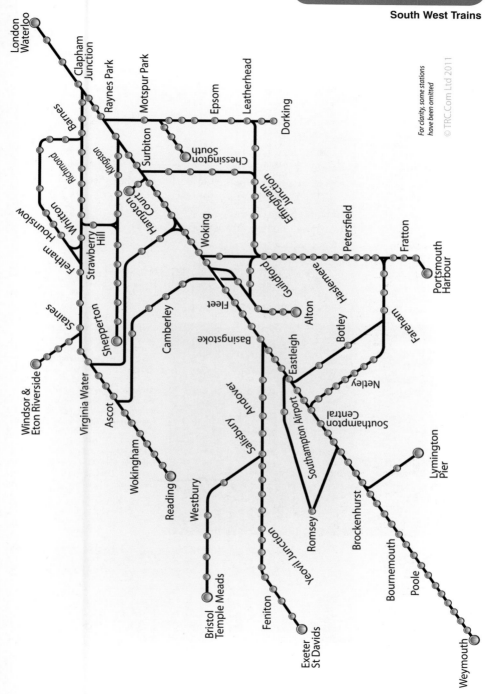

Passenger Train Operating Companies - South West Trains

For clarity, some stations have been omitted

© TRC.Com Ltd 2011

South West Trains

Class 159/0

Vehicle Length: 76ft 1¾in (23.21m)	Engine: 1 x Cummins NTA855R of 400hp per vehicle				
Height: 12ft 6in (3.81m)	Horsepower: 1,200hp (895kW)				
Width: 9ft 3¼in (2.82m)	Seats (total/car): 24F-172S, 24F-28S/72S/72S				

Number	Formation DMCL+MSL+DMSL	Depot	Livery	Owner	Operator	Name
159001	52873+58718+57873	SA	SWM	PTR	SWT	*City of Exeter*
159002	52874+58719+57874	SA	SWM	PTR	SWT	*City of Salisbury*
159003	52875+58720+57875	SA	SWM	PTR	SWT	*Templecombe*
159004	52876+58721+57876	SA	SWM	PTR	SWT	*Basingstoke and Deane*
159005	52877+58722+57877	SA	SWM	PTR	SWT	
159006	52878+58723+57878	SA	SWM	PTR	SWT	
159007	52879+58724+57879	SA	SWM	PTR	SWT	
159008	52880+58725+57880	SA	SWM	PTR	SWT	
159009	52881+58726+57881	SA	SWM	PTR	SWT	
159010	52882+58727+57882	SA	SWM	PTR	SWT	
159011	52883+58728+57883	SA	SWM	PTR	SWT	
159012	52884+58729+57884	SA	SWM	PTR	SWT	
159013	52885+58730+57885	SA	SWM	PTR	SWT	
159014	52886+58731+57886	SA	SWM	PTR	SWT	
159015	52887+58732+57887	SA	SWM	PTR	SWT	
159016	52888+58733+57888	SA	SWM	PTR	SWT	
159017	52889+58734+57889	SA	SWM	PTR	SWT	
159018	52890+58735+57890	SA	SWM	PTR	SWT	
159019	52891+58736+57891	SA	SWM	PTR	SWT	
159020	52892+58737+57892	SA	SWM	PTR	SWT	
159021	52893+58738+57893	SA	SWM	PTR	SWT	
159022	52894+58739+57894	SA	SWM	PTR	SWT	

Left: The South West Trains Class 159 fleet allocated to Salisbury depot is responsible for services on the now hourly Waterloo to Exeter route, operating in either three, six or nine car formations to cope with passenger demands on this ever popular route. The 22 members of Class 159/0 were the original build for the route, which has now been supplemented by Class 159/1 sets. Class 159/0 No. 159020 is seen inside the 2009 opened fuelling shed at Salisbury depot. The Class 159s usually operate the Exeter line services with their DMCL vehicle at the London end. **CJM**

Class 159/1

Vehicle Length: 76ft 1¾in (23.21m)	Engine: 1 x Cummins NTA855R of 350hp per vehicle				
Height: 12ft 6in (3.81m)	Horsepower: 1,050hp (782kW)				
Width: 9ft 3¼in (2.82m)	Seats (total/car): 24F-170S, 24F-28S/70S/72S				

Number	Formation DMCL+MSL+DMSL	Depot	Livery	Owner	Operator
159101 (158800)	52800+58717+57800	SA	SWM	PTR	SWT
159102 (158803)	52803+58703+57803	SA	SWM	PTR	SWT
159103 (158804)	52804+58704+57804	SA	SWM	PTR	SWT
159104 (158805)	52805+58705+57805	SA	SWM	PTR	SWT
159105 (158807)	52807+58707+57807	SA	SWM	PTR	SWT
159106 (158909)	52809+58709+57809	SA	SWM	PTR	SWT
159107 (158811)	52811+58711+57811	SA	SWM	PTR	SWT
159108 (158801)	52801+58701+57801	SA	SWM	PTR	SWT

Right: *With major passenger growth on the Waterloo to Exeter route and the desire to operate an hourly service over the length of the line, extra Class 159 sets were sought. These came from a huge rebuild of eight existing three-car Class 158s, with Wabtec of Doncaster bringing the sets up to Class 159 standards. The Class 159/0 and Class 159/1 sets operate as a common pool. Set No. 159107 is seen departing from Woking with an Exeter St Davids bound service. CJM*

Class 444
Desiro

Vehicle Length: 77ft 3in (23.57m)		Horsepower: 2,682hp (2,000kW)		
Height: 12ft 1½in (3.7m)		Seats (total/car): 35F-299S, 35F-24S/47S/76S/76S/76S		
Width: 9ft 2in (2.7m)				

Number	Formation DMCO+TSO+TSO+TSRMB+DMSO	Depot	Livery	Owner	Operator	Name
444001	63801+67101+67151+67201+63851	NT	SWM	ANG	SWT	*Naomi House*
444002	63802+67102+67152+67202+63852	NT	SWM	ANG	SWT	
444003	63803+67103+67153+67203+63853	NT	SWM	ANG	SWT	
444004	63804+67104+67154+67204+63854	NT	SWM	ANG	SWT	
444005	63805+67105+67155+67205+63855	NT	SWM	ANG	SWT	
444006	63806+67106+67156+67206+63856	NT	SWM	ANG	SWT	
444007	63807+67107+67157+67207+63857	NT	SWM	ANG	SWT	
444008	63808+67108+67158+67208+63858	NT	SWM	ANG	SWT	
444009	63809+67109+67159+67209+63859	NT	SWM	ANG	SWT	
444010	63810+67110+67160+67210+63860	NT	SWM	ANG	SWT	
444011	63811+67111+67161+67211+63861	NT	SWM	ANG	SWT	
444012	63812+67112+67162+67212+63862	NT	SWM	ANG	SWT	*Destination Weymouth*
444013	63813+67113+67163+67213+63863	NT	SWM	ANG	SWT	
444014	63814+67114+67164+67214+63864	NT	SWM	ANG	SWT	
444015	63815+67115+67165+67215+63865	NT	SWM	ANG	SWT	
444016	63816+67116+67166+67216+63866	NT	SWM	ANG	SWT	
444017	63817+67117+67167+67217+63867	NT	SWM	ANG	SWT	
444018	63818+67118+67168+67218+63868	NT	SWM	ANG	SWT	*The FAB 444*
444019	63819+67119+67169+67219+63869	NT	SWM	ANG	SWT	
444020	63820+67120+67170+67220+63870	NT	SWM	ANG	SWT	
444021	63821+67121+67171+67221+63871	NT	SWM	ANG	SWT	
444022	63822+67122+67172+67222+63872	NT	SWM	ANG	SWT	
444023	63823+67123+67173+67223+63873	NT	SWM	ANG	SWT	
444024	63824+67124+67174+67224+63874	NT	SWM	ANG	SWT	
444025	63825+67125+67175+67225+63875	NT	SWM	ANG	SWT	
444026	63826+67126+67176+67226+63876	NT	SWM	ANG	SWT	
444027	63827+67127+67177+67227+63877	NT	SWM	ANG	SWT	
444028	63828+67128+67178+67228+63878	NT	SWM	ANG	SWT	
444029	63829+67129+67179+67229+63879	NT	SWM	ANG	SWT	
444030	63830+67130+67180+67230+63880	NT	SWM	ANG	SWT	
444031	63831+67131+67181+67231+63881	NT	SWM	ANG	SWT	
444032	63832+67132+67182+67232+63882	NT	SWM	ANG	SWT	
444033	63833+67133+67183+67233+63883	NT	SWM	ANG	SWT	
444034	63834+67134+67184+67234+63884	NT	SWM	ANG	SWT	
444035	63835+67135+67185+67235+63885	NT	SWM	ANG	SWT	
444036	63836+67136+67186+67236+63886	NT	SWM	ANG	SWT	
444037	63837+67137+67187+67237+63887	NT	SWM	ANG	SWT	
444038	63838+67138+67188+67238+63888	NT	SWM	ANG	SWT	
444039	63839+67139+67189+67239+63889	NT	SWM	ANG	SWT	
444040	63840+67140+67190+67240+63890	NT	SWM	ANG	SWT	

South West Trains

444041	63841+67141+67191+67241+63891	NT	SWM	ANG	SWT
444042	63842+67142+67192+67242+63892	NT	SWM	ANG	SWT
444043	63843+67143+67193+67243+63893	NT	SWM	ANG	SWT
444044	63844+67144+67194+67244+63894	NT	SWM	ANG	SWT
444045	63845+67145+67195+67245+63895	NT	SWM	ANG	SWT

Left: *Modernisation of the South West lines from Waterloo came with the Stagecoach franchise of South West Trains. A large fleet of Austrian and German-built 'Desiro' units of two designs were ordered and are now the backbone of outer suburban and main line routes. The 45 members of Class 444 operate the main line services on the Waterloo-Portsmouth/ Bournemouth and Weymouth lines. These are high-quality five-car sets. Set No. 444026 passes Vauxhall with a service to Poole in April 2010.* **CJM**

Class 450/0
Desiro

Vehicle Length: 66ft 9in (20.4m)	Horsepower: 2,682hp (2,000kW)
Height: 12ft 1½in (3.7m)	Seats (total/car): 24F-237S, 70S/24F-36S/61S/70S
Width: 9ft 2in (2.7m)	

Number	Formation DMSO+TCO+TSO+DMSO	Depot	Livery	Owner	Operator	Name
450001	63201+64201+68101+63601	NT	SWO	ANG	SWT	
450002	63202+64202+68102+63602	NT	SWO	ANG	SWT	
450003	63203+64203+68103+63603	NT	SWO	ANG	SWT	
450004	63204+64204+68104+63604	NT	SWO	ANG	SWT	
450005	63205+64205+68205+63605	NT	SWO	ANG	SWT	
450006	63206+64206+68206+63606	NT	SWO	ANG	SWT	
450007	63207+64207+68207+63607	NT	SWO	ANG	SWT	
450008	63208+64208+68108+63608	NT	SWO	ANG	SWT	
450009	63209+64209+68109+63609	NT	SWO	ANG	SWT	
450010	63210+64210+68110+63610	NT	SWO	ANG	SWT	
450011	63211+64211+68111+63611	NT	SWO	ANG	SWT	
450012	63212+64212+68112+63612	NT	SWO	ANG	SWT	
450013	63213+64213+68113+63613	NT	SWO	ANG	SWT	
450014	63214+64214+68114+63614	NT	SWO	ANG	SWT	
450015	63215+64215+68115+63615	NT	SWO	ANG	SWT	Desiro
450016	63216+64216+68116+63616	NT	SWO	ANG	SWT	
450017	63217+64217+68117+63617	NT	SWO	ANG	SWT	
450018	63218+64218+68118+63618	NT	SWO	ANG	SWT	
450019	63219+64219+68119+63619	NT	SWO	ANG	SWT	
450020	63220+64220+68120+63620	NT	SWO	ANG	SWT	
450021	63221+64221+68121+63621	NT	SWO	ANG	SWT	
450022	63222+64222+68122+63622	NT	SWO	ANG	SWT	
450023	63223+64223+68123+63623	NT	SWO	ANG	SWT	
450024	63224+64224+68124+63624	NT	SWO	ANG	SWT	
450025	63225+64225+68125+63625	NT	SWO	ANG	SWT	
450026	63226+64226+68126+63626	NT	SWO	ANG	SWT	
450027	63227+64227+68127+63627	NT	SWO	ANG	SWT	
450028	63228+64228+68128+63628	NT	SWO	ANG	SWT	
450029	63229+64229+68129+63629	NT	SWO	ANG	SWT	
450030	63230+64230+68130+63630	NT	SWO	ANG	SWT	
450031	63231+64231+68131+63631	NT	SWO	ANG	SWT	
450032	63232+64232+68132+63632	NT	SWO	ANG	SWT	
450033	63233+64233+68133+63633	NT	SWO	ANG	SWT	
450034	63234+64234+68134+63634	NT	SWO	ANG	SWT	
450035	63235+64235+68135+63635	NT	SWO	ANG	SWT	
450036	63236+64236+68136+63636	NT	SWO	ANG	SWT	

450037	63237+64237+68137+63637	NT	SWO	ANG	SWT	
450038	63238+64238+68138+63638	NT	SWO	ANG	SWT	
450039	63239+64239+68139+63639	NT	SWO	ANG	SWT	
450040	63240+64240+68140+63640	NT	SWO	ANG	SWT	
450041	63241+64241+68141+63641	NT	SWO	ANG	SWT	
450042	63242+64242+68142+63642	NT	SWO	ANG	SWT	*Treloar College*
450071	63271+64271+68171+63671	NT	SWO	ANG	SWT	
450072	63272+64272+68172+63672	NT	SWO	ANG	SWT	
450073	63273+64273+68173+63673	NT	SWO	ANG	SWT	
450074	63274+64274+68174+63674	NT	SWO	ANG	SWT	
450075	63275+64275+68175+63675	NT	SWO	ANG	SWT	
450076	63276+64276+68176+63676	NT	SWO	ANG	SWT	
450077	63277+64277+68177+63677	NT	SWO	ANG	SWT	
450078	63278+64278+68178+63678	NT	SWO	ANG	SWT	
450079	63279+64279+68179+63679	NT	SWO	ANG	SWT	
450080	63280+64280+68180+63680	NT	SWO	ANG	SWT	
450081	63281+64281+68181+63681	NT	SWO	ANG	SWT	
450082	63282+64282+68182+63682	NT	SWO	ANG	SWT	
450083	63283+64283+68183+63683	NT	SWO	ANG	SWT	
450084	63284+64284+68184+63684	NT	SWO	ANG	SWT	
450085	63285+64285+68185+63685	NT	SWO	ANG	SWT	
450086	63286+64286+68186+63686	NT	SWO	ANG	SWT	
450087	63287+64287+68187+63687	NT	SWO	ANG	SWT	
450088	63288+64288+68188+63688	NT	SWO	ANG	SWT	
450089	63289+64289+68189+63689	NT	SWO	ANG	SWT	
450090	63290+64290+68190+63690	NT	SWO	ANG	SWT	
450091	63291+64291+68191+63691	NT	SWO	ANG	SWT	
450092	63292+64292+68192+63692	NT	SWO	ANG	SWT	
450093	63293+64293+68193+63693	NT	SWO	ANG	SWT	
450094	63294+64294+68194+63694	NT	SWO	ANG	SWT	
450095	63295+64295+68195+63695	NT	SWO	ANG	SWT	
450096	63296+64296+68196+63696	NT	SWO	ANG	SWT	
450097	63297+64297+68197+63697	NT	SWO	ANG	SWT	
450098	63298+64298+68198+63698	NT	SWO	ANG	SWT	
450099	63299+64299+68199+63699	NT	SWO	ANG	SWT	
450100	63300+64300+68200+63700	NT	SWO	ANG	SWT	
450101	63701+66851+66801+63751	NT	SWO	ANG	SWT	
450102	63702+66852+66802+63752	NT	SWO	ANG	SWT	
450103	63703+66853+66803+63753	NT	SWO	ANG	SWT	
450104	63704+66854+66804+63754	NT	SWO	ANG	SWT	
450105	63705+66855+66805+63755	NT	SWO	ANG	SWT	
450106	63706+66856+66806+63756	NT	SWO	ANG	SWT	
450107	63707+66857+66807+63757	NT	SWO	ANG	SWT	
450108	63708+66858+66808+63758	NT	SWO	ANG	SWT	
450109	63709+66859+66809+63759	NT	SWO	ANG	SWT	
450110	63710+66860+66810+63750	NT	SWO	ANG	SWT	
450111	63901+66921+66901+63921	NT	SWO	ANG	SWT	
450112	63902+66922+66902+63922	NT	SWO	ANG	SWT	
450113	63903+66923+66903+63923	NT	SWO	ANG	SWT	
450114	63904+66924+66904+63924	NT	SWO	ANG	SWT	*Fairbridge - investing in the Future*
450115	63905+66925+66905+63925	NT	SWO	ANG	SWT	
450116	63906+66926+66906+63926	NT	SWO	ANG	SWT	
450117	63907+66927+66907+63927	NT	SWO	ANG	SWT	
450118	63908+66928+66908+63928	NT	SWO	ANG	SWT	
450119	63909+66929+66909+63929	NT	SWO	ANG	SWT	
450120	63910+66930+66910+63930	NT	SWO	ANG	SWT	
450121	63911+66931+66911+63931	NT	SWO	ANG	SWT	
450122	63912+66932+66912+63932	NT	SWO	ANG	SWT	
450123	63913+66933+66913+63933	NT	SWO	ANG	SWT	
450124	63914+66934+66914+63934	NT	SWO	ANG	SWT	
450125	63915+66935+66915+63935	NT	SWO	ANG	SWT	
450126	63916+66936+66916+63936	NT	SWO	ANG	SWT	
450127	63917+66937+66917+63937	NT	SWO	ANG	SWT	

Passenger Train Operating Companies - South West Trains

Above: *The outer-suburban SWT routes are operated by four-car Class 450/0 sets. Each set has a small first class area in an intermediate TCO vehicle. An eight-car formation of Class 450/0 stock, led by set No. 450106, approaches Woking with a Southampton to London Waterloo service.* **CJM**

DESIRO

Left: *The nameplate* Desiro *as applied to set No. 450015.* **CJM**

Class 450/5
Desiro

Vehicle Length: 66ft 9in (20.4m)	Horsepower: 2,682hp (2,000kW)
Height: 12ft 1½in (3.7m)	Seats (total/car): 240S, 64S/56S/56S/64S
Width: 9ft 2in (2.7m)	

Number	Formation DMSO+TSO+TSO+DMSO	Depot	Livery	Owner	Operator
450543 (450043)	63243+64243+68143+63643	NT	SWO	ANG	SWT
450544 (450044)	63244+64244+68144+63644	NT	SWO	ANG	SWT
450545 (450045)	63245+64245+68145+63645	NT	SWO	ANG	SWT
450546 (450046)	63246+64246+68146+63646	NT	SWO	ANG	SWT
450547 (450047)	63247+64247+68147+63647	NT	SWO	ANG	SWT
450548 (450048)	63248+64248+68148+63648	NT	SWO	ANG	SWT
450549 (450049)	63249+64249+68149+63649	NT	SWO	ANG	SWT
450550 (450050)	63250+64250+68150+63650	NT	SWO	ANG	SWT
450551 (450051)	63251+64251+68151+63651	NT	SWO	ANG	SWT
450552 (450052)	63252+64252+68152+63652	NT	SWO	ANG	SWT
450553 (450053)	63253+64253+68153+63653	NT	SWO	ANG	SWT
450554 (450054)	63254+64254+68154+63654	NT	SWO	ANG	SWT
450555 (450055)	63255+64255+68155+63655	NT	SWO	ANG	SWT
450556 (450056)	63256+64256+68156+63656	NT	SWO	ANG	SWT
450557 (450057)	63257+64257+68157+63657	NT	SWO	ANG	SWT
450558 (450058)	63258+64258+68158+63658	NT	SWO	ANG	SWT
450559 (450059)	63259+64259+68159+63659	NT	SWO	ANG	SWT
450560 (450060)	63260+64260+68160+63660	NT	SWO	ANG	SWT
450561 (450061)	63261+64261+68161+63661	NT	SWO	ANG	SWT
450562 (450062)	63262+64262+68162+63662	NT	SWO	ANG	SWT
450563 (450063)	63263+64263+68163+63663	NT	SWO	ANG	SWT
450564 (450064)	63264+64264+68164+63664	NT	SWO	ANG	SWT
450565 (450065)	63265+64265+68165+63665	NT	SWO	ANG	SWT
450566 (450066)	63266+64266+68166+63666	NT	SWO	ANG	SWT
450567 (450067)	63267+64267+68167+63667	NT	SWO	ANG	SWT
450568 (450068)	63268+64268+68168+63668	NT	SWO	ANG	SWT
450569 (450069)	63269+64269+68169+63669	NT	SWO	ANG	SWT
450570 (450070)	63270+64270+68170+63670	NT	SWO	ANG	SWT

Right: *Soon after introduction it was found that capacity issues on 'Windsor' line services radiating from London Waterloo were causing a problem. To address this and provide extra standing room, 28 Class 450/0 sets had their trailer composite vehicle modified to a trailer standard and revised seating provided throughout the trains, this increasing space in the door vestibule areas. Sets were renumbered in the 450/5 series and have 'HC' applied above the unit number. Set No. 450548 is seen at Weybridge.* **CJM**

Class 455/7

Vehicle Length: (Driving) 65ft 0½in (19.83m)
(Inter) 65ft 4½in (19.92m)
Height: 12ft 1½in (3.79m) [TSO- 11ft 6½in (3.58m)
Width: 9ft 3¼in (2.82m)
Horsepower: 1,000hp (746kW)
Seats (total/car): 244S, 54S/68S/68S/54S

Number	Formation DMSO(A)+MSO+TSO+DTSO(B)	Depot	Livery	Owner	Operator
(45)5701	77727+62783+71545+77728	WD	SWS	PTR	SWT
(45)5702	77729+62784+71547+77730	WD	SWS	PTR	SWT
(45)5703	77731+62785+71540+77732	WD	SWS	PTR	SWT
(45)5704	77733+62786+71548+77734	WD	SWS	PTR	SWT
(45)5705	77735+62787+71565+77736	WD	SWS	PTR	SWT
(45)5706	77737+62788+71534+77738	WD	SWS	PTR	SWT
(45)5707	77739+62789+71536+77740	WD	SWS	PTR	SWT
(45)5708	77741+62790+71560+77742	WD	SWS	PTR	SWT
(45)5709	77743+62791+71532+77744	WD	SWS	PTR	SWT
(45)5710	77745+62792+71566+77746	WD	SWS	PTR	SWT
(45)5711	77747+62793+71542+77748	WD	SWS	PTR	SWT
(45)5712	77749+62794+71546+77750	WD	SWS	PTR	SWT
(45)5713	77751+62795+71567+77752	WD	SWS	PTR	SWT
(45)5714	77753+62796+71539+77754	WD	SWS	PTR	SWT
(45)5715	77755+62796+71535+77756	WD	SWS	PTR	SWT
(45)5716	77757+62798+71564+77758	WD	SWS	PTR	SWT
(45)5717	77759+62799+71528+77760	WD	SWS	PTR	SWT
(45)5718	77761+62800+71557+77762	WD	SWS	PTR	SWT
(45)5719	77763+62801+71558+77764	WD	SWS	PTR	SWT
(45)5720	77765+62802+71568+77766	WD	SWS	PTR	SWT
(45)5721	77767+62803+71553+77768	WD	SWS	PTR	SWT
(45)5722	77769+62804+71533+77770	WD	SWS	PTR	SWT
(45)5723	77771+62805+71526+77772	WD	SWS	PTR	SWT
(45)5724	77773+62806+71561+77774	WD	SWS	PTR	SWT
(45)5725	77775+62807+71541+77776	WD	SWS	PTR	SWT
(45)5726	77777+62608+71556+77778	WD	SWS	PTR	SWT
(45)5727	77779+62809+71562+77780	WD	SWS	PTR	SWT
(45)5728	77781+62810+71527+77782	WD	SWS	PTR	SWT
(45)5729	77783+62811+71550+77784	WD	SWS	PTR	SWT
(45)5730	77785+62812+71551+77786	WD	SWS	PTR	SWT
(45)5731	77787+62813+71555+77788	WD	SWS	PTR	SWT
(45)5732	77789+62814+71552+77790	WD	SWS	PTR	SWT
(45)5733	77791+62815+71549+77792	WD	SWS	PTR	SWT
(45)5734	77793+62816+71531+77794	WD	SWS	PTR	SWT
(45)5735	77795+62817+71563+77796	WD	SWS	PTR	SWT
(45)5736	77797+62818+71554+77798	WD	SWS	PTR	SWT
(45)5737	77799+62819+71544+77800	WD	SWS	PTR	SWT
(45)5738	77801+62820+71529+77802	WD	SWS	PTR	SWT
(45)5739	77803+62821+71537+77804	WD	SWS	PTR	SWT
(45)5740	77805+62822+71530+77806	WD	SWS	PTR	SWT
(45)5741	77807+62823+71559+77808	WD	SWS	PTR	SWT
(45)5742	77809+62824+71543+77810	WD	SWS	PTR	SWT
(45)5750*	77811+62825+71538+77812	WD	SWS	PTR	SWT	*Originally numbered (45)5743*

Above: *Three different batches of Class 455 operate on the South West Trains suburban routes from Waterloo. Class 455/7 No. (45)5709 approaches Clapham Junction.* **CJM**

Class 455/8

	Vehicle Length: (Driving) 65ft 0½in (19.83m)	Width: 9ft 3¼in (2.82m)
	(Inter) 65ft 4½in (19.92m)	Horsepower: 1,000hp (746kW)
	Height: 12ft 1½in (3.79m)	Seats (total/car): 223S, 50S/84S/84S/50S

Number	Formation DMSO(A)+MSO+TSO+DTSO(B)	Depot	Livery	Owner	Operator
(45)5847	77671+62755+71683+77672	WD	SWS	PTR	SWT
(45)5848	77673+62756+71684+77674	WD	SWS	PTR	SWT
(45)5849	77675+62757+71685+77676	WD	SWS	PTR	SWT
(45)5850	77677+62758+71686+77678	WD	SWS	PTR	SWT
(45)5851	77679+62759+71687+77680	WD	SWS	PTR	SWT
(45)5852	77681+62760+71688+77682	WD	SWS	PTR	SWT
(45)5853	77683+62761+71689+77684	WD	SWS	PTR	SWT
(45)5854	77685+62762+71690+77686	WD	SWS	PTR	SWT
(45)5855	77687+62763+71691+77688	WD	SWS	PTR	SWT
(45)5856	77689+62764+71692+77690	WD	SWS	PTR	SWT
(45)5857	77691+62765+71693+77692	WD	SWS	PTR	SWT
(45)5858	77693+62766+71694+77694	WD	SWS	PTR	SWT
(45)5859	77695+62767+71695+77696	WD	SWS	PTR	SWT
(45)5860	77697+62768+71696+77698	WD	SWS	PTR	SWT
(45)5861	77699+62769+71697+77700	WD	SWS	PTR	SWT
(45)5862	77701+62770+71698+77702	WD	SWS	PTR	SWT
(45)5863	77703+62771+71699+77704	WD	SWS	PTR	SWT
(45)5864	77705+62772+71700+77706	WD	SWS	PTR	SWT
(45)5865	77707+62773+71701+77708	WD	SWS	PTR	SWT
(45)5866	77709+62774+71702+77710	WD	SWS	PTR	SWT
(45)5867	77711+62775+71703+77712	WD	SWS	PTR	SWT
(45)5868	77713+62776+71704+77714	WD	SWS	PTR	SWT
(45)5869	77715+62777+71705+77716	WD	SWS	PTR	SWT
(45)5870	77717+62778+71706+77718	WD	SWS	PTR	SWT
(45)5871	77719+62779+71707+77720	WD	SWS	PTR	SWT
(45)5872	77721+62780+71708+77722	WD	SWS	PTR	SWT
(45)5873	77723+62781+71709+77724	WD	SWS	PTR	SWT
(45)5874	77725+62782+71710+77726	WD	SWS	PTR	SWT

Left: *The SWT Class 455 fleet are painted in Stagecoach suburban red livery, off-set with blue passenger doors. All Class 455 sets are allocated to Wimbledon depot and form the majority of London area branch line services. Set No. (45)5847 heads towards Waterloo at Clapham Junction.* **CJM**

Class 455/9

	Vehicle Length: (Driving) 65ft 0½in (19.83m)	Width: 9ft 3¼in (2.82m)
	(Inter) 65ft 4½in (19.92m)	Horsepower: 1,000hp (746kW)
	Height: 12ft 1½in (3.79m)	Seats (total/car): 236S, 50S/68S/68S/50S

Number	Formation DMSO(A)+MSO+TSO+DTSO(B)	Depot	Livery	Owner	Operator
(45)5901	77813+62826+71714+77814	WD	SWS	PTR	SWT
(45)5902	77815+62827+71715+77816	WD	SWS	PTR	SWT
(45)5903	77817+62828+71716+77818	WD	SWS	PTR	SWT
(45)5904	77819+62829+71717+77820	WD	SWS	PTR	SWT
(45)5905	77821+62830+71725+77822	WD	SWS	PTR	SWT
(45)5906	77823+62831+71719+77824	WD	SWS	PTR	SWT
(45)5907	77825+62832+71720+77826	WD	SWS	PTR	SWT
(45)5908	77827+62833+71721+77828	WD	SWS	PTR	SWT
(45)5909	77829+62834+71722+77830	WD	SWS	PTR	SWT
(45)5910	77831+62835+71723+77832	WD	SWS	PTR	SWT
(45)5911	77833+62836+71724+77834	WD	SWS	PTR	SWT
(45)5912	77835+62837+67400+77836	WD	SWS	PTR	SWT
(45)5913	77837+62838+71726+77838	WD	SWS	PTR	SWT
(45)5914	77839+62839+71727+77840	WD	SWS	PTR	SWT
(45)5915	77841+62840+71728+77842	WD	SWS	PTR	SWT
(45)5916	77843+62841+71729+77844	WD	SWS	PTR	SWT
(45)5917	77845+62842+71730+77846	WD	SWS	PTR	SWT
(45)5918	77847+62843+71732+77848	WD	SWS	PTR	SWT
(45)5919	77849+62844+71718+77850	WD	SWS	PTR	SWT
(45)5920	77851+62845+71733+77852	WD	SWS	PTR	SWT

Right: *Twenty members of Class 455/9 exist; these were the final derivative of the design to enter service. On 28 September 2009, the 13.24 South West Trains service from Waterloo to Dorking, via Epsom, arrives at Worcester Park formed of set numbers (45)5905 leading and (45)5910 on the rear.* **Brian Morrison**

Class 458
Juniper

	Vehicle Length: (Driving) 69ft 6in (21.16m)	Width: 9ft 2in (2.79m)
	(Inter) 65ft 4in (19.91m)	Horsepower: 2,172hp (1,620kW)
	Height: 12ft 3in (3.73m)	Seats (total/car): 24F-250S, 12F-63S/49S/75S/12F-63S

Number	Formation DMCO(A)+TSO+MSO+DTCO(B)	Depot	Livery	Owner	Operator
(45)8001	67601+74001+74101+67701	WD	SWM	PTR	SWT
(45)8002	67602+74002+74102+67702	WD	SWM	PTR	SWT
(45)8003	67603+74003+74103+67703	WD	SWM	PTR	SWT
(45)8004	67604+74004+74104+67704	WD	SWM	PTR	SWT
(45)8005	67605+74005+74105+67705	WD	SWM	PTR	SWT
(45)8006	67606+74006+74106+67706	WD	SWM	PTR	SWT
(45)8007	67607+74007+74107+67707	WD	SWM	PTR	SWT
(45)8008	67608+74008+74108+67708	WD	SWM	PTR	SWT
(45)8009	67609+74009+74109+67709	WD	SWM	PTR	SWT
(45)8010	67610+74010+74110+67710	WD	SWM	PTR	SWT
(45)8011	67611+74011+74111+67711	WD	SWM	PTR	SWT
(45)8012	67612+74012+74112+67712	WD	SWM	PTR	SWT
(45)8013	67613+74013+74113+67713	WD	SWM	PTR	SWT
(45)8014	67614+74014+74114+67714	WD	SWM	PTR	SWT
(45)8015	67615+74015+74115+67715	WD	SWM	PTR	SWT
(45)8016	67616+74016+74116+67716	WD	SWM	PTR	SWT

South West Trains

(45)8017	67617+74017+74117+67717	WD	SWM	PTR	SWT
(45)8018	67618+74018+74118+67718	WD	SWM	PTR	SWT
(45)8019	67619+74019+74119+67719	WD	SWM	PTR	SWT
(45)8020	67620+74020+74120+67720	WD	SWM	PTR	SWT
(45)8021	67621+74021+74121+67721	WD	SWM	PTR	SWT
(45)8022	67622+74022+74122+67722	WD	SWM	PTR	SWT
(45)8023	67623+74023+74123+67723	WD	SWM	PTR	SWT
(45)8024	67624+74024+74124+67724	WD	SWM	PTR	SWT
(45)8025	67625+74025+74125+67725	WD	SWM	PTR	SWT
(45)8026	67626+74026+74126+67726	WD	SWM	PTR	SWT
(45)8027	67627+74027+74127+67727	WD	SWM	PTR	SWT
(45)8028	67628+74028+74128+67728	WD	SWM	PTR	SWT
(45)8029	67629+74029+74129+67729	WD	SWM	PTR	SWT
(45)8030	67630+74030+74130+67730	WD	SWM	PTR	SWT

Above: *Soon after the South West passenger route radiating from London was franchised to Stagecoach new train orders were placed. At the time Alstom were offering their 'Juniper' product and South West Trains in partnership with Porterbrook ordered 30 sets for deployment on outer-suburban services. All are allocated to Wimbledon and are painted in the operator's white livery with orange/red swirl ends. The fleet are used exclusively on the Waterloo to Reading route. Set No. (45)8012 is illustrated at Clapham Junction.* **Brian Morrison**

Left: *In having a front end gangway, the driving cab on this design was only able to occupy one third of the body width, giving a very cramped operating space for the driver. The cab is set out for left hand operation, with a single power (pull), brake (push) handle. Instrumentation is on the inclined panel in front of the driver and side panels left and right incorporate door controls and radio equipment. The scope of front vision is very limited.* **CJM**

South Eastern

Address: ✉ Friars Bridge Court, 41-45 Blackfriars Road, London, SE1 8NZ
✎ info@southeasternrailway.co.uk
✆ 08700 000 2222
ⓘ www.southeasternrailway.co.uk

Managing Director: Charles Horton
Franchise Dates: 1 April 2006 - 31 March 2012
Principal Routes: London to Kent and parts of East Sussex, domestic services on HS1
Depots: Slade Green (SG), Ramsgate (RM), Ashford (AD*)
Parent Company: Govia
* Operated by Hitachi

Class 375/3
Electrostar

Vehicle Length: (Driving) 66ft 9in (20.3m) | Width: 9ft 2in (2.79m)
(Inter) 65ft 6in (19.96m) | Horsepower: 1,341hp (1,000kW)
Height: 12ft 4in (3.75m) | Seats (total/car): 24F-152S, 12F-48S/56S/12F-48S

Number	Formation DMCO(A)+TSO+DMCO(B)	Depot	Livery	Owner	Operator	Name
375301	67921+74351+67931	RM	SET	HSB	SET	
375302	67922+74352+67932	RM	SET	HSB	SET	
375303	67923+74353+67933	RM	SET	HSB	SET	
375304	67924+74354+67934	RM	SET	HSB	SET	Medway Valley Line 1856-2006
375305	67925+74355+67935	RM	SET	HSB	SET	
375306	67926+74356+67936	RM	SET	HSB	SET	
375307	67927+74357+67937	RM	SET	HSB	SET	
375308	67928+74358+67938	RM	SET	HSB	SET	
375309	67929+74359+67939	RM	SET	HSB	SET	
375310	67930+74360+67940	RM	SET	HSB	SET	

Class 375/6
Electrostar

Vehicle Length: (Driving) 66ft 9in (20.3m) | Width: 9ft 2in (2.79m)
(Inter) 65ft 6in (19.96m) | Horsepower: 2,012hp (1,500kW)
Height: 12ft 4in (3.75m) | Seats (total/car): 24F-218S, 12F-48S/66S/56S/12F-48S

Number	Formation DMCO(A)+MSO+TSO+DMCO(B)	Depot	Livery	Owner	Operator	Name
375601	67801+74251+74201+67851	RM	SET	HSB	SET	
375602	67802+74252+74202+67852	RM	SET	HSB	SET	
375603	67803+74253+74203+67853	RM	SET	HSB	SET	
375604	67804+74254+74204+67854	RM	SET	HSB	SET	
375605	67805+74255+74205+67855	RM	SET	HSB	SET	
375606	67806+74256+74206+67856	RM	SET	HSB	SET	
375607	67807+74257+74207+67857	RM	SET	HSB	SET	
375608	67808+74258+74208+67858	RM	SET	HSB	SET	Bromley Travelwise
375609	67809+74259+74209+67859	RM	SET	HSB	SET	
375610	67810+74260+74210+67860	RM	SET	HSB	SET	Royal Tunbridge Wells
375611	67811+74261+74211+67861	RM	SET	HSB	SET	Dr William Harvey
375612	67812+74262+74212+67862	RM	SET	HSB	SET	
375613	67813+74263+74213+67863	RM	SET	HSB	SET	
375614	67814+74264+74214+67864	RM	SET	HSB	SET	
375615	67815+74265+74215+67865	RM	SET	HSB	SET	
375616	67816+74266+74216+67866	RM	SET	HSB	SET	
375617	67817+74267+74217+67867	RM	SET	HSB	SET	
375618	67818+74268+74218+67868	RM	SET	HSB	SET	
375619	67819+74269+74219+67869	RM	SET	HSB	SET	Driver John Neve

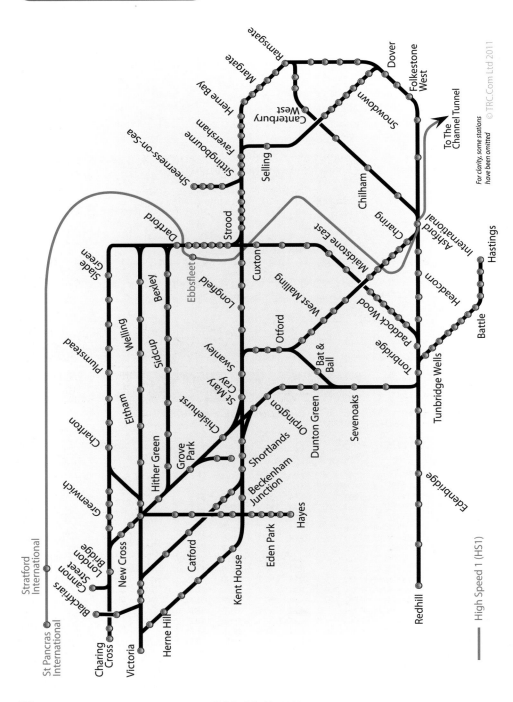

Passenger Train Operating Companies - South Eastern

For clarity, some stations have been omitted
© TRC.Com Ltd 2011

St Pancras International
Stratford International

High Speed 1 (HS1)

375620	67820+74270+74220+67870	RM	SET	HSB	SET	
375621	67821+74271+74221+67871	RM	SET	HSB	SET	
375622	67822+74272+74222+67872	RM	SET	HSB	SET	
375623	67823+74273+74223+67873	RM	SET	HSB	SET	
375624	67824+74274+74224+67874	RM	SET	HSB	SET	*Hospice in the Weald*
375625	67825+74275+74225+67875	RM	SET	HSB	SET	
375626	67826+74276+74226+67876	RM	SET	HSB	SET	
375627	67827+74277+74227+67877	RM	SET	HSB	SET	
375628	67828+74278+74228+67878	RM	SET	HSB	SET	
375629	67829+74279+74229+67879	RM	SET	HSB	SET	
375630	67830+74280+74230+67880	RM	SET	HSB	SET	

Class 375/7
Electrostar

Vehicle Length: (Driving) 66ft 9in (20.3m) (Inter) 65ft 6in (19.96m)   Width: 9ft 2in (2.79m)   Horsepower: 2,012hp (1,500kW)
Height: 12ft 4in (3.75m)   Seats (total/car): 24F-218S, 12F-48S/66S/56S/12F-48S

Number	Formation	Depot	Livery	Owner	Operator	Name
	DMCO(A)+MSO+TSO+DMCO(B)					
375701	67831+74281+74231+67881	RM	SET	HSB	SET	*Kent Air Ambulance Explorer*
375702	67832+74282+74232+67882	RM	SET	HSB	SET	
375703	67833+74283+74233+67883	RM	SET	HSB	SET	
375704	67834+74284+74234+67884	RM	SET	HSB	SET	
375705	67835+74285+74235+67885	RM	SET	HSB	SET	
375706	67836+74286+74236+67886	RM	SET	HSB	SET	
375707	67837+74287+74237+67887	RM	SET	HSB	SET	
375708	67838+74288+74238+67888	RM	SET	HSB	SET	
375709	67839+74289+74239+67889	RM	SET	HSB	SET	
375710	67840+74290+74240+67890	RM	SET	HSB	SET	
375711	67841+74291+74241+67891	RM	SET	HSB	SET	
375712	67842+74292+74242+67892	RM	SET	HSB	SET	
375713	67843+74293+74243+67893	RM	SET	HSB	SET	
375714	67844+74294+74244+67894	RM	SET	HSB	SET	
375715	67845+74295+74245+67895	RM	SET	HSB	SET	

Class 375/8
Electrostar

Vehicle Length: (Driving) 66ft 9in (20.3m) (Inter) 65ft 6in (19.96m)   Width: 9ft 2in (2.79m)   Horsepower: 2,012hp (1,500kW)
Height: 12ft 4in (3.75m)   Seats (total/car): 24F-218S, 12F-48S/66S/56S/12F-48S

Number	Formation	Depot	Livery	Owner	Operator	Name
	DMCO(A)+MSO+TSO+DMCO(B)					
375801	73301+79001+78201+73701	RM	SET	HSB	SET	
375802	73302+79002+78202+73702	RM	SET	HSB	SET	
375803	73303+79003+78203+73703	RM	SET	HSB	SET	
375804	73304+79004+78204+73704	RM	SET	HSB	SET	
375805	73305+79005+78205+73705	RM	SET	HSB	SET	
375806	73306+79006+78206+73706	RM	SET	HSB	SET	
375807	73307+79007+78207+73707	RM	SET	HSB	SET	
375808	73308+79008+78208+73708	RM	SET	HSB	SET	
375809	73309+79009+78209+73709	RM	SET	HSB	SET	
375810	73310+79010+78210+73710	RM	SET	HSB	SET	
375811	73311+79011+78211+73711	RM	SET	HSB	SET	
375812	73312+79012+78212+73712	RM	SET	HSB	SET	
375813	73313+79013+78213+73713	RM	SET	HSB	SET	
375814	73314+79014+78214+73714	RM	SET	HSB	SET	
375815	73315+79015+78215+73715	RM	SET	HSB	SET	
375816	73316+79016+78216+73716	RM	SET	HSB	SET	
375817	73317+79017+78217+73717	RM	SET	HSB	SET	
375818	73318+79018+78218+73718	RM	SET	HSB	SET	
375819	73319+79019+78219+73719	RM	SET	HSB	SET	
375820	73320+79020+78220+73720	RM	SET	HSB	SET	
375821	73321+79021+78221+73721	RM	SET	HSB	SET	
375822	73322+79022+78222+73722	RM	SET	HSB	SET	
375823	73323+79023+78223+73723	RM	SET	HSB	SET	
375824	73324+79024+78224+73724	RM	SET	HSB	SET	
375825	73325+79025+78225+73725	RM	SET	HSB	SET	

South Eastern

375826	73326+79026+78226+73726	RM	SET	HSB	SET		
375827	73327+79027+78227+73727	RM	SET	HSB	SET		
375828	73328+79028+78228+73728	RM	SET	HSB	SET		
375829	73329+79029+78229+73729	RM	SET	HSB	SET		
375830	73330+79030+78230+73730	RM	SET	HSB	SET	*City of London*

Class 375/9
Electrostar

Vehicle Length: (Driving) 66ft 9in (20.3m)
(Inter) 65ft 6in (19.96m)
Height: 12ft 4in (3.75m)
Width: 9ft 2in (2.79m)
Horsepower: 2,012hp (1,500kW)
Seats (total/car): 24F-250S, 12F-59S/73S/59S/12F-59S

Number	Formation *DMCO(A)+MSO+TSO+DMCO(B)*	Depot	Livery	Owner	Operator
375901	73331+79031+79061+73731	RM	SET	HSB	SET
375902	73332+79032+79062+73732	RM	SET	HSB	SET
375903	73333+79033+79063+73733	RM	SET	HSB	SET
375904	73334+79034+79064+73734	RM	SET	HSB	SET
375905	73335+79035+79065+73735	RM	SET	HSB	SET
375906	73336+79036+79066+73736	RM	SET	HSB	SET
375907	73337+79037+79067+73737	RM	SET	HSB	SET
375908	73338+79038+79068+73738	RM	SET	HSB	SET
375909	73339+79039+79069+73739	RM	SET	HSB	SET
375910	73340+79040+79070+73740	RM	SET	HSB	SET
375911	73341+79041+79071+73741	RM	SET	HSB	SET
375912	73342+79042+79072+73742	RM	SET	HSB	SET
375913	73343+79043+79073+73743	RM	SET	HSB	SET
375914	73344+79044+79074+73744	RM	SET	HSB	SET
375915	73345+79045+79075+73745	RM	SET	HSB	SET
375916	73346+79046+79076+73746	RM	SET	HSB	SET
375917	73347+79047+79077+73747	RM	SET	HSB	SET
375918	73348+79048+79078+73748	RM	SET	HSB	SET
375919	73349+79049+79079+73749	RM	SET	HSB	SET
375920	73350+79050+79080+73750	RM	SET	HSB	SET
375921	73351+79051+79081+73751	RM	SET	HSB	SET
375922	73352+79052+79082+73752	RM	SET	HSB	SET
375923	73353+79053+79083+73753	RM	SET	HSB	SET
375924	73354+79054+79084+73754	RM	SET	HSB	SET
375925	73355+79055+79085+73755	RM	SET	HSB	SET
375926	73356+79056+79086+73756	RM	SET	HSB	SET
375927	73357+79057+79087+73757	RM	SET	HSB	SET

Below: *Five different sub-classes of the Bombardier 'Electrostar' are in operation with South Eastern; different power collection and seating styles call for the different classifications. All sets are allocated to Ramsgate and operate the entire South Eastern outer suburban and main line network. All sets are owned by Eversholt Leasing and are painted in various versions of South Eastern white livery. Class 375/8 No. 375819 is illustrated at London Bridge. The Class 375/8 sub-class are identified by SET as dc only express sets fitted with modified shoe gear.* **Chris Perkins**

Class 376
Electrostar

Vehicle Length: (Driving) 66ft 9in (20.3m)		Width: 9ft 2in (2.79m)		
(Inter) 65ft 6in (19.96m)		Horsepower: 2,682hp (2,000kW)		
Height: 12ft 4in (3.75m)		Seats (total/car): 216S, 36S/48S/48S/48S/36S + 116 perch		

Number	Formation DMSO(A)+MSO+TSO+MSO+DMSO(B)	Depot	Livery	Owner	Operator
376001	61101+63301+64301+63501+61601	SG	SET	HSB	SET
376002	61102+63302+64302+63502+61602	SG	SET	HSB	SET
376003	61103+63303+64303+63503+61603	SG	SET	HSB	SET
376004	61104+63304+64304+63504+61604	SG	SET	HSB	SET
376005	61105+63305+64305+63505+61605	SG	SET	HSB	SET
376006	61106+63306+64306+63506+61606	SG	SET	HSB	SET
376007	61107+63307+64307+63507+61607	SG	SET	HSB	SET
376008	61108+63308+64308+63508+61608	SG	SET	HSB	SET
376009	61109+63309+64309+63509+61609	SG	SET	HSB	SET
376010	61110+63310+64310+63510+61610	SG	SET	HSB	SET
376011	61111+63311+64311+63511+61611	SG	SET	HSB	SET
376012	61112+63312+64312+63512+61612	SG	SET	HSB	SET
376013	61113+63313+64313+63513+61613	SG	SET	HSB	SET
376014	61114+63314+64314+63514+61614	SG	SET	HSB	SET
376015	61115+63315+64315+63515+61615	SG	SET	HSB	SET
376016	61116+63316+64316+63516+61616	SG	SET	HSB	SET
376017	61117+63317+64317+63517+61617	SG	SET	HSB	SET
376018	61118+63318+64318+63518+61618	SG	SET	HSB	SET
376019	61119+63319+64319+63519+61619	SG	SET	HSB	SET
376020	61120+63320+64320+63520+61620	SG	SET	HSB	SET
376021	61121+63321+64321+63521+61621	SG	SET	HSB	SET
376022	61122+63322+64322+63522+61622	SG	SET	HSB	SET
376023	61123+63323+64323+63523+61623	SG	SET	HSB	SET
376024	61124+63324+64324+63524+61624	SG	SET	HSB	SET
376025	61125+63325+64325+63525+61625	SG	SET	HSB	SET
376026	61126+63326+64326+63526+61626	SG	SET	HSB	SET
376027	61127+63327+64327+63527+61627	SG	SET	HSB	SET
376028	61128+63328+64328+63528+61628	SG	SET	HSB	SET
376029	61129+63329+64329+63529+61629	SG	SET	HSB	SET
376030	61130+63330+64330+63530+61630	SG	SET	HSB	SET
376031	61131+63331+64331+63531+61631	SG	SET	HSB	SET
376032	61132+63332+64332+63532+61632	SG	SET	HSB	SET
376033	61133+63333+64333+63533+61633	SG	SET	HSB	SET
376034	61134+63334+64334+63534+61634	SG	SET	HSB	SET
376035	61135+63335+64335+63535+61635	SG	SET	HSB	SET
376036	61136+63336+64336+63536+61636	SG	SET	HSB	SET

Below: *For high-density suburban operation South Eastern operate a fleet of 36 five-car high-capacity Bombardier Class 376 sets. These are very austere, with few seats and large open spaces for standing passengers. The sets are gangwayed within units only. All are allocated to Slade Green depot. Set No. 376001 is illustrated departing south from London Bridge.* **Chris Perkins**

South Eastern

Class 395
Javelin

Vehicle Length: (Driving) 67ft 7in (20.6m)	Width: 9ft 2in (2.79m)
(Inter) 67ft 6in (20.5m)	Horsepower: 2,252hp (1,680kW)
Height: 12ft 6in (3.81m)	Seats (total/car): 340S, 28S/66S/66S/66S/66S/48S

Number	Formation DMSO(A)+MSO(A)+MSO(B)+ MSO(C)+MSO(D)+DMSO(B)	Depot	Livery	Owner	Operator	Name
395001	39011+39012+39013+39014+39015+39016	AD	HS1	HSB	SET	*Dame Kelly Holmes*
395002	39021+39022+39023+39024+39025+39026	AD	HS1	HSB	SET	*Sebastian Coe*
395003	39031+39032+39033+39034+39035+39036	AD	HS1	HSB	SET	*Sir Steve Redgrave*
395004	39041+39042+39043+39044+39045+39046	AD	HS1	HSB	SET	*Sir Chris Hoy*
395005	39051+39052+39053+39054+39055+39056	AD	HS1	HSB	SET	*Dame Tanni Grey-Thompson*
395006	39061+39062+39063+39064+39065+39066	AD	HS1	HSB	SET	*Daley Thompson*
395007	39071+39072+39073+39074+39075+39076	AD	HS1	HSB	SET	*Steve Backley*
395008	39081+39082+39083+39084+39085+39086	AD	HS1	HSB	SET	*Ben Ainslie*
395009	39091+39092+39093+39094+39095+39096	AD	HS1	HSB	SET	*Rebecca Adlington*
395010	39101+39102+39103+39104+39105+39106	AD	HS1	HSB	SET	
395011	39111+39112+39113+39114+39115+39116	AD	HS1	HSB	SET	
395012	39121+39122+39123+39124+39125+39126	AD	HS1	HSB	SET	
395013	39131+39132+39133+39134+39135+39136	AD	HS1	HSB	SET	
395014	39141+39142+39143+39144+39145+39146	AD	HS1	HSB	SET	
395015	39151+39152+39153+39154+39155+39156	AD	HS1	HSB	SET	
395016	39161+39162+39163+39164+39165+39166	AD	HS1	HSB	SET	*Jamie Staff*
395017	39171+39172+39173+39174+39175+39176	AD	HS1	HSB	SET	
395018	39181+39182+39183+39184+39185+39186	AD	HS1	HSB	SET	
395019	39191+39192+39193+39194+39195+39196	AD	HS1	HSB	SET	
395020	39201+39202+39203+39204+39205+39206	AD	HS1	HSB	SET	
395021	39211+39212+39213+39214+39215+39216	AD	HS1	HSB	SET	
395022	39221+39222+39223+39224+39225+39226	AD	HS1	HSB	SET	
395023	39231+39232+39233+39234+39235+39236	AD	HS1	HSB	SET	
395024	39241+39242+39243+39244+39245+39246	AD	HS1	HSB	SET	
395025	39251+39252+39253+39254+39255+39256	AD	HS1	HSB	SET	
395026	39261+39262+39263+39264+39265+39266	AD	HS1	HSB	SET	
395027	39271+39272+39273+39274+39275+39276	AD	HS1	HSB	SET	
395028	39281+39282+39283+39284+39285+39286	AD	HS1	HSB	SET	
395029	39291+39292+39293+39294+39295+39296	AD	HS1	HSB	SET	

Below: *A fleet of 29 Ashford-based Class 395 Hitachi six-car sets operate domestic South Eastern services over High Speed 1 and on Kent domestic routes. The trains were built in Japan and are maintained under contract by Hitachi in new facilities at Ashford, Kent. All are painted in dark blue with South Eastern branding. Sets Nos. 395006 and 395002 pass Broombridge Wood, near Ashford.* **Brian Morrison**

Class 465/0
Networker

Vehicle Length: (Driving) 68ft 6½in (20.89m)			Width: 9ft 3in (2.81m)		
(Inter) 65ft 9¾in (20.05m)			Horsepower: 2,252hp (1,680kW)		
Height: 12ft 4½in (3.77m)			Seats (total/car): 348S, 86S/90S/86S/86S		

Number	Formation DMSO(A)+TSO+TSO+DMSO(B)	Depot	Livery	Owner	Operator
465001	64759+72028+72029+64809	SG	SET	HSB	SET
465002	64760+72030+72031+64810	SG	SET	HSB	SET
465003	64761+72032+72033+64811	SG	SET	HSB	SET
465004	64762+72034+72035+64812	SG	SET	HSB	SET
465005	64763+72036+72037+64813	SG	SET	HSB	SET
465006	64764+72038+72039+64814	SG	SET	HSB	SET
465007	64765+72040+72041+64815	SG	SET	HSB	SET
465008	64766+72042+72043+64816	SG	SET	HSB	SET
465009	64767+72044+72045+64817	SG	SET	HSB	SET
465010	64768+72046+72047+64818	SG	SET	HSB	SET
465011	64769+72048+72049+64819	SG	SET	HSB	SET
465012	64770+72050+72051+64820	SG	SET	HSB	SET
465013	64771+72052+72053+64821	SG	SET	HSB	SET
465014	64772+72054+72055+64822	SG	SET	HSB	SET
465015	64773+72056+72057+64823	SG	SET	HSB	SET
465016	64774+72058+72059+64824	SG	SET	HSB	SET
465017	64775+72060+72061+64825	SG	SET	HSB	SET
465018	64776+72062+72063+64826	SG	SET	HSB	SET
465019	64777+72064+72065+64827	SG	SET	HSB	SET
465020	64778+72066+72067+64828	SG	SET	HSB	SET
465021	64779+72068+72069+64829	SG	SET	HSB	SET
465022	64780+72070+72071+64830	SG	SET	HSB	SET
465023	64781+72072+72073+64831	SG	SET	HSB	SET
465024	64782+72074+72075+64832	SG	SET	HSB	SET
465025	64783+72076+72077+64833	SG	SET	HSB	SET
465026	64784+72078+72079+64834	SG	SET	HSB	SET
465027	64785+72080+72081+64835	SG	SET	HSB	SET
465028	64786+72082+72083+64836	SG	SET	HSB	SET
465029	64787+72084+72085+64837	SG	SET	HSB	SET
465030	64788+72086+72087+64838	SG	SET	HSB	SET
465031	64789+72088+72089+64839	SG	SET	HSB	SET
465032	64790+72090+72091+64840	SG	SET	HSB	SET
465033	64791+72092+72093+64841	SG	SET	HSB	SET
465034	64792+72094+72095+64842	SG	SET	HSB	SET
465035	64793+72096+72097+64843	SG	SET	HSB	SET
465036	64794+72098+72099+64844	SG	SET	HSB	SET
465037	64795+72100+72101+64845	SG	SET	HSB	SET
465038	64796+72102+72103+64846	SG	SET	HSB	SET
465039	64797+72104+72105+64847	SG	SET	HSB	SET
465040	64798+72106+72107+64848	SG	SET	HSB	SET
465041	64799+72108+72109+64849	SG	SET	HSB	SET
465042	64800+72110+72111+64850	SG	SET	HSB	SET
465043	64801+72112+72113+64851	SG	SET	HSB	SET
465044	64802+72114+72115+64852	SG	SET	HSB	SET
465045	64803+72116+72117+64853	SG	SET	HSB	SET
465046	64804+72118+72119+64854	SG	SET	HSB	SET
465047	64805+72120+72121+64855	SG	SET	HSB	SET
465048	64806+72122+72123+64856	SG	SET	HSB	SET
465049	64807+72124+72125+64857	SG	SET	HSB	SET
465050	64808+72126+72127+64858	SG	SET	HSB	SET

Class 465/1
Networker

Vehicle Length: (Driving) 68ft 6½in (20.89m)			Width: 9ft 3in (2.81m)		
(Inter) 65ft 9¾in (20.05m)			Horsepower: 2,252hp (1,680kW)		
Height: 12ft 4½in (3.77m)			Seats (total/car): 348S, 86S/90S/86S/86S		

Number	Formation DMSO(A)+TSO+TSO+DMSO(B)	Depot	Livery	Owner	Operator
465151	65800+72900+72901+65847	SG	SET	HSB	SET
465152	65801+72902+72903+65848	SG	SET	HSB	SET

Passenger Train Operating Companies - South Eastern

South Eastern

465153	65802+72904+72905+65849	SG	SET	HSB	SET
465154	65803+72906+72907+65850	SG	SET	HSB	SET
465155	65804+72908+72909+65851	SG	SET	HSB	SET
465156	65805+72910+72911+65852	SG	SET	HSB	SET
465157	65806+72912+72913+65853	SG	SET	HSB	SET
465158	65807+72914+72915+65854	SG	SET	HSB	SET
465159	65808+72916+72917+65855	SG	SET	HSB	SET
465160	65809+72918+72919+65856	SG	SET	HSB	SET
465161	65810+72920+72921+65857	SG	SET	HSB	SET
465162	65811+72922+72923+65858	SG	SET	HSB	SET
465163	65812+72924+72925+65859	SG	SET	HSB	SET
465164	65813+72926+72927+65860	SG	SET	HSB	SET
465165	65814+72928+72929+65861	SG	SET	HSB	SET
465166	65815+72930+72931+65862	SG	SET	HSB	SET
465167	65816+72932+72933+65863	SG	SET	HSB	SET
465168	65817+72934+72935+65864	SG	SET	HSB	SET
465169	65818+72936+72937+65865	SG	SET	HSB	SET
465170	65819+72938+72939+65866	SG	SET	HSB	SET
465171	65820+72940+72941+65867	SG	SET	HSB	SET
465172	65821+72942+72943+65868	SG	SET	HSB	SET
465173	65822+72944+72945+65869	SG	SET	HSB	SET
465174	65823+72946+72947+65870	SG	SET	HSB	SET
465175	65824+72948+72949+65871	SG	SET	HSB	SET
465176	65825+72950+72951+65872	SG	SET	HSB	SET
465177	65826+72952+72952+65873	SG	SET	HSB	SET
465178	65827+72954+72955+65874	SG	SET	HSB	SET
465179	65828+72956+72957+65875	SG	SET	HSB	SET
465180	65829+72958+72959+65876	SG	SET	HSB	SET
465181	65830+72960+72961+65877	SG	SET	HSB	SET
465182	65831+72962+72963+65878	SG	SET	HSB	SET
465183	65832+72964+72965+65879	SG	SET	HSB	SET
465184	65833+72966+72967+65880	SG	SET	HSB	SET
465185	65834+72968+72969+65881	SG	SET	HSB	SET
465186	65835+72970+72971+65882	SG	SET	HSB	SET
465187	65836+72972+72973+65883	SG	SET	HSB	SET
465188	65837+72974+72975+65884	SG	SET	HSB	SET
465189	65838+72976+72977+65885	SG	SET	HSB	SET
465190	65839+72978+72979+65886	SG	SET	HSB	SET
465191	65840+72980+72981+65887	SG	SET	HSB	SET
465192	65841+72982+72983+65888	SG	SET	HSB	SET
465193	65842+72984+72985+65889	SG	SET	HSB	SET
465194	65843+72986+72987+65890	SG	SET	HSB	SET
465195	65844+72988+72989+65891	SG	SET	HSB	SET
465196	65845+72990+72991+65892	SG	SET	HSB	SET
465197	65846+72992+72993+65893	SG	SET	HSB	SET

Class 465/2
Networker

Vehicle Length: (Driving) 68ft 6½in (20.89m)
(Inter) 65ft 9¾in (20.05m)
Height: 12ft 4½in (3.77m)

Width: 9ft 3in (2.81m)
Horsepower: 2,252hp (1,680kW)
Seats (total/car): 348S, 86S/90S/86S/86S

Number	Formation	Depot	Livery	Owner	Operator
	DMSO(A)+TSO+TSO+DMSO(B)				
465235	65734+72787+72788+65784	SG	SET	ANG	SET
465236	65735+72789+72790+65785	SG	SET	ANG	SET
465237	65736+72791+72792+65786	SG	SET	ANG	SET
465238	65737+72793+72794+65787	SG	SET	ANG	SET
465239	65738+72795+72796+65788	SG	SET	ANG	SET
465240	65739+72797+72798+65789	SG	SET	ANG	SET
465241	65740+72799+72800+65790	SG	SET	ANG	SET
465242	65741+72801+72802+65791	SG	SET	ANG	SET
465243	65742+72803+72804+65792	SG	SET	ANG	SET
465244	65743+72805+72806+65793	SG	SET	ANG	SET
465245	65744+72807+72808+65794	SG	SET	ANG	SET
465246	65745+72809+72810+65795	SG	SET	ANG	SET
465247	65746+72811+72812+65796	SG	SET	ANG	SET

465248	65747+72813+72814+65797	SG	SET	ANG	SET		
465249	65748+72815+72816+65798	SG	SET	ANG	SET		
465250	65749+72817+72818+65799	SG	SET	ANG	SET		

Class 465/9
Networker

Vehicle Length: (Driving) 68ft 6½in (20.89m) Width: 9ft 3in (2.81m)
(Inter) 65ft 9¾in (20.05m) Horsepower: 2,252hp (1,680kW)
Height: 12ft 4½in (3.77m) Seats (total/car): 24F-302S, 12F-68S/76S/90S/12F-68S

Number	Formation DMCO(A)+TSO+TSO+DMCO(B)	Depot	Livery	Owner	Operator	Name
465901 (465201)	65700+72719+72720+65750	SG	SET	ANG	SET	
465902 (465202)	65701+72721+72722+65751	SG	SET	ANG	SET	
465903 (465203)	65702+72723+72724+65752	SG	SET	ANG	SET	*Remembrance*
465904 (465204)	65703+72725+72726+65753	SG	SET	ANG	SET	
465905 (465205)	65704+72727+72728+65754	SG	SET	ANG	SET	
465906 (465206)	65705+72729+72730+65755	SG	SET	ANG	SET	
465907 (465207)	65706+72731+72732+65756	SG	SET	ANG	SET	
465908 (465208)	65707+72733+72734+65757	SG	SET	ANG	SET	
465909 (465209)	65708+72735+72736+65758	SG	SET	ANG	SET	
465910 (465210)	65709+72737+72738+65759	SG	SET	ANG	SET	
465911 (465211)	65710+72739+72740+65760	SG	SET	ANG	SET	
465912 (465212)	65711+72741+72742+65761	SG	SET	ANG	SET	
465913 (465213)	65712+72743+72744+65762	SG	SET	ANG	SET	
465914 (465214)	65713+72745+72746+65763	SG	SET	ANG	SET	
465915 (465215)	65714+72747+72748+65764	SG	SET	ANG	SET	
465916 (465216)	65715+72749+72750+65765	SG	SET	ANG	SET	
465917 (465217)	65716+72751+72752+65766	SG	SET	ANG	SET	
465918 (465218)	65717+72753+72754+65767	SG	SET	ANG	SET	
465919 (465219)	65718+72755+72756+65768	SG	SET	ANG	SET	
465920 (465220)	65719+72757+72758+65769	SG	SET	ANG	SET	
465921 (465221)	65720+72759+72760+65770	SG	SET	ANG	SET	
465922 (465222)	65721+72761+72762+65771	SG	SET	ANG	SET	
465923 (465223)	65722+72763+72764+65772	SG	SET	ANG	SET	
465924 (465224)	65723+72765+72766+65773	SG	SET	ANG	SET	
465925 (465225)	65724+72767+72768+65774	SG	SET	ANG	SET	
465926 (465226)	65725+72769+72770+65775	SG	SET	ANG	SET	
465927 (465227)	65726+72771+72772+65776	SG	SET	ANG	SET	
465928 (465228)	65727+72773+72774+65777	SG	SET	ANG	SET	
465929 (465229)	65728+72775+72776+65778	SG	SET	ANG	SET	
465930 (465230)	65729+72777+72778+65779	SG	SET	ANG	SET	
465931 (465231)	65730+72779+72780+65780	SG	SET	ANG	SET	
465932 (465232)	65731+72781+72782+65781	SG	SET	ANG	SET	
465933 (465233)	65732+72783+72784+65782	SG	SET	ANG	SET	
465934 (465234)	65733+72785+72786+65783	SG	SET	ANG	SET	

Right: *South Eastern suburban services are operated by a large fleet of Class 465 'Networker' units introduced under the Network SouthEast banner to replace ageing slam door stock. The sets are allocated to Slade Green depot and are painted in various versions of SET white livery. The original Class 465/0 and 465/1 sets were built by BREL at York, while the Class 465/2 sets were built by Alstom of Birmingham. The present Class 465/9 units were modified from Class 465/2s at Wabtec, Doncaster. Set No. 465171 is shown approaching Waterloo East from the south.* **Chris Perkins**

South Eastern

Passenger Train Operating Companies - South Eastern

Class 466
Networker

Vehicle Length: (Driving) 68ft 6½in (20.89m)	Horsepower: 1,126hp (840kW)
Height: 12ft 4½in (3.77m)	Seats (total/car): 168S, 86S/82S
Width: 9ft 3in (2.81m)	

Number	Formation DMSO+DTSO	Depot	Livery	Owner	Operator
466001	64860+78312	SG	SET	ANG	SET
466002	64861+78313	SG	SET	ANG	SET
466003	64862+78314	SG	SET	ANG	SET
466004	64863+78315	SG	SET	ANG	SET
466005	64864+78316	SG	SET	ANG	SET
466006	64865+78317	SG	SET	ANG	SET
466007	64866+78318	SG	SET	ANG	SET
466008	64867+78319	SG	SET	ANG	SET
466009	64868+78320	SG	SET	ANG	SET
466010	64869+78321	SG	SET	ANG	SET
466011	64870+78322	SG	SET	ANG	SET
466012	64871+78323	SG	SET	ANG	SET
466013	64872+78324	SG	SET	ANG	SET
466014	64873+78325	SG	SET	ANG	SET
466015	64874+78326	SG	SET	ANG	SET
466016	64875+78327	SG	SET	ANG	SET
466017	64876+78328	SG	SET	ANG	SET
466018	64877+78329	SG	SET	ANG	SET
466019	64878+78330	SG	SET	ANG	SET
466020	64879+78331	SG	SET	ANG	SET
466021	64880+78332	SG	SET	ANG	SET
466022	64881+78333	SG	SET	ANG	SET
466023	64882+78334	SG	SET	ANG	SET
466024	64883+78335	SG	SET	ANG	SET
466025	64884+78336	SG	SET	ANG	SET
466026	64885+78337	SG	SET	ANG	SET
466027	64886+78338	SG	SET	ANG	SET
466028	64887+78339	SG	SET	ANG	SET
466029	64888+78340	SG	SET	ANG	SET
466030	64889+78341	SG	SET	ANG	SET
466031	64890+78342	SG	SET	ANG	SET
466032	64891+78343	SG	SET	ANG	SET
466033	64892+78344	SG	SET	ANG	SET
466034	64893+78345	SG	SET	ANG	SET
466035	64894+78346	SG	SET	ANG	SET
466036	64895+78347	SG	SET	ANG	SET
466037	64896+78348	SG	SET	ANG	SET
466038	64897+78349	SG	SET	ANG	SET
466039	64898+78350	SG	SET	ANG	SET
466040	64899+78351	SG	SET	ANG	SET
466041	64900+78352	SG	SET	ANG	SET
466042	64901+78353	SG	SET	ANG	SET
466043	64902+78354	SG	SET	ANG	SET

Above: *To provide formation flexibility on SouthEastern, a batch of 43 two-car Class 466 'Networker' units were built by Alstom, permitting for formation of two, six and ten car trains. The two-car sets are allocated to Slade Green and owned by Angel Trains. All are painted in South Eastern white livery. Set No. 466022 is seen departing south from London Bridge.* **CJM**

Southern

Address: ✉ Go-Ahead House, 26-28 Addiscombe Road, Croydon, CR9 5GA
📠 info@southernrailway.com
☎ 08451 272920
ⓘ www.southernrailway.com

Managing Director: Chris Burchell
Franchise Dates: 1 March 2003 - 25 July 2015
Principal Routes: London Victoria/London Bridge to Brighton, Coastway route, Uckfield/East Grinstead. Services to Surrey, Sussex and Brighton to Ashford route
Depots: Brighton (BI), Selhurst (SU)
Parent Company: Govia

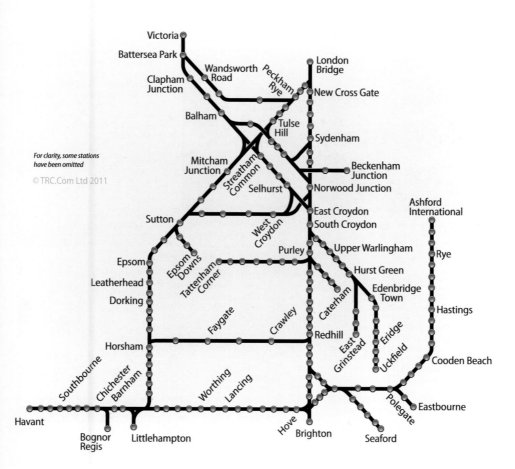

For clarity, some stations have been omitted

© TRC.Com Ltd 2011

Passenger Train Operating Companies - Southern

Southern

Class 171/7
Turbostar

Vehicle Length: 77ft 6in (23.62m)
Height: 12ft 4½in (3.77m)
Width: 8ft 10in (2.69m)
Engine: 1 x MTU 6R 183TD13H 422hp per vehicle
Horsepower: 844hp (629kW)
Seats (total/car): 9F-107S 9F-43S/64S

Number	Formation DMCL+DMSL	Depot	Livery	Owner	Operator
171721	50721+79721	SU	SOU	PTR	SOU
171722	50722+79722	SU	SOU	PTR	SOU
171723	50723+79723	SU	SOU	PTR	SOU
171724	50724+79724	SU	SOU	PTR	SOU
171725	50725+79725	SU	SOU	PTR	SOU
171726	50726+79726	SU	SOU	PTR	SOU
171727	50727+79727	SU	SOU	PTR	SOU
171728	50728+79728	SU	SOU	PTR	SOU
171729	50729+79729	SU	SOU	PTR	SOU
171730	50392+79392	SU	SOU	PTR	SOU

171730 Previously numbered 170392

Class 171/8
Turbostar

Vehicle Length: 77ft 6in (23.62m)
Height: 12ft 4½in (3.77m)
Width: 8ft 10in (2.69m)
Engine: 1 x MTU 6R 183TD13H 422hp per vehicle
Horsepower: 1,688hp (1,259kW)
Seats (total/car): 18F-241S 9F-43S/74S/74S/9F-50SS

Number	Formation DMCL(A)+MS+MS+DMCL(B)	Depot	Livery	Owner	Operator
171801	50801+54801+56801+79801	SU	SOU	PTR	SOU
171802	50802+54802+56802+79802	SU	SOU	PTR	SOU
171803	50803+54803+56803+79803	SU	SOU	PTR	SOU
171804	50804+54804+56804+79804	SU	SOU	PTR	SOU
171805	50805+54805+56805+79805	SU	SOU	PTR	SOU
171806	50806+54806+56806+79806	SU	SOU	PTR	SOU

Left: *A fleet of 16 Bombardier Turbostar units (10 two-car and six four-car) of Class 171 are operated by Southern for non-electrified line use. All are allocated to Selhurst and are finished in Southern white and green livery. Set No 171726, a two-car unit, leads a train at London Bridge.*
Ian Docwra

Class 313/2

Vehicle Length: (Driving) 64ft 11½in (20.75m)
(Inter) 65ft 4¼in (19.92m)
Height: 11ft 9in (3.58m)
Width: 9ft 3in (2.82m)
Horsepower: 880hp (656kW)
Seats (total/car): 202S, 66S/70S/66S

Number	Formation DMSO+PTSO+BDMSO	Depot	Livery	Owner	Operator
313201 (313101)	62529+71213+62593	BI	SOU	HSB	SOU
313202 (313102)	62530+71214+62594	BI	SOU	HSB	SOU
313203 (313103)	62531+71215+62595	BI	SOU	HSB	SOU
313204 (313104)	62532+71216+62596	BI	SOU	HSB	SOU
313205 (313105)	62533+71217+62597	BI	SOU	HSB	SOU
313206 (313106)	62534+71218+62598	BI	SOU	HSB	SOU
313207 (313107)	62535+71219+62599	BI	SOU	HSB	SOU
313208 (313108)	62536+71220+62600	BI	SOU	HSB	SOU
313209 (313109)	62537+71221+62601	BI	SOU	HSB	SOU
313210 (313110)	62538+71222+62602	BI	SOU	HSB	SOU
313211 (313111)	62539+71223+62603	BI	SOU	HSB	SOU
313212 (313112)	62540+71224+62604	BI	SOU	HSB	SOU
313213 (313113)	62541+71225+62605	BI	SOU	HSB	SOU
313214 (313114)	62542+71226+62606	BI	SOU	HSB	SOU
313215 (313115)	62543+71227+62607	BI	SOU	HSB	SOU
313216 (313116)	62544+71228+62608	BI	SOU	HSB	SOU
313217 (313117)	62545+71229+61609	BI	SOU	HSB	SOU
313219 (313119)	62547+71231+61611	BI	SOU	HSB	SOU
313220 (313120)	62548+71232+61612	BI	SOU	HSB	SOU

Right: *To operate on the Coastway route radiating from Brighton, Southern have recently introduced a fleet of Class 313/2 units, displaced from London Overground services by introduction of Class 378 stock. The sets are allocated to Brighton and have been re-branded in Southern colours and received interior facelift work. Some sets carry route pictogram branding. Set No. 313210 is seen at Wabtec, Doncaster following overhaul.*
Derek Porter

Class 377/1
Electrostar

Vehicle Length: (Driving) 66ft 9in (20.3m) Width: 9ft 2in (2.79m)
(Inter) 65ft 6in (19.96m) Horsepower: 2,012hp (1,500kW)
Height: 12ft 4in (3.75m) Seats (total/car): 24F-218S, 12F-48(56S)/62S(70S)/52S(62S)/12F-48(56S)

Number	Formation DMCO(A)+MSO+TSO+DMCO(B)	Depot	Livery	Owner	Operator
377101	78501+77101+78901+78701	BI	SOU	PTR	SOU
377102	78502+77102+78902+78702	BI	SOU	PTR	SOU
377103	78503+77103+78903+78703	BI	SOU	PTR	SOU
377104	78504+77104+78904+78704	BI	SOU	PTR	SOU
377105	78505+77105+78905+78705	BI	SOU	PTR	SOU
377106	78506+77106+78906+78706	BI	SOU	PTR	SOU
377107	78507+77107+78907+78707	BI	SOU	PTR	SOU
377108	78508+77108+78908+78708	BI	SOU	PTR	SOU
377109	78509+77109+78909+78709	BI	SOU	PTR	SOU
377110	78510+77110+78910+78710	BI	SOU	PTR	SOU
377111	78511+77111+78911+78711	BI	SOU	PTR	SOU
377112	78512+77112+78912+78712	BI	SOU	PTR	SOU
377113	78513+77113+78913+78713	BI	SOU	PTR	SOU
377114	78514+77114+78914+78714	BI	SOU	PTR	SOU
377115	78515+77115+78915+78715	BI	SOU	PTR	SOU
377116	78516+77116+78916+78716	BI	SOU	PTR	SOU
377117	78517+77117+78917+78717	BI	SOU	PTR	SOU
377118	78518+77118+78918+78718	BI	SOU	PTR	SOU
377119	78519+77119+78919+78719	BI	SOU	PTR	SOU
377120	78520+77120+78920+78720	SU	SOU	PTR	SOU
377121	78521+77121+78921+78721	SU	SOU	PTR	SOU
377122	78522+77122+78922+78722	SU	SOU	PTR	SOU
377123	78523+77123+78923+78723	SU	SOU	PTR	SOU
377124	78524+77124+78924+78724	SU	SOU	PTR	SOU
377125	78525+77125+78925+78725	SU	SOU	PTR	SOU
377126	78526+77126+78926+78726	SU	SOU	PTR	SOU
377127	78527+77127+78927+78727	SU	SOU	PTR	SOU
377128	78528+77128+78928+78728	SU	SOU	PTR	SOU
377129	78529+77129+78929+78729	SU	SOU	PTR	SOU
377130	78530+77130+78930+78730	SU	SOU	PTR	SOU
377131	78531+77131+78931+78731	SU	SOU	PTR	SOU
377132	78532+77132+78932+78732	SU	SOU	PTR	SOU
377133	78533+77133+78933+78733	SU	SOU	PTR	SOU
377134	78534+77134+78934+78734	SU	SOU	PTR	SOU
377135	78535+77135+78935+78735	SU	SOU	PTR	SOU
377136	78536+77136+78936+78736	SU	SOU	PTR	SOU
377137	78537+77137+78937+78737	SU	SOU	PTR	SOU
377138	78538+77138+78938+78738	SU	SOU	PTR	SOU
377139	78539+77139+78939+78739	SU	SOU	PTR	SOU
377140	78540+77140+78940+78740	SU	SOU	PTR	SOU

Southern

377141	78541+77141+78941+78741	SU	SOU	PTR	SOU
377142	78542+77142+78942+78742	SU	SOU	PTR	SOU
377143	78543+77143+78943+78743	SU	SOU	PTR	SOU
377144	78544+77144+78944+78744	SU	SOU	PTR	SOU
377145	78545+77145+78945+78745	SU	SOU	PTR	SOU
377146	78546+77146+78946+78746	SU	SOU	PTR	SOU
377147	78547+77147+78947+78747	SU	SOU	PTR	SOU
377148	78548+77148+78948+78748	SU	SOU	PTR	SOU
377149	78549+77149+78949+78749	SU	SOU	PTR	SOU
377150	78550+77150+78950+78750	SU	SOU	PTR	SOU
377151	78551+77151+78951+78751	SU	SOU	PTR	SOU
377152	78552+77152+78952+78752	SU	SOU	PTR	SOU
377153	78553+77153+78953+78753	SU	SOU	PTR	SOU
377154	78554+77154+78954+78754	SU	SOU	PTR	SOU
377155	78555+77155+78955+78755	SU	SOU	PTR	SOU
377156	78556+77156+78956+78756	SU	SOU	PTR	SOU
377157	78557+77157+78957+78757	SU	SOU	PTR	SOU
377158	78558+77158+78958+78758	SU	SOU	PTR	SOU
377159	78559+77159+78959+78759	SU	SOU	PTR	SOU
377160	78560+77160+78960+78760	SU	SOU	PTR	SOU
377161	78561+77161+78961+78761	SU	SOU	PTR	SOU
377162	78562+77162+78962+78762	SU	SOU	PTR	SOU
377163	78563+77163+78963+78763	SU	SOU	PTR	SOU
377164	78564+77164+78964+78764	SU	SOU	PTR	SOU

Class 377/2
Electrostar

Vehicle Length: (Driving) 66ft 9in (20.3m) Width: 9ft 2in (2.79m)
(Inter) 65ft 6in (19.96m) Horsepower: 2,012hp (1,500kW)
Height: 12ft 4in (3.75m) Seats (total/car): 24F-222S, 12F-48/69S/57S/12F-48S

Number	Formation	Depot	Livery	Owner	Operator
	DMCO(A)+MSO+PTSO+DMCO(B)				
377201	78571+77171+78971+78771	BI	SOU	PTR	SOU
377202	78572+77172+78972+78772	BI	SOU	PTR	SOU
377203	78573+77173+78973+78773	BI	SOU	PTR	SOU
377204	78574+77174+78974+78774	BI	SOU	PTR	SOU
377205	78575+77175+78975+78775	SU	SOU	PTR	SOU
377206	78576+77176+78976+78776	SU	SOU	PTR	SOU
377207	78577+77177+78977+78777	BI	SOU	PTR	SOU
377208	78578+77178+78978+78778	BI	SOU	PTR	SOU
377209	78579+77179+78979+78779	BI	SOU	PTR	SOU
377210	78580+77180+78980+78780	SU	SOU	PTR	SOU
377211	78581+77181+78981+78781	SU	SOU	PTR	SOU
377212	78582+77182+78982+78782	SU	SOU	PTR	SOU
377213	78583+77183+78983+78783	BI	SOU	PTR	SOU
377214	78584+77184+78984+78784	SU	SOU	PTR	SOU
377215	78585+77185+78985+78785	BI	SOU	PTR	SOU

Class 377/3
Electrostar

Vehicle Length: (Driving) 66ft 9in (20.3m) Width: 9ft 2in (2.79m)
(Inter) 65ft 6in (19.96m) Horsepower: 2,012hp (1,500kW)
Height: 12ft 4in (3.75m) Seats (total/car): 24F-152S, 12F-48/56S/12F-48S

Number		Formation	Depot	Livery	Owner	Operator
		DMCO(A)+TSO+DMCO(B)				
377301	(375311)	68201+74801+68401	BI	SOU	PTR	SOU
377302	(375312)	68202+74802+68402	BI	SOU	PTR	SOU
377303	(375313)	68203+74803+68403	BI	SOU	PTR	SOU
377304	(375314)	68204+74804+68404	BI	SOU	PTR	SOU
377305	(375315)	68205+74805+68405	BI	SOU	PTR	SOU
377306	(375316)	68206+74806+68406	BI	SOU	PTR	SOU
377307	(375317)	68207+74807+68407	BI	SOU	PTR	SOU
377308	(375318)	68208+74808+68408	BI	SOU	PTR	SOU
377309	(375319)	68209+74809+68409	BI	SOU	PTR	SOU
377310	(375320)	68210+74810+68410	BI	SOU	PTR	SOU
377311	(375321)	68211+74811+68411	BI	SOU	PTR	SOU
377312	(375322)	68212+74812+68412	BI	SOU	PTR	SOU

377313	(375323)	68213+74813+68413	BI	SOU	PTR	SOU	
377314	(375324)	68214+74814+68414	BI	SOU	PTR	SOU	
377315	(375325)	68215+74815+68415	BI	SOU	PTR	SOU	
377316	(375326)	68216+74816+68416	BI	SOU	PTR	SOU	
377317	(375327)	68217+74817+68417	BI	SOU	PTR	SOU	
377318	(375328)	68218+74818+68418	BI	SOU	PTR	SOU	
377319	(375329)	68219+74819+68419	BI	SOU	PTR	SOU	
377320	(375330)	68220+74820+68420	BI	SOU	PTR	SOU	
377321	(375331)	68221+74821+68421	BI	SOU	PTR	SOU	
377322	(375332)	68222+74822+68422	BI	SOU	PTR	SOU	
377323	(375333)	68223+74823+68423	BI	SOU	PTR	SOU	
377324	(375334)	68224+74824+68424	BI	SOU	PTR	SOU	
377325	(375335)	68225+74825+68425	BI	SOU	PTR	SOU	
377326	(375336)	68226+74826+68426	BI	SOU	PTR	SOU	
377327	(375337)	68227+74827+68427	BI	SOU	PTR	SOU	
377328	(375338)	68228+74828+68428	BI	SOU	PTR	SOU	

Right: *The post privatisation modernisation of the South Central franchise has seen the railway re-named as Southern, with outer suburban and main line slam door trains replaced by Bombardier Class 377 'Electrostar' units. Four different sub-classes exist reflecting formation and power collection. Class 377/1 set No. 377142 is illustrated at Clapham Junction.* **CJM**

Class 377/4
Electrostar

Vehicle Length: (Driving) 66ft 9in (20.3m) Width: 9ft 2in (2.79m)
(Inter) 65ft 6in (19.96m) Horsepower: 2,012hp (1,500kW)
Height: 12ft 4in (3.75m) Seats (total/car): 20F-221S, 10F-48/69S/56S/10F-48S

Number	Formation DMCO(A)+MSO+TSO+DMCO(B)	Depot	Livery	Owner	Operator
377401	73401+78801+78601+73801	BI	SOU	PTR	SOU
377402	73402+78802+78602+73802	BI	SOU	PTR	SOU
377403	73403+78803+78603+73803	BI	SOU	PTR	SOU
377404	73404+78804+78604+73804	BI	SOU	PTR	SOU
377405	73405+78805+78605+73805	BI	SOU	PTR	SOU
377406	73406+78806+78606+73806	BI	SOU	PTR	SOU
377407	73407+78807+78607+73807	BI	SOU	PTR	SOU
377408	73408+78808+78608+73808	BI	SOU	PTR	SOU
377409	73409+78809+78609+73809	BI	SOU	PTR	SOU
377410	73410+78810+78610+73810	BI	SOU	PTR	SOU
377411	73411+78811+78611+73811	BI	SOU	PTR	SOU
377412	73412+78812+78612+73812	BI	SOU	PTR	SOU
377413	73413+78813+78613+73813	BI	SOU	PTR	SOU
377414	73414+78814+78614+73814	BI	SOU	PTR	SOU
377415	73415+78815+78615+73815	BI	SOU	PTR	SOU
377416	73416+78816+78616+73816	SU	SOU	PTR	SOU
377417	73417+78817+78617+73817	BI	SOU	PTR	SOU
377418	73418+78818+78618+73818	BI	SOU	PTR	SOU
377419	73419+78819+78619+73819	BI	SOU	PTR	SOU
377420	73420+78820+78620+73820	BI	SOU	PTR	SOU
377421	73421+78821+78621+73821	BI	SOU	PTR	SOU
377422	73422+78822+78622+73822	BI	SOU	PTR	SOU
377423	73423+78823+78623+73823	BI	SOU	PTR	SOU
377424	73424+78824+78624+73824	BI	SOU	PTR	SOU
377425	73425+78825+78625+73825	BI	SOU	PTR	SOU
377426	73426+78826+78626+73826	BI	SOU	PTR	SOU
377427	73427+78827+78627+73827	BI	SOU	PTR	SOU

Southern

377428	73428+78828+78628+73828	BI	SOU	PTR	SOU
377429	73429+78829+78629+73829	SU	SOU	PTR	SOU
377430	73430+78830+78630+73830	BI	SOU	PTR	SOU
377431	73431+78831+78631+73831	BI	SOU	PTR	SOU
377432	73432+78832+78632+73832	BI	SOU	PTR	SOU
377433	73433+78833+78633+73833	BI	SOU	PTR	SOU
377434	73434+78834+78634+73834	BI	SOU	PTR	SOU
377435	73435+78835+78635+73835	BI	SOU	PTR	SOU
377436	73436+78836+78636+73836	BI	SOU	PTR	SOU
377437	73437+78837+78637+73837	BI	SOU	PTR	SOU
377438	73438+78838+78638+73838	BI	SOU	PTR	SOU
377439	73439+78839+78639+73839	BI	SOU	PTR	SOU
377440	73440+78840+78640+73840	BI	SOU	PTR	SOU
377441	73441+78841+78641+73841	BI	SOU	PTR	SOU
377442	73442+78842+78642+73842	BI	SOU	PTR	SOU
377443	73443+78843+78643+73843	BI	SOU	PTR	SOU
377444	73444+78844+78644+73844	BI	SOU	PTR	SOU
377445	73445+78845+78645+73845	BI	SOU	PTR	SOU
377446	73446+78846+78646+73846	BI	SOU	PTR	SOU
377447	73447+78847+78647+73847	SU	SOU	PTR	SOU
377448	73448+78848+78648+73848	BI	SOU	PTR	SOU
377449	73449+78849+78649+73849	BI	SOU	PTR	SOU
377450	73450+78850+78650+73850	BI	SOU	PTR	SOU
377451	73451+78851+78651+73851	BI	SOU	PTR	SOU
377452	73452+78852+78652+73852	SU	SOU	PTR	SOU
377453	73453+78853+78653+73853	BI	SOU	PTR	SOU
377454	73454+78854+78654+73854	BI	SOU	PTR	SOU
377455	73455+78855+78655+73855	BI	SOU	PTR	SOU
377456	73456+78856+78656+73856	BI	SOU	PTR	SOU
377457	73457+78857+78657+73857	BI	SOU	PTR	SOU
377458	73458+78858+78658+73858	BI	SOU	PTR	SOU
377459	73459+78859+78659+73859	BI	SOU	PTR	SOU
377460	73460+78860+78660+73860	SU	SOU	PTR	SOU
377461	73461+78861+78661+73861	BI	SOU	PTR	SOU
377462	73462+78862+78662+73862	BI	SOU	PTR	SOU
377463	73463+78863+78663+73863	BI	SOU	PTR	SOU
377464	73464+78864+78664+73864	BI	SOU	PTR	SOU
377465	73465+78865+78665+73865	BI	SOU	PTR	SOU
377466	73466+78866+78666+73866	BI	SOU	PTR	SOU
377467	73467+78867+78667+73867	BI	SOU	PTR	SOU
377468	73468+78868+78668+73868	BI	SOU	PTR	SOU
377469	73469+78869+78669+73869	BI	SOU	PTR	SOU
377470	73470+78870+78670+73870	BI	SOU	PTR	SOU
377471	73471+78871+78671+73871	BI	SOU	PTR	SOU
377472	73472+78872+78672+73872	BI	SOU	PTR	SOU
377473	73473+78873+78673+73873	BI	SOU	PTR	SOU
377474	73474+78874+78674+73874	BI	SOU	PTR	SOU
377475	73475+78875+78675+73875	BI	SOU	PTR	SOU

Left: *The Southern 'Electrostar' fleet are allocated to Selhurst and Brighton depots and are some of the most reliable sets in traffic. Class 377/4 No. 377446 is illustrated at Clapham Junction forming a Brighton to London Victoria semi-fast service. On the right a South West Trains Class 455 unit can be seen.* **CJM**

Class 442

	Vehicle Length: (Driving) 75ft 11½in (23.15m)			Width: 8ft 11½in (2.73m)		
	(Inter) 75ft 5½in (22.99m)			Horsepower: 1,608hp (1,200kW)		
	Height: 12ft 4in (3.81m)			Seats (total/car): 24F-318S, 74S/76S/24F-28S/66S/74S		

Number	Formation DTSO(A)+TSO+MBC+TSO+DTSO(B)	Depot	Livery	Owner	Operator
442401	77382+71818+62937+71841+77406	BI	SGX	ANG	SOU
442402	77383+71819+62938+71842+77407	BI	SGX	ANG	SOU
442403	77384+71820+62941+71843+77408	BI	SGX	ANG	SOU
442404	77385+71821+62939+71844+77409	BI	SGX	ANG	SOU
442405	77386+71822+62944+71845+77410	BI	SGX	ANG	SOU
442406	77389+71823+62942+71846+77411	BI	SGX	ANG	SOU
442407	77388+71824+62943+71847+77412	BI	SGX	ANG	SOU
442408	77387+71825+62945+71848+77413	BI	SGX	ANG	SOU
442409	77390+71826+62946+71849+77414	BI	SGX	ANG	SOU
442410	77391+71827+62948+71850+77415	BI	SGX	ANG	SOU
442411	77392+71828+62940+71851+77422	BI	SGX	ANG	SOU
442412	77393+71829+62947+71858+77417	BI	SGX	ANG	SOU
442413	77394+71830+62949+71853+77418	BI	SGX	ANG	SOU
442414	77395+71831+62950+71854+77419	BI	SGX	ANG	SOU
442415	77396+71832+62951+71855+77420	BI	SGX	ANG	SOU
442416	77397+71833+62952+71856+77421	BI	SGX	ANG	SOU
442417	77398+71834+62953+71857+77416	BI	SGX	ANG	SOU
442418	77399+71835+62954+71852+77423	BI	SGX	ANG	SOU
442419	77400+71836+62955+71859+77424	BI	SGX	ANG	SOU
442420	77401+71837+62956+71860+77425	BI	SGX	ANG	SOU
442421	77402+71838+62957+71861+77426	BI	SGX	ANG	SOU
442422	77403+71839+62958+71862+77427	BI	SGX	ANG	SOU
442423	77404+71840+62959+71863+77428	BI	SGX	ANG	SOU
442424	77405+71841+62960+71864+77429	BI	SGX	ANG	SOU

Right: *Following the decision by South West Trains to withdraw the Class 442 'Wessex' electric sets from use, the fleet were stored. After a long period they were gradually taken over by Southern/Gatwick Express to launch a revised London Victoria to Gatwick Airport service, with trains extended to Brighton and the South Coast. All 24 sets are now operated by Southern and painted in Gatwick Express livery. Set No. 442407 is shown leading another unit of the same class towards London Victoria at Clapham Junction.* **CJM**

Class 455/8

	Vehicle Length: (Driving) 65ft 0½in (19.83m)			Width: 9ft 3¼in (2.82m)		
	(Inter) 65ft 4½in (19.92m)			Horsepower: 1,000hp (746kW)		
	Height: 12ft 1½in (3.79m)			Seats (total/car): 310S, 74S/78S/84S/74S		

Number	Formation DTSO(A)+MSO+TSO+DTSO(B)	Depot	Livery	Owner	Operator
455801	77627+62709+71657+77580	SU	SOU	HSB	SOU
455802	77581+62710+71664+77582	SU	SOU	HSB	SOU
455803	77583+62711+71639+77584	SU	SOU	HSB	SOU
455804	77585+62712+71640+77586	SU	SOU	HSB	SOU
455805	77587+62713+71641+77588	SU	SOU	HSB	SOU
455806	77589+62714+71642+77590	SU	SOU	HSB	SOU
455807	77591+62715+71643+77592	SU	SOU	HSB	SOU
455808	77637+62716+71644+77594	SU	SOU	HSB	SOU
455809	77623+62717+71648+77602	SU	SOU	HSB	SOU
455810	77597+62718+71646+77598	SU	SOU	HSB	SOU
455811	77599+62719+71647+77600	SU	SOU	HSB	SOU
455812	77595+62720+71645+77626	SU	SOU	HSB	SOU

Passenger Train Operating Companies - Southern

Southern

455813	77603+62721+71649+77604	SU	SOU	HSB	SOU
455814	77605+62722+71650+77606	SU	SOU	HSB	SOU
455815	77607+62723+71651+77608	SU	SOU	HSB	SOU
455816	77609+62724+71652+77633	SU	SOU	HSB	SOU
455817	77611+62725+71653+77612	SU	SOU	HSB	SOU
455818	77613+62726+71654+77632	SU	SOU	HSB	SOU
455819	77615+62727+71637+77616	SU	SOU	HSB	SOU
455820	77617+62728+71656+77618	SU	SOU	HSB	SOU
455821	77619+62729+71655+77620	SU	SOU	HSB	SOU
455822	77621+62730+71658+77622	SU	SOU	HSB	SOU
455823	77601+62731+71659+77596	SU	SOU	HSB	SOU
455824	77593+62732+71660+77624	SU	SOU	HSB	SOU
455825	77579+62733+71661+77628	SU	SOU	HSB	SOU
455826	77630+62734+71662+77629	SU	SOU	HSB	SOU
455827	77610+62735+71663+77614	SU	SOU	HSB	SOU
455828	77631+62736+71638+77634	SU	SOU	HSB	SOU
455829	77635+62737+71665+77636	SU	SOU	HSB	SOU
455830	77625+62743+71666+77638	SU	SOU	HSB	SOU
455831	77639+62739+71667+77640	SU	SOU	HSB	SOU
455832	77641+62740+71668+77642	SU	SOU	HSB	SOU
455833	77643+62741+71669+77644	SU	SOU	HSB	SOU
455834	77645+62742+71670+77646	SU	SOU	HSB	SOU
455835	77647+62738+71671+77648	SU	SOU	HSB	SOU
455836	77649+62744+71672+77650	SU	SOU	HSB	SOU
455837	77651+62745+71673+77652	SU	SOU	HSB	SOU
455838	77653+62746+71674+77654	SU	SOU	HSB	SOU
455839	77655+62747+71675+77656	SU	SOU	HSB	SOU
455840	77657+62748+71676+77658	SU	SOU	HSB	SOU
455841	77659+62749+71677+77660	SU	SOU	HSB	SOU
455842	77661+62750+71678+77662	SU	SOU	HSB	SOU
455843	776636+2751+71679+77664	SU	SOU	HSB	SOU
455844	776656+2752+71680+77666	SU	SOU	HSB	SOU
455845	776676+2753+71681+77668	SU	SOU	HSB	SOU
455846	776696+2754+71682+77670	SU	SOU	HSB	SOU

Left: *A fleet of 46 four-car Class 455/8 suburban units are operated by Southern, allocated to Selhurst depot. All have been refurbished and this group have had their original front gangway connection removed and sealed up, stopping inter-unit access en route. All sets are painted in Southern livery. Set No. 455822 departs from Clapham Junction.* **CJM**

Class 456

Vehicle Length: (Driving) 65ft 3¼in (19.89m)	Horsepower: 500hp (370kW)
Height: 12ft 4½in (3.77m)	Seats (total/car): 152S, 79S/73S
Width: 9ft 3in (2.81m)	

Number	Formation DMSO+DTSO	Depot	Livery	Owner	Operator
456001	64735+78250	SU	SOU	PTR	SOU
456002	64736+78251	SU	SOU	PTR	SOU
456003	64737+78252	SU	SOU	PTR	SOU
456004	64738+78253	SU	SOU	PTR	SOU
456005	64739+78254	SU	SOU	PTR	SOU
456006	64740+78255	SU	SOU	PTR	SOU
456007	64741+78256	SU	SOU	PTR	SOU
456008	64742+78257	SU	SOU	PTR	SOU
456009	64743+78258	SU	SOU	PTR	SOU
456010	64744+78259	SU	SOU	PTR	SOU
456011	64745+78260	SU	SOU	PTR	SOU
456012	64746+78261	SU	SOU	PTR	SOU
456013	64747+78262	SU	SOU	PTR	SOU
456014	64748+78263	SU	SOU	PTR	SOU
456015	64749+78264	SU	SOU	PTR	SOU
456016	64750+78265	SU	SOU	PTR	SOU
456017	64751+78266	SU	SOU	PTR	SOU
456018	64752+78267	SU	SOU	PTR	SOU
456019	64753+78268	SU	SOU	PTR	SOU
456020	64754+78269	SU	SOU	PTR	SOU
456021	64755+78270	SU	SOU	PTR	SOU
456022	64756+78271	SU	SOU	PTR	SOU
456023	64757+78272	SU	SOU	PTR	SOU
456024	64758+78273	SU	SOU	PTR	SOU

Name applied
456024   Sir Cosmo Bonsor

Right: *BREL built 24 two-car Class 456s to either operate alone on low-patronage routes or to allow strengthening of trains to six or ten-car formations. The sets were built without end gangways, with a messy jumper air pipe arrangement on the front end. All sets are allocated to Selhurst and carry Southern livery. Set No. 456012 is shown from its DTSO end.* **CJM**

Class 460
Juniper

Vehicle Length: (Driving) 68ft 11½in (21.01m) Width: 9ft 2¼in (2.80m)
(Inter) 65ft 4¾in (19.93m) Horsepower: 3,626hp (2,704kW)
Height: 12ft 4½in (3.77m) Seats (total/car): 48F-316S, 10F/28F/9F-42S/60S/60S/38S/60S/56S

Number	Formation	Depot	Livery	Owner	Operator
	DMFLO+TFO+TCO+MSO+TSO+MSO+DMSO				
460001	67901+74401+74411+74421+74431+74441+74451+67911	SL	GAT	PTR	SOU
460002	67902+74402+74412+74422+74432+74442+74452+67912	SL	GAT	PTR	SOU
460003	67903+74403+74413+74423+74433+74443+74453+67913	SL	GAT	PTR	SOU
460004 (S)	67904+74404+74414+74424+74434+74444+74454+67914	SL/AF	GAT	PTR	-
460005	67905+74405+74415+74425+74435+74445+74455+67915	SL	GAT	PTR	SOU
460006 (S)	67906+74406+74416+74426+74436+74446+74456+67916	SL/AF	GAT	PTR	-
460007	67907+74407+74417+74427+74437+74447+74457+67917	SL	GAT	PTR	SOU
460008	67908+74408+74418+74428+74438+74448+74458+67918	SL	GAT	PTR	SOU

Right: *The eight 8-car Class 460 'Juniper' sets built for Gatwick Express use are allocated to Stewarts Lane and are still to be found operating on the London Victoria to Gatwick Airport route. However, these units are scheduled to come off lease in May 2011 and donate their vehicles to strengthen South West Trains Class 458 stock to five car formations. Set No. '06' (460006) is shown.* **CJM.**

Class 73/2

Vehicle Length: 53ft 8in (16.35m) Power: 750V dc third rail or English Electric 6K
Height: 12ft 5⁵⁄₁₆in (3.79m) Horsepower: electric - 1,600hp (1,193kW)
Width: 8ft 8in (2.64m) Horsepower: diesel - 600hp (447kW)
  Electrical Equipment: English Electric

Number	Depot	Pool	Livery	Owner	Operator	Name
73202 (73137)	SL	IVGA	GAT	PTR	SOU	*Dave Berry*

Right: *Southern, through its Gatwick Express operation, is the operator of one locomotive - Class 73/2 No. 73202, based at Stewarts Lane for 'Thunderbird' duties. The loco is painted in a version of Gatwick Express colours. It is owned by Porterbrook, and is viewed at Redhill when engaged in driver's route learning.*
Mark V. Pike

Virgin Trains

Address: ✉ 85 Smallbrook Queensway, Birmingham, B5 4HA

✎ info@virgintrains.co.uk

✆ 0845 000 8000

ⓘ www.virgintrains.co.uk

Managing Director:	Chris Gibb
Franchise Dates:	12 December 2006 - 31 March 2012
Principal Routes:	London Euston-Birmingham, Holyhead, Manchester Liverpool, Glasgow and Edinburgh
Depots:	Edge Hill* (LL), Longsight** (MA), Oxley** (OY), Wembley** (WB), Central Rivers (CZ) ** Operated by Alstom Transportation
Parent Company:	Virgin Group

Class 57/3

Vehicle Length: 63ft 6in (19.38m)   *Engine: EMD 645-12F3B*
Height: 12ft 10½in (3.91m)   *Horsepower: 2,750hp (2,051kW)*
Width: 9ft 2in (2.79m)   *Electrical Equipment: Brush*

Number	Depot	Pool	Livery	Owner	Operator	Name/Notes
57301 (47845)	MA	-	VWC	PBR	- (warm store)	*Scott Tracy*
57302 (47827)	MA	IWCA	VWC	PBR	VWC	*Virgil Tracy*
57303 (47705)	MA	-	VWC	PBR	- (warm store)	*Alan Tracy*
57304 (47807)	MA	IWCA	VWC	PBR	VWC	*Gordon Tracy*
57305 (47822)	MA	-	VWC	PBR	- (warm store)	*John Tracy*
57306 (47814)	MA	-	VWC	PBR	- (warm store)	*Jeff Tracy*
57307 (47225)	MA	IWCA	VWC	PBR	VWC	*Lady Penelope*
57308 (47846)	MA	IWCA	VWC	PBR	VWC	*Tin Tin*
57309 (47806)	MA	IWCA	VWC	PBR	VWC	*Brains*
57310 (47831)	MA	-	VWC	PBR	- (warm store)	*Kyrano*
57311 (47817)	MA	IWCA	VWC	PBR	VWC	*Parker*
57312 (47330)	MA	-	VWC	PBR	- (warm store)	*The Hood*
57313 (47371)	MA	IWCA	BLU	PBR	ATW	*Used by Arriva Trains Wales*
57314 (47372)	MA	IWCA	ATE	PBR	ATW	*Used by Arriva Trains Wales*
57315 (47234)	MA	IWCA	ATE	PBR	ATW	*Used by Arriva Trains Wales*
57316 (47290)	MA	IWCA	BLU	PBR	ATW	*Used by Arriva Trains Wales*

Below: *Originally a fleet of 16 Class 57/3 locos were on the books of Virgin Trains to act as 'Thunderbird' locos to the operators Pendolino and Voyager fleets. Today 12 remain operational allocated to Manchester and painted in full VT colours. No. 57309* Brains *is shown at Cardiff while on loan to First Great Western.* **CJM**

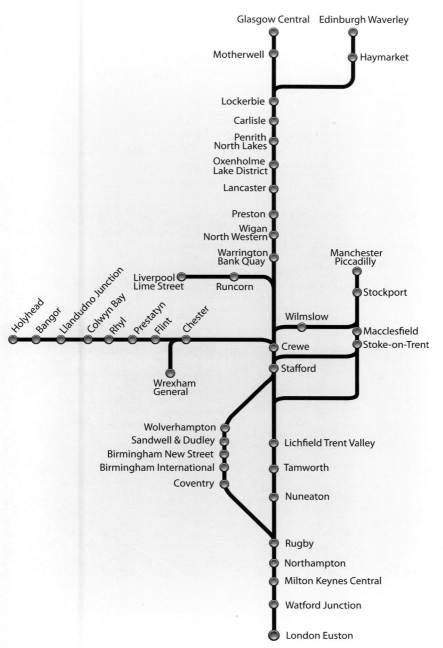

Passenger Train Operating Companies - Virgin Trains

Virgin Trains

Class 221
Super Voyager

Vehicle Length: 77ft 6in (23.62m)
Height: 12ft 4in (3.75m)
Width: 8ft 11in (2.73m)
Engine: 1 x Cummins 750hp per vehicle
Horsepower: 5-car - 3,750hp (2,796kW). 4-car - 3,000hp (2,237kW)
Seats (total/car): 26F/214S 42S/60S/60S/52S*/26F (*not in 4-car set)

Number	Formation	Depot	Livery	Owner	Operator	Name
	221101 - 221118 - DMS+MS+MS+MSRMB+DMF					
221101	60351+60951+60851+60751+60451	CZ	VWC	HBS	VWC	*Louis Bleriot*
221102	60352+60952+60852+60752+60452	CZ	VWC	HBS	VWC	*John Cabot*
221103	60353+60953+60853+60753+60453	CZ	VWC	HBS	VWC	*Christopher Columbus*
221104	60354+60954+60854+60754+60454	CZ	VWC	HBS	VWC	*Sir John Franklin*
221105	60355+60955+60855+60755+60455	CZ	VWC	HBS	VWC	*William Baffin*
221106	60356+60956+60856+60756+60456	CZ	VWC	HBS	VWC	*William Barents*
221107	60357+60957+60857+60757+60457	CZ	VWC	HBS	VWC	*Sir Martin Frobisher*
221108	60358+60958+60858+60758+60458	CZ	VWC	HBS	VWC	*Sir Ernest Shackleton*
221109	60359+60959+60859+60759+60459	CZ	VWC	HBS	VWC	*Marco Polo*
221110	60360+60960+60860+60760+60460	CZ	VWC	HBS	VWC	*James Cook*
221111	60361+60961+60861+60761+60461	CZ	VWC	HBS	VWC	*Roald Amundsen*
221112	60362+60962+60862+60762+60462	CZ	VWC	HBS	VWC	*Ferdinand Magellan*
221113	60363+60963+60863+60763+60463	CZ	VWC	HBS	VWC	*Sir Walter Raleigh*
221114	60364+60964+60864+60764+60464	CZ	VWC	HBS	VWC	
221115	60365+60965+60865+60765+60465	CZ	VWC¤	HBS	VWC	*Polmadie Depot*
221116	60366+60966+60866+60766+60466	CZ	VWC	HBS	VWC	
221117	60367+60967+60867+60767+60467	CZ	VWC	HBS	VWC	
221118	60368+60968+60868+60768+60468	CZ	VWC	HBS	VWC	
221142	60392+60992+60994ø+60792+60492	CZ	VWC	HBS	VWC	*Bombardier Voyager*
221143	60393+60993+60794+60793+60493	CZ	VWC	HBS	VWC	*Auguste Picard*

¤ One driving car carries Bombardier branding. ø MRSMB vehicle
Cars 60394 and 60494 from set 211144 are spare vehicles in warm store

Above: *Virgin Trains currently operates a fleet of 20 five-car Super Voyager sets. All are allocated to Central Rivers depot near Burton. Today the sets operate on non-electrified West Coast services. All sets are painted in Virgin Trains silver and red livery. Set No. 221112* Ferdinand Magellan *passes South Kenton with a London Euston to Holyhead service.* **CJM**

● A proposal exists for all Class 220-222 sets to receive an additional intermediate pantograph coach, allowing dual diesel-electric operation. The project calls for the building of 123 new pantograph carriages and the rebuilding of 21 existing intermediate vehicles to accommodate a pantograph pick up. No agreement for this project has yet been reached. If the project was to go ahead, vehicle construction would be undertaken by Bombardier at Derby.

Class 390
Pendolino

Vehicle Length Driving: 75ft 6in (23.01m)
Height: 11ft 6in (3.50m)
Width: 8ft 11in (2.71m)
Horsepower: 6,840hp (5,100kW)
Seats (total/car): 147F/300S, 18F/39F/44F/46F/76S/66S/48S/64S/46S
31 sets are to be strengthened to eleven vehicles and four extra Class 390 sets are to be built by Virgin Rail Projects

Number	Formation DMRFO+MFO+PTFO+MFO+TSO+MSO+PTSRMB+MSO+DMSO	Depot	Livery	Owner	Operator	Name
390001	69101+69401+69501+69601+68801+69701+69801+69901+69201	MA	VWC	ANG	VWC	*Virgin Pioneer*
390002	69102+69402+69502+69602+68802+69702+69802+69902+69202	MA	VWC	ANG	VWC	*Virgin Angel*
390003	69103+69403+69503+69603+68803+69703+69803+69903+69203	MA	VWC	ANG	VWC	*Virgin Hero*
390004	69104+69404+69504+69604+68804+69704+69804+69904+69204	MA	VWC	ANG	VWC	*Alstom Pendolino*
390005	69105+69405+69505+69605+68805+69705+69805+69905+69205	MA	VWC	ANG	VWC	*City of Wolverhampton*
390006	69106+69406+69506+69606+68806+69706+69806+69906+69206	MA	VWC	ANG	VWC	*Tate Liverpool*
390007	69107+69407+69507+69607+68807+69707+69807+69907+69207	MA	VWC	ANG	VWC	*Virgin Lady*
390008	69108+69408+69508+69608+68808+69708+69808+69908+69208	MA	VWC	ANG	VWC	*Virgin King*
390009	69109+69409+69509+69609+68809+69709+69809+69909+69209	MA	VWC	ANG	VWC	*Treaty of Union*
390010	69110+69410+69510+69610+68810+69710+69810+69910+69210	MA	VWC	ANG	VWC	*A Decade of Progress*
390011	69111+69411+69511+69611+68811+69711+69811+69911+69211	MA	VWC	ANG	VWC	*City of Lichfield*
390012	69112+69412+69512+69612+68812+69712+69812+69912+69212	MA	VWC	ANG	VWC	*Virgin Star*
390013	69113+69413+69513+69613+68813+69713+69813+69913+69213	MA	VWC	ANG	VWC	*Virgin Spirit*
390014	69114+69414+69514+69614+68814+69714+69814+69914+69214	MA	VWC	ANG	VWC	*City of Manchester*
390015	69115+69415+69515+69615+68815+69715+69815+69915+69215	MA	VWC	ANG	VWC	*Virgin Crusader*
390016	69116+69416+69516+69616+68816+69716+69816+69916+69216	MA	VWC	ANG	VWC	*Virgin Champion*
390017	69117+69417+69517+69617+68817+69717+69817+69917+69217	MA	VWC	ANG	VWC	*Virgin Prince*
390018	69118+69418+69518+69618+68818+69718+69818+69918+69218	MA	VWC	ANG	VWC	*Virgin Princess*
390019	69119+69419+69519+69619+68819+69719+69819+69919+69219	MA	VWC	ANG	VWC	*Virgin Warrior*
390020	69120+69420+69520+69620+68820+69720+69820+69920+69220	MA	VWC	ANG	VWC	*Virgin Cavalier*
390021	69121+69421+69521+69621+68821+69721+69821+69921+69221	MA	VWC	ANG	VWC	*Virgin Dream*
390022	69122+69422+69522+69622+68822+69722+69822+69922+69222	MA	VWC	ANG	VWC	*Penny the Pendolino*
390023	69123+69423+69523+69623+68823+69723+69823+69923+69223	MA	VWC	ANG	VWC	*Virgin Glory*
390024	69124+69424+69524+69624+68824+69724+69824+69924+69224	MA	VWC	ANG	VWC	*Virgin Venturer*
390025	69125+69425+69525+69625+68825+69725+69825+69925+69225	MA	VWC	ANG	VWC	*Virgin Stagecoach*
390026	69126+69426+69526+69626+68826+69726+69826+69926+69226	MA	VWC	ANG	VWC	*Virgin Enterprise*
390027	69127+69427+69527+69627+68827+69727+69827+69927+69227	MA	VWC	ANG	VWC	*Virgin Buccaneer*
390028	69128+69428+69528+69628+68828+69728+69828+69928+69228	MA	VWC	ANG	VWC	*City of Preston*
390029	69129+69429+69529+69629+68829+69729+69829+69929+69229	MA	VWC	ANG	VWC	*City of Stoke-on-Trent*
390030	69130+69430+69530+69630+68830+69730+69830+69930+69230	MA	VWC	ANG	VWC	*City of Edinburgh*
390031	69131+69431+69531+69631+68831+69731+69831+69931+69231	MA	VWC	ANG	VWC	*City of Liverpool*
390032	69132+69432+69532+69632+68832+69732+69832+69932+69232	MA	VWC	ANG	VWC	*City of Birmingham*
390034	69134+69434+69534+69634+68834+69734+69834+69934+69234	MA	VWC	ANG	VWC	*City of Carlisle*
390035	69135+69435+69535+69635+68835+69735+69835+69935+69235	MA	VWC	ANG	VWC	*City of Lancaster*
390036	69136+69436+69536+69636+68836+69736+69836+69936+69236	MA	VWC	ANG	VWC	*City of Coventry*
390037	69137+69437+69537+69637+68837+69737+69837+69937+69237	MA	VWC	ANG	VWC	*Virgin Difference*
390038	69138+69438+69538+69638+68838+69738+69838+69938+69238	MA	VWC	ANG	VWC	*City of London*
390039	69139+69439+69539+69639+68839+69739+69839+69939+69239	MA	VWC	ANG	VWC	*Virgin Quest*
390040	69140+69440+69540+69640+68840+69740+69840+69940+69240	MA	VWC	ANG	VWC	*Virgin Pathfinder*

Virgin Trains

Passenger Train Operating Companies - Virgin Trains

Set	Cars					Name
390041	69141+69441+69541+69641+69841+68841+69741+69941+69241	MA	VWC	ANG	VWC	City of Chester
390042	69142+69442+69542+69642+68842+69742+69842+69942+69242	MA	VWC	ANG	VWC	City of Bangor / Dinas Bangor
390043	69143+69443+69543+69643+69843+69743+69843+69943+69243	MA	VWC	ANG	VWC	Virgin Explorer
390044	69144+69444+69544+69644+68844+69744+69844+69944+69244	MA	VWC	ANG	VWC	Virgin Lionheart
390045	69145+69445+69545+69645+68845+69745+69845+69945+69245	MA	VWC	ANG	VWC	101 Squadron
390046	69146+69446+69546+69646+68846+69746+69846+69946+69246	MA	VWC	ANG	VWC	Virgin Soldiers
390047	69147+69447+69547+69647+68847+69747+69847+69947+69247	MA	VWC	ANG	VWC	Clic Sargent
390048	69148+69448+69548+69648+68848+69748+69848+69948+69248	MA	VWC	ANG	VWC	Virgin Harrier
390049	69149+69449+69549+69649+68849+69749+69849+69949+69249	MA	VWC	ANG	VWC	Virgin Express
390050	69150+69450+69550+69650+68850+69750+69850+69950+69250	MA	VWC	ANG	VWC	Virgin Invader
390051	69151+69451+69551+69651+68851+69751+69851+69951+69251	MA	VWC	ANG	VWC	Virgin Ambassador
390052	69152+69452+69552+69652+68852+69752+69852+69952+69252	MA	VWC	ANG	VWC	Virgin Knight
390053	69153+69453+69553+69653+68853+69753+69853+69953+69253	MA	VWC	ANG	VWC	Mission Accomplished
390054	69154+69454+69554+69654+68354+68954+69754+65854+65954+69254	MA	VWC	ANG	VWC §	
390055	69155+69455+69555+69655+68355+68955+69755+65855+65955+69255	MA	VWC	ANG	VWC	(Under construction due 01/11) §
390056	69156+69456+69556+69656+68356+68956+69756+65856+65956+69256	MA	VWC	ANG	VWC	(Under construction due 08/11) §
390057	69157+69457+69557+69657+68357+68957+69757+65857+65957+69257	MA	VWC	ANG	VWC	(Under construction due 12/11) §

§ It is expected that these sets will operate on the East Coast between end 2011 and March 2012

■ The additional vehicles under construction for 31 sets will be an additional TSO 653xx series and an MSO 689xx series. These will be inserted after the 696xx MFO vehicle.

■ Pendolino set No. 390033 *City of Glasgow*, which was involved in the Grayrigg derailment on 23 February 2007 was withdrawn from service. After spending a period stored at Long Marston, some of the vehicles have now seen further use.

Cars 69133 and 69833 have been rebuilt as static training vehicles for use at the Virgin Trains training school in Crewe.

69933 and 69733 are in use at the fire training school in Morton-in-Marsh, while Nos. 69533, 68833 and 69433 remain in store at Long Marston owned by Virgin Group. Vehicle No. 69233 has been broken up.

Above: *The 52 Virgin Pendolino sets allocated to Manchester depot are the backbone of Virgin services on all electrified routes. Sets usually operate with their first class accommodation at the London end. All sets are owned by Angel Trains. Set No. 390025 Virgin Stagecoach passes South Kenton in May 2010 with a London Euston bound express.* **CJM**

Mk3 Hauled Stock

Vehicle Length: 75ft 0in (22.86m)   Width: 8ft 11in (2.71m)
Height: 12ft 9in (3.88m)   Bogie Type: BT10

AJ1G - RFB *Seating 18F*

Number	Depot	Livery	Owner
10212	WB	VWC	PTR
10217	WB	VWC	PTE

AD1G - FO *Seating 48F*

Number	Depot	Livery	Owner
11007	WB	VWC	PTR
11018	WB	VWC	PTR

11048	WB	VWC	PTR

AC2G - TS0 (*TSOD) *Seating 76/70*S*

Number	Depot	Livery	Owner
12011	WB	VWC	PTR
12078	WB	VWC	PTR
12122*	WB	VWC	PTR
12133	WB	VWC	PTR
12138	WB	VWC	PTR

NL - DVT

Number	Depot	Livery	Owner
82101	WB	VWC	PTR§
82126	WB	VWC	PTR

§ Spare vehicle

■ The Virgin West Coast loco-hauled set is operated on an 'as required' basis to cover for a shortfall in Pendolino stock. Motive power is provided by DBS in the form of a Class 90/0 or a VWC Class 57/3.

Above Right: *Rebuilt from Virgin West Coast stock at Wabtec of Doncaster, the Virgin loco-hauled set is maintained at Wembley. The set is painted in full Virgin West Coast silver and red livery, offset by black and white striped passenger doors. The interior has been refurbished as far as possible in keeping with the Pendolino fleet. In the upper view the entire train, led by Mk3 DVT No. 82126 is seen powering the 13.30 Birmingham New Street to London Euston at Carpenders Park on 30 January 2010.* **Brian Morrison**

Middle Right : *Virgin West Coast Mk3 RFB No. 10212 seen from the first class seating end.* **Nathan Williamson**

Below Right: *Virgin West Coast Mk3 FO No. 11018.* **Nathan Williamson**

The following vehicles are assigned as spare and could be used to form a second West Coast loco hauled train if required in the future:
DB Regio owned TSOs 12017/054/059/ 094/124. Cargo-D owned FOs 11064/084/086, Porterbrook-owned DVT 82101.

Passenger Train Operating Companies - Wrexham & Shropshire Railway

Wrexham & Shropshire Railway

Address: ✉ The Pump House, Cotton Hill, Shrewsbury, SY1 2DP
🖰 info@wrexhamandshropshire.co.uk
📞 0845 260 5233
ⓘ www.wrexhamandshropshire.co.uk

Managing Director: Andy Hamilton
Franchise Dates: Open access operator
Principal Routes: London Marylebone to Wrexham
Parent Company: Wrexham, Shropshire & Marylebone Railway Co - originally a joint venture between Renaissance Trains, Laing Rail and DB Regio.
From January 2010 the Renaissance Trains and Laing Rail share was transferred to DB Regio and the WSR business was operated by Chiltern Railways.

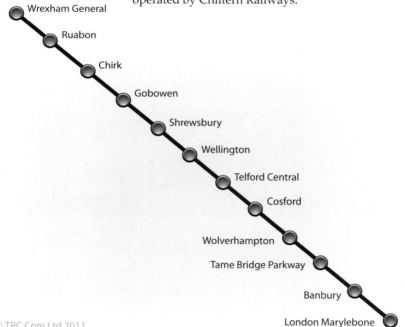

Wrexham General
Ruabon
Chirk
Gobowen
Shrewsbury
Wellington
Telford Central
Cosford
Wolverhampton
Tame Bridge Parkway
Banbury
London Marylebone

© TRC.Com Ltd 2011

Class 67

Vehicle Length: 64ft 7in (19.68m)	Engine: EMD 12N-710G3B-EC
Height: 12ft 9in (3.88m)	Horsepower: 2,980hp (2,223kW)
Width: 8ft 9in (2.66m)	Electrical Equipment: EMD

Number	Depot	Pool	Livery	Owner	Operator	Name
67010	TO	WAWN	WSR	ANG	DBS/WSR	
67012	TO	WAWN	WSR	ANG	DBS/WSR	*A Shropshire Lad*
67013	TO	WAWN	WSR	ANG	DBS/WSR	*Dyfrbont Pontcysyllte*
67014	TO	WAWN	WSR	ANG	DBS/WSR	*Thomas Telford*
67015	TO	WAWN	WSR	ANG	DBS/WSR	*David J. Lloyd*

Right: *DB Schenker are the providers of motive power for the Wrexham & Shropshire Railway services, with a batch of five Class 67s allocated to the service. These are operated as a separate pool from the core locos and painted in Wrexham & Shropshire two-tone grey livery. The locos remain based at Toton and frequently return to the Nottinghamshire depot for maintenance. No. 67014* Thomas Telford *is illustrated.* **Chris Perkins**

Mk3 Hauled Stock (Passenger)

Vehicle Length: 75ft 0in (22.86m)
Height: 12ft 9in (3.88m)   Width: 8ft 11in (2.71m)
Bogie Type: BT10

AJ1G - RFM *Seating 30F*

Number	Depot	Livery	Owner
10208 (40517)	AL	WSR	DBR
10230 (10021)	AL	WSR	DBR
10236 (10018)	AL	WSR	DBR
10255 (10010)	AL	WSR	DBR

AC2G - TSO *Seating 72S*

Number	Depot	Livery	Owner
12048	AL	WSR	DBR

12059	AL	WSR	DBR
12069	AL	WSR	DBR
12072	AL	WSR	DBR
12117	AL	WSR	DBR
12127	AL	WSR	DBR
12131	AL	WSR	DBR
12145	AL	WSR	DBR
12169	AL	WSR	DBR
12173¤	AL	WSR	DBR
12174¤	AL	WSR	DBR

12175¤	AL	WSR	DBR

¤ 12173-75 renumbered from 11042/50/52

Stored vehicles
12054, 12094, 12124 at WN/AL

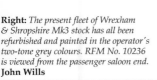

Right: *The present fleet of Wrexham & Shropshire Mk3 stock has all been refurbished and painted in the operator's two-tone grey colours. RFM No. 10236 is viewed from the passenger saloon end.* **John Wills**

Mk3 Hauled Stock (NPCCS)

Vehicle Length: 75ft 0in (22.86m)
Height: 12ft 9in (3.88m)
Width: 8ft 11in (2.71m)
Bogie Type: BT7

NZAG - DVT

Number	Depot	Livery	Owner
82301 (82117)	CE	WSR	DBR
82302 (82151)	CE	CRW	DBR

82303 (82135)	CE	WSR	DBR
82304 (82130)	CE	WSR	DBR
82305 (82134)	CE	WSR	DBR

Right: *Five Mk3 DVTs are available for Wrexham & Shropshire use, allocated to Crewe depot for maintenance. All are painted in WSR two-tone grey livery with the exception of No. 82302 which is outshopped in blue and white Chiltern colours.* **Brian Morrison**

Colas Rail

Address:	✉ Dacre House, 19 Dacre Street, London, SW1H 0DJ
	✎ enquiries@colasrail.co.uk
	✆ 0207 593 5353
	ⓘ www.colasrail.co.uk
Chairman:	Charles-Albert Giral
Depots:	Washwood Heath (AW), Rugby (RU), Eastleigh Works (ZG)

Class 47/7

Vehicle Length: 63ft 6in (19.35m)	Engine: Sulzer 12LDA28C
Height: 12ft 10⅜in (3.91m)	Horsepower: 2,580hp (1,922kW)
Width: 9ft 2in (2.79m)	Electrical Equipment: Brush
Electric Train Heat fitted	

Number	Depot	Pool	Livery	Owner	Operator	Name
47727 (47569)	AW	COLO	COL	COL	COL	*Rebecca*
47739 (47594)	AW	COLO	COL	COL	COL	*Robin of Templecombe*
47749 (47625)	AW	COLO	COL	COL	COL	*Demelza*

Left: *Colas operate a fleet of three Class 47s for general freight and spot hire use. After a period of allocation at Tavistock Junction, Plymouth, the three are now maintained at Washwood Heath, Birmingham. All are painted in the green and orange Colas house colours. No. 47739* Robin of Templecombe *is viewed at Carlisle.* **Bill Wilson**

Below: *Colas Nos. 47727 and 47749 pass through Oxford with a freight on 25 June 2009. These locos retain their green spot multiple control equipment allowing one driver to operate both locos.* **Nathan Williamson**

Class 66/8

Vehicle Length: 70ft 0½in (21.34m)			Engine: EMD 12N-710G3B-EC		
Height: 12ft 10in (3.91m)			Horsepower: 3,300hp (2,462kW)		
Width: 8ft 8¼in (2.65m)			Electrical Equipment: EMD		

Number		Depot	Pool	Livery	Owner	Operator
66841	(66406)	RU	COLO	COL	PTR	COL
66842	(66407)	RU	COLO	COL	PTR	COL
66843	(66408)	RU	COLO	COL	PTR	COL
66844	(66409)	RU	COLO	COL	PTR	COL
66845	(66410)	RU	COLO	COL	PTR	COL

Above: *After working for DRS and a short time with Advenza Freight, Class 66/8s Nos. 66841-845 are now leased to Colas from owner Porterbrook. The locos power general Colas rail freight flows. The batch are officially allocated to Rugby but often receive maintenance by DRS. No. 66843 is viewed at Carlisle while powering a Chirk bound log train. It has been suggested that further Class 66s might transfer to Colas in the future.* **Stacey Thew**

Class 960

Length: 64ft 6in (19.66m)			Engine: 2 x Leyland 150hp	
Height: 12ft 8½in (3.87m)			Horsepower: 300hp (224kW)	
Width: 9ft 3in (2.81m)				

Number	Depot	Livery	Owner	Operator	Note
977968(S)	RU	YEL	COL	COL	Ex Class 121 55029, Route Training Unit

Right: *Former Class 121 'Bubble' car No. 55029 is in service with Colas. Based at Rugby, the vehicle is often used as a route training vehicle. The double-cabbed saloon is seen passing along the Dawlish Sea Wall bound for Paignton.* **CJM**

Freight Operating Companies

DB Schenker - EWS

Address (UK): ✉ Lakeside Business Park, Caroline Way, Doncaster, DN4 5PN

✆ info@rail.dbschenker.co.uk

☎ 0870 140 5000

ⓘ www.rail.dbschenker.co.uk

Chief Executive: Alain Thauvette

Class 08

Vehicle Length: 29ft 3in (8.91m)			Engine: English Electric 6K		
Height: 12ft 8⅝in (3.87m)			Horsepower: 400hp (298kW)		
Width: 8ft 6in (2.59m)			Electrical Equipment: English Electric		

Number	Depot	Pool	Livery	Owner	Operator
08389	TO	WNTS	EWS	DBS	DBS
08393(S)	BS	WNTS	EWS	DBS	-
08405¤	TO	WSSI	EWS	DBS	DBS
08428	TO	WSSK	EWS	DBS	DBS
08442(S)	WQ	WSXX	BRT	DBS	-
08480*	TO	WSSK	EWS	DBS	DBS
08495¤	TO	WSSK	EWS	DBS	DBS
08499(S)	WQ	WSXX	BLU	DBS	PUL
08500(S)	WQ	WNTS	EWS	DBS	-
08514(S)	WQ	WNTS	EWS	DBS	-
08516(S)	WQ	WSXX	EWS	DBS	-
08567	TO	WNYX	EWS	DBS	DBS
08578	TO	WSSI	EWS	DBS	DBS
08580(S)	WQ	WNXX	EWS	DBS	-
08593(S)	WQ	WNTS	EWS	DBS	-
08605(S)¤	TO	WSSK	EWS	DBS	-
08623	TO	WSSK	EWS	DBS	DBS
08630(S)	WQ	WNTS	EWS	DBS	-
08632(S)	TO	WNYX	EWS	DBS	-
08633(S)	WA	WSSK	EWS	DBS	-
08646(S)	MG	WNTS	BRT	DBS	-
08653	BS	WNTR	EWS	DBS	-
08662(S)	WQ	WNTS	EWS	DBS	-
08664(S)	DR	WNTS	EWS	DBS	-
08676	TO	WSSK	EWS	DBS	DBS
08685	TO	WSSI	EWS	DBS	DBS
08701¤	TO	WNTS	PCL	DBS	-
08703	TO	WNYX	EWS	DBS	-
08706¤	TO	WSSI	EWS	DBS	DBS
08709	WQ	WNTS	EWS	DBS	-
08711	DR	WSSK	PCL	DBS	DBS
08714	TO	WSSA	EWS	DBS	DBS
08735¤	EH	WSSK	EWS	DBS	DBS
08737(S)	TO	WNYX	EWS	DBS	-
08742¤(S)	TO	WNYX	PCL	DBS	-
08752(S)	TO	WNYX	EWS	DBS	-
08757¤	TO	WSSK	RES	DBS	DBS
08782	MG	WSSK	BLK	DBS	-
08783(S)	WQ	WNTS	EWS	DBS	-
08784¤	TO	WSSK	EWS	DBS	-
08798	TO	WNTS	EWS	DBS	DBS
08799	TO	WNTX	EWS	DBS	DBS
08802	TO	WSSK	EWS	DBS	DBS
08804¤	TO	WSSI	EWS	DBS	-
08824(S)	WQ	WSXX	BLK	DBS	-
08842(S)	WQ	WNTS	EWS	DBS	-
08844	BS	WNTS	EWS	DBS	DBS
08854(S)	WQ	WNTS	EWS	DBS	-
08865	TO	WSSK	EWS	DBS	DBS
08866(S)	WQ	WNTS	EWS	DBS	-
08877(S)	WQ	WSXX	BRD	DBS	-
08879¤	TO	WSSK	EWS	DBS	DBS
08886(S)	BS	WSSK	EWS	DBS	-
08888¤	TO	WNYX	EWS	DBS	-
08904(S)	TO	WNYX	EWS	DBS	-
08905	WQ	WNTS	EWS	DBS	-
08907	TO	WSSK	EWS	DBS	DBS
08909	TO	WSSK	EWS	DBS	DBS
08918(S)	TO	WNTS	BRD	DBS	-
08921(S)	TO	WSSI	EWS	DBS	-
08922(S)	CE	WNTR	BRD	DBS	-
08951(S)	TO	WNTS	EWS	DBS	-
08993+	TO	WSSK	EWS	DBS	DBS
08994+	DR	WSSK	EWS	DBS	DBS
08995+(S)	TO	WNYX	EWS	DBS	-

+ Numbered - Toton No. 1, 08993 was previously No. 08592, 08994 was previously No. 08562, 08995 was previously No. 08687.
¤ Remote Control fitted.

Names applied

08442	*Richard J Wenham Eastleigh Depot December 1989 - July 1999*
08495	*Noel Kirton OBE*
08630	*Bob Brown*
08701	*Type 100*
08799	*Andy Bower*
08844	*Chris Wren 1955-2002*
08905	*Danny Daniels*
08951	*Fred*

Left: *DB Schenker (EWS) have vastly reduced the number of Class 08s in operation, preferring to use train locos to perform shunting. Carrying former Res red livery No. 08757 is shown at Westbury. This loco is one of the remote control batch, identified by extra lights on the cab end.*
Tony Christie

Class 09/0

Vehicle Length: 29ft 3in (8.91m)			Engine: English Electric 6K		
Height: 12ft 8⅝in (3.87m)			Horsepower: 400hp (298kW)		
Width: 8ft 6in (2.59m)			Electrical Equipment: English Electric		

Number	Depot	Pool	Livery	Owner	Operator
09006(S)	WQ	WNTS	EWS	DBS	-
09011(S)	WQ	WNTS	BRD	DBS	-
09017(S)+	TO	WNTR	EWS	DBS	-
09020(S)	TO	WNYX	EWS	DBS	-

Number	Depot	Pool	Livery	Owner	Operator
09022	TO	WSSI	EWS	DBS	DBS
09023	IM	WNTR	EWS	DBS	DBS
09024(S)	WQ	WNTS	MLF	DBS	-

+ 09017 previously numbered 97806

Right: *Originally the Class 09 fleet were the higher speed version of the Class 08 and used on the Southern Region. Many were fitted with waist height air connections for coupling to EMU stock. Today the remaining members of the fleet are operated in the general freight pool. No. 09017 is shown passing Newport powering a main line freight train. The loco carries EWS maroon and gold livery.*
Brian Garrett

Class 09/1

Vehicle Length: 29ft 3in (8.91m)			Engine: English Electric 6K		
Height: 12ft 8⅝in (3.87m)			Horsepower: 400hp (298kW)		
Width: 8ft 6in (2.59m)			Electrical Equipment: English Electric		

Number		Depot	Pool	Livery	Owner	Operator
09106	(08759)	TO	WSSI	BRD	DBS	DBS
09107(S)	(08845)	TO	WNTR	EWS	DBS	-

Class 09/2

Vehicle Length: 29ft 3in (8.91m)			Engine: English Electric 6K		
Height: 12ft 8⅝in (3.87m)			Horsepower: 400hp (298kW)		
Width: 8ft 6in (2.59m)			Electrical Equipment: English Electric		

Number		Depot	Pool	Livery	Owner	Operator
09201(S)	(08421)	WQ	WNYX	BRD	DBS	-
09203(S)	(08781)	WQ	WNXX	BRD	DBS	-
09204(S)	(08717)	WQ	WNXX	BRD	DBS	-
09205(S)	(08620)	WQ	WNTS	BRD	DBS	-

Below: *Two small batches of standard Class 08s were modified as Class 09s in the 1980s. No. 09101 (now withdrawn) is illustrated painted in general freight grey.* **Tony Christie**

DB Schenker

Freight Operating Companies - DB Schenker

Class 37/4

Vehicle Length: 61ft 6in (18.74m)
Height: 13ft 0¼in (3.96m)
Width: 8ft 11⅝in (2.73m)
Electric Train Heat fitted

Engine: English Electric 12CSVT
Horsepower: 1,750hp (1,304kW)
Electrical Equipment: English Electric

Number		Depot	Pool	Livery	Owner	Operator	Name
37401(S)	(37268)	CE	WNXX	EWS	DBS	-	
37402(S)	(37274)	TO	WNXX	TLF	DBS	-	Bont-Y-Bermo
37405(S)	(37282)	TO	WNXX	EWS	DBS	-	Strathclyde Region
37406(S)	(37295)	CD	WNXX	EWS	DBS	-	The Saltire Society
37410(S)	(37273)	ZW	WNXX	EWS	DBS	-	
37411(S)	(37290)*	EH	WNXX	GRN	DBS	-	Caerphilly Castle/Castell Caerffili
37416(S)	(37302)	EH	WNXX	GSW	DBS	-	
37417(S)	(37269)	EH	WNXX	EWS	DBS	-	
37419(S)	(37291)	TO	WNXX	DBS	DBS	-	
37422(S)	(37266)	TO	WNXX	EWS	DBS	-	Cardiff Canton
37425(S)	(37292)	TO	WNXX	BLL	DBS	-	Pride of the Valleys/Balchder y Cymoedd
37427(S)	(37288)	TY	WNXX	EWS	DBS	-	

■ All DBS Class 37/4s were offered for sale by tender in December 2010.

Left: *At the end of 2010, DB Schenker still held on to a batch of Class 37/4 locos - but none were in traffic; all were stored and the long term future for the fleet does not look good. The 12 locos still on the books are stored at various sites in the UK and sport a varied collection of liveries, including BR blue, EWS red, Trainload Freight, Green, Blue Large Logo and DB Schenker red. One of the most popular locos of the fleet No. 37425* Pride of the Valleys/Balchder y Cymoedd *is illustrated.* **Tony Christie**

Class 37/7

Vehicle Length: 61ft 6in (18.74m)
Height: 13ft 0¼in (3.96m)
Width: 8ft 11⅝in (2.73m)

Engine: English Electric 12CSVT
Horsepower: 1,750hp (1,304kW)
Electrical Equipment: English Electric

Number		Hire No.	Depot	Pool	Livery	Owner	Operator
37703	(37067)	L25	CON/SS	WZKS	CON	DBS	CON
37714	(37024)	L26	CON/SS	WZKS	CON	DBS	CON
37716	(37094)	L23	CON/SS	WZKS	CON	DBS	CON
37718	(37084)	L22	CON/SS	WZKS	CON	DBS	CON
37800	(37143)	L33	CON/SS	WZKS	CON	DBS	CON
37884	(37183)	L34	CON/SS	WZKS	CON	DBS	CON

Left: *Several years ago a batch of Class 37s were upgraded by EWS at Toton and exported to Spain to take part in high speed line construction, powering engineering works trains on the new standard gauge system. Several locos have been disposed of but six still remain on the roster, but it is understood none were in active service in late 2010. Now withdrawn No. L28 (37883) is illustrated at Vilafranca del Penedes on 3 July 2006.* **Gavin Lake**

Class 47/4

	Vehicle Length: 63ft 6in (19.35m)	Engine: Sulzer 12LDA28C
	Height: 12ft 10⅜in (3.91m)	Horsepower: 2,580hp (1,922kW)
	Width: 9ft 2in (2.79m)	Electrical Equipment: Brush
	Electric Train Heat fitted	

Number	Depot	Pool	Livery	Owner	Operator	
47799 (47835)	EH	WNXX	ROY	DBS	DBS	Used for coach pre-heating at Eastleigh

Class 58

	Vehicle Length: 62ft 9½in (19.13m)	Engine: Ruston Paxman 12RK3ACT
	Height: 12ft 10in (3.91m)	Horsepower: 3,300hp (2,460kW)
	Width: 9ft 1in (2.72m)	Electrical Equipment: Brush

Right: *Through their Axiom Rail arm, DB Schenker have successfully operated a large number of Class 58s in mainland Europe, with contracts in Holland, Spain and France. Currently only Spain has an operational fleet, working on infrastructure projects for Continental Rail. No. 58047 is seen at one of the high speed line construction bases at Requena, near Valencia.*
Enrique Dopico

Number	Hire No.	Depot	Pool	Livery	Owner	Location	Operator	Name
58001	-		WZFF	ETF	DBS	France	ETF	
58004§	-		WZFF	TSO	DBS	France	TSO	
58005	-		WZFF	ETF	DBS	France	ETF	
58006§	-		WZFF	ETF	DBS	France	ETF	
58007	-		WZFF	TSO	DBS	France	TSO	
58008(S)	EH		WNXX	MLF	DBS	UK	-	
58009	-		WZFF	TSO	DBS	France	TSO	
58010	-		WZFF	FER	DBS	France	TSO	
58011§	-		WZFF	TSO	DBS	France	TSO	
58012(S)	TO		WNXX	MLG	DBS	UK	-	
58013	-		WZFF	ETF	DBS	France	ETF	
58015	L54	CON/SS	WZFS	CON	DBS	Spain	CON	
58017(S)	EH		WZTS	MLG	DBS	UK	-	
58018	EH		WZFF	TSO	DBS	France	TSO	
58020	L43	CON/SS	WZFS	CON	DBS	Spain	CON	
58021	-		WZFF	TSO	DBS	France	TSO	
58022(S)	CD		WNXX	MLG	DBS	UK	-	
58023(S)	TO		WNXX	MLF	DBS	UK	-	
58024	L42	CON/SS	WZFS	CON	DBS	Spain	CON	
58025	L41	CON/SS	WZFS	CON	DBS	Spain	CON	
58026§	-		WZTS	TSO	DBS	France	TSO	
58027	L52	CON/SS	WZFS	CON	DBS	Spain	CON	
58029	L44	CON/SS	WZFS	CON	DBS	Spain	CON	
58030	L46	CON/SS	WZFS	CON	DBS	Spain	CON	
58031	L45	CON/SS	WZFS	CON	DBS	Spain	CON	
58032	-		WZFF	ETF	DBS	France	ETF	Cabellero Ferroviaro
58033	-		WZFF	TSO	DBS	France	TSO	
58034	-		WZFF	TSO	DBS	France	TSO	
58035	-		WZFF	TSO	DBS	France	TSO	
58036	-		WZFF	ETF	DBS	France	ETF	
58037(S)	EH		WNXX	EWS	DBS	UK	-	
58038	58-038	-	WZFF	ETF	DBS	France	ETF	
58039	58-039	-	WZFF	ETF	DBS	France	ETF	
58040§	-		WZFF	TSO	DBS	France	TSO	
58041	L36	CON/SS	WZFS	CON	DBS	Spain	CON	
58042	-		WZFF	TSO	DBS	France	TSO	

DB Schenker

58043	L37	CON/SS	WZFS	CON	DBS	Spain	CON
58044	58-044	-	WZFF	ETF	DBS	France	ETF
58046		-	WZFF	TSO	DBS	France	TSO
58047	L51	CON/SS	WZFS	CON	DBS	Spain	CON
58048(S)		CE	WNXX	EWS	DBS	UK	-
58049§		-	WZFF	TSO	DBS	France	ETF
58050	L53	CON/SS	WZFS	CON	DBS	Spain	CON

§ Stored at Alizay (Rouen)

Class 59/2

Vehicle Length: 70ft 0½in (21.34m)
Height: 12ft 10in (3.91m)
Width: 8ft 8¼in (2.65m)

Engine: EMD 16-645 E3C
Horsepower: 3,000hp (2,462kW)
Electrical Equipment: EMD

Number	Depot	Pool	Livery	Owner	Operator	Name
59201	TO	WDAM	EWS	DBS	DBS	*Vale of York*
59202	TO	WDAM	EWS	DBS	DBS	*Vale of White Horse*
59203(S)	CE	WFMS	EWS	DBS	-	*Vale of Pickering*
59204	TO	WDAK	EWS	DBS	DBS	*Vale of Glamorgan*
59205	TO	WDAM	EWS	DBS	DBS	*L Keith McNair*
59206	TO	WDAI	DBS	DBS	DBS	*John F. Yeoman Rail Pioneer*

Above: *Six Class 59/2s originally built for National Power are now operated by DB Schenker and officially allocated to Toton depot, but receive most maintenance at Merehead. One loco, No. 59206, is painted in the latest DB Schenker red livery.* **Brian Morrison**

Class 60

■ Some Class 60s are scheduled to receive a Genrral overhaul in 2011, loco identified are 60007/054/091.

Vehicle Length: 70ft 0½in (21.34m)
Height: 12ft 10⅝in (3.92m)
Width: 8ft 8in (2.64m)

Engine: Mirrlees MB275T
Horsepower: 3,100hp (2,240kW)
Electrical Equipment: Brush

Number	Depot	Pool	Livery	Owner	Operator	Name
60002(S)	TO	WNTS	EWS	DBS	-	*High Peak*
60003(S)	TO	WNTR	EWS	DBS	-	*Freight Transport Association*
60004(S)	TO	WNTS	EWS	DBS	-	
60005(S)	TO	WNTS	EWS	DBS	-	
60007(S)	TO	WNTS	LHL	DBS	-	
60009(S)	TO	WNTS	EWS	DBS	-	
60010	TO	WCBI	EWS	DBS	DBS	
60011(S)	TO	WCAI	DBS	DBS	-	
60012(S)	TO	WNTS	EWS	DBS	-	
60013(S)	TO	WNTR	RFE	DBS	-	*Robert Boyle*
60015	TO	WCBK	RFE	DBS	DBS	*Bow Fell*
60017(S)	TO	WNTS	EWS	DBS	-	*Shotton Works Centenary Year 1996*
60018(S)	TO	WNTS	EWS	DBS	-	
60019(S)	TO	WNTR	EWS	DBS	-	*Pathfinder Tours 30 Years of Railtouring 1973-2003*
60020(S)	TO	WNTS	EWS	DBS	-	
60021(S)	TO	WNTS	EWS	DBS	-	
60022(S)	TO	WNTR	EWS	DBS	-	

60024(S)	TO	WNTR	EWS	DBS	-	
60025(S)	TO	WNTS	EWS	DBS	-	
60026(S)	TO	WNTR	EWS	DBS	-	
60027(S)	TO	WNTR	EWS	DBS	-	
60028(S)	TO	WNTR	RFE	DBS	-	John Flamsteed
60029(S)	TO	WNTS	EWS	DBS	-	Clitheroe Castle
60030(S)	TO	WNTS	EWS	DBS	-	
60032(S)	TO	WNTS	EWS	DBS	-	
60033(S)	TO	WNTS	COR	DBS	-	Tees Steel Express
60034(S)	TO	WNTS	RFE	DBS	-	Carnedd Llewelyn
60035(S)	TO	WNTR	EWS	DBS	-	
60036(S)	TO	WNTS	EWS	DBS	-	GEFCO
60037(S)	TO	WNTS	EWS	DBS	-	
60039	TO	WCAK	EWS	DBS	DBS	
60040(S)	TO	WNTR	DBM	DBS	-	The Territorial Army Centenary
60041(S)	TO	WNTR	EWS	DBS	-	
60043(S)	TO	WNTR	EWS	DBS	-	
60044(S)	TO	WNTS	MLF	DBS	-	
60045	TO	WCAI	EWS	DBS	DBS	The Permanent Way Institution
60046(S)	TO	WNTR	RFE	DBS	-	William Wilberforce
60047(S)	TO	WNTR	EWS	DBS	-	
60048(S)	TO	WNTR	EWS	DBS	-	
60049(S)	TO	WNTR	EWS	DBS	-	
60051(S)	TO	WNTS	EWS	DBS	-	
60052(S)	TO	WNTS	EWS	DBS	-	Glofa Twr - The last deep mine in Wales - Tower Colliery
60053(S)	TO	WNTS	EWS	DBS	-	
60054(S)	TO	WNTR	RFP	DBS	-	Charles Babbage
60056(S)	TO	WNTR	RFE	DBS	-	William Beveridge
60057(S)	TO	WNTS	RFE	DBS	-	Adam Smith
60059(S)	TO	WNTS	LHL	DBS	-	Swinden Dalesman
60060(S)	TO	WNTS	RFE	DBS	-	
60061(S)	TO	WNTS	RFE	DBS	-	
60062(S)	TO	WNTS	EWS	DBS	-	
60063(S)	TO	WNTR	RFE	DBS	-	James Murray
60064(S)	TO	WNTS	RFE	DBS	-	Back Tor
60065(S)	TO	WNTS	EWS	DBS	-	Spirit of Jaguar
60066(S)	TO	WNTS	RFE	DBS	-	John Logie Baird
60067(S)	TO	WNTS	RFE	DBS	-	
60069(S)	TO	WNTS	EWS	DBS	-	Slioch
60071	TO	WCAI	EWS	DBS	DBS	Ribblehead Viaduct
60072(S)	TO	WNTS	RFE	DBS	-	Cairn Toul
60073(S)	TO	WNTR	RFE	DBS	-	Cairn Gorm
60074	TO	WCAI	DBB	DBS	DBS	Teenage Spirit
60076(S)	TO	WNTR	RFE	DBS	-	
60077(S)	TO	WNTR	RFE	DBS	-	
60079(S)	TO	WNTS	RFE	DBS	-	Foinaven
60083(S)	TO	WNTS	EWS	DBS	-	
60084(S)	TO	WNTR	RFE	DBS	-	Cross Fell
60085(S)	TO	WNTR	EWS	DBS	-	Mini - Pride of Oxford
60086(S)	TO	WNTS	RFE	DBS	-	
60087(S)	TO	WNTS	EWS	DBS	-	
60088(S)	TO	WNTS	MLG	DBS	-	
60090(S)	TO	WNTS	RFE	DBS	-	Quinag
60091(S)	TO	WNTR	RFE	DBS	-	An Teallach
60092(S)	CD	WNTR	RFE	DBS	-	Reginald Munns
60093(S)	TO	WNTS	EWS	DBS	-	
60094(S)	CD	WNTR	EWS	DBS	-	Rugby Flyer
60095(S)	TO	WNTR	RFE	DBS	-	
60096(S)	TO	WNTS	EWS	DBS	-	
60097(S)	TO	WNTS	EWS	DBS	-	
60099(S)	TO	WNTR	TAT	DBS	-	
60100(S)	TO	WNTS	EWS	DBS	-	
60500(S)*	TO	WNTS	EWS	DBS	-	

* Previously numbered 60016

Freight Operating Companies - DB Schenker

DB Schenker

Above: *Only a handful of Class 60s still remain operational and in autumn 2010 a number of withdrawn members were offered for sale to scrap dealers, ending speculation of a rebuild programme. Painted in light blue Teenage Cancer Trust livery, No. 60074 Teenage Spirit passes Newport with an oil train bound for Westerleigh.* **CJM**

Class 66

Vehicle Length: 70ft 0½in (21.34m)	Engine: EMD 12N-710G3B-EC	
Height: 12ft 10in (3.91m)	Horsepower: 3,300hp (2,462kW)	
Width: 8ft 8¼in (2.65m)	Electrical Equipment: EMD	

Number	Depot	Pool	Livery	Owner	Operator
66001	TO	WBAK	EWS	ANG	DBS
66002	TO	WBAN	EWS	ANG	DBS
66003	TO	WBAN	EWS	ANG	DBS
66004	TO	WBAK	EWS	ANG	DBS
66005	TO	WBAN	EWS	ANG	DBS
66006	TO	WBAK	EWS	ANG	DBS
66007	TO	WBAI	EWS	ANG	DBS
66008	TO	WBSN	EWS	ANG	DBS
66009	TO	WBAM	EWS	ANG	DBS
66010 E	TO	WBEN	EWS	ANG	DBS
66011	TO	WBAM	EWS	ANG	DBS
66012	TO	WFMU	EWS	ANG	DBS
66013	TO	WBSN	EWS	ANG	DBS
66014	TO	WBAM	EWS	ANG	DBS
66015	TO	WBAN	EWS	ANG	DBS
66016	TO	WBAM	EWS	ANG	DBS
66017	TO	WBAK	EWS	ANG	DBS
66018	TO	WFMU	EWS	ANG	DBS
66019	TO	WBAK	EWS	ANG	DBS
66020	TO	WBAI	EWS	ANG	DBS
66021	TO	WBAN	EWS	ANG	DBS
66022 E	TO	WBEN	EWS	ANG	DBS
66023	TO	WBAI	EWS	ANG	DBS
66024	TO	WBAN	EWS	ANG	DBS
66025	TO	WBAN	EWS	ANG	DBS
66026 E	TO	WBEN	EWS	ANG	DBS
66027	TO	WFMU	EWS	ANG	DBS
66028 E	TO	WBEN	EWS	ANG	DBS
66029 E	TO	WBEN	EWS	ANG	DBS
66030	TO	WBAI	EWS	ANG	DBS
66031 E	TO	WFMU	EWS	ANG	DBS
66032 E	TO	WBEN	EWS	ANG	DBS
66033 E	TO	WBEN	EWS	ANG	DBS
66034	TO	WBAN	EWS	ANG	DBS
66035	TO	WBAN	EWS	ANG	DBS
66036 E	TO	WBEN	EWS	ANG	DBS
66037	TO	WBAK	EWS	ANG	DBS
66038 E	TO	WBEN	EWS	ANG	DBS
66039	TO	WBAK	EWS	ANG	DBS
66040	TO	WBAI	EWS	ANG	DBS
66041	TO	WBAI	EWS	ANG	DBS
66042 E	TO	WBEN	EWS	ANG	DBS
66043	TO	WBAN	EWS	ANG	DBS
66044	TO	WBAK	EWS	ANG	DBS
66045 E	TO	WBEN	EWS	ANG	DBS
66046	TO	WBAM	EWS	ANG	DBS
66047	TO	WBAN	EWS	ANG	DBS
66048(S)	TO	WFMU	STO	ANG	-
66049 E	TO	WBEN	EWS	ANG	DBS
66050	TO	WBAI	EWS	ANG	DBS
66051	TO	WBAN	EWS	ANG	DBS
66052 E	TO	WBEN	EWS	ANG	DBS
66053	TO	WBAI	EWS	ANG	DBS
66054	TO	WBAI	EWS	ANG	DBS
66055	TO	WBAN	EWS	ANG	DBS
66056	TO	WFMU	EWS	ANG	DBS
66057	TO	WBLI	EWS	ANG	DBS
66058	TO	WBAM	EWS	ANG	DBS
66059	TO	WBAK	EWS	ANG	DBS
66060	TO	WBAN	EWS	ANG	DBS
66061	TO	WBAN	EWS	ANG	DBS
66062 E	TO	WBEN	EWS	ANG	DBS
66063	TO	WFMU	EWS	ANG	DBS
66064 E	TO	WBEN	EWS	ANG	DBS
66065	TO	WBAK	EWS	ANG	DBS
66066	TO	WBAM	EWS	ANG	DBS
66067	TO	WBAN	EWS	ANG	DBS
66068	TO	WFMU	EWS	ANG	DBS
66069	TO	WBAN	EWS	ANG	DBS
66070	TO	WBAN	EWS	ANG	DBS
66071 E	TO	WBEN	EWS	ANG	DBS
66072 E	TO	WBEN	EWS	ANG	DBS
66073 E	TO	WBEN	EWS	ANG	DBS

DB Schenker

66074	TO	WBAK	EWS	ANG	DBS	66138	TO	WBAN	EWS	ANG	DBS
66075	TO	WBAM	EWS	ANG	DBS	66139	TO	WBAN	EWS	ANG	DBS
66076	TO	WBAM	EWS	ANG	DBS	66140	TO	WBAK	EWS	ANG	DBS
66077	TO	WFMU	EWS	ANG	DBS	66141	TO	WBAN	EWS	ANG	DBS
66078	TO	WBAM	EWS	ANG	DBS	66142	TO	WBAI	EWS	ANG	DBS
66079	TO	WBAI	EWS	ANG	DBS	66143	TO	WBAM	EWS	ANG	DBS
66080	TO	WBAM	EWS	ANG	DBS	66144	TO	WBAM	EWS	ANG	DBS
66081	TO	WBAM	EWS	ANG	DBS	66145	TO	WFMU	EWS	ANG	DBS
66082	TO	WBAM	EWS	ANG	DBS	66146	TO	WBAK	EWS	ANG	DBS
66083	TO	WBAN	EWS	ANG	DBS	66147	TO	WBAN	EWS	ANG	DBS
66084	TO	WBAN	EWS	ANG	DBS	66148	TO	WBAN	EWS	ANG	DBS
66085	TO	WBAN	EWS	ANG	DBS	66149	TO	WBAK	EWS	ANG	DBS
66086	TO	WBAN	EWS	ANG	DBS	66150	TO	WBAM	EWS	ANG	DBS
66087	TO	WBAM	EWS	ANG	DBS	66151	TO	WBAM	EWS	ANG	DBS
66088	TO	WBAM	EWS	ANG	DBS	66152	TO	WBAN	DBS	ANG	DBS
66089	TO	WBAI	EWS	ANG	DBS	66153	TO	WBAN	EWS	ANG	DBS
66090	TO	WBAN	EWS	ANG	DBS	66154	TO	WBAI	EWS	ANG	DBS
66091	TO	WBAI	EWS	ANG	DBS	66155	TO	WBAM	EWS	ANG	DBS
66092	TO	WBAN	EWS	ANG	DBS	66156	TO	WBAN	EWS	ANG	DBS
66093	TO	WBSN	EWS	ANG	DBS	66157	TO	WBAI	EWS	ANG	DBS
66094	TO	WBAK	EWS	ANG	DBS	66158	TO	WBAK	EWS	ANG	DBS
66095	TO	WFMU	EWS	ANG	DBS	66159	TO	WBAN	EWS	ANG	DBS
66096	TO	WBAN	EWS	ANG	DBS	66160	TO	WBAN	EWS	ANG	DBS
66097	TO	WBAI	EWS	ANG	DBS	66161	TO	WBAN	EWS	ANG	DBS
66098	TO	WBAM	EWS	ANG	DBS	66162	TO	WBAN	EWS	ANG	DBS
66099	TO	WBAN	EWS	ANG	DBS	66163 P	TO	WBAI	EWS	ANG	DBS
66100	TO	WBBN	EWS	ANG	DBS	66164	TO	WBAM	EWS	ANG	DBS
66101	TO	WBSN	EWS	ANG	DBS	66165	TO	WBAN	EWS	ANG	DBS
66102	TO	WBBN	EWS	ANG	DBS	66166	TO	WBAM	EWS	ANG	DBS
66103	TO	WBAM	EWS	ANG	DBS	66167	TO	WBAI	EWS	ANG	DBS
66104	TO	WBBN	EWS	ANG	DBS	66168	TO	WBAN	EWS	ANG	DBS
66105	TO	WBAM	EWS	ANG	DBS	66169	TO	WBAK	EWS	ANG	DBS
66106	TO	WBBI	EWS	ANG	DBS	66170	TO	WBAN	EWS	ANG	DBS
66107	TO	WBAN	EWS	ANG	DBS	66171	TO	WBAI	EWS	ANG	DBS
66108	TO	WFMU	EWS	ANG	DBS	66172	TO	WFMU	EWS	ANG	DBS
66109	TO	WBAI	EWS	ANG	DBS	66173	TO	WBAN	EWS	ANG	DBS
66110 E	TO	WBAI	EWS	ANG	DBS	66174	TO	WBAN	EWS	ANG	DBS
66111	TO	WBBK	EWS	ANG	DBS	66175	TO	WBAM	EWS	ANG	DBS
66112	TO	WBBN	EWS	ANG	DBS	66176	TO	WBAM	EWS	ANG	DBS
66113	TO	WFMU	EWS	ANG	DBS	66177	TO	WBAK	EWS	ANG	DBS
66114	TO	WBBN	EWS	ANG	DBS	66178	TO	WBAM	EWS	ANG	DBS
66115	TO	WBAN	EWS	ANG	DBS	66179 E	TO	WBEN	EWS	ANG	DBS
66116	TO	WBAN	EWS	ANG	DBS	66180	TO	WBAN	EWS	ANG	DBS
66117	TO	WFMU	EWS	ANG	DBS	66181	TO	WBAM	EWS	ANG	DBS
66118	TO	WBSN	EWS	ANG	DBS	66182	TO	WBAM	EWS	ANG	DBS
66119	TO	WBAK	EWS	ANG	DBS	66183	TO	WBAN	EWS	ANG	DBS
66120	TO	WBSN	EWS	ANG	DBS	66184	TO	WBAI	EWS	ANG	DBS
66121	TO	WBAN	EWS	ANG	DBS	66185	TO	WBAM	EWS	ANG	DBS
66122	TO	WBAN	EWS	ANG	DBS	66186	TO	WBAI	EWS	ANG	DBS
66123 E	TO	WBEN	EWS	ANG	DBS	66187	TO	WBAN	EWS	ANG	DBS
66124	TO	WBAM	EWS	ANG	DBS	66188	TO	WBAN	EWS	ANG	DBS
66125	TO	WBSN	EWS	ANG	DBS	66189	TO	WBAN	EWS	ANG	DBS
66126	TO	WBAN	EWS	ANG	DBS	66190 E	TO	WBEN	EWS	ANG	DBS
66127	TO	WBAN	EWS	ANG	DBS	66191 E	TO	WBEN	EWS	ANG	DBS
66128	TO	WBAK	EWS	ANG	DBS	66192	TO	WBAK	EWS	ANG	DBS
66129	TO	WBAM	EWS	ANG	DBS	66193	TO	WBAI	EWS	ANG	DBS
66130	TO	WBAM	EWS	ANG	DBS	66194	TO	WBAM	EWS	ANG	DBS
66131	TO	WBAN	EWS	ANG	DBS	66195 E	TO	WBEN	EWS	ANG	DBS
66132	TO	WBAM	EWS	ANG	DBS	66196	TO	WBAI	EWS	ANG	DBS
66133	TO	WBAI	EWS	ANG	DBS	66197	TO	WFMU	EWS	ANG	DBS
66134	TO	WBAM	EWS	ANG	DBS	66198	TO	WBAK	EWS	ANG	DBS
66135	TO	WBAI	EWS	ANG	DBS	66199	TO	WBAM	EWS	ANG	DBS
66136	TO	WBAN	EWS	ANG	DBS	66200	TO	WBAK	EWS	ANG	DBS
66137	TO	WBAI	EWS	ANG	DBS	66201	TO	WBAN	EWS	ANG	DBS

Freight Operating Companies - DB Schenker

DB Schenker

66202 E	TO	WBEN	EWS	ANG	DBS		66227 P	TO	WBAM	EWS	ANG	DBS
66203 E	TO	WBEN	EWS	ANG	DBS		66228 E	TO	WBEN	EWS	ANG	DBS
66204	TO	WBSN	EWS	ANG	DBS		66229 E	TO	WBEN	EWS	ANG	DBS
66205 E	TO	WBEN	EWS	ANG	DBS		66230	TO	WBAI	EWS	ANG	DBS
66206	TO	WBAN	EWS	ANG	DBS		66231 E	TO	WBEN	EWS	ANG	DBS
66207	TO	WBAK	EWS	ANG	DBS		66232	TO	WBAN	EWS	ANG	DBS
66208 E	TO	WBEN	EWS	ANG	DBS		66233 E	TO	WBEN	EWS	ANG	DBS
66209 E	TO	WBEN	EWS	ANG	DBS		66234 E	TO	WBEN	EWS	ANG	DBS
66210 E	TO	WBEN	EWS	ANG	DBS		66235 E	TO	WBEN	EWS	ANG	DBS
66211 E	TO	WBEN	EWS	ANG	DBS		66236 E	TO	WBEN	EWS	ANG	DBS
66212 E	TO	WBEN	EWS	ANG	DBS		66237	TO	WBAK	EWS	ANG	DBS
66213	TO	WFMU	EWS	ANG	DBS		66238	TO	WBAN	EWS	ANG	DBS
66214 E	TO	WBEN	EWS	ANG	DBS		66239 P	TO	WBEN	EWS	ANG	DBS
66215 E	TO	WBEN	EWS	ANG	DBS		66240 E	TO	WBEN	EWS	ANG	DBS
66216 E	TO	WBEN	EWS	ANG	DBS		66241 E	TO	WBEN	EWS	ANG	DBS
66217 E	TO	WBEN	EWS	ANG	DBS		66242 E	TO	WBEN	EWS	ANG	DBS
66218 E	TO	WBEN	EWS	ANG	DBS		66243 E	TO	WBEN	EWS	ANG	DBS
66219 E	TO	WBEN	EWS	ANG	DBS		66244 E	TO	WBEN	EWS	ANG	DBS
66220 P	TO	WBEN	EWS	ANG	DBS		66245 E	TO	WBEN	EWS	ANG	DBS
66221	TO	WBAM	EWS	ANG	DBS		66246 E	TO	WBEN	EWS	ANG	DBS
66222 E	TO	WBEN	EWS	ANG	DBS		66247 E	TO	WBEN	EWS	ANG	DBS
66223 E	TO	WBEN	EWS	ANG	DBS		66248 P	TO	WBEN	EWS	ANG	DBS
66224 E	TO	WBEN	EWS	ANG	DBS		66249 E	TO	WBEN	EWS	ANG	DBS
66225 E	TO	WBEN	EWS	ANG	DBS		66250	TO	WBAK	EWS	ANG	DBS
66226 E	TO	WBEN	EWS	ANG	DBS							

Names applied

66002	*Lafarge Quorn*
66048	*James the Engine*
66050	*EWS Energy*
66077	*Benjamin Gimbert GC*
66079	*James Nightall GC*
66152	*Derek Holmes Railway Operator*
66172	*Paul Melleney*
66200	*Railway Heritage Committee*
66250	*Robert K. Romak* (not standard nameplate)

■ DBS Class 66/0s operated by Euro Cargo Rail in France, marked 'E' on the above listing, are usually maintained at Sotteville, France.

■ Locomotives marked with a 'P' are operated in or scheduled to transfer to Poland for operation by DB Schenker Polska. A total of 40 locos will move to Poland, 13 in 2011 and the balance in 2012-13. Locos will be from the series 66146-250.

Below: *Immediately after privatisation of the UK railways in 1996, the new owner of the freight business sought replacement traction. This came with a fleet of 250 Class 66s, similar to the Class 59 but with upgraded equipment. All 250 locos are allocated to Toton, with today a number operating in France for Euro Cargo Rail and some in Poland for DB Schenker Polska. Sporting original EWS maroon and gold livery, No. 66128 is viewed at Didcot.* **CJM**

Class 67

Vehicle Length: 64ft 7in (19.68m)		Engine: EMD 12N-710G3B-EC			
Height: 12ft 9in (3.88m)		Horsepower: 2,980hp (2,223kW)			
Width: 8ft 9in (2.66m)		Electrical Equipment: EMD			

Number	Depot	Pool	Livery	Owner	Operator	Name
67001	CE	WAAN	EWS	ANG	DBS	
67002	CE	WAAN	EWS	ANG	DBS	Special Delivery
67003	CE	WAAN	EWS	ANG	DBS	
67004	CE	WABN	EWS	ANG	DBS	Post Haste
67005	CE	WAAN	ROY	ANG	DBS	Queen's Messenger
67006	CE	WAAN	ROY	ANG	DBS	Royal Sovereign
67007	CE	WABN	EWS	ANG	DBS	
67008	CE	WAAN	EWS	ANG	DBS	
67009	CE	WFMU	EWS	ANG	DBS	
67010	TO	WAWN	WSR	ANG	DBS/WSR	
67011	CE	WABN	EWS	ANG	DBS	
67012	TO	WAWN	WSR	ANG	DBS/WSR	A Shropshire Lad
67013	TO	WAWN	WSR	ANG	DBS/WSR	Dyfrbont Pontcysyllte
67014	TO	WAWN	WSR	ANG	DBS/WSR	Thomas Telford
67015	TO	WAWN	WSR	ANG	DBS/WSR	David J. Lloyd
67016	CE	WAFN	EWS	ANG	DBS	
67017	CE	WAFN	EWS	ANG	DBS	Arrow
67018	CE	WAFN	DBS	ANG	DBS	Keith Heller
67019	CE	WAAN	EWS	ANG	DBS	
67020	CE	WAAN	EWS	ANG	DBS	
67021	CE	WAAN	EWS	ANG	DBS	
67022	CE	WFMU	EWS	ANG	DBS	
67023	CE	WAAN	EWS	ANG	DBS	
67024	CE	WAAN	EWS	ANG	DBS	
67025	CE	WAAN	EWS	ANG	DBS	Western Star
67026	CE	WAAN	EWS	ANG	DBS	
67027	CE	WAAN	EWS	ANG	DBS	Rising Star
67028	CE	WAAN	EWS	ANG	DBS	
67029	CE	WAAN	EWE	ANG	DBS	Royal Diamond
67030	CE	WABN	EWS	ANG	DBS	

Below: *The replacement passenger or higher speed loco for EWS came in the form of a batch of 30 Spanish-built Class 67s. All are allocated to Crewe and today five are operated as part of the Wrexham & Shropshire fleet, allocated to Toton. Two locos (67005/006) are painted in Royal Train claret livery, 67029 is painted in VIP silver and No. 67018* Keith Heller *(illustrated) is painted in a modified version of DB Schenker red including a Canadian maple leaf logo.* **CJM**

Freight Operating Companies – DB Schenker

DB Schenker

Class 90

Vehicle Length: 61ft 6in (18.74m)			Power Collection: 25kV ac overhead			
Height: 13ft 0¼in (3.96m)			Horsepower: 7,860hp (5,860kW)			
Width: 9ft 0in (2.74m)			Electrical Equipment: GEC			

Number		Depot	Pool	Livery	Owner	Operator	Name
90017(S)		CE	WNTS	EWS	DBS	-	
90018		CE	WEFE	EWS	DBS	DBS	
90019		CE	WFMU	FGS	DBS	DBS	
90020		CE	WEFE	EWS	DBS	DBS	Collingwood
90021	(90221)	CE	WEFE	FGS	DBS	DBS	
90022(S)	(90222)	CE	WNTS	RFE	DBS	-	Freightconnection
90023(S)	(90223)	CE	WNTS	EWS	DBS	-	
90024	(90224)	CE	WEFE	FGS	DBS	DBS	
90025(S)	(90225)	CE	WNTS	FGS	DBS	-	
90026(S)		CE	WNTR	EWS	DBS	-	
90027(S)	(90227)	CE	WNTS	RFD	DBS	-	Allerton T&RS Depot Quality Approved
90028(S)		CE	WNTS	EWS	DBS	DBS	
90029(S)		CE	WNTS	EWS	DBS	-	The Institution of Civil Engineers
90030(S)	(90130)	CE	WNTR	EWS	DBS	-	Crewe Locomotive Works
90031(S)	(90131)	CE	WNTS	EWS	DBS	-	The Railway Children Partnership – Working for Street Children Worldwide
90032(S)	(90132)	CE	WNTS	EWS	DBS	-	
90033(S)	(90233)	CE	WNTS	RFI	DBS	-	
90034(S)	(90134)	CE	WNTS	EWS	DBS	-	
90035	(90135)	CE	WEFE	EWS	DBS	DBS	
90036	(90136)	CE	WEFE	RFE	DBS	DBS	
90037(S)	(90137)	CE	WNTS	EWS	DBS	-	Spirit of Dagenham
90038(S)	(90238)	CE	WNTS	RFI	DBS	-	
90039	(90239)	CE	WEFE	EWS	DBS	DBS	
90040(S)	(90140)	CE	WNTS	EWS	DBS	-	The Railway Mission
90050(S)	(90050)	CE	WNTS	FLG	DBS	-	

■ Ten DBS-operated Class 90s are scheduled for modification and export to Poland and Bulgaria.

Left: *A fleet of 25 Class 90s are operated by DB Schenker; however, a number are stored out of use. Four of the batch are painted in First Scotrail colours and used on overnight sleeper services between Edinburgh/Glasgow and London Euston. No. 90021 is seen departing from London Euston at the head of a charter train.*
Brian Morrison

Class 92

Vehicle Length: 70ft 1in (21.34m)		Power Collection: 25kV ac overhead / 750V dc third rail			
Height: 13ft 0in (3.95m)		Horsepower: ac – 6,700hp (5,000kW) / dc 5,360hp (4,000kW)			
Width: 8ft 8in (2.66m)		Electrical Equipment: Brush			

Number	Depot	Pool	Livery	Owner	Operator	Name
92001	CE	WTAE	EWS	HAL	DBS	Victor Hugo
92002 (S)	CE	WNTS	RFE	HAL	-	H G Wells
92003	CE	WTAE	RFE	HAL	DBS	Beethoven
92004 (S)	CE	WNTS	RFE	HAL	-	Jane Austen
92005	CE	WTAE	RFE	HAL	DBS	Mozart
92007	CE	WTAE	RFE	HAL	DBS	Schubert
92008 (S)	CE	WNTR	RFE	HAL	-	Jules Verne
92009	CE	WTAE	RFE	HAL	DBS	Elgar
92011 (S)	CE	WNTS	RFE	HAL	-	Handel
92012	CE	WTAE	RFE	HAL	DBS	Thomas Hardy
92013	CE	WFMU	RFE	HAL	DBS	Puccini
92015	CE	WFMU	RFE	HAL	DBS	D H Lawrence
92016 (S)	CE	WNTS	RFE	HAL	DBS	Brahms

92017	CE	WTAE	STO	HAL	DBS	*Bart the Engine*
92019	CE	WTAE	RFE	HAL	-	*Wagner*
92022	CE	WTAE	RFE	HAL	DBS	*Charles Dickens*
92024 (S)	CE	WNTS	RFE	HAL	-	*J S Bach*
92025 (S)	CE	WNTS	RFE	HAL	-	*Oscar Wilde*
92026	CE	WTAE	RFE	HAL	DBS	*Britten*
92027 (S)	CE	WNTS	RFE	HAL	-	*George Eliot*
92029 (S)	CE	WNTS	RFE	HAL	-	*Dante*
92030 (S)	CE	WNTR	RFE	HAL	-	*Ashford*
92031 (S)	CE	WNTR	EWS	HAL	-	*The Institute of Logistics and Transport*
92034	CE	WTAE	RFE	HAL	DBS	*Kipling*
92035 (S)	CE	WNTS	RFE	HAL	-	*Mendelssohn*
92036	CE	WFMU	RFE	HAL	DBS	*Bertolt Brecht*
92037 (S)	CE	WNTR	RFE	HAL	DBS	*Sullivan*
92039 (S)	CE	WNTS	RFE	HAL	-	*Johann Strauss*
92041	CE	WFMU	RFE	HAL	DBS	*Vaughan Williams*
92042	CE	WFMU	RFE	HAL	DBS	*Honegger*

Right: *Designed and built for Anglo-French freight and passenger traffic, the EWS-operated Class 92s, of which many are stored, operate the limited freight flows through the Channel Tunnel and some domestic UK freight. Two of the fleet, Nos. 92001 and 92031, are painted in full EWS livery. No. 92001* Victor Hugo *is shown powering a southbound intermodal train at Old Linslade on the West Coast Main Line.* **Michael J. Collins**

Freight Operating Companies - DB Schenker

Hauled Stock (Passenger)

AJ41 - RBR

Number	Depot	Livery	Owner
1658(S)	EH	MAR	DBR
1679	EH	LNE	DBR
1680	EH	LNE	DBR

AD1D - FO

Number	Depot	Livery	Owner
3186	DY	INT	DBR

AD1E - FOT

Number	Depot	Livery	Owner
3255 (3525)	EH	MAR	DBR

AD1F - FO

Number	Depot	Livery	Owner
3269	EH	MAR	DBR
3292	EH	MAR	DBR
3318	EH	MAR	DBR
3331	EH	MAR	DBR
3338(S)	EH	MAR	DBR
3358	EH	MAR	DBR
3368(S)	EH	MAR	DBR
3375(S)	EH	MAR	DBR
3388	EH	MAR	DBR

Mk1	
Vehicle Length: 64ft 6in (19.65m)	Height: 12ft 9½in (3.89m) Width: 9ft 3in (2.81m)

Mk2	
Vehicle Length: 66ft 0in (20.11m)	Height: 12ft 9½in (3.89m) Width: 9ft 3in (2.81m)

Mk 3	
Vehicle Length: 75ft 0in (22.86m)	Height: 12ft 9in (3.88m) Width: 8ft 11in (2.71m)

3399(S)	EH	MAR	DBR
3400	EH	MAR	DBR
3414	EH	MAR	DBR
3424	EH	MAR	DBR

AC21 - TSO

Number	Depot	Livery	Owner
4925(S)	EH	GRN	DBR *(for sale)*
4956(S)	EH	BLG	DBR *(for sale)*
5005(S)	EH	BLG	DBR *(for sale)*
5037(S)	EH	GRN	DBR *(for sale)*

AC2A - TSO

Number	Depot	Livery	Owner
5331	EH	MAR	DBR
5386(S)	EH	MAR	DBR

AC2B - TSO

Number	Depot	Livery	Owner
5482	TO	MAR	DBR

DB Schenker

Freight Operating Companies - DB Schenker

AC2D - TSO

Number	Depot	Livery	Owner
5631	MH	MAR	DBR
5632	MH	MAR	DBR
5657	MH	MAR	DBR

AC2F - TSO

Number	Depot	Livery	Owner
5922	MH	MAR	DBR
5924	MH	MAR	DBR
5954	MH	MAR	DBR
5959	MH	MAR	DBR
6036	MH	MAR	DBR
6110	MH	MAR	DBR
6139	MH	MAR	DBR
6152	MH	MAR	DBR

AX51 - GEN

Number	Depot	Livery	Owner
6311 (92911)	TO	BLU	DBR *(for sale)*

AN1D - RMBF

Number	Depot	Livery	Owner
6720 (6602)	CE	MAR	DBR

AE2D - BSO

Number	Depot	Livery	Owner
9494	CE	MAR	DBR

AE2F - BSO

Number	Depot	Livery	Owner
9522	MH	MAR	DBR
9529	MH	MAR	DBR
9531	MH	MAR	DBR

AJ1G - RFM

Number		Depot	Livery	Owner
10205(S)	(40503)	AL	SPL	DBR
10211	(40510)	TO	EWE	DBS
10215	(11032)	CE	BLG	DBR
10226(S)	(11015)	LM	VIR	DBR
10233(S)	(10013)	LM	VIR	DBR
10235	(10015)	CE	BLG	DBR
10237	(10022)	BY	DRU	DBR
10250(S)	(10020)	ZW	VIR	DBR
10257	(10007)	WN	BLG	DBR

AU4G - SLEP

Number	Depot	Livery	Owner
10540	AL	-	DBR
10546	TO	EWE	DBS

AS4G - SLE

Number	Depot	Livery	Owner
10647(S)	LM	INT	DBR
10710(S)	LM	CWR	DBR
10731(S)	LM	INT	DBR

AD1G - FO

Number	Depot	Livery	Owner
11005(S)	LM	VIR	DBR
11013	WN	DRU	DBR
11019	BY	DRU	DBR
11027	BY	BLU	DBR/DRS
11029	AL	BLG	DBR
11030	BY	DRU	DBR
11031	CE	BLG	DBR/WS
11033	WN	DRU	DBR
11039	TO	EWE	DBS
11040	WN	BLG	DBR/CAG
11041(S)	LM	VIR	DBR
11044	BY	DRU	DBR
11046	BY	DRU	DBR
11052(S)	LM	VIR	DBR
11054	BY	DRU	DBR
11058(S)	LM	VIR	DBR
11097	CE	BLG	DBR

AC2G - TSO

Number	Depot	Livery	Owner
12053	AL	BLG	DBR/CAG

AB21 - BSK

Number	Depot	Livery	Owner
35290(S)	CP	CAR	DBR

GK2G - TRSB

Number	Depot	Livery	Owner
40402 (40002)	LM	VIR	DBR
40403 (40003)	LM	VIR	DBR
40416 (40016)	LM	VIR	DBR
40419 (40019)	LM	VIR	DBR
40434 (40234)	LM	VIR	DBR

Saloon

Number	Depot	Livery	Owner
45020	ML	MAR	DBR
45029(S)	ML	EWS	DBR

Below: *DBS-owned former Virgin Trains TRSB No. 40416 is seen stored at Long Marston.* **Brian Garrett**

Hauled Stock (NPCCS)

Mk 3 (DVT)	Height: 12ft 9in (3.88m)
Vehicle Length: 61ft 9in (18.83m)	Width: 8ft 11in (2.71m)

NZAG - DVT

Number	Depot	Livery	Owner
82106(S)	LM	VIR	DBR
82108(S)	LM	VIR	DBR
82110(S)	LM	VIR	DBR
82113(S)	LM	VIR	DBR
82116(S)	LM	VIR	DBR
82120(S)	LM	VIR	DBR
82122(S)	LM	VIR	DBR
82131(S)	LM	VIR	DBR
82137(S)	LM	VIR	DBR
82138(S)	LM	VIR	DBR
82141(S)	LM	VIR	DBR
82144(S)	LM	VIR	DBR
82146	TO	DBE	DBS
82148(S)	LM	VIR	DBR
82150(S)	LM	VIR	DBR
82301 (82117)	CE	WSR	DBR
82302 (82151)	CE	WSR	DBR
82303 (82135)	CE	WSR	DBR
82304 (82130)	CE	WSR	DBR
82305 (82134)	CE	WSR	DBR

NKA1 - H-GUV

Number	Depot	Livery	Owner
92203 (S)	CP	RES	DBS
94103 (W) (95103)	CX	RES	DBS
94104 (S) (95104)	TO	RES	DBS
94106 (S) (95106)	MH	RES	DBS
94113 (S) (95113)	OM	RES	DBS
94116 (S) (95116)	TY	RES	DBS
94121 (S) (95121)	TO	RES	DBS
94137 (S) (95137)	ML	RES	DBS
94147 (S) (95147)	ML	RES	DBS
94150 (S) (95150)	SP	RES	DBS
94153 (S) (95153)	WE	RES	DBS
94155 (S) (95155)	SP	RES	DBS
94160 (S) (95160)	MH	RES	DBS
94166 (S) (95166)	BS	RES	DBS
94170 (S) (95170)	MH	RES	DBS
94176 (S) (95176)	ML	RES	DBS
94177 (S) (95177)	TO	RES	DBS
94191 (S) (95351)	SP	RES	DBS
94192 (S) (95352)	MY	RES	DBS
94195 (S) (95355)	BS	RES	DBS
94197 (S) (95357)	BS	RES	DBS
94203 (S) (95363)	SP	RES	DBS
94207 (S) (95367)	TO	RES	DBS
94208 (S) (95368)	TO	RES	DBS
94209 (W) (95369)	CX	RES	DBS
94213 (S) (95373)	MY	RES	DBS
94214 (S) (95374)	MH	RES	DBS
94217 (S) (93131)	MH	RES	DBS
94221 (S) (93905)	MH	RES	DBS
94222 (S) (93474)	MH	RES	DBS
94225 (S) (93849)	MH	RES	DBS
94227 (S) (93585)	TE	RES	DBS
94229 (S) (93720)	MH	RES	DBS

NAA1 - PCV

Number	Depot	Livery	Owner
94302 (S) (75124)	TY	RES	DBS
94303 (S) (75131)	TY	RES	DBS
94304 (S) (75107)	MH	RES	DBS
94306 (S) (75112)	TY	RES	DBS
94307 (S) (75127)	CX	RES	DBS
94308 (S) (75125)	MH	RES	DBS
94310 (S) (75119)	WE	RES	DBS
94311 (S) (75105)	WE	RES	DBS
94313 (S) (75129)	WE	RES	DBS
94316 (S) (75108)	TO	RES	DBS
94317 (S) (75117)	TO	RES	DBS
94318 (S) (75115)	CX	RES	DBS
94322 (S) (75111)	MH	RES	DBS
94323 (S) (75110)	TY	RES	DBS
94326 (S) (75123)	TY	RES	DBS
94331 (S) (75022)	CX	RES	DBS
94332 (S) (75011)	TY	RES	DBS
94333 (S) (75016)	TY	RES	DBS
94334 (S) (75017)	CD	RES	DBS
94335 (S) (75032)	TY	RES	DBS
94336 (S) (75031)	TY	RES	DBS
94338 (S) (75008)	WE	RES	DBS
94340 (S) (75012)	CD	RES	DBS
94343 (S) (75027)	MH	RES	DBS
94344 (S) (75014)	TO	RES	DBS

NBA1, NOA1, NQA, NRA1 - BVHS

Number	Depot	Livery	Owner
94400 (92524)	CX	RES	DBS
94406 (92956)	MH	RES	DBS
94408 (92981)	TY	RES	DBS
94410 (92941)	WE	RES	DBS
94411 (92945)	CX	RES	DBS
94412 (92945)	ML	RES	DBS
94413 (92236)	ML	RES	DBS
94416 (92746)	MY	RES	DBS
94420 (92263)	MH	RES	DBS
94422 (92651)	TO	RES	DBS
94423 (92914)	BS	RES	DBS
94427 (92754)	WE	RES	DBS
94428 (92166)	MY	RES	DBS
94429 (92232)	TE	RES	DBS
94431 (92604)	MH	RES	DBS
94432 (92999)	MY	RES	DBS
94433 (92643)	MH	RES	DBS
94434 (92584)	TY	RES	DBS
94435 (92134)	TO	RES	DBS
94438 (92251)	TO	RES	DBS
94440 (92645)	MY	RES	DBS
94445 (92615)	WE	RES	DBS
94451 (92257)	WE	RES	DBS
94458 (92974)	CX	RES	DBS
94462 (92270)	CD	RES	DBS
94463 (92995)	TY	RES	DBS

DB Schenker

94470	(92113)	TO	RES	DBS	94525	(92229)	TY	RES	DBS
94479	(92132)	TO	RES	DBS	94526	(92518)	TY	RES	DBS
94481	(92641)	CX	RES	DBS	94527	(92728)	TY	RES	DBS
94482	(92639)	MH	RES	DBS	94528	(92252)	ML	RES	DBS
94488	(92105)	CD	RES	DBS	94529	(92267)	CD	RES	DBS
94490	(92230)	MH	RES	DBS	94530	(94409)	MY	RES	DBS
94492	(92721)	WE	RES	DBS	94531	(94456)	TY	RES	DBS
94495	(92755)	TY	RES	DBS	94532	(94489)	LM	RES	DBS
94497	(92717)	ML	RES	DBS	94534	(94430)	MY	RES	DBS
94498	(92555)	MH	RES	DBS	94536	(94491)	MY	RES	DBS
94499	(92577)	CD	BLG	DBS	94538	(94426)	MH	RES	DBS
94501	(92725)	TO	RES	DBS	94539	(92302)	MH	RES	DBS
94504	(92748)	TY	RES	DBS	94540	(92860)	TJ	RES	DBS
94512	(92582)	TY	RES	DBS	94541	(92316)	ML	RES	DBS
94514	(92122)	MY	RES	DBS	94542	(92330)	TY	RES	DBS
94515	(92513)	CE	DBS	DBS	94543	(92389)	MY	RES	DBS
94518	(92258)	MY	RES	DBS	94544	(92345)	MH	RES	DBS
94519	(92916)	ML	RES	DBS	94545	(92329)	TE	RES	DBS
94520	(92917)	TY	RES	DBS	94546	(92804)	TY	RES	DBS
94521	(92917)	CD	RES	DBS	94547	(92392)	MH	RES	DBS
94522	(92907)	TY	RES	DBS	94548	(92344)	TY	RES	DBS

NAA1 - PCV

Number		Depot	Livery	Owner
95300	(94300)	MH	RES	DBS
95301	(94301)	MH	RES	DBS

NRA1 - BAA

Number		Depot	Livery	Owner
95400	(95203)	MH	EWS	DBS
95410	(95213)	MH	EWS	DBS

NOA1 - H-GUV

Number		Depot	Livery	Owner
95727	(95127)	WE	RES	DBS
95754	(95154)	TY	RES	DBS
95758	(95158)	SP	RES	DBS
95761	(95161)	WE	RES	DBS
95763	(95163)	BS	RES	DBS

NX5G - NGV

Number		Depot	Livery	Owner
96371(S)	(10545)	WB	EPS	DBS
96372(S)	(10564)	LM	EPS	DBS
96373(S)	(10568)	LM	EPS	DBS
96374(S)	(10585)	LM	EPS	DBS
96375(S)	(10587)	LM	EPS	DBS

Above: *DBS own an extensive collection of van and passenger vehicles. The van stock is largely stored, while the passenger fleets are used for charter work. Stored PCV No. 95300 is illustrated in full EWS livery.* **Tony Christie**

Below: *The DBS Executive train formed of DVT 82146 and Mk3s 10211, 10546 and 11039 with Class 67 No. 67029 on the rear head to Plymouth through Dawlish.* **CJM**

Euro Cargo Rail A part of DB Schenker

Address: ✉ Immeuble la Palacio, 25-29 Place de la Madeleine, Paris, 75008

📠 info@eurocargorail.com

✆ +33 977 400000

ⓘ www.eurocargorail.com

Class 08

Vehicle Length: 29ft 3in (8.91m)	Engine: English Electric 6K
Height: 12ft 8⅜in (3.87m)	Horsepower: 400hp (298kW)
Width: 8ft 6in (2.59m)	Electrical Equipment: English Electric

Number	Depot	Pool	Livery	Owner	Operator	Name
08738	FN	WSEN	ECR	DBS	ECR (at Vallourec Steel, Amiens)	Silver Fox
08939	TO	WSEN	ECR	DBS	ECR (at Vallourec Steel, Amiens)	

Class 21

Vehicle Length: (21/5) 48ft 2in (14.70m), (21/6) 46ft 3in (14.13m)	Engine: (21/5) Caterpiller 3512B DI-TA of 2,011hp
Height: (21/5) 13ft 8in (4.16m), (21/6) 13ft 9in (4.19m)	Engine: (21/6) MTU 8V 4000 R41L of 1,475hp
Width: 8ft 8¼in (2.65m)	Hydraulic Equipment: Voith

Number	Depot	Pool	Livery	Owner	Operator
21544	DM	WLAN	MAR	ANG	ECR
21545	DM	WLAN	MAR	ANG	ECR
21546	DM	WLAN	MAR	ANG	ECR
21547	DM	WLAN	MAR	ANG	ECR
21610	DM	WLAN	MAR	ANG	ECR
21611	DM	WLAN	MAR	ANG	ECR

Class 77
(JT42CWRM)

Vehicle Length: 70ft 0½in (21.34m)	Engine: EMD 12N-710G3B-EC
Height: 12ft 10in (3.91m)	Horsepower: 3,300hp (2,462kW)
Width: 8ft 8¼in (2.65m)	Electrical Equipment: EMD

Number	Depot	Livery	Owner	Opt'r
77001	ND	ELR	DBS	ECR
77002	ND	ELR	DBS	ECR
77003	ND	ELR	DBS	ECR
77004	ND	ELR	DBS	ECR
77005	ND	ELR	DBS	ECR
77006	ND	ELR	DBS	ECR
77007	ND	ELR	DBS	ECR
77008	ND	ELR	DBS	ECR
77009	ND	ELR	DBS	ECR
77010	ND	ELR	DBS	ECR
77011	ND	ELR	DBS	ECR
77012	ND	ELR	DBS	ECR
77013	ND	ELR	DBS	ECR
77014	ND	ELR	DBS	ECR
77015	ND	ELR	DBS	ECR
77016	ND	ELR	DBS	ECR
77017	ND	ELR	DBS	ECR
77018	ND	ELR	DBS	ECR
77019	ND	ELR	DBS	ECR
77020	ND	ELR	DBS	ECR
77021	ND	ELR	DBS	ECR
77022	ND	ELR	DBS	ECR
77023	ND	ELR	DBS	ECR
77024	ND	ELR	DBS	ECR
77025	ND	ELR	DBS	ECR
77026	ND	ELR	DBS	ECR
77027	ND	ELR	DBS	ECR
77028	ND	ELR	DBS	ECR
77029	ND	ELR	DBS	ECR
77030	ND	ELR	DBS	ECR
77031	ND	ELR	DBS	ECR
77032	ND	ELR	DBS	ECR
77033	ND	ELR	DBS	ECR
77034	ND	ELR	DBS	ECR
77035	ND	ELR	DBS	ECR
77036	ND	ELR	DBS	ECR
77037	ND	ELR	DBS	ECR
77038	ND	ELR	DBS	ECR
77039	ND	ELR	DBS	ECR
77040	ND	ELR	DBS	ECR
77041	ND	ELR	DBS	ECR
77042	ND	ELR	DBS	ECR
77043	ND	ELR	DBS	ECR
77044	ND	ELR	DBS	ECR
77045	ND	ELR	DBS	ECR
77046	ND	ELR	DBS	ECR
77047	ND	ELR	DBS	ECR
77048	ND	ELR	DBS	ECR
77049	ND	ELR	DBS	ECR
77050	ND	ELR	DBS	ECR
77051	ND	ELR	DBS	ECR
77052	ND	ELR	DBS	ECR
77053	ND	ELR	DBS	ECR
77054	ND	ELR	DBS	ECR
77055	ND	ELR	DBS	ECR
77056	ND	ELR	DBS	ECR
77057	ND	ELR	DBS	ECR
77058	ND	ELR	DBS	ECR
77059	ND	ELR	DBS	ECR
77060	ND	ELR	DBS	ECR

■ 20 members of this fleet are scheduled to be transferred to DBS in Germany and re-classified as Class 247.

Right: *DB subsidiary Euro Cargo Rail operate a number of locos in mainland Europe, including a batch of UK Class 66s. The operator also has two ex-BR Class 08s, Class 21 single cab road locos and a batch of Euro Class 66s, classified as Class 77. Euro '66' No. 77003 is shown.*
Rogier Immers

Direct Rail Services

Address (UK): ✉ Kingmoor Depot, Etterby Road, Carlisle, Cumbria, CA3 9NZ
📠 info@directrailservices.com
✆ 01228 406600
ⓘ www.directrailservices.com

Managing Director: Neil McNicholas
Depots: Carlisle Kingmoor (KM), Crewe Gresty Bridge (CG)

Class 20/3

Vehicle Length: 46ft 9¼in (14.26m)				Engine: English Electric 8SVT Mk2			
Height: 12ft 7⅝in (3.84m)				Horsepower: 1,000hp (745kW)			
Width: 8ft 9in (2.66m)				Electrical Equipment: English Electric			

Number		Depot	Pool	Livery	Owner	Operator	Name
20301	(20047)	KM	GBEE	DRU	DRS	GBR	Max Joule 1958 - 1999
20302	(20084)	KM	GBEE	DRU	DRS	GBR	
20303(S)	(20127)	KM	XHNC	DRU	DRS	-	
20304	(20120)	KM	GBEE	DRU	DRS	GBR	
20305	(20095)	KM	GBEE	DRU	DRS	GBR	Gresty Bridge
20306(S)	(20131)	KM	XHNC	DRS	DRS	-	
20307(S)	(20128)	KM/CS	XHSS	DRS	DRS	-	
20308	(20187)	KM	GBEE	DRC	DRS	GBR	
20309(S)	(20075)	KM	XHSS	DRC	DRS	-	
20310(S)	(20190)	KM/CS	XHSS	DRS	DRS	-	
20311(S)	(20102)	KM/CS	XHSS	DRS	DRS	-	
20312(S)	(20042)	KM/CS	XHSS	DRC	DRS	-	
20313(S)	(20194)	KM/CS	XHSS	DRS	DRS	-	
20314(S)	(20117)	KM/CS	XHSS	DRC	DRS	-	
20315(S)	(20104)	KM/CS	XHSS	DRS	DRS	-	

■ Nos. 20301/302/304/305/308 fitted with trip cock equipment to allow operation over LUL tracks.

Left: *Direct Rail Services has 15 Class 20/3 locos on its books, although all are out of DRS service at the end of 2010 and stored. Five locos are however working on lease to GBRf for powering new London Underground stock between Derby, Old Dalby and the LUL network. Two of the DRS fleet Nos. 20314 and 20305 stand side by side showing the different end designs.* **Brian Morrison**

Class 37/0

Vehicle Length: 61ft 6in (18.74m)				Engine: English Electric 12CSVT		
Height: 13ft 0¼in (3.96m)				Horsepower: 1,750hp (1,304kW)		
Width: 8ft 11⅝in (2.73m)				Electrical Equipment: English Electric		

Number	Depot	Pool	Livery	Owner	Operator	Name
37038	KM	XHSS	DRS	DRS	DRS	
37059	KM	XHNC	DRC	DRS	DRS	
37069	KM	XHNC	DRC	DRS	DRS	
37087	KM	XHNC	DRS	DRS	DRS	Keighley & Worth Valley Railway
37194	KM	XHNC	DRC	DRS	DRS	
37197(S)	BH	XHNC	BLU	DRS	-	
37218	KM	XHNC	DRS	DRS	DRS	
37229	KM	XHNC	DRC	DRS	DRS	Jonty Jarvis
37259	KM	XHNC	DRC	DRS	DRS	
37261(S)	KM/CS	XHSS	DRS	DRS	-	

Class 37/4

Vehicle Length: 61ft 6in (18.74m)				*Engine: English Electric 12CSVT*		
Height: 13ft 0¼in (3.96m)				*Horsepower: 1,750hp (1,304kW)*		
Width: 8ft 11⅝in (2.73m)				*Electrical Equipment: English Electric*		
Electric Train Heat fitted						

Number		Depot	Pool	Livery	Owner	Operator	Name
37409	(37270)	KM	XHNC	DRC	DRS	DRS	**Lord Hinton**
37423	(37296)	KM	XHNC	DRC	DRS	DRS	**Spirit of the Lakes**

Class 37/5

Vehicle Length: 61ft 6in (18.74m)			*Engine: English Electric 12CSVT*	
Height: 13ft 0¼in (3.96m)			*Horsepower: 1,750hp (1,304kW)*	
Width: 8ft 11⅝in (2.73m)			*Electrical Equipment: English Electric*	

Number		Depot	Pool	Livery	Owner	Operator	Name/Notes
37510		KM	XHNC	DRC	DRS	DRS	
37667	(37151)	KM	XHNC	DRC	DRS	DRS	
37682(S)	(37236)	KM	XHHP	DRC	DRS	-	
37683(S)	(37187)	CG	XHSS	DRS	DRS	-	*(At Waterman Railways Crewe - training loco)*
37688	(37205)	KM	XHNC	DRC	DRS	DRS	**Kingmoor TMD**

Class 37/6

Vehicle Length: 61ft 6in (18.74m)			*Engine: English Electric 12CSVT*	
Height: 13ft 0¼in (3.96m)			*Horsepower: 1,750hp (1,304kW)*	
Width: 8ft 11⅝in (2.73m)			*Electrical Equipment: English Electric*	

Number		Depot	Pool	Livery	Owner	Operator	Name
37601	(37501)	KM	XHNC	DRC	DRS	DRS	*Class 37 – 'Fifty'*
37602	(37502)	KM	XHSS	DRS	DRS	-	
37603	(37504)	KM	XHNC	DRC	DRS	DRS	
37604	(37506)	KM	XHNC	DRC	DRS	DRS	
37605(S)	(37507)	KM/CS	XHXX	DRS	DRS	-	
37606(S)	(37508)	KM	XHSS	DRS	DRS	-	
37607	(37511)	KM	XHNC	DRS	DRS	DRS	
37608	(37512)	KM	XHNC	DRC	DRS	DRS	
37609	(37514)	KM	XHNC	DRS	DRS	DRS	
37610(S)	(37687)	KM	XHSS	DRC	DRS	-	*T. S. (Ted) Cassady 14.5.61-6.4.08*
37611	(37690)	KM	XHNC	DRC	DRS	DRS	
37612(S)	(37691)	KM/CS	XHSS	DRS	DRS	-	

Below: *Direct Rail Services operate a substantial fleet of Class 37s on flask and freight flows all are based at Carlisle Kingmoor and can be found throughout the freight network. Class 37/0 No. 37087* Keighley & Worth Valley Railway, *passes light through Stratford station in East London in May 2010. The loco's No. 1 or cooler group end is nearest the camera. This loco displays the older DRS livery.* **CJM**

Direct Rail Services

Class 47/4

Vehicle Length: 63ft 6in (19.35m)
Height: 12ft 10⅓in (3.91m)
Width: 9ft 2in (2.79m)
Electric Train Heat fitted

Engine: Sulzer 12LDA28C
Horsepower: 2,580hp (1,922kW)
Electrical Equipment: Brush

Number		Depot	Pool	Livery	Owner	Operator	Name
47501		KM	XHAC	DRC	DRS	DRS	*Craftsman*
47802	(47552)	KM	XHAC	DRC	DRS	DRS	*Pride of Cumbria*
47810	(47247/655)	BH	XHAC	DRC	DRS	DRS	
47818	(47240/663)	BH	XHHP	DRU	DRS	DRS	
47832	(47560)	KM	XHAC	DRC	DRS	DRS	*Solway Princess*
47841	(47622)	KM	XHNC	DRC	DRS	DRS	

Class 47/7

Number		Depot	Pool	Livery	Owner	Operator	Name
47703(S)	(47514)	KM	XHSS	FRB	DRS	-	
47709(S)	(47499)	KM/ZG	XHHP	DRC	DRS	-	
47712	(47505)	KM	XHAC	DRC	DRS	DRS	*Pride of Carlisle*
47790	(47673)	KM	XHAC	DRC	DRS	DRS	
47791(S)	(47675)	KM	XHSS	RES	DRS	-	

Left: *Examples of both Class 47/4 and 47/7 operate within the DRS pool, and further examples of the Class 47/4 fleet were added to stock in late 2010. Painted in the latest DRS Compass colours, No. 47832* Solway Princess *is recorded together with a National Express blue liveried Class 90 No. 90005 at Kelvedon.*
Michael J. Collins

Class 57/0

Vehicle Length: 63ft 6in (19.38m)
Height: 12ft 10⅓in (3.91m)
Width: 9ft 2in (2.79m)

Engine: EMD 645-12E3
Horsepower: 2,500hp (1,864kW)
Electrical Equipment: Brush

Number		Depot	Pool	Livery	Owner	Operator	Name/Notes
57002	(47322)	KM	XHCK	DRC*	PTR	DRS	* with Colas branding
57003	(47317)	KM	XHCK	DRC	PTR	DRS	
57004	(47347)	KM	XHCK	DRC	PTR	DRS	
57007	(47332)	KM	XHCK	DRC	PTR	DRS	
57008	(47060)	KM	XHCK	DRC	PTR	DRS	*Telford International Railfreight Park June - 2009*
57009	(47079)	KM	XHCK	DRC	PTR	DRS	
57010	(47231)	KM	XHNC	DRC	PTR	DRS	
57011	(47329)	KM	XHCK	DRC	PTR	DRS	
57012	(47204)	KM	XHCK	DRC	PTR	DRS	

Left: *Nine Class 57s are operated by Direct Rail Services, all allocated to Carlisle Kingmoor and painted in the latest Compass livery style. No. 57012, rebuilt from Class 47 No. 47204 is seen at Paignton while engaged in driver's route training. The loco is viewed from its No. 2 end.* **Stacey Thew**

Class 66/4

	Vehicle Length: 70ft 0½in (21.34m)	Engine: EMD 12N-710G3B-EC
	Height: 12ft 10in (3.91m)	Horsepower: 3,300hp (2,462kW)
	Width: 8ft 8¼in (2.65m)	Electrical Equipment: EMD

Number	Depot	Pool	Livery	Owner	Operator	Name
66411	KM	XHIM	STO	HAL	DRS	*Eddie the Engine*
66412	KM	XHIM	MAL	HAL	DRS	
66413	KM	XHIM	DRC	HAL	DRS	
66414	KM	XHIM	TES	HAL	DRS	*James the Engine*
66415	KM	XHIM	DRC	HAL	DRS	
66416	KM	XHIM	DRC	HAL	DRS	
66417	KM	XHIM	DRC	HAL	DRS	
66418	KM	XHIM	DRC	HAL	DRS	
66419	KM	XHIM	DRC	HAL	DRS	
66420	KM	XHIM	DRC	HAL	DRS	
66421	KM	XHIM	DRC	HAL	DRS	
66422	KM	XHIM	DRC	HAL	DRS	
66423	KM	XHIM	DRC	HAL	DRS	
66424	KM	XHIM	DRC	HAL	DRS	
66425	KM	XHIM	DRC	HAL	DRS	
66426	KM	XHIM	DRC	HAL	DRS	
66427	KM	XHIM	DRC	HAL	DRS	
66428	KM	XHIM	DRC	HAL	DRS	
66429	KM	XHIM	DRC	HAL	DRS	
66430	KM	XHIM	DRC	HAL	DRS	
66431	KM	XHIM	DRC	HAL	DRS	
66432	KM	XHIM	DRC	HAL	DRS	
66433	KM	XHIM	DRC	HAL	DRS	
66434	KM	XHIM	FLF	HAL	DRS	

Above: *The most modern fleet of locomotives operated by Direct Rail Services are 27 Class 66s, built by Electro Motive and owned by Halifax Assets Finance. No. 66426 is illustrated passing Gospel Oak, powering the daily Tilbury to Daventry intermodal service on 2 September 2010.* **CJM**

Direct Rail Services

Coaching Stock

Mk2	
Vehicle Length: 66ft 0in (20.11m)	Height: 12ft 9½in (3.89m)
	Width: 9ft 3in (2.81m)

AC2 - BSO

Number	Depot	Livery	Owner
9419	KM	DRS	DRS
9428	KM	DRS	DRS

AB1D - BFK

Number	Depot	Livery	Owner
17159	ZG	DRO	DRS

Left: *Direct Rail Services operate a small number of passenger vehicles, mainly as support coaches for loaded flask trains. Mk2c BSO No. 9428 is shown carrying the latest DRS Compass livery. Note the grille in the forward window of the original brake van, providing ventilation to an onboard generator.* **Tony Christie**

Royal Mail (operations contracted to DBS)

Address: ✉ 148 Old Street, London, EC1V 9HQ

✎ press.office@royalmail.com ✆ 0207 250 2468 ⓘ www.royalmailgroup.com

Class 325

Vehicle Length: (Driving) 65ft 0¾in (19.82m)	Width: 9ft 2in (2.82m)
(Inter) 65ft 4¼in (19.92m)	Horsepower: 1,278hp (990kW)
Height: 12ft 4½in (3.76m)	Seats (total/car): None - luggage space

Number	Formation DTPMV+MPMV+TPMV+DTPMV	Depot	Livery	Owner	Operator	Name
325001	68300+68340+68360+68301	CE	RML	RML	DBS	
325002	68302+68341+68361+68303	CE	RML	RML	DBS	*Royal Mail North Wales & North West*
325003	68304+68342+68362+68305	CE	RML	RML	DBS	
325004	68306+68343+68363+68307	CE	RML	RML	DBS	
325005	68308+68344+68364+68309	CE	RML	RML	DBS	*John Grierson*
325006	68310+68345+68365+68311	CE	RML	RML	DBS	
325007	68312+68346+68366+68313	CE	RML	RML	DBS	*Peter Howarth C.B.E*
325008	68314+68347+68367+68315	CE	RML	RML	DBS	
325009	68316+68348+68368+68317	CE	RML	RML	DBS	
325010(S)	68318+68349+68369+68319	CE/IL	RML	RML	DBS	
325011	68320+68350+68370+68321	CE	RML	RML	DBS	
325012	68322+68351+68371+68323	CE	RML	RML	DBS	
325013	68324+68352+68372+68325	CE	RML	RML	DBS	
325014	68326+68353+68373+68327	CE	RML	RML	DBS	
325015	68328+68354+68374+68329	CE	RML	RML	DBS	
325016	68330+68355+68375+68331	CE	RML	RML	DBS	

The 16 Royal Mail owned Class 325 mail and parcels EMUs are operated under contract by EWS on behalf of Royal Mail on a restricted number of West Coast services radiating from the Princess Royal Distribution Centre in Wembley, London. The 17.42 Mail from Shieldmuir to Warrington passes Abington on 9 April 2010, formed of units Nos. 325015, 325003 and 325013. **Brian Morrison**

Europorte – GB Railfreight (GBRf)

Address:	✉ 15-25 Artillery Lane, London, E1 7HA
	📠 gbrfinfo@gbrailfreight.com
	✆ 0207 983 5177
	① www.gbrailfreight.com
Managing Director:	John Smith
Depots:	Peterborough (PT), Wembley (SV), St Leonards (SE)
	Coquelles (CQ), Ashford Hitachi (AD)

Class 20/3

DRS traction operated under contract by GBRf

Vehicle Length: 46ft 9¼in (14.26m)
Height: 12ft 7⅝in (3.84m)
Width: 8ft 9in (2.66m)

Engine: English Electric 8SVT Mk2
Horsepower: 1,000hp (745kW)
Electrical Equipment: English Electric

Number		Depot	Pool	Livery	Owner	Operator	Name
20301	(20047)	KM	GBEE	DRU	DRS	GBR	*Max Joule 1958 – 1999*
20302	(20084)	KM	GBEE	DRU	DRS	GBR	
20304	(20120)	KM	GBEE	DRU	DRS	GBR	
20305	(20095)	KM	GBEE	DRU	DRS	GBR	*Gresty Bridge*
20308	(20187)	KM	GBEE	DRC	DRS	GBR	

Right: *To facilitate the transfer of new London Underground 'S' stock between Bombardier Derby Litchurch Lane and the Old Dalby test track and between Old Dalby and the LUL network, GBRailfreight won a contract to power the train. GBRf then sub-leased from Direct Rail Services five Class 20/3s to operate the trains. The locos were debranded and fitted with 'trip-cocks' to allow operation over LUL tracks. A Derby to LUL delivery run is seen near Wychnor Junction on 14 July 2010 top and tailed by Nos. 20304/302 and 20301/305.* **Stacey Thew**

Class 66/4 & 66/7

Vehicle Length: 70ft 0½in (21.34m)
Height: 12ft 10in (3.91m)
Width: 8ft 8¼in (2.65m)

Engine: EMD 12N-710G3B-EC
Horsepower: 3,300hp (2,462kW)
Electrical Equipment: EMD

Number	Depot	Pool	Livery	Owner	Operator
66401	PT	GBRT	BLU	PTR	GBR
66402	PT	GBRT	BLU	PTR	GBR
66403	PT	GBRT	BLU	PTR	GBR
66404	PT	GBRT	BLU	PTR	GBR
66405	PT	GBRT	BLU	PTR	GBR

Number	Depot	Pool	Livery	Owner	Operator	Name
66701	PT	GBRT	GBR	HSB	GBR	*Whitemoor*
66702	PT	GBRT	GBR	HSB	GBR	*Blue Lightning*
66703	PT	GBCM	GBR	HSB	GBR	*Doncaster PSB 1981 - 2002*
66704	PT	GBCM	GBR	HSB	GBR	*Colchester Power Signalbox*
66705	PT	GBCM	GBR	HSB	GBR	*Golden Jubilee*
66706	PT	GBCM	GBR	HSB	GBR	*Nene Valley*
66707	PT	GBCM	GBR	HSB	GBR	*Sir Sam Fay / Great Central Railway*
66708	PT	GBRT	GBR	HSB	GBR	
66709	PT	GBRT	MED	HSB	GBR	*Joseph Arnold Davies*
66710	PT	GBCM	GBR	HSB	GBR	*Phil Packar*
66711	PT	GBCM	GBR	HSB	GBR	
66712	PT	GBCM	GBR	HSB	GBR	*Peterborough Power Signalbox*
66713	PT	GBCM	GBR	HSB	GBR	*Forest City*
66714	PT	GBCM	GBR	HSB	GBR	*Cromer Lifeboat*
66715	PT	GBCM	GBR	HSB	GBR	*Valour*

Europorte – GBRf

66716	PT	GBCM	GBR	HSB	GBR	
66717	PT	GBCM	GBR	HSB	GBR	Good Old Boy
66718	PT	GBCM	GBM	HSB	GBR	Gwyneth Dunwoody
66719	PT	GBCM	GBM	HSB	GBR	Metro-Land
66720	PT	GBCM	GBM	HSB	GBR	Metronet Pathfinder
66721	PT	GBCM	GBM	HSB	GBR	Harry Beck
66722	PT	GBCM	GBM	HSB	GBR	Sir Edward Watkin
66723	PT	GBSD	GBF	HSB	GBR	Chinook
66724	PT	GBSD	GBF	HSB	GBR	Drax Power Station
66725	PT	GBSD	GBF	HSB	GBR	Sunderland
66726	PT	GBCM	GBF	HSB	GBR	Sheffield Wednesday
66727	PT	GBSD	GBF	HSB	GBR	Andrew Scott CBE
66728	PT	GBMU	GBF	PTR	GBR	Institution of Railway Operators
66729	PT	GBMU	GBF	PTR	GBR	Derby County
66730	PT	GBMU	GBF	PTR	GBR	
66731	PT	GBMU	GBE	PTR	GBR	
66732	PT	GBMU	GBF	PTR	GBR	GBRf The First Decade 1999-2009 John Smith - MD

Left: *A fleet of 32 EMD-built Class 66s form the main GBRf motive power fleet. The locos are painted in various livery schemes and all are allocated to Peterborough depot. The batch 66718-722 are painted in a special Metronet livery for powering London Underground engineering trains. No. 66722 is illustrated.* **CJM**

Class 73

Vehicle Length: 53ft 8in (16.35m)		Power: 750V dc third rail or English Electric 6K
Height: 12ft 5⅝in (3.79m)		Horsepower: electric - 1,600hp (1,193kW)
Width: 8ft 8in (2.64m)		Horsepower: diesel - 600hp (447kW)
		Electrical Equipment: English Electric

Number		Depot	Pool	Livery	Owner	Operator	Name
73141		SE	GBED	FGF	GBR	GBR	Charlotte
73204	(73125)	SE	GBED	GBR	GBR	GBR	Janice
73205	(73124)	SE	GBED	GBR	GBR	GBR	Jeanette
73206	(731230)	SE	GBED	GBR	GBR	GBR	Lisa
73207	(73122)	SE	GBED	BLL	GBR	GBR	
73208	(73121)	SE	GBED	BLU	GBR	GBR	Kirsten
73209(S)	(73120)	SE	GBZZ	GBR	GBR	GBR	Alison
73212	(73102)	SE	GBED	GBU	GBR	GBR	
73213	(73112)	SE	GBED	FGU	GBR	GBR	

Left: *The largest operator of Class 73 electro-diesels is GB Railfreight, who deploy the fleet on engineering trains especially those operating over the third rail network. As most locos are fitted with buck-eye couplers, the locos are sometimes used as coupling barriers between conventional coupling fitted stock and vehicles using the buck- eye coupler. Painted in plain GBRf blue livery No. 73212 is illustrated. This example fitted with three section snowploughs has lost its buck-eye coupler at the No. 1 end.* **CJM**

Class 92

Vehicle Length: 70ft 1in (21.34m)				Power Collection: 25kV ac overhead / 750V dc third rail			
Height: 13ft 0in (3.95m)				Horsepower: ac - 6,700hp (5,000kW) / dc 5,360hp (4,000kW)			
Width: 8ft 8in (2.66m)				Electrical Equipment: Brush			

Number	Depot	Pool	Livery	Owner	Operator	Name
92010(S)	CO	PTXX	EU2	EU2	-	Moliere
92020(S)	CO/DM	PTXX	EU2	EU2	-	Milton
92021(S)	CO	PTXX	EU2	EU2	-	Purcell
92028	CO	GBET	EU2	EU2	GBR	Saint Saens
92032	CO	GBET	EU2	EU2	GBR	Cesar Franck
92038	CO	GBET	EU2	EU2	GBR	Voltaire
92040(S)	CO/DM	PTXX	EU2	EU2	-	Goethe
92043	CO	GBET	EU2	EU2	GBR	Debussy
92044	CO	GBET	EU2	EU2	GBR	Couperin
92045(S)	CO	PTXX	EU2	EU2	-	Chaucer
92046(S)	CO	PTXX	EU2	EU2	-	Sweelinck

Below: *Following the sale of GB Railfreight by First Group to EuroTunnel in early 2010, the Europorte Class 92s came under the GBRf banner. Sporting Europorte branding, No. 92038 is captured passing Kensington Olympia on 5 August 2010 powering a Willesden to Dollands Moor training run.* **Michael J. Collins**

■ GBRf also operates Class 08 No. 08934 at either Peterborough or Whitemoor. The loco is owned by Alstom and is listed in that section of *Rail Guide 2011*.

Coaching Stock

Barrier Vans

Mk1				
Vehicle Length: 64ft 6in (19.65m)		Height: 12ft 9½in (3.89m)		
		Width: 9ft 3in (2.81m)		

AW51

Number	Depot	Livery	Owner
6376 (ADB975973, 1021)	WB	BLU	PTR
6377 (ADB975975, 1042)	WB	BLU	PTR
6378 (ADB975971, 1054)	AD	BLU	PTR
6379 (ADB975972, 1039)	AD	BLU	PTR

The Future

Right: *The next orders for main line diesel power for GBRf and most other UK operators are unlikely to come from the home market. This is one option, or a scaled down version for the UK: the Vossloh Euro4000, of which Beacon Rail Leasing, a subsidiary of the Bank of Tokyo, now has four on lease to the French arm of Europorte. No. 4002 (92-87-0004-002-7-F-BRLL) was shown at Innotrans 2010 held in Berlin. A striking loco which incorporates the same prime mover as the Class 66, an EMD710!* **CJM**

Freightliner

Address:	✉ 3rd Floor, The Podium, 1 Eversholt Street, London, NW1 2FL
	✆ pressoffice@freightliner.co.uk
	✆ 0207 200 3900
	ⓘ www.freightliner.com

Chief Executive:	Peter Maybury
Managing Director Intermodal:	Adam Cunliffe
Managing Director Heavy Haul:	Paul Smart
Depots:	Freightliner Diesels (FD), Freightliner Electrics (FE), Freightliner Shunters (FS), Ipswich* (IP), Leeds Midland Road (LD), Southampton Maritime (SZ)
	* Stabling point
Parent Company:	Arcapita

Class 08/0

Vehicle Length: 29ft 3in (8.91m)
Height: 12ft 8⅝in (3.87m)
Width: 8ft 6in (2.59m)
Engine: English Electric 6K
Horsepower: 400hp (298kW)
Electrical Equipment: English Electric

Number	Depot	Pool	Livery	Owner	Operator
08077(S)	FS/LH	DHLT	FLR	FLR	FLR
08530(S)	FS	DFLS	FLR	PTR	FLR
08531(S)	FS	DFLS	FLR	PTR	FLR
08575	SZ	DHLT	FLR	PTR	FLR
08585	SZ¤	DFLS	FLR	PTR	FLR
08624	SZ*	DFLS	BLU	PTR	FLR
08691	SZ	DHLT	FLR	FLR	FLR
08785	FD	DFLS	FLR	PTR	FLR
08891	FD	DFLS	FLR	PTR	FLR

* 08624 Working at Tilbury
¤ 08585 At L H Services

Names applied

08585	*Vicky*
08691	*Terri*
08891	*J. R. 1951 - 2005*

Left: *For shunting locos and stock within Freightliner terminals a fleet of Class 08s are deployed. Most are finished in Freightliner green and yellow livery. No. 08891 J. R. 1951-2005 is seen at Southampton.*
Brian Garrett

Class 47/4

Vehicle Length: 63ft 6in (19.35m)
Height: 12ft 10³⁄₈in (3.91m)
Width: 9ft 2in (2.79m)
Electric Train Heat fitted
Engine: Sulzer 12LDA28C
Horsepower: 2,580hp (1,922kW)
Electrical Equipment: Brush

Number		Depot	Pool	Livery	Owner	Operator
47811(S)	(47656)	BH	DFLH	GRN	FLR	-
47816(S)		FD	DFLH	GRN	FLR	-
47830(S)		BH	DFLH	GRN	FLR	-

Class 66/5

Vehicle Length: 70ft 0½in (21.34m)			Engine: EMD 12N-710G3B-EC			
Height: 12ft 10in (3.91m)			Horsepower: 3,300hp (2,462kW)			
Width: 8ft 8¼in (2.65m)			Electrical Equipment: EMD			

Number	Depot	Pool	Livery	Owner	Operator	Name
66501	FD	DFGM	FLR	PTR	FLR	*Japan 2001*
66502	FD	DFGM	FLR	PTR	FLR	*Basford Hall Centenary 2001*
66503	FD	DFGM	FLR	PTR	FLR	*The Railway Magazine*
66504	FD	DFGM	FLR	PTR	FLR	
66505	FD	DFRT	FLR	PTR	FLR	
66506	FD	DFHH	FLR	HSB	FLR	*Crewe Regeneration*
66507(S)	FD	DFRT	FLR	HSB	-	
66508	FD	DFRT	FLR	HSB	FLR	
66509	FD	DFHH	FLR	HSB	FLR	
66510	FD	DFRT	FLR	HSB	FLR	
66511	FD	DFRT	FLR	HSB	FLR	
66512	FD	DFHH	FLR	HSB	FLR	
66513	FD	DFHH	FLR	HSB	FLR	
66514	FD	DFRT	FLR	HSB	FLR	
66515	FD	DFGM	FLR	HSB	FLR	
66516	FD	DFGM	FLR	HSB	FLR	
66517	FD	DFGM	FLR	HSB	FLR	
66518	FD	DFRT	FLR	HSB	FLR	
66519	FD	DFHH	FLR	HSB	FLR	
66520	FD	DFRT	FLR	HSB	FLR	
66522	LD	DFRT	FLR	HSB	FLR	*east london express*
66523	FD	DFRT	FLR	HSB	FLR	
66524	FD	DFHH	FLR	HSB	FLR	
66525	FD	DFHH	FLR	HSB	FLR	
66526	LD	DFHH	FLR	PTR	FLR	*Driver Steve Dunn (George)*
66527	LD	DFHH	FLR	HSB	FLR	*Don Raider*
66528	FD	DFHH	FLR	PTR	FLR	
66529	FD	DFHH	FLR	PTR	FLR	
66530	FD	DFGM	FLR	PTR	FLR	
66531	FD	DFHH	FLR	PTR	FLR	
66532	FD	DFGM	FLR	PTR	FLR	*P&O Nedlloyd Atlas*
66533	FD	DFGM	FLR	PTR	FLR	*Hanjin Express / Senator Express*
66534	FD	DFGM	FLR	PTR	FLR	*OOCL Express*
66535	FD	DFGM	FLR	PTR	FLR	
66536	FD	DFGM	FLR	PTR	FLR	
66537	FD	DFGM	FLR	PTR	FLR	
66538	FD	DFIM	FLR	HSB	FLR	
66539	FD	DFIM	FLR	HSB	FLR	
66540	FD	DFIM	FLR	HSB	FLR	*Ruby*
66541	FD	DFIM	FLR	HSB	FLR	
66542	FD	DFIM	FLR	HSB	FLR	
66543	FD	DFIM	FLR	HSB	FLR	
66544	FD	DFHG	FLR	PTR	FLR	
66545	FD	DFHG	FLR	PTR	FLR	
66546	FD	DFHG	FLR	PTR	FLR	
66547	FD	DFHG	FLR	PTR	FLR	
66548	FD	DFHG	FLR	PTR	FLR	
66549	FD	DFHG	FLR	PTR	FLR	
66550	FD	DFHG	FLR	PTR	FLR	
66551	FD	DFHG	FLR	PTR	FLR	
66552	FD	DFHG	FLR	PTR	FLR	*Maltby Raider*
66553	FD	DFHG	FLR	PTR	FLR	
66554	FD	DFHG	FLR	HSB	FLR	
66555	FD	DFHG	FLR	HSB	FLR	
66556	FD	DFHG	FLR	HSB	FLR	
66557	FD	DFHG	FLR	HSB	FLR	
66558	FD	DFIM	FLR	HSB	FLR	
66559	FD	DFIM	FLR	HSB	FLR	
66560	FD	DFHG	FLR	HSB	FLR	
66561	FD	DFHG	FLR	HSB	FLR	

Freightliner

66562	FD	DFIM	FLR	HSB	FLR	
66563	FD	DFIM	FLR	HSB	FLR	
66564	FD	DFIM	FLR	HSB	FLR	
66565	FD	DFIM	FLR	HSB	FLR	
66566	FD	DFIM	FLR	HSB	FLR	
66567	FD	DFIM	FLR	HSB	FLR	
66568	FD	DFIM	FLR	HSB	FLR	
66569	FD	DFIM	FLR	HSB	FLR	
66570	FD	DFIM	FLR	HSB	FLR	
66571	FD	DFIM	FLR	HSB	FLR	
66572	FD	DFIM	FLR	HSB	FLR	
66575	FD	DFIM	FLR	HSB	FLR	
66576	FD	DFIM	FLR	HSB	FLR	*Hamburg Sud Advantage*
66577	FD	DFIM	FLR	HSB	FLR	
66578(S)	FD	DFTZ	FLR	HSB	-	
66579(S)	FD	DFTZ	FLR	HSB	-	
66580(S)	FD/SZ	DFTZ	FLU	HSB	-	
66581(S)	FD/SZ	DFTZ	FLU	HSB	-	
66582	*Exported, working in Poland for Freightliner Poland as 66009FPL*					
66583	*Exported, working in Poland for Freightliner Poland as 66010FPL*					
66584	*Exported, working in Poland for Freightliner Poland as 66011FPL*					
66585	FD	DFHG	FLR	HAL	FLR	*The Drax Flyer*
66586	*Exported, working in Poland for Freightliner Poland as 66008FPL*					
66587	FD	DFFT	FLR	HAL	FLR	
66588	FD	DFIN	FLR	HAL	FLR	
66589	FD	DFIN	FLR	HAL	FLR	
66590	FD	DFIN	FLR	HAL	FLR	
66591	FD	DFIN	FLR	LTS	FLR	
66592	FD	DFIN	FLR	LTS	FLR	*Johnson Stevens Agencies*
66593	FD	DFIN	FLR	LTS	FLR	*3MG Mersey Multimodal Gateway*
66594	FD	DFIN	FLR	LTS	FLR	*NYK Spirit of Kyoto*
66595	FD	DFHG	FLR	BEA	FLR	
66596	FD	DFHG	FLR	BEA	FLR	
66597	FD	DFHG	FLR	BEA	FLR	
66598	FD	DFHG	FLR	BEA	FLR	
66599	FD	DFHG	FLR	BEA	FLR	

Above: *EMD-built Class 66s became the core motive power for Freightliner after privatisation in the mid 1990s, with members of Class 66/5, 66/6 and 66/9 now in operation. All locos are allocated to Freightliner Diesel (FD) and receive maintenance at Crewe, Midland Road (Leeds) or Southampton. Class 66/5 No 66572 passes southbound through South Kenton with an intermodal service bound for Felixstowe.* **CJM**

Class 66/6

Some stored members of Class 66/6 have operated after being placed in stored status.

Number	Depot	Pool	Livery	Owner	Operator	Name
66601(S)	FD	DFTZ	FLR	PTR	-	The Hope Valley
66602(S)	FD	DFTZ	FLR	PTR	-	
66603(S)	FD	DFTZ	FLR	PTR	-	
66604(S)	FD	DFTZ	FLR	PTR	-	
66605(S)	FD	DFTZ	FLR	PTR	-	
66606(S)	FD	DFTZ	FLR	PTR	-	
66607	FD	DFHG	FLR	PTR	FLR	
66608 *Awaiting export to Poland for Freightliner Poland as 66603FPL*						
66609	FD	DFHG	FLR	PTR	FLR	
66610	FD	DFHG	FLR	PTR	FLR	
66611	FD	DFHG	FLR	PTR	FLR	
66612	FD	DFHG	FLG	PTR	FLR	Forth Raider
66613(S)	FD	DFTZ	FLR	PTR	-	
66614	FD	DFHG	FLR	PTR	FLR	
66615	FD	DFHG	FLR	PTR	FLR	
66616	FD	DFHG	FLR	PTR	FLR	
66617	FD	DFHG	FLR	PTR	FLR	
66618	FD	DFHG	FLR	PTR	FLR	Railways Illustrated Annual Photographic Awards - Alan Barnes
66619	FD	DFHG	FLR	PTR	FLR	Derek W. Johnson MBE
66620	FD	DFHG	FLR	PTR	FLR	
66621	FD	DFHG	FLR	PTR	FLR	
66622	FD	DFHG	FLR	PTR	FLR	
66623	FD	DFHG	AIN	HSB	FLR	Bill Bolsover
66624 *Exported, working in Poland for Freightliner Poland as 66602FPL*						
66625 *Exported, working in Poland for Freightliner Poland as 66601FPL*						

Originally 25 Freightliner Class 66s were fitted with improved tractive effort for operating heavier trains. By 2011 two of the batch have been exported to Poland. No. 66607 is shown powering a heavy cement train. **Tony Christie**

Class 66/9

Number	Depot	Pool	Livery	Owner	Operator	Name
66951	FD	DFHG	FLR	HSB	FLR	
66952	FD	DFHG	FLR	HSB	FLR	
66953	FD	DFHG	FLR	BEA	FLR	
66954	FD	DFIN	FLR	BEA	FLR	
66955	FD	DFIN	FLR	BEA	FLR	
66956	FD	DFIN	FLR	BEA	FLR	
66957	FD	DFIN	FLR	BEA	FLR	Stephenson Locomotive Society 1909-2009

Freight Operating Companies - Freightliner

Freightliner

Class 70 - PH37ACmi

Vehicle Length: 71ft 2½in (21.71m)	Engine: GE V16-cyliner PowerHaul 616
Height: 12ft 10in (3.91m)	Horsepower: 3,700hp (2,750kW)
Width: 8ft 8in (2.64m)	Electrical Equipment: General Electric

Number	Depot	Pool	Livery	Owner	Operator	Name/Notes
70001	FD	DFGI	FLP	LTS	FLR	*PowerHaul*
70002	FD	DFGH	FLP	LTS	FLR	
70003	FD	DFGH	FLP	LTS	FLR	
70004	FD	DFGH	FLP	LTS	FLR	
70005	FD	DFGH	FLP	LTS	FLR	
70006	FD	DFGH	FLP	LTS	FLR	
70007	FD	DFGI	FLP	LTS	FLR	
70008	FD	DFGI	FLP	LTS	FLR	
70009	FD	DFGI	FLP	LTS	FLR	
70010	FD	DFGH	FLP	LTS	FLR	
70011	FD	DFGH	FLP	LTS	FLR	
70012	FD	DHLT	FLP	LTS	-	*Stored due to accident damage on delivery*
70013	FD	DHLT	FLP	LTS	FLR	*Due for delivery Autumn 2011*
70014	FD	DHLT	FLP	LTS	FLR	*Due for delivery Autumn 2011*
70015	FD	DHLT	FLP	LTS	FLR	*Due for delivery Autumn 2011*
70016	FD	DHLT	FLP	LTS	FLR	*Due for delivery Autumn 2011*
70017	FD	DHLT	FLP	LTS	FLR	*Due for delivery Autumn 2011*
70018	FD	DHLT	FLP	LTS	FLR	*Due for delivery Autumn 2011*
70019	FD	DHLT	FLP	LTS	FLR	*Due for delivery Autumn 2011*
70020	FD	DHLT	FLP	LTS	FLR	*Due for delivery Autumn 2011*

Above: *The six Class 70s operational in the UK in 2010 had a slow start in service with many problems reported. However, by the end of the year reliability had improved and the batch 70007-70012 incorporated a number of modifications. On 16 March 2010 No. 70003 is seen near Cam & Dursley powering a Stoke Gifford bound empty coal train.* **Nathan Williamson**

■ *Originally 30 locomotives were ordered in 2007 for delivery in 2009-10. 12 locos were delivered by January 2011. Locos 70013-020 are scheduled for delivery in Autumn 2011, and the balance in 2012.*

Class 86/5 & 86/6

Vehicle Length: 58ft 6in (17.83m)	Power Collection: 25kV ac overhead
Height: 13ft 0⅝in (3.97m)	Horsepower: 5,900hp (4,400kW)
Width: 8ft 8¼in (2.64m)	Electrical Equipment: GEC

Number		Depot	Pool	Livery	Owner	Operator
86501	(86608/86408)	FE	DFGC	FLR	FLR	FLR
86604	(86404)	FE	DFNC	FLR	FLR	FLR
86605	(86405)	FE	DFNC	FLR	FLR	FLR
86607	(86407)	FE	DFNC	FLR	FLR	FLR
86609	(86409)	FE	DFNC	FLR	PTR	FLR

86610	(86410)	FE	DFNC	FLR	PTR	FLR
86612	(86412)	FE	DFNC	FLR	PTR	FLR
86613	(86413)	FE	DFNC	FLR	PTR	FLR
86614(S)	(86414)	CP	DHLT	FLR	PTR	FLR
86621	(86421)	FE	DFNC	FLR	PTR	FLR
86622	(86422)	FE	DFNC	FLP	PTR	FLR
86627	(86427)	FE	DFNC	FLR	PTR	FLR
86628	(86428)	FE	DFNC	FLR	PTR	FLR
86632	(86432)	FE	DFNC	FLR	PTR	FLR
86637	(86437)	FE	DFNC	FLP	PTR	FLR
86638	(86438)	FE	DFNC	FLR	PTR	FLR
86639	(86439)	FE	DFNC	FLR	PTR	FLR

Below: *One Class 86/5 and 16 Class 86/6s are operated by Freightliner, based at Crewe and working on the West Coast and Great Eastern lines. The unique Class 86/5 No. 86501 is shown between duties at Ipswich.* **Tony Christie**

Freight Operating Companies - Freightliner

Class 90

Vehicle Length: 61ft 6in (18.74m)	Power Collection: 25kV ac overhead
Height: 13ft 0¼in (3.96m)	Horsepower: 7,860hp (5,860kW)
Width: 9ft 0in (2.74m)	Electrical Equipment: GEC

Number	Depot	Pool	Livery	Owner	Operator
90016	CP	DFLC	FLR	PTR	FLR
90041	CP	DFLC	FLR	PTR	FLR
90042	CP	DFLC	FLY	PTR	FLR
90043	CP	DFLC	FLY	PTR	FLR
90044	CP	DFLC	FLY	PTR	FLR
90045	CP	DFLC	FLP	PTR	FLR
90046	CP	DFLC	FLR	PTR	FLR
90047	CP	DFLC	FLY	PTR	FLR
90048	CP	DFLC	FLP	PTR	FLR
90049	CP	DFLC	FLP	PTR	FLR

Name applied

90043 *Freightliner Coatbridge*

Above: *In 2010 a start was made at repainting both Class 86 and 90 locos into the new Freightliner PowerHaul livery, giving a very striking and smart appearance to the fleet. The new livery is shown on Class 90/0 No. 90045 near Lichfield on 2 September 2010.* **Stacey Thew**

Mendip Rail

Address:	✉ Torr Works, East Cranmore, Shepton Mallet, Somerset, BA4 5SQ
	✍ info@mendip-rail.co.uk
	✆ 01749 880672
	ⓘ www.mendip-rail.co.uk
Managing Director:	Alan Taylor
Depots:	Merehead (MD), Whatley (WH)
Parent Company:	Aggregate Industries and Hanson

Class 08

Vehicle Length: 29ft 3in (8.91m)
Height: 12ft 8⅝in (3.87m)
Width: 8ft 6in (2.59m)

Engine: English Electric 6K
Horsepower: 400hp (298kW)
Electrical Equipment: English Electric

Number	Depot	Pool	Livery	Owner	Operator		Number					
08643	MD	MBDL	GRN	FOS	MRL		08652	WH	MBDL	HAN	HAN	MRL
08650	MD	MBDL	FOS	FOS	MRL		08731	MD	MBDL	BLU	FOS	MRL
							08947	WH	MBDL	BLU	FOS	MRL

Class 59/0

Vehicle Length: 70ft 0½in (21.34m)
Height: 12ft 10in (3.91m)
Width: 8ft 8¼in (2.65m)

Engine: EMD 16-645 E3C
Horsepower: 3,000hp (2,462kW)
Electrical Equipment: EMD

Number	Depot	Pool	Livery	Owner	Operator	Name
59001	MD	XYPO	AGI	FOS	MRL	*Yeoman Endeavour*
59002	MD	XYPO	FOS	FOS	MRL	*Alan J Day*
59003	-	-	HHP	HHP	HHP	*Yeoman Highlander*
59004	MD	XYPO	FOS	FOS	MRL	*Paul A Hammond*
59005	MD	XYPO	AGI	FOS	MRL	*Kenneth J Painter*

■ Loco No. 59003 Yeoman Highlander, *originally used by Foster Yeoman in the UK, is now owned and operated by Heavy Haul Power International and based in Germany.*

Above: *Four Class 59/0 locos, the first American main line diesel locos to work in the UK, are operated by Foster Yeoman/ Aggregate Industries and work on Mendip aggregate trains. No. 59005* Kenneth J. Painter *shows the latest Aggregate Industries livery at Westbury.* **Tony Christie**

Class 59/1

Number	Depot	Pool	Livery	Owner	Operator	Name
59101	MD	XYPA	HAN	HAN	MRL	*Village of Whatley*
59102	MD	XYPA	HAN	HAN	MRL	*Village of Chantry*
59103	MD	XYPA	HAN	HAN	MRL	*Village of Mells*
59104	MD	XYPA	HAN	HAN	MRL	*Village of Great Elm*

SW1001 'Switcher'

Vehicle Length: 40ft 6in (12.34m)				Engine: GM 8-645E		
Height: 14ft 3in (4.34m)				Horsepower: 1,000hp (746kW)		
Width: 10ft 0in (3.04m)				Electrical Equipment: EMD		

Number	Depot	Pool	Livery	Owner	Operator	Name
44	MD	-	FOS	FOS	MRL	*Yeoman Endeavour II*
120	WH	-	HAN	HAN	MRL	

Right: *For shunting aggregate wagons at Merehead and Whatley quarries two US designed and built 'switchers' are operated. Due to gauge restrictions the locos are unable to operate on the main line network. General Motors built modified SW1001 No. 44 Yeoman Endeavour II seen in the yard at Merehead.* **Tony Christie**

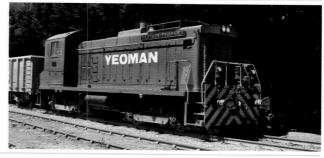

SNCF - French Railways

Address: ✉ Fret-SNCF, 10 Palace de Budapest, Paris, 75009

📠 info@fret-sncf.com

ⓘ www.fret-sncf.com

Class 92

Vehicle Length: 70ft 1in (21.34m)				Power Collection: 25kV ac overhead / 750V dc third rail		
Height: 13ft 0in (3.95m)				Horsepower: ac - 6,700hp (5,000kW) / dc 5,360hp (4,000kW)		
Width: 8ft 8in (2.66m)				Electrical Equipment: Brush		

Number	Depot	Pool	Livery	Owner	Operator	Name
92006 (S)	CE	WNWX	SNF	SNF	-	*Louis Armand*
92014 (S)	CE	WNWX	SNF	SNF	-	*Emile Zola*
92018 (S)	CE	WNWX	SNF	SNF	-	*Stendhal*
92023 (S)	CE	WNWX	SNF	SNF	-	*Ravel*
92033 (S)	CE	WNWX	SNF	SNF	-	*Berlioz*

Above: *French Railways officially own five Class 92s, built as part of the core Class 92 build, which was originally owned by Railfreight (now EWS), European Passenger Services (EPS) and French Railways (SNCF). The five are allocated to Crewe International depot but are presently stored. No. 92006 Louis Armand is seen at North Pole depot.* **CJM**

Eurotunnel

Address (UK): ✉ The Channel Tunnel Group Ltd, UK Terminal,
Ashford Road, Folkestone, CT18 8XX

✎ info@eurotunnel.com

✆ 01303 282222

ⓘ www.eurotunnel.com

Chairman & CEO: Jacques Gounon

Depot: Coquelles, France (CO)

Shuttle

All locomotives are allocated to the Eurotunnel Maintenance Facility in Coquelles, France, but can be stabled and receive light repair at Cheriton terminal in the UK.

Class 9/0

Vehicle Length: 72ft 2in (22m)	Power Collection: 25kV ac overhead
Height: 13ft 9in (4.20m)	Horsepower: 7,720hp (5,760kW)
Width: 9ft 9in (3.01m)	Electrical Equipment: Brush

Original loco order, many now rebuilt and upgraded to Class 9/8.

9005	*Jessye Norman*	9018	*Wilhelmena Fernandez*	9033	*Montserrat Caballe*
9007	*Dame Joan Sutherland*	9022	*Dame Janet Baker*	9036	*Alan Fondary*
9011	*José Van Dam*	9024	*Gotthard 1882*	9037	*Gabriel Bacquier*
9013	*Maria Callas*	9026	*Furkatunnel 1982*	9040	
9015	*Lötschberg 1913*	9029	*Thomas Allan*		

Left: *When the Channel Tunnel opened a fleet of Berne Gauge Tri-Bo locos were introduced for powering passenger and freight shuttle services on the self-contained network between Coquelles in France and Cheriton in England. The locos were built by Brush Traction of Loughborough. One of the batch of 13 Class 9/1 locos, No. 9102, is viewed at Coquelles depot in France. This loco is now renumbered to 9712.* **CJM**

Class 9/1

Class 9/1 locos presently under refurbishment and upgrade, being renumbered in 9711-9723 series.

Vehicle Length: 72ft 2in (22m)	Power Collection: 25kV ac overhead
Height: 13ft 9in (4.20m)	Horsepower: 7,720hp (5,760kW)
Width: 9ft 9in (3.01m)	Electrical Equipment: Brush

9105	9106	9108	9109	9110	9111	9112	9113

Class 9/7

Vehicle Length: 72ft 2in (22m)	Power Collection: 25kV ac overhead
Height: 13ft 9in (4.20m)	Horsepower: 9,387hp (7,000kW)
Width: 9ft 9in (3.01m)	Electrical Equipment: Brush

9701	9702	9703	9704	9705	9706	9707
9711 (9101)	9712 (9102)	9713 (9103)	9714 (9104)	9717 (9107)		

Class 9/8

Rebuilt from Class 9/0 locos, 800 added to original running number on conversion.

Vehicle Length: 72ft 2in (22m)	Power Collection: 25kV ac overhead
Height: 13ft 9in (4.20m)	Horsepower: 9,387hp (7,000kW)
Width: 9ft 9in (3.01m)	Electrical Equipment: Brush

9801	*Lesley Garrett*	9808	*Elisabeth Soderstrom*	9816	*Willard White*
9802	*Stuart Burrows*	9809	*Francois Pollet*	9817	*José Carreras*
9803	*Benjamin Luxon*	9810	*Jean-Philippe Courtis*	9819	*Maria Ewing*
9804	*Victoria de Los Angeles*	9812	*Luciano Pavarotti*	9820	*Nicolai Ghiaurov*
9806	*Regine Crespin*	9814	*Lucia Pop*	9821	*Teresa Berganza*

9823	*Dame Elisabeth Legge-*	9828	*Dame Kiri Te Kanawa*	9835	*Nicolai Gedda*
	Schwarzkopf	9831		9838	*Hildegard Behrens*
9825		9832	*Renata Tebaldi*		
9827	*Barbara Hendricks*	9834	*Mirella Freni*		

Right: *Channel Tunnel Class 9/8 shuttle loco No. 9803* Benjamin Luxon *rounds the loop to the Cheriton Terminal platforms on 11 May 2010, with a car transporter service from Coquelles. A number of the original Class 9/0 locos have now been rebuilt as Class 9/8s with more powerful electrical equipment and renumbered, with the second digit of their number changing from a '0' to an '8'. No. 9805 shows the latest blue and silver EuroTunnel livery with large Euro tunnel branding on the bodyside.*
Brian Morrison

MaK DE1004

Vehicle Length: 54ft 2in (16.50m)
Diesel Engine: MTU 12V396tc
Horsepower: 1,260hp (939.5kW)
Electrical Equipment: BBC

0001 (21901)	0002 (21902)	0003 (21903)	0004 (21904)	0005 (21905)

Allocated to TOPS pool PTXX

Right: *Five MaK built Bo-Bo locos are owned by Euro Tunnel and allocated to Coquelles. These are used for either engineering trains or to rescue/assist Shuttle, Eurostar or Channel Tunnel freight trains. They are fitted with drop-head Scharfenberg couplers and are authorised to operate over HS1 as far as London St Pancras. The centre cab design has an output of 1,260hp and for assisting purposes they usually operate in pairs. No. 0003 (TOPS No. 21903) is seen inside the maintenance shed at Coquelles.* **CJM**

■ Two additional locos are to be added to stock in 2011, these will be rebuilt from NS 6400 class Nos. 6456 and 6457, with provisional numbering allocated as 0006 (21906) and 0007 (21907).

Hunslet/Schöma

Diesel Engine: Deutz
Horsepower: 200hp (270kW)
Mechanical Equipment: Hunslet

0031	*Frances*	0034	*Amanda*	0037	*Lydie*	0040	*Jill*
0032	*Elisabeth*	0035	*Mary*	0038	*Jenny*	0041	*Kim*
0033	*Silke*	0036	*Lawrence*	0039	*Pacita*	0042	*Nicole*

Network Rail

Address: ✉ Kings Place, 90 York Way, London, N1 9AG
✎ enquiries@networkrail.co.uk
℗ Helpline: 08457 114141, Switchboard: 0203 356 9595
ⓘ www.networkrail.co.uk

Chief Executive: Iain Coucher*   **Director Operations:** Robin Gisby
Depots: Heaton (HT), Barrow Hill (BH), Derby (DF), Rugby (RU)
* Replaced by David Higgins from February 2011

Class 08

	Vehicle Length: 29ft 3in (8.91m)	Engine: English Electric 6K
	Height: 12ft 8⅝in (3.87m)	Horsepower: 400hp (298kW)
	Width: 8ft 6in (2.59m)	Electrical Equipment: English Electric

Number	Depot	Pool	Livery	Owner	Operator						
08417	DF	QADD	SEC	NRL	NRL	08956	DF	QADD	BLU	NRL	NRL

Class 31/1 & 31/4

	Vehicle Length: 56ft 9in (17.29m)	Engine: English Electric 12SVT
	Height: 12ft 7in (3.91m)	Horsepower: 1,470hp (1,097kW)
	Width: 8ft 9in (2.65m)	Electrical Equipment: Brush
	31/4 Fitted with electric train heat	

Number	Depot	Pool	Livery	Owner	Operator					
31105	DF	QADD	NRL	NRL	NRL	31285	DF	QADD	NRL	NRL	NRL
31233	DF	QADD	NRL	NRL	NRL	31465*	DF	QADD	NRL	NRL	NRL

* Previously numbered 31565, 31213

Left: *A very important part of the UK rail network is the operation of infrastructure test trains, ensuring track, power supplies and lineside equipment are in good order. To power these trains several locos are maintained by RVEL in Derby. Four Class 31s are in operation painted in high visibility yellow. No. 31465 is shown on the rear of a track assessment train at Honiton.* **Stacey Thew**

Class 37 & 97/3

	Vehicle Length: 61ft 6in (18.74m)	Engine: English Electric 12CSVT
	Height: 13ft 0¼in (3.96m)	Horsepower: 1,750hp (1,304kW)
	Width: 8ft 11⅝in (2.73m)	Electrical Equipment: English Electric

Number	Depot	Pool	Livery	Owner	Operator	Name
37198	BH	MBDL	NRL	NRL	NRL	
97301 (37100)	ZA	QETS	NRL	NRL	NRL	
97302 (37170)	ZA	QETS	NRL	NRL	NRL	
97303 (37178)	ZA	QETS	NRL	NRL	NRL	
97304 (37217)	ZA	QETS	NRL	NRL	NRL	John Tiley

Left: *Five Class 37s are operated by Network Rail, four of these - classified as 97/3 - are dedicated to development trains in association with ERTMS on the Cambrian route in Wales. In this rare view Nos. 97301, 97302 and 97303 pose in the yard at the RTC Derby, alongside Class 31 No. 31459, DBSO No. 9701 and NMT power car No. 43013.* **Andy Royle**

Class 43

					Engine: MTU 16V4000 R31R	
	Vehicle Length: 58ft 5in (18.80m)				Horsepower: 2,250hp (1,680kW)	
	Height: 12ft 10in (3.90m)				Electrical Equipment: Brush	
	Width: 8ft 11in (2.73m)					

Number	Depot	Pool	Livery	Owner	Operator	Name
43013	HT	QCAR	NRL	PTR	NRL	
43014	HT	QCAR	NRL	PTR	NRL	
43062	HT	QCAR	NRL	PTR	NRL	*John Armitt*

Right: *The HST-based New Measurement Train or NMT operates over most main lines on a semi-timetabled basis analysing the rail and track bed condition for any defects which could affect the safety of the railway. One coach in the train is also equipped with a non power collecting pantograph for inspecting the overhead contact wire. While on a Plymouth to London run, the train is led by power car No. 43062 and seen passing Dawlish.* **CJM**

Class 73/1

Vehicle Length: 53ft 8in (16.35m)				Power: 750V dc third rail or English Electric 6K	
Height: 12ft 5⅞in (3.79m)				Horsepower: electric - 1,600hp (1,193kW)	
Width: 8ft 8in (2.64m)				Horsepower: diesel - 600hp (447kW)	
				Electrical Equipment: English Electric	

Number	Depot	Pool	Livery	Owner	Operator
73138	DF	QADD	NRL	NRL	NRL

Below: *Recently introduced electro-diesel No. 73138 shows its revised front end at Woking.* **Stacey Thew**

Class 86/9

		Vehicle Length: 58ft 6in (17.83m)			Power Collection: 25kV ac overhead	
		Height: 13ft 0⅝in (3.97m)			Horsepower: 2,950hp (2,200kW)	
		Width: 8ft 8¼in (2.64m)			Electrical Equipment: GEC	

Number		Depot	Pool	Livery	Owner	Operator	Name
86901	(86253)	RU	QACL	NRL	NRL	NRL	*Chief Engineer*
86902	(86210)	RU	QACL	NRL	NRL	NRL	*Rail Vehicle Engineering*

Right: *A pair of former Class 86/2s are operated by Network Rail as mobile load bank locomotives and classified as 86/9. The locos are used to draw current from the overhead to gauge performance of the system. Each loco retains one operational bogie to allow self propulsion. In winter months the pair are sometimes used for East Coast de-icing duties. The locos are seen stabled at Rugby.* **Brian Morrison**

Infrastructure Companies - Network Rail

Class 950

Vehicle Length: 64ft 9¾in (19.74m)	Engine: 1 x NT855R5 of 285hp per vehicle	
Height: 12ft 4½in (3.77m)	Horsepower: 570hp (425kW)	
Width: 9ft 3⅛in (2.82m)	Seats (total/car): 124S, 59S/65S	

Number	Formation	Depot	Livery	Owner	Operator	Note
950001	999600+999601	ZA	NRL	NRL	NRL	Track assessment train (Class 150 outline)

Left: *Network Rail set No. 950001 is based on a Class 150, with its body shells built alongside the production Class 150/1 sets at BREL York. No. 950001 is a track assessment train and travels over the entire railway studying track and rail conditions. The set is seen stabled at Bristol Temple Meads.* **Brian Garrett**

Class 960

Length: 64ft 6in (19.66m)	Engine: 2 x Leyland 150hp	
Height: 12ft 8½in (3.87m)	Horsepower: 300hp (224kW)	
Width: 9ft 3in (2.81m)	Seats (total/car): None	

Number	Formation	Depot	Livery	Owner	Operator	Notes
960201(S)	977975	CF	NRL	NRL	(ATW)	Ex Class 121 55027, Severn Tunnel Train
960202(S)	977976	CF	NRL	NRL	(ATW)	Ex Class 121 55031, Severn Tunnel Train

Left: *Although stored out of use at Cardiff Canton, the two former Network Rail Class 960 Severn Tunnel emergency train units No. 960201 and 960202 are still visible. The former Class 121 'Bubble' cars were rebuilt with side opening doors to assist in evacuation of passengers and staff from the Severn Tunnel in case of an accident. This operation is now undertaken by special road/rail units kept at Severn Tunnel Junction.* **CJM**

De-Icing Cars

Vehicle Length: 66ft 4in (20.22m)	Horsepower: 500hp (370kW)	
Height: 12ft 4in (3.75m)	Seats (total/car): None	
Width: 9ft 2in (2.82m)		

Number	Vehicle	Depot	Livery	Owner	Operator	Notes
489102	68501 (977975)	TN	NRL	NRL	NRL	De-icing vehicle modified from Class 489 DMBS
489105	68504	TN	NRL	GBR	GBR	De-icing vehicle modified from Class 489 DMBS
489106	68505	TN	NRL	GBR	GBR	De-icing vehicle modified from Class 489 DMBS
489109	68508 (977976)	TN	NRL	NRL	NRL	De-icing vehicle modified from Class 489 DMBS

Left: *Icing on the surface of the third rail on South Eastern, Southern and South West Trains routes can cause serious problems with the power collection pick up of EMU trains. Network Rail operate a fleet of four former Class 489 DMBS vehicles for de-icing which operate on a GBRf safety case and are kept at Tonbridge. Nos. 489106, 489105, Class 73 No. 73204 and 489109 are shown passing Ashford.* **Brian Stephenson**

Hauled Stock

Royal Train

Mk2				Height: 12ft 9½in (3.89m)	
Vehicle Length: 66ft 0in (20.11m)				Width: 9ft 3in (2.81m)	
Mk 3				Height: 12ft 9in (3.88m)	
Vehicle Length: 75ft 0in (22.86m)				Width: 8ft 11in (2.71m)	

Number	Type	Depot	Livery	Operator	Use
2903 (11001)	AT5G	ZN	ROY	NRL/DBS	HM The Queen's Saloon
2904 (12001)	AT5G	ZN	ROY	NRL/DBS	HRH The Duke of Edinburgh's Saloon
2915 (10735)	AT5G	ZN	ROY	NRL/DBS	Royal Household Sleeping Coach
2916 (40512)	AT5G	ZN	ROY	NRL/DBS	HRH The Prince of Wales's Dining Coach
2917 (40514)	AT5G	ZN	ROY	NRL/DBS	Kitchen Car and Royal Household Dining Coach
2918 (40515)	AT5G	ZN	ROY	NRL/DBS	Royal Household Coach
2919 (40518)	AT5G	ZN	ROY	NRL/DBS	Royal Household Coach
2920 (17109)	AT5B	ZN	ROY	NRL/DBS	Generator Coach and Household Sleeping Coach
2921 (17107)	AT5B	ZN	ROY	NRL/DBS	Brake, Coffin Carrier and Household Accommodation
2922	AT5G	ZN	ROY	NRL/DBS	HRH The Prince of Wales's Sleeping Coach
2923	AT5G	ZN	ROY	NRL/DBS	Royal Passenger Saloon

Right: *Eleven Royal Train vehicles are currently in stock. These are allocated to Wolverton and operate as required for the conveyance of HM The Queen, HRH Prince Philip, and HRH The Prince of Wales. Saloon No. 2915, a Royal Household sleeping coach, rebuilt from Mk3 sleeper No. 10735 is seen formed in the Royal set passing Dawlish on 11 March 2010 while en route from Newton Abbot to Exeter St Davids.* **CJM**

Hauled Stock

Number	Type	Depot	Livery	Operator	Use
1205 (6348)	AJ1F/RFO	ZA	VIR	NRL	Out of use
1256 (3296)	AJ1F/RFO	ZA	NRL	NRL	Special vehicle
5981	AC2F/TSO	ZA	NRL	NRL	Special vehicle
6260 (92116)	AX51/GEN	ZA(S)	RTK	NRL	Generator
6261 (92988)	AX51/GEN	ZA	NRL	NRL	Generator
6262 (92928)	AX51/GEN	ZA(S)	NRL	NRL	Generator
6263 (92961)	AX51/GEN	ZA	NRL	NRL	Generator
6264 (92923)	AX51/GEN	ZA	NRL	NRL	Generator
9481	AE2D/BSO	ZA	NRL	NRL	Radio survey coach
9701 (9528)	AF2F/DBSO	ZA	NRL	NRL	Remote driving car (Mentor train)
9702 (9510)	AF2F/DBSO	ZA	NRL	NRL	Remote driving car
9703 (9517)	AF2F/DBSO	ZA	NRL	NRL	Remote driving car
9708 (9530)	AF2F/DBSO	ZA	NRL	NRL	Remote driving car (Structure Gauging)
9714 (9536)	AF2F/DBSO	ZA	NRL	NRL	Remote driving car
72612 (6156)	Mk2f/TSO	ZA	RTB	NRL	Brake force runner
72616 (6007)	Mk2f/TSO	ZA	NRL	NRL	Brake force runner
72630 (6094)	Mk2f/TSO	ZA	NRL	NRL	Brake force runner
72631 (6096)	Mk2f/TSO	ZA	NRL	NRL	Brake force runner
72639 (6070)	Mk2f/TSO	ZA	NRL	NRL	Brake force runner
80211(S)	Mk1/COU	ZA	NRL	NRL	Special vehicle
82115	MK3/DVT	ZA	VIR	NRL	Driving Van Trailer
92114 (81443)	Mk1/BG	ZA	NRL	NRL	Special vehicle
92939 (92039)	Mk1/BG	ZA	INT	NRL	Special vehicle
99666 (3250)	Mk2e/FO	ZA	NRL	NRL	Ultrasonic Test Train
971001 (94150)	Mk1/NKA	BS	NRL	NRL	Tool Van
971002 (94190)	Mk1/NKA	WA	NRL	NRL	Tool Van

Network Rail

971003	(94191)	Mk1/NKA	BS	NRL	NRL	Tool Van
971004	(94168)	Mk1/NKA	WA	NRL	NRL	Tool Van
975025	(60755)	6B Buffet	ZA	GRN	NRL	Control Inspection Saloon *Caroline*
975081	(35313)	Mk1/BSK	ZA	NRL	NRL	Structure Gauging Train
975091	(34615)	Mk1/BSK	ZA	NRL	NRL	Overhead line test coach - *Mentor*
975280	(21263)	Mk1/BCK	ZA	NRL	NRL	Staff coach
975464	(35171)	Mk1/BSK	IS	NRL	NRL	Snowblower coach *Ptarmigan*
975486	(34100)	Mk1/BSK	IS	NRL	NRL	Snowblower coach *Polar Bear*
975494	(35082)	Mk1/BSK	MG	NRL	NRL	Re-Railing Train (Margam)
975573	(34729)	Mk1/BSK	MG	NRL	NRL	Re-Railing Train (Margam)
975574	(34599)	Mk1/BSK	TO	NRL	NRL	Re-Railing Train (Toton)
975611	(80915)	Mk1/BG	TO	NRL	NRL	Re-Railing Train (Toton)
975612	(80922)	Mk1/BG	MG	NRL	NRL	Re-Railing Train (Margam)
975613	(80918)	Mk1/BG	TO	NRL	NRL	Re-Railing Train (Toton)
975814	(41000)	HST/TF	EC	NRL	NRL	NMT Conference coach
975984	(40000)	HST/TRUB	EC	NRL	NRL	NMT Lecture coach
977337	(9395)	Mk2/BSO	ZA	NRL	NRL	Track recording - Staff coach
977868	(5846)	Mk2e/TSO	ZA	NRL	NRL	Radio Survey coach
977869	(5858)	Mk2e/TSO	ZA	NRL	NRL	Radio Survey coach
977969	(14112)	Mk2/BFK	ZA	NRL	NRL	Staff coach (Former Royal Saloon 2906)
977974	(5854)	Mk2e/TSO	ZA	NRL	NRL	Laboratory coach (Owned by Delta Rail)
977983	(3407)	Mk2f/FO	ZA	NRL	NRL	Hot Box Detection coach
977984	(40501)	HST/TRFK	EC	NRL	NRL	NMT Staff coach
977985	(6019)	Mk2f/TSO	ZA	NRL	NRL	Structure Gauging Train
977986	(3189)	Mk2d/FO	ZA	NRL	NRL	Track Recording coach
977990	(92937)	Mk1/BG	SP	NRL	NRL	Tool Van
977991	(92991)	Mk1/BG	SP	NRL	NRL	Tool Van
977993	(44053)	HST/TGS	EC	NRL	NRL	NMT Overhead Line Test coach
977994	(44087)	HST/TGS	EC	NRL	NRL	NMT Recording coach
977995	(40719)	HST/TRFM	EC	NRL	NRL	NMT Generator coach
977996	(44062)	HST/TGS	EC	NRL	NRL	NMT Battery coach
977997	(72613)	Mk2f/TSO	ZA	NRL	NRL	Radio Survey Test Vehicle (originally TSO 6126)
999508		Saloon	ZA	NRL	NRL	Track Recording coach - UTU3
999550		Mk2	ZA	NRL	NRL	Track Recording coach (Purpose built)
999602	(62483)	Mk1/REP	ZA	NRL	SEC	Ultrasonic Test coach - UTU3
999605	(62482)	Mk1/REP	ZA	NRL	NRL	Ultrasonic Test coach - UTU2
999606	(62356)	Mk1/REP	ZA	NRL	NRL	Ultrasonic Test coach - UTU4

Left: *Former Hastings line buffet car No. 60755 was rebuilt in the late 1960s as the Southern Region General Manager's saloon and numbered DB975025. The vehicle after privatisation transferred to Network Rail and it is now used as an inspection saloon, based at Derby. It is currently painted in mock Southern green livery and named* Caroline. *It is fitted with blue star multiple control equipment and is seen powered by a DRS Class 37 passing Dawlish Warren.* **CJM**

Right: *After being displaced from Great Eastern line use by Mk3 DVTs on the London-Norwich route, several DBSOs were transferred to Network Rail for use at the remote ends of test trains. The vehicles were heavily modified for their new role and each now has specific equipment for working with different test cars. DBSO No. 9714 leads one of the ultrasonic test trains towards Starcross powered by Class 31 No. 31106 on the rear.* **Michael J. Collins**

Right: *Former Southern Region 4REP motor car No. 62356, now Network Rail No. 999606, is an ultrasonic test coach, identified as UTU4. The coach is usually formed as the middle coach of a three vehicle test set powered by a Class 31. In this view the coach is seen at Bristol Temple Meads.*
Nathan Williamson

Snowploughs

Independent Drift Ploughs – ZZA

Number	Allocation
ADB965203	Thornaby
ADB965206	Doncaster
ADB965208	Inverness
ADB965209	Bristol Barton H
ADB965210	Tonbridge
ADB965211	Wigan
ADB965217	Mossend
ADB965219	Mossend
ADB965223	Margam
ADB965224	Carlisle
ADB965230	Carlisle
ADB965231	Bristol Barton H
ADB965232	Peterborough
ADB965233	Peterborough
ADB965234	Mossend
ADB965235	Margam
ADB965236	Tonbridge

ADB965237	Wigan
ADB965240	Inverness
ADB965241	Doncaster
ADB965242	Thornaby
ADB965243	Mossend

Below: *Independent 'Drift Plough' No. 965230 is seen in black livery stabled at Carlisle.* **Stacey Thew**

Beilhack Patrol Ploughs (ex-Class 40 bogies) – ZZA

Number	Allocation
ADB965576	Mossend
ADB965577	Mossend
ADB965578	Carlisle
ADB965579	Carlisle
ADB965580	Wigan
ADB965581	Wigan
ADB966096	Doncaster

ADB866097	Doncaster
ADB966098	Peterborough
ADB966099	Peterborough

Right: *Ten ex-Class 40 bogies fitted with Beilhack ploughs are in operation. No. ADB965578 of the Carlisle allocation is illustrated.* **Tony Christie**

Beilhack Snow Blowers – ZWA

Number	Allocation
ADB968500	Rutherglen
ADB968501	Rutherglen

Right: *With the UK not experiencing many major snow falls, very few snowploughs are to be found on the network. Railways in the UK tend to stop running if snow gets more than an inch or two above rail height, unlike most other countries in the world. However, two heavy duty snow blowers, built by Beilhack and originally allocated to the Southern Region and Scottish Region, are still available to Network Rail. Both are allocated to Rutherglen in Scotland and used in various locations as needed. No. ADB968501 is illustrated.* **CJM**

Infrastructure Companies - Network Rail

Network Rail ø Vehicles owned by Fastline are in the process of sale to new operators

Track Machines (On-Track Plant)

Plasser & Theurer DTS-62-N – Dynamic Track Stabiliser – ZWA

DR72201	Fastline ø	DR72208	Fastline ø	DR72214*	Fastline ø
DR72203	Fastline ø	DR72209	Fastline ø		
DR72205	Fastline ø	DR72211	Balfour Beatty	* Previously DR72210	
DR72206	Fastline ø	DR72213	Balfour Beatty		

Plasser & Theurer 09-16-CSM – Tamper/Liner – ZWA

DR73001	Fastline ø	DR73301	Fastline ø

Plasser & Theurer 09-32-CSM – Tamper/Liner – ZWA

DR73101	Fastline ø	DR73104	Fastline ø	DR73106	Fastline ø
DR73103	Colas	DR73105	Colas	DR73107	Fastline ø

Plasser & Theurer 09-32-RT – Tamper/Liner – ZWA

DR73108	*Tiger*		Amey

Plasser & Theurer 09-3X – Tamper/Liner – ZWA

DR73109		SB Rail	DR73110	*Peter White* SB Rail

Plasser & Theurer 09-3X-D-RT – Tamper/Liner ZWA

DR73111 *Reading Panel 1965 - 2005*	Network Rail	DR73116	Network Rail
DR73113	Network Rail	DR73117	Network Rail
DR73114 *Ron Henderson*	Network Rail	DR73118	Network Rail
DR73115	Network Rail		

Above: *Plasser & Theurer 09-3X-D-RT Tamper/liner No. DR73111 Reading Panel 1965 - 2005, stands at Bristol Temple Meads.* **Right:** *Plasser & Theurer makers' plate. Both:* **CJM**

Plasser & Theurer 07-16 – Universal Tamper/Liner – ZWA

DR73216		Fastline ø	DR73265		Fastline ø
DR73238	*Brian Langley*	Fastline ø	DR73266		Balfour Beatty
DR73243		Fastline ø	DR73267		Fastline ø
DR73244		Fastline ø	DR73269		Fastline ø
DR73246		Balfour Beatty	DR73270	*Alan Chamberlain*	Fastline ø
DR73248		Fastline ø	DR73271		Fastline ø
DR73251		Balfour Beatty	DR73272		Fastline ø
DR73256		Fastline ø	DR73273		Balfour Beatty
DR73257		Balfour Beatty	DR73276		Balfour Beatty
DR73261		Balfour Beatty	DR73278		Balfour Beatty
DR73263		Balfour Beatty			

Infrastructure Companies - Network Rail

Plasser & Theurer 07-275 – Switch/Crossing Tamper – ZWA

DR73307		Fastline ø	
DR73309		Fastline ø	
DR73310		Fastline ø	
DR73311	*Cyril Dryland*	Balfour Beatty	
DR73312		Fastline ø	

DR73314	Fastline ø
DR73316	Fastline ø
DR73318 *Peter Atkinson*	Balfour Beatty
DR73321	Fastline ø

Plasser & Theurer 07-32 – Duomatic Tamper/Liner – ZWA

DR73403	Fastline ø	DR73419	Fastline ø	DR73428	Fastline ø
DR73404	Fastline ø	DR73420	Fastline ø	DR73431	Fastline ø
DR73413	Fastline ø	DR73421	Fastline ø	DR73432	Fastline ø
DR73414	Fastline ø	DR73423	Fastline ø	DR73433	Fastline ø
DR73415	Fastline ø	DR73424	Balfour Beatty	DR73434	Balfour Beatty
DR73416	Fastline ø	DR73425	Fastline ø	DR73435	Fastline ø
DR73418	Fastline ø	DR73427	Fastline ø		

Plasser & Theurer 08-16/90 – Tamper/Liner – ZWA

DR73502	Balfour Beatty	DR73503	Balfour Beatty

Plasser & Theurer 07-32 – Duomatic Tamper/Liner – ZWA

DR73601	Fastline ø

Plasser & Theurer 08-16 – Universal Tamper/Liner – ZWA

DR73802	Fastline ø

Plasser & Theurer 08-32U RT – Plain Line Tamper – ZWA

DR73803 *Alexander Graham Bell*	SBRail

Plasser & Theurer 08-16U RT – Plain Line Tamper – ZWA

DR73804 *James Watt* SBRail	

Plasser & Theurer 08-16(32)U RT – Plain Line Tamper – ZWA

DR73805	Colas	DR73805 *Karine* Colas	

Right: *Painted in Colas orange and yellow livery, Plasser & Theurer 08-16(32)U-RT plain line tamper No. DR73805 passes through Newport station in May 2010 bound for Bristol.* **CJM**

Plasser & Theurer 08-275 – Switch/Crossing Tamper – ZWA

DR73901	Colas	DR73903	*George Mullineux* Fastline ø
DR73902	Fastline ø		

Plasser & Theurer 08-4x4/4S - RT – Switch/Crossing Tamper – ZWA

DR73904	*Thomas Telford* SBRail	DR73909	*Saturn* Colas
DR73905	*Eddie King* Amey	DR73910	*Jupiter* Colas
DR73906	*Panther* Amey		
DR73908	Colas		

Infrastructure Companies - Network Rail

Left: *Amey Railway owned Plasser & Theurer 08-4x4/4S - RT switch and crossing tamper No. DR73905 Eddie King is allocated to the West Country and is seen passing along the sea wall near Dawlish in March 2009.* **CJM**

Plasser & Theurer 08-16/4x4C - RT – Switch/Crossing Tamper – ZWA

DR73911	*Puma*	Amey	DR73913		Colas
DR73912	*Lynx*	Amey			

Plasser & Theurer 08-4x4S - RT – Switch/Crossing Tamper – ZWA

DR73914	*Robert McAlpine*	SBRail

Plasser & Theurer 08-4x4S - RT – Switch/Crossing Tamper – ZWA

DR73923	*Mercury*	Colas

Plasser & Theurer 08-16/4x4C100 - RT – Tamper – ZWA

DR73924	*Atlas*	Colas	DR73927		Balfour Beatty
DR73925	*Europa*	Colas	DR73928		Balfour Beatty
DR73926	*Stephen Keith Blanchard*	Balfour Beatty			

Plasser & Theurer 08-4x4S - RT – Switch/Crossing Tamper – ZWA

DR73929	Colas	DR73930	Colas	

Left: *Colas Rail yellow and white liveried Plasser & Theurer 08-4x4S RT switch and crossing tamper is recorded passing Preston.* **CJM**

Plasser & Theurer 08-16/4x4C100 - RT – Tamper

DR73931	Colas

Plasser & Theurer 08-4x4/4S - RT – Switch/Crossing Tamper

DR73932	SBRail

Plasser & Theurer 08-16/4x4C - RT – Switch/Crossing Tamper – ZWA

DR73915	*William Arrol*	SBRail	DR73916	*First Engineering*	SBRail

Plasser & Theurer 08-4x4/4S - RT – Switch/Crossing Tamper – ZWA

DR73919	Colas

Plasser & Theurer 08-16/4x4C80 - RT – Tamper – ZWA

DR73920	Amey		DR93922	*John Snowdon*	Amey
DR73921	Amey				

Right: *One of three Plasser & Theurer 08-16/4x4C80 - RT tampers operated by Amey Railways No. DR73920 was captured running through Starcross in Devon in June 2010 en route from Exeter to Plymouth.* **CJM**

Plasser & Theurer 08-16/4x4C100-RT – Tamper – ZWA

DR73933	SBRail	DR73934	SB Rail

Plasser & Theurer 08-4x4/4S - RT – Switch/Crossing Tamper – ZWA

DR73935	Colas	DR73936	Colas

Plasser & Theurer 08-16/4x4C100-RT – Tamper – ZWA

DR73937	Balfour Beatty	DR73938	Balfour Beatty	DR73939	Balfour Beatty

Plasser & Theurer 08-4x4/4S-RT – Switch/Crossing Tamper – ZWA

DR73940	SBRail	DR73941	SBRail	DR73942	Colas

Right: *Displaying SB Rail white, orange and blue livery, Plasser & Theurer 08-4x4/4S-RT switch and crossing tamper No. DR73940 is seen stabled at Derby.* **Tony Christie**

Plasser & Theurer 08-16/4x4C100-RT – Tamper – ZWA

DR73943	Balfour Beatty	DR73944	Balfour Beatty	DR73945	Balfour Beatty

Plasser & Theurer Euromat 08-4x4/4S – ZWA

DR73946	Volker Rail

Plasser & Theurer 08-4x4/4S-RT – Switch/Crossing Tamper ZWA

DR73947	Colas

Plasser & Theurer 08-16/90 – Special Tamper/Liner – ZWA

DR75001	Fastline ø

Plasser & Theurer 08-16/90 275 – Switch/Crossing Tamper – ZWA

DR75201	Balfour Beatty	DR75202	Balfour Beatty

Network Rail

Plasser & Theurer 08-16/90 SP-T – Switch/Crossing Tamper – ZWA

DR75203	Fastline ø

Plasser & Theurer 08-75ZW – Switch/Crossing Tamper – ZWY

DR75204	Trackwork

Matisa B45 Tamper – ZWA

DR75301	Volker Rail	DR75302	Volker Rail	DR75303	Volker Rail

Matisa B41UE Tamper – ZWA

DR75401	Volker Rail	DR75404	Volker Rail	DR75407	Colas
DR75402	Volker Rail	DR75405	Volker Rail	DR75408	Balfour Beatty
DR75403	Volker Rail	DR75406	Colas	DR75409	Balfour Beatty

Left: *Matisa B41UE Tamper No. 75406 displaying Colas Rail orange and yellow livery rests between duties at Exeter St Davids. Eight vehicles of this design are currently in operational use on Network Rail.* **CJM**

Plasser & Theurer RM74 – Ballast Cleaner – ZWB

DR76304	Fastline ø	DR76311	Fastline ø
DR76308	Fastline ø	DR76318	Fastline ø

Plasser & Theurer RM95RT – Ballast Cleaner – ZWA

DR76323	Network Rail	DR76324	Network Rail

Plasser & Theurer RM900RT Ballast Cleaner – ZWA / ZWQ

DR76501	Network Rail	DR76502	Network Rail	DR76503	Network Rail

Left: *One of the largest bases for on-track plant in the West Country is Fairwater Yard, Taunton, where the HOBC train and TRT are currently out-based. No. DR 76501 shown left is a Network Rail-owned Plasser & Theurer RM900RT Ballast Cleaner. Note the mesh over the cab windows to prevent breakage from flying ballast.* **CJM**

Plasser & Theurer RM90 Ballast Cleaner – ZWA

DR76601	*Olwen*		Colas

Plasser & Theurer VM80 NR – ZWA

DR76701	Network Rail

Plasser & Theurer 09-16 CM NR – ZWA

DR76801	Network Rail

Plasser & Theurer AFM 2000 RT – Rail Finishing Machine – ZWA

DR77001	SBRail	DR77002	SBRail

Above: *SB Rail-owned, white-liveried Plasser & Theurer AFM 2000 RT Rail Finishing Machine No. DR 77001 is seen stabled between work at Fairwater Yard, Taunton.* **CJM**

Plasser & Theurer USP 5000C – Ballast Regulator – ZWA

DR77311	Fastline ø	DR77321	Fastline ø	DR77329	Fastline ø
DR77313	Fastline ø	DR77322	Balfour Beatty	DR77330	Fastline ø
DR77315	Balfour Beatty	DR77323	Fastline ø	DR77331	Fastline ø
DR77316	Balfour Beatty	DR77325	Fastline ø	DR77332	Fastline ø
DR77317	Fastline ø	DR77326	Fastline ø	DR77333	Fastline ø
DR77319	Colas	DR77327	Colas	DR77335	Colas
DR77320	Fastline ø	DR77328	Fastline ø	DR77336	Balfour Beatty

Matisa R24S – Ballast Regulator – ZWA

DR77801	Volker Rail	DR77802	Volker Rail

Plasser & Theurer USP 5000RT – Ballast Regulator – ZWA

DR77901		Colas	DR77906		Network Rail
DR77903	*Frank Jones*	Network Rail	DR77907		Network Rail
DR77904		Network Rail	DR77908*		SBRail
DR77905		Network Rail	* Previously DR77902		

Plasser & Theurer Self Propelled Heavy Duty Twin Jib Crane – YJB

DR78211	Fastline ø	DR78216	Balfour Beatty	DR78222	Balfour Beatty
DR78212	Fastline ø	DR78217	Fastline ø	DR78223	Balfour Beatty
DR78213	Volka Rail	DR78218	Balfour Beatty	DR78224	Balfour Beatty
DR78214	Fastline ø	DR78219	Fastline ø		
DR78215	Fastline ø	DR78221	Balfour Beatty		

Cowens Sheldon Self Propelled Heavy Duty Twin Jib Crane – YJB

DR78225	Fastline ø	DR78230	Fastline ø	DR78234	Fastline ø
DR78226	Fastline ø	DR78231	Fastline ø	DR78235	Fastline ø
DR78227	Fastline ø	DR78232	Fastline ø	DR78237	Fastline ø
DR78229	Fastline ø	DR78233	Fastline ø		

Donelli PD250 Single Line Track Relayer

DR78406	Fastline ø	DR78413	Fastline ø	DR78422	Fastline ø
DR78407	Fastline ø	DR78416	Fastline ø	DR78423	Fastline ø
DR78410	Fastline ø	DR78417	Fastline ø	DR78426	Fastline ø
DR78411	Fastline ø	DR78420	Fastline ø	DR78427	Fastline ø
DR78412	Fastline ø	DR78421	Fastline ø	GR5092	Volker Rail

Network Rail

Donelli PTH350 Single Line Track Relayer

SLG78490	Volker Rail	SLG78491	Volker Rail

Harsco Track Technologies NTC Power Wagon – YJA

DR78701	Balfour Beatty	DR78702	Balfour Beatty

Matisa B95 Track Renewal Train – YJA

DR78801	Network Rail	DR78821	Network Rail
DR78811	Network Rail	DR78831	Network Rail

Left: *All four vehicles of the Matisa B95 Track Renewal Train, which in 2010 was based at Taunton Fairwater, are different. This series of illustrations shows all four constituent parts of the set. From top to bottom the vehicles are DR78821, DR78831, DR78801 and DR78811. All:* **CJM**

Infrastructure Companies - Network Rail

Schweebau SPM L15 – Rail Grinder – ZWA

DR79200	Loram

Schweebau SPM L17 – Rail Grinder – ZWA

DR79201	Loram

Speno RPS 32-2 – Rail Grinder – ZWA

DR79221	Speno	DR79223	Speno	DR79225	Speno
DR79222	Speno	DR79224	Speno	DR79226	Speno

Loram C21 – Rail Grinder – ZWA

Set 01		Set 02		Set 03	
DR79231	Loram	DR79241	Loram	DR79251	Loram
DR79232	Loram	DR79242	Loram	DR79252	Loram
DR79233	Loram	DR79243	Loram	DR79253	Loram
DR79234	Loram	DR79244	Loram	DR79254	Loram
DR79235	Loram	DR79245	Loram	DR79255	Loram
DR79236	Loram	DR79246	Loram	DR79256	Loram
DR79237	Loram	DR79247	Loram	DR79257	Loram

Harsco Track Technologies RGH-20C Switch/Crossing Rail Grinder – ZWA

DR79261 + DR79271	Network Rail	DR79264 + DR79274	Network Rail
DR79262 + DR79272	Network Rail	DR79265 + DR79275	Network Rail
DR79263 + DR79273	Network Rail	DR79266 + DR79276	Network Rail

Pandrol Jackson – Stoneblower – YZA

DR80200	Network Rail	DR80205	Network Rail	DR80210	Network Rail
DR80201	Network Rail	DR80206	Network Rail	DR80211	Network Rail
DR80202	Network Rail	DR80207	Network Rail	DR80212	Network Rail
DR80203	Network Rail	DR80208	Network Rail		
DR80204	Network Rail	DR80209	Network Rail		

Harsco Track Technologies – Stoneblower – YZA

DR80213	Network Rail	DR80215	Network Rail	DR80217	Network Rail
DR80214	Network Rail	DR80216	Network Rail		

Harsco Track Technologies – Switch/Crossing Stoneblower – YZA

DR80301	*Stephen Cornish*	Network Rail	DR80303	Network Rail
DR80302		Network Rail		

Plasser & Theurer Heavy Duty Diesel Hydraulic Crane – YOB

DR81505	Balfour Beatty	DR81515	Fastline ø	DR81523	Fastline ø
DR81507	Balfour Beatty	DR81516	Fastline ø	DR81525	Balfour Beatty
DR81508	Balfour Beatty	DR51517	Balfour Beatty	DR81527	Fastline ø
DR81511	Balfour Beatty	DR81519	Balfour Beatty	DR81528	Fastline ø
DR81513	Balfour Beatty	DR81521	Fastline ø	DR81529	Fastline ø
DR81514	Fastline ø	DR81522	Balfour Beatty	DR81532	Balfour Beatty

Cowans Sheldon Heavy Duty Diesel Hydraulic Crane

DR81533	Fastline ø

Kirow KRC810UK 100 tonne Diesel Hydraulic Crane – ZOA

DR81601	*Nigel Chester*	Volker Rail	DR81602	Balfour Beatty

Kirow KRC1200UK 125 tonne Diesel Hydraulic Crane – ZOA

DR81611	*Malcolm L Pearce*	Balfour Beatty	DR81613	Volker Rail
DR81612		Colas		

Kirow KRC250UK Heavy Duty Diesel Hydraulic Crane – ZOA

DR81621	Volker Rail	DR81622	Volker Rail	DR81623	SBRail

Infrastructure Companies - Network Rail

Network Rail

DR81624	SBRail	DR81625	SBRail

Plasser & Theurer 08-16 Universal Tamper/Liner

DR86101	Balfour Beatty

Plasser & Theurer Loading Station

DR88101	Network Rail

Starfer Single Line Spoil Handling System Train

DR92201	Network Rail	DR92205	Network Rail	DR92209	Network Rail
DR92202	Network Rail	DR92206	Network Rail	DR92210	Network Rail
DR92203	Network Rail	DR92207	Network Rail	DR92211	Network Rail
DR92204	Network Rail	DR92208	Network Rail	DR92212	Network Rail

Skako Ballast Distribution Train – YDA 'Octopus'

DR92213	Network Rail	DR92217	Network Rail	DR92221	Network Rail
DR92214	Network Rail	DR92218	Network Rail	DR92222	Network Rail
DR92215	Network Rail	DR92219	Network Rail		
DR92216	Network Rail	DR92220	Network Rail		

Plasser & Theurer NFS-D Ballast Distribution Train Hopper – YDA

DR92223	Network Rail	DR92229	Network Rail	DR92235	Network Rail
DR92224	Network Rail	DR92230	Network Rail	DR92236	Network Rail
DR92225	Network Rail	DR92231	Network Rail	DR92237	Network Rail
DR92226	Network Rail	DR92232	Network Rail	DR92238	Network Rail
DR92227	Network Rail	DR92233	Network Rail	DR92239	Network Rail
DR92228	Network Rail	DR92234	Network Rail	DR92240	Network Rail

Plasser & Theurer MFS-D Ballast Distribution Train Hopper – YDA

DR92241	Network Rail	DR92246	Network Rail	DR92251	Network Rail
DR92242	Network Rail	DR92247	Network Rail	DR92252	Network Rail
DR92243	Network Rail	DR92248	Network Rail	DR92253	Network Rail
DR92244	Network Rail	DR92249	Network Rail	DR92254	Network Rail
DR92245	Network Rail	DR92250	Network Rail		

Plasser & Theurer MFS-SB Swivel Conveyer Wagon – YDA

DR92259	Network Rail	DR92261	Network Rail
DR92260	Network Rail	DR92262	Network Rail

Plasser & Theurer MFS-PW Single Line Handling Train Power Wagon – YOA

DR92263	Network Rail

Plasser & Theurer NB-PW Ballast Distribution Train Power Wagon – YOA

DR92264	Network Rail

Plasser & Theurer MFS-D Ballast Distribution Train Hopper – YDA

DR92265	Network Rail	DR92270	Network Rail	DR92275	Network Rail
DR92266	Network Rail	DR92271	Network Rail	DR92276	Network Rail
DR92267	Network Rail	DR92272	Network Rail	DR92277	Network Rail
DR92268	Network Rail	DR92273	Network Rail	DR92278	Network Rail
DR92269	Network Rail	DR92274	Network Rail	DR92279	Network Rail

Plasser & Theurer MFS-SB Swivel Conveyer Wagon – YDA

DR92280	Network Rail	DR92281	Network Rail

Plasser & Theurer MFS-A Materials Handling Train Interface Wagon – YDA

DR92282	Network Rail	DR92283	Network Rail

Plasser & Theurer PW-RT Materials Handling Train Power Wagon – YOA

DR92285	Network Rail

Plasser & Theurer NPW-RT Materials Handling Train Power Wagon – YOA

DR92286	Network Rail

Plasser & Theurer MFS-SB Swivel Conveyer Wagon – YDA

DR92287	Network Rail	DR92290	Network Rail	DR92293	Network Rail
DR92288	Network Rail	DR92291	Network Rail	DR92294	Network Rail
DR92289	Network Rail	DR92292	Network Rail		

Plasser & Theurer MFS-D Ballast Distribution Train Hopper – YDA

DR92295	Network Rail	DR92311	Network Rail	DR92321	Network Rail
DR92296	Network Rail	DR92312	Network Rail	DR92322	Network Rail
DR92297	Network Rail	DR92313	Network Rail	DR92323	Network Rail
DR92298	Network Rail	DR92314	Network Rail	DR92324	Network Rail
DR92299	Network Rail	DR92315	Network Rail	DR92325	Network Rail
DR92300	Network Rail	DR92316	Network Rail	DR92326	Network Rail
DR92301	Network Rail	DR92317	Network Rail	DR92327	Network Rail
DR92302	Network Rail	DR92318	Network Rail	DR92328	Network Rail
DR92303	Network Rail	DR92319	Network Rail	DR92329	Network Rail
DR92304	Network Rail	DR92320	Network Rail	DR92330	Network Rail
DR92305	Network Rail				
DR92306	Network Rail				
DR92307	Network Rail				
DR92308	Network Rail				
DR92309	Network Rail				
DR92310	Network Rail				

Right: *Plasser & Theurer MFS-D Ballast Distribution Train hopper wagon No. DR92299 stands within a train consist at Taunton.*
Tony Christie

Left: *Plasser & Theurer MFS-A Materials Handling Train interface wagon No. DR92282 at Taunton.*
Tony Christie

Plasser & Theurer PW-RT Materials Handling Train Power Wagon – YOA

DR92331	Network Rail

Plasser & Theurer NPW-RT Materials Handling Train Power Wagon – YOA

DR92332	Network Rail

Plasser & Theurer MFS-SB Swivel Conveyer Wagon – YDA

DR92333	Network Rail	DR92336	Network Rail	DR92339	Network Rail
DR92334	Network Rail	DR92337	Network Rail	DR92340	Network Rail
DR92335	Network Rail	DR92338	Network Rail		

Infrastructure Companies - Network Rail

Network Rail

Plasser & Theurer MFS-D Ballast Distribution Train Hopper – YDA

DR92341	Network Rail	DR92354	Network Rail	DR92367	Network Rail
DR92342	Network Rail	DR92355	Network Rail	DR92368	Network Rail
DR92343	Network Rail	DR92356	Network Rail	DR92369	Network Rail
DR92344	Network Rail	DR92357	Network Rail	DR92370	Network Rail
DR92345	Network Rail	DR92358	Network Rail	DR92371	Network Rail
DR92346	Network Rail	DR92359	Network Rail	DR92372	Network Rail
DR92347	Network Rail	DR92360	Network Rail	DR92373	Network Rail
DR92348	Network Rail	DR92361	Network Rail	DR92374	Network Rail
DR92349	Network Rail	DR92362	Network Rail	DR92375	Network Rail
DR92350	Network Rail	DR92363	Network Rail	DR92376	Network Rail
DR92351	Network Rail	DR92364	Network Rail	DR92377	Colas
DR92352	Network Rail	DR92365	Network Rail		
DR92353	Network Rail	DR92366	Network Rail		

Plasser & Theurer MFS-A Materials Handling Train Interface Wagon – YDA

DR92400	Colas

Plasser & Theurer PW-RT Materials Handling Train Power Wagon

DR92431	Network Rail

Plasser & Theurer NPW-RT Materials Handling Train Power Wagon

DR92432	Network Rail

Plasser & Theurer MFS-SB Swivel Conveyer Wagon

DR92433	Network Rail	DR92436	Network Rail	DR92439	Network Rail
DR92434	Network Rail	DR92437	Network Rail	DR92440	Network Rail
DR92435	Network Rail	DR92438	Network Rail		

Plasser & Theurer MFS-D Ballast Distribution Train Hopper – YDA

DR92441	Network Rail	DR92453	Network Rail	DR92465	Network Rail
DR92442	Network Rail	DR92454	Network Rail	DR92466	Network Rail
DR92443	Network Rail	DR92455	Network Rail	DR92467	Network Rail
DR92444	Network Rail	DR92456	Network Rail	DR92468	Network Rail
DR92445	Network Rail	DR92457	Network Rail	DR92469	Network Rail
DR92446	Network Rail	DR92458	Network Rail	DR92470	Network Rail
DR92447	Network Rail	DR92459	Network Rail	DR92471	Network Rail
DR92448	Network Rail	DR92460	Network Rail	DR92472	Network Rail
DR92449	Network Rail	DR92461	Network Rail	DR92473	Network Rail
DR92450	Network Rail	DR92462	Network Rail	DR92474	Network Rail
DR92451	Network Rail	DR92463	Network Rail	DR92475	Network Rail
DR92452	Network Rail	DR92464	Network Rail	DR92476	Network Rail

Sleeper Delivery Train – Generator Wagon – YFA

DR92501	Fastline ø	DR92502	Fastline ø	DR92503	Fastline ø

Twin Jib Rail Recovery Train 'Slinger' – YFA

DR92504	Fastline ø	DR92507	Fastline ø	DR92510	Fastline ø
DR92505	Fastline ø	DR92508	Fastline ø	DR92511	Fastline ø
DR92506	Fastline ø	DR92509	Fastline ø	DR92512	Fastline ø

Single Jib Rail Recovery Train 'Slinger' – YFA

DR92513	Fastline ø	DR92515	Fastline ø	DR92517	Fastline ø
DR92514	Fastline ø	DR92516	Fastline ø	DR92518	Fastline ø

Sleeper Delivery Train – Twin Crane 'Slinger' – YFA

DR92519	Fastline

Sleeper Delivery Train – Generator Wagon 'Slinger' – YFA

DR92520	Fastline ø	DR92522	Fastline ø	DR92524	Fastline ø
DR92521	Fastline ø	DR92523	Fastline ø	DR92525	Fastline ø

Sleeper Delivery Train – Twin Crane 'Slinger' – YFA

DR92526	Fastline ø	DR92529	Fastline ø	DR92532	Fastline ø
DR92527	Fastline ø	DR92530	Fastline ø		
DR92528	Fastline ø	DR92531	Fastline ø		

Sleeper Delivery Train – Generator Wagon 'Slinger' – YFA

DR92533	Fastline ø	DR92534	Fastline ø

Sleeper Delivery Train – Twin Crane 'Slinger' – YFA

DR92535	Fastline ø	DR92539	Fastline ø	DR92543	Fastline ø
DR92536	Fastline ø	DR92540	Fastline ø	DR92544	Fastline ø
DR92537	Fastline ø	DR92541	Fastline ø	DR92545	Fastline ø
DR92538	Fastline ø	DR92542	Fastline ø	DR92546	Fastline ø

Sleeper Delivery Train – Generator Wagon 'Slinger' – YFA

DR92547	Fastline ø	DR92548	Fastline ø	DR92549	Fastline ø

Sleeper Delivery Train – Twin Crane 'Slinger' – YFA

DR92550	Fastline ø	DR92558	Fastline ø	DR92566	Fastline ø
DR92551	Fastline ø	DR92559	Fastline ø	DR92567	Fastline ø
DR92552	Fastline ø	DR92560	Fastline ø	DR92568	Fastline ø
DR92553	Fastline ø	DR92561	Fastline ø	DR92569	Fastline ø
DR92554	Fastline ø	DR92562	Fastline ø	DR92570	Fastline ø
DR92555	Fastline ø	DR92563	Fastline ø	DR92571	Fastline ø
DR92556	Fastline ø	DR92564	Fastline ø		
DR92557	Fastline ø	DR92565	Fastline ø		

W H Davis Sleeper Wagons – YXA

DR92601	Network Rail	DR92623	Network Rail	DR92645	Network Rail
DR92602	Network Rail	DR92624	Network Rail	DR92646	Network Rail
DR92603	Network Rail	DR92625	Network Rail	DR92647	Network Rail
DR92604	Network Rail	DR92626	Network Rail	DR92648	Network Rail
DR92605	Network Rail	DR92627	Network Rail	DR92649	Network Rail
DR92606	Network Rail	DR92628	Network Rail	DR92650	Network Rail
DR92607	Network Rail	DR92629	Network Rail	DR92651	Network Rail
DR92608	Network Rail	DR92630	Network Rail	DR92652	Network Rail
DR92609	Network Rail	DR92631	Network Rail	DR92653	Network Rail
DR92610	Network Rail	DR92632	Network Rail	DR92654	Network Rail
DR92611	Network Rail	DR92633	Network Rail	DR92655	Network Rail
DR92612	Network Rail	DR92634	Network Rail	DR92656	Network Rail
DR92613	Network Rail	DR92635	Network Rail	DR92657	Network Rail
DR92614	Network Rail	DR92636	Network Rail	DR92658	Network Rail
DR92615	Network Rail	DR92637	Network Rail	DR92659	Network Rail
DR92616	Network Rail	DR92638	Network Rail	DR92660	Network Rail
DR92617	Network Rail	DR92639	Network Rail	DR92661	Network Rail
DR92618	Network Rail	DR92640	Network Rail	DR92662	Network Rail
DR92619	Network Rail	DR92641	Network Rail	DR92663	Network Rail
DR92620	Network Rail	DR92642	Network Rail	DR92664	Network Rail
DR92621	Network Rail	DR92643	Network Rail	DR92665	Network Rail
DR92622	Network Rail	DR92644	Network Rail		

Below: *W. H. Davis-built Sleeper Wagon DR 92622 stabled in Taunton FairwaterYard.* **CJM**

Infrastructure Companies - Network Rail

Network Rail

W H Davis Flat/Workshop/Barrier Wagons – YSA

DR92701	Network Rail	DR92703	Network Rail	DR92705	Network Rail
DR92702	Network Rail	DR92704	Network Rail	DR92706	Network Rail

Cowans Sheldon 75 tonne Diesel Hydraulic Recovery Crane – ZIA* ZIB¤

ARDC96710¤ Network Rail (BS)	ARDC96714* Network Rail (MG)
ARDC96713¤ Network Rail (SP)	ARDC96715¤ Network Rail (TO)

Left: *Cowans Sheldon 75 tonne recovery crane No. ADRC96715 based at Toton is viewed at Fairwater Yard, Taunton.* **Brian Garrett**

Below: *Cowans Sheldon 75 tonne recovery crane No. ADRC96714 based at Margam is seen during the re-railing of a derailed ballast train at Fairwater Yard, Taunton.* **Brian Garrett**

Eiv de Brieve DU94BA – TRAMM – ZWA

DR97001	High Speed 1 (HS1)

Windhoff Overhead Line – MPV – YXA

DR97011	High Speed 1 (HS1)	DR97013	High Speed 1 (HS1)
DR97012	High Speed 1 (HS1)	DR97014	High Speed 1 (HS1)

Windhoff Overhead Line – MPV – YXA

DR98001	Network Rail	DR98005	Network Rail	DR98009	Network Rail	DR98013	Network Rail
DR98002	Network Rail	DR98006	Network Rail	DR98010	Network Rail	DR98014	Network Rail
DR98003	Network Rail	DR98007	Network Rail	DR98011	Network Rail		
DR98004	Network Rail	DR98008	Network Rail	DR98012	Network Rail		

Plasser & Theurer General Purpose Machine (GP-TRAMM) – ZWA

DR98210	Amey	DR98216	Balfour Beatty	DR98218	Balfour Beatty	DR98220	Balfour Beatty
DR98215	Balfour Beatty	DR98217	Balfour Beatty	DR98219	Balfour Beatty		

Geismar General Purpose Machine (GP-TRAMM)

DR98300	Fastline ø	DR98302	Fastline ø	DR98303	Fastline ø

Geismar VMT860 PL/UM – ZWA

DR98305	Network Rail	DR98307	Colas
DR98306	Network Rail	DR98308	Colas

Right: DR98307 is one of four Colas-operated Geismar VMT860 PL/UM general purpose track machines. In March 2009 the two-vehicle set is seen passing west through Dawlish en route to Tavistock Junction. **CJM**

Windhoff Multi Purpose Vehicle (MPV) – YXA

Right: A total of 32 two-vehicle MPV sets are operated by Network Rail. These self-contained unit Multi Purpose Vehicles carry a variety of 'pods' on the flat part of their structure and can be used for a multitude of operations, including weed control and rail head treatment in periods of low adhesion. DR98958 + DR98908 are viewed at Taunton during adhesion improvement runs. **Tony Christie**

Infrastructure Companies - Network Rail

Network Rail

DR98901 + DR98951 Network Rail	DR98912 + DR98962 Network Rail	DR98923 + DR98973 Network Rail
DR98902 + DR98952 Network Rail	DR98913 + DR98963 Network Rail	DR98924 + DR98974 Network Rail
DR98903 + DR98953 Network Rail	DR98914 + DR98964 Network Rail	DR98925 + DR98975 Network Rail
DR98904 + DR98954 Network Rail	DR98915 + DR98965 Network Rail	DR98926 + DR98976 Network Rail
DR98905 + DR98955 Network Rail	DR98916 + DR98966 Network Rail	DR98927 + DR98977 Network Rail
DR98906 + DR98956 Network Rail	DR98917 + DR98967 Network Rail	DR98928 + DR98978 Network Rail
DR98907 + DR98957 Network Rail	DR98918 + DR98968 Network Rail	DR98929 + DR98979 Network Rail
DR98908 + DR98958 Network Rail	DR98919 + DR98969 Network Rail	DR98930 + DR98980 Network Rail
DR98909 + DR98959 Network Rail	DR98920 + DR98970 Network Rail	DR98931 + DR98981 Network Rail
DR98910 + DR98960 Network Rail	DR98921 + DR98971 Network Rail	DR98932 + DR98982 Network Rail
DR98911 + DR98961 Network Rail	DR98922 + DR98972 Network Rail	

Continuous Welded Rail Wagon – YEA 'Perch'

DR979001 Network Rail	DR979035 Network Rail	DR979069 Network Rail	DR979103 Network Rail
DR979002 Network Rail	DR979036 Network Rail	DR979070 Network Rail	DR979104 Network Rail
DR979003 Network Rail	DR979037 Network Rail	DR979071 Network Rail	DR979105 Network Rail
DR979004 Network Rail	DR979038 Network Rail	DR979072 Network Rail	DR979106 Network Rail
DR979005 Network Rail	DR979039 Network Rail	DR979073 Network Rail	DR979107 Network Rail
DR979006 Network Rail	DR979040 Network Rail	DR979074 Network Rail	DR979108 Network Rail
DR979007 Network Rail	DR979041 Network Rail	DR979075 Network Rail	DR979109 Network Rail
DR979008 Network Rail	DR979042 Network Rail	DR979076 Network Rail	DR979110 Network Rail
DR979009 Network Rail	DR979043 Network Rail	DR979077 Network Rail	DR979111 Network Rail
DR979010 Network Rail	DR979044 Network Rail	DR979078 Network Rail	DR979112 Network Rail
DR979011 Network Rail	DR979045 Network Rail	DR979079 Network Rail	DR979113 Network Rail
DR979012 Network Rail	DR979046 Network Rail	DR979080 Network Rail	DR979114 Network Rail
DR979013 Network Rail	DR979047 Network Rail	DR979081 Network Rail	DR979115 Network Rail
DR979014 Network Rail	DR979048 Network Rail	DR979082 Network Rail	DR979116 Network Rail
DR979015 Network Rail	DR979049 Network Rail	DR979083 Network Rail	DR979117 Network Rail
DR979016 Network Rail	DR979050 Network Rail	DR979084 Network Rail	DR979118 Network Rail
DR979017 Network Rail	DR979051 Network Rail	DR979085 Network Rail	DR979119 Network Rail
DR979018 Network Rail	DR979052 Network Rail	DR979086 Network Rail	DR979120 Network Rail
DR979019 Network Rail	DR979053 Network Rail	DR979087 Network Rail	DR979121 Network Rail
DR979020 Network Rail	DR979054 Network Rail	DR979088 Network Rail	DR979122 Network Rail
DR979021 Network Rail	DR979055 Network Rail	DR979089 Network Rail	DR979123 Network Rail
DR979022 Network Rail	DR979056 Network Rail	DR979090 Network Rail	DR979124 Network Rail
DR979023 Network Rail	DR979057 Network Rail	DR979091 Network Rail	DR979125 Network Rail
DR979024 Network Rail	DR979058 Network Rail	DR979092 Network Rail	DR979126 Network Rail
DR979025 Network Rail	DR979059 Network Rail	DR979093 Network Rail	DR979127 Network Rail
DR979026 Network Rail	DR979060 Network Rail	DR979094 Network Rail	DR979128 Network Rail
DR979027 Network Rail	DR979061 Network Rail	DR979095 Network Rail	DR979129 Network Rail
DR979028 Network Rail	DR979062 Network Rail	DR979096 Network Rail	DR979130 Network Rail
DR979029 Network Rail	DR979063 Network Rail	DR979097 Network Rail	DR979131 Network Rail
DR979030 Network Rail	DR979064 Network Rail	DR979098 Network Rail	DR979132 Network Rail
DR979031 Network Rail	DR979065 Network Rail	DR979099 Network Rail	DR979133 Network Rail
DR979032 Network Rail	DR979066 Network Rail	DR979100 Network Rail	DR979134 Network Rail
DR979033 Network Rail	DR979067 Network Rail	DR979101 Network Rail	
DR979034 Network Rail	DR979068 Network Rail	DR979102 Network Rail	

Continuous Welded Rail Clamping Wagon – YEA 'Perch'

DR979409 Network Rail	DR979412 Network Rail	DR979415 Network Rail

Continuous Welded Rail End of Train Wagon – YEA 'Porpoise'

DR979505 Network Rail	DR979509 Network Rail	DR979513 Network Rail	DR979515 Network Rail
DR979506 Network Rail	DR979511 Network Rail	DR979514 Network Rail	

Continuous Welded Rail 'Chute' Wagon – YEA 'Porpoise'

DR979500 Network Rail	DR979502 Network Rail	DR979507 Network Rail	DR979510 Network Rail
DR979501 Network Rail	DR979503 Network Rail	DR979508 Network Rail	DR979512 Network Rail

Continuous Welded Rail Gantry Wagon – YEA 'Perch'

DR979604 Network Rail	DR979611 Network Rail	DR979614 Network Rail
DR979607 Network Rail	DR979612 Network Rail	
DR979609 Network Rail	DR979613 Network Rail	

Above: *The business end of one of the Network Rail continuous welded rail train, showing a 'Gantry' and 'Shute' wagon. The cranes on the nearer vehicle position the rail sections for delivery to the track from the end wagon.* **CJM**

Below: *Network Rail continuous welded rail carrier, YEA No. 979057.* **Nathan Williamson**

Balfour Beatty Rail Services

Address: ✉ 130 Wilton Road, London, SW1V 4LQ
📠 info@bbrail.com
📞 0207 216 6800
ⓘ www.bbrail.com

Managing Director: Peter Anderson **Depot:** Ashford (AD)

Hauled Stock

	Mk1		
	Vehicle Length: 64ft 6in (19.65m)	Height: 12ft 9½in (3.89m)	Width: 9ft 3in (2.81m)

Number		Type	Depot	Livery	Operator	Use
977163	(35487)	Mk1/BSK	AD	BBR	BBR	Staff & Generator coach
977165	(35408)	Mk1/BSK	AD	BBR	BBR	Staff & Generator coach
977166	(35419)	Mk1/BSK	AD	BBR	BBR	Staff & Generator coach
977167	(35400)	Mk1/BSK	AD	BBR	BBR	Staff & Generator coach
977168	(35289)	Mk1/BSK	AD	BBR	BBR	Staff & Generator coach

Alstom Transport

Address: ✉ PO Box 70, Newbold Road, Rugby, Warwickshire, CV21 2WR
🖳 info@transport.alstom.com, ✆ 01788 577111, ⓘ www.transport.alstom.com
Managing Director: Paul Robinson
Depots: Chester (CH), Liverpool - Edge Hill (LL), Manchester - Longsight (MA),
Wolverhampton - Oxley (OY), Wembley (WB)

Class 08

Vehicle Length: 29ft 3in (8.91m)		Engine: English Electric 6K	
Height: 12ft 8⅝in (3.87m)		Horsepower: 400hp (298kW)	
Width: 8ft 6in (2.59m)		Electrical Equipment: English Electric	

Number	Depot	Pool	Livery	Owner	Operator						
08451(S)	AT	ATZZ	GBF	ALS	-	08696	AT	ATLO	GRN	ALS	ALS
08454	WB	ATLO	BLK	ALS	ALS	08721	AT	ATLO	BLU	ALS	ALS
08611	AT	ATLO	VT1	ALS	ALS	08790	AT	ATLO	BLU	ALS	ALS
08617	WB	ATLO	BLK	ALS	ALS	08887(S)	AT	ATZZ	BLK	ALS	-
						08934	PB	GBWM	BLK	ALS	GBF

Names applied **08696** *Longsight TMD,* **08721** *M A Smith,* **08790** *Starlet*

Bombardier Transportation

Address: ✉ Litchurch Lane, Derby, DE24 8AD
🖳 info@bombardier.com, ✆ 01332 344666, ⓘ www.bombardier.com
Chief Country Representative: Colin Walton
Works: Derby (ZD), Crewe (ZC)

Class 08

Vehicle Length: 29ft 3in (8.91m)		Engine: English Electric 6K	
Height: 12ft 8⅝in (3.87m)		Horsepower: 400hp (298kW)	
Width: 8ft 6in (2.59m)		Electrical Equipment: English Electric	

Number	Depot	Pool	Livery	Owner	Operator	Name
08682 (D3849)	ZD	INDL	GRN	BOM	BOM	*Lionheart*
08846	ZD	INDL	BOM	BOM	BOM	

Class 423 (4VEP)

Vehicle Length: 64ft 6in (19.65m)		Horsepower: 1000hp (745.7kW)	
Height: 12ft 11in (3.93m)		Seats (total/car): Nil	
Width: 9ft 0in (2.74m)		Tractor unit for internal use	

Number	Formation DTC+TSO+MBS+DTC	Depot	Livery	Owner	Operator
(42)3905	76397+70904+62266+76398	AF	COX	BOM	BOM (Chart Leaon depot pilot)
(42)3918	76527+70950+62321+76528	AF	COX	BOM	BOM (Chart Leaon depot pilot)

Above: Bombardier Transportation still operate a small facility at Chart Leacon, Ashford (Kent). Two former Class 423 (4VEP) sets remain at the depot for shunting duties. Both sets are seen parked up in autumn 2010. **Tony Christie**

Class 424
Classic

Vehicle Length: 64ft 6in (19.65m)		Horsepower: Un-powered	
Height: 12ft 11in (3.93m)		Seats (total/car): 64S	
Width: 9ft 0in (2.74m)		Demonstrator vehicle	

Number	Formation	Depot	Livery	Owner	Operator	Use
424001(S)	76112	ZB	SIL	BOM	-	Networker Classic demonstrator

Brush-Barclay Ltd

Address: ✉ Caledonia Works, West Langlands Street, Kilmarnock, Ayrshire, Scotland, KA1 2QD

✆ sales@brushtraction.com ✆ 01563 523573, ⓘ www.brushtraction.com

Managing Director: John Bidewell

Right: One of the most important vehicle repair and modification plants in the UK is the former Hunslet-Barclay site at Kilmarnock, now operated by Brush. The facility has major engineering facilities and can handle any form of traction. In this view a Mk3 passenger coach is under conversion for departmental use within the New Measurement Train. **CJM**

For Brush Traction - See Train Builders section

Knights Rail Services

Address: ✉ Shoeburyness: Building D23, MoD Shoeburyness, Blackgate Road, Shoeburyness, Essex, SS3 9SR

Eastleigh: Eastleigh Rail Works, Campbell Road, Eastleigh, Hampshire, SO50 5AD

✆ gosborne@knightsrail.co.uk ✆ 01702 299631, ⓘ www.rail-services.net

Managing Director: Bruce Knights

Depots: Eastleigh (ZG), Shoeburyness (SN)

Class 07

Vehicle Length: 26ft 9½in (8.16m)			Engine: Paxman 6RPHL MkIII		
Height: 12ft 10in (3.91m)			Horsepower: 275hp (205kW)		
Width: 8ft 6in (2.59m)			Electrical Equipment: AEI		

Number	Depot	Pool	Livery	Owner	Operator
07007 (D2991) ZG		MBDL	BLU	KRS	KRS

Right: Knights Rail Services now operate the larger part of the former Eastleigh Works and offer a high quality engineering service, as well as warm store facilities for off-lease rolling stock. For pilot purposes the site operates former BR Class 07 No. 07007. **Stacey Thew**

Knights Rail Services

Class 73/1

Vehicle Length: 53ft 8in (16.35m)		Power: 750V dc third rail or English Electric 6K	
Height: 12ft 5⅝in (3.79m)		Horsepower: electric - 1,600hp (1,193kW)	
Width: 8ft 8in (2.64m)		Horsepower: diesel - 600hp (447kW)	
		Electrical Equipment: English Electric	

Number	Depot	Pool	Livery	Owner	Operator	Name
73119	ZG	MBDL	BLU	KRS	KRS	*Borough of Eastleigh*

Left: Knights Rail own Class 73 No. 73119 Borough of Eastleigh which in 2010 was used for passenger service on the Swanage Railway. Here it is seen in multiple with a Class 37.
Tony Christie

Class 421 (4-CIG)

Vehicle Length: 64ft 9½in (19.75m)	Horsepower: 1,000hp (740kW)	
Height: 12ft 9¼in (3.89m)	Seats (total/car): 42F-192S, 18F-36S/56S/72S/24F-28S	
Width: 9ft 3in (2.81m)		

Number	Formation DTC+DTC	Depot	Livery	Owner	Operator
(42)1884(S)	76838+76767	ZG	SWT	KRS	-

Railcare Ltd

Address: ✉ Wolverton Works, Stratford Road, Wolverton, Milton Keynes, MK12 5NT
✒ info@railcare.com ✆ 08000 741122, ① www.railcare.com

Managing Director: Colin Love

Depots: Glasgow (ZH), Wolverton (ZN)

Class 08

Vehicle Length: 29ft 3in (8.91m)	Engine: English Electric 6K	
Height: 12ft 8⅝in (3.87m)	Horsepower: 400hp (298kW)	
Width: 8ft 6in (2.59m)	Electrical Equipment: English Electric	

Number	Depot	Pool	Livery	Owner	Operator	Name
08568	ZH	RCZH	ALS	RCL	RCL	*St Rollox*
08629	ZN	RCZN	ROY	RCL	RCL	
08649	ZN	RCZN	WEX	RCL	RCL	*G H Stratton*
08730	ZH	RCZH	ALS	RCL	RCL	*The Caley*

Left: Railcare Ltd, the operators of the engineering sites at Glasgow and Wolverton, have four Class 08 0-6-0 shunters on their books, two working at each site. No. 08568 painted in Railcare livery and sporting the name St Rollox is seen at the Glasgow complex.
Bill Wilson

Rail Vehicle Engineering Ltd

Address: ✉ Vehicles Workshop, RTC Business Park, London Road, Derby, DE24 8UP
☏ enquiries@rvel.co.uk ✆ 01332 331210, ⓘ www.rvel.co.uk
Managing Director: Andy Lynch
Depot: Derby (DF)

Class 08

Vehicle Length: 29ft 3in (8.91m)			Engine: English Electric 6K	
Height: 12ft 8⅝in (3.87m)			Horsepower: 400hp (298kW)	
Width: 8ft 6in (2.59m)			Electrical Equipment: English Electric	

Number	Depot	Pool	Livery	Owner	Operator
08536	DF	HISE	EMT	EMT	RVE
08697	DF	EMSL	EMT	EMT	RVE

Class 31/1, 31/4, 31/6

Vehicle Length: 56ft 9in (17.29m)	Engine: English Electric 12SVT
Height: 12ft 7in (3.91m)	Horsepower: 1,470hp (1,097kW)
Width: 8ft 9in (2.65m)	Electrical Equipment: Brush
Class 31/4 - Fitted with electric train heat.	Class 31/6 - Fitted with through wiring

Number		Depot	Pool	Livery	Owner	Operator	Name
31106		DF	RVLO	BLU	HJA	RVE	
31454	(31554, 31228)	DF	RVLO	ICS	BAR	RVE	
31459	(31256)	DF	RVLO	BLK	RVE	RVE	Cerberus
31468(S)	(31568, 31321)	DF	RVLS	BLK	BAR	RVE	Hydra
31601	(31186)	DF	RVLO	DCG	BAR	RVE	
31602	(31191)	DF	RVLO	NRL	BAR	RVE	Driver Dave Green 19B

Above: *Rail Vehicle Engineering Ltd, based in the original Engineering Development Unit building at Derby RTC, operates a number of Class 31 locos and one Class 56 which operate under contract for Network Rail or are available for spot hire. Owned by British American Railroad, No. 31601 is painted in Devon & Cornwall Railway green and is seen with a Network Rail track inspection train at Plymouth.* **Tony Christie**

Class 56/3

Vehicle Length: 63ft 6in (19.35m)			Engine: Ruston Paxman 16RK3CT	
Height: 13ft 0in (3.96m)			Horsepower: 3,250hp (2,420kW)	
Width: 9ft 2in (2.79m)			Electrical Equipment: Brush	

Number	Depot	Pool	Livery	Owner	Operator	
56303 (56125)	DF	RVLO	GRN	RVE	RVE	(For sale)

Siemens Transportation

Address: ✉ Kings Heath Traincare Facility, Heathfield Way, Kings Heath,
Northampton, NN5 7QP
✆ enquiries@siemenstransportation.co.uk ✆ 01604 594500
ⓘ www.siemenstransportation.co.uk

Managing Director UK: Steve Scrimshaw
Depots: Ardwick, Manchester (AK), Kings Heath, Northampton (NN),
Northam, Southampton (NT)

Class 01.5

Number	Depot	Pool	Livery	Owner	Operator
01551 (H016)	AK	MBDL	WAB	WAB	SIE

Barrier Wagons

Number	Depot	Pool	Livery	Owner	Operator	Notes
6321 (96385, 86515)	NN	SIEM	BLU	SIE	FLR	Desiro stock barrier wagon
6322 (93686, 86859)	NN	SIEM	BLU	SIE	FLR	Desiro stock barrier wagon
6323 (96387, 86973)	NN	SIEM	BLU	SIE	FLR	Desiro stock barrier wagon
6324 (96388, 86562)	NN	SIEM	BLU	SIE	FLR	Desiro stock barrier wagon
6325 (96389, 86135)	NN	SIEM	BLU	SIE	FLR	Desiro stock barrier wagon

Left: *Detail of Scharfenberg coupling
fitted to one end of each of the Siemens
barrier coaches to enable connection
with Desiro-type rolling stock.* **CJM**

Wabtec

Address: ✉ PO Box 400, Doncaster Works, Hexthorpe Road, Doncaster, DN1 1SL
✆ wabtecrail@wabtec.com ✆ 01302 340700, ⓘ www.wabtecrail.co.uk

Managing Director: John Meehan
Depot: Doncaster (ZB)

Class 08

*Vehicle Length: 29ft 3in (8.91m)
Height: 12ft 8⅝in (3.87m)
Width: 8ft 6in (2.59m)*

*Engine: English Electric 6K
Horsepower: 400hp (298kW)
Electrical Equipment: English Electric*

Number	Depot	Pool	Livery	Owner	Operator	Name
08472	ZB	RFSH	GNE	WAB	NXE	
08571	ZB	RFSH	WAB	WAB	NXE	

08596(S)	ZB	RFSH	WAB	WAB	NXE		
08615	ZB	RFSH	WAB	WAB	NXE		
08669	ZB	RFSH	WAB	WAB	WAB	*Bob Machin*	
08724	ZB	RFSH	WAB	WAB	WAB		
08764	ZB	MBDL	BLU	WAB	TRN	*Old Tom*	
08853	ZB	RFSH	BLU	WAB	WAB		
08871	EC	RFSH	COT	WAB	WAB		
08927(S)	ZB	TTLS	EWS	WAB	DBS		

Above: *Painted in Wabtec Rail black livery with wasp ends and a red connecting rod, No. 08571 is seen shunting at the East Coast depot at Bounds Green. The East Coast operator has an ongoing contract with Doncaster-based Wabtec Rail to provide shunting locomotives for its principal depots at Bounds Green and Edinburgh Craigentinny.* **Tony Christie**

Pullman Group

Address: ✉ Train Maintenance Depot, Leckwith Road, Cardiff, CF11 8HP
✎ sales@pullmans.net ✆ 029 2036 8850, ⓘ www.pullmans.net

Managing Director: Colin Robinson
Depot: Cardiff Canton (CF)

Class 08

Vehicle Length: 29ft 3in (8.91m)	Engine: English Electric 6K
Height: 12ft 8⅜in (3.87m)	Horsepower: 400hp (298kW)
Width: 8ft 6in (2.59m)	Electrical Equipment: English Electric

Number	Depot	Pool	Livery	Owner	Operator
08499	CF	WSXX	BLU	DBS	PUL

Right: *Painted in all over blue livery and with its running number applied on the fuel tank inspection plate, No. 08499 operated by Pullman Rail is seen at Cardiff Canton depot.* **CJM**

Europhoenix Ltd

Address: ✉ 58A High Street, Stony Stratford, Milton Keynes, MK11 1AX

✍ info@europhoenix.eu ✆ 01467 624366, ⓘ www.europhoenix.eu

Facilities: Europhoenix purchased the redundant Class 86/87 locos released from traffic by introduction of new multiple unit rolling stock. The locos are offered to Continental European operators fully refurbished and modified to suit customer needs.

Class 86

Vehicle Length: 58ft 6in (17.83m)	Power Collection: 25kV ac overhead
Height: 13ft 0⅝in (3.97m)	Horsepower: 5,900hp (4,400kW)
Width: 8ft 8¼in (2.64m)	Electrical Equipment: GEC

Number	Location	Hire to
86215	LM	-
86217	LM	-
86218	XX	Floyd (Hungary)
86226	LM	-
86228	LM	-
86229	LM	-
86231	LM	-

Number	Location	Hire to
86232	LM	-
86233	XX	Floyd (Hungary)
86234	LM	-
86235	LM	-
86242	LM	-
86246	LM	-
86247	LM	-
86248	XX	Floyd (Hungary)

Number	Location	Hire to
86250	XX	Floyd (Hungary)
86251	LM	-
86424 (Now with AC Loco Group)		
86701 (86205)		CP* ETL
86702 (86260)		CP* ETL

Names applied

86701 *Orion*
86702 *Cassiopeia*

* Spot hire loco, operated by Electric Traction Services

Left: *Europhoenix have purchased a number of withdrawn Class 86 locomotives with the intention of refurbishing them and offering them for sale to mainland European operators. Demonstrator No. 86247 with revised front end and carrying an attractive Europhoenix livery is seen at Long Marston.* **CJM**

Class 87

Vehicle Length: 58ft 6in (17.83m)	Power Collection: 25kV ac overhead
Height: 13ft 1¼in (3.99m)	Horsepower: 7,860hp (5,680kW)
Width: 8ft 8¼in (2.64m)	Electrical Equipment: GEC

Number	Owner	Location						
87009	EPX	LM	87017	EPX	LM	87023	EPX	LM

Porterbrook

Address: ✉ Burdett House, Becket Street, Derby, DE1 1JP

✍ enquiries@porterbrook.co.uk ✆ 01332 262405, ⓘ www.porterbrook.co.uk

Managing Director: Paul Francis

Facilities: Porterbrook Leasing have made available the off-lease Class 87s to mainland European operators, with a significant number being exported to operate in Bulgaria.

Stored in the UK

Number	Owner	Location
87025	PTR	LM

Exported

Number	Present operator
87003	BZK Bulgaria
87004	BZK Bulgaria
87006	BZK Bulgaria
87007	BZK Bulgaria
87008	BZK Bulgaria

Number	Present operator
87010	BZK Bulgaria
87012	BZK Bulgaria
87013	BZK Bulgaria
87014	BZK Bulgaria
87019	BZK Bulgaria
87020	BZK Bulgaria

Number	Present operator
87022	BZK Bulgaria
87026	BZK Bulgaria
87028	BZK Bulgaria
87029	BZK Bulgaria
87033	BZK Bulgaria
87034	BZK Bulgaria

Alstom

Address: ✉ PO Box 70, Newbold Road, Rugby, Warwickshire, CV21 2WR

〠 info@transport.alstom.com ✆ 01788 577111, ⓘ www.transport.alstom.com

Managing Director: Paul Robinson

Facilities: Following the assembly of the Virgin Trains Class 390 Pendolino stock, Alstom closed down its UK production facility at Washwood Heath, Birmingham. However, the company still operates from many specialist sites in mainland Europe and if Alstom win further new build contracts in the UK, these will be assembled in Europe.

Bombardier

Address: ✉ Litchurch Lane, Derby, DE24 8AD

〠 info@bombardier.com ✆ 01332 344666, ⓘ www.bombardier.com

Chief Country Representative: Colin Walton

Facilities: Bombardier Transportation is one of the largest transport builders in the world, with offices and building facilities in many countries. Its product range extends well beyond rail vehicles and includes aircraft, boats and leisure equipment.

In terms of the UK two main sites are located in Derby (Litchurch Lane) and Crewe. New build work is undertaken at the Derby site, which mainly concentrates on electric and diesel multiple unit designs.

Brush Traction

Address: ✉ PO Box 17, Loughborough, Leicestershire, LE11 1HS

〠 sales@brushtraction.com ✆ 01509 617000, ⓘ www.brushtraction.com

Managing Director: John Bidewell

Facilities: Brush Traction is now part of the FKI Group and in recent years has been responsible for the majority of UK loco building. The company has been synonymous with loco building for the UK and overseas markets for many years. Although recent main line loco builds have been awarded overseas, the facilities at the Loughborough plant where the Class 31, 47, 60, Eurotunnel Shuttle locos and the Class 57s emerged are still available for new build work. Recently the site has concentrated on re-build operations including the highly successful re-engining of the HST fleet with MTU power units.

Right: *Brush Traction, one of the most established names in locomotive building and refurbishment, operates a facility in Loughborough, Leicestershire. In recent years, rather than new build work, the site has concentrated on refurbishment of locos for Eurotunnel, First Great Western, CrossCountry Trains, East Coast, Grand Central, Freightliner, and DRS to name but a few. In immaculate condition, Class 20/3 No. 20303 is seen inside the main erecting shop undergoing a major overhaul.* **CJM**

Electro-Motive

Address: ✉ Electro-Motive Diesels Inc, 9301 West 55th Street, LaGrange, Illinois, USA 60525

Electro-Motive Diesels Inc, Oxford Street, London, Ontario, Canada

📠 info@emdiesels.com ✆ +1 (800) 255 5355, ⓘ www.emdiesels.com

Facilities: Formerly part of General Motors, Electro-Motive is one of the two largest loco builders in the world. Its main production facility is in London, Ontario, Canada. Production from this site sees locos transported throughout the world, including the UK and mainland Europe. In terms of the UK the JT42CWRM or Class 66 has been built in copious numbers for many different users. The design has also been built for mainland European operators including DBS subsidiary Euro Cargo Rail. Most recently the JT42CWRM design has been built for use in Egypt.

EMD is now owned by Progress Rail, a part of the Caterpillar Group.

General view of the EMD Caterpillar plant in London, Ontario, Canada. This plant has been responsible for the entire Class 66 build. **CJM**

General Electric

Address: ✉ GE Transportation Rail, 2901 East Lake Road, Erie, Pennsylvania, USA, 16531

UK office: Inspira House, Martinfield, Welwyn Garden City, Herts, AL7 1GW

📠 info@getransportation.com ✆ 01707 383700 ⓘ www.getransportation.com

Chief Executive Officer: Lorenzo Simonelli

Facilities: General Electric have only recently entered the UK loco arena, and are currently fulfilling an order for 'PowerHaul' locomotives for Freightliner. The company operates a huge construction facility in Erie, Pennsylvania, USA where the UK locos are being built.

Hitachi Europe Ltd

Address: ✉ 16 Upper Woburn Place, London, WC1H 0AF

📠 hirofumi.ojima@hitachi-eu.com ✆ 0207 970 2700, ⓘ www.hitachi-rail.com

Facilities: Hitachi Rail is a relatively new name to the UK rail scene. It won the contract to design, build, test and manage the fleet of Class 395 EMUs for use on the new high speed service from Kent to London St Pancras International using HS1. In 2009 the company formed the construction arm of the consortium awarded the IEP project to design, build and introduce the next generation of high speed passenger trains in the UK.

Hitachi at present do not have construction facilities in the UK and the Class 395s together with the first 60 vehicles of the IEP have been and will be constructed in Japan and shipped to the UK. Hitachi intends to open a construction site in the UK.

Siemens Transportation Ltd

Address: ✉ Ashby Park, Ashby de la Zouch, Leicestershire, LE65 1JD
✍ uk.mobility@siemens.com ✆ 01530 258000
ⓘ www.siemens.co.uk/mobility

Managing Director UK: Steve Scrimshaw

Facilities: Siemens are now an established provider of UK EMU and DMU rolling stock with various derivatives of their 'Desiro' product line. Siemens while having maintenance facilities in the UK, perform all new build work in mainland Europe at their Krefeld/Uerdingen factory in Germany. Testing of vehicles is performed in Germany before delivery at the world famous test track at Wildenrath.

Above & Right: *One of the most important suppliers of new rolling stock is Siemens, who have their main erection and test facility in Germany. After assembly of all locomotives and multiple unit trains they are taken to the company's test track at Wildenrath where dynamic testing can take place. Huge engineering workshops are also available at this location for modification and upgrade work. In the above view one of the new Vectron electric locos for mainland Europe No. 193 921 is seen. In the view right, a new 'Desiro' EMU for First Scotrail No. 380002 stands next to Belgian Class 18 EuroSprinter No. 1822. This is one of an order for 120 locos of type ES60U3. Both:* **CJM**

Angel Trains

Address: ✉ Portland House, Bressenden Place, London, SW1E 5BH
✆ reception@angeltrains.co.uk © 0207 592 0500, ⓘ www.angeltrains.co.uk
Chief Executive: Malcolm Brown
Owned by: Babcock Brown, AMP Capital & Deutsche Bank

British American Railway Services

Incorporating: RMS Locotec, RT Rail, Dartmoor Railway, Devon & Cornwall Railways, Weardale Railway, Ealing Community Transport and Hanson Rail

Address: ✉ London Riverside, London, SE1 2AQ
President: Ed Ellis
Depots: RMS Wakefield (ZS), Washwood Heath (WH)

UK operation is part of Iowa Pacific Holdings. BARS is also a Train Operating Company.

Class 08

Vehicle Length: 29ft 3in (8.91m)
Height: 12ft 8⅜in (3.87m)
Width: 8ft 6in (2.59m)
Engine: English Electric 6K
Horsepower: 400hp (298kW)
Electrical Equipment: English Electric

Number	Depot	Pool	Livery	Owner	Operator	Number	Depot	Pool	Livery	Owner	Operator
08308	IS	MRSO	FSR	ECT	FSR	08754	ZB	MRSO	BLU	ECT	IND
08423	ZS	INDL	RMS	RMS	IND	08756	MR	MRSO	GRY	ECT	GBR
08573	ZB	MRSO	BLK	ECT	BOM	08762	ZB	MRSO	BLK	ECT	WAB
08588	ZB	MRSO	BLK	ECT	IND	08870	ZS	MBDL	BLG	RMS	IND
08613	BH	MOLO	BLU	RMS	IND	08873	ZB	MRSO	HUN	ECT	FLR
08622	ZS	INDL	BLU	RMS	IND	08885	ZS	INDL	GBR	RMS	GBR
08750	ZB	MRSO	BLK	ECT	FCC	08936	ZS	MBDL	BLU	RMS	IND

Above: *British American Railway (BAR) are the supplier of a number of pilot locos to depots. No. 08573, painted in black livery and officially owned by ECT is seen operating at Bombardier Ilford depot, where it is used to shunt vehicles either loco hauled or multiple units into and out of the repair shop. The loco is seen attached to a barrier wagon.* **CJM**

Class 20

Vehicle Length: 46ft 9¼in (14.26m)
Height: 12ft 7⅝in (3.84m)
Width: 8ft 9in (2.66m)
Engine: English Electric 8SVT Mk2
Horsepower: 1,000hp (745kW)
Electrical Equipment: English Electric

Number	Depot	Pool	Livery	Owner	Operator	Number	Depot	Pool	Livery	Owner	Operator
20189	WR	MOLO	GRN	C20	BAR	20227	WR	MOLO	RFG	C20	BAR

Class 31/1, 31/4 & 31/6

Vehicle Length: 56ft 9in (17.29m)			Engine: English Electric 12SVT		
Height: 12ft 7in (3.91m)			Horsepower: 1,470hp (1,097kW)		
Width: 8ft 9in (2.65m)			Electrical Equipment: Brush		
31/4 Fitted with electric train heat, 31/6 through wired					

Number	Depot	Pool	Livery	Owner	Operator	Name
31190	WH	HTLX	GRN	BAR	- (Spot hire)	
31452 (31552/279)	DF	RVLO	DCG	ECT	ECT	
31602 (31191)	DF	RVLO	NRL	BAR	RVE	Driver Dave Green 19B

31454, 31468, 31601 - See Rail Vehicle Engineering (RVEL), section owned by ECT, operated by RVEL

Class 56

Vehicle Length: 63ft 6in (19.35m)			Engine: Ruston Paxman 16RK3CT		
Height: 13ft 0in (3.96m)			Horsepower: 3,250hp (2,420kW)		
Width: 9ft 2in (2.79m)			Electrical Equipment: Brush		

Number		Depot	Pool	Livery	Owner	Operator	Name
56311	(56057)	WH	HTLX	GRY	BAR	BAR	
56312	(56003)	WH	HTLX	PUR	BAR	BAR	Artemis
(56313) (S)	56128	WH	HTLX	FRB	BAR	-	
(56314) (S)	56114	WF	HTLX	-	BAR	-	

Right: *BAR merged with Hanson Traction in late 2010, expanding the capacity and facilities of both operators. The two former Hanson Class 56s, Nos. 56311 and 56312, are seen powering a westbound charter through Dawlish on 26 June 2010 bound for Penzance. These Class 56s are based at Washwood Heath.* **CJM**

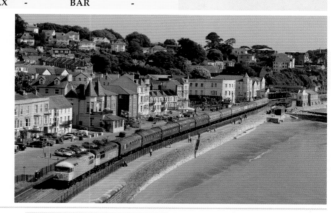

Class 73

Vehicle Length: 53ft 8in (16.35m)			Power: 750V dc third rail or English Electric 6K		
Height: 12ft 5⅛in (3.79m)			Horsepower: electric - 1,600hp (1,193kW)		
Width: 8ft 8in (2.64m)			Horsepower: diesel - 600hp (447kW)		
			Electrical Equipment: English Electric		

Number	Depot	Pool	Livery	Owner	Operator	Name
73107	SE	MBED	GRY	RTR	ECT	Redhill 1844 - 1994
73201 (73142)	SE	MBED	BLU	PTR	ECT	Broadlands

Right: *Electro-diesel No. 73107, painted in triple grey livery and usually outbased at St Leonards depot and used to power Network Rail inspection trains, was reunited with its* Redhill 1844-1994 *nameplate at the end of 2010, having its* Spitfire *plates removed. On 22 April 2010, No. 73107 is seen bringing up the rear of a southbound Network Rail test train at Clapham Junction.* **CJM**

Cargo-D

Address: ✉ 32 Sydney Road, Haywards Heath, West Sussex, RH16 1QA
✉ info@cargo-d.co.uk   📞 07970 344046, ⓘ www.cargo-d.co.uk
Commercial Director: Mark Honey
Cargo-D also owns the rail passenger charter business Rail Blue Charters

Hauled stock

Number	Type	Depot	Livery	Operator
Mk2 Vehicle Length: 66ft 0in (20.11m)			Height: 12ft 9½in (3.89m) Width: 9ft 3in (2.81m)	
1252 (3280)	AJ1F/RFO	LM	VIR	CAD
1254 (3391)	AJ1F/RFO	BH	BLG	WCR
1657	AJ41/RBR	BH	BLG	CAD
3241	AD1F/FO	BH	BLG	CAD
3366	AD1F/FO	BH	BLG	CAD
3374	AD1F/FO	BH	BLG	WCR
5787	AD2E/TSO	BH	BLG	CAD
5797	AD2E/TSO	BH	BLG	CAD
5810	AC2E/TSO	BH	BLG	CAD
5866	AC2E/TSO	WN	BLG	CAD
5876	AC2E/TSO	BH	BLG	CAD
5901	AC2F/TSO	BH	BLG	CAD
5906	AC2F/TSO	WN	BLG	CAD
5919	AC2F/TSO	BH	BLG	CAD
5925	AC2F/TSO	BH	BLG	CAD
5941	AC2F/TSO	BH	BLG	CAD
5958	AC2F/TSO	BH	BLG	CAD
5971	AC2F/TSO	BH	BLG	WCR
5995	AC25/TSO	BH	BLG	CAD
6001	AC2F/TSO	BH	BLG	CAD
6008	AC2F/TSO	BH	BLG	FGW
6045	AC2F/TSO	BH	VIR	CAD
6046	AC2F/TSO	BH	BLG	CAD
6064	AC2F/TSO	BK	BLG	FGW
6117	AC2F/TSO	BH	BLG	FGW
6122	AC2F/TSO	BH	BLG	WCR
6134	AC2F/TSO	KT	ICS	CAD
6151	AC2F/TSO	BH	BLG	CAD
6168	AC2F/TSO	WN	BLG	CAD

Number	Type	Depot	Livery	Operator
Mk3 Vehicle Length: 75ft 0in (22.86m)			Height: 12ft 9in (3.88m) Width: 8ft 11in (2.71m)	
6173	AC2F/TSO	BH	BLG	WCR
9497	AC2E/BSO	WN	BLG	CAD
9506	AE2E/BSO	BH	BLG	CAD
9508	AE2E/BSO	BH	BLG	FGW
9525	AE2E/BSO	BH	BLG	CAS
10202 (40504)	AJ1G/RFM	WN	BLG	CAD
10242 (10002)	AJ1G/RFM	CE	BLG	WSR
10245 (10019)	AJ1G/RFM	AL	BLG	CAD
10246 (10014)	AJ1G/RFM	BH	BLG	WSR
10249 (10012)	AJ1G/RFM	CF	ATW	ATW
10588	AU4G/SLEP	WN	BLG	CAD
11064	AD1H/FO	BH	BLG	CAD
11065	AD1H/FO	WN	BLG	CAD
11071	AD1H/FO	WN	BLG	WSR
11079	AD1H/FO	CE	VIR	CAD
11083	AD1H/FOD	WN	BLG	WSR
11084	AD1H/FO	WN	BLG	CAD/VWC
11086	AD1H/FO	WN	BLG	CAD
11089	AD1H/FO	WN	BLG	CAD
12014	AC2G/TSO	AL	BLG	WSR
12017	AC2G/TSO	WB	VIR	WSR/VWC
12038	AC2G/TSO	WN	BLG	WSR
12043	AC2G/TSO	AL	BLG	WSR
12059	AC2G/TSO	WB	VIR	WSR/VWC
12094	AC2G/TSO	WB	VIR	WSR/VWC
12119	AC2G/TSO	WN	BLG	WSR
80042 (1646)	AJ41/RK	BH	BLG	CAD
96603(S)	Motorail	LM	GRN	-
96604(S)	Motorail	LM	GRN	-

Left: *Now a major player in the provision of quality rolling stock to both national operators and charter companies Cargo-D is based at Barrow Hill. Most of this operator's stock has been repainted in the 1970s blue/grey Inter-City colours and maintained to a high standard both technically and internally. AC2f TSO No. 6117 is illustrated.* **Brian Garrett**

Electric Traction Limited

Address: ⊠ Woodlands, Manse Road, Inverurie, Scotland, AB51 3UJ
Depot: Long Marston (LM)
Electric Traction Ltd provide spot hire of Class 86 and 87 traction, as well as providing engineering and graphic design services to the rail industry.

Class 86

Vehicle Length: 58ft 6in (17.83m)				Power Collection: 25kV ac overhead		
Height: 13ft 0⅝in (3.97m)				Horsepower: 5,900hp (4,400kW)		
Width: 8ft 8¼in (2.64m)				Electrical Equipment: GEC		

Number	Depot	Pool	Livery	Owner	Operator	Name
86101	WA	ACAC	BLU	ETL	ETL	
86701 (86205)	CP	ETLO	ETL	ETL	ETL	Orion
86702 (86260)	CP	ETLO	ETL	ETL	ETL	Cassiopeia

Right: *The two refurbished Class 86/7s owned by Electric Traction Ltd are usually based at Crewe and made available for spot hire. 'Topped and tailed' by Class 86/7s Nos. 86702* Cassiopeia *and No. 86701* Orion, *the 08.00 charter from Newcastle to London King's Cross passes through Welwyn Garden City at speed on 17 October 2009.* **Brian Morrison**

Class 87

Vehicle Length: 58ft 6in (17.83m)				Power Collection: 25kV ac overhead		
Height: 13ft 1¼in (3.99m)				Horsepower: 7,860hp (5,680kW)		
Width: 8ft 8¼in (2.64m)				Electrical Equipment: GEC		

Number	Depot	Pool	Livery	Owner	Operator	Name
87002	CP	ETLO	BLU	ETL	ETL	Royal Sovereign

Right: *Operated by Electric Traction Ltd, the immaculate No. 87002* Royal Sovereign *is seen at Long Marston, where it was restored to main line condition.* **CJM**

Eversholt Rail Group (Previously HSBC Rail)

Address: ⊠ PO Box 29499, 1 Eversholt Street, London, NW1 2ZF
            ✆ info@eversholtrail.co.uk ☏ 0207 380 5040, ⓘ www.eversholtrail.co.uk
Chief Operating Officer: Mary Kenny

Harry Needle Railroad Company

Address: ✉ Harry Needle Railway Shed, Barrow Hill Roundhouse, Campbell Drive, Chesterfield, Derbyshire, S43 2PR

Managing Director: Harry Needle

Depot: Barrow Hill (BH)

Harry Needle Railroad Company also operates as a scrap dealer in dismantling locomotives and rolling stock. ø Reported for sale

Class 01

Number	Depot	Pool	Livery	Owner	Operator
01552 (TH167V)	BH	HNRL	IND	HNR	IND
01564 (12088)	BH	HNRL	BLK	HNR	IND

Class 07

Vehicle Length: 26ft 9½in (8.16m)	Engine: Paxman 6RPHL MkIII
Height: 12ft 10in (3.91m)	Horsepower: 275hp (205kW)
Width: 8ft 6in (2.59m)	Electrical Equipment: AEI

Number	Depot	Pool	Livery	Owner	Operator
07001	BH	HNRS	HNR	HNR	IND

Class 08 & 09

Vehicle Length: 29ft 3in (8.91m)	Engine: English Electric 6K
Height: 12ft 8⅜in (3.87m)	Horsepower: 400hp (298kW)
Width: 8ft 6in (2.59m)	Electrical Equipment: English Electric

Number	Depot	Pool	Livery	Owner	Operator
08492	BH	HNRL	BLU	HNR	HNR
08502	BH	HNRL	NOR	HNR	NOR
08507	CZ	HNRL	HNR	HNR	BOM
08517(S)	LM	HNRS	BLU	HNR	-
08527(S)	BH	HNRL	JAR	HNR	IND
08665	BH	HNRL	?	HNR	?
08818	BH	HNRL	HNR	HNR	IND
08827(S)	LM	HNRS	BLU	HNR	-
08834	BH	HNRL	DRS	HNR	OLD
08868	CP	HNRL	LNW	HNR	LNW

Number	Depot	Pool	Livery	Owner	Operator
08892	BH	HNRL	DRS	HNR	RVE
08929(S)	LM	HNRS	BLK	HNR	-
08943	SH‡	MBDL	HNR	HNR	NRM
09003(S)	WH	HNRS	EWS	HNR	-
09012	BH	HNRS	EWS	HNR	HNT
09014	-	HNRS	EWS	HNR	-
09018(S)	BH	HNRS	EWS	HNR	-
09019	-	HNRS	EWS	HNR	-

‡ At Waterloo International (Railway Children)

Left: *Owned by the Harry Needle Railroad Company, No. 08868 is painted in LNWR two-tone grey and red livery and is used as depot pilot at the operator's Crewe base. It is unusual on a shunter that black and yellow 'wasp' ends are not applied.* **Nathan Williamson**

Class 20/0

Vehicle Length: 46ft 9¼in (14.26m)	Engine: English Electric 8SVT Mk2
Height: 12ft 7⅝in (3.84m)	Horsepower: 1,000hp (745kW)
Width: 8ft 9in (2.66m)	Electrical Equipment: English Electric

Number	Depot	Pool	Livery	Owner	Operator
20016(S) ø	LM	HNRS	BLU	HNR	-
20032(S) ø	LM	HNRS	BLU	HNR	-
20056	BH	HNRL	COR	HNR	TAT
20057(S) ø	LM	HNRS	BLU	HNR	-
20066	BH	HNRL	TAT	HNR	TAT
20072(S) ø	LM	HNRS	BLU	HNR	-
20081(S) ø	LM	HNRS	BLU	HNR	-
20088(S) ø	LM	HNRS	RFG	HNR	-
20092(S)	BH	HNRS	LAF	HNR	-
20096	BH	HNRL	BLU	HNR	HNR
20107(S)	BH	HNRS	BLU	HNR	-
20121(S)	BH	HNRS	BLU	HNR	-
20132(S)	CP	HNRS	GRN	HNR	-
20138(S)	LM	HNRS	RFT	HNR	-
20168	EA	HNRL	LAF	HNR	LAF

Right: *Looking very foreign, former BR Class 20 No. 20066 is now hired by HNRL to Tata Steel at Scunthorpe and carried this operator's No. 82. Seen at Barrow Hill after restoration, note the high level marker/tail lights and roof mounted lights on the cab.*
Bill Wilson

Name applied
20168   Sir George Earle

20056 carries Corus Steel No. 81.
20066 carries Tata Rail No. 82.

Class 20/9

Vehicle Length: 46ft 9¼in (14.26m)				*Engine: English Electric 8SVT Mk2*		
Height: 12ft 7⅝in (3.84m)				*Horsepower: 1,000hp (745kW)*		
Width: 8ft 9in (2.66m)				*Electrical Equipment: English Electric*		

Number		Depot	Pool	Livery	Owner	Operator
20901	(20101)	BH	HNRL	TLG	HNR	HNR
20902(S)	(20060)	LM	HNRS	DRS	HNR	-
20903(S)	(20083)	LM	HNRS	DRS	HNR	-
20904(S)	(20041)	LM	HNRS	DRS	HNR	-
20905	(20225)	BH	HNRL	TLG	HNR	HNR
20906	(20219)	WH	HNRL	DRS	HNR	HNR

Class 37/0

Vehicle Length: 61ft 6in (18.74m)			*Engine: English Electric 12CSVT*		
Height: 13ft 0¼in (3.96m)			*Horsepower: 1,750hp (1,304kW)*		
Width: 8ft 11⅝in (2.73m)			*Electrical Equipment: English Electric*		

Number		Depot	Pool	Livery	Owner	Operator
37029		BH	HNRS	GRN	HNR	HNR *(At Epping & Ongar Railway)*
37165(S)	(37374)	CS	HNRS	CIV	HNR	-

Class 37/4

Vehicle Length: 61ft 6in (18.74m)			*Engine: English Electric 12CSVT*		
Height: 13ft 0¼in (3.96m)			*Horsepower: 1,750hp (1,304kW)*		
Width: 8ft 11⅝in (2.73m)			*Electrical Equipment: English Electric*		
Electric Train Heat fitted					

Number		Depot	Pool	Livery	Owner	Operator/Notes
37412(S)	(37301)	CS	HNRS	TLF	HNR	Stored at WCRC Carnforth
37415(S)	(37277)	LM	HNRS	EWS	HNR	-
37428 ø	(37281)	LM	HNRS	MAR	HNR	-

Class 37/5

Vehicle Length: 61ft 6in (18.74m)			*Engine: English Electric 12CSVT*		
Height: 13ft 0¼in (3.96m)			*Horsepower: 1,750hp (1,304kW)*		
Width: 8ft 11⅝in (2.73m)			*Electrical Equipment: English Electric*		

Number		Depot	Pool	Livery	Owner	Operator
37696(S)	(37228) ø	BH	HNRS	TGG	HNR	-

Class 47

Vehicle Length: 63ft 6in (19.35m)			*Engine: Sulzer 12LDA28C*		
Height: 12ft 10⅜in (3.91m)			*Horsepower: 2,580hp (1,922kW)*		
Width: 9ft 2in (2.79m)			*Electrical Equipment: Brush*		
Electric Train Heat fitted to Class 47/4 and 47/7					

Number		Depot	Pool	Livery	Owner	Opertor
47237(S)		GL	HNRL	ADV	HNR	-
47295(S)		LM	HNRL	FL1	HNR	-
47714	(47511)	OD	HNRL	ANG	HNR	SEC*

Rolling Stock Hire Companies

HNRC

47761 (47038/564)	BH	HNRL	RES	HNR	-
47813 (47129/658)	BH	XHHP	CWR	HNR	(for DRS)
47828 (47266/629)	BH	XHHP	CWR	HNR	(for DRS)
47829(S) (47264/619) ø LM		HNRL	POL	HNR	-

* Working at Old Dalby

Left: *Following the demise of Cotswold Rail and Advenza Freight HNRC purchased a number of the quality assets, including Class 47/0 No. 47237 which in 2010 was stored out of use at Gloucester carry its former Advenza blue livery.* **CJM**

Class 57/0

Vehicle Length: 63ft 6in (19.38m)	Engine: EMD 645-12E3	
Height: 12ft 10½in (3.91m)	Horsepower: 2,500hp (1,864kW)	
Width: 9ft 2in (2.79m)	Electrical Equipment: Brush	

Number	Depot	Pool	Livery	Owner	Operator	Notes
57005 (47350)	BH(CF)	HNRL	ADV	-	-	Stored at Cardiff
57006 (47187)	BH(HT)	HNRL	ADV	-	-	Stored at Heaton

Left: *Towards the end of 2010, HNRC took over on paper the two ex-Advenza Freight Class 57/0s, Nos. 57005/006, which were stored at Cardiff and Heaton respectively. No. 57005 is illustrated at Cardiff in summer 2010. It is understood that HNRC will not be overhauling or using these locomotives.* **CJM**

Nemesis Rail

Address: ✉ Nemesis Rail Ltd, Barrow Hill Roundhouse, Campbell Drive, Chesterfield, Derbyshire, S43 2PR

✍ enquiries@ nemesisrail.com ✆ 01246 472331, ⓘ www.nemesisrail.com

Formed from the demise of FM Rail

Depot: Barrow Hill (BH)

Class 31/1

Vehicle Length: 56ft 9in (17.29m)	Engine: English Electric 12SVT	
Height: 12ft 7in (3.91m)	Horsepower: 1,470hp (1,097kW)	
Width: 8ft 9in (2.65m)	Electrical Equipment: Brush	

Number	Depot	Pool	Livery	Owner	Operator	Name
31128	NY	NRLO	BLU	NEM	NYM	*Charybdis*

Rolling Stock Hire Companies – HNRC, Nemesis Rail

Right: *Owned by Nemesis Rail, Class 31/1 No. 31128 painted in rail blue with full yellow ends is presently operated on the North Yorkshire Moors Railway. It is main line certified and can operate trains over the section of line between Grosmont and Whitby.* **Tony Christie**

Class 33/1

Vehicle Length: 50ft 9in (15.47m)				Engine: Sulzer 8LDA28A		
Height: 12ft 8in (3.86m)				Horsepower: 1,550hp (1,156kW)		
Width: 9ft 3in (2.81m)				Electrical Equipment: Crompton Parkinson		

Number	Depot	Pool	Livery	Owner	Operator	Name
33103	BH	MBDL	BLU	NEM	NEM	*Swordfish*

On loan to Swanage Railway

Class 45/1

Vehicle Length: 67ft 11in (20.70m)				Engine: Sulzer 12LDA28B		
Height: 12ft 10½in (3.91m)				Horsepower: 2,500hp (1,862kW)		
Width: 9ft 1½in (2.78m)				Electrical Equipment: Crompton Parkinson		

Number	Depot	Pool	Livery	Owner	Operator	Name
45112	BH	MBDL	BLU	NEM	NEM	*Royal Army Ordnance Corps*

Class 47

Vehicle Length: 63ft 6in (19.35m)				Engine: Sulzer 12LDA28C		
Height: 12ft 10⅜in (3.91m)				Horsepower: 2,580hp (1,922kW)		
Width: 9ft 2in (2.79m)				Electrical Equipment: Brush		
Electric Train Heat fitted to Class 47/4 and 47/7						

Number	Depot	Pool	Livery	Owner	Opertor					
47375	BH	MBDL	BLU	NEM	NEM	47716	BH	MBDL	RES	NEM	NEM
47488	BH	MBDL	GRN	NEM	NEM	47744	BH	MBDL	EWS	NEM	NEM

Porterbrook

Address: ✉ Ivatt House, The Point, Pinnacle Way, Pride Park, Derby, DE24 8ZS
📧 enquiries@porterbrook.co.uk ☎ 01332 285050, ⓘ www.porterbrook.co.uk

Managing Director: Paul Francis
Owned by: Antin Infrastructure Partners, Deutsche Bank & OP Trust

Transmart Trains

Address: ✉ Green Farm House, Falfield, Wootton-under-Edge, Gloucestershire. GL12 8DL
Managing Director: Oliver Buxton
Depots: Selhurst (SU), Stewarts Lane (SL)

Part of Cambrian Transport

Class 73

‡ *At Barry Railway*
• *Not main line certified*

Vehicle Length: 53ft 8in (16.35m)				Power: 750V dc third rail or English Electric 6K		
Height: 12ft 5⅝in (3.79m)				Horsepower: electric - 1,600hp (1,193kW)		
Width: 8ft 8in (2.64m)				Horsepower: diesel - 600hp (447kW)		
				Electrical Equipment: English Electric		

Number	Depot	Pool	Livery	Owner	Operator	Name	
73109	SU	MBED	SWT	TTS	TTS		■ *Former Gatwick Express Class*
73118	‡	-	GRY	TTS	TTS		*488 vehicles Nos. 72505, 72620,*
73133 •	SU	-	GRN	TTS	TTS		*72621, 72629, 72710 from sets*
73136	SU	MBED	GRN	TTS	TTS	*Perseverance*	*488206 and 488311 are also owned*
73211 (spares)	SL	-	ICS	TTS	TTS		*by Transmart Trains.*

Rolling Stock Hire Companies – Nemesis Rail, Porterbrook, Transmart Trains

Listings provide details of locomotives and stock authorised for operation on the UK National Rail network and that can be seen operating special and charter services.
Preserved locomotives authorised for main line operation are found in the preserved section.

Bo'ness and Kinneil Railway

Number	Type	Depot	Livery	Operator	Use
464	AO3/BCK	BT	CAL	BOK	Charter train use
1375 (99803)	AO2/TK	BT	CAL	BOK	Charter train use
3096 (99827)	AD11/FO	BT	MAR	BOK	Charter train use
3115	AD11/FO	BT	MAR	BOK	Charter train use
3150	AD11/FO	BT	MAR	BOK	Charter train use
4831 (99824)	AC21/TSO	BT	MAR	BOK	Charter train use
4832 (99823)	AC21/TSO	BT	CHC	BOK	Charter train use
4836 (99831)	AC21/TSO	BT	MAR	BOK	Charter train use
4856 (99829)	AC21/TSO	BT	MAR	BOK	Charter train use
5028 (99830)	AC21/TSO	BT	CAR	BOK	Charter train use
5412	AC2A/TSO	BT	MAR	BOK	Charter train use
13229 (99826)	AA11/FK	BT	MAR	BOK	Charter train use
13230 (99828)	AA11/FK	BT	MAR	BOK	Charter train use

Flying Scotsman Railway Ltd

Number	Type	Depot	Livery	Operator	Notes/Name
316 (S) (975608)	AO11/PFK	CS	PUL	FSL	Pullman *Magpie*
321 (S)	AO11/PFK	CS	PUL	FSL	Pullman *Swift*
337 (S)	AO11/PSK	CS	PUL	FSL	Pullman Car No. 337

Great Scottish & Western Railway Co

Number	Type	Depot	Livery	Operator	Notes/Name
313 (S) (99964)	AO11/PFK	CS	MAR	GSW	Royal Scotsman - *Finch*
317 (99967)	AO11/PFK	CS	MAR	GSW	Royal Scotsman - *Raven*
319 (99965)	AO11/PFK	CS	MAR	GSW	Royal Scotsman - *Snipe*
324 (99961)	AO11/PFP	CS	MAR	GSW	Royal Scotsman - *Amber*
329 (99962)	AO11/PFP	CS	MAR	GSW	Royal Scotsman - *Pearl*
331 (99963)	AO11/PFP	CS	MAR	GSW	Royal Scotsman - *Topaz*
1999 (99131)	AO10/SAL	CS	MAR	GSW	Royal Scotsman - *Lochaber*

Jeremy Hoskins

Number	Type	Depot	Livery	Operator	Notes/Name
3125 (S)	AD11/FO	TM	CHC	JHS	*Loch Shiel*
3148 (S) (3610)	AD11/FO	CS	MAR	JHS	

Mid-Hants Railway

Number	Type	Depot	Livery	Operator
1105 (99531/302)	AJ41/RG	RL	GRN	MHR
21252	AB31/BCK	RL	GRN	MHR

North Yorkshire Moors Railway

Class 25

Vehicle Length: 50ft 6in (15.39m)
Height: 12ft 8in (3.86m)
Width: 9ft 1in (2.76m)
Engine: Sulzet 6LDA28B
Horsepower: 1,250hp (932kW)
Electrical Equipment: Brush

Number	Depot	Pool	Livery	Owner	Operator	Name	Notes
25278	NY	MBDL	GRN	NYM	NYM	*Sybilia*	*Restricted main line use*

Coaching Stock

Number	Type	Depot	Livery	Operator	
1823	AN21/RMB	NY	MAR	NYM	
3860	AC21/TSO	NY	MAR	NYM	
3872	AC21/TSO	NY	CAR	NYM	
3948	AC21/TSO	NY	CAR	NYM	Spare vehicle
4198	AC21/TSO	NY	CAR	NYM	
4252	AC21/TSO	NY	CAR	NYM	
4290	AC21/TSO	NY	MAR	NYM	
4455	AC21/TSO	NY	CAR	NYM	
4786	AC21/TSO	NY	MAR	NYM	
4817	AC21/TSO	NY	CHC	NYM	
5000	AC21/TSO	NY	MAR	NYM	
5029	AC21/TSO	NY	CHC	NYM	
9267	AE21/BSO	NY	CHC	NYM	
9274	AE21/BSO	NY	CHC	NYM	
16156 (7156)	AA31/CK	NY	MAR	NYM	
35089	AB2I/BSK	NY	MAR	NYM	

Railfilms Limited

Number	Type	Depot	Livery	Operator	Notes/Name
84 (99884)		EH	PUL	RAF	
310 (99107)	AO11/PFL	EH	PUL	RAF	Pegasus
1659 (16509)	AJ41/RBR	EH	PUL	RAF	
3188	AD1D/FO	EH	PUL	RAF	Sovereign
3231	AD1E/FO	EH	PUL	RAF	Apollo
5067 (99993)	AC21/TSO	CP	MAR	RAF	
9004	GWR	EH	GWR	RAF	
13508 (S)	AA1B/FK	CS	MAR	RAF	
17080	AO3/BCK	EH	PUL	RAF	

Above: *Owned by Railfilms and painted in Pullman umber and cream livery is former BR Mk1 RBR No. 1659. The coach is viewed from its kitchen end.* **Tony Christie**

Ridings Railtours

Number	Type	Depot	Livery	Operator
5520 (S)	AC2C/TSO	SV	PUL	RRS
13581 (S)	AA1D/FK	SV	ICS	RRS
13583 (S)	AA1D/FK	SV	ICS	RRS

Private Train Operators – NYMR, Railfilms, Ridings

Riviera Trains

Class 47

Vehicle Length: 63ft 6in (19.35m)
Height: 12ft 10⅜in (3.91m)
Width: 9ft 2in (2.79m)
Electric Train Heat fitted

Engine: Sulzer 12LDA28C
Horsepower: 2,580hp (1,922kW)
Electrical Equipment: Brush

Number	Depot	Pool	Livery	Owner	Operator	Name
47747 (47615)	CP	RTLO	EWS	RIV	RIV	
47769 (47491)	CP	RTLO	VIR	RIV	RIV	
47805 (47650)	CP	RTLO	RIV	RIV	RIV	Talisman
47812 D1916 (47657)	CP	RTLO	GRN	RIV	RIV	
47815 D1748 (47660)	CP	RTLO	GRN	RIV	RIV	Great Western
47839 (47621)	CP	RTLO	RIV	RIV	RIV	Pegasus
47843 (47623)	CP	RTLO	RIV	RIV	RIV	Vulcan
47847 (47577)	CP	RTLO	RIV	RIV	RIV	
47848 (47632)	CP	RTLO	RIV	RIV	RIV	Titan Star
47853 (47614)	CP	RTLO	XP6	RIV	RIV	Rail Express

Left: Although the prime workload for Riviera Trains locomotives is to power charter specials over the National Network, occasionally locos are hired for freight and other use. One such duty was on 17 September 2009, when No. 47812 powered Colas train 6Z47, the 09.55 Tavistock Junction to Rugby formed of ZWA DR76601, YDA DR92377, YDA DR92400 and KFA TIPH9344. The train is seen passing Dawlish. **CJM**

Coaching Stock

Number	Type	Depot	Livery	Operator	Notes/Name
1200 (6459)	AJ1F/RFO	EH	RIV	RIV	Set 04 - The Great Briton - Amber
1203 (3291)	AJ1F/RFO	EH	RIV	RIV	
1212 (6453)	AJ1F/RFO	EH	VIR	RIV	Set 05 - The Norfolkman
1250 (3372)	AJ1F/RFO	EH	VIR	RIV	Set 07 - The West Coast Set
1651	AJ41/RBR	EH	MAR	RIV	Set 02 - The Royal Scot Set
1671	AJ41/RBR	EH	MAR	RIV	Set 02 - The Royal Scot Set
1683	AJ41/RBR	BH	BLU	RIV	Set 04 - The Great Briton - Carol
1691	AJ41/RBR	CP	CCM	RIV	Set 02 - The Royal Scot Set
1692	AJ41/RBR	CP	CHC	RIV	Set 01 - The British Classic Set
1699	AJ41/RBR	CP	BLU	RIV	Set 04 - The Great Briton
1813	AN21/RMB	CP	MAR	RIV	Set 03
1832	AN21/RMB	EH	CCM	RIV	
1842	AN21/RMB	EH	CCM	RIV	Set 02 - The Royal Scot Set
1863	AN21/RMB	EH	CHC	RIV	Set 01 - British Classic Set
2834 (S) (21267)	AU51/SLSC	EH	LNR	RIV	
3066 (99566)	AD11/FO	EH	CCM	RIV	Set 02 - The Royal Scot Set
3068 (99568)	AD11/FO	EH	CCM	RIV	Set 02 - The Royal Scot Set
3069 (99540)	AD11/FO	EH	CCM	RIV	Set 02 - The Royal Scot Set
3097	AD11/FO	EH	CCM	RIV	Set 02 - The Royal Scot Set
3098	AD11/FO	EH	CHC	RIV	Set 01 - The British Classic Set
3107	AD11/FO	EH	CHC	RIV	Set 01 - The British Classic Set
3110 (99124)	AD11/FO	EH	CHC	RIV	Set 01 - The British Classic Set
3112 (99357)	AD11/FO	EH	CHC	RIV	Set 01 - The British Classic Set
3114 (S)	AD11/FO	EH	GRN	RIV	

3119	AD11/FO	EH	CCM	RIV	Set 02 - The Royal Scot Set
3120	AD11/FO	EH	CCM	RIV	Set 03
3121	AD11/FO	EH	LNE	RIV	Set 02 - The Royal Scot Set
3122	AD11/FO	EH	CHC	RIV	Set 01 - British Classic Set
3123	AD11/FO	EH	LNE	RIV	Set 03
3124 (S)	AD11/FO	EH	GRN	RIV	
3127 (S)	AD11/FO	EH	GRN	RIV	
3131 (S) (99190)	AD11/FO	EH	MAR	RIV	
3132 (S) (99191)	AD11/FO	EH	MAR	RIV	
3133 (S) (99192)	AD11/FO	EH	MAR	RIV	
3140	AD11/FO	EH	CHC	RIV	Set 01 - British Classic Set
3141 (3608)	AD11/FO	EH	MRN	RIV	Set 03
3144 (3602)	AD11/FO	EH	MRN	RIV	Set 03
3146	AD11/FO	EH	MRN	RIV	Set 03
3147 (3604)	AD11/FO	EH	LNE	RIV	Set 03
3149	AD11/FO	EH	CCM	RIV	Set 02 - The Royal Scot Set
3181 (S)	AD1D/FO	EH	RIV	RIV	*Topaz*
3223 (S)	AD1E/FO	EH	RIV	RIV	*Diamond*
3240 (S)	AD1E/FO	EH	RIV	RIV	*Sapphire*
3277	AD1F/FO	EH	ANG	RIV	Set 05 - The Norfolkman
3279	AD1F/FO	EH	MAR	RIV	Set 05 - The Norfolkman
3295	AD1F/FO	EH	ANG	RIV	Set 05 - The Norfolkman
3304	AD1F/FO	EH	VIR	RIV	Set 07 - West Coast Set
3314	AD1F/FO	EH	VIR	RIV	Set 07 - West Coast Set
3325	AD1F/FO	EH	VIR	RIV	Set 07 - West Coast Set
3330	AD1F/FO	EH	RIV	RIV	Set 04 - The Great Briton - *Brunel*
3333	AD1F/FO	EH	VIR	RIV	Set 07 - The West Coast Set
3334	AD1F/FO	EH	ANG	RIV	Set 05 - The Norfolkman
3336	AD1F/FO	CD	ANG	RIV	Set 05 - The Norfolkman
3340	AD1F/FO	EH	VIR	RIV	Set 07 - The West Coast Set
3344	AD1F/FO	EH	RIV	RIV	Set 07 - The West Coast Set
3345	ADIF/FO	EH	VIR	RIV	Set 07 - The West Coast Set
3348	AD1F/FO	EH	RIV	RIV	Set 04 - The Great Briton - *Gainsborough*
3356	AD1F/FO	EH	RIV	RIV	Set 04 - The Great Briton - *Tennyson*
3364	AD1F/FO	EH	RIV	RIV	Set 04 - The Great Briton - *Shakespeare*
3379	AD1F/FO	EH	ANG	RIV	
3384	AD1F/FO	EH	RIV	RIV	Set 04 - The Great Briton - *Dickens*
3386	AD1F/FO	EH	VIR	RIV	Set 07 - The West Coast Set
3390	AD1F/FO	EH	RIV	RIV	Set 04 - The Great Briton - *Constable*
3397	AD1F/FO	EH	RIV	RIV	Set 04 - The Great Briton - *Wordsworth*
3417	AD1F/FO	EH	ANG	RIV	
3426	AD1F/FO	EH	RIV	RIV	Set 04 - The Great Briton - *Elgar*
4902	AC21/TSO	EH	CHC	RIV	Set 01 - British Classic Set
4927	AC21/TSO	EH	CHC	RIV	Set 01 - British Classic Set
4946 (S) (99000)	AC21/TSO	EH	MAR	RIV	(at Minehead)
4949	AC21/TSO	ZA	CHC	RIV	Set 03
4959	AC21/TSO	ZA	CHC	RIV	
4986	AC21/TSO	EH	GRN	RIV	Set 03
4991	AC21/TSO	ZA	CHC	RIV	
4996 (S) (99001)	AC21/TSO	EH	MAR	RIV	(at Minehead)
4998	AC21/TSO	EH	MAR	RIV	Set 03
4999 (S)	AC21/TSO	EH	BLG	RIV	
5007 (S)	AC21/TSO	EH	GRN	RIV	
5008 (99002)	AC21/TSO	EH	MAN	RIV	(at Minehead)
5009	AC21/TSO	EH	CHC	RIV	Set 01 - British Classic Set
5023	AC21/TSO	EH	RIV	RIV	Set 03
5027 (S)	AC21/TSO	EH	GRN	RIV	
5040	AC21/TSO	EH	CHC	RIV	Set 01 - British Classic Set
5276	AC2A/TSO	EH	RIV	RIV	Set 02 - The Royal Scot Set
5292	AC2A/TSO	EH	CHC	RIV	Set 02 - The Royal Scot Set
5309 (S)	AC2A/TSO	EH	CHC	RIV	
5322	AC2A/TSO	EH	RIV	RIV	Set 02 - The Royal Scot Set
5341	AC2A/TSO	EH	CCM	RIV	Set 02 - The Royal Scot Set
5350	AC2A/TSO	EH	CHC	RIV	Set 01 - British Classic Set - *Dawn*
5366	AC2A/TSO	ZA	CHC	RIV	Set 02 - The Royal Scot Set
5494 (S)	AC2B/TSO	SV	NSE	RIV	
5647 (S)	AC2D/TSO	EH	RIV	RIV	

Riviera

5739 (S)	AC2D/TSO	SV	NWM	RIV	
5748	AC2E/TSO	EH	INT	RIV	
5769	AC2E/TSO	EH	INT	RIV	
5792	AC2E/TSO	EH	VIR	RIV	
5910	AC2F/TSO	EH	VIR	RIV	Set 07 - The West Coast Set
5921	AC2F/TSO	EH	RIV	RIV	Set 05 - The Norfolkman
5929	AC2F/TSO	EH	ANG	RIV	Set 05 - The Norfolkman
5937	AC2F/TSO	EH	VIR	RIV	
5945	AC2F/TSO	EH	VIR	RIV	Set 07 - The West Coast Set
5946	AC2F/TSO	EH	VIR	RIV	Set 07 - The West Coast Set
5950	AC2F/TSO	EH	RIV	RIV	
5952 (S)	AC2F/TSO	EH	VIR	RIV	
5955 (S)	AC2F/TSO	EH	VIR	RIV	
5961	AC2F/TSO	EH	VIR	RIV	Set 07 - The West Coast Set
5964	AC2F/TSO	EH	ANG	RIV	
5985	AC2F/TSO	EH	ANG	RIV	Set 05 - The Norfolkman
5987	AC2F/TSO	EH	VIR	RIV	Set 07 - The West Coast Set
5997	AC2F/TSO	EH	VIR	RIV	Set 07 - The West Coast Set
5998	AC2F/TSO	EH	ANG	RIV	Set 05 - The Norfolkman
6006	AC2F/TSO	CF	ANG	RIV	Set 05 - The Norfolkman
6024 (S)	AC2F/TSO	EH	VIR	RIV	
6027	AC2F/TSO	EH	RIV	RIV	Set 07 - The West Coast Set
6042	AC2F/TSO	EH	ANG	RIV	Set 05 - The Norfolkman
6051	AC2F/TSO	EH	VIR	RIV	Set 07 - The West Coast Set
6054	AC2F/TSO	EH	VIR	RIV	Set 07 - The West Coast Set
6067 (S)	AC2F/TSO	EH	VIR	RIV	
6107	AC2F/TSO	EH	RIV	RIV	
6141	AC2F/TSO	EH	RIV	RIV	Set 07 - The West Coast Set
6153 (S)	AC2F/TSO	ZG	VIR	RIV	
6158	AC2F/TSO	EH	VIR	RIV	Set 07 - The West Coast Set
6176 (S)	AC2F/TSO	EH	VIR	RIV	
6177	AC2F/TSO	EH	RIV	RIV	
6310 (81448)	AX51/GEN	EH	CHC	RIV	
6320	AZ5Z/SAL	SK	MRN	RIV	
6720 (6602)	AN1D/RMBF	EH	MRN	RIV	
9504	AC2E/BSO	EH	VIR	RIV	Set 07 - The West Coast Set
9507	AC2E/BSO	EH	RIV	RIV	
9520	AE2F/BSO	EH	RIV	RIV	Set 07 - The West Coast Set
9526	AC2F/BSO	EH	INT	RIV	
9527	AC2F/BSO	EH	ANG	RIV	
9537	AE2F/BSO	EH	RIV	RIV	Set 07 - The West Coast Set
17015 (14015)	AB11/BFK	EH	CHC	RIV	Set 02 - The Royal Scot Set
17056 (S) (14056)	AB1A/BFK	EH	MAR	RIV	
17077 (14077)	AB1A/BFK	EH	RIV	RIV	Set 04 - The Great Briton - *Catherine*
17105 (2905)	AX5B/BFK	EH	RIV	RIV	Set 02 - Staff Couchette
21224	AB31/BCK	EH	MAR	RIV	Directors saloon
21245 (99356)	AB31/BCK	EH	MAR	RIV	Set 03
21269	AB31/BCK	EH	LNE	RIV	
21272 (99129)	AB31/BCK	EH	CHC	RIV	Set 01 - British Classic Set
35469 (99763)	AB21/BSK	EH	CCM	RIV	Set 03
80041 (1690)	AK51/RK	EH	MAR	RIV	Set 03 - Pride of the Nation

Left: *Painted in Anglia turquoise livery, Riviera trains Mk2F TSO No. 5964 stands at Cardiff while on hire to First Great Western to operate on the Cardiff to Taunton corridor in 2010.*
CJM

Right: *Mk2F BSO No. 9526, owned by Riviera Trains was still painted in original InterCity livery when photographed with a Class 67 at Taunton in summer 2010. This coach has received a replacement black door sometime during its recent career.* **Tony Christie**

Scottish Railway Preservation Society

Number	Type	Depot	Livery	Operator
1859 (99822)	AN21/RMB	BT	MAR	SRP
21241	AB31/BCK	BT	CHC	SRP
35185	AB21/BSK	BT	MAR	SRP

Stratford Class 47 Group

Vehicle Length: 63ft 6in (19.35m)	*Engine: Sulzer 12LDA28C*
Height: 12ft 10⅝in (3.91m)	*Horsepower: 2,580hp (1,922kW)*
Width: 9ft 2in (2.79m)	*Electrical Equipment: Brush*
Electric Train Heat fitted	

Number	Depot	Pool	Livery	Owner	Operator	Name
47580 (47732)	TM	MBDL	LLB	S4G	S4G	*County of Essex*

Right: *One of the most popular main line certified Class 47s is No. 47580 County of Essex, owned by the Stratford Class 47 Group and usually kept at Tyseley. The loco sports Stratford style large logo blue livery and is made available for spot hire and charter train use. It is seen passing Dawlish running light to Paignton to power a return charter.* **CJM**

Venice Simplon Orient Express (VSOE)

Number	Name	Type	Depot	Livery	Operator	Notes
213 (99535)	*Minerva*	AO40/PFP	SL	PUL	VSO	
239 (S)	*Agatha*	AO40/PFP	SL	PUL	VSO	
243 (99541)	*Lucille*	AO40/PFP	SL	PUL	VSO	
245 (99534)	*Ibis*	AO40/PFK	SL	PUL	VSO	
254 (99536)	*Zena*	AO40/PFP	SL	PUL	VSO	
255 (99539)	*Ione*	AO40/PFK	SL	PUL	VSO	
261 (S)	Car No. 83	AO40/PTP	SL	PUL	VSO	
264 (S)	*Ruth*	AO40/PCK	SL	PUL	VSO	

VSOE

280 (99537)	Audrey	AO40/PFK	SL	PUL	VSO
281 (99546)	Gwen	AO40/PFK	SL	PUL	VSO
283 (S)	Mona	AO40/PFK	SL	PUL	VSO
284 (99543)	Vera	AO40/PFK	SL	PUL	VSO
285 (S)	Car No. 85	AO40/PTP	SL	PUL	VSO
286 (S)	Car No. 86	AO40/PTP	SL	PUL	VSO
288 (S)	Car No. 88	AO40/PTB	SL	PUL	VSO
292 (S)	Car No. 92	AO40/PTB	SL	PUL	VSO
293 (S)	Car No. 93	AO40/PTB	SL	PUL	VSO
301 (99530)	Perseus	AO41/PFP	SL	PUL	VSO
302 (99531)	Phoenix	AO41/PFP	SL	PUL	VSO
307 (S)	Carina	AO41/PFK	SL	PUL	VSO
308 (99532)	Cygnus	AO41/PFP	SL	PUL	VSO
325 (2907)		AJ11/RFO	CP	PUL	VSO
1207 (6422)		AJ11/RFO	CP	-	VSO
1221 (3371)		AJ11/RFO	CP	-	VSO
1566		AK51/RKB	CP	VSN	VSO
1953		AJ41/RBR	CP	VSN	VSO
3174	Glamis	AD1D/FO	CP	VSN	VSO
3182	Warwick	AD1D/FO	CP	VSN	VSO
3232		AD1E/FO	BH	BLG	VSO
3247	Chatsworth	AD1E/FO	CP	VSN	VSO
3267	Belvoir	AD1E/FO	CP	VSN	VSO
3273	Alnwick	AD1E/FO	CP	VSN	VSO
3275	Harlech	AD1E/FO	CP	VSN	VSO
6313 (92167)		AX51/GEN	SL	PUL	VSO
9502		AE2E/BSO	SL	PUL	VSO
10541 (99968)		AO4G/SSV	CS	MRN	VSO	Royal Scotsman - State Car 5
10556 (99969)		AO4G/SSV	CS	MRN	VSO	Royal Scotsman - Service Car
10569 (S)	Leviathan	AU4G/SLEP	CP	PUL	VSO
10729	Crewe	AS4G/SLE	CP	VSN	VSO
10734 (2914)	Balmoral	AS4G/SLE	CP	VSN	VSO
17167 (14167)		AB1D/BFK	CP	VSN	VSO
35466 (99545)		AB21/BSK	SL	PUL	VSO
92904		NBA	CP	PUL	VSO

Left: *The wonderful restored VSOE heritage Pullman stock is kept at Stewarts Lane depot in South London. The vehicles are maintained to the highest standard of any train in the UK and operate main line specials several times each week. Pullman car* Cygnus *No. 308 is illustrated at Taunton.*
Brian Garrett

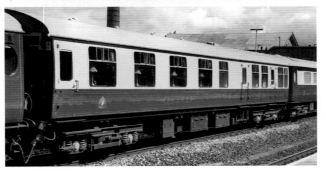

Left: *VSOE also operate the Northern Belle train, based at Crewe which is formed of a number of superbly restored Mk1 and Mk2 vehicles. Former Royal Train coach No. 2907 is one vehicle in the fleet, which now operates as RFO No. 325 and is painted in Northern Belle maroon and cream. The kitchen car is seen within the Northern Belle set at Totnes in July 2010.*
Nathan Williamson

Vintage Trains

Class 47

Vehicle Length: 63ft 6in (19.35m)	Engine: Sulzer 12LDA28C
Height: 12ft 10⅜in (3.91m)	Horsepower: 2,580hp (1,922kW)
Width: 9ft 2in (2.79m)	Electrical Equipment: Brush
Electric Train Heat fitted	

Number	Depot	Pool	Livery	Owner	Operator
47773 (47541)	TM	MBDL	GRN	VTN	VTN

Coaching Stock

Number	Type	Depot	Livery	Owner	Operator
335 (99361)	AO11/PSK	TM	PUL	VTN	VTN
349 (99349)	AO11/PSP	TM	PUL	VTN	VTN
353 (99353)	AO11/PSP	TM	PUL	VTN	VTN
5928	AC2F/TSO	TM	CHC	VTN	VTN
17018 (99108)	AB11/BFK	TM	CHC	VTN	VTN

West Coast Railway Company

Class 03

Vehicle Length: 26ft 3in (7.92m)	Engine: Gardner 8L3
Height: 12ft 7⅟₁₆in (3.72m)	Horsepower: 204hp (149kW)
Width: 8ft 6in (2.59m)	Mechanical Equipment: Wilson-Drewry

Number	Depot	Pool	Livery	Owner	Operator	Name
03196	CS	MBDL	GRN	WCR	WCR	Joyce
D2381	CS	MBDL	BLK	WCR	WCR	

Right: *Two ex-BR Class 03s are on the books of the West Coast Railway Co at Carnforth and when operational can be used for depot and work shop pilotage. No. 03381 painted in non-authentic lined green livery with its number on the front in steam loco style is seen in the depot yard.* **Tony Christie**

Class 08

Vehicle Length: 29ft 3in (8.91m)	Engine: English Electric 6K
Height: 12ft 8⅜in (3.87m)	Horsepower: 400hp (298kW)
Width: 8ft 6in (2.59m)	Electrical Equipment: English Electric

Number	Depot	Pool	Livery	Owner	Operator	Name
08418	CS	MBDL	EWS	WCR	WCR	
08485	CS	MBDL	BLU	WCR	WCR	
08678	CS	MBDL	GLX	WCR	WCR	Artila

Class 33

Vehicle Length: 50ft 9in (15.47m)	Engine: Sulzer 8LDA28A
Height: 12ft 8in (3.86m)	Horsepower: 1,550hp (1,156kW)
Width: 33/0, 33/1 9ft 3in (2.81m) 33/2 8ft 8in (2.64m)	Electrical Equipment: Crompton P'n

Number	Depot	Pool	Livery	Owner	Operator	Name
33025	CS	MBDL	WCR	WCR	WCR	Glen Falloch
33029	CS	MBDL	WCR	WCR	WCR	Glen Roy
33030 (S)	CS	MBDL	DRS	WCR	-	
33207	CS	MBDL	WCR	WCR	WCR	Jim Martin

WCRC

Class 37

Vehicle Length: 61ft 6in (18.74m)
Height: 13ft 0¼in (3.96m)
Width: 8ft 11⅝in (2.73m)

Engine: English Electric 12CSVT
Horsepower: 1,750hp (1,304kW)
Electrical Equipment: English Electric

Number	Depot	Pool	Livery	Owner	Operator	Name
37214	CS	MBDL	WCR	WCR	WCR	Loch Laidon
37248 (S)	CS	MBDL	WCR	TTT	WCR	
37516 (S) (37086)	CS	MBDL	WCR	WCR	-	
37517 (S) (37018)	CS	MBDL	LHL	WCR	-	
37668 (S) (37257)	CS	MBDL	EWS	WCR	-	Loch Rannoch
37676 (37126)	CS	MBDL	WCR	WCR	WCR	
37685 (37234)	CS	MBDL	WCR	WCR	WCR	
37706 (37016)	CS	MBDL	WCR	WCR	WCR	
37710 (S) (37044)	CS	MBDL	LHL	WCR	-	
37712 (37102)	CS	MBDL	WCR	WCR	WCR	

Class 47

Vehicle Length: 63ft 6in (19.35m)
Height: 12ft 10⅜in (3.91m)
Width: 9ft 2in (2.79m)
Electric Train Heat fitted to Class 47/4, 47/7 and 47/8

Engine: Sulzer 12LDA28C
Horsepower: 2,580hp (1,922kW)
Electrical Equipment: Brush

Number	Depot	Pool	Livery	Owner	Operator	Name
47194 (S)	CS	MBDL	TLF	WCR	-	
47245	CS	MBDL	WCR	WCR	WCR	
47270	CS	MBDL	BLU	WCR	WCR	Swift
47355 (S)	CS	MBDL	WCR	WCR	-	
47492	CS	MBDL	RES	WCR	WCR	
47500 (47770)	CS	MBDL	WCR	WCR	WCR	
47526 (S)	CS	MBDL	BLU	WCR	-	
47760 (47562)	CS	MBDL	WCR	WCR	WCR	
47772 (S) (47537)	CS	MBDL	RES	WCR	-	
47776 (S) (47578)	CS	MBDL	RES	WCR	-	
47786 (47821)	CS	MBDL	WCR	WCR	WCR	Roy Castle OBE
47787 (47823)	CS	MBDL	WCR	WCR	WCR	Windsor Castle
47804 (47792)	CS	MBDL	WCR	WCR	WCR	
47826 (47637)	CS	MBDL	WCR	WCR	WCR	
47851/D1648 (47639)	CS	MBDL	WCR	WCR	WCR	
47854 (47674)	CS	MBDL	WCR	WCR	WCR	

Left: The prime West Coast Railway Co traction fleet is maintained in a first class condition and displays the operator's maroon livery with small yellow warning end and a neat bodyside branding. Stabled in the middle road at Carlisle No. 47826 is seen from its No. 2 end.
Tony Christie

Class 57/6

Vehicle Length: 63ft 6in (19.38m)
Height: 12ft 10½in (3.91m)
Width: 9ft 2in (2.79m)

Engine: EMD 645-12E3
Horsepower: 2,500hp (1,860kW)
Electrical Equipment: Brush

Number	Depot	Pool	Livery	Owner	Operator
57601 (47825)	CS	MBDL	WCR	WCR	WCR

Coaching Stock

Number	Name	Type	Depot	Livery	Operator	Notes
159 (99980)		AO10/SAL	CS	-	WCR	Former LNWR saloon
326 (S) (99402)	Emerald	AO11/PFP	CS	PUL	WCR	
347	Car No. 347	AO11/PSO	CS	WCR	WCR	
348 (99348)	Car No. 348	AO11/PSP	CS	WCR	WCR	
350 (99350)	Car No. 350	AO11/PSP	CS	GRN	WCR	
352 (99352)	Car No. 352	AO11/PSP	CS	PUL	WCR	
354 (99354)	The Hadrian Bar	AO11/PSP	CS	PUL	WCR	
504 (99678)	Ullswater	AP1Z/PFK	CS	PUL	WCR	
506 (99679)	Windermere	AP1Z/PFK	CS	PUL	WCR	
546 (S) (99670)	City of Manchester	AQ1Z/PFP	CS	PUL	WCR	
548 (99671)	Grasmere	AQ1Z/PFP	CS	PUL	WCR	
549 (99672)	Bassenthwaite	AQ1Z/PFP	CS	PUL	WCR	
550 (99673)	Rydal Water	AQ1Z/PFP	CS	PUL	WCR	
551 (99674)	Buttermere	AQ1Z/PFP	CS	PUL	WCR	
552 (99675)	Ennerdale Water	AQ1Z/PFP	CS	PUL	WCR	
553 (99676)	Crummock Water	AQ1Z/PFP	CS	PUL	WCR	
586 (99677)	Derwent Water	AR1Z/PFB	CS	PUL	WCR	
807 (99881)		AO10/SAL	CS	-	WCR	Former GNR Saloon
1644 (S)		AJ41/RBR	CS	ICS	WCR	
1650 (S)		AJ41/RBR	CS	ICS	WCR	
1652 (S)		AJ41/RBR	CS	ICS	WCR	
1655 (S)		AJ41/RBR	CS	ICS	WCR	
1663 (S)		AJ41/RBR	CS	ICS	WCR	
1670 (S)		AJ41/RBR	CS	ICS	WCR	
1730		AJ41/RBR	CS	WCR	WCR	
1800 (5970)	Tintagel	AN2F/RSS	CS	CHC	WCR	
1840		AN21/RMB	CS	GRN	WCR	Set - The Green Train
1860		AN21/RMB	CS	WCR	WCR	
1861 (99132)		AN21/RMB	CS	WCR	WCR	
1882 (99311)		AN21/RMB	CS	WCR	WCR	
1961		AJ41/RBR	CS	GRN	WCR	Set - The Green Train
2127 (S)		AO11/SLF	CS	MAR	WCR	
2833 (21270)		AU51/SLSC	CS	BLU	WCR	
3093 (977594)	Paula	AD11/FO	CS	WCR	WCR	
3105 (99121)	Julia	AD11/FO	CS	WCR	WCR	
3106 (99122)	Alexandra	AD11/FO	CS	WCR	WCR	
3113 (99125)	Jessica	AD11/FO	CS	WCR	WCR	
3117 (99127)	Christina	AD11/FO	CS	WCR	WCR	
3128 (99371)	Victoria	AD11/FO	CS	WCR	WCR	
3130 (99128)	Pamela	AD11/FO	CS	WCR	WCR	
3136 (3605)	Diana	AD11/FO	CS	WCR	WCR	
3143 (3609)	Patricia	AD11/FO	CS	WCR	WCR	
3309		AD1F/FO	CS	ICS	WCR	
3313		AD1F/FO	CS	WCR	WCR	
3326		AD1F/FO	CS	WCR	WCR	
3350		AD1F/FO	CS	WCR	WCR	
3352		AD1F/FO	CS	WCR	WCR	
3359		AD1F/FO	CS	WCR	WCR	
3360		AD1F/FO	CS	ICS	WCR	
3362		AD1F/FO	CS	ICS	WCR	
3392 (S)		AD1F/FO	CS	BPM	WCR	Blue Pullman vehicle
3395		AD1F/FO	CS	WCR	WCR	
3408		AD1F/FO	CS	WCR	WCR	
3416		AD1F/FO	CS	ICS	WCR	
3431		AD1F/FO	CS	WCR	WCR	
3766 (99317)		AC21/SO	CS	WCR	WCR	
4860 (S) (99193)		AC21/TSO	CS	MAR	WCR	
4905		AC21/TSO	CS	WCR	WCR	
4912 (99318)		AC21/TSO	CS	WCR	WCR	
4931 (99329)		AC21/TSO	CS	WCR	WCR	
4932 (S)		AC21/TSO	CS	BLG	WCR	
4940		AC21/TSO	CS	WCR	WCR	
4951		AC21/TSO	CS	WCR	WCR	
4954 (99326)		AC21/TSO	CS	WCR	WCR	
4958		AC21/TSO	CS	WCR	WCR	
4960		AC21/TSO	CS	WCR	WCR	

Private Train Operators – WCRC

WCRC

4973		AC21/TSO	CS	WCR	WCR	
4984		AC21/TSO	CS	WCR	WCR	
4994		AC21/TSO	CS	WCR	WCR	
4997 (S)		AC21/TSO	CS	BLG	WCR	
5032 (99194)		AC21/TSO	CS	WCR	WCR	
5033 (99328)		AC21/TSO	CS	WCR	WCR	
5035 (99195)		AC21/TSO	CS	WCR	WCR	
5044 (99327)		AC21/TSO	CS	WCR	WCR	
5125 (S)		AC2Z/TSO	BH	GRN	WCR	
5171		AC2Z/TSO	CS	GRN	WCR	
5200		AC2Z/TSO	CS	GRN	WCR	
5216		AC2Z/TSO	CS	GRN	WCR	
5222		AC2Z/TSO	CS	MAR	WCR	
5229	*The Green Knight*	AC2Z/SO	CS	MAR	WTN	
5236		AC2Z/SO	CS	GRN	WCR	
5237		AD2Z/SO	CS	GRN	WCR	
5239	*The Red Knight*	AD2Z/SO	CS	MAR	WTN	
5249		AD2Z/SO	CS	GRN	WCR	
5278	*Melisande*	AC2A/TSO	CS	CHC	WTN	
5419	*Sir Launcelot*	AC2A/TSO	CS	CHC	WTN	
5453		AC2B/TSO	CS	WCR	WCR	
5463 (S)		AC2B/TSO	CS	WCR	WCR	
5478		AC2B/TSO	CS	WCR	WCR	
5487		AC2B/TSO	CS	WCR	WCR	
5491		AC2B/TSO	CS	WCR	WCR	
5569		AC2C/TSO	CS	WCR	WCR	
5669 (S)		AC2D/TSO	EM	BPM	CWR	Blue Pullman vehicle
5756 (S)		AC2E/TSO	CS	WCR	WCR	
6000		AC2F/TSO	CS	WCR	WCR	
6014 (S)		AC2F/TSO	CS	ICS	WCR	At Hellifield
6022		AC2F/TSO	CS	WCR	WCR	
6041		AC2F/TSO	CS	WCR	WCR	
6103		AC2F/TSO	CS	WCR	WCR	
6115 (S)		AC2F/TSO	CS	WCR	WCR	
6135 (S)		AC2F/TSO	CS	ICS	WCR	At Hellifield
6312 (92925)		AX51/GEN	CS	WCR	WCR	
6528 (5592)		AG2C/TSOT	CS	WCR	WCR	
6723		AN1D/RMBF	CS	WCR	WCR	
6724		AN1D/RMBF	CS	WCR	WCR	
9104 (S) (9401)		AH2Z/BSOT	CS	WCR	WCR	
9391	*Pendragon*	AE2Z/BSO	CS	PUL	WTN	
9392		AE2Z/BSO	CS	WCR	WCR	Set - The Green Train
9440		AE2C/BSO	CS	WCR	WCR	
9448 (S)		AE2C/BSO	CS	WCR	WCR	
9493 (S)		AE2D/BSO	EM	BPM	CWR	Blue Pullman vehicle
13227		AA11/FK	CS	WCR	WCR	
13306 (S)		AA11/FK	CS	WCR	WCR	
13320 (S)		AA11/FK	CS	WCR	WCR	
13321 (99316)		AA11/FK/RBR	CS	WCR	WCR	
13440 (S)		AA1A/FK	CS	GRN	WCR	Set - The Green Train
17102 (99680)		AB1A/BFK	CS	MAB	WCR	
17168 (S) (99319)		AB1D/BFK	CS	WCR	WCR	
18756 (99721)		AA21/SK	CS	WCR	WCR	
18767 (99710)		AA21/SK	CS	WCR	WCR	
18806 (99722)		AA21/SK	CS	WCR	WCR	
18808 (99706)		AA21/SK	CS	WCR	WCR	
18862 (99718)		AA21/SK	CS	WCR	WCR	
18893 (S) (99712)		AA21/SK	CS	CHC	WCR	
19208 (99884)	Car No. 84	AA21/SK	CS	WCR	WCR	
21256 (99304)		AB31/BCK	CS	WCR	WCR	
21266		AB31/BCK	CS	WCR	WCR	
34525 (S) (99966)		AR51/GEN	CS	WCR	WCR	
35407 (99886)		AB21/BSK	CJ	-	WCR	Finished in LNWR livery
45018 (99052)		AO10/SAL	CJ	QOS	WCR	
45026 (S)		SAL	CS	MAR	WCR	LMS Inspection Saloon
96175		GUV	CS	MAR	WCR	Water carrier
99723 (35459)		AB21/BSK	CS	WCR	WCR	

Above: *Rebuilt from BG No. 92925, West Coast now operates this vehicle as generator coach 6312, painted in standard lined maroon livery. In WCRC use the coach had one of its door sets replaced by a roller shutter, while an underslung fuel tank has been fitted. The immaculate coach is seen at Carlisle.* **Tony Christie**

Below: *The public image of the WCRC fleet is excellent. In immaculate condition Mk1 BSK No. 99723 (35459) is illustrated from the compartment end. This vehicle is usually used for staff travel.* **Tony Christie**

Loco Support Coaches

Most preserved locomotives authorised for main line operation, either steam or diesel, operate with a support coach conveying owners' representatives, engineering staff and light maintenance equipment. Support coaches can be allocated to a specific locomotive or operate with a pool of locos.

Number	Type	Depot	Livery	Support Coach for
14007 (99782) *Mercator*	AB11/BSK	BH	MAR	61264
14099 (17099)	AB11/BSK	BQ	MAR	44871, 45305 or 70013
17013 (14013) *Botaurus*	AB11/BFK	SH	PUL	60019
17019 (99792)	AB11/BFK	CS	MAR	30777 or 70013
17025 (14025)	AB11/BFK	CS	MAR	45690
17041 (99141)	AB1Z/BFK	BQ	MAR	71000
17096	AB1B/BFK	SL	CHC	35028
21096 (99080)	AB31/BCK	NY	MAR	60007
21232 (99040)	AB31/BCK	SK	MAR	46233
21236 (99120)	AB31/BCK	ZG	GRN	30828
21249 (S)	AB21/BCK	-	MAR	60163
21268	AB31/BCK	SH	MAR	46100
35317	AD21/BSK	BQ	GRN	30850
35322 (99035)	AB21/BSK	CJ	MAR	70000
35329	AB21/BSK	RL	GRN	Mid Hants fleet
35333 (99180)	AB21/BSK	DI	CHC	6024
35449 (99241)	AB21/BSK	BQ	MAR	45231
35457 (99995)	AB21/BSK	NY	MAR	60532
35461 (99720)	AB21/BSK	TM	CHC	5029
35463 (99312)	AB21/BSK	CS	WCR	WCR fleet
35464	AB21/BSK	PR	MAR	Swanage Railway
35465 (99991)	AB21/BSK	BQ	CCM	46201
35468 (99953)	AB21/BSK	NY	MAR	NYMR fleet
35470	AB21/BSK	TM	CHC	Vintage Trains fleet
35476 (99041)	AB21/BSK	SK	MAR	46233
35486 (99405)	AB21/BSK	--	MAR	60009 or 61994
35508	AB1C/BSK	BQ	MAR	East Lancs fleet
35517 (17088)	ABIK/BSKk	BQ	MAR	East Lancs fleet
35518 (17097)	AB11/BFK	SH	GRN	34067
80204 (35297)	NNX	CS	MAR	WCRC fleet
80217 (35299)	NNX	CS	MAR	WCRC fleet
80220 (35276)	NNX	NY	MAR	62005

Below: *Officially based at Bury on the East Lancs Railway, BSK No. E14099 is the official support coach for either 'Black 5' No. 44871 or 'Britannia' No. 70013* Oliver Cromwell. *This type of brake vehicle is ideal for the role of a support coach, as it has both seating for staff and a luggage van to transport maintenance items and consumables. No. E14099 is seen at Totnes from its compartment end.* **Nathan Williamson**

Private Train Operators – Loco Support Coaches

Locomotives

Number	Class	Owner	Location
56301	56/3	JAR	HI
56302	56/3	JAR	HI
57001	57/0	PTR	BA
57301	57/3	PTA	MA
57303	57/3	PTA	MA
57305	57/3	PTA	MA
57306	57/3	PTA	MA

Number	Class	Owner	Location
57310	57/3	PTA	MA
57312	57/3	PTA	MA
66544	66/5	PTR	LD
66546	66/5	PTR	LD
66547	66/5	PTR	LD
66551	66/5	PTR	LD
66552	66/5	PTR	LD
66573	66/5	HSB	LD
66574	66/5	HSB	LD

Number	Class	Owner	Location
66578	66/5	HSB	ZG
66579	66/5	HSB	ZG
66580	66/5	HSB	ZG
66581	66/5	HSB	ZG
66301	66/3	BEA	CG
66302	66/3	BEA	CG
66303	66/3	BEA	CG
66304	66/3	BEA	CG
66305	66/3	BEA	CG

Above: *The amazing and saddening sight of almost new locos being taken out of service and stored. Here Freightliner Class 66/5 66579, 66578, 66580 and 66581 pass Southampton on 21 October 2010 running as the 0Z90, 14.13 Southampton Maritime to Eastleigh Works for 'warm storage'.* **Mark V. Pike**

Diesel Multiple Units

At the time of writing no DMU stock was off-lease

Electric Multiple Units

Number	Class	Owner	Location
313121	313/1	HSB	WN
365526	365	HSB	ZC*
508201	508	ANG	DO
508202	508	ANG	DO

Number	Class	Owner	Location
508203	508	ANG	DO
508204	508	ANG	AF
508205	508	ANG	DO
508206	508	ANG	AF
508207	508	ANG	SL
508208	508	ANG	DO
508209	508	ANG	DO

Number	Class	Owner	Location
508210	508	ANG	DO
508211	508	ANG	DO
508212	508	ANG	GI
508301	508	ANG	ZG
508302	508	ANG	ZG
508303	508	ANG	ZG
* Collision damage			

Coaching Stock - Passenger

Number	Type	Owner	Location
1204 (3401)	RFO	HSB	PY
1209 (6457)	RFO	HSB	ZH
1211 (3305)	RFO	HSB	LM
1214 (6433)	RFO	HSB	KT
1219 (3418)	RFO	HSB	KT
1253 (3432)	RFO	HSB	LM

Number	Type	Owner	Location
1258 (3322)	RFO	HSB	KT
3229	FO	HSB	KT
3351	FO	HSB	TM
3434	FO	HSB	OY
3438	FO	HSB	LM

Number	Type	Owner	Location
5148	TSO	HSB	TM
5179	TSO	HSB	TM
5183	TSO	HSB	TM
5186	TSO	HSB	TM
5193	TSO	HSB	TM
5194	TSO	HSB	TM
5212	TSO	HSB	TM

Off-lease Rolling Stock

Off-lease Rolling Stock

5221	TSO	HSB	TM
5636	TSO	HSB	PM
5679	TSO	HSB	KT
5737	TSO	HSB	KT
5740	TSO	HSB	KT
5745	TSO	HSB	KT
5750	TSO	HSB	KT
5754	TSO	HSB	KT
5788	TSO	HSB	KT
5793	TSO	HSB	KT
5821	TSO	HSB	KT
5881	TSO	HSB	KT
5886	TSO	HSB	KT
5888	TSO	HSB	KT
5899	TSO	HSB	KT
5900	TSO	HSB	KT
5903	TSO	HSB	KT
5905	TSO	HSB	KT
5908	TSO	HSB	ZG
5912	TSO	HSB	KT
5930	TSO	HSB	KT
5933	TSO	HSB	ZG
5936	TSO	HSB	LM
5940	TSO	HSB	ZG
5943	TSO	HSB	ZG¤
5947	TSO	HSB	ZG¤
5948	TSO	HSB	ZG¤
5949	TSO	HSB	ZG¤
5957	TSO	HSB	ZG¤
5960	TSO	HSB	KT
5962	TSO	HSB	KT
5969	TSO	HSB	ZG
5977	TSO	HSB	ZG¤
5978	TSO	HSB	ZG
5980	TSO	HSB	ZG¤
5981	TSO	HSB	ZA
5983	TSO	HSB	KT
5991	TSO	HSB	KT
6009	TSO	HSB	ZG¤
6012	TSO	HSB	ZG¤
6016	TSO	HSB	ZG
6021	TSO	HSB	ZG
6028	TSO	HSB	ZG
6029	TSO	HSB	ZG¤
6031	TSO	HSB	ZG¤

6037	TSO	HSB	ZG¤
6049	TSO	HSB	KT
6050	TSO	HSB	ZG
6052	TSO	HSB	KT
6053	TSO	HSB	KT
6059	TSO	HSB	KT
6061	TSO	HSB	ZG¤
6073	TSO	HSB	KT
6101	TSO	HSB	ZG
6120	TSO	HSB	KT
6121	TSO	HSB	KT
6136	TSO	HSB	ZG
6150	TSO	HSB	ZG
6151	TSO	HSB	ZG
6160	TSO	HSB	LM
6164	TSO	HSB	KT
6175	TSO	HSB	ZG¤
6179	TSO	HSB	ZG¤

¤ For export to New Zealand

9480	BSO	HSB	KT
9490	BSO	HSB	KT
9496	BSO	HSB	TM
9498	BSO	HSB	KT
9500	BSO	HSB	LM
9505	BSO	HSB	LM
9516	BSO	HSB	KT
9522	BSO	HSB	CE
9523	BSO	HSB	KT
9538	BSO	HSB	KT

9704	DBSOHSB	ZG
9705	DBSOHSB	ZG
9707	DBSOHSB	ZG
9709	DBSOHSB	ZG
9710	DBSOHSB	ZG

10204 (40502)	RFM	PTR	3M
10231 (10016)	RFM	PTR	LM
10240 (10003)	RFM	PTR	LM
10253 (10026)	RFM	PTR	LM
10256 (10028)	RFM	PTR	YO¶
10260 (10001)	RFM	PTR	YO¶

¶ Instruction vehicle - Yoker

10547	SLE	PTR	IS
10596	SLE	PTR	LM
10661 Concept vehicle at Wolverton			
10667	SLE	-	LM
10682	SLE	PTR	TO
10698	SLE	-	LM
10733	SLE	-	MM

11006	FO	PTR	LM
11011	FO	PTR	LM
11026	FO	PTR	LM

12008	TSO	PTR	ZB
12022	TSO	PTR	ZB
12029	TSO	PTR	LM
12036	TSO	PTR	LM
12047	TSO	PTR	LM
12063	TSO	PTR	LM
12065	TSO	PTR	LM
12083	TSO	PTR	LM
12087	TSO	PTR	LM
12092	TSO	PTR	LM
12095	TSO	PTR	LM
12101	TSO	PTR	LM
12134	TSO	PTR	LM
12139	TSO	PTR	LM
12142	TSO	PTR	LM
12144	TSO	PTR	LM
12156	TSO	PTR	LM
12158	TSO	PTR	BN
12160	TSO	PTR	LM
12163	TSO	PTR	BN

Coaching Stock - HST

Number	Type	Owner	Location
40208 (40008)	TRSB	ANG	ZG
40209 (40009)	TRSB	ANG	ZG
40228 (40028)	TRSB	ANG	ZG
40402 (40002)	TRSB	PTR	LM
40403 (40003)	TRSB	PTR	LM
40416 (40016)	TRSB	PTR	LM
40417 (40017)	TRSB	PTR	ZK
40419 (40019)	TRSB	PTR	LM
40425 (40025)	TRSB	PTR	ZK
40434 (40034)	TRSB	PTR	LM
40709 (40309)	TRSB	ANG	ZG
40712 (40312)	TRSB	ANG	LM
40714 (40314)	TRSB	ANG	LM
40717 (40317)	TRSB	ANG	ZG
40725 (40325)	TRSB	ANG	ZG
40726 (40326)	TRSB	ANG	ZG
40731 (40331)	TRSB	ANG	ZG
40736 (40336)	TRSB	ANG	ZG
40738 (40338)	TRSB	ANG	ZG
40744 (40344)	TRSB	ANG	ZG
40745 (40345)	TRSB	ANG	ZG
40747 (40347)	TRSB	ANG	ZG

Coaching Stock - NPCCS

Number	Type	Owner	Location
82109	DVT	PTR	ZB
82110	DVT	PTR	LM
82111	DVT	PTR	LM
82124	DVT	PTR	LM
82125	DVT	PTR	LM
82128	DVT	PTR	LM
82129	DVT	PTR	LM
82140	DVT	PTR	LM
82141	DVT	PTR	LM
82145	DVT	PTR	LM
82149	DVT	PTR	FC
92159 (81534)	BG	HSB	KT
92901 (92001)	BG	HSB	WB
92931 (92031)	BG	HSB	PY
96100 (93734)	GUV	HSB	TM
96139 (93751)	GUV	HSB	WB
96181 (93875)	GUV	HSB	LM
96602 (96150)	NV	HSB	LM
96603 (96155)	NV	HSB	LM
96604 (96156)	NV	HSB	LM
96605 (96157)	NV	HSB	LM
96606 (96213)	NV	HSB	LM
96607 (96215)	NV	HSB	LM
96608 (96216)	NV	HSB	LM
96609 (96217)	NV	HSB	LM

Preserved motive power is listed in this section. Those in a red type face are authorised for main line operation. For information on preserved steam traction and railway centres, please refer to our sister publication *Railways Restored*, edited by Alan Butcher and published by Ian Allan Publishing.

Locomotives

Main line certified shown in red

Number	Operator/Base	Status
Prototype Locomotives		
LMS7050	NRM	STC
LMS7051	MID	OPR
LMS7069	GWR	RES
D0226	KWV	OPR
18000	GWR	STC
DELTIC	NRM	STC
Non Classified		
D2511	KWV	OPR
D2767	BKR	OPR
D2774	STR	RES
DS75	NRS	STC
Class 01		
D2953	PRL	OPR
D2956	ELR	OPR
Class 02		
D2854	PRL	OPR
D2858	MRC	RES
D2860	NRM	OPR
D2866	PRL	RES
D2867	BAT	OPR
D2868	PRL	OPR
Class 03		
03018	MFM	RES
03020	LDL	STO
03022	SWI	OPR
D2023	KES	OPR
D2024	KES	STO
03027	PRL	RES
03037	PRL	OPR
D2041	COL	OPR
D2046	PVR	RES
D2051	NNR	STO
03059	IOW	OPR
03062	ELR	OPR
03063	NNR	OPR
03066	BHR	OPR
03069	GWR	OPR
03072	LHR	OPR
03073	RAC	OPR
03078	TYN	OPR
03079	DER	OPR
03081	MFM	RES
03084	ECC	OPR
03089	MFM	OPR
03090	NRS	OPR
03094	CRT	OPR
03099	PRL	OPR
03113	PRL	RES
D2117	LHR	OPR
D2118	PRL	RES
03119	WSR	OPR
03120	FHL	OPR
03128	APF	STO
D2133	WSR	OPR
03134	DEE	OPR
D2138	MRC	OPR
D2139	PRL	RES
03141	PRB	RES
03144	WEN	OPR
03145	MOL	OPR
D2148	RIB	OPR
03152	SWI	OPR
03158	LWR	OPR
03162	LAN	OPR
03170	BAT	OPR
D2178	GWI	OPR
D2182	GWR	OPR
D2184	COL	OPR
D2189	RIB	RES
D2192	PDR	OPR
03197	LDL	Res
D2199	PRL	OPR
03371	ROW	OPR
03399	MFM	OPR
Class 04		
D2203	EMB	OPR
D2205	WSR	STO
D2207	NYM	OPR
D2229	PRL	RES
D2245	BAT	STO
D2246	SDR	OPR
D2271	WSR	STO
D2272	PRL	RES
D2279	EAR	OPR
D2280	NNR	RES
D2284	PRL	OPR
D2298	BRC	OPR
D2302	BHR	OPR
D2310	BAT	OPR
D2324	BHR	STO
D2325	MFM	OPR
D2334	CVR	OPR
D2337	PRL	RES
Class 05		
05001	IOW	OPR
D2578	MOL	OPR
D2587	PRL	RES
D2595	RIB	OPR
Class 06		
06003	PRL	OPR
Class 07		
07005	GCR	RES
07010	AVR	OPR
07011	SEL	OPR
07012	APF	RES
07013	PRL	RES
Class 08		
D3000	APF	RES
D3002	PVR	OPR
D3014	PDR	OPR
08011	CPR	OPR
08012	CRT	OPR
08015	SVR	OPR
08016	PRL	OPR
08021	BRM	OPR
08022	CWR	OPR
08032	MHR	OPR
08046	CRB	OPR
08054	EMB	OPR
08060	CWR	OPR
08064	NRS	OPR
D3101	GCR	OPR
08102	LWR	OPR
08108	KES	OPR
08114	GCR	OPR
08123	CWR	OPR
08133	SVR	OPR
08164	ELR	OPR
08168	BAT	OPR
D3261	SWI	RES
08195	LAN	OPR
08202	GWR	OPR
08220	NHC	STO
08238	DFR	OPR
08266	KWV	OPR
08288	MHR	OPR
08359	TSR	OPR
08377	WSR	OPR
08388	NHD	STO
08436	SWN	OPR
08443	BKR	RES
08444	BWR	OPR
08471	SVR	OPR
08473	DFR	STO
08476	SWN	OPR
08479	ELR	OPR
08481	VOG	RES
08490	STR	OPR
08528	BAT	OPR
08556	NYM	OPR
08590	MRC	OPR
08598	IND	OPR
08604	DID	OPR
08631	MNR	OPR
08635	SVR	RES
08683	GWR	RES
08694	GCR	RES
08700	ELR	OPR
08734	DFR	STO
08767	NNR	OPR
08769	SVR	OPR
08772	NNR	OPR
08773	EMB	OPR
08780	SOU	OPR
08830	RAC	OPR
08850	NYM	OPR§
08891	SVR	RES
08896	SVR	OPR
08911	NRM	OPR

Above, Left & Below: *The quality of UK diesel loco preservation is quite outstanding, with many locos now in better condition than in BR days. Above we see Class 47/3 No. 47376* Freightliner 1995 *owned by the Brush Type 4 Fund on the Gloucestershire & Warwickshire Railway. Left is Class 33/1 No. 33110 and Class 47 No. 47306* The Sapper *on the Bodmin & Wenford Railway. The '33' sports General grey livery while the '47' carries Railfreight Distribution. Below is Class 45 'Peak' No. 45060* Sherwood Forester, *usually based at Barrow Hill, operating on the Swanage line. All:* **Tony Christie**

08937	DAR	OPR	20087	ELR	OPR	27066	DFR	OPR
08944	ELR	OPR	20098	GCR	RES			

§ *Battersby-Whitby only*

			20110	SDR	OPR	**Class 28**		
			20118	SDR	OPR	D5705	ELR	RES

Class 09

09002	SDR	RES	20137	GWR	OPR			
09004	SPV	OPR	20142	BHR	OPR	**Class 31**		
09010	SDR	RES	20154	GCR	OPR	D5500	NRM	OPR
09025	SWI	OPR	20169	SRC	RES	31101	BAT	RES
			20177	SVR	STO	31108	MRC	OPR

Class 10

D3452	BWR	OPR	20188	SVR	OPR	31119	EMB	OPR
D3489	SPV	OPR	20189	MRC	OPR	31130	BAT	OPR
D4067	GCR	OPR	20205	MRC	RES	31144	NHD	RES
D4092	BHR	RES	20214	LHR	OPR	31162	EHC	OPR
			20227	MRC	OPR	31163	CPR	OPR

Class 11

12052	CRB	STO	20228	BIR	OPR	31203	PBR	OPR
12061	PRL	RES				31206	RST	OPR
12077	MRC	OPR	**Class 24**			31207	NNR	OPR
12082	MHR	OPR	24032	NYM	RES	31210	DFR	RES
(Runs as 12049)			24054	ELR	OPR	31235	MNR	OPR
12093	CRB	OPR	24061	NYM	RES	31255	COL	OPR
12099	SVR	OPR	24082	GWR	OPR	31270	PRL	OPR
12131	NNR	OPR				31271	NVR	OPR

Class 12

15224	SPV	OPR	**Class 25**			31289	NLR	OPR
			25035	GCR	OPR	31327	STR	OPR

Class 14

D9500	PRL	RES	25057	NNR	OPR	31410	SRC	RES
D9502	PRL	STO	25059	KWV	OPR	31414	ECC	OPR
D9504	NVR	OPR	25067	BAT	OPR	31415	BHR	RES
D9513	EMB	OPR	25072	CRB	RES	31418	MRC	RES
D9516	NVR	OPR	25083	CRB	RES	31422	RVE	RES
D9518	NVR	OPR	25173	WSR	OPR	31435	EMB	OPR
D9520	NVR	OPR	25185	PDR	OPR	31438	MNR	OPR
D9521	DFR	OPR	25191	NYM	STO	31461	BAT	STO
D9523	NVR	OPR	25235	BKR	RES	31463	GCR	OPR
D9524	EHC	RES	25244	EKR	STO	31466	DFR	OPR
D9525	PRL	OPR	25262	SDR	OPR	31530	MNR	RES
D9526	WSR	OPR	25265	GCR	RES			
D9529	NVR	OPR	25278	NYM	OPR	**Class 33**		
D9531	ELR	RES	25279	GCR	OPR	33002	SDR	OPR
D9537	RIP	RES	25283	DFR	RES	33008	BAT	RES
D9539	RIB	OPR	25309	WCR	RES	33012	SWN	OPR
D9551	DEE	OPR	25313	WEN	RES	33018	MRC	STO
D9553	GWR	STO	25321	MRC	OPR	33019	BAT	OPR
D9555	DFR	OPR	25322	CVR	RES	33021	BRM	RES
						33034	SWN	RES

Class 15

D8233	ELR	RES	**Class 26**			33035	BHR	RES
			26001	CRB	OPR	33046	MRC	STO

Class 17

D8568	CPR	RES	26002	STR	RES	33048	WSR	OPR
			26004	BKR	STO	33052	KES	OPR

Class 20

D8000	NRM	OPR	26007	GCR	OPR	33053	MHR	OPR
20001	ECC	OPR	26010	LAN	OPR	33057	WSR	RES
20007	GCR	OPR	26011	BHR	RES	33063	SPV	OPR
20020	BKR	RES	26014	CRB	OPR	33065	SPV	RES
20031	KWV	OPR	26024	BKR	OPR	33102	CVR	RES
20035	CVR	STO	26025	STR	RES	33103	BHR	RES
20048	MRC	RES	26035	CRB	RES	33108	BHR	RES
20059	BRM	RES	26038	CAN	RES	33109	ELR	OPR
20063	GWR	STO	26040	MET	RES	33110	BWR	RES
20069	MNR	OPR	26043	GWR	RES	33111	SWN	OPR
						33116	GCR	OPR
			Class 27			33117	ELR	RES
			27001	BKR	OPR	33201	MRC	OPR
			27005	BKR	STO	33202	MFM	OPR
			27007	MHR	RES	33208	MHR	OPR
			27024	LHR	OPR			
			27050	STR	RES	**Class 35**		
			27056	GCR	OPR	D7017	WSR	OPR
			27059	SVR	RES	D7018	WSR	RES

Preserved Motive Power

D7029	SVR	RES
D7076	ELR	OPR

Class 37

D6700	NRM	OPR
37003	MNR	OPR
37009	GCR	RES
37023	ALY	RES
37025	BKR	RES
37032	NNR	RES
37037	SDR	OPR
37075	CVR	OPR
37097	CRB	OPR
37108	RAC	OPR
37109	ELR	OPR
37116	CPR	OPR
37142	BWR	OPR
37146	SRC	RES
37152	PRL	RES
37175	BKR	RES
37188	PRL	RES
37207	PVR	RES
37215	GWR	OPR
37216	PBR	OPR
37219	CPR	OPR
37227	BAT	OPR
37240	LAN	OPR
37250	EDR	RES
37254	SPV	OPR
37255	GCR	OPR
37263	DFR	RES
37264	BRM	RES
37275	BHR	OPR
37294	EMB	RES
37308	EHD	RES
37314	MRC	OPR
37324	GWR	OPR
37372	BHR	RES
37403	BKR	RES
37407	CVR	STO
37413	BKR	RES
37418	ELR	RES
37421	PBR	RES
37424	CVR	STO
37518	NVR	OPR
37674	SRC	RES
37679	NLR	RES
37901	ELR	OPR
37905	BAT	OPR
37906	SVR	OPR

Class 40

D200	NRM	RES
40012	MRC	OPR
40013	BHR	OPR
40106	NVR	OPR
40118	BRM	RES
40135	ELR	OPR
40145	ELR	OPR

Class 41

41001	NRM	STC

Class 42

D821	SVR	OPR
D832	WSR	OPR

Class 44

D4	MRC	RES
44008	PRL	OPR

Class 45

45014	BAT	STO
45041	MRC	OPR
45060	BHR	OPR
45105	BHR	RES
45108	MRC	RES
45118	NLR	RES
45125	GCR	OPR
45132	MHR	RES
45133	MRC	RES
45135	ELR	RES
45149	GWR	RES

Class 46

46010	GCN	OPR
46035	RAC	STO
46045	MRC	OPR

Class 47

47004	EMB	OPR
47105	GWR	OPR
47117	GCR	OPR
47192	DAR	OPR
47205	NLR	OPR
47292	GCR	OPR
47306	BWR	OPR
47367	NNR	OPR
47376	GWR	RES
47401	MRC	OPR
47402	ELR	OPR
47417	MRC	RES
47449	LAN	OPR
47484	GDM	STO
47524	CVR	RES
47540	WEN	STO
47596	MNR	RES
47635	PRL	OPR
47640	BAT	OPR
47643	BKR	OPR
47701	DAR	OPR
47703	WEN	OPR
47715	WEN	OPR
47765	GCR	RES
47768	BIR	OPR
47771	COL	RES
47773	BRM	OPR
47785	ECC	RES
47793	MFM	OPR
47798	NRM	OPR
47840	WST	OPR

Class 50

50002	SDR	RES
50007	MRC	OPR
50008	ELR	OPR
50015	ELR	OPR
50017	PVR	RES
50019	MNR	OPR
50021	BRM	RES
50026	EHD	RES
50027	NYM	OPR
50029	PRL	STO
50030	PRL	RES
50031	SVR	RES
50033	BRM	STO
50135	EHD	OPR
50042	BWR	OPR
50044	SVR	OPR
50049	SVR	OPR

50050	YEO	RES

Class 52

D1010	WSR	OPR
D1013	SVR	OPR
D1015	EHD	OPR
D1023	NRM	OPR
D1041	ELR	STO
D1048	MRC	RES
D1062●	SVR	OPR

Class 55

55002	NRM	RES
55009	BHR	OPR
55015	BHR	RES
55016	BHR	OPR
55019	BHR	OPR
55022	ELR	OPR

Class 56

56006	BHR	OPR
56040	MNR	OPR
56086	BAT	RES
56097	GCR	OPR
56098	BAT	RES
56101	BHR	RES

Class 58

58016	BHR	RES

Class 97

97650	LWR	OPR
97651	STR	OPR
97654	PRL	OPR

Class 71

71001	NRM	STO

Class 73

73001	DFR	OPR
73003	SWI	OPR
73005	SVR(EH)	RES
73006	SVR	OPR
73101	AVR	OPR
73103	ALY	STO
73104	WED	STO
73110	GCR	OPR
73114	BAT	OPR
73117	BHR	OPR
73128	PBR	OPR
73129	GWR	OPR
73130	FIN	OPR
73134	BHR	OPR
73139	WED	OPR
73140	SPV	OPR
73210	MNR	OPR

Class 76

E26020	NRM	STC

Class 77

E27000	MRC	STC
E27001	MSM	STC

Class 81

81002	BHR	STC

Class 82

82008	BHR	STC

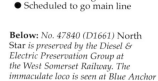

Class 83		
83012	BHR	STC

Class 84		
84001	BHR	STC

Class 85		
85101	BHR	STC

Class 86		
86101	BHR	OPR
86213¤	WB	OPR/WB

86233	MLM	STC
86259	BRM	OPR
86401¤	MLM	OPR/WB

Class 87		
87001	NRM	STC
87002	MLM	OPR
87035	RAC	RES

Class 89		
89001	BHR	STC

London Transport

12	LUL	OPR

¤ In use as a carriage heater
● Scheduled to go main line

Below: *No. 47840 (D1661) North Star is preserved by the Diesel & Electric Preservation Group at the West Somerset Railway. The immaculate loco is seen at Blue Anchor on 14 June 2008.* **CJM**

Diesel Units

Number	Base

Unclassified

APT-E	NRS
LEV1	NNR
RB004	TEL
79018	MRC
79612	MRC
79900	ECC
79960	NNR
79962	KWV
79963	NNR
79964	KWV
79976	GCR
79978	COL

Class 100

56301	MNR

Class 101

50222	BIR
50256	EKR
50338	BIR
51505	ECC
51187	CRT
51188	ECC
51189	KWV
51192	ELR
51205	CRT
51210	WEN
51226	MNR
51228	NNR
51247	WEN

51427	GCR
51434	MNR
51499	MNR
51503	MNR
51505	EAR
51511	NYM
51512	CRT
51213	EAR
51803	KWV
53160	CHS
53164	CHS
53170	MRC
53193	GCR
53203	GCR
53204	NYM
53253	MRC
53266	GCR
53321	GCR
53746	WEN
54055	CRT
54062	NNR
54365	EAR
54408	SPV
56343	EKR
56352	ELR
56358	EAR
59117	MNR
59539	NYM

Class 104

50447	LAN
50454	LAN

50455	TEL
50479	TEL
50494	CVR
50517	CVR
50528	LAN
50531	TEL
50547	CVR
50556	TEL
56182	CVR
59137	CVR
59228	TEL

Class 105

51485	ELR
56121	ELR
56456	LAN

Class 107

51990	STR
52005	NVR
52006	AVR
52008	STR
52025	AVR
52030	STR
59791	NVR

Class 108

50599	EAR
50619	DFR
50632	PBR
50929	KWV
50980	BWR

51562	NRM
51565	KWV
51566	DFR
51567	MRC
51568	KEI
51571	KES
51572	WEN
51907	LAN
51909	AVR
51914	DFR
51919	BVR
51922	NRM
51933	DFR
51941	SVR
51942	PBR
51947	BWR
51950	GWR
51973	MRC
52044	PBR
52048	BVR
52053	KEI
52054	BWR
52062	GWR
52064	SVR
53628	KEI
53645	GCR
53926	GCR
53971	KES
54223	EAR
54270	PBR
54279	LDL
54490	LAN

Preserved Motive Power

54504	SWN	59719	SDR	59508	GWI
56208	SVR	59740	SDR	59509	WEN
56224	ECC	59761	BRC	59510	MHR
56271	AVR			59513	PDR
56484	MRC	**Class 116**		59514	SWI
56491	KEI	51131	BAT	59516	SWN
56492	DFR	51138	GCR	59517	PDR
56495	KLR	51151	GCR	59520	PBR
59245	APF	51321	BAT	59521	MRC
59250	SVR	59003	PDR	59522	CHS
59387	DFR	59004	PDR	59603	CHS
59389	GCR	59444	CHS		

Class 109

50416	LAN
56171	LAN

Class 110

51813	WEN
51842	WEN
52071	LHR
52077	LHR
59701	WEN

Class 111

59575	MRC

Class 114

50015	MRC
50019	MRC
54057	STR
56006	MRC
56015	MRC

Class 115

51655	(BIR)¤
51663	WSR
51669	SPV
51677	(BIR)¤
51849	SPV
51852	WSR
51859	WSR
51880	WSR
51886	BRC
51887	WSR
51899	BRC
59659	SDR
59664	(BIR)¤
59678	WSR

Class 117

51339	LHG
51341	MRC
51342	EPO
51346	SWN
51347	GWI
51351	PBR
51353	MRC
51356	SWN
51359	NLR
51360	ECC
51363	MHR
51365	PVR
51367	STR
51372	TIT
51381	MFM
51382	LHG
51384	EPO
51388	SWN
51392	SWN
51395	MRC
51397	PBR
51398	MRC
51400	WEN
51401	GWI
51402	STR
51405	MHR
51407	PVR
59486	MRC
59488	PDR
59492	SWN
59494	PDR
59500	WEN
59503	PDR
59506	WSR
59507	PDR

Class 119

51073	ECC
51074	SWI
51104	SWI

Class 120

59276	GCR

Class 121

55023	CPR
55028	SWN
55033	COL
54289	ECC
56287	COL

Class 122

55000	SDR
55001	ELR
55003	MHR
55005	BAT
55006	ECC
55009	MNR
55012	SHI

Class 126

51017	BKR
51043	BKR
59404	BKR
79443	BKR

Class 127

51592	SDR
51604	SDR
51616	GCR
51618	LAN
51622	GCR
55966	MRC

55976	MRC
59609	MRC

Class 140
140001 - 55500/01   KEI

Class 141

141103	WED
141108	COL
141110	WED
141113	MRC

Class 201, 202 & 203

60116	HAD
60118	HAD
60501	HAD
60529	HAD
60750	WPH
201001	HAD

Class 205

60117	PBR
60822	LDL
60828	PBR
60154 X 1101	EKR
60800 X 1101	EKR
70549	ELR
Set 205009	EDR
Set 205025	MHR
Set 205028	DAR
Set 205033	DAR
Set 205033	LDL
Set 205205	EPO

Class 207

60127	SWI
60130 X 207202	ELR
60138	WPH
60142	SPV
60145	SEL
60149	SEL
60616	SPV
60901	SWI
60904 X 207202	ELR
60916	SPV
901001	CVR

Left: *Restored former Birmingham RC&W Class 104 cars Nos. 50455 and 50517 pose on the Churnet Valley Railway at Cheddleton.* **Cliff Beeton**

Electric Units

Unclassified
28249	NRM
29666	MRC
29670	MRC
79998	DEE
79999	DEE

BEL
85	SOU
87	KEI
91	RAM

BIL
10656 (2090)	NRS
12123 (2090)	NRS

COR
10096	EKR
11161	EKR
11179	NRM
11201	BLU
11825	EKR

DD
13004	NIR

Class 302
75033	MFM
75250	MFM

Class 303
303032	SHP

Class 306
306017	KIN

Class 307
75023	WPH

Class 308
75881	WPH

Class 309
309616	COV
309624	COV

Class 405 (SUB)
S8143S	NRM
4732	COV

Class 411/412 (CEP)
61742	DAR
61743	DAR
61798	EVR
61799	EVR
61804	EVR
61805	EVR
70229	EVR
70257	GCR
70273	DFR
70284	NIR
70292	SMP
70296	NIR
70354	EVR
70527	WRN
70531	SMP
70539	EVR
70576	SNI
70607	EVR
Set 1198	PBR
Set 7105	EKR

Class 414 (HAP)
61275	NRM
61287 (4311)	COV
75395	NRM
75407 (4311)	COV

Class 415 (EPB)
14351 (5176)	NIR
14352 (5176)	NIR
15345	COV
15396 (5176)	NIR

Class 416 (EPB)
65302	FIN
65304	FIN
65373 (5759)	EKR
77558 (5759)	EKR
14573 (6307)	COV
16117 (6307)	COV
65321 (5791)	COV
77112 (5793)	COV

Class 419 (MLV)
68001	EKR
68002	EKR
68003	EVR
68004	MNR
68005	EVR
68008	EKR
68009	EKR

Class 421 (CIG)
62364	DFR
62378	DFR
62384	GCR
62887	LWR
69339	GCR
76726	DFR
76740	DFR
76746	GCR
76797	DFR
76811	DFR
76812	DAR
76817	GCR
Set 1497	MNF
Set 1498	EPO
Set 1399	PBR
Set 1881	BEL

Class 422 (BEP)
69304	NIR
69310	DAR
69318	COL

69332	DAR
69333	LDL
69337	HAD

Class 423 (VEP)
(42)3417	BLU
76875	NRM

Class 457
67300	COV

Class 488
72501	ECC
72617	ECC

Class 489
68500	ECC
68506	ECC

Class 501
61183	COV
75186	COV

Class 502
28361	TEB
29896	TEB

Class 503
28690	COV
29298	COV
29720	COV

Class 504
65451	ELR
77172	ELR

Right: *The National Collection at the National Railway Museum, York has London North Western Open Brake Third No. 28249 as used on the Euston-Watford line. Built in 1916, the vehicle is restored to LMS maroon.* **CJM**

UK Power Exported

These lists give details of former UK diesel and electric locos exported for further use overseas and understood to still be operational.

Class 03
D2013	Italy
D2032	Italy
D2033	Italy
D2036	Italy

Class 04
D2216	Italy
D2232	Italy
D2289	Italy
D2295	Italy

Class 08
D3047	Lamco Liberia
D3092	Lamco Liberia
D3094	Lamco Liberia
D3098	Lamco Liberia
D3100	Lamco Liberia

Class 10
D3639	Conakry (Guinea)
D3649	Conakry (Guinea)

Class 14
D9534	Bruges

Class 37
37702	Continental Rail, Spain
37703	Continental Rail, Spain
37714	Continental Rail, Spain
37716	Continental Rail, Spain
37718	Continental Rail, Spain
37800	Continental Rail, Spain
37883	Continental Rail, Spain
37884	Continental Rail, Spain
37888	Continental Rail, Spain

Class 58
58001	ETF France
58004§	TSO France
58005	ETF France
58006§	ETF France
58007	TSO France
58009	TSO France
58010	TSO France
58011§	TSO France
58013	ETF France
58015	Continental Rail, Spain
58018	TSO France
58020	Continental Rail, Spain
58021	TSO France
58024	Continental Rail, Spain
58025	Continental Rail, Spain
58026§	TSO France
58027	Continental Rail, Spain
58029	Continental Rail, Spain
58030	Continental Rail, Spain
58031	Continental Rail, Spain
58032	ETF France
58033	TSO France
58034	TSO France
58035	TSO France
58036	ETF France
58038	ETF France
58039	ETF France
58040§	TSO France
58041	Continental Rail, Spain
58042	TSO France
58043	Continental Rail, Spain
58044	ETF France
58046	TSO France
58047	Continental Rail, Spain
58049§	ETF France
58050	Continental Rail, Spain

§ Stored at Alizay (Rouen)

Class 59
59003	HHPI, Germany

Class 66
66010	ECR, France
66013	ECR, France
66022	ECR, France
66026	ECR, France
66028	ECR, France
66029	ECR, France
66031	ECR, France
66032	ECR, France
66033	ECR, France
66036	ECR, France

Left: *With less work in the UK, a batch of EWS, now DBS Class 66/0s, were modified for use in mainland Europe. The EWS branding was replaced with the Euro Cargo Rail logo and full international numbers have been applied. No. 66246 is seen at Grande Synthe, Dunkirk on 17 November 2009. This loco also carries the number GB 92-70-0-066246-4.* **Michael J. Collins**

Left: *Originally operating in Germany under a joint contract between DB and Foster Yeoman, Class 59/0 No. 59003* **Yeoman Highlander** *is now operated by Heavy Haul Power International and can be seen powering heavy block trains mostly on the German - Poland corridor. No. 59003 is seen at Genshagener Heide near Berlin on 24 September 2008.* **CJM**

UK Power Exported

66038	ECR, France	66219	ECR, France	**Class 86**	
66042	ECR, France	66220	DBS, Poland	86218	Floyd, Hungary
66045	ECR, France	66222	ECR, France		As 0450-004-1
66049	ECR, France	66223	ECR, France	86232	Floyd, Hungary
66052	ECR, France	66224	ECR, France		As 0450-003-3
66062	ECR, France	66225	ECR, France	86248	Floyd, Hungary
66064	ECR, France	66226	ECR, France		As 0450-001-7
66071	ECR, France	66228	ECR, France	86250	Floyd, Hungary
66072	ECR, France	66229	ECR, France		As 0450-002-5
66073	ECR, France	66231	ECR, France		
66110	ECR, France	66233	ECR, France	**Class 87**	
66123	ECR, France	66234	ECR, France	87003	BZK Bulgaria
66179	ECR, France	66235	ECR, France	87004	BZK Bulgaria
66190	ECR, France	66236	ECR, France	87006	BZK Bulgaria
66191	ECR, France	66239	DBS, Poland	87007	BZK Bulgaria
66195	ECR, France	66240	ECR, France	87008	BZK Bulgaria
66202	ECR, France	66241	ECR, France	87010	BZK Bulgaria
66203	ECR, France	66242	ECR, France	87012	BZK Bulgaria
66205	ECR, France	66243	ECR, France	87013	BZK Bulgaria
66208	ECR, France	66244	ECR, France	87014	BZK Bulgaria
66209	ECR, France	66245	ECR, France	87019	BZK Bulgaria
66210	ECR, France	66246	ECR, France	87020	BZK Bulgaria
66211	ECR, France	66247	ECR, France	87022	BZK Bulgaria
66212	ECR, France	66249	ECR, France	87026	BZK Bulgaria
66214	ECR, France	66582	Freightliner, Poland	87028	BZK Bulgaria
66215	ECR, France	66583	Freightliner, Poland	87029	BZK Bulgaria
66216	ECR, France	66584	Freightliner, Poland	87033	BZK Bulgaria
66217	ECR, France	66586	Freightliner, Poland	87034	BZK Bulgaria
66218	ECR, France	66625	Freightliner, Poland		

Below: *Carrying BR rail blue livery and BR logo, Class 87/0 No. 87004 is seen working passenger services in Bulgaria in summer 2010. The loco retains its original BR name* Britannia, *but now sports Bulgarian style horns and light clusters, plus wing mirrors.* **Philip Wormald**

A number of preserved modern traction locomotives have been allocated five-digit Class 89 TOPS numbers to allow their operation either under power or dead over the National Network. The numbers allocated are shown below; not all locos may currently be authorised for use on Network Rail metals.

The first two digits are the class, the third is the power type while the final two digits are the final two of the original running number. If two locos clash with the same number the second to be registered will have 1 added to the number.

Class 89 TOPS No.	BR No.	Type	Name
89100	20050	Class 20	-
89101	20001	Class 20	-
89110	20110	Class 20	-
89127	20227	Class 20	-
89166	20166	Class 20	-
89188	20188	Class 20	-
89200	31018	Class 31	-
89204	26004	Class 26	-
89210	27059	Class 27	-
89212	LT 12	Met Loco	Sarah Siddons
89223	25173	Class 25	-
89233	25283	Class 25	-
89247	27001	Class 27	-
89254	24054	Class 24	-
89259	25309	Class 25	-
89261	24061	Class 24	-
89262	25262	Class 25	-
89280	31162	Class 31	-
89317	D7017	Class 35	-
89400	E27000	Class 77	Electra
89401	47401	Class 47	North Eastern
89402	50002	Class 50	Superb
89403	71001	Class 71	-
89404	44004	Class 44	Great Gable
89405	47105	Class 47	-
89407	50007	Class 50	Sir Edward Elgar
89408	50008	Class 50	Thunderer
89412	40012	Class 40	Aureol
89413	D1013	Class 52	Western Ranger
89415	50015	Class 50	Valiant
89416	D1015	Class 52	Western Champion
89417	50017	Class 50	Royal Oak
89420	45108	Class 45	-
89421	D821	Class 42	Greyhound
89423	45125	Class 45	-
89424	D1023	Class 52	Western Fusilier
89427	50027	Class 50	Lion
89431	50031	Class 50	Hood
89432	D832	Class 42	Onslaught
89435	40135	Class 40	-
89440	45133	Class 45	-
89441	D1041	Class 52	Western Prince
89442	47192	Class 47	-
89443	50042	Class 50	Triumph
89444	50044	Class 50	Exeter
89445	40145	Class 40	-
89448	D1048	Class 52	Western Lady
89449	50049	Class 50	Defiance
89453	45041	Class 45	Royal Tank Regiment
89460	45060	Class 45	Sherwood Forester
89462	D1062	Class 52	Western Courier
89466	47449	Class 47	-
89472	46035	Class 46	Ixion
89500	55022	Class 55	Royal Scots Grey
89502	55002	Class 55	The Kings Own Yorkshire Light Infantry
89503	81002	Class 81	-
89509	55009	Class 55	Alycidon
89515	55015	Class 55	Tulyar
89516	55016	Class 55	Gordon Highlander
89519	55019	Class 55	Royal Highland Fusilier
89523	DP1	Proto	Deltic
89535	83012	Class 83	-
89561	85101	Class 85	-

Left: *To allow preserved locomotives to be reported on the Network Rail computer system TOPS, all preserved locos are allocated a TOPS five-digit number. For diesels and electrics this is under the classification 89, with the third digit representing the power classification and the final two digits wherever possible the last two numbers of the original number. Preserved 'Western' No. D1015* Western Champion *is allocated the TOPS identity 89416 (the loco used 16 as its final two digits as 15 was previously issued to preserved Class 50 No. 50015).* Western Champion, *painted in maroon livery, is seen passing Langstone Rock, Devon on 7 April 2010.* **CJM**

Several preserved steam locomotives have been allocated five-digit TOPS numbers to allow their operation over the National Network. The numbers allocated are shown below; not all locos may currently be authorised for use on Network Rail metals.

TOPS No.	Railway No.	Type	Name
98150	1450	GWR 14xx	
98166	1466	GWR 14xx	
98186	686	0-6-0T	Lady Armaghdale
98212	41312	LMS 2MT	
98219	55189	CR 0-4-4T	
98221	46521	LMS 2MT	
98238	1638	GWR 16xx	
98240	3440	GWR 34xx	City of Truro
98241	46441	LMS 2MT	
98243	46443	LMS 2MT	
98253	30053	SR M7	
98254	58926	LNWR 2F	
98273	65243	NBR J36	Maude
98315	7715	GWR 57xx	
98321	69621	GER N7	A. J. Hill
98372	30072	SR USA	
98400	41000	LMS 4P	
98406	43106	LMS 4MT	
98414	75014	BR 4MT	
98425	7325	GWR 7321	
98426	31625	SR U	
98427	44027	LMS 4F	
98435	80135	BR 4MT	
98455	4555	GWR 45xx	
98457	9600	GWR 8750	
98460	7760	GWR 57xx	
98466	9466	GWR 94xx	
98469	75069	BR 4MT	
98472	5572	GWR 4575	
98476	76079	BR 4MT	
98478	68078	WD 4F	
98479	80079	BR 4MT	
98480	80080	BR 4MT	
98482	3882	0-6-0ST	Barbara
98488	4588	GWR 4575	
98494	65894	LNER J27	
98498	80098	BR 4MT	
98500	45000	LMS 5MT	
98502	7802	GWR 78xx	Bradley Manor
98505	45305	LMS 5MT	Alderman A E Draper
98507	45407	LMS 5MT	Lancashire Fusilier
98510	45110	LMS 5MT	
98512	7812	GWR 78xx	Erlestoke Manor
98519	7819	GWR 78xx	Hinton Manor
98525	45025	LMS 5MT	
98526	30925	SR V	Cheltenham
98529	73129	BR 5MT	
98530	4930	GWR 49xx	Hagley Hall
98531	45231	LMS 5MT	Sherwood Forester
98532	44932	LMS 5MT	
98536	4936	GWR 49xx	Kinlet Hall
98549	4965	GWR 49xx	Rood Ashton Hall
98553	4953	GWR 49xx	Pitchford Hall
98560	6960	GWR 6959	Raveningham Hall
98564	61264	LNER B1	

TOPS No.	Railway No.	Type	Name
98565	42765	LMS 6P5F	
98567	44767	LMS 5MT	George Stephenson
98568	42968	LMS 5MT	
98571	44871	LMS 5MT	
98572	5972	GWR 49xx	Olton Hall
98577	30777	SR N15	Sir Lamiel
98596	73096	BR 5MT	
98598	6998	GWR 6959	Burton Agnes Hall
98605	62005	LNER K1	
98628	30828	SR S15	
98641	30841	SR S15	
98642	61994	LNER K4	The Great Marquess
98690	45690	LMS 6P5F	Leander
98693	45593	LMS 6P5F	Kolhapur
98696	45596	LMS 6P5F	Bahamas
98700	70000	BR 7P	Britannia
98701	34101	SR WC	Hartland
98709	53809	SDJR 7F	
98713	70013	BR 7P	Oliver Cromwell
98715	46115	LMS 7P	Scots Guardsman
98716	34016	SR WC	Bodmin
98727	34027	SR WC	Taw Valley
98728	5029	GWR 4073	Nunney Castle
98729	7029	GWR 4073	Clun Castle
98750	30850	SR LN	Lord Nelson
98751	5051	GWR 4073	Earl Bathurst
98767	34067	SR BB	Tangmere
98771	60800	LNER V2	Green Arrow
98772	34072	SR BB	257 Squadron
98780	5080	GWR 4073	Defiant
98792	34092	SR WC	City of Wells
98800	6000	GWR 60xx	King George V
98801	46201	LMS 8P	Princess Elizabeth
98802	71000	BR 8P	Duke of Gloucester
98803	46203	LMS 8P	Princess Margaret Rose
98805	35005	SR MN	Canadian Pacific
98809	60009	LNER A4	Union of South Africa
98824	6024	GWR 60xx	King Edward I
98828	35028	SR MN	Clan Line
98829	46229	LMS 8P	Duchess of Hamilton
98832	60532	LNER A2	Blue Peter
98834	46233	LMS 8P	Duchess of Sutherland
98851	48151	LMS 8F	
98857	2857	GWR 28xx	
98863	60163	LNER A1	Tornado
98868	60022	LNER A4	Mallard
98872	60103	LNER A3	Flying Scotsman
98873	48773	LMS 8F	
98898	60007	LNER A4	Sir Nigel Gresley
98920	92220	BR 9F	Evening Star

Above: LNER Class A4 No. 60007 Sir Nigel Gresley is allocated the TOPS number of 98898 and is seen at Barrow Hill. **Chris Perkins**

Coupling Codes & Couplings

With the introduction of modern traction from the 1950s a number of different methods of multiple operation were introduced, covering the different control principle of locomotives, for example those using electro-pneumatic or electro-magnetic systems.

Six main systems are in operation today:

Blue Star ★ using the electro-pneumatic system and fitted to Classes 20, 25, 31, 33, 37, 40 and 73.

Green Spot ● a unique system installed on some Class 47s operated by the freight sector.

Orange Square ■ an English Electric system used only on the Class 50s.

Red Diamond ◆ a 1970s system developed for the modern freight locos of Classes 56 and 58.

In addition to the above coded systems, the American developed main line locos of Classes 59, 66, 67 and 70 use the US standard AAR (Association of American Railroads) system. Direct Rail Services (DRS) have also developed a unique system which is installed on some of the company's Class 20, 37, 47 and 57 locos.

A number of locomotives have either been built with or modified to incorporate Time Division Multiplex (TDM) remote operation equipment, which uses coach lighting type Railway Clearing House (RCH) nose end jumper cables.

Some of the surviving first generation DMMU sets carry a **Blue Square** ■ multiple operation system.

Details of the main coupling systems in operation in the UK are included in the accompanying illustrations.

Standard Coupling

Above: Class 59 and 66 front end layout (non-DBS operated). 1-Coupling hook, 2-Coupling shackle, 3-Air brake pipe (red), 4-Main reservoir pipe (yellow), 5-Buffer, 6-Association of American Railroads (AAR) jumper socket. No. 66726 illustrated. **CJM**

Standard Coupling

Above: Standard coupling arrangement to be found on many classes of UK loco. 1-Electric Train Supply (ETS) jumper socket, 2-Main reservoir air pipe (yellow), 3-Vacuum brake pipe, 4-Coupling hook and shackle, 5-Air brake pipe (red), 6-Electric Train Supply (ETS) jumper cable. Loco No. 47580 illustrated. **CJM**

Drop Head Buck-Eye with TDM Coupling

Above: The unique front end layout of the Royal Mail Class 325. 1-Brake pipe (red), 2-Main reservoir pipe (yellow), 3-Electric Train Supply (ETS) socket, 4-Time Division Multiplex (TDM) jumper socket, 5-Drop-head buck-eye coupling, 6-Electric Train Supply (ETS) cable. **CJM**

Couplings

Drop Head Dellner Coupling

Above: *Following the introduction of Virgin Trains 'Voyager' and 'Pendolino' stock, a fleet of 16 Class 57/3s were introduced with drop head Dellner couplers and cabling to provide 'hotel power'. The coupling is seen in this illustration in the raised position. 1-Electric Train Supply (ETS) jumper socket, 2-Main reservoir pipe (yellow), 3-Air brake pipe (red), 4-Coupling hook, 5-Dellner coupling face, 6-Electric Train Supply (ETS) jumper cable.* **CJM**

BSI Coupling

Above: *With the birth of modern multiple unit trains came the Bergische Stahi Industrie (BSI) automatic coupling, first seen in the UK on the Tyne & Wear metro vehicles in 1978. The modern generation of UK DMUs now concentrate on the Compact BSI coupler with a CK2 coupling interface. The couplers are engaged by the compression of the two coupling faces which completes a physical connection which also opens a watertight cover to an electrical connection box. The full train air connection is made during the coupling compression process. The coupling is complete by the driver pressing a 'couple' button in the driving cab. 1-Emergency air connection, 2-Coupling face, 3-Electric connection (behind plate), 4-Air connection. The coupling shown is on a Class 166.* **CJM**

Tightlock with Drum Connection

Above: *The Tightlock coupler is a derivative of the Association of American Railroads (AAR) type H coupler, later under the control of American Public Transportation Association (APTA). A modified Type H coupler was introduced in the UK from the early 1970s and has become a standard fitting on many of the later BR and several post privatisation EMUs. The UK Tightlock design can be supplied with or without an electrical connection box and with or without a pneumatic connection. This view shows a fully automated version as fitted to the 'Networker' fleet. Attachment is achieved by driving the two vehicles together which physically connects the vehicles, while a 'roll-cover' box opens to connect electric and pneumatic services. 1-Emergency air connector, 2-Manual release handle, 3-Semi-rotary electric/pneumatic cover, 4-Physical coupler.* **CJM**

Tightlock with Nose End Connections

Above: *The BR Southern Region-designed Class 455 and 456 units have a semi automatic Tightlock used for physical connections, while air and electrical connections are made by waist height flexible pipes. 1-Main reservoir pipe (yellow), 2-Control jumper, 3-Tightlock coupler, 4-Couple/Uncouple drum switch, 5-Manual release handle, 6-Control jumper receptacle.* **CJM**

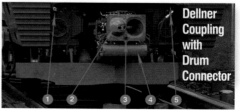

Dellner Coupling with Drum Connector

Above: *Dellner couplers have become the standard in the UK and much of Europe; these are fully automatic and come in various forms. 1-Emergency air supply, 2-Dellner coupling plate, 3-Pneumatic connection, 4-Roll-cover to electrical connections, 5-Air supply. Coupling of Class 360 illustrated.* **CJM**

Couplings

Coupling Codes & Couplings

Dellner Coupling

Dellner Coupling

Above: *A large number of different design of Dellner couplers exist on UK rolling stock some feature full automatic operation including pneumatic and electrical connections, while others only provide physical coupling. This view shows a pair of Voyager units coupled together with Dellner couplers. The electrical connection box is above the physical coupler. After trains are 'pushed' together the driver operates a 'couple' button in the cab to complete the attachment. Uncoupling is achieved by the driver pressing an 'uncouple' button and driving the trains apart.* **CJM**

Left: *The Virgin Trains 'Pendolino' stock use Dellner couplers with a rotary covered electrical connector plate above. These couplers are supplemented by electric train supply connections either side to provide 'hotel power' to Class 390 sets from attached Class 57 locos. 1-Electric Train Supply (ETS) socket, 2-Emergency air connector, 3-Electrical connector plate under semi-rotary cover, 4-Dellner physical coupler, 5-Pneumatic connections. In normal use the Dellner coupler on 'Pendolino' stock is covered by a front fairing.* **CJM**

Dellner Coupling Without Electric Connector

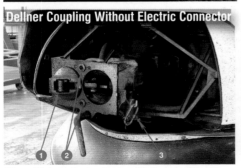

Above: *Under the front end fairing of the Eurostar Class 373 stock a standard Scharfenberg is located for assistance purposes and shunting. No electrical provision is made and the couplers are seldom used. 1-Scharfenberg coupling face, 2 Pneumatic connections, 3-Manual uncoupling handle.* **CJM**

Dellner Coupling With Electric Connector

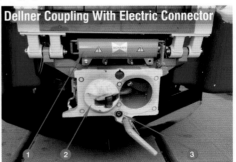

Above: *In as-installed condition and having never been coupled to another set, a Class 380 Scharfenberg coupler is viewed, showing the auto opening electrical connection box above. 1-Electrical connection box, 2-Coupling face plate, 3-Pneumatic connection.* **CJM**

Over the years a number of former BR locomotives have after withdrawal from normal duties taken up use for industrial operators. The list below represents those which are understood to still be in existence in late 2010. Some locos operated at preservation sites are deemed to be 'industrial' but these are grouped in the preserved section.

Class 03

03112 (D2112)	Port of Boston
03179 *Clive*	First Capital Connect, Hornsey Depot

Class 08

08202	Gloucestershire - Warwickshire Railway
08331 (H001)	Cemex, Washwood Heath
08375	Ketton Cement Works
08398 (402D) *Annabel*	Imerys Clay Company, Bugle
08411	LH Group, Burton - owned by Classic Traction
08441	Colne Valley Railway
08445	Castle Cement, Stamford
08447	John G. Russell Transit, Hillington, Glasgow
08460	Felixstowe Dock & Railway
08484 *Captain Nathaniel Darell*	Felixstowe Dock & Railway
08503	Rye Farm, Wishaw
08511	Felixstowe Dock & Railway
08523	Celtic Energy, Onllwyn Washery
08535	Corus, Shotton
08598	The Potter Group, Ely
08600	LH Group Services, Barton-under-Needwood
08613	Corus, Shotton Works
08622 (H028) (7)	P & D Ports Teesport
08643	Aggregate Industries, Whatley
08650 *Isle of Grain*	Aggregate Industries, Isle of Grain
08652	Hanson Aggregates, Whatley Quarry
08668	St. Modwen Storage, Long Marston
08670	Colne Valley Railway
08699	Corus, Shotton
08704 (D3871)	Port of Boston, Boston Docks
08728	St. Modwen Storage, Long Marston
08731	Aggregate Industries, Merehead
08743 *Bryan Turner*	SembCorp Utilities Teesside, Wilton
08774 *Arthur Vernon Dawson*	AV Dawson, Middlesbrough
08787	Hanson Aggregates, Machen
08807	AV Dawson, Middlesbrough
08809	Corus, Shotton (at Washwood Heath 12/10)
08813	St. Modwen Storage, Long Marston
08818 *Molly*	Faber Prest Ports, Flixborough Wharf
08823 (D3991)	Thames Steel, Isle of Sheppey
08827	St. Modwen Storage, Long Marston
08847	Stored at Norwich Crown Point (Cotswold Rail - for sale)
08870 (H024)	Castle Cement, Ketton
08873	Freightliner Terminal, Southampton
08881 (D4095)	Lafarge Aggregates, Mountsorrel
08903 *John W. Antill*	SembCorp Utilities Teesside, Wilton
08912	AV Dawson, Middlesbrough
08913	W H Malcolm (Owned by Hunslet)
08915	Stephenson Railway Museum
08933	Aggregate Industried, Merehead
08936	Corus, Shotton Works
08937 *Bluebell Mel*	Aggregate Industries, Meldon Quarry
08947	Aggregate Industries, Merehead

Class 11

12088	John G Russell Transport, Hillington

Class 14

D9529 (14029)	Aggregate Industries, Bardon Quarry

Class 56

56009 (56201)	Brush Traction, Loughborough

Light Rail Operators

Transport for London
London Underground

Address: ✉ Floor 11, Windsor House, 50 Victoria Street, London SW1H 0TL
✍ pressoffice@tfl.gov.uk
☎ 0845 604 4141
ⓘ www.tfl.gov.uk

Managing Director: Mike Brown

Operations: The London Underground system, now operated by Transport for London (TfL), operates services on 10 lines in and around the capital and uses a mix of surface and tunnel stock.

Bakerloo Line	Tube Line. Operates services between Elephant & Castle and Harrow & Wealdstone. **Rolling Stock:** 1972 Mk2, livery - red, white and blue, allocated to Stonebridge Park. Scheduled for replacement in 2018.
Central Line	Tube Line. Operates services between West Ruislip/Ealing and Epping **Rolling Stock:** 1992, livery - red, white and blue, allocated to Hainault.
Circle Line	Sub-Surface Line. Operates circle network in Central London and the branch from Edgware Road to Hammersmith. **Rolling Stock:** 'C' stock, introduced 1969-78, livery - red, white and blue, allocated to Hammersmith.
District Line	Sub-Surface Line. Operates services between Wimbledon, Richmond, Ealing, Edgware Road, Kensington Olympia and Upminster. **Rolling Stock:** 'C' and 'D' stock, livery - red, white and blue, allocated to Ealing Common and Upminster.
Jubilee Line	Tube Line. Operates services between Stanmore and Stratford. **Rolling Stock:** 1996, livery - red, white and blue, allocated to Wembley Park.
Metropolitan Line	Sub-Surface Line. Operates services from Amersham, Chesham, Watford and Uxbridge to Aldgate. **Rolling Stock:** 'A' stock, livery - red, white and blue, allocated to Wembley Park, due for replacement with 'S' stock in 2010-2011.
Northern Line	Tube Line. Operates services between Morden and Edgware, Mill Hill East and High Barnet. **Rolling Stock:** 1995 Stock, livery - red, white and blue, allocated to Morden.
Piccadilly Line	Tube Line. Operates services between Heathrow Airport / Uxbridge and Cockfosters. **Rolling Stock:** 1973 Stock, livery - red, white and blue, allocated to Northfields and Cockfosters. Stock due for replacement in 2014.
Victoria Line	Tube Line. Operates services between Brixton and Walthamstow Central **Rolling Stock:** 1967 and 2009 Stock, livery - red, white and blue, allocated to Northumberland Park.
Waterloo & City Line	Tube Line. Operates services between Waterloo and Bank **Rolling Stock:** 1992 Stock, livery - red, white and blue, allocated to Waterloo.

Light Rail

Above: *The London Underground 'surface' Metropolitan Line is currently phasing out the 'A' line stock with the new 'S' type illustrated below. An eight car formation of 'A' stock is illustrated, led by driving car No. 5010.* **Tony Christie**

Below: *Thumbs up from the cab, on the first official day in service of London Underground's 'S' stock eight car continuous coach tube train. With three complete sets delivered to Neasden depot by late summer 2010, Monday 2 August saw No. 21003 operating between Wembley Park and Watford. These are the first air conditioned trains for London Underground, and will have replaced the existing 'A' stock on the Metropolitan line by the end of 2011. The train is seen here departing Northwood.* **Colin Cooke**

For space reasons, we are unable in this publication to provide vehicle numbers for London Underground stock.

Transport for London
Docklands Light Railway

Contact details as London Underground.

Operations: The Docklands Light Railway operates between Bank and Tower Gateway and Woolwich Arsenal, Beckton and Stratford, as well as a Lewisham to Stratford service.

Class B90 (twin)

Train Length: 94ft 5in (28.80m)		Seating: 52 + 4 tip-up	
Width: 8ft 7in (2.65m)		Horsepower: 375hp (280kW)	
Power Supply: 750V dc third rail		Electrical Equipment: Brush	

22	25	28	31	34	37	40	43
23	26	29	32	35	38	41	44
24	27	30	33	36	39	42	

Class B92 (twin)

Train Length: 94ft 5in (28.80m)		Seating: 54 + 4 tip-up	
Width: 8ft 7in (2.65m)		Horsepower: 375hp (280kW)	
Power Supply: 750V dc third rail		Electrical Equipment: Brush	

45	51	57	63	69	75	81	87
46	52	58	64	70	76	82	88
47	53	59	65	71	77	83	89
48	54	60	66	72	78	84	90
49	55	61	67	73	79	85	91
50	56	62	68	74	80	86	

Class B2K (twin)

Train Length: 94ft 5in (28.80m)		Seating: 52 + 4 tip-up	
Width: 8ft 7in (2.65m)		Horsepower: 375hp (280kW)	
Power Supply: 750V dc third rail		Electrical Equipment: Brush	

01	04	07	10	13	16	94	97
02	05	08	11	14	92	95	98
03	06	09	12	15	93	96	99

Class B07 (twin)

Train Length: 94ft 5in (28.80m)		Seating: 52 + 4 tip-up	
Width: 8ft 7in (2.65m)		Horsepower: 375hp (280kW)	
Power Supply: 750V dc third rail		Electrical Equipment: Bombardier	
To be extended to three-car sets in time for 2012 Olympic Games			

101	108	115	122	129	136	143	150
102	109	116	123	130	137	144	151
103	110	117	124	131	138	145	152
104	111	118	125	132	139	146	153
105	112	119	126	133	140	147	154
106	113	120	127	134	141	148	155
107	114	121	128	135	142	149	

Left: *Class B2K twin set No. 02 leads another unit of the same class on the Docklands Light Railway at Poplar on 27 March 2010.* **Stacy Thew**

Light Rail

Transport for London
Croydon Tramlink

Contact details as London Underground.
Operations: The Croydon Tramlink operates between Croydon and Wimbledon, New Addington, Beckenham, and Elmers End.

Six-axle stock

Train Length: 98ft 9in (30.1m)		Seating: 70
Width: 8ft 7in (2.65m)		Horsepower: 643hp (480kW)
Power Supply: 750V dc overhead		Electrical Equipment: Bombardier

2530	2533	2536	2539	2542	2545	2548	2551
2531	2534	2537	2540	2543	2546	2549	2552
2532	2535	2538	2541	2544	2547	2550	2553

Name applied
2535   **Stephen Parascandolo**
        1980-2007

Right: *Painted in the Croydon Tramlink colours of green, white, grey and blue, set No. 2551 is seen at West Croydon station on 2 September 2010 forming a service to New Addington.*
CJM

Manchester Metrolink

Address: ✉ Greater Manchester PTE, 2 Piccadilly Gardens, Manchester, M1 3BG
           Metrolink House, Queens Road, Manchester, M6 0RY
    ✍ customerservices@metrolink.co.uk
    ✆ 0161 224 1000
    ⓘ www.metrolink.co.uk

Metrolink is operated for GMPTE by Stagecoach Group.
Operations: Manchester Metrolink operates a street and dedicated track tram system around Manchester. Services operate from the city centre to Bury, Altrincham and Eccles via MediaCity UK.

Six-axle stock

Train Length: 95ft 1in (29m)		Seating: 82 + 4 tip-up
Width: 8ft 7in (2.65m)		Horsepower: 697hp (520kW)
Power Supply: 750V dc overhead		Electrical Equipment: Firema

1001		1010		1019	
1002	*Da Vinci*	1011	*VANS . The original since 1966*	1020	*Lancashire Fusilier*
1003	*VANS . The original since 1966*	1012		1021	
1004	*VANS . The original since 1966*	1013		1022	*Poppy Appeal*
1005	*The Railway Mission*	1014	*The Great Manchester Runner*	1023	
1006	*VANS . The original since 1966*	1015	*Burma Star*	1024	
1007	*East Lancashire Railway*	1016		1025	
1008		1017	*Bury Hospice*	1026	
1009		1018			

Light Rail

Above: *Twenty-six of the first generation of trams are still in operation on the Manchester tram system, providing an excellent service in the Manchester area. Set No. 1005 is illustrated.* **John Binch**

Six-axle stock

Train Length: 95ft 1in (29m)				*Seating: 82 + 4 tip-up*	
Width: 8ft 7in (2.65m)				*Horsepower: 697hp (520kW)*	
Power Supply: 750V dc overhead				*Electrical Equipment: Ansaldo*	

2001(S)	2002	2003	2004	2005	2006

M5000 stock

Train Length: 93ft 1in (28.4m)				*Seating: 52 + 8 tip-up*	
Width: 8ft 7in (2.65m)				*Horsepower: 643hp (480kW)*	
Power Supply: 750V dc overhead				*Electrical Equipment: Bombardier*	

3001	3010	3019	3028	3037	3046	3055
3002	3011	3020	3029	3038	3047	3056
3003	3012	3021	3030	3039	3048	3057
3004	3013	3022	3031	3040	3049	3058
3005	3014	3023	3032	3041	3050	3059
3006	3015	3024	3033	3042	3051	3060
3007	3016	3025	3034	3043	3052	3061
3008	3017	3026	3035	3044	3053	3062
3009	3018	3027	3036	3045	3054	

■ *In December 2010, deliveries had reached No. 3025. Sets 3014 onwards were stored as signalling was not compatible with the existing lines.*

Left: *A fleet of new Bombardier-built M5000 series trams are now being introduced in Manchester. Set No. 3004 is illustrated.* **Brian Arnold**

Nottingham Express Transit

Address: ✉ Transdev Tram UK Ltd, Garrick House, 74 Chiswick High Road, London, W4 1SY

Nottingham City Transport Ltd, Lower Parliament Street, Nottingham, NG1 1GG

✆ info@thetram.net ✆ 0115 942 7777, ⓘ www.thetram.net

Operations: Nottingham Express Transit (NET) operate trams between Hucknall and Nottingham.

Six-axle stock

Train Length: 108ft 3in (29m)	Seating: 54 + 4 tip-up
Width: 7ft 9in (2.4m)	Horsepower: 697hp (520kW)
Power Supply: 750V dc overhead	Electrical Equipment: Bombardier

201	
202	*DH Lawrence*
203	*Bendigo Thompson*
204	*Erica Beardsmore*
205	*Lord Byron*
206	*Angela Alcock*
207	*Mavis Worthington*
208	*Dinah Minton*
209	*Sid Standard*
210	*Sir Jesse Boot*
211	*Robin Hood*
212	*William Booth*
213	*Mary Potter*
214	*Dennis McCarthy*
215	*Brian Clough*

Right: *Nottingham Tram set No. 201 in Nottingham Contemporary livery is seen at Lace Market on 17 September 2010.* **John Binch**

Midland Metro

Address: ✉ Travel West Midlands, PO Box 3565, Birmingham, B1 3JR

✆ info@travelmetro.co.uk ✆ 0121 254 7272, ⓘ www.travelmetro.co.uk

Operations: Midland Metro operates trams between Birmingham Snow Hill and Wolverhampton.

Six-axle stock

Train Length: 108ft 3in (29m)	Seating: 54 + 4 tip-up
Width: 7ft 9in (2.4m)	Horsepower: 697hp (520kW)
Power Supply: 750V dc overhead	Electrical Equipment: Bombardier

01(S)	*Sir Frank Whittle*	07	*Billy Wright*	13	*Anthony Nolan*
02		08	*Joseph Chamberlain*	14	*Jim Eames*
03	*Ray Lewis*	09	*Jeff Astle*	15	*Agenoria*
04		10	*John Stanley Webb*	16	*Gerwyn John*
05	*Sister Dora*	11	*Theresa Stewart*		
06	*Alan Garner*	12			

Right: *Painted in Midland Metro pink and silver livery, set No. 05 is seen at Wolverhampton on 4 August 2010.* **Stacey Thew**

Sheffield Super Tram

Address: ✉ Stagecoach Supertram, Nunnery Depot, Woodburn Road, Sheffield, S9 3LS

🖳 enquiries@supertram.com

✆ 0114 272 8282

ⓘ www.supertram.com

Operations: Sheffield Super Tram operates services within Sheffield city centre and to Herdings Park, Halfway, Meadowhall Interchange, Middlewood and Malin Bridge.

Six-axle stock

Train Length: 113ft 6in (34.75m)	Seating: 80 + 6 tip-up
Width: 8ft 7in (2.65m)	Horsepower: 800hp (596kW)
Power Supply: 750V dc overhead	Electrical Equipment: Siemens

101	105	109	113	117	121	125
102	106	110	114	118	122	
103	107	111	115	119	123	
104	108	112	116	120	124	

Left: *On the afternoon of Tuesday 25 May 2010, Duewag eight-axle articulated Sheffield Super Tram No. 120, sporting a light blue advertising livery promoting East Midlands Trains stands at the Middlewood terminus on the Sheffield Supertram system with a yellow route service to Meadowhall. Following their refreshment programme in 2009, this is now the only Sheffield Supertram vehicle to carry advertising livery, the rest of the 25-strong fleet having now received Stagecoach blue colours.* **John Binch**

Tyne & Wear Metro

Address: ✉ Tyne & Wear Passenger Transport Executive (NEXUS), Nexus House, 33 St James Boulevard, Newcastle upon Tyne, NE1 4AX

🖳 enquiries@nexus.co.uk

✆ 0191 203 3333

ⓘ www.nexus.org.uk

Operations: Tyne & Wear Metro operates tram services within Newcastle city centre and to Whitley Bay, Newcastle Airport, South Shields, Sunderland and South Hylton.

Six-axle stock

Train Length: 91ft 3in (27.80m)	Seating: 68 tip-up
Width: 8ft 7in (2.65m)	Horsepower: 500hp (374kW)
Power Supply: 1500V dc overhead	Electrical Equipment: Siemens

4001	4011	4021	4031	4041	4051	4061
4002	4012	4022	4032	4042	4052	4062
4003	4013	4023	4033	4043	4053	4063
4004	4014	4024	4034	4044	4054	4064
4005	4015	4025	4035	4045	4055	4065
4006	4016	4026	4036	4046	4056	4066
4007	4017	4027	4037	4047	4057	4067
4008	4018	4028	4038	4048	4058	4068
4009	4019	4029	4039	4049	4059	4069
4010	4020	4030	4040	4050	4060	4070

4071	4074	4077	4080	4083	4086	4089
4072	4075	4078	4081	4084	4087	4090
4073	4076	4079	4082	4085	4088	

Name applied
4026 *George Stephenson*
4041 *Harry Cowans*
4060 *Thomas Bewick*
4064 *Michael Campbell*
4065 *Dame Catherine Cookson*
4073 *Danny Marshall*
4077 *Robert Stephenson*
4078 *Ellen Wilkinson*

Right: *Tyne & Wear set No. 4034 is seen at Whitley Bay on 27 September 2009.* **John Law**

Glasgow Subway

Address: ✉ SPT, Consort House, 12 West George Street, Glasgow, G2 1HN
 ✉ enquiry@spt.co.uk
 ✆ 0141 332 6811
 ⓘ www.spt.co.uk

Glasgow Subway is operated by Strathclyde Partnership for Transport (SPT)
Operations: Circular network around Glasgow city centre.

Single Power Cars

Length: 42ft 2in (12.81m)
Width: 7ft 7in (2.34m)
Power Supply: 600V dc third rail
Seating: 36S
Horsepower: 190hp (142.4kW)
Electrical Equipment: GEC

101	105	109	113	117	121	125	129	133
102	106	110	114	118	122	126	130	
103	107	111	115	119	123	127	131	
104	108	112	116	120	124	128	132	

Trailer Cars

Length: 41ft 6in (12.70m)
Width: 7ft 7in (2.34m)
Seating: 40S

| 201 | 202 | 203 | 204 | 205 | 206 | 207 | 208 |

Right: *Outside its normal environment underground, Glasgow 'Clockwork Orange' trailer car No. 207 is seen on the back of a low loader being returned to the network from Railcare Glasgow. The vehicle is painted in Strathclyde PTE carmine and cream with the 'subway' legend on the bodyside.* **Bill Wilson**

Livery Codes

ABL	Arriva Trains Blue
ADV	Advenza Freight, blue with yellow branding
AGI	Aggregate Industries green, silver and green
AIN	Aggregate Industries - blue
ALS	Alstom Transportation
ANG	Anglia - mid blue
ANN	Anglia - turquoise/white with National Express East Anglia branding
ATE	Arriva Trains Executive- turquoise/cream with branding
ATW	Arriva Trains Wales - turquoise/cream
AXC	Arriva Cross Country - brown, silver, pink
BBR	Balfour Beatty Rail blue/white
BLG	Blue and Grey
BLK	Black
BLL	BR rail blue with large logo
BLU	Blue
BLW	Carillion Rail blue/white
BOM	Bombardier Transportation
BPM	Blue Pullman - Nankin blue and white
BRD	BR Departmental mid grey
BRT	BR Trainload two-tone grey
c2c	c2c - blue/pink
CAL	Caledonian Railway
CAR	Carmine & Cream
CEN	Central Trains blue and two-tone green
CHC	Chocolate & Cream
CIV	BR Civil Engineers - grey and yellow
COL	Colas - Orange, lime green and black
CON	Continental Rail - light/mid blue
COR	Corus Steel - light blue or yellow
COX	Connex white and yellow
CRW	Chilton Railways - while/blue
CTL	Central Trains blue, green with yellow doors
CWR	Cotswold Rail - silver with branding
DBB	DB Schenker - light blue
DBM	DB Schenker - maroon
DBS	DB Schenker - red
DCG	Devon & Cornwall Railway - green
DRC	Direct Rail Services - blue compass branding
DRO	Direct Rail Services - Ocean Liner blue
DRS	Direct Rail Services - blue
DRU	Direct Rail Services - unbranded blue
ECR	European Cargo Rail - grey
ECS	East Coast - silver
ECT	East Coast branded National Express livery
EMT	East Midlands Trains, white, blue, swirl cab ends
EPS	European Passenger Services
EPX	Europhoenix red/silver
ETF	ETF Rail - yellow with green band
EU2	Eurotunnel - Europort2
EUS	Eurostar - white, yellow and blue
EWE	English Welsh Scottish Executive
EWS	English Welsh Scottish - red with gold band
FCC	First Capital Connect, First Group Urban Lights - mauve/blue with pink, blue and white lower branding
FER	Fertis - grey with branding
FGB	First Great Western blue
FGF	First Group - GBRf (Barbie)
FGL	First Great Western local lines
FGN	First Great Western branded Northern blue
FGS	First Group Scotrail with EWS branding
FGT	First Great Western, Thames/London area branding
FGW	First Great Western, as FST with FGW branding
FHT	First Hull Trains, as FST with Hull Trains branding
FLF	Fastline Freight - grey with yellow/white chevrons
FLG	Freightliner green unbranded
FLP	Freightliner - green/yellow - Powerhaul
FLR	Freightliner - green/yellow - original
FLU	Freightliner - green/yellow - unbranded
FLY	Freightliner grey
FNA	First livery with National Express East Anglia branding
FOS	Foster Yeoman
FRB	Fragonset black
FSN	Northern branded First Group
FSP	First Scotrail Strathclyde carmine and cream (some with turquoise band)
FSR	First Scotrail, as FST with FSR branding
FSS	First Scotrail, blue with white Saltire branding
FST	First Group - dark blue, pink and white swirl
FSW	First Group - green and white with gold branding
FTP	First TransPennine, as FST with FTP branding
GAT	Gatwick Express, white, mid-grey and red with red doors
GBE	GB Railfreight - Europorte branding
GBF	GB Railfreight - swirl
GBM	GB Railfreight Metronet
GBR	GB Railfreight - blue
GBU	GB Railfreight swirl (no First branding)
GLX	Glaxochem - grey, blue and black
GNE	Great North Eastern Railway - blue
GRN	Green
GRY	Grey
GSW	Great Scottish & Western Railway - maroon
GTL	Grand Central Railway - black
GTO	Grand Central Railway - black with orange
GWG	First Great Western - green
GWR	Great Western Railway - green
HAN	Hanson
HEC	Heathrow Connect - grey, orange
HEL	Heathrow Connect - Terminal 4 'Link'
HEX	Heathrow Express - silver, grey
HNR	Harry Needle Railroad - yellow/grey
HS1	High Speed 1 - blue with powder blue doors
HUN	Hunslet
ICS	InterCity Swallow - two-tone grey off-set with red and white body band
IND	Industrial colours of operator
INT	InterCity two-tone grey off-set with red and white body band
JAR	Jarvis maroon
LAF	Lafarge Aggregates - green/white
LHL	Loadhaul Freight - black and orange
LLB	Large Logo Blue

LMI	London Midland grey, green and black	SCT	Scotrail Caledonian Sleeper - mauve/ white
LNE	LNER tourist green/cream	SEC	Serco
LOG	London Overground, white and blue with orange doors	SET	South Eastern Trains - white with branding
LUL	London Underground red	SGK	Southern Gatwick Express - blue, white and red with swirl ends
MAB	Statesman Pullman - maroon/beige	SIL	Silver
MAI	MainTrain - blue with branding	SKL	Silverlink London Overground, SLK with London Overground branding
MAL	Malcolm Rail	SLF	Silverlink, with First Great Western branding
MAR	Maroon	SLK	Silverlink, mauve, green and white
MED	Medite - black	SNF	Railfreight grey with SNCF branding
MER	Merseyrail - silver and yellow	SNT	SNCF domestic on Eurostar, silver, while and yellow
MLF	Mainline Freight - aircraft blue		
MLG	Mainline Freight - branded double grey	SOU	Southern - white, black and green
MML	Midland Main Line - turquoise/white	SPL	Special livery
NE2	National Express with c2c branding	STN	Stansted Express
NGE	First Great Eastern grey/blue with cab end swirl, branded National Express	STO	Stobart Rail
		SWM	South West Trains main line white and blue
NOM	Northern Rail - blue Metro branded	SWO	South West Trains outer suburban blue
NOR	Northern - blue, purple, grey	SWS	South West Trains suburban red
NOU	Northern unbranded	SWT	South West Trains blue, red, grey
NRL	Network Rail - yellow with branding	TAT	Tata Steel - blue
NSE	Network SouthEast - red, white and blue	TES	Tesco
NUB	Northern Rail blue - unbranded ScotRail	TEX	TransPennine Express - As FST with TPE brand
NWT	North West Trains - dark blue	TGG	Transrail Grey with 'T' branding
NXA	National Express East Anglia	THM	Thameslink - blue, white, yellow
NXE	National Express East Coast	TLF	Trainload Freight - grey
NXG	National Express East Coast branding on GNER blue livery	TLL	Trainload grey with Loadhaul branding
		TLP	Thameslink promotional multi-coloured stripes
NXS	National Express brand on Silverlink		
NXU	National Express unbranded white/grey	TPD	Trans Pennine/Central Trains logo
ONE	One Anglia mid-blue	TSO	Travaux du Sud Ouest - yellow
ORN	One Railway with National Express branding	TTG	Two-tone grey
PCL	BR Parcels red/grey	VIR	Virgin - red/grey
POL	Police livery	VSN	VSOE Northern
PTR	Porterbrook	VT1	Virgin - red/grey unbranded
PUL	Pullman - umber/cream	VWC	Virgin West Coast, silver, red, white and black
PUR	Artemis purple		
QOS	Queen of Scots Pullman	WAB	Wabtec Rail - black
RES	Rail express systems - red and graphite	WAG	West Anglia Great Northern - purple
RFD	Railfreight Distribution	WAL	Wales & Borders 'Alphaline' silver/grey
RFE	Railfreight grey with EWS branding	WCR	West Coast Railway - maroon
RFG	Railfreight grey	WES	Wessex Trains - maroon
RFI	Railfreight International	WET	Wessex Trains - silver, maroon/pink doors
RFP	Railfreight with Petroleum branding	WEX	Wessex Rail Engineering
RFT	BR Railfreight - grey, red and yellow, with large logo and numbers	WHT	White
		WMD	West Midlands Network, light blue and green
RIV	Riviera Trains - maroon	WSR	Wrexham & Shropshire two-tone grey
RML	Royal Mail Limited - red	XCM	AXC branding on MML or CTR livery
ROY	Royal Train - claret	XP4	BR XP64 colours
RTB	Railtrack - blue	YEL	Yellow
RTK	Railtrack - grey/brown		
SCE	Stagecoach - white with East Midlands branding		

Right: *Modern EMU power at Clapham Junction on 22 April 2010. On the left is a South West Trains Class 444 'Desiro' set, while on the right three Southern-operated Bombardier Class 377 'Electrostar' sets can be seen.* **CJM**

Data Tables

Rail Data Tables

Operational Pool Codes

ADFL	Advenza Freight - Freight locos
ATLO	West Coast Traincare - Locomotives
ATTB	West Coast Traincare - Class 57/3 with Dellner
ATZZ	West Coast Traincare - Locos for disposal
CDJD	Serco Railtest - Shunting locos
COLO	Colas Rail - Operational locomotives
CREL	Cotswold Rail - Locomotives
DFFT	Freightliner - Restricted duties
DFGC	Freightliner Class 86/5 trials locomotive
DFGH	Freightliner - Heavy Haul Class 70
DFGI	Freightliner - Intermodal Class 70
DFGM	Freightliner - Intermodal Class 66/5
DFHG	Freightliner - Heavy Haul Class 66/5 & 66/6
DFHH	Freightliner - Heavy Haul Class 66/5 & 66/6
DFIM	Freightliner - Intermodal Class 66/5
DFIN	Freightliner - Intermodal - low emission
DFLC	Freightliner - Class 90
DFLS	Freightliner - Class 08
DFNC	Freightliner - Class 86/6
DFRT	Freightliner - Class 66 Infrastructure contracts
DFTZ	Freightliner - Stored Class 66
DHLT	Freightliner - Awaiting repairs
EFOO	First Great Western - Class 57
EFPC	First Great Western - HST power cars
EFSH	First Great Western - Class 08
EHPC	CrossCountry Trains - HST power cars
EJLO	London Midland - Class 08
EMPC	East Midlands Trains - HST power cars
EMSL	East Midlands Trains - Class 08
EPXX	Europhoenix Class 86
GBCM	Europort/GBRf - Class 66 commercial contracts
GBED	Europort/GBRf- Class 73
GBET	Europort/GBRf - Class 92
GBMU	Europort/GBRf - Class 66 modified for MU
GBRT	Europort/GBRf - Class 66 Infrastructure
GBSD	Europort/GBRf - Class 66 RETB
GBZZ	Europort/GBRf - Stored locomotives
GCHP	Grand Central - HST power cars
GPSS	Eurostar UK - Class 08
HNRL	Harry Needle Railroad - Class 08, 20 hire locos
HNRS	Harry Needle Railroad - Stored locomotives
HTCX	Hanson Traction - Class 56
HYWD	South West Trains - Class 73
IANA	National Express East Anglia - Class 90
IECA	National Express East Coast - Class 91
IECP	National Express East Coast - HST power cars
INDL	Industrial (unofficial code)
IVGA	Gatwick Express - Class 73/2
IWCA	Virgin West Coast - Class 57/3
MBDL	Private operators - Diesel traction
MBED	Private operators - Class 73
MRSO	Mainline Rail - Class 08
PTXX	Eurotunnel - Europort2 Class 92
QACL	Network Rail - Class 86 load banks
QADD	Network Rail - Class 31
QCAR	Network Rail - HST power cars
QETS	Network Rail - Class 97/3
QSTR	Network Rail - stored locos
RCZH	Railcare Springburn - Class 08
RCZN	Railcare Wolverton - Class 08
RFSH	Wabtec Rail Doncaster - Class 08
RVLO	Rail Vehicle Engineering Derby - Locos
RVLS	Rail Vehicle Engineering Derby - Stored locos
SIEM	Siemens Transportation - Barriers
TTLS	Traditional Traction - Locomotives
WAAN	DB Schenker - Class 67
WABN	DB Schenker - Class 67 RETB fitted
WAFN	DB Schenker - Class 67 hire to FGW
WAWN	Wrexham & Shropshire Railway - Class 67
WBAI	DB Schenker - Class 66 Industrial
WBAK	DB Schenker - Class 66 Construction
WBAM	DB Schenker - Class 66 Energy
WBAN	DB Schenker - Class 66 Network
WBBI	DB Schenker - Class 66 Industrial RETB fitted
WBBM	DB Schenker - Class 66 Energy RETB fitted
WBBN	DB Schenker - Class 66 Network RETB fitted
WBEI	DB Schenker - Class 66 Euro in the UK
WBEN	DB Schenker - Class 66 Euro Cargo Rail
WBEP	DB Schenker - Class 66 Poland
WBES	DB Schenker - Class 66 ECR RHTT
WBLI	DB Schenker - Class 66 Industrial Auto coupler
WCAI	DB Schenker - Class 60 Industrial 990 gal fuel
WCAK	DB Schenker - Class 60 Construction 990 gal fuel
WCAM	DB Schenker - Class 60 Energy 990 gal fuel
WCBI	DB Schenker - Class 60 Industrial 1150 gal fuel
WCBK	DB Schenker - Class 60 Construct'n 1150 gal fuel
WDAI	DB Schenker - Class 59/2 Industrial
WDAK	DB Schenker - Class 59/2 Construction
WDAM	DB Schenker - Class 59/2 Liverpool Bulk
WEFE	DB Schenker - Class 90
WFMS	DB Schenker - Class 60 Fleet Management
WFMU	DB Schenker - Fleet Management
WKBN	DB Schenker - Class 37 Network RETB fitted
WLAN	DB Schenker - Euro Cargo Rail Class 21
WNTR	DB Schenker - Stored locos - reserve
WNTS	DB Schenker - Stored locos - serviceable
WNXX	DB Schenker - Stored locos - unserviceable
WNYX	DB Schenker - Stored locos - parts recovery
WNZX	DB Schenker - Awaiting Disposal
WRLN	DB Schenker - Class 08, 09 - North London
WSEN	DB Schenker - Euro Cargo Rail - Class 08
WSSA	DB Schenker - Class 08, 09 - Axiom Rail
WSSI	DB Schenker - Class 08, 09 Industrial
WSSM	DB Schenker - Class 08, 09 Energy
WSSK	DB Schenker - Class 08, 09 Network/Const'n
WSXX	DB Schenker - Class 08, 09 Stored
WTAE	DB Schenker - Class 92 Network
WZFF	DB Schenker - Class 58 France
WZFS	DB Schenker - Class 58 Spain
WZGF	DB Schenker - Class 56, 92 France
WZTS	DB Schenker - Class 08, 56, 58 Stored (hire pool)
XHAC	Direct Rail Services - Class 47
XHCK	Direct Rail Services - Class 57
XHHP	Direct Rail Services - Holding Pool
XHIM	Direct Rail Services - Class 66 - Intermodal
XHNC	Direct Rail Services - Nuclear Traffic
XHSS	Direct Rail Services - Stored
XYPA	Mendip Rail - Hanson Group
XYPO	Mendip Rail - Foster Yeoman (Aggregate Inds)

■ Pools are given only for locomotive groups which are included in this book. Pool codes for multiple units are not included.

Data Tables

Preserved site codes

ACL	AC Locomotive Group
ALY	Allelys, Studley
APF	Appleby-Frodingham RPS
AVR	Avon Valley Railway
BAT	Battlefield Line
BEL	5Bel Trust Barrow Hill
BHR	Barrow Hill Roundhouse
BIR	Barry Island Railway
BKR	Bo'ness & Kinneil Railway
BLU	Bluebell Railway
BRC	Buckinghamshire Railway Centre
BRM	Birmingham Railway Museum, Tyseley
BVR	Bridgend Valleys Railway
BWR	Bodmin & Wenford Railway
CAN	Canton (Pullman Rail)
CHS	Chasewater Railway
COL	Colne Valley Railway
COV	Coventry Electric Railway Museum
CPR	Chinnor & Princes Risborough Railway
CRB	Caledonian Railway, Brechin
CRT	Cambrian Railway Trust
CVR	Churnet Valley Railway
CWR	Cholsey & Wallingford Railway
DAR	Dartmoor Railway
DEE	Royal Deeside Railway
DER	Derwent Valley Railway
DFR	Dean Forest Railway
DID	Didcot Railway Centre
EAR	East Anglian Railway Museum
ECC	Ecclesbourne Valley Railway
EDR	Eden Valley Railway
EHC	Elsecar Heritage Centre
EHD	Eastleigh DBS Depot
EKR	East Kent Railway
ELR	East Lancashire Railway
EMB	Embsay Steam Railway
EPO	Epping - Ongar Railway
FHL	Fawley Hall (Private)
FIN	Finmere Station, Oxfordshire
GCN	Great Central Railway (North)
GCR	Great Central Railway
GKR	Graham Kirk Rail
GWI	Gwili Railway
GWR	Gloucestershire & Warwickshire Railway
HAD	Hastings Diesels
IOW	Isle of Wight Railway
KEI	Keith & Dufftown Railway
KES	Kent & East Sussex Railway
KIN	MoD Kineton
KWV	Keighley & Worth Valley Railway
LAN	Llangollen Railway
LDL	Lavender Line
LHG	L H Group Services, Burton
LHR	Lakeside & Haverthwaite Railway
LNW	London North Western, Crewe
LWR	Lincolnshire Wolds Railway
MET	Methill (Private)
MFM	Mangapps Farm Railway Museum
MHR	Mid Hants Railway

MID	Middleton Railway
MLM	Motorail - Long Marston
MNF	Mid Norfolk Railway
MOR	Moreton-on-Lugg
MRC	Middleton Railway Centre
MSM	Museum of Science & Industry, Manchester
NHD	Newton Heath Depot
NIR	Northamptonshire Ironstone Railway
NLR	Northampton & Lamport Railway
NNR	North Norfolk Railway
NRM	National Railway Museum, York
NRS	National Railway Museum, Shildon
NYM	North Yorkshire Moors Railway
PBR	Pontypool & Blaenavon Railway
PDR	Paignton & Dartmouth Railway
PRL	Peak Rail
PVR	Plym Valley Railway
RAC	Railway Age, Crewe
RAM	Rampart, Derby
RIB	Ribble Steam Railway
RIP	Rippingdale Station
ROW	Rowley Mill
RST	Rushden Station Transport Museum
SEL	St Leonards Railway Engineering
SHP	Summerlee Heritage Park
SLN	Stewarts Lane Depot
SNI	Snibston Railway
SPV	Spa Valley Railway
SRC	Stainmore Railway Co
STR	Strathspey Railway
SVR	Severn Valley Railway
SWI	Swindon & Cricklade Railway
SWN	Swanage Railway
TEB	Friends of 502 Group, Tebay
TEL	Telford Horsehay Steam Trust
TIT	Titley Junction
TSR	Telford Steam Railway
TYN	North Tyneside Railway
VOG	Vale of Glamorgan Railway
WCR	West Coast Railway Co
WED	Weardale Railway
WEN	Wensleydale Railway
WPH	Walthamstow Pump House
WSR	West Somerset Railway
XXX	Private unspecified site
YEO	Yeovil Railway Centre

Status	
OPR	Operational
OPR	Operational Main Line certified
RES	Under restoration
STC	Static exhibit
STO	Stored

Data Tables

Depot Codes

Code	Facility	Name	Operator
AB	SD	Aberdeen Guild Street	DBS
AC	CSD	Aberdeen Clayhills	ICE
AD	EMUD	Ashford Hitachi	HIT/SET
AF	T&RSMD	Ashford Chart Leacon	BOM
AH	MoD	Ashchurch	MoD
AK	DMUD	Ardwick	SIE/FTP
AL	DMUD	Aylesbury	CRW
AN	TMD/WRD	Allerton, Liverpool	DBS
AP	TMD	Ashford Rail Plant	BBR
AS	Store	Allelys	ALL
AT	TMD	Various sites	ALS
AW	SD	Washwood Heath	Hanson
AY	SD	Ayr	DBS
AZ	TMD	Ashford	BBR
BA	TMD	Crewe Basford Hall	FLR, DBS
BC	MoD	Bicester	MoD
BD	T&RSMD	Birkenhead North	MER
BF	EMUD	Bedford Cauldwell Walk	FCC
BG	SD	Hull Botanic Gardens	NOR
BH	Eng	Barrow Hill Roundhouse	BHE
BI	EMUD	Brighton	SOU
BK	T&RSMD	Barton Hill	DBS
BM	T&RSMD	Bournemouth	SWT
BN	T&RSMD	Bounds Green	ICE
BP	SD	Blackpool CS	NOR
BQ	TMD	Bury	ELR
BR	SD	Bristol Kingsland Road	NRL, FLR
BS	TMD	Bescot	DBS
BT	TMD	Bo'ness	BOK
BW	SD	Barrow-in-Furness	NOR
BZ	T&RSMD	St Blazey	DBS
CA	SD	Cambridge Coldhams Ln	AXI
CB	STORE	Crewe Brook Sidings	DBS
CC	T&RSMD	Clacton	NXA
CD	SD	Crewe Diesel	RIV, DBS
CE	IEMD	Crewe Electric	DBS
CF	DMUD	Cardiff Canton	PUL, ATW
CG	TMD	Crewe Gresty Bridge	DRS
CH	DMUD	Chester	ALS, ATW
CJ	SD	Clapham Junction	SWT
CK	DMUD	Corkerhill	FSR
CL	Store	Carlisle Upperby	DBS
CM	SD	Camden	LMI
CO	IEMD	Coquelles (France)	EUR
CP	CARMD	Crewe Carriage Shed	LNW
CQ	T&RSMD	Crewe Railway Age	CHC
CR	SD	Colchester	NXA
CS	T&RSMD	Carnforth	WCR
CT	SD	Cleethorpes	FTP
CW	MoD	Caerwent	MoD
CX	Store	Cardiff Tidal	DBS
CY	Store	Crewe Coal/South Yards	DRS
CZ	TMD	Central Rivers	BOM
DD	SD	Doncaster Wood Yard	DBS
DF	T&RSMD	Rail Vehicle Engineering	RVE
DI	Pres	Didcot Railway Centre	GWS
DM	TMD	Dollands Moor	DBS
DO	Store	Donnington Railfreight	-
DR	TMD	Doncaster Carr	DBS
DT	SD	Didcot Triangle	DBS
DV	SD	Dover	SET
DW	SD	Doncaster West Yard	NRL, WAB
DY	T&RSMD	Derby Etches Park	EMT
EA	SD	Earles Sidings	DBS
EC	T&RSMD	Craigentinny (Edinburgh)	ICE
ED	DMUD	Eastfield	FSR
EF	MPVD	Effingham Junction	AMS
EH	SD	Eastleigh	DBS
EM	EMUD	East Ham	c2c
EN	CARMD	Euston Downside	NRL
EU	SD	Euston Station Sidings	VWC
EZ	DMUD	Exeter	FGW
FB	Store	Ferrybridge	DBS
FC*		Fire College (Moreton-on-Lugg)	
FD	Mobile	Diesel loco	FLR
FE	Mobile	Electric loco	FLR
FF	TRSMD	Forest - Brussels	SNCB, NMBS, EUS
FH	TRACK	Frodingham	GRP
FN	Hire	France	ECR
FP	CSD	Ferme Park	ICE
FR	EMUD	Fratton	SWT
FS	Mobile	Diesel Shunter	FLR
FW	SD	Fort William	DBS
FX	TMD	Felixstowe	FDH
GI	EMUD	Gillingham	SET
GL	TMD	Gloucester	CWR, ADV
GP	SD	Grove Park	SET
GW	EMUD	Glasgow Shields	FSR
HA	TMD	Haymarket	FSR
HD	SD	Holyhead	ATW
HE	EMUD	Hornsey	FCC
HF	SD	Hereford	DBS
HG	Store	Hither Green	DBS
HI	TM	Hitchin	BBR
HJ	SD	Hoo Junction	DBS
HM	SD/WRD	Healey Mills	DBS
HT	T&RSMD	Heaton	NOR, GTL
HY	SD	Oxford Hinksey Yard	NRL
IL	T&RSMD	Ilford	NXA
IM	SD	Immingham	DBS
IP	SD	Ipswich	FLR
IS	TMD	Inverness	FSR
KC	Store	Carlisle Currock WRD	DBS
KD	SD	Kingmoor Yard	DRS
KK	EMUD	Kirkdale	MER
KM	TMD	Carlisle Kingmoor	DRS
KR	T&RSMD	Kidderminster	SVR
KT	MoD	Kineton	MoD
KY	SD/WRD	Knottingley	DBS
LA	T&RSMD	Laira	FGW
LB	Eng	Loughborough	BTL
LD	TMD	Leeds Midland Road	FLR
LE	T&RSMD	Landore	FGW
LG	T&RSMD	Longsight Electric	ALT
LH	Eng	LH Group	LHG
LL	CSD	Liverpool Edge Hill	ALS
LM	Store	Long Marston	MLS
LO	T&RSMD	Longsight Diesel	NOR
LP*	Eng	EMD Longport	EMD

LR	SD	Leicester	DBS
LT	MoD	Longtown	MoD
LU	MoD	Ludgershall	MoD
LY	T&RSMD	Le Landy - Paris	SNCF, EUS
MA	CARMD	Manchester International	ALS
MD	TMD	Merehead	MRL
MG	TMD	Margam	DBS
MH	SD	Millerhill	DBS
ML	SD	Motherwell	DBS
MM	Store	Moreton in Marsh	-
MN	DMUD	Machynlleth	ATW
MQ	Store	Meldon Quarry	BAR
MR	SD	March	GBR
MW	MoD	Marchwood Military Port	MoD
MY	SD/Store	Mossend Yard	DBS, FLR
NB	SD	New Brighton	MER
NC	T&RSMD	Norwich Crown Point	NXA
ND	Works	NedTrans, Tilburg	NDZ
NG	T&RSMD	New Cross Gate	LOL
NH	DMUD	Newton Heath	NOR
NL	T&RSMD	Neville Hill (Leeds)	EMT, ICE
NM	SD	Nottingham Eastcroft	EMT
NN	EMUD	Northampton, Kings Heath	SIE, LMI
NT	EMUD	Northam	SIE, SWT
NY	T&RSMD	Grosmont	NYM
OD	Eng	Old Dalby	ALS
OH	EMUD	Old Oak Common Electric	SIE
ON	SD	Orpington	SET
OO	HSTMD	Old Oak Common HST	FGW
OX	CSD	Oxford Carriage Sidings	FGW
OY	CARMD	Oxley	ALS
PB	SD	Peterborough	DBS
PC	TRSMD	Polmadie	ALS
PE	SD	Peterborough Nene	FCC
PF	SD	Peak Forest	DBS
PG	TRSMD	Peterborough	GBR
PH	SD	Perth	FSR
PM	TRSMD	St Philip's Marsh (Bristol)	FGW
PN	SD	Preston Station	NOR
PQ	SD	Harwich Parkeston Quay	DBS
PT	SD	Peterborough	GBR
PY	MoD	Shoeburyness (Pigs Bay)	MoD, KRS
PZ	TRSMD	Penzance (Long Rock)	FGW
RE	EMUD	Ramsgate	SET
RG	DMUD	Reading	FGW
RH	SD	Redhill	DBS
RL	TRSMD	Ropley	MHR
RO	SD	Rotherham Steel	DBS
RU	TMD	Rugby Rail Plant	GRP
RY	EMUD	Ryde	SWT
SA	DMUD	Salisbury	SWT
SB	TMD	Shrewsbury	NOR
SE	TRSMD	St Leonards	SLR
SG	EMUD	Slade Green	SET
SH	CARMD	Southall Railway Centre	WCR
SI	EMUD	Soho	LMI
SJ	TRSMD	Stourbridge Junction	LMI
SK	TRSMD	Swanwick	MRC
SL	TRSMD	Stewarts Lane	DBS, VSO, SOU
SM	SD	Sheffield Station	NOR
SN	SD	Shoeburyness	c2c
SO*		Southend	
SP	CRDC	Springs Branch	DBS
SQ	SD	Stockport	NOR
ST	SD	Southport	MER
SU	TRSMD	Selhurst	SOU
SX	SD	Shrewsbury	ATW
SZ	TMD	Southampton Maritime	FLR
TB	SD	Three Bridges	DBS
TE	TMD	Thornaby/Tees Yard	DBS
TF	SD	Orient Way	NXA
TG	SD	Tonbridge	GBR
TI	TRSMD	Temple Mills	EUS
TJ	TMD	Tavistock Junction	COL
TM	SD	Tyseley Loco Works	BRM
TN	SD	Taunton Fairwater	NRL, FLR
TO	TMD	Toton	DBS
TS	DMUD	Tyseley	LMI
TT	Store	Toton Training Compound	DBS
TY	Store	Tyne Yard	DBS
VI	SD	Victoria	SET
VR	SD	Aberystwyth	ATW
VZ	EMUD	Strawberry Hill	SIE, SWT
WA	SD	Warrington Arpley	DBS
WB	TRSMD	Wembley	ALS
WD	EMUD	East Wimbledon	SWT
WE	SD	Willesden Brent	DBS
WF	SD	Wansford	NVR
WH	Eng	Whatley	MRL
WH*	TMD	Washwood Heath	HAN
WK	SD	West Kirby	MER
WN	EMUD	Willesden	LOG
WO	TMD	Wolsingham	WER
WP	SD	Worksop	DBS
WS	SD	Worcester	LMI
WW	SD	West Worthing	SOU
WY	SD/CSD	Westbury Yard	DBS
WZ*	TRSMD	Washwood Heath	HAN
XW	TMD	Crofton	BOM
XX	-	Exported	-
YK	DMUD	Siemens York	SIE, FTP
YL	TMD	York Leeman Road	JAR, FLF
YM	Store	National Railway Museum	NRM
YN	SD	York North Yard	DBS
YO	SD	Yoker	FSR
ZA	Eng	RTC Derby	SER, NRL, AEA
ZB	Eng	Doncaster	WAB
ZC	Eng	Crewe	BOM
ZD	Eng	Derby Litchurch Lane	BOM
ZG	Eng	Eastleigh Works	KRS
ZH	Eng	Glasgow	RCL
ZI	Eng	Ilford	BOM
ZK	Eng	Kilmarnock	BTL
ZL	Eng	Cardiff Canton	PUL
ZN	Eng	Wolverton	RCL
ZS	Eng	Locotech Wakefield	BAR
ZW	Eng	Stoke-on-Trent (Marcroft)	AXI
3M*		3M Industries, Bracknell	

* Unofficial code

Data Tables

Operator Codes

ADV	Advenza Freight
ALL	Allelys Heavy Haul
ALS	Alstom
AMS	Amec Spie Rail
ATW	Arriva Trains Wales
AXC	Arriva Cross Country
AXI	Axiom Rail
BAR	British American Railway Services
BBR	Balfour Beatty
BHE	Barrow Hill Roundhouse
BOK	Bo'ness and Kinneil
BOM	Bombardier
BRM	Birmingham Railway Museum
BTL	Brush Traction Limited
C2C	C2C Rail
CAD	Cargo-D
CAR	Carillion
CHS	Crewe Heritage Centre
COL	Colas Rail
CON	Continental Rail (Spain)
COR	Corus Steel
CRW	Chiltern Railways
CWR	Cotswold Rail
DBS	DB Schenker West
DRS	Direct Rail Services
ECR	Euro Cargo Rail (DBS)
ELR	East Lancashire Railway
EMT	East Midlands Trains
ETF	ETF Freight (France)
ETL	Electric Traction Ltd
EU2	Eurotunnel Europort2
EUR	Eurotunnel
EUS	Eurostar
FCC	First Capital Connect
FDH	Felixstowe Dock & Harbour
FGW	First Great Western
FHT	First Hull Trains
FLF	Fastline Freight
FLR	Freightliner
FMR	FM Rail
FSL	Flying Scotsman Railway Ltd
FSR	First ScotRail
FTP	First TransPennine
GBR	GB Railfreight
GRP	Grant Rail Plant
GTL	Grand Central Railway
GWS	Great Western Society
HEC	Heathrow Connect
HEX	Heathrow Express
HIT	Hitachi

HNR	Harry Needle Railroad
ICE	Inter City East Coast
IND	Industrial operator
JAR	Jarvis
JHS	Jeremy Hoskins
KRS	Knights Rail Services
LAF	Lafarge Aggregates
LMI	London Midland
LNW	L&WR Railway Co
LOG	London Overground
LUL	London Underground Ltd
MER	Merseyrail
MHR	Mid Hants Railway
MoD	Ministry of Defence
MRC	Midland Railway Centre
MRL	Mendip Rail Ltd
MRS	Motorail Logistics
NDZ	NedTrains
NOR	Northern Rail
NRL	Network Rail
NRM	National Railway Museum
NVR	Nene Valley Railway
NXA	National Express East Anglia
NYM	North Yorkshire Moors Railway
OLD	Old Dalby Test Track
PUL	Pullman Group
RAF	Railfilms Ltd
RCL	Railcare Ltd
RIV	Riviera Trains
RRS	Ridings Railtours
RVE	Rail Vehicle Engineering
S4G	Stratford 47 Group
SET	Southeastern Trains
SIE	Siemens
SIL	Stagecoach Island Line
SLR	St Leonards Rail Engineering
SNB	Société Nationale des Chemins de fer Belges
SNF	Société Nationale des Chemins de fer Francais
SOU	Southern
SRP	Scottish Railway Preservation Society
SVR	Severn Valley Railway
SWT	South West Trains
TRN	Transfessa
TSO	Travaux du Sud Ouest (France)
TTS	Transmart Trains
VSO	Venice Simplon Orient Express
VTN	Vintage Trains
VWC	Virgin West Coast
WAB	Wabtec
WCR	West Coast Railway Co
WSR	Wrexham & Shropshire Railway
WTN	Wessex Trains

Owner Codes

AEA	AEA Rail Technology
ALS	Alstom
ANG	Angel Trains
ATW	Arriva Trains Wales
BAA	British Airports Authority
BCC	Bridgend County Council
BEA	Beacon Rail
BOM	Bombardier
BOT	Bank of Tokyo (Mitsubishi)
BTM	BTMU Capital Corporation
C20	Class 20 Locomotive Ltd
CAD	Cargo-D
CCC	Cardiff County Council
COL	Colas Rail
CRW	Chiltern Railways
CWR	Cotswold Rail
DBR	DB Regio
DBS	DB Schenker West
DRS	Direct Rail Services
ECR	Euro Cargo Rail (DBS)
ECT	ECT Main Line Rail
EMT	East Midlands Trains
ETL	Electric Traction Ltd
EU2	Eurotunnel Europort2
EUR	Eurotunnel
EUS	Eurostar
FGP	First Group
FLF	Fastline Freight
FLR	Freightliner
FOS	Foster Yeoman

GBR	GB Railfreight
GTL	Grand Central Railway Ltd
HAL	Halifax Assets Finance Ltd
HAN	Hanson Traction
HBS	Halifax-Bank of Scotland
HJA	Howard Johnson Associates
HNR	Harry Needle Railroad
HSB	HSBC Bank (Eversholt Leasing)
JAR	Jarvis
KRS	Knights Rail Services
LTS	Lloyds TSB Finance
NRL	Network Rail
NYM	North Yorkshire Moors Railway
PTR	Porterbrook
QWR	QW Rail Leasing
RCL	Railcare Limited
RIV	Riviera Trains
RML	Royal Mail
RMS	RMS Locotech
RTR	RT Rail
RVE	Rail Vehicle Engineering
S4G	Stratford Class 47 Group
SEC	Serco
SIE	Siemens
SNB	Societe National des Chemins de fer de Belges
SNF	Societe National des Chemins de fer Francais
SOU	Southern (Govia)
SWT	South West Trains (Stagecoach)
TTS	Transmart Trains
VTN	Vintage Trains
WAB	Wabtec
WCR	West Coast Railway Co
WYP	West Yorkshire PTE

Below: *One of the most successful of the modern EMU designs is the Siemens 'Desiro', now operated in different configurations by Heathrow Connect, National Express East Anglia, South West Trains, London Midland and First Scotrail. SWT Class 450 outer suburban set No. 450126 approaches Southampton on 3 August 2010 with a stopping service to London Waterloo.* **CJM**

Data Tables

Rail Data Tables

Station three-letter Codes

Station	Code	Station	Code	Station	Code	Station	Code
Abbey Wood	ABW	Appley Bridge	APB	Banstead	BAD	Bere Alston	BAS
Aber	ABE	Apsley	APS	Barassie	BSS	Bere Ferrers	BFE
Abercynon	ACY	Arbroath	ARB	Barbican	ZBB	Berkhamsted	BKM
Aberdare	ABA	Ardgay	ARD	Bardon Mill	BLL	Berkswell	BKW
Aberdeen	ABD	Ardlui	AUI	Bare Lane	BAR	Berney Arms	BYA
Aberdour	AUR	Ardrossan Harbour	ADS	Bargeddie	BGI	Berry Brow	BBW
Aberdovey	AVY	Ardrossan South Beach	ASB	Bargoed	BGD	Berrylands	BRS
Abererch	ABH	Ardrossan Town	ADN	Barking	BKG	Berwick	BRK
Abergavenny	AGV	Ardwick	ADK	Barking Underground	ZBK	Berwick-upon-Tweed	BWK
Abergele & Pensarn	AGL	Argyle Street	AGS	Barlaston	BRT	Bescar Lane	BES
Aberystwyth	AYW	Arisaig	ARG	Barming	BMG	Bescot Stadium	BSC
Accrington	ACR	Arlesey	ARL	Barmouth	BRM	Betchworth	BTO
Achanalt	AAT	Armathwaite	AWT	Barnehurst	BNH	Bethnal Green	BET
Achnasheen	ACN	Arnside	ARN	Barnes	BNS	Betws-y-Coed	BYC
Achnashellach	ACH	Arram	ARR	Barnes Bridge	BNI	Beverley	BEV
Acklington	ACK	Arrochar & Tarbet	ART	Barnetby	BTB	Bexhill	BEX
Acle	ACL	Arundel	ARU	Barnham	BAA	Bexley	BXY
Acocks Green	ACG	Ascot	ACT	Barnhill	BNL	Bexleyheath	BXH
Acton Bridge	ACB	Ascott-u-Wychwood	AUW	Barnsley	BNY	Bicester North	BCS
Acton Central	ACC	Ash	ASH	Barnstaple	BNP	Bicester Town	BIT
Acton Main Line	AML	Ash Vale	AHV	Barnt Green	BTG	Bickley	BKL
Adderley Park	ADD	Ashburys	ABY	Barrhead	BRR	Bidston	BID
Addiewell	ADW	Ashchurch	ASC	Barrhill	BRL	Biggleswade	BIW
Addlestone	ASN	Ashfield	ASF	Barrow Haven	BAV	Bilbrook	BBK
Adisham	ADM	Ashford International	AFK	Barrow Upon Soar	BWS	Billericay	BIC
Adlington (Cheshire)	ADC	Ashford (Eurostar)	ASI	Barrow-in-Furness	BIF	Billingham	BIL
Adlington (Lancs)	ADL	Ashford (Surrey)	AFS	Barry	BRY	Billingshurst	BIG
Adwick	AWK	Ashley	ASY	Barry Docks	BYD	Bingham	BIN
Aigburth	AIG	Ashtead	AHD	Barry Island	BYI	Bingley	BIY
Ainsdale	ANS	Ashton-under-Lyne	AHN	Barry Links	BYL	Birchgrove	BCG
Aintree	AIN	Ashurst	AHS	Barton-on-Humber	BAU	Birchington-on-Sea	BCH
Airbles	AIR	Ashurst New Forest	ANF	Basildon	BSO	Birchwood	BWD
Airdrie	ADR	Ashwell & Morden	AWM	Basingstoke	BSK	Birkbeck	BIK
Albany Park	AYP	Askam	ASK	Bat & Ball	BBL	Birkdale	BDL
Albrighton	ALB	Aslockton	ALK	Bath Spa	BTH	Birkenhead Central	BKC
Alderley Edge	ALD	Aspatria	ASP	Bathgate	BHG	Birkenhead North	BKN
Aldermaston	AMT	Aspley Guise	APG	Batley	BTL	Birkenhead Park	BKP
Aldershot	AHT	Aston	AST	Battersby	BTT	Birmingham Int	BHI
Aldrington	AGT	Atherstone	ATH	Battersea Park	BAK	Birmingham Moor St	BMO
Alexandra Palace	AAP	Atherton	ATN	Battle	BAT	Birmingham New St	BHM
Alexandra Parade	AXP	Attadale	ATT	Battlesbridge	BLB	Birmingham Snow Hill	BSW
Alexandria	ALX	Attenborough	ATB	Bayford	BAY	Bishop Auckland	BIA
Alfreton	ALF	Attleborough	ATL	Beaconsfield	BCF	Bishopbriggs	BBG
Allens West	ALW	Auchinleck	AUK	Bearley	BER	Bishops Stortford	BIS
Alloa	ALO	Audley End	AUD	Bearsden	BRN	Bishopstone	BIP
Alness	ASS	Aughton Park	AUG	Bearsted	BSD	Bishopton	BPT
Alnmouth	ALM	Aviemore	AVM	Beasdale	BSL	Bitterne	BTE
Alresford	ALR	Avoncliff	AVF	Beaulieu Road	BEU	Blackburn	BBN
Alsager	ASG	Avonmouth	AVN	Beauly	BEL	Blackheath	BKH
Althorne	ALN	Axminster	AXM	Bebington	BEB	Blackhorse Road	BHO
Althorpe	ALP	Aylesbury	AYS	Beccles	BCC	Blackpool North	BPN
Altnabreac	ABC	Aylesbury Parkway	AVP	Beckenham Hill	BEC	Blackpool P Beach	BPB
Alton	AON	Aylesford	AYL	Beckenham Junction	BKJ	Blackpool South	BPS
Altrincham	ALT	Aylesham	AYH	Bedford	BDM	Blackrod	BLK
Alvechurch	ALV	Ayr	AYR	Bedford St Johns	BSJ	Blackwater	BAW
Ambergate	AMB	Bache	BAC	Bedhampton	BDH	Blaenau Ffestiniog	BFF
Amberley	AMY	Baglan	BAJ	Bedminster	BMT	Blair Atholl	BLA
Amersham	AMR	Bagshot	BAG	Bedworth	BEH	Blairhill	BAI
Ammanford	AMF	Baildon	BLD	Bedwyn	BDW	Blake Street	BKT
Ancaster	ANC	Baillieston	BIO	Beeston	BEE	Blakedown	BKD
Anderston	AND	Balcombe	BAB	Bekesbourne	BKS	Blantyre	BLT
Andover	ADV	Baldock	BDK	Belle Vue	BLV	Blaydon	BLO
Anerley	ANZ	Balham	BAL	Bellgrove	BLG	Bleasby	BSB
Angel Road	AGR	Balloch	BHC	Bellingham	BGM	Bletchley	BLY
Angmering	ANG	Balmossie	BSI	Bellshill	BLH	Bloxwich	BLX
Annan	ANN	Bamber Bridge	BMB	Belmont	BLM	Bloxwich North	BWN
Anniesland	ANL	Bamford	BAM	Belper	BLP	Blundellsands & Crosby	BLN
Ansdell & Fairhaven	AFV	Banavie	BNV	Beltring	BEG	Blythe Bridge	BYB
Appleby	APP	Banbury	BAN	Belvedere	BVD	Bodmin Parkway	BOD
Appledore (Kent)	APD	Bangor (Gwynedd)	BNG	Bempton	BEM	Bodorgan	BOR
Appleford	APF	Bank Hall	BAH	Ben Rhydding	BEY	Bognor Regis	BOG
				Benfleet	BEF	Bogston	BGS
				Bentham	BEN	Bolton	BON
				Bentley	BTY	Bolton-on-Dearne	BTD
				Bentley (South Yorks)	BYK	Bookham	BKA

Data Tables

Station	Code	Station	Code	Station	Code	Station	Code
Bootle	BOC	Brough	BUH	Carlton	CTO	Chorleywood	CLW
Bootle New Strand	BNW	Broughty Ferry	BYF	Carluke	CLU	Christchurch	CHR
Bootle Oriel Road	BOT	Broxbourne	BXB	Carmarthen	CMN	Christs Hospital	CHH
Bordesley	BBS	Bruce Grove	BCV	Carmyle	CML	Church & Oswaldtwistle	CTW
Borough Green	BRG	Brundall	BDA	Carnforth	CNF	Church Fenton	CHF
Borth	BRH	Brundall Gardens	BGA	Carnoustie	CAN	Church Stretton	CTT
Bosham	BOH	Brunstane	BSU	Carntyne	CAY	Cilmeri	CIM
Boston	BSN	Brunswick	BRW	Carpenders Park	CPK	City Thameslink	CTK
Botley	BOE	Bruton	BRU	Carrbridge	CAG	Clacton on Sea	CLT
Bottesford	BTF	Bryn	BYN	Carshalton	CSH	Clandon	CLA
Bourne End	BNE	Buckenham	BUC	Carshalton Beeches	CSB	Clapham High Street	CLP
Bournemouth	BMH	Buckley	BCK	Carstairs	CRS	Clapham Junction	CLJ
Bournville	BRV	Bucknell	BUK	Cartsdyke	CDY	Clapham (Yorkshire)	CPY
Bow Brickhill	BWB	Bugle	BGL	Castle Bar Park	CBP	Clapton	CPT
Bowes Park	BOP	Builth Road	BHR	Castle Cary	CLC	Clarbeston Road	CLR
Bowling	BWG	Bulwell	BLW	Castleford	CFD	Clarkston	CKS
Boxhill & Westhumble	BXW	Bures	BUE	Castleton	CAS	Claverdon	CLV
Bracknell	BCE	Burgess Hill	BUG	Castleton Moor	CSM	Claygate	CLG
Bradford Forster Sq	BDQ	Burley Park	BUY	Caterham	CAT	Cleethorpes	CLE
Bradford Interchange	BDI	Burley-in-Wharfedale	BUW	Catford	CTF	Cleland	CEA
Bradford-on-Avon	BOA	Burnage	BNA	Catford Bridge	CFB	Clifton	CLI
Brading	BDN	Burneside	BUD	Cathays	CYS	Clifton Down	CFN
Braintree	BTR	Burnham	BNM	Cathcart	CCT	Clitheroe	CLH
Braintree Freeport	BTP	Burnham-on-Crouch	BUU	Cattal	CTL	Clock House	CLK
Bramhall	BML	Burnley Barracks	BUB	Causeland	CAU	Clunderwen	CUW
Bramley	BLE	Burnley Central	BNC	Cefn-y-Bedd	CYB	Clydebank	CYK
Bramley (Hants)	BMY	Burnley Manchester Rd	BYM	Chadwell Heath	CTH	Coatbridge Central	CBC
Brampton (Cumbria)	BMP	Burnside	BUI	Chafford Hundred	CFH	Coatbridge Sunnyside	CBS
Brampton (Suffolk)	BRP	Burntisland	BTS	Chalfont & Latimer	CFO	Coatdyke	COA
Branchton	BCN	Burscough Bridge	BCB	Chalkwell	CHW	Cobham & Stoke d'An	CSD
Brandon	BND	Burscough Junction	BCJ	Chandlers Ford	CFR	Codsall	CSL
Branksome	BSM	Bursledon	BUO	Chapel-en-le-Frith	CEF	Cogan	CGN
Braystones	BYS	Burton Joyce	BUJ	Chapelton	CPN	Colchester	COL
Bredbury	BDY	Burton-on-Trent	BUT	Chapeltown	CLN	Colchester Town	CET
Breich	BRC	Bury St Edmunds	BSE	Chappel & Wakes Colne	CWC	Coleshill Parkway	CEH
Brentford	BFD	Busby	BUS	Charing	CHG	Collingham	CLM
Brentwood	BRE	Bush Hill Park	BHK	Charing Cross (FSR)	CHC	Collington	CLL
Bricket Wood	BWO	Bushey	BSH	Charlbury	CBY	Colne	CNE
Bridge of Allan	BEA	Butlers Lane	BUL	Charlton	CTN	Colwall	CWL
Bridge of Orchy	BRO	Buxted	BXD	Chartham	CRT	Colwyn Bay	CWB
Bridgend	BGN	Buxton	BUX	Chassen Road	CSR	Combe	CME
Bridgeton	BDG	Byfleet & New Haw	BFN	Chatelherault	CTE	Commondale	COM
Bridgwater	BWT	Bynea	BYE	Chatham	CTM	Congleton	CNG
Bridlington	BDT	Cadoxton	CAD	Chathill	CHT	Conisbrough	CNS
Brierfield	BRF	Caergwrle	CGW	Cheadle Hulme	CHU	Connel Ferry	CON
Brigg	BGG	Caerphilly	CPH	Cheam	CHE	Cononley	CEY
Brighouse	BGH	Caersws	CWS	Cheddington	CED	Conway Park	CNP
Brighton	BTN	Caldicot	CDT	Chelford	CEL	Conwy	CNW
Brimsdown	BMD	Caledonian Rd & Bby	CIR	Chelmsford	CHM	Cooden Beach	COB
Brinnington	BNT	Calstock	CSK	Chelsfield	CLD	Cookham	COO
Bristol Parkway	BPW	Cam & Dursley	CDU	Cheltenham Spa	CNM	Cooksbridge	CBR
Bristol Temple Meads	BRI	Camberley	CAM	Chepstow	CPW	Coombe Halt	COE
Brithdir	BHD	Camborne	CBN	Cherry Tree	CYT	Copplestone	COP
British Steel Redcar	RBS	Cambridge	CBG	Chertsey	CHY	Corbridge	CRB
Briton Ferry	BNF	Cambridge Heath	CBH	Cheshunt	CHN	Corby	COR
Brixton	BRX	Cambuslang	CBL	Chessington North	CSN	Corkerhill	CKH
Broad Green	BGE	Camden Road	CMD	Chessington South	CSS	Corkickle	CKL
Broadbottom	BDB	Camelon	CMO	Chester	CTR	Corpach	CPA
Broadstairs	BSR	Canley	CNL	Chester Road	CRD	Corrour	CRR
Brockenhurst	BCU	Cannock	CAO	Chesterfield	CHD	Coryton	COY
Brockholes	BHS	Canonbury	CNN	Chester-le-Street	CLS	Coseley	CSY
Brockley	BCY	Canterbury East	CBE	Chestfield & Swalecliffe	CSW	Cosford	COS
Bromborough	BOM	Canterbury West	CBW	Chetnole	CNO	Cosham	CSA
Bromborough Rake	BMR	Cantley	CNY	Chichester	CCH	Cottingham	CGM
Bromley Cross	BMC	Capenhurst	CPU	Chilham	CIL	Cottingley	COT
Bromley North	BMN	Carbis Bay	CBB	Chilworth	CHL	Coulsdon South	CDS
Bromley South	BMS	Cardenden	CDD	Chingford	CHI	Coventry	COV
Bromsgrove	BMV	Cardiff Bay	CDB	Chinley	CLY	Cowden	CWN
Brondesbury	BSY	Cardiff Central	CDF	Chippenham	CPM	Cowdenbeath	COW
Brondesbury Park	BSP	Cardiff Queen Street	CDQ	Chipstead	CHP	Cradley Heath	CRA
Brookmans Park	BPK	Cardonald	CDO	Chirk	CRK	Craigendoran	CGD
Brookwood	BKO	Cardross	CDR	Chislehurst	CIT	Cramlington	CRM
Broome	BME	Carfin	CRF	Chiswick	CHK	Craven Arms	CRV
Broomfleet	BMF	Cark	CAK	Cholsey	CHO	Crawley	CRW
Brora	BRA	Carlisle	CAR	Chorley	CRL	Crayford	CRY

Data Tables

Station	Code	Station	Code	Station	Code	Station	Code
Crediton	CDI	Dent	DNT	Dyce	DYC	Exmouth	EXM
Cressing	CES	Denton	DTN	Dyffryn Ardudwy	DYF	Exton	EXN
Cressington	CSG	Deptford	DEP	Eaglescliffe	EAG	Eynsford	EYN
Creswell	CWD	Derby	DBY	Ealing Broadway	EAL	Failsworth	FLS
Crewe	CRE	Derby Road	DBR	Earlestown	ERL	Fairbourne	FRB
Crewkerne	CKN	Derker	DKR	Earley	EAR	Fairfield	FRF
Crews Hill	CWH	Devonport	DPT	Earlsfield	EAD	Fairlie	FRL
Crianlarich	CNR	Dewsbury	DEW	Earlswood (Surrey)	ELD	Fairwater	FRW
Criccieth	CCC	Didcot Parkway	DID	Earlswood (Midlands)	EWD	Falconwood	FCN
Cricklewood	CRI	Digby & Sowton	DIG	East Croydon	ECR	Falkirk Grahamston	FKG
Croftfoot	CFF	Dilton Marsh	DMH	East Didsbury	EDY	Falkirk High	FKK
Crofton Park	CFT	Dinas Powys	DNS	East Dulwich	EDW	Falls of Cruachan	FOC
Cromer	CMR	Dinas Rhondda	DMG	East Farleigh	EFL	Falmer	FMR
Cromford	CMF	Dingle Road	DGL	East Garforth	EGF	Falmouth Docks	FAL
Crookston	CKT	Dingwall	DIN	East Grinstead	EGR	Falmouth Town	FMT
Cross Gates	CRG	Dinsdale	DND	East Kilbride	EKL	Fareham	FRM
Crossflatts	CFL	Dinting	DTG	East Malling	EML	Farnborough (Main)	FNB
Crosshill	COI	Disley	DSL	East Midlands Parkway	EMD	Farnborough North	FNN
Crosskeys	CKY	Diss	DIS	East Tilbury	ETL	Farncombe	FNC
Crossmyloof	CMY	Dockyard	DOC	East Worthing	EWR	Farnham	FNH
Croston	CSO	Dodworth	DOD	Eastbourne	EBN	Farningham Road	FNR
Crouch Hill	CRH	Dolau	DOL	Eastbrook	EBK	Farnworth	FNW
Crowborough	COH	Doleham	DLH	Easterhouse	EST	Farringdon	ZFD
Crowhurst	CWU	Dolgarrog	DLG	Eastham Rake	ERA	Fauldhouse	FLD
Crowle	CWE	Dolwyddelan	DWD	Eastleigh	ESL	Faversham	FAV
Crowthorne	CRN	Doncaster	DON	Eastrington	EGN	Faygate	FGT
Croy	CRO	Dorchester South	DCH	Ebbw Vale Parkway	EBV	Fazakerley	FAZ
Crystal Palace	CYP	Dorchester West	DCW	Eccles	ECC	Fearn	FRN
Cuddington	CUD	Dore	DOR	Eccles Road	ECS	Featherstone	FEA
Cuffley	CUF	Dorking	DKG	Eccleston Park	ECL	Felixstowe	FLX
Culham	CUM	Dorking Deepdene	DPD	Edale	EDL	Feltham	FEL
Culrain	CUA	Dorking West	DKT	Eden Park	EDN	Feniton	FNT
Cumbernauld	CUB	Dormans	DMS	Edenbridge	EBR	Fenny Stratford	FEN
Cupar	CUP	Dorridge	DDG	Edenbridge Town	EBT	Fernhill	FER
Curriehill	CUH	Dove Holes	DVH	Edge Hill	EDG	Ferriby	FRY
Cuxton	CUX	Dover Priory	DVP	Edinburgh Park	EDP	Ferryside	FYS
Cwmbach	CMH	Dovercourt	DVC	Edinburgh Waverley	EDB	Ffairfach	FFA
Cwmbran	CWM	Dovey Junction	DVY	Edmonton Green	EDR	Filey	FIL
Cynghordy	CYN	Downham Market	DOW	Effingham Junction	EFF	Filton Abbey Wood	FIT
Dagenham Dock	DDK	Drayton Green	DRG	Eggesford	EGG	Finchley Rd & Frognal	FNY
Daisy Hill	DSY	Drayton Park	DYP	Egham	EGH	Finsbury Park	FPK
Dalgety Bay	DAG	Drem	DRM	Egton	EGT	Finstock	FIN
Dalmally	DAL	Driffield	DRF	Elephant & Castle	EPH	Fishbourne (Sussex)	FSB
Dalmarnock	DAK	Drigg	DRI	Elgin	ELG	Fishersgate	FSG
Dalmeny	DAM	Droitwich Spa	DTW	Ellesmere Port	ELP	Fishguard Harbour	FGH
Dalmuir	DMR	Dronfield	DRO	Elmers End	ELE	Fiskerton	FSK
Dalreoch	DLR	Drumchapel	DMC	Elmstead Woods	ESD	Fitzwilliam	FZW
Dalry	DLY	Drumfrochar	DFR	Elmswell	ESW	Five Ways	FWY
Dalston	DLS	Drumgelloch	DRU	Elsecar	ELR	Fleet	FLE
Dalston Kingsland	DLK	Drumry	DMY	Elsenham	ESM	Flimby	FLM
Dalton	DLT	Dublin Ferryport	DFP	Elstree & Borehamwood	ELS	Flint	FLN
Dalwhinnie	DLW	Dublin Port - Stena	DPS	Eltham	ELW	Flitwick	FLT
Danby	DNY	Duddeston	DUD	Elton & Orston	ELO	Flixton	FLI
Danescourt	DCT	Dudley Port	DDP	Ely	ELY	Flowery Field	FLF
Danzey	DZY	Duffield	DFI	Emerson Park	EMP	Folkestone Central	FKC
Darlington	DAR	Duirinish	DRN	Emsworth	EMS	Folkestone West	FKW
Darnall	DAN	Duke Street	DST	Enfield Chase	ENC	Ford	FOD
Darsham	DSM	Dullingham	DUL	Enfield Lock	ENL	Forest Gate	FOG
Dartford	DFD	Dumbarton Central	DBC	Enfield Town	ENF	Forest Hill	FOH
Darton	DRT	Dumbarton East	DBE	Entwistle	ENT	Formby	FBY
Darwen	DWN	Dumbreck	DUM	Epsom	EPS	Forres	FOR
Datchet	DAT	Dumfries	DMF	Epsom Downs	EPD	Forsinard	FRS
Davenport	DVN	Dumpton Park	DMP	Erdington	ERD	Fort Matilda	FTM
Dawlish	DWL	Dunbar	DUN	Eridge	ERI	Fort William	FTW
Dawlish Warren	DWW	Dunblane	DBL	Erith	ERH	Four Oaks	FOK
Deal	DEA	Duncraig	DCG	Esher	ESH	Foxfield	FOX
Dean	DEN	Dundee	DEE	Essex Road	EXR	Foxton	FXN
Dean Lane	DNN	Dunfermline Q'n Margaret	DFL	Etchingham	ETC	Frant	FRT
Deansgate	DGT	Dunfermline Town	DFE	Euxton Balshaw Lane	EBA	Fratton	FTN
Deganwy	DGY	Dunkeld & Birnam	DKD	Evesham	EVE	Freshfield	FRE
Deighton	DHN	Dunlop	DNL	Ewell East	EWE	Freshford	FFD
Delamere	DLM	Dunrobin Castle	DNO	Ewell West	EWW	Frimley	FML
Denby Dale	DBD	Dunston	DOT	Exeter Central	EXC	Frinton on Sea	FRI
Denham	DNM	Dunton Green	DNG	Exeter St Davids	EXD	Frizinghall	FZH
Denham Golf Club	DGC	Durham	DHM	Exeter St Thomas	EXT	Frodsham	FRD
Denmark Hill	DMK	Durrington-on-Sea	DUR	Exhibition Centre	EXG	Frome	FRO

Data Tables

Station	Code	Station	Code	Station	Code	Station	Code
Fulwell	FLW	Great Malvern	GMV	Harringay Green Lanes	HRY	High St (Glasgow)	HST
Furness Vale	FNV	Great Missenden	GMN	Harrington	HRR	High Street Kensington	ZHS
Furze Platt	FZP	Great Yarmouth	GYM	Harrogate	HGT	High Wycombe	HWY
Gainsborough Central	GNB	Green Lane	GNL	Harrow & Wealdstone	HRW	Higham	HGM
Gainsborough Lea Rd	GBL	Green Road	GNR	Harrow-on-the-Hill	HOH	Highams Park	HIP
Garelochhead	GCH	Greenbank	GBK	Hartford	HTF	Highbridge & Burnham	HIG
Garforth	GRF	Greenfaulds	GRL	Hartlebury	HBY	Highbury & Islington	HHY
Gargrave	GGV	Greenfield	GNF	Hartlepool	HPL	Hightown	HTO
Garrowhill	GAR	Greenford	GFD	Hartwood	HTW	Hildenborough	HLB
Garscadden	GRS	Greenhithe for Bluewater	GNH	Harwich International	HPQ	Hillfoot	HLF
Garsdale	GSD	Greenock Central	GKC	Harwich Town	HWC	Hillington East	HLE
Garston (Hertfordshire)	GSN	Greenock West	GKW	Haslemere	HSL	Hillington West	HLW
Garswood	GSW	Greenwich	GNW	Hassocks	HSK	Hillside	HIL
Gartcosh	GRH	Gretna Green	GEA	Hastings	HGS	Hilsea	HLS
Garth (Bridgend)	GMG	Grimsby Docks	GMD	Hatch End	HTE	Hinchley Wood	HYW
Garth (Powys)	GTH	Grimsby Town	GMB	Hatfield	HAT	Hinckley	HNK
Garve	GVE	Grindleford	GRN	Hatfield & Stainforth	HFS	Hindley	HIN
Gathurst	GST	Grosmont	GMT	Hatfield Peverel	HAP	Hinton Admiral	HNA
Gatley	GTY	Grove Park	GRP	Hathersage	HSG	Hitchin	HIT
Gatwick Airport	GTW	Guide Bridge	GUI	Hatton	HTN	Hither Green	HGR
Georgemas Junction	GGJ	Guildford	GLD	Havant	HAV	Hockley	HOC
Gerrards Cross	GER	Guiseley	GSY	Havenhouse	HVN	Hollingbourne	HBN
Gidea Park	GDP	Gunnersbury	GUN	Haverfordwest	HVF	Hollinwood	HOD
Giffnock	GFN	Gunnislake	GSL	Hawarden	HWD	Holmes Chapel	HCH
Giggleswick	GIG	Gunton	GNT	Hawarden Bridge	HWB	Holmwood	HLM
Gilberdyke	GBD	Gwersyllt	GWE	Hawkhead	HKH	Holton Heath	HOL
Gilfach Fargoed	GFF	Gypsy Lane	GYP	Haydon Bridge	HDB	Holyhead	HHD
Gillingham (Dorset)	GIL	Habrough	HAB	Haydons Road	HYR	Holytown	HLY
Gillingham (Kent)	GLM	Hackbridge	HCB	Hayes & Harlington	HAY	Homerton	HMN
Gilshochill	GSC	Hackney Central	HKC	Hayes (Kent)	HYS	Honeybourne	HYB
Gipsy Hill	GIP	Hackney Downs	HAC	Hayle	HYL	Honiton	HON
Girvan	GIR	Hackney Wick	HKW	Haymarket	HYM	Honley	HOY
Glaisdale	GLS	Haddenham & T Parkway	HDM	Haywards Heath	HHE	Honor Oak Park	HPA
Glan Conwy	GCW	Haddiscoe	HAD	Hazel Grove	HAZ	Hook	HOK
Glasgow Central	GLC	Hadfield	HDF	Headcorn	HCN	Hooton	HOO
Glasgow Queen Street	GLQ	Hadley Wood	HDW	Headingley	HDY	Hope (Derbyshire)	HOP
Glasshoughton	GLH	Hag Fold	HGF	Headstone Lane	HDL	Hope (Flintshire)	HPE
Glazebrook	GLZ	Hagley	HAG	Heald Green	HDG	Hopton Heath	HPT
Gleneagles	GLE	Hairmyres	HMY	Healing	HLI	Horley	HOR
Glenfinnan	GLF	Hale	HAL	Heath High Level	HHL	Hornbeam Park	HBP
Glengarnock	GLG	Halesworth	HAS	Heath Low Level	HLL	Hornsey	HRN
Glenrothes with Thornton	GLT	Halewood	HED	Heathrow Airport T123	HXX	Horsforth	HRS
Glossop	GLO	Halifax	HFX	Heathrow Airport T4	HAF	Horsham	HRH
Gloucester	GCR	Hall Green	HLG	Heathrow Terminal 5	HWV	Horsley	HSY
Glynde	GLY	Hall I 'Th' Wood	HID	Heaton Chapel	HTC	Horton-in-Ribblesdale	HIR
Gobowen	GOB	Hall Road	HLR	Hebden Bridge	HBD	Horwich Parkway	HWI
Godalming	GOD	Halling	HAI	Heckington	HEC	Hoscar	HSC
Godley	GDL	Haltwhistle	HWH	Hedge End	HDE	Hough Green	HGN
Godstone	GDN	Ham Street	HMT	Hednesford	HNF	Hounslow	HOU
Goldthorpe	GOE	Hamble	HME	Heighington	HEI	Hove	HOV
Golf Street	GOF	Hamilton Central	HNC	Helensburgh Central	HLC	Hoveton & Wroxham	HXM
Golspie	GOL	Hamilton Square	BKQ	Helensburgh Upper	HLU	How Wood	HWW
Gomshall	GOM	Hamilton West	HNW	Hellifield	HLD	Howden	HOW
Goodmayes	GMY	Hammerton	HMM	Helmsdale	HMS	Howwood (Renfrew)	HOZ
Goole	GOO	Hampden Park	HMD	Helsby	HSB	Hoylake	HYK
Goostrey	GTR	Hampstead Heath	HDH	Hemel Hempstead	HML	Hubberts Bridge	HBB
Gordon Hill	GDH	Hampton	HMP	Hendon	HEN	Hucknall	HKN
Goring & Streatley	GOR	Hampton Court	HMC	Hengoed	HNG	Huddersfield	HUD
Goring-by-Sea	GBS	Hampton Wick	HMW	Henley-in-Arden	HNL	Hull Paragon	HUL
Gorton	GTO	Hampton-in-Arden	HIA	Henley-on-Thames	HOT	Humphrey Park	HUP
Gospel Oak	GPO	Hamstead	HSD	Hensall	HEL	Huncoat	HCT
Gourock	GRK	Hamworthy	HAM	Hereford	HFD	Hungerford	HGD
Gowerton	GWN	Hanborough	HND	Herne Bay	HNB	Hunmanby	HUB
Goxhill	GOX	Handforth	HTH	Herne Hill	HNH	Huntingdon	HUN
Grange Park	GPK	Hanwell	HAN	Hersham	HER	Huntly	HNT
Grange-Over-Sands	GOS	Hapton	HPN	Hertford East	HFE	Hunts Cross	HNX
Grangetown	GTN	Harlech	HRL	Hertford North	HFN	Hurst Green	HUR
Grantham	GRA	Harlesden	HDN	Hessle	HES	Hutton Cranswick	HUT
Grateley	GRT	Harling Road	HRD	Heswall	HSW	Huyton	HUY
Gravelly Hill	GVH	Harlington	HLN	Hever	HEV	Hyde Central	HYC
Gravesend	GRV	Harlow Mill	HWM	Heworth	HEW	Hyde North	HYT
Grays	GRY	Harlow Town	HWN	Hexham	HEX	Hykeham	HKM
Great Ayton	GTA	Harold Wood	HRO	Heyford	HYD	Hyndland	HYN
Great Bentley	GRB	Harpenden	HPD	Heysham Port	HHB	Hythe	HYH
Great Chesterford	GRC	Harrietsham	HRM	High Brooms	HIB	IBM	IBM
Great Coates	GCT	Harringay	HGY			Ifield	IFI

Data Tables

Station	Code	Station	Code	Station	Code	Station	Code
Ilford	IFD	Kingston	KNG	Leuchars (St Andrews)	LEU	London Fenchurch St	FST
Ilkley	ILK	Kingswood	KND	Levenshulme	LVM	London Fields	LOF
Imperial Wharf	IMW	Kingussie	KIN	Lewes	LWS	London King's Cross	KGX
Ince	INC	Kintbury	KIT	Lewisham	LEW	London Liverpool St	LST
Ince & Elton	INE	Kirby Cross	KBX	Leyland	LEY	London Marylebone	MYB
Ingatestone	INT	Kirk Sandall	KKS	Leyton Midland Road	LEM	London Paddington	PAD
Insch	INS	Kirkby	KIR	Leytonstone High Road	LER	London Road (Brighton)	LRB
Invergordon	IGD	Kirkby in Ashfield	KKB	Lichfield City	LIC	London Road (Guildford)	LRD
Invergowrie	ING	Kirkby Stephen	KSW	Lichfield Trent Valley	LTV	London St Pancras	STP
Inverkeithing	INK	Kirkby-in-Furness	KBF	Lidlington	LID	London Victoria	VIC
Inverkip	INP	Kirkcaldy	KDY	Limehouse	LHS	London Waterloo	WAT
Inverness	INV	Kirkconnel	KRK	Lincoln Central	LCN	London Waterloo East	WAE
Invershin	INH	Kirkdale	KKD	Lingfield	LFD	Long Buckby	LBK
Inverurie	INR	Kirkham & Wesham	KKM	Lingwood	LGD	Long Eaton	LGE
Ipswich	IPS	Kirkhill	KKH	Linlithgow	LIN	Long Preston	LPR
Irlam	IRL	Kirknewton	KKN	Liphook	LIP	Longbeck	LGK
Irvine	IRV	Kirkwood	KWD	Liskeard	LSK	Longbridge	LOB
Isleworth	ISL	Kirton Lindsey	KTL	Liss	LIS	Longcross	LNG
Islip	ISP	Kiveton Bridge	KIV	Lisvane & Thornhill	LVT	Longfield	LGF
Iver	IVR	Kiveton Park	KVP	Little Kimble	LTK	Longniddry	LND
Ivybridge	IVY	Knaresborough	KNA	Little Sutton	LTT	Longport	LPT
Jewellery Quarter	JEQ	Knebworth	KBW	Littleborough	LTL	Longton	LGN
Johnston	JOH	Knighton	KNI	Littlehampton	LIT	Looe	LOO
Johnstone	JHN	Knockholt	KCK	Littlehaven	LVN	Lostock	LOT
Jordanhill	JOR	Knottingley	KNO	Littleport	LTP	Lostock Gralam	LTG
Kearsley	KSL	Knucklas	KNU	Liverpool Central	LVC	Lostock Hall	LOH
Kearsney	KSN	Knutsford	KNF	Liverpool James Street	LVJ	Lostwithiel	LOS
Keighley	KEI	Kyle of Lochalsh	KYL	Liverpool Lime Street	LIV	Loughborough	LBO
Keith	KEH	Ladybank	LDY	Liverpool South Parkway	LPY	Loughborough Junction	LGJ
Kelvedon	KEL	Ladywell	LAD	Livingston North	LSN	Lowdham	LOW
Kelvindale	KVD	Laindon	LAI	Livingston South	LVG	Lower Sydenham	LSY
Kemble	KEM	Lairg	LRG	Llanaber	LLA	Lowestoft	LWT
Kempston Hardwick	KMH	Lake	LKE	Llanbedr	LBR	Ludlow	LUD
Kempton Park	KMP	Lakenheath	LAK	Llanbister Road	LLT	Luton	LUT
Kemsing	KMS	Lamphey	LAM	Llanbradach	LNB	Luton Airport Parkway	LTN
Kemsley	KML	Lanark	LNK	Llandaf	LLN	Luxulyan	LUX
Kendal	KEN	Lancaster	LAN	Llandanwg	LDN	Lydney	LYD
Kenley	KLY	Lancing	LAC	Llandecwyn	LLC	Lye	LYE
Kennett	KNE	Landywood	LAW	Llandeilo	LLL	Lymington Pier	LYP
Kennishead	KNS	Langbank	LGB	Llandovery	LLV	Lymington Town	LYT
Kensal Green	KNL	Langho	LHO	Llandrindod	LLO	Lympstone Commando	LYC
Kensal Rise	KNR	Langley	LNY	Llandudno	LLD	Lympstone Village	LYM
Kensington Olympia	KPA	Langley Green	LGG	Llandudno Junction	LLJ	Lytham	LTM
Kent House	KTH	Langley Mill	LGM	Llandybie	LLI	Macclesfield	MAC
Kentish Town	KTN	Langside	LGS	Llanelli	LLE	Machynlleth	MCN
Kentish Town West	KTW	Langwathby	LGW	Llanfairfechan	LLF	Maesteg	MST
Kenton	KNT	Langwith-Whaley Thorns	LAG	Llanfairpwll	LPG	Maesteg (Ewenny Rd)	MEW
Kents Bank	KBK	Lapford	LAP	Llangadog	LLG	Maghull	MAG
Kettering	KET	Lapworth	LPW	Llangammarch	LLM	Maiden Newton	MDN
Kew Bridge	KWB	Larbert	LBT	Llangennech	LLH	Maidenhead	MAI
Kew Gardens	KWG	Largs	LAR	Llangynllo	LGO	Maidstone Barracks	MDB
Keyham	KEY	Larkhall	LRH	Llanharan	LLR	Maidstone East	MDE
Keynsham	KYN	Lawrence Hill	LWH	Llanhilleth	LTH	Maidstone West	MDW
Kidbrooke	KDB	Layton	LAY	Llanishen	LLS	Malden Manor	MAL
Kidderminster	KID	Lazonby & Kirkoswald	LZB	Llanrwst	LWR	Mallaig	MLG
Kidsgrove	KDG	Lea Green	LEG	Llansamlet	LAS	Malton	MLT
Kidwelly	KWL	Lea Hall	LEH	Llantwit Major	LWM	Malvern Link	MVL
Kilburn High Road	KBN	Leagrave	LEA	Llanwrda	LNR	Manchester Airport	MIA
Kildale	KLD	Lealholm	LHM	Llanwrtyd	LNW	Manchester Oxford Rd	MCO
Kildonan	KIL	Leamington Spa	LMS	Llwyngwril	LLW	Manchester Piccadilly	MAN
Kilgetty	KGT	Leasowe	LSW	Llwynypia	LLY	Manchester United FC	MUF
Kilmarnock	KMK	Leatherhead	LHD	Loch Awe	LHA	Manchester Victoria	MCV
Kilmaurs	KLM	Ledbury	LED	Loch Eil Outward Bound	LHE	Manea	MNE
Kilpatrick	KPT	Lee	LEE	Lochailort	LCL	Manningtree	MNG
Kilwinning	KWN	Leeds	LDS	Locheilside	LCS	Manor Park	MNP
Kinbrace	KBC	Leicester	LEI	Lochgelly	LCG	Manor Road	MNR
Kingham	KGM	Leigh (Kent)	LIH	Lochluichart	LCC	Manorbier	MRB
Kinghorn	KGH	Leigh-on-Sea	LES	Lochwinnoch	LHW	Manors	MAS
Kings Langley	KGL	Leighton Buzzard	LBZ	Lockerbie	LOC	Mansfield	MFT
King's Lynn	KLN	Lelant	LEL	Lockwood	LCK	Mansfield Woodhouse	MSW
Kings Norton	KNN	Lelant Saltings	LTS	London Blackfriars	BFR	March	MCH
Kings Nympton	KGN	Lenham	LEN	London Bridge	LBG	Marden	MRN
Kings Park	KGP	Lenzie	LNZ	London Cannon Street	CST	Margate	MAR
Kings Sutton	KGS	Leominster	LEO	London Charing Cross	CHX	Market Harborough	MHR
Kingsknowe	KGE	Letchworth Garden City	LET	London Euston	EUS	Market Rasen	MKR

Markinch	MNC	Morfa Mawddach	MFA	Newton (Lanarks)	NTN	Pantyffynnon	PTF
Marks Tey	MKT	Morley	MLY	Newton St Cyres	NTC	Par	PAR
Marlow	MLW	Morpeth	MPT	Newton-le-Willows	NLW	Parbold	PBL
Marple	MPL	Mortimer	MOR	Newtonmore	NWR	Park Street	PKT
Marsden	MSN	Mortlake	MTL	Newton-on-Ayr	NOA	Parkstone (Dorset)	PKS
Marske	MSK	Moses Gate	MSS	Newtown (Powys)	NWT	Parson Street	PSN
Marston Green	MGN	Moss Side	MOS	Ninian Park	NNP	Partick	PTK
Martin Mill	MTM	Mossley	MSL	Nitshill	NIT	Parton	PRN
Martins Heron	MAO	Mossley Hill	MSH	Norbiton	NBT	Patchway	PWY
Marton	MTO	Mosspark	MPK	Norbury	NRB	Patricroft	PAT
Maryhill	MYH	Moston	MSO	Normans Bay	NSB	Patterton	PTT
Maryland	MYL	Motherwell	MTH	Normanton	NOR	Peartree	PEA
Maryport	MRY	Motspur Park	MOT	North Berwick	NBW	Peckham Rye	PMR
Matlock	MAT	Mottingham	MTG	North Camp	NCM	Pegswood	PEG
Matlock Bath	MTB	Mottisfont & Dunbridge	DBG	North Dulwich	NDL	Pemberton	PEM
Mauldeth Road	MAU	Mouldsworth	MLD	North Fambridge	NFA	Pembrey & Burry Port	PBY
Maxwell Park	MAX	Moulsecoomb	MCB	North Llanrwst	NLR	Pembroke	PMB
Maybole	MAY	Mount Florida	MFL	North Queensferry	NQU	Pembroke Dock	PMD
Maze Hill	MZH	Mount Vernon	MTV	North Road	NRD	Penally	PNA
Meadowhall	MHS	Mountain Ash	MTA	North Sheen	NSH	Penarth	PEN
Meldreth	MEL	Muir of Ord	MOO	North Walsham	NWA	Pencoed	PCD
Melksham	MKM	Muirend	MUI	North Wembley	NWB	Pengam	PGM
Melton	MES	Musselburgh	MUB	Northallerton	NTR	Penge East	PNE
Melton Mowbray	MMO	Mytholmroyd	MYT	Northampton	NMP	Penge West	PNW
Menheniot	MEN	Nafferton	NFN	Northfield	NFD	Penhelig	PHG
Menston	MNN	Nailsea & Backwell	NLS	Northfleet	NFL	Penistone	PNS
Meols	MEO	Nairn	NRN	Northolt Park	NLT	Penkridge	PKG
Meols Cop	MEC	Nantwich	NAN	Northumberland Park	NUM	Penmaenmawr	PMW
Meopham	MEP	Narberth	NAR	Northwich	NWI	Penmere	PNM
Merrytown	MEY	Narborough	NBR	Norton Bridge	NTB	Penrhiwceiber	PER
Merstham	MHM	Navigation Road	NVR	Norwich	NRW	Penrhyndeudraeth	PRH
Merthyr Tydfil	MER	Neath	NTH	Norwood Junction	NWD	Penrith	PNR
Merthyr Vale	MEV	Needham Market	NMT	Nottingham	NOT	Penryn	PYN
Metheringham	MGM	Neilston	NEI	Nuneaton	NUN	Pensarn (Gwynedd)	PES
MetroCentre	MCE	Nelson	NEL	Nunhead	NHD	Penshurst	PHR
Mexborough	MEX	Neston	NES	Nunthorpe	NNT	Pentre-Bach	PTB
Micheldever	MIC	Netherfield	NET	Nutbourne	NUT	Pen-y-Bont	PNY
Micklefield	MIK	Nethertown	NRT	Nutfield	NUF	Penychain	BPC
Middlesbrough	MBR	Netley	NTL	Oakengates	OKN	Penyffordd	PNF
Middlewood	MDL	New Barnet	NBA	Oakham	OKM	Penzance	PNZ
Midgham	MDG	New Beckenham	NBC	Oakleigh Park	OKL	Perranwell	PRW
Milford Haven	MFH	New Brighton	NBN	Oban	OBN	Perry Barr	PRY
Milford (Surrey)	MLF	New Clee	NCE	Ockendon	OCK	Pershore	PSH
Mill Hill Broadway	MIL	New Cross	NWX	Ockley	OLY	Perth	PTH
Mill Hill (Lancashire)	MLH	New Cross Gate	NXG	Old Hill	OHL	Peterborough	PBO
Millbrook (Bedfordshire)	MLB	New Cumnock	NCK	Old Roan	ORN	Petersfield	PTR
Millbrook (Hants)	MBK	New Eltham	NEH	Old Street	OLD	Petts Wood	PET
Milliken Park	MIN	New Hey	NHY	Oldfield Park	OLF	Pevensey & Westham	PEV
Millom	MLM	New Holland	NHL	Oldham Mumps	OLM	Pevensey Bay	PEB
Mills Hill	MIH	New Hythe	NHE	Oldham Werneth	OLW	Pewsey	PEW
Milngavie	MLN	New Lane	NLN	Olton	OLT	Pilning	PIL
Milnrow	MLR	New Malden	NEM	Ore	ORE	Pinhoe	PIN
Milton Keynes Central	MKC	New Mills Central	NMC	Ormskirk	OMS	Pitlochry	PIT
Minffordd	MFF	New Mills Newtown	NMN	Orpington	ORP	Pitsea	PSE
Minster	MSR	New Milton	NWM	Orrell	ORR	Pleasington	PLS
Mirfield	MIR	New Pudsey	NPD	Orrell Park	OPK	Plockton	PLK
Mistley	MIS	New Southgate	NSG	Otford	OTF	Pluckley	PLC
Mitcham Eastfields	MTC	Newark Castle	NCT	Oulton Broad North	OUN	Plumley	PLM
Mitcham Junction	MIJ	Newark North Gate	NNG	Oulton Broad South	OUS	Plumpton	PMP
Mobberley	MOB	Newbridge	NBE	Outwood	OUT	Plumstead	PLU
Monifieth	MON	Newbury	NBY	Overpool	OVE	Plymouth	PLY
Monks Risborough	MRS	Newbury Racecourse	NRC	Overton	OVR	Pokesdown	POK
Montpelier	MTP	Newcastle	NCL	Oxenholme Lake District	OXN	Polegate	PLG
Montrose	MTS	Newcraighall	NEW	Oxford	OXF	Polesworth	PSW
Moorfields	MRF	Newhaven Harbour	NVH	Oxshott	OXS	Pollokshaws East	PWE
Moorgate	ZMG	Newhaven Town	NVN	Oxted	OXT	Pollokshaws West	PWW
Moorside	MSD	Newington	NGT	Paddock Wood	PDW	Pollokshields East	PLE
Moorthorpe	MRP	Newmarket	NMK	Padgate	PDG	Pollokshields West	PLW
Morar	MRR	Newport (Essex)	NWE	Paignton	PGN	Polmont	PMT
Morchard Road	MRD	Newport (S. Wales)	NWP	Paisley Canal	PCN	Polsloe Bridge	POL
Morden South	MDS	Newquay	NQY	Paisley Gilmour Street	PYG	Ponders End	PON
Morecambe	MCM	Newstead	NSD	Paisley St James	PYJ	Pontarddulais	PTD
Moreton (Dorset)	MTN	Newton Abbot	NTA	Palmers Green	PAL	Pontefract Baghill	PFR
Moreton (Merseyside)	MRT	Newton Aycliffe	NAY	Pangbourne	PAN	Pontefract Monkhill	PFM
Moreton-in-Marsh	MIM	Newton for Hyde	NWN	Pannal	PNL	Pontefract Tanshelf	POT

Station	Code	Station	Code	Station	Code	Station	Code
Pontlottyn	PLT	Redhill	RDH	Sanderstead	SNR	Shotts	SHS
Pontyclun	PYC	Redland	RDA	Sandhills	SDL	Shrewsbury	SHR
Pont-y-Pant	PYP	Redruth	RED	Sandhurst	SND	Sidcup	SID
Pontypool & New Inn	PPL	Reedham (Norfolk)	REE	Sandling	SDG	Sileby	SIL
Pontypridd	PPD	Reedham (Surrey)	RHM	Sandown	SAN	Silecroft	SIC
Poole	POO	Reigate	REI	Sandplace	SDP	Silkstone Common	SLK
Poppleton	POP	Renton	RTN	Sandwell & Dudley	SAD	Silver Street	SLV
Port Glasgow	PTG	Retford	RET	Sandwich	SDW	Silverdale	SVR
Port Sunlight	PSL	Rhiwbina	RHI	Sandy	SDY	Singer	SIN
Port Talbot Parkway	PTA	Rhoose Cardiff Int Airport	RIA	Sankey for Penketh	SNK	Sittingbourne	SIT
Portchester	PTC	Rhosneigr	RHO	Sanquhar	SQH	Skegness	SKG
Porth	POR	Rhyl	RHL	Sarn	SRR	Skewen	SKE
Porthmadog	PTM	Rhymney	RHY	Saundersfoot	SDF	Skipton	SKI
Portlethen	PLN	Ribblehead	RHD	Saunderton	SDR	Slade Green	SGR
Portslade	PLD	Rice Lane	RIL	Sawbridgeworth	SAW	Slaithwaite	SWT
Portsmouth & Southsea	PMS	Richmond	RMD	Saxilby	SXY	Slateford	SLA
Portsmouth Arms	PMA	Rickmansworth	RIC	Saxmundham	SAX	Sleaford	SLR
Portsmouth Harbour	PMH	Riddlesdown	RDD	Scarborough	SCA	Sleights	SLH
Possilpark & Parkhouse	PPK	Ridgmont	RID	Scotscalder	SCT	Slough	SLO
Potters Bar	PBR	Riding Mill	RDM	Scotstounhill	SCH	Small Heath	SMA
Poulton-le-Fylde	PFY	Risca & Pontymister	RCA	Scunthorpe	SCU	Smallbrook Junction	SAB
Poynton	PYT	Rishton	RIS	Sea Mills	SML	Smethwick Galton Bridge	SGB
Prees	PRS	Robertsbridge	RBR	Seaford	SEF	Smethwick Rolfe Street	SMR
Prescot	PSC	Roby	ROB	Seaforth & Litherland	SFL	Smitham	SMI
Prestatyn	PRT	Rochdale	RCD	Seaham	SEA	Smithy Bridge	SMB
Prestbury	PRB	Roche	ROC	Seamer	SEM	Snaith	SNI
Preston	PRE	Rochester	RTR	Seascale	SSC	Snodland	SDA
Preston Park	PRP	Rochford	RFD	Seaton Carew	SEC	Snowdown	SWO
Prestonpans	PST	Rock Ferry	RFY	Seer Green & Jordans	SRG	Sole Street	SOR
Prestwick International Airport	PRA	Rogart	ROG	Selby	SBY	Solihull	SOL
Prestwick Town	PTW	Rogerstone	ROR	Selhurst	SRS	Somerleyton	SYT
Priesthill & Darnley	PTL	Rolleston	ROL	Sellafield	SEL	South Acton	SAT
Princes Risborough	PRR	Roman Bridge	RMB	Selling	SEG	South Bank	SBK
Prittlewell	PRL	Romford	RMF	Selly Oak	SLY	South Bermondsey	SBM
Prudhoe	PRU	Romiley	RML	Settle	SET	South Croydon	SCY
Pulborough	PUL	Romsey	ROM	Seven Kings	SVK	South Elmsall	SES
Purfleet	PFL	Roose	ROO	Seven Sisters	SVS	South Greenford	SGN
Purley	PUR	Rose Grove	RSG	Sevenoaks	SEV	South Gyle	SGL
Purley Oaks	PUO	Rose Hill Marple	RSH	Severn Beach	SVB	South Hampstead	SOH
Putney	PUT	Rosyth	ROS	Severn Tunnel Junction	STJ	South Kenton	SOK
Pwllheli	PWL	Rotherham Central	RMC	Shalford	SFR	South Merton	SMO
Pyle	PYL	Roughton Road	RNR	Shanklin	SHN	South Milford	SOM
Quakers Yard	QYD	Rowlands Castle	RLN	Shaw & Crompton	SHA	South Ruislip	SRU
Queenborough	QBR	Rowley Regis	ROW	Shawford	SHW	South Tottenham	STO
Queens Park (Glasgow)	QPK	Roy Bridge	RYB	Shawlands	SHL	South Wigston	SWS
Queens Park (London)	QPW	Roydon	RYN	Sheerness-on-Sea	SSS	South Woodham Ferrers	SOF
Queens Road, Peckham	QRP	Royston	RYS	Sheffield	SHF	Southall	STL
Queenstown Road	QRB	Ruabon	RUA	Shelford	SED	Southampton Airport	SOA
Quintrell Downs	QUI	Rufford	RUF	Shenfield	SNF	Southampton Central	SOU
Radcliffe (Notts)	RDF	Rugby	RUG	Shenstone	SEN	Southbourne	SOB
Radlett	RDT	Rugeley Town	RGT	Shepherd's Bush	SPB	Southbury	SBU
Radley	RAD	Rugeley Trent Valley	RGL	Shepherds Well	SPH	Southease	SEE
Radyr	RDR	Runcorn	RUN	Shepley	SPY	Southend Central	SOC
Rainford	RNF	Runcorn East	RUE	Shepperton	SHP	Southend East	SOE
Rainham (Essex)	RNM	Ruskington	RKT	Shepreth	STH	Southend Victoria	SOV
Rainham (Kent)	RAI	Ruswarp	RUS	Sherborne	SHE	Southminster	SMN
Rainhill	RNH	Rutherglen	RUT	Sherburn-in-Elmet	SIE	Southport	SOP
Ramsgate	RAM	Ryde St Johns Road	RYR	Sheringham	SHM	Southwick	SWK
Ramsgreave & Wilpshire	RGW	Ryde Esplanade	RYD	Shettleston	SLS	Sowerby Bridge	SOW
Rannoch	RAN	Ryde Pier Head	RYP	Shieldmuir	SDM	Spalding	SPA
Rauceby	RAU	Ryder Brow	RRB	Shifnal	SFN	Spean Bridge	SBR
Ravenglass for Eskdale	RAV	Rye	RYE	Shildon	SHD	Spital	SPI
Ravensbourne	RVB	Rye House	RYH	Shiplake	SHI	Spondon	SPO
Ravensthorpe	RVN	Salford Central	SFD	Shipley	SHY	Spooner Row	SPN
Rawcliffe	RWC	Salford Crescent	SLD	Shippea Hill	SPP	Spring Road	SRI
Rayleigh	RLG	Salfords	SAF	Shipton	SIP	Springburn	SPR
Raynes Park	RAY	Salhouse	SAH	Shirebrook	SHB	Springfield	SPF
Reading	RDG	Salisbury	SAL	Shirehampton	SHH	Squires Gate	SQU
Reading West	RDW	Saltaire	SAE	Shireoaks	SRO	St Albans	SAC
Rectory Road	REC	Saltash	STS	Shirley	SRL	St Albans Abbey	SAA
Redbridge	RDB	Saltburn	SLB	Shoeburyness	SRY	St Andrews Road	SAR
Redcar Central	RCC	Saltcoats	SLT	Sholing	SHO	St Annes-on-the-Sea	SAS
Redcar East	RCE	Saltmarshe	SAM	Shoreham (Kent)	SEH	St Austell	SAU
Reddish North	RDN	Salwick	SLW	Shoreham-by-Sea	SSE	St Bees	SBS
Reddish South	RDS	Sandal & Agbrigg	SNA	Shortlands	SRT	St Budeaux Ferry Road	SBF
Redditch	RDC	Sandbach	SDB	Shotton	SHT	St Budeaux Victoria Rd	SBV

St Columb Road	SCR	Sudbury Hill Harrow	SDH	Tile Hill	THL	Wallyford	WAF
St Denys	SDN	Sugar Loaf	SUG	Tilehurst	TLH	Walmer	WAM
St Erth	SER	Summerston	SUM	Tipton	TIP	Walsall	WSL
St Germans	SGM	Sunbury	SUU	Tir-Phil	TIR	Walsden	WDN
St Helens Central	SNH	Sunderland	SUN	Tisbury	TIS	Waltham Cross	WLC
St Helens Junction	SHJ	Sundridge Park	SUP	Tiverton Parkway	TVP	Walthamstow Central	WHC
St Helier	SIH	Sunningdale	SNG	Todmorden	TOD	Walthamstow Queen's Rd	WMW
St Ives (Cornwall)	SIV	Sunnymeads	SNY	Tolworth	TOL	Walton (Merseyside)	WAO
St James Park	SJP	Surbiton	SUR	Ton Pentre	TPN	Walton on the Naze	WON
St James Street	SJS	Sutton Coldfield	SUT	Tonbridge	TON	Walton-on-Thames	WAL
St Johns	SAJ	Sutton Common	SUC	Tondu	TDU	Wanborough	WAN
St Keyne	SKN	Sutton Parkway	SPK	Tonfanau	TNF	Wandsworth Common	WSW
St Leonards Warrior Sq	SLQ	Sutton (Surrey)	SUO	Tonypandy	TNP	Wandsworth Road	WWR
St Margarets (London)	SMG	Swale	SWL	Tooting	TOO	Wandsworth Town	WNT
St Margarets (Herts)	SMT	Swanley	SAY	Topsham	TOP	Wanstead Park	WNP
St Mary Cray	SMY	Swanscombe	SWM	Torquay	TQY	Warblington	WBL
St Michaels	STM	Swansea	SWA	Torre	TRR	Ware	WAR
St Neots	SNO	Swanwick	SNW	Totnes	TOT	Wareham	WRM
St Pancras International	SPX	Sway	SWY	Tottenham Hale	TOM	Wargrave	WGV
Stafford	STA	Swaythling	SWG	Totton	TTN	Warminster	WMN
Staines	SNS	Swinderby	SWD	Town Green	TWN	Warnham	WNH
Stallingborough	SLL	Swindon	SWI	Trafford Park	TRA	Warrington Bank Quay	WBQ
Stalybridge	SYB	Swineshead	SWE	Trefforest	TRF	Warrington Central	WAC
Stamford	SMD	Swinton (Gr Manchester)	SNN	Trefforest Estate	TRE	Warwick	WRW
Stamford Hill	SMH	Swinton (Yorks)	SWN	Trehafod	TRH	Warwick Parkway	WRP
Stanford-le-Hope	SFO	Sydenham	SYD	Treherbert	TRB	Water Orton	WTO
Stanlow & Thornton	SNT	Sydenham Hill	SYH	Treorchy	TRY	Waterbeach	WBC
Stansted Airport	SSD	Syon Lane	SYL	Trimley	TRM	Wateringbury	WTR
Stansted Mountfitchet	SST	Syston	SYS	Tring	TRI	Waterloo (Merseyside)	WLO
Staplehurst	SPU	Tackley	TAC	Troed-y-rhiw	TRD	Watford High Street	WFH
Stapleton Road	SRD	Tadworth	TAD	Troon	TRN	Watford Junction	WFJ
Starbeck	SBE	Taffs Well	TAF	Trowbridge	TRO	Watford North	WFN
Starcross	SCS	Tain	TAI	Truro	TRU	Watlington	WTG
Staveley (Cumbria)	SVL	Talsarnau	TAL	Tulloch	TUL	Watton-at-Stone	WAS
Stechford	SCF	Talybont	TLB	Tulse Hill	TUH	Waun-Gron Park	WNG
Steeton & Silsden	SON	Tal-y-Cafn	TLC	Tunbridge Wells	TBW	Wavertree Tech Park	WAV
Stepps	SPS	Tame Bridge Parkway	TAB	Turkey Street	TUR	Wedgwood	WED
Stevenage	SVG	Tamworth	TAM	Tutbury & Hatton	TUT	Weeley	WEE
Stevenston	STV	Taplow	TAP	Twickenham	TWI	Weeton	WET
Stewartby	SWR	Tattenham Corner	TAT	Twyford	TWY	Welham Green	WMG
Stewarton	STT	Taunton	TAU	Ty Croes	TYC	Welling	WLI
Stirling	STG	Taynuilt	TAY	Ty Glas	TGS	Wellingborough	WEL
Stockport	SPT	Teddington	TED	Tygwyn	TYG	Wellington (Shropshire)	WLN
Stocksfield	SKS	Tees-side Airport	TEA	Tyndrum Lower	TYL	Welshpool	WLP
Stocksmoor	SSM	Teignmouth	TGM	Tyseley	TYS	Welwyn Garden City	WGC
Stockton	STK	Telford Central	TFC	Tywyn	TYW	Welwyn North	WLW
Stoke Mandeville	SKM	Templecombe	TMC	Uckfield	UCK	Wem	WEM
Stoke Newington	SKW	Tenby	TEN	Uddingston	UDD	Wembley Central	WMB
Stoke-on-Trent	SOT	Teynham	TEY	Ulceby	ULC	Wembley Stadium	WCX
Stone	SNE	Thames Ditton	THD	Ulleskelf	ULL	Wemyss Bay	WMS
Stone Crossing	SCG	Thatcham	THA	Ulverston	ULV	Wendover	WND
Stonebridge Park	SBP	Thatto Heath	THH	Umberleigh	UMB	Wennington	WNN
Stonegate	SOG	The Hawthorns	THW	University	UNI	West Allerton	WSA
Stonehaven	STN	The Lakes	TLK	Uphall	UHA	West Brompton	WBP
Stonehouse	SHU	Theale	THE	Upholland	UPL	West Byfleet	WBY
Stoneleigh	SNL	Theobalds Grove	TEO	Upminster	UPM	West Calder	WCL
Stourbridge Junction	SBJ	Thetford	TTF	Upper Halliford	UPH	West Croydon	WCY
Stourbridge Town	SBT	Thirsk	THI	Upper Holloway	UHL	West Drayton	WDT
Stowmarket	SMK	Thornaby	TBY	Upper Tyndrum	UTY	West Dulwich	WDU
Stranraer	STR	Thorne North	TNN	Upper Warlingham	UWL	West Ealing	WEA
Stratford (London)	SRA	Thorne South	TNS	Upton	UPT	West Ham	WEH
Stratford-upon-Avon	SAV	Thornford	THO	Upwey	UPW	West Hampstead	WHD
Strathcarron	STC	Thornliebank	THB	Urmston	URM	West Hampstead T'link	WHP
Strawberry Hill	STW	Thornton Abbey	TNA	Uttoxeter	UTT	West Horndon	WHR
Streatham	STE	Thornton Heath	TTH	Valley	VAL	West Kilbride	WKB
Streatham Common	SRC	Thorntonhall	THT	Vauxhall	VXH	West Kirby	WKI
Streatham Hill	SRH	Thorpe Bay	TPB	Virginia Water	VIR	West Malling	WMA
Streethouse	SHC	Thorpe Culvert	TPC	Waddon	WDO	West Norwood	WNW
Strines	SRN	Thorpe-le-Soken	TLS	Wadhurst	WAD	West Ruislip	WRU
Stromeferry	STF	Three Bridges	TBD	Wainfleet	WFL	West Runton	WRN
Strood	SOO	Three Oaks	TOK	Wakefield Kirkgate	WKK	West St Leonards	WLD
Stroud	STD	Thurgarton	THU	Wakefield Westgate	WKF	West Sutton	WSU
Sturry	STU	Thurnscoe	THC	Walkden	WKD	West Wickham	WWI
Styal	SYA	Thurso	THS	Wallasey Grove Road	WLG	West Worthing	WWO
Sudbury	SUY	Thurston	TRS	Wallasey Village	WLV	Westbury (Wilts)	WSB
Sudbury & Harrow Road	SUD	Tilbury Town	TIL	Wallington	WLT	Westcliff	WCF

Data Tables

Westcombe Park	WCB	Whittlesford Parkway	WLF	Winsford	WSF	Workington	WKG		
Westenhanger	WHA	Whitton	WTN	Wishaw	WSH	Worksop	WRK		
Wester Hailes	WTA	Whitwell	WWL	Witham	WTM	Worle	WOR		
Westerfield	WFI	Whyteleafe	WHY	Witley	WTY	Worplesdon	WPL		
Westerton	WES	Whyteleafe South	WHS	Witton	WTT	Worstead	WRT		
Westgate-on-Sea	WGA	Wick	WCK	Wivelsfield	WVF	Worthing	WRH		
Westhoughton	WHG	Wickford	WIC	Wivenhoe	WIV	Wrabness	WRB		
Weston Milton	WNM	Wickham Market	WCM	Woburn Sands	WOB	Wraysbury	WRY		
Weston-super-Mare	WSM	Widdrington	WDD	Woking	WOK	Wrenbury	WRE		
Wetheral	WRL	Widnes	WID	Wokingham	WKM	Wressle	WRS		
Weybridge	WYB	Widney Manor	WMR	Woldingham	WOH	Wrexham Central	WXC		
Weymouth	WEY	Wigan North Western	WGN	Wolverhampton	WVH	Wrexham General	WRX		
Whaley Bridge	WBR	Wigan Wallgate	WGW	Wolverton	WOL	Wye	WYE		
Whalley	WHE	Wigton	WGT	Wombwell	WOM	Wylam	WYM		
Whatstandwell	WTS	Wildmill	WMI	Wood End	WDE	Wylde Green	WYL		
Whifflet	WFF	Willesden Junction	WIJ	Wood Street	WST	Wymondham	WMD		
Whimple	WHM	Williamwood	WLM	Woodbridge	WDB	Wythall	WYT		
Whinhill	WNL	Willington	WIL	Woodgrange Park	WGR	Yalding	YAL		
Whiston	WHN	Wilmcote	WMC	Woodhall	WDL	Yardley Wood	YRD		
Whitby	WTB	Wilmslow	WML	Woodhouse	WDH	Yarm	YRM		
Whitchurch (Cardiff)	WHT	Wilnecote	WNE	Woodlesford	WDS	Yate	YAE		
Whitchurch (Hants)	WCH	Wimbledon	WIM	Woodley	WLY	Yatton	YAT		
Whitchurch (Shropshire)	WTC	Wimbledon Chase	WBO	Woodmansterne	WME	Yeoford	YEO		
White Hart Lane	WHL	Winchelsea	WSE	Woodsmoor	WSR	Yeovil Junction	YVJ		
White Notley	WNY	Winchester	WIN	Wool	WOO	Yeovil Pen Mill	YVP		
Whitecraigs	WCR	Winchfield	WNF	Woolston	WLS	Yetminster	YET		
Whitehaven	WTH	Winchmore Hill	WIH	Woolwich Arsenal	WWA	Ynyswen	YNW		
Whitland	WTL	Windermere	WDM	Woolwich Dockyard	WWD	Yoker	YOK		
Whitley Bridge	WBD	Windsor & Eton Central	WNC	Wootton Wawen	WWW	York	YRK		
Whitlocks End	WTE	Windsor & Eton Riverside	WNR	Worcester Foregate St	WOF	Yorton	YRT		
Whitstable	WHI	Winnersh	WNS	Worcester Park	WCP	Ystrad Mynach	YSM		
Whittlesea	WLE	Winnersh Triangle	WTI	Worcester Shrub Hill	WOS	Ystrad Rhondda	YSR		

Left: *Much criticism has been levelled at the 'Pacer' design of DMU over the years, but on more lightly used routes these sets do provide a good service. First Great Western Class 143 No. 143612 departs from Dawlish Warren on 4 July 2009 with an evening Exmouth to Paignton service.* **CJM**

DMU and EMU Vehicle Codes

BDMSO	Battery Driving Motor Standard Open	MFL	Motor First Lavatory
DM	Driving Motor	MPMV	Motor Parcels Mail Van
DMBS	Driving Motor Brake Standard	MS	Motor Standard
DMCL	Driving Motor Composite Lavatory	MSL	Motor Standard Lavatory
DMCO	Driving Motor Composite Open	MSLRB	Motor Standard Lavatory Restaurant Buffet
DMF	Driving Motor First	MSO	Motor Standard Open
DMFO	Driving Motor Brake Open	MSRMB	Motor Standard Restaurant Micro Buffet
DMFLO	Driving Motor First Luggage Open	PTSO	Pantograph Trailer Standard Open
DMRFO	Driving Motor Restaurant First Open	RB	Restaurant Buffet
DMS	Driving Motor Standard	TBFO	Trailer Brake First Open
DMSL	Driving Motor Standard Lavatory	TCO	Trailer Composite Open
DMSO	Driving Motor Standard Open	TFO	Trailer First Open
DTCO	Driving Trailer Composite Open	TPMV	Trailer Parcels Mail Van
DTPMV	Driving Trailer Parcels Mail Van	TSO	Trailer Standard Open
DTSO	Driving Trailer Standard Open	TSRMB	Trailer Standard Restaurant Micro Buffet
MBC	Motor Brake Composite		
MBSO	Motor Brake Standard Open	(A) - A Car	
MC	Motor Composite	(B) - B Car	

This cross number checklist indicates in which section of the ABC Rail Guide 2011 full details of rolling stock can be found.

Number Cross-Link Codes

Code	Name		Code	Name		Code	Name
			FLR	Freightliner		PRE	Preserved
			FMR	FM Rail		PUL	Pullman Rail
3MP	3M Productions		FSL	Flying Scotsman Railway Ltd		RAF	Railfilms
ALS	Alstom		FSR	First ScotRail		RCL	Railcare
ATW	Arriva Trains Wales		FTP	First TransPennine		RIV	Riviera
AXC	Arriva Cross Country		GBR	GB Railfreight		RRS	Ridings Railtours
BAR	British American Railway		GSW	Great Scottish & Western Rly		RVE	Rail Vehicle Engineering
BOK	Bo'ness & Kinneil Railway		GTL	Grand Central Railway		S47	Stratford Class 47 Group
BOM	Bombardier Transportation		HAN	Hanson Traction		SEC	Serco Railtest
C2C	c2c Railway		HEC	Heathrow Connect		SET	South Eastern Trains
CAD	Cargo - D		HEX	Heathrow Express		SIE	Siemens
COL	Colas		HNR	Harry Needle Railroad Co		SIL	Stagecoach Island Line
CRW	Chiltern Railways		IND	Industrial		SNF	SNCF (French Railways)
CWR	Cotswold Rail		JAR	Jarvis		SOU	Southern
DBS	DB Schenker		JHS	Jeremy Hoskins		SRP	Scottish Railway Preservation Soc
DRS	Direct Rail Services		KRS	Knights Rail Services		SUP	Support Coaches
ECR	Euro Cargo Rail		LMI	London Midland		SWT	South West Trains
EMT	East Midlands Trains		LOG	London Overground		TTS	Transmart Trains
EPX	Euro Phoenix Ltd		MER	Merseyrail		VSO	Venice Simplon Orient Express
ETL	Electric Traction Ltd		MHR	Mid Hants Railway		VTN	Vintage Trains
EUR	Eurotunnel		MRL	Mendip Rail Ltd		VWC	Virgin West Coast
EUR	Europort2		NEM	Nemesis Rail		WAB	Wabtec
EUS	Eurostar UK		NOR	Northern		WCR	West Coast Railway
EXP	Exported		NRL	Network Rail Limited		WSR	Wrexham & Shropshire Railway
FCC	First Capital Connect		NXA	National Express East Anglia		WTN	Wessex Trains
FGW	First Great Western		NXE	National Express East Coast			
FHT	First Hull Trains		NYM	North Yorkshire Moors Railway			
FLF	Fastline Freight		OLS	Off Lease			

Locomotives - Diesel & Electric

Number	Code	Number	Code	Number	Code	Number	Code	Number	Code
❏ D0226	PRE	❏ D2178	PRE	❏ D2774	PRE	❏ D7029	PRE	❏ LMS7050	PRE
		❏ D2182	PRE	❏ D2854	PRE	❏ D7076	PRE	❏ LMS7051	PRE
❏ D4	PRE	❏ D2184	PRE	❏ D2858	PRE			❏ LMS7069	PRE
		❏ D2192	PRE	❏ D2860	PRE	❏ D8000	PRE		
❏ D200	PRE	❏ D2199	PRE	❏ D2866	PRE			❏ E26020	PRE
				❏ D2867	PRE	❏ D8233	PRE		
❏ D821	PRE	❏ D2203	PRE	❏ D2868	PRE			❏ E27000	PRE
❏ D832	PRE	❏ D2205	PRE			❏ D8568	PRE	❏ E27001	PRE
		❏ D2207	PRE	❏ D2953	PRE				
❏ D1010	PRE	❏ D2229	PRE	❏ D2956	PRE	❏ D9500	PRE	❏ 9005	EUR
❏ D1013	PRE	❏ D2245	PRE			❏ D9502	PRE	❏ 9006	EUR
❏ D1015	PRE	❏ D2246	PRE	❏ D3000	PRE	❏ D9504	PRE	❏ 9007	EUR
❏ D1023	PRE	❏ D2271	PRE	❏ D3002	PRE	❏ D9513	PRE	❏ 9011	EUR
❏ D1041	PRE	❏ D2272	PRE	❏ D3014	PRE	❏ D9516	PRE	❏ 9013	EUR
❏ D1048	PRE	❏ D2279	PRE	❏ D3101	PRE	❏ D9520	PRE	❏ 9015	EUR
❏ D1062	PRE	❏ D2280	PRE	❏ D3255	PRE	❏ D9521	PRE	❏ 9018	EUR
		❏ D2284	PRE	❏ D3261	PRE	❏ D9523	PRE	❏ 9022	EUR
		❏ D2298	PRE	❏ D3452	PRE	❏ D9524	PRE	❏ 9023	EUR
		❏ D2302	PRE	❏ D3489	PRE	❏ D9525	PRE	❏ 9024	EUR
❏ D2023	PRE	❏ D2310	PRE	❏ D4067	PRE	❏ D9526	PRE	❏ 9026	EUR
❏ D2024	PRE	❏ D2324	PRE	❏ D4092	PRE	❏ D9529	IND	❏ 9027	EUR
❏ D2041	PRE	❏ D2325	PRE			❏ D9531	PRE	❏ 9029	EUR
❏ D2046	PRE	❏ D2334	PRE	❏ D5500	PRE	❏ D9537	PRE	❏ 9031	EUR
❏ D2051	PRE	❏ D2337	PRE			❏ D9539	PRE	❏ 9033	EUR
❏ D2117	PRE			❏ D5705	PRE	❏ D9551	PRE	❏ 9036	EUR
❏ D2118	PRE	❏ D2511	PRE			❏ D9553	PRE	❏ 9037	EUR
❏ D2133	PRE	❏ D2578	PRE	❏ D6700	PRE	❏ D9555	PRE	❏ 9040	EUR
❏ D2138	PRE	❏ D2587	PRE					❏ 9101	EUR
❏ D2139	PRE	❏ D2595	PRE	❏ D7017	PRE	❏ DELTIC	PRE	❏ 9103	EUR
❏ D2148	PRE	❏ D2767	PRE	❏ D7018	PRE	❏ DS75	PRE	❏ 9105	EUR

Data Tables

☐ 9106	EUR	☐ 03113	PRE	☐ 08393	DBS	☐ 08600	IND	☐ 08752	DBS
☐ 9107	EUR	☐ 03119	PRE	☐ 08398	IND	☐ 08604	PRE	☐ 08754	BAR
☐ 9108	EUR	☐ 03120	PRE	☐ 08405	DBS	☐ 08605	DBS	☐ 08756	BAR
☐ 9109	EUR	☐ 03128	PRE	☐ 08410	FGW	☐ 08611	ALS	☐ 08757	DBS
☐ 9110	EUR	☐ 03134	PRE	☐ 08411	IND	☐ 08613	BAR	☐ 08762	BAR
☐ 9111	EUR	☐ 03141	PRE	☐ 08417	NRL	☐ 08615	WAB	☐ 08764	WAB
☐ 9112	EUR	☐ 03144	PRE	☐ 08418	WCR	☐ 08616	LMI	☐ 08767	PRE
☐ 9113	EUR	☐ 03145	PRE	☐ 08423	BAR	☐ 08617	ALS	☐ 08769	PRE
☐ 9701	EUR	☐ 03152	PRE	☐ 08428	DBS	☐ 08622	BAR	☐ 08772	PRE
☐ 9702	EUR	☐ 03158	PRE	☐ 08436	PRE	☐ 08623	DBS	☐ 08773	PRE
☐ 9703	EUR	☐ 03162	PRE	☐ 08441	IND	☐ 08624	FLR	☐ 08774	IND
☐ 9704	EUR	☐ 03170	PRE	☐ 08442	DBS	☐ 08629	RCL	☐ 08780	PRE
☐ 9705	EUR	☐ 03179	IND	☐ 08443	PRE	☐ 08630	DBS	☐ 08782	DBS
☐ 9706	EUR	☐ 03189	PRE	☐ 08444	PRE	☐ 08631	PRE	☐ 08783	DBS
☐ 9707	EUR	☐ 03196	WCR	☐ 08445	IND	☐ 08632	DBS	☐ 08784	DBS
☐ 9712	EUR	☐ 03371	PRE	☐ 08447	IND	☐ 08633	DBS	☐ 08785	FLR
☐ 9714	EUR	☐ 03381	WCR	☐ 08451	ALS	☐ 08635	PRE	☐ 08787	IND
☐ 9801	EUR	☐ 03399	PRE	☐ 08454	ALS	☐ 08641	FGW	☐ 08790	ALS
☐ 9802	EUR			☐ 08460	IND	☐ 08643	MRL	☐ 08795	FGW
☐ 9803	EUR	☐ 05001	PRE	☐ 08471	PRE	☐ 08644	FGW	☐ 08798	DBS
☐ 9804	EUR			☐ 08472	WAB	☐ 08645	FGW	☐ 08799	DBS
☐ 9808	EUR	☐ 06003	PRE	☐ 08473	PRE	☐ 08646	DBS	☐ 08802	DBS
☐ 9809	EUR			☐ 08476	PRE	☐ 08649	RCL	☐ 08804	DBS
☐ 9810	EUR	☐ 07001	HNR	☐ 08479	PRE	☐ 08650	MRL	☐ 08805	LMI
☐ 9812	EUR	☐ 07005	PRE	☐ 08480	DBS	☐ 08652	MRL	☐ 08807	IND
☐ 9814	EUR	☐ 07007	KRS	☐ 08481	PRE	☐ 08653	DBS	☐ 08809	IND
☐ 9816	EUR	☐ 07010	PRE	☐ 08483	FGW	☐ 08662	DBS	☐ 08818	HNR
☐ 9817	EUR	☐ 07011	PRE	☐ 08484	IND	☐ 08663	FGW	☐ 08822	FGW
☐ 9819	EUR	☐ 07012	PRE	☐ 08485	WCR	☐ 08664	DBS	☐ 08823	IND
☐ 9820	EUR	☐ 07013	PRE	☐ 08490	PRE	☐ 08665	HNR	☐ 08824	DBS
☐ 9821	EUR			☐ 08492	HNR	☐ 08669	WAB	☐ 08827	HNR
☐ 9825	EUR	☐ 08011	PRE	☐ 08495	DBS	☐ 08670	IND	☐ 08830	PRE
☐ 9828	EUR	☐ 08012	PRE	☐ 08499	PUL	☐ 08676	DBS	☐ 08834	HNR
☐ 9832	EUR	☐ 08015	PRE	☐ 08500	DBS	☐ 08678	WCR	☐ 08836	FGW
☐ 9834	EUR	☐ 08016	PRE	☐ 08502	HNR	☐ 08682	BOM	☐ 08842	DBS
☐ 9835	EUR	☐ 08021	PRE	☐ 08503	IND	☐ 08683	PRE	☐ 08844	DBS
☐ 9838	EUR	☐ 08022	PRE	☐ 08507	HNR	☐ 08685	DBS	☐ 08846	BOM
		☐ 08032	PRE	☐ 08511	IND	☐ 08690	EMT	☐ 08847	IND
☐ 01509	CRW	☐ 08046	PRE	☐ 08514	DBS	☐ 08691	FLR	☐ 08850	PRE
☐ 01551	SIE	☐ 08054	PRE	☐ 08516	DBS	☐ 08694	PRE	☐ 08853	WAB
☐ 01552	HNR	☐ 08060	PRE	☐ 08517	HNR	☐ 08696	ALS	☐ 08854	DBS
☐ 01564	HNR	☐ 08064	PRE	☐ 08523	IND	☐ 08697	RVE	☐ 08865	DBS
		☐ 08077	FLR	☐ 08525	EMT	☐ 08699	IND	☐ 08866	DBS
☐ 03018	PRE	☐ 08102	PRE	☐ 08527	HNR	☐ 08700	PRE	☐ 08868	HNR
☐ 03020	PRE	☐ 08108	PRE	☐ 08528	PRE	☐ 08701	DBS	☐ 08870	BAR
☐ 03022	PRE	☐ 08114	PRE	☐ 08530	DBS	☐ 08703	DBS	☐ 08871	WAB
☐ 03027	PRE	☐ 08123	PRE	☐ 08531	FLR	☐ 08704	IND	☐ 08873	BAR
☐ 03037	PRE	☐ 08133	PRE	☐ 08535	IND	☐ 08706	DBS	☐ 08877	DBS
☐ 03059	PRE	☐ 08164	PRE	☐ 08536	RVE	☐ 08709	DBS	☐ 08879	DBS
☐ 03062	PRE	☐ 08168	PRE	☐ 08556	PRE	☐ 08711	DBS	☐ 08881	IND
☐ 03066	PRE	☐ 08195	PRE	☐ 08567	DBS	☐ 08714	DBS	☐ 08885	BAR
☐ 03069	PRE	☐ 08202	PRE	☐ 08568	RCL	☐ 08721	ALS	☐ 08887	ALS
☐ 03072	PRE	☐ 08220	PRE	☐ 08571	WAB	☐ 08724	WAB	☐ 08886	DBS
☐ 03073	PRE	☐ 08238	PRE	☐ 08573	BAR	☐ 08728	IND	☐ 08888	DBS
☐ 03078	PRE	☐ 08266	PRE	☐ 08575	FLR	☐ 08730	RCL	☐ 08891	FLR
☐ 03079	PRE	☐ 08266	PRE	☐ 08578	DBS	☐ 08731	MRL	☐ 08892	HNR
☐ 03081	PRE	☐ 08308	BAR	☐ 08580	DBS	☐ 08734	PRE	☐ 08896	PRE
☐ 03084	PRE	☐ 08331	IND	☐ 08585	FLR	☐ 08735	DBS	☐ 08899	EMT
☐ 03089	PRE	☐ 08359	PRE	☐ 08588	BAR	☐ 08737	DBS	☐ 08903	IND
☐ 03090	PRE	☐ 08375	IND	☐ 08590	PRE	☐ 08738	ECR	☐ 08904	DBS
☐ 03094	PRE	☐ 08377	PRE	☐ 08593	DBS	☐ 08742	DBS	☐ 08905	DBS
☐ 03099	PRE	☐ 08388	PRE	☐ 08596	WAB	☐ 08743	IND	☐ 08907	DBS
☐ 03112	IND	☐ 08389	DBS	☐ 08598	IND	☐ 08750	BAR	☐ 08908	EMT

Data Tables

08909	DBS	20016	HNR	21611	ECR	31144	PRE	37003	PRE
08911	PRE	20020	PRE	21901	EUR	31162	PRE	37009	PRE
08912	IND	20031	PRE	21902	EUR	31163	PRE	37023	PRE
08913	IND	20032	HNR	21903	EUR	31190	BAR	37025	PRE
08915	IND	20048	PRE	21904	EUR	31203	PRE	37029	HNR
08918	DBS	20056	HNR	21905	EUR	31206	PRE	37032	PRE
08921	DBS	20057	HNR			31207	PRE	37037	PRE
08922	DBS	20059	PRE	24032	PRE	31210	PRE	37038	DRS
08927	WAB	20066	HNR	24054	PRE	31233	NRL	37059	DRS
08929	HNR	20069	PRE	24061	PRE	31235	PRE	37069	DRS
08933	IND	20072	HNR	24082	PRE	31270	PRE	37075	PRE
08934	ALS	20081	HNR			31271	PRE	37087	DRS
08936	BAR	20087	PRE	25035	PRE	31285	NRL	37097	PRE
08937	PRE	20088	HNR	25057	PRE	31289	PRE	37108	PRE
08939	ECR	20092	HNR	25059	PRE	31327	PRE	37109	PRE
08943	HNR	20096	HNR	25067	PRE	31410	PRE	37116	PRE
08944	PRE	20098	PRE	25072	PRE	31414	PRE	37142	PRE
08947	MRL	20107	HNR	25083	PRE	31415	PRE	37146	PRE
08948	EUS	20110	PRE	25173	PRE	31418	PRE	37152	PRE
08950	EMT	20118	PRE	25185	PRE	31422	PRE	37165	HNR
08951	DBS	20121	HNR	25191	PRE	31435	PRE	37175	PRE
08956	NRL	20132	HNR	25235	PRE	31438	PRE	37188	PRE
08993	DBS	20137	PRE	25244	PRE	31452	BAR	37194	DRS
08994	DBS	20138	HNR	25262	PRE	31454	RVE	37197	DRS
08995	DBS	20142	PRE	26265	PRE	31459	RVE	37198	NRL
		20154	PRE	25278	NYM	31461	PRE	37207	PRE
09002	PRE	20166	PRE	25279	PRE	31463	PRE	37214	WCR
09003	HNR	20168	HNR	25283	PRE	31465	NRL	37215	PRE
09004	PRE	20169	PRE	25309	PRE	31466	PRE	37216	PRE
09006	DBS	20177	PRE	25311	PRE	31468	RVE	37218	DRS
09007	LOG	20188	PRE	25321	PRE	31530	PRE	37219	PRE
09010	PRE	20189	BAR	25322	PRE	31601	RVE	37227	PRE
09011	DBS	20205	PRE			31602	RVE	37229	DRS
09012	HNR	20214	PRE	26001	PRE			37240	PRE
09017	DBS	20227	BAR	26002	PRE	33002	PRE	37248	WCR
09018	HNR	20301	GBR	26004	PRE	33008	PRE	37250	PRE
09020	DBS	20302	GBR	26007	PRE	33012	PRE	37254	PRE
09022	DBS	20303	DRS	26010	PRE	33018	PRE	37255	PRE
09023	DBS	20304	GBR	26011	PRE	33019	PRE	37259	DRS
09024	DBS	20305	GBR	26014	PRE	33021	PRE	37261	DRS
09025	PRE	20306	DRS	26024	PRE	33025	WCR	37263	PRE
09106	DBS	20307	DRS	26025	PRE	33029	WCR	37264	PRE
09107	DBS	20308	GBR	26035	PRE	33030	WCR	37275	PRE
09201	DBS	20309	DRS	26038	PRE	33035	PRE	37294	PRE
09203	DBS	20310	DRS	26040	PRE	33046	PRE	37308	PRE
09204	DBS	20311	DRS	26043	PRE	33048	PRE	37314	PRE
09205	DBS	20312	DRS			33052	PRE	37324	PRE
		20313	DRS	27001	PRE	33053	PRE	37372	PRE
12052	PRE	20314	DRS	27005	PRE	33057	PRE	37401	DBS
12061	PRE	20315	DRS	27007	PRE	33063	PRE	37402	DBS
12077	PRE	20901	HNR	27024	PRE	33065	PRE	37403	PRE
12082	PRE	20902	HNR	27050	PRE	33102	PRE	37405	DBS
12088	IND	20903	HNR	27056	PRE	33103	NEM	37406	DBS
12093	PRE	20904	HNR	27059	PRE	33108	PRE	37407	PRE
12099	PRE	20905	HNR	27066	PRE	33109	PRE	37409	DRS
12131	PRE	20906	HNR			33110	PRE	37410	DBS
				31101	PRE	33111	PRE	37411	DBS
15224	PRE	21544	ECR	31105	NRL	33116	PRE	37412	HNR
		21545	ECR	31106	RVE	33117	PRE	37413	PRE
18000	PRE	21546	ECR	31108	PRE	33201	PRE	37415	HNR
		21547	ECR	31119	PRE	33202	PRE	37416	DBS
20001	PRE			31128	NEM	33207	WCR	37417	DBS
20007	PRE	21610	ECR	31130	PRE	33208	PRE	37418	PRE

Data Tables

37419	DBS	43013	NRL	43088	FGW	43183	FGW	45014	PRE
37421	PRE	43014	NRL	43089	EMT	43185	FGW	45041	PRE
37422	DBS	43015	FGW	43091	FGW	43186	FGW	45060	PRE
37423	DRS	43016	FGW	43092	FGW	43187	FGW	45105	PRE
37424	PRE	43017	FGW	43093	FGW	43188	FGW	45108	PRE
37425	DBS	43018	FGW	43094	FGW	43189	FGW	45112	NEM
37427	DBS	43020	FGW	43097	FGW	43190	FGW	45118	PRE
37428	HNR	43021	FGW	43098	FGW	43191	FGW	45125	PRE
37510	DRS	43022	FGW	43122	FGW	43192	FGW	45132	PRE
37516	WCR	43023	FGW	43124	FGW	43193	FGW	45133	PRE
37517	WCR	43024	FGW	43125	FGW	43194	FGW	45135	PRE
37518	PRE	43025	FGW	43126	FGW	43195	FGW	45149	PRE
37601	DRS	43026	FGW	43127	FGW	43196	FGW		
37602	DRS	43027	FGW	43128	FGW	43197	FGW	46010	PRE
37603	DRS	43028	FGW	43129	FGW	43198	FGW	46035	PRE
37604	DRS	43029	FGW	43130	FGW			46045	PRE
37605	DRS	43030	FGW	43131	FGW	43206	ICE		
37606	DRS	43031	FGW	43132	FGW	43207	AXC	47004	PRE
37607	DRS	43032	FGW	43133	FGW	43208	ICE	47105	PRE
37608	DRS	43033	FGW	43134	FGW	43238	ICE	47117	PRE
37609	DRS	43034	FGW	43135	FGW	43239	ICE	47192	PRE
37610	DRS	43035	FGW	43136	FGW	43251	ICE	47194	WCR
37611	DRS	43036	FGW	43137	FGW	43257	ICE	47205	PRE
37612	DRS	43037	FGW	43138	FGW	43277	ICE	47237	HNR
37667	DRS	43040	FGW	43139	FGW	43285	AXC	47245	WCR
37668	WCR	43041	FGW	43140	FGW	43290	ICE	47270	WCR
37674	PRE	43042	FGW	43141	FGW	43295	ICE	47292	PRE
37676	WCR	43043	EMT	43142	FGW	43296	ICE	47295	HNR
37679	PRE	43044	EMT	43143	FGW	43299	ICE	47306	PRE
37682	DRS	43045	EMT	43144	FGW	43300	ICE	47355	WCR
37683	DRS	43046	EMT	43145	FGW	43301	AXC	47367	PRE
37685	WCR	43047	EMT	43146	FGW	43302	ICE	47375	NEM
37688	DRS	43048	EMT	43147	FGW	43303	AXC	47376	PRE
37696	HNR	43049	EMT	43148	FGW	43304	AXC	47401	PRE
37703	DBS	43050	EMT	43149	FGW	43305	ICE	47402	PRE
37706	WCR	43052	EMT	43150	FGW	43306	ICE	47417	PRE
37710	WCR	43053	FGW	43151	FGW	43307	ICE	47449	PRE
37712	WCR	43054	EMT	43152	FGW	43308	ICE	47484	PRE
37714	DBS	43055	EMT	43153	FGW	43309	ICE	47488	NEM
37716	DBS	43056	FGW	43154	FGW	43310	ICE	47492	WCR
37718	DBS	43058	EMT	43155	FGW	43311	ICE	47500	WCR
37800	DBS	43059	EMT	43156	FGW	43312	ICE	47501	DRS
37884	DBS	43060	EMT	43158	FGW	43313	ICE	47524	PRE
37901	PRE	43061	EMT	43159	FGW	43314	ICE	47526	WCR
37905	PRE	43062	NRL	43160	FGW	43315	ICE	47580	S47
37906	PRE	43063	FGW	43161	FGW	43316	ICE	47596	PRE
		43064	EMT	43162	FGW	43317	ICE	47635	PRE
40012	PRE	43066	EMT	43163	FGW	43318	ICE	47640	PRE
40013	PRE	43069	FGW	43164	FGW	43319	ICE	47643	PRE
40106	PRE	43070	FGW	43165	FGW	43320	ICE	47701	PRE
40118	PRE	43071	FGW	43168	FGW	43321	AXC	47703	DRS
40135	PRE	43072	EMT	43169	FGW	43357	AXC	47709	DRS
40145	PRE	43073	EMT	43170	FGW	43366	AXC	47712	DRS
		43074	EMT	43171	FGW	43367	ICE	47714	HNR
41001	PRE	43075	EMT	43172	FGW	43378	AXC	47715	PRE
		43076	EMT	43174	FGW	43384	AXC	47716	NEM
43002	FGW	43078	FGW	43175	FGW	43465	GTL	47727	COL
43003	FGW	43079	FGW	43176	FGW	43467	GTL	47739	COL
43004	FGW	43081	EMT	43177	FGW	43468	GTL	47744	NEM
43005	FGW	43082	EMT	43179	FGW	43480	GTL	47746	PRE
43009	FGW	43083	EMT	43180	FGW	43484	GTL	47747	RIV
43010	FGW	43086	FGW	43181	FGW	43523	GTL	47749	COL
43012	FGW	43087	FGW	43182	FGW	44008	PRE	47760	WCR

No.	Code	No.	Code	No.	Code	No.	Code	No.	Code
47761	HNR	55015	PRE	58013	DBS	60018	DBS	60096	DBS
47763	PRE	55016	PRE	58015	DBS	60019	DBS	60097	DBS
47765	PRE	55019	PRE	58016	PRE	60020	DBS	60099	DBS
47768	PRE	55022	PRE	58017	DBS	60021	DBS	60100	DBS
47769	RIV			58018	DBS	60022	DBS	60500	DBS
47771	PRE	56009	IND	58020	DBS	60024	DBS		
47772	WCR	56040	PRE	58021	DBS	60025	DBS	66001	DBS
47773	VTN	56086	PRE	58022	DBS	60026	DBS	66002	DBS
47776	WCR	56097	PRE	58023	DBS	60027	DBS	66003	DBS
47785	PRE	56098	PRE	58024	DBS	60028	DBS	66004	DBS
47786	WCR	56101	PRE	58025	DBS	60029	DBS	66005	DBS
47787	WCR	56301	OLS	58026	DBS	60030	DBS	66006	DBS
47790	DRS	56302	OLS	58027	DBS	60032	DBS	66007	DBS
47791	DRS	56303	RVE	58029	DBS	60033	DBS	66008	DBS
47793	PRE	56311	BAR	58030	DBS	60034	DBS	66009	DBS
47798	PRE	56312	BAR	58031	DBS	60035	DBS	66010	DBS
47799	DBS	56313	BAR	58032	DBS	60036	DBS	66011	DBS
47802	DRS	56314	BAR	58033	DBS	60037	DBS	66012	DBS
47804	WCR			58034	DBS	60039	DBS	66013	DBS
47805	RIV	57001	OLS	58035	DBS	60040	DBS	66014	DBS
47810	DRS	57002	DRS	58036	DBS	60041	DBS	66015	DBS
47811	FLR	57003	DRS	58037	DBS	60043	DBS	66016	DBS
47812	RIV	57004	DRS	58038	DBS	60044	DBS	66017	DBS
47813	HNR	57005	HNR	58039	DBS	60045	DBS	66018	DBS
47815	RIV	57006	NHR	58040	DBS	60046	DBS	66019	DBS
47816	FLR	57007	DRS	58041	DBS	60047	DBS	66020	DBS
47818	DRS	57008	DRS	58042	DBS	60048	DBS	66021	DBS
47826	WCR	57009	DRS	58043	DBS	60049	DBS	66022	DBS
47828	HNR	57010	DRS	58044	DBS	60051	DBS	66023	DBS
47829	HNR	57011	DRS	58046	DBS	60052	DBS	66024	DBS
47830	FLR	57012	DRS	58047	DBS	60053	DBS	66025	DBS
47832	DRS	57301	OLS	58048	DBS	60054	DBS	66026	DBS
47839	RIV	57302	VWC	58049	DBS	60056	DBS	66027	DBS
47840	PRE	57303	OLS	58050	DBS	60057	DBS	66028	DBS
47841	DRS	57304	VWC			60059	DBS	66029	DBS
47843	RIV	57305	OLS	59001	MRL	60060	DBS	66030	DBS
47847	RIV	57306	OLS	59002	MRL	60061	DBS	66031	DBS
47848	RIV	57307	VWC	59003	EXP	60062	DBS	66032	DBS
47851	WCR	57308	VWC	59004	MRL	60063	DBS	66033	DBS
47853	RIV	57309	VWC	59005	MRL	60064	DBS	66034	DBS
47854	WCR	57310	OLS	59101	MRL	60065	DBS	66035	DBS
		57311	VWC	59102	MRL	60066	DBS	66036	DBS
50002	PRE	57312	OLS	59103	MRL	60067	DBS	66037	DBS
50007	PRE	57313	ATW	59104	MRL	60069	DBS	66038	DBS
50008	PRE	57314	ATW	59201	DBS	60071	DBS	66039	DBS
50015	PRE	57315	ATW	59202	DBS	60072	DBS	66040	DBS
50017	PRE	57316	ATW	59203	DBS	60073	DBS	66041	DBS
50019	PRE	57601	WCR	59204	DBS	60074	DBS	66042	DBS
50021	PRE	57602	FGW	59205	DBS	60076	DBS	66043	DBS
50026	PRE	57603	FGW	59206	DBS	60077	DBS	66044	DBS
50027	PRE	57604	FGW			60079	DBS	66045	DBS
50029	PRE	57605	FGW	60002	DBS	60083	DBS	66046	DBS
50030	PRE			60003	DBS	60084	DBS	66047	DBS
50031	PRE	58001	DBS	60004	DBS	60085	DBS	66048	DBS
50033	PRE	58004	DBS	60005	DBS	60086	DBS	66049	DBS
50135	PRE	58005	DBS	60007	DBS	60087	DBS	66050	DBS
50042	PRE	58006	DBS	60009	DBS	60088	DBS	66051	DBS
50044	PRE	58007	DBS	60010	DBS	60090	DBS	66052	DBS
50049	PRE	58008	DBS	60011	DBS	60091	DBS	66053	DBS
50050	PRE	58009	DBS	60012	DBS	60092	DBS	66054	DBS
		58010	DBS	60013	DBS	60093	DBS	66055	DBS
55002	PRE	58011	DBS	60015	DBS	60094	DBS	66056	DBS
55009	PRE	58012	DBS	60017	DBS	60095	DBS	66057	DBS

Data Tables

❏ 66058	DBS	❏ 66121	DBS	❏ 66184	DBS	❏ 66247	DBS	❏ 66527	FLR
❏ 66059	DBS	❏ 66122	DBS	❏ 66185	DBS	❏ 66248	DBS	❏ 66528	FLR
❏ 66060	DBS	❏ 66123	DBS	❏ 66186	DBS	❏ 66249	DBS	❏ 66529	FLR
❏ 66061	DBS	❏ 66124	DBS	❏ 66187	DBS	❏ 66250	DBS	❏ 66530	FLR
❏ 66062	DBS	❏ 66125	DBS	❏ 66188	DBS	❏ 66301	OLS	❏ 66531	FLR
❏ 66063	DBS	❏ 66126	DBS	❏ 66189	DBS	❏ 66302	OLS	❏ 66532	FLR
❏ 66064	DBS	❏ 66127	DBS	❏ 66190	DBS	❏ 66303	OLS	❏ 66533	FLR
❏ 66065	DBS	❏ 66128	DBS	❏ 66191	DBS	❏ 66304	OLS	❏ 66534	FLR
❏ 66066	DBS	❏ 66129	DBS	❏ 66192	DBS	❏ 66305	OLS	❏ 66535	FLR
❏ 66067	DBS	❏ 66130	DBS	❏ 66193	DBS	❏ 66401	GBR	❏ 66536	FLR
❏ 66068	DBS	❏ 66131	DBS	❏ 66194	DBS	❏ 66402	GBR	❏ 66537	FLR
❏ 66069	DBS	❏ 66132	DBS	❏ 66195	DBS	❏ 66403	GBR	❏ 66538	FLR
❏ 66070	DBS	❏ 66133	DBS	❏ 66196	DBS	❏ 66404	GBR	❏ 66539	FLR
❏ 66071	DBS	❏ 66134	DBS	❏ 66197	DBS	❏ 66405	GBR	❏ 66540	FLR
❏ 66072	DBS	❏ 66135	DBS	❏ 66198	DBS	❏ 66411	DRS	❏ 66541	FLR
❏ 66073	DBS	❏ 66136	DBS	❏ 66199	DBS	❏ 66412	DRS	❏ 66542	FLR
❏ 66074	DBS	❏ 66137	DBS	❏ 66200	DBS	❏ 66413	DRS	❏ 66543	FLR
❏ 66075	DBS	❏ 66138	DBS	❏ 66201	DBS	❏ 66414	DRS	❏ 66544	OLS
❏ 66076	DBS	❏ 66139	DBS	❏ 66202	DBS	❏ 66415	DRS	❏ 66545	FLR
❏ 66077	DBS	❏ 66140	DBS	❏ 66203	DBS	❏ 66416	DRS	❏ 66546	OLS
❏ 66078	DBS	❏ 66141	DBS	❏ 66204	DBS	❏ 66417	DRS	❏ 66547	OLS
❏ 66079	DBS	❏ 66142	DBS	❏ 66205	DBS	❏ 66418	DRS	❏ 66548	FLR
❏ 66080	DBS	❏ 66143	DBS	❏ 66206	DBS	❏ 66419	DRS	❏ 66549	FLR
❏ 66081	DBS	❏ 66144	DBS	❏ 66207	DBS	❏ 66420	DRS	❏ 66550	FLR
❏ 66082	DBS	❏ 66145	DBS	❏ 66208	DBS	❏ 66421	DRS	❏ 66551	OLS
❏ 66083	DBS	❏ 66146	DBS	❏ 66209	DBS	❏ 66422	DRS	❏ 66552	OLS
❏ 66084	DBS	❏ 66147	DBS	❏ 66210	DBS	❏ 66423	DRS	❏ 66553	FLR
❏ 66085	DBS	❏ 66148	DBS	❏ 66211	DBS	❏ 66424	DRS	❏ 66554	FLR
❏ 66086	DBS	❏ 66149	DBS	❏ 66212	DBS	❏ 66425	DRS	❏ 66555	FLR
❏ 66087	DBS	❏ 66150	DBS	❏ 66213	DBS	❏ 66426	DRS	❏ 66556	FLR
❏ 66088	DBS	❏ 66151	DBS	❏ 66214	DBS	❏ 66427	DRS	❏ 66557	FLR
❏ 66089	DBS	❏ 66152	DBS	❏ 66215	DBS	❏ 66428	DRS	❏ 66558	FLR
❏ 66090	DBS	❏ 66153	DBS	❏ 66216	GBR	❏ 66429	DRS	❏ 66559	FLR
❏ 66091	DBS	❏ 66154	DBS	❏ 66217	DBS	❏ 66430	DRS	❏ 66560	FLR
❏ 66092	DBS	❏ 66155	DBS	❏ 66218	DBS	❏ 66431	DRS	❏ 66561	FLR
❏ 66093	DBS	❏ 66156	DBS	❏ 66219	DBS	❏ 66432	DRS	❏ 66562	FLR
❏ 66094	DBS	❏ 66157	DBS	❏ 66220	DBS	❏ 66433	DRS	❏ 66563	FLR
❏ 66095	DBS	❏ 66158	DBS	❏ 66221	DBS	❏ 66434	DRS	❏ 66564	FLR
❏ 66096	DBS	❏ 66159	DBS	❏ 66222	DBS	❏ 66501	FLR	❏ 66565	FLR
❏ 66097	DBS	❏ 66160	DBS	❏ 66223	DBS	❏ 66502	FLR	❏ 66566	FLR
❏ 66098	DBS	❏ 66161	DBS	❏ 66224	DBS	❏ 66503	FLR	❏ 66567	FLR
❏ 66099	DBS	❏ 66162	DBS	❏ 66225	DBS	❏ 66504	FLR	❏ 66568	FLR
❏ 66100	DBS	❏ 66163	DBS	❏ 66226	DBS	❏ 66505	FLR	❏ 66569	FLR
❏ 66101	DBS	❏ 66164	DBS	❏ 66227	DBS	❏ 66506	FLR	❏ 66570	FLR
❏ 66102	DBS	❏ 66165	DBS	❏ 66228	DBS	❏ 66507	OLS	❏ 66571	FLR
❏ 66103	DBS	❏ 66166	DBS	❏ 66229	DBS	❏ 66508	FLR	❏ 66572	FLR
❏ 66104	DBS	❏ 66167	DBS	❏ 66230	DBS	❏ 66509	FLR	❏ 66573	FLR
❏ 66105	DBS	❏ 66168	DBS	❏ 66231	DBS	❏ 66510	FLR	❏ 66574	FLR
❏ 66106	DBS	❏ 66169	DBS	❏ 66232	DBS	❏ 66511	FLR	❏ 66575	FLR
❏ 66107	DBS	❏ 66170	DBS	❏ 66233	DBS	❏ 66512	FLR	❏ 66576	FLR
❏ 66108	DBS	❏ 66171	DBS	❏ 66234	DBS	❏ 66513	FLR	❏ 66577	FLR
❏ 66109	DBS	❏ 66172	DBS	❏ 66235	DBS	❏ 66514	FLR	❏ 66578	OLS
❏ 66110	DBS	❏ 66173	DBS	❏ 66236	DBS	❏ 66515	FLR	❏ 66579	OLS
❏ 66111	DBS	❏ 66174	DBS	❏ 66237	DBS	❏ 66516	FLR	❏ 66580	OLS
❏ 66112	DBS	❏ 66175	DBS	❏ 66238	DBS	❏ 66517	FLR	❏ 66581	OLS
❏ 66113	DBS	❏ 66176	DBS	❏ 66239	DBS	❏ 66518	FLR	❏ 66582	EXP
❏ 66114	DBS	❏ 66177	DBS	❏ 66240	DBS	❏ 66519	FLR	❏ 66583	EXP
❏ 66115	DBS	❏ 66178	DBS	❏ 66241	DBS	❏ 66520	FLR	❏ 66584	EXP
❏ 66116	DBS	❏ 66179	DBS	❏ 66242	DBS	❏ 66522	FLR	❏ 66585	FLR
❏ 66117	DBS	❏ 66180	DBS	❏ 66243	DBS	❏ 66523	FLR	❏ 66586	EXP
❏ 66118	DBS	❏ 66181	DBS	❏ 66244	DBS	❏ 66524	FLR	❏ 66587	FLR
❏ 66119	DBS	❏ 66182	DBS	❏ 66245	DBS	❏ 66525	FLR	❏ 66588	FLR
❏ 66120	DBS	❏ 66183	DBS	❏ 66246	DBS	❏ 66526	FLR	❏ 66589	FLR

Data Tables

❏ 66590	FLR	❏ 66729	GBR	❏ 73003	PRE	❏ 77028	ECR	❏ 86259	PRE
❏ 66591	FLR	❏ 66730	GBR	❏ 73005	PRE	❏ 77029	ECR	❏ 86401	PRE
❏ 66592	FLR	❏ 66731	GBR	❏ 73006	PRE	❏ 77030	ECR	❏ 86424	ETL
❏ 66593	FLR	❏ 66841	COL	❏ 73101	PRE	❏ 77031	ECR	❏ 86501	FLR
❏ 66594	FLR	❏ 66842	COL	❏ 73103	PRE	❏ 77032	ECR	❏ 86602	FLR
❏ 66595	FLR	❏ 66843	COL	❏ 73104	PRE	❏ 77033	ECR	❏ 86604	FLR
❏ 66596	FLR	❏ 66844	COL	❏ 73107	BAR	❏ 77034	ECR	❏ 86605	FLR
❏ 66597	FLR	❏ 66845	COL	❏ 73109	TTS	❏ 77035	ECR	❏ 86607	FLR
❏ 66598	FLR	❏ 66951	FLR	❏ 73110	PRE	❏ 77036	ECR	❏ 86609	FLR
❏ 66599	FLR	❏ 66952	FLR	❏ 73114	PRE	❏ 77037	ECR	❏ 86610	FLR
❏ 66601	FLR	❏ 66953	FLR	❏ 73117	PRE	❏ 77038	ECR	❏ 86612	FLR
❏ 66602	FLR	❏ 66954	FLR	❏ 73118	TTS	❏ 77039	ECR	❏ 86613	FLR
❏ 66603	FLR	❏ 66955	FLR	❏ 73119	KRS	❏ 77040	ECR	❏ 86614	FLR
❏ 66604	FLR	❏ 66956	FLR	❏ 73128	PRE	❏ 77041	ECR	❏ 86621	FLR
❏ 66605	FLR	❏ 66957	FLR	❏ 73129	PRE	❏ 77042	ECR	❏ 86622	FLR
❏ 66606	FLR			❏ 73130	PRE	❏ 77043	ECR	❏ 86623	FLR
❏ 66607	FLR	❏ 67001	DBS	❏ 73133	TTS	❏ 77044	ECR	❏ 86627	FLR
❏ 66608	FLR	❏ 67002	DBS	❏ 73134	PRE	❏ 77045	ECR	❏ 86628	FLR
❏ 66609	FLR	❏ 67003	DBS	❏ 73136	TTS	❏ 77046	ECR	❏ 86632	FLR
❏ 66610	FLR	❏ 67004	DBS	❏ 73138	NRL	❏ 77047	ECR	❏ 86633	FLR
❏ 66611	FLR	❏ 67005	DBS	❏ 73139	PRE	❏ 77048	ECR	❏ 86635	FLR
❏ 66612	FLR	❏ 67006	DBS	❏ 73140	PRE	❏ 77049	ECR	❏ 86637	FLR
❏ 66613	OLS	❏ 67007	DBS	❏ 73141	GBR	❏ 77050	ECR	❏ 86638	FLR
❏ 66614	FLR	❏ 67008	DBS	❏ 73201	BAR	❏ 77051	ECR	❏ 86639	FLR
❏ 66615	FLR	❏ 67009	DBS	❏ 73202	SOU	❏ 77052	ECR	❏ 86701	ETL
❏ 66616	FLR	❏ 67010	WSR	❏ 73204	GBR	❏ 77053	ECR	❏ 86702	ETL
❏ 66617	FLR	❏ 67011	DBS	❏ 73205	GBR	❏ 77054	ECR	❏ 86901	NRL
❏ 66618	FLR	❏ 67012	WSR	❏ 73206	GBR	❏ 77055	ECR	❏ 86902	NRL
❏ 66619	FLR	❏ 67013	WSR	❏ 73207	GBR	❏ 77056	ECR		
❏ 66620	FLR	❏ 67014	WSR	❏ 73208	GBR	❏ 77057	ECR	❏ 87001	PRE
❏ 66621	FLR	❏ 67015	WSR	❏ 73209	GBR	❏ 77058	ECR	❏ 87002	ETL
❏ 66622	FLR	❏ 67016	DBS	❏ 73210	PRE	❏ 77059	ECR	❏ 87003	EXP
❏ 66623	FLR	❏ 67017	DBS	❏ 73211	TTS	❏ 77060	ECR	❏ 87004	EXP
❏ 66624	EXP	❏ 67018	DBS	❏ 73212	GBR			❏ 87006	EXP
❏ 66625	EXP	❏ 67019	DBS	❏ 73213	GBR	❏ 81002	PRE	❏ 87007	EXP
❏ 66701	GBR	❏ 67020	DBS					❏ 87008	EXP
❏ 66702	GBR	❏ 67021	DBS	❏ 77001	ECR	❏ 82008	PRE	❏ 87009	EPX
❏ 66703	GBR	❏ 67022	DBS	❏ 77002	ECR			❏ 87010	EXP
❏ 66704	GBR	❏ 67023	DBS	❏ 77003	ECR	❏ 83012	PRE	❏ 87012	EXP
❏ 66705	GBR	❏ 67024	DBS	❏ 77004	ECR			❏ 87013	EXP
❏ 66706	GBR	❏ 67025	DBS	❏ 77005	ECR	❏ 84001	PRE	❏ 87014	EXP
❏ 66707	GBR	❏ 67026	DBS	❏ 77006	ECR			❏ 87017	EPX
❏ 66708	GBR	❏ 67027	DBS	❏ 77007	ECR	❏ 85101	PRE	❏ 87019	EXP
❏ 66709	GBR	❏ 67028	DBS	❏ 77008	ECR			❏ 87020	EXP
❏ 66710	GBR	❏ 67029	DBS	❏ 77009	ECR	❏ 86101	ETL	❏ 87022	EXP
❏ 66711	GBR	❏ 67030	DBS	❏ 77010	ECR	❏ 86213	PRE	❏ 87023	EPX
❏ 66712	GBR			❏ 77011	ECR	❏ 86215	EPX	❏ 87025	OLS
❏ 66713	GBR	❏ 70001	FLR	❏ 77012	ECR	❏ 86217	EPX	❏ 87026	EXP
❏ 66714	GBR	❏ 70002	FLR	❏ 77013	ECR	❏ 86218	EPX	❏ 87028	EXP
❏ 66715	GBR	❏ 70003	FLR	❏ 77014	ECR	❏ 86226	EPX	❏ 87029	EXP
❏ 66716	GBR	❏ 70004	FLR	❏ 77015	ECR	❏ 86228	EPX	❏ 87033	EXP
❏ 66717	GBR	❏ 70005	FLR	❏ 77016	ECR	❏ 86229	EPX	❏ 87034	EXP
❏ 66718	GBR	❏ 70006	FLR	❏ 77017	ECR	❏ 86231	EPX	❏ 87035	PRE
❏ 66719	GBR	❏ 70007	FLR	❏ 77018	ECR	❏ 86232	EPX		
❏ 66720	GBR	❏ 70008	FLR	❏ 77019	ECR	❏ 86233	PRE	❏ 89001	PRE
❏ 66721	GBR	❏ 70009	FLR	❏ 77020	ECR	❏ 86234	EPX		
❏ 66722	GBR	❏ 70010	FLR	❏ 77021	ECR	❏ 86235	EPX	❏ 90001	NXA
❏ 66723	GBR	❏ 70011	FLR	❏ 77022	ECR	❏ 86242	EPX	❏ 90002	NXA
❏ 66724	GBR	❏ 70012	FLR	❏ 77023	ECR	❏ 86246	EPX	❏ 90003	NXA
❏ 66725	GBR			❏ 77024	ECR	❏ 86247	EPX	❏ 90004	NXA
❏ 66726	GBR	❏ 71001	PRE	❏ 77025	ECR	❏ 86248	EPX	❏ 90005	NXA
❏ 66727	GBR			❏ 77026	ECR	❏ 86250	EXP	❏ 90006	NXA
❏ 66728	GBR	❏ 73001	PRE	❏ 77027	ECR	❏ 86251	EPX	❏ 90007	NXA

Data Tables

Number Cross-Link

❏ 90008	NXA	❏ 91120	ICE	❏ 97304	NRL	❏ 51382	PRE	❏ 52030	PRE
❏ 90009	NXA	❏ 91121	ICE			❏ 51384	PRE	❏ 52044	PRE
❏ 90010	NXA	❏ 91122	ICE	❏ 97650	PRE	❏ 51388	PRE	❏ 52048	PRE
❏ 90011	NXA	❏ 91124	ICE	❏ 97651	PRE	❏ 51392	PRE	❏ 52053	PRE
❏ 90012	NXA	❏ 91125	ICE	❏ 97654	PRE	❏ 51395	PRE	❏ 52054	PRE
❏ 90013	NXA	❏ 91126	ICE			❏ 51397	PRE	❏ 52062	PRE
❏ 90014	NXA	❏ 91127	ICE	**Diesel Multiple**		❏ 51398	PRE	❏ 52064	PRE
❏ 90015	NXA	❏ 91128	ICE	**Units**		❏ 51400	PRE	❏ 52071	PRE
❏ 90016	FLR	❏ 91129	ICE	❏ APT-E	PRE	❏ 51401	PRE	❏ 52077	PRE
❏ 90017	DBS	❏ 91130	ICE	❏ LEV1	PRE	❏ 51402	PRE		
❏ 90018	DBS	❏ 91131	ICE	❏ RB004	PRE	❏ 51405	PRE	❏ 53160	PRE
❏ 90019	DBS	❏ 91132	ICE			❏ 51407	PRE	❏ 53164	PRE
❏ 90020	DBS			❏ 50015	PRE	❏ 51434	PRE	❏ 53170	PRE
❏ 90021	DBS	❏ 92001	DBS	❏ 50019	PRE	❏ 51485	PRE	❏ 53193	PRE
❏ 90022	DBS	❏ 92002	DBS	❏ 50222	PRE	❏ 51499	PRE	❏ 53203	PRE
❏ 90023	DBS	❏ 92003	DBS	❏ 50256	PRE	❏ 51503	PRE	❏ 53204	PRE
❏ 90024	DBS	❏ 92004	DBS	❏ 50338	PRE	❏ 51505	PRE	❏ 53253	PRE
❏ 90025	DBS	❏ 92005	DBS	❏ 50416	PRE	❏ 51511	PRE	❏ 53266	PRE
❏ 90026	DBS	❏ 92006	SNF	❏ 50447	PRE	❏ 51512	PRE	❏ 53321	PRE
❏ 90027	DBS	❏ 92007	DBS	❏ 50454	PRE	❏ 51513	PRE	❏ 53628	PRE
❏ 90028	DBS	❏ 92008	DBS	❏ 50479	PRE	❏ 51562	PRE	❏ 53645	PRE
❏ 90029	DBS	❏ 92009	DBS	❏ 50528	PRE	❏ 51565	PRE	❏ 53746	PRE
❏ 90030	DBS	❏ 92010	GRB	❏ 50531	PRE	❏ 51566	PRE	❏ 53926	PRE
❏ 90031	DBS	❏ 92011	DBS	❏ 50556	PRE	❏ 51567	PRE	❏ 53971	PRE
❏ 90032	DBS	❏ 92012	DBS	❏ 50599	PRE	❏ 51568	PRE		
❏ 90033	DBS	❏ 92013	DBS	❏ 50619	PRE	❏ 51571	PRE	❏ 54055	PRE
❏ 90034	DBS	❏ 92014	SNF	❏ 50632	PRE	❏ 51572	PRE	❏ 54057	PRE
❏ 90035	DBS	❏ 92015	DBS	❏ 50929	PRE	❏ 51592	PRE	❏ 54062	PRE
❏ 90036	DBS	❏ 92016	DBS	❏ 50980	PRE	❏ 51604	PRE	❏ 54207	PRE
❏ 90037	DBS	❏ 92017	DBS			❏ 51616	PRE	❏ 54223	PRE
❏ 90038	DBS	❏ 92018	SNF	❏ 51017	PRE	❏ 51618	PRE	❏ 54270	PRE
❏ 90039	DBS	❏ 92019	DBS	❏ 51043	PRE	❏ 51622	PRE	❏ 54279	PRE
❏ 90040	DBS	❏ 92020	GBR	❏ 51073	PRE	❏ 51655	PRE	❏ 54289	PRE
❏ 90041	FLR	❏ 92021	GBR	❏ 51074	PRE	❏ 51663	PRE	❏ 54365	PRE
❏ 90042	FLR	❏ 92022	SNF	❏ 51104	PRE	❏ 51669	PRE	❏ 54408	PRE
❏ 90043	FLR	❏ 92023	DBS	❏ 51131	PRE	❏ 51677	PRE	❏ 54490	PRE
❏ 90044	FLR	❏ 92024	DBS	❏ 51138	PRE	❏ 51803	PRE	❏ 54504	PRE
❏ 90045	FLR	❏ 92025	DBS	❏ 51151	PRE	❏ 51813	PRE		
❏ 90046	FLR	❏ 92026	DBS	❏ 51187	PRE	❏ 51842	PRE	❏ 55000	PRE
❏ 90047	FLR	❏ 92027	DBS	❏ 51188	PRE	❏ 51849	PRE	❏ 55001	PRE
❏ 90048	FLR	❏ 92028	GBR	❏ 51189	PRE	❏ 51852	PRE	❏ 55003	PRE
❏ 90049	FLR	❏ 92029	DBS	❏ 51192	PRE	❏ 51859	PRE	❏ 55005	PRE
❏ 90050	FLR	❏ 92030	DBS	❏ 51205	PRE	❏ 51880	PRE	❏ 55006	PRE
		❏ 92031	DBS	❏ 51210	PRE	❏ 51886	PRE	❏ 55009	PRE
❏ 91101	ICE	❏ 92032	GBR	❏ 51226	PRE	❏ 51887	PRE	❏ 55012	PRE
❏ 91102	ICE	❏ 92033	SNF	❏ 51228	PRE	❏ 51899	PRE	❏ 55023	PRE
❏ 91103	ICE	❏ 92034	DBS	❏ 51247	PRE	❏ 51907	PRE	❏ 55028	PRE
❏ 91104	ICE	❏ 92035	DBS	❏ 51321	PRE	❏ 51909	PRE	❏ 55032	ATW
❏ 91105	ICE	❏ 92036	DBS	❏ 51339	PRE	❏ 51914	PRE	❏ 55033	PRE
❏ 91106	ICE	❏ 92037	DBS	❏ 51341	PRE	❏ 51919	PRE	❏ 55966	PRE
❏ 91107	ICE	❏ 92038	GBR	❏ 51342	PRE	❏ 51922	PRE	❏ 55976	PRE
❏ 91108	ICE	❏ 92039	DBS	❏ 51346	PRE	❏ 51933	PRE		
❏ 91109	ICE	❏ 92040	GBR	❏ 51347	NRL	❏ 51941	PRE	❏ 56006	PRE
❏ 91110	ICE	❏ 92041	DBS	❏ 51351	PRE	❏ 51942	PRE	❏ 56015	PRE
❏ 91111	ICE	❏ 92042	DBS	❏ 51353	PRE	❏ 51947	PRE	❏ 56121	PRE
❏ 91112	ICE	❏ 92043	EUR	❏ 51356	PRE	❏ 51950	PRE	❏ 56171	PRE
❏ 91113	ICE	❏ 92044	EUR	❏ 51359	PRE	❏ 51973	PRE	❏ 56208	PRE
❏ 91114	ICE	❏ 92045	EUR	❏ 51360	PRE	❏ 51990	PRE	❏ 56224	PRE
❏ 91115	ICE	❏ 92046	EUR	❏ 51363	PRE	❏ 52005	PRE	❏ 56271	PRE
❏ 91116	ICE			❏ 51365	PRE			❏ 56287	PRE
❏ 91117	ICE	❏ 97301	NRL	❏ 51367	PRE	❏ 52006	PRE	❏ 56301	PRE
❏ 91118	ICE	❏ 97302	NRL	❏ 51372	PRE	❏ 52008	PRE	❏ 56343	PRE
❏ 91119	ICE	❏ 97303	NRL	❏ 51381	PRE	❏ 52025	PRE	❏ 56352	PRE

Data Tables

No.		No.		No.		No.		No.	
56358	PRE	79612	PRE	142047	NOR	143615	ATW	150127	FGW
56456	PRE	79900	PRE	142048	NOR	143617	FGW	150128	FGW
56484	PRE	79960	PRE	142049	NOR	143618	FGW	150129	FGW
56491	PRE	79962	PRE	142050	NOR	143619	FGW	150130	FGW
56492	PRE	79963	PRE	142051	NOR	143620	FGW	150131	FGW
56495	PRE	79964	PRE	142052	NOR	143621	FGW	150132	LMI
		79976	PRE	142053	NOR	143622	ATW	150133	NOR
59003	PRE	79978	PRE	142054	NOR	143623	ATW	150134	NOR
59004	PRE			142055	NOR	143624	ATW	150135	NOR
59117	PRE	121020	CRW	142056	NOR	143625	ATW	150136	NOR
59228	PRE	121032	ATW	142057	NOR			150137	NOR
59245	PRE	121034	CRW	142058	NOR	144001	NOR	150138	NOR
59250	PRE			142060	NOR	144002	NOR	150139	NOR
59276	PRE	139001	LMI	142061	NOR	144003	NOR	150140	NOR
59387	PRE	139002	LMI	142062	NOR	144004	NOR	150141	NOR
59389	PRE			142063	FGW	144005	NOR	150142	NOR
59404	PRE	140001	PRE	142064	FGW	144006	NOR	150143	NOR
59444	PRE			142065	NOR	144007	NOR	150144	NOR
59486	PRE	142001	FGW	142066	NOR	144008	NOR	150145	NOR
59488	PRE	142002	ATW	142067	NOR	144009	NOR	150146	NOR
59492	PRE	142003	NOR	142068	FGW	144010	NOR	150147	NOR
59494	PRE	142004	NOR	142069	ATW	144011	NOR	150148	NOR
59500	PRE	142005	NOR	142070	NOR	144012	NOR	150149	NOR
59503	PRE	142006	ATW	142071	NOR	144013	NOR	150150	NOR
59506	PRE	142007	NOR	142072	ATW	144014	NOR	150201	NOR
59507	PRE	142009	FGW	142073	ATW	144015	NOR	150203	NOR
59508	PRE	142010	ATW	142074	ATW	144016	NOR	150205	NOR
59509	PRE	142011	NOR	142075	ATW	144017	NOR	150207	NOR
59510	PRE	142012	NOR	142076	ATW	144018	NOR	150208	ATW
59513	PRE	142013	NOR	142077	ATW	144019	NOR	150211	NOR
59514	PRE	142014	NOR	142078	NOR	144020	NOR	150214	LMI
59516	PRE	142015	NOR	142079	NOR	144021	NOR	150215	NOR
59517	PRE	142016	NOR	142080	ATW	144022	NOR	150216	LMI
59520	PRE	142017	NOR	142081	ATW	144023	NOR	150218	NOR
59521	PRE	142018	NOR	142082	ATW			150219	FGW
59522	PRE	142019	NOR	142083	ATW	150001	LMI	150221	FGW
59539	PRE	142020	NOR	142084	NOR	150002	LMI	150222	NOR
59575	PRE	142021	NOR	142085	ATW	150003	LMI	150223	NOR
59603	PRE	142022	NOR	142086	NOR	150005	LMI	150224	NOR
59609	PRE	142023	NOR	142087	NOR	150007	LMI	150225	NOR
59659	PRE	142024	NOR	142088	NOR	150009	LMI	150228	NOR
59664	PRE	142025	NOR	142089	NOR	150010	LMI	150232	FGW
59678	PRE	142026	NOR	142090	NOR	150011	LMI	150233	FGW
59701	PRE	142027	NOR	142091	NOR	150012	LMI	150234	FGW
59719	PRE	142028	NOR	142092	NOR	150013	LMI	150236	ATW
59740	PRE	142029	FGW	142093	NOR	150014	LMI	150238	FGW
59761	PRE	142030	FGW	142094	NOR	150015	LMI	150239	FGW
59791	PRE	142031	NOR	142095	NOR	150016	LMI	150240	ATW
		142032	NOR	142096	NOR	150017	LMI	150241	ATW
60117	PRE	142033	NOR			150018	LMI	150242	ATW
60127	PRE	142034	NOR	143601	ATW	150019	LMI	150243	FGW
60142	PRE	142035	NOR	143602	ATW	150101	LMI	150244	FGW
60145	PRE	142036	NOR	143603	FGW	150102	LMI	150245	ATW
60149	PRE	142037	NOR	143604	ATW	150104	LMI	150246	FGW
60616	PRE	142038	NOR	143605	ATW	150106	LMI	150247	FGW
60822	PRE	142039	NOR	143606	ATW	150108	LMI	150248	FGW
60828	PRE	142040	NOR	143607	ATW	150120	FGW	150249	FGW
60901	PRE	142041	NOR	143608	ATW	150121	FGW	150250	ATW
60904	PRE	142042	NOR	143609	ATW	150122	LMI	150251	ATW
60916	PRE	142043	NOR	143610	ATW	150123	FGW	150252	ATW
		142044	NOR	143611	FGW	150124	LMI	150253	ATW
70549	PRE	142045	NOR	143612	FGW	150125	LMI	150254	ATW
79018	PRE	142046	NOR	143614	ATW	150126	LMI	150256	ATW

Data Tables

No.	Code	No.	Code	No.	Code	No.	Code	No.	Code
150258	ATW	153335	NXA	156419	NXA	156482	NOR	158730	FSR
150259	ATW	153351	NOR	156420	NOR	156483	NOR	158731	FSR
150260	ATW	153352	NOR	156421	NOR	156484	NOR	158732	FSR
150261	FGW	153353	ATW	156422	NXA	156485	FSR	158733	FSR
150262	ATW	153354	LMI	156423	NOR	156486	NOR	158734	FSR
150263	FGW	153355	EMT	156424	NOR	156487	NOR	158735	FSR
150264	ATW	153356	LMI	156425	NOR	156488	NOR	158736	FSR
150265	FGW	153357	EMT	156426	NOR	156489	NOR	158737	FSR
150266	FGW	153358	NOR	156427	NOR	156490	NOR	158738	FSR
150267	ATW	153359	NOR	156428	NOR	156491	NOR	158739	FSR
150268	NOR	153360	NOR	156429	NOR	156492	FSR	158740	FSR
150269	NOR	153361	FGW	156430	FSR	156493	FSR	158741	FSR
150270	NOR	153362	ATW	156431	FSR	156494	FSR	158749	FGW
150271	NOR	153363	NOR	156432	FSR	156495	FSR	158752	NOR
150272	NOR	153364	LMI	156433	FSR	156496	FSR	158753	NOR
150273	NOR	153365	LMI	156434	FSR	156497	NOR	158754	NOR
150274	NOR	153366	LMI	156435	FSR	156498	NOR	158755	NOR
150275	NOR	153367	ATW	156436	FSR	156499	FSR	158756	NOR
150276	NOR	153368	FGW	156437	FSR	156500	FSR	158757	NOR
150277	NOR	153369	FGW	156438	NOR	156501	NOR	158758	NOR
150278	ATW	153370	FGW	156439	FSR	156502	FSR	158759	NOR
150279	ATW	153371	LMI	156440	NOR	156503	FSR	158763	FGW
150280	ATW	153372	FGW	156441	NOR	156504	FSR	158766	FGW
150281	ATW	153373	FGW	156442	FSR	156505	FSR	158767	FGW
150282	ATW	153374	EMT	156443	NOR	156506	FSR	158769	FGW
150283	ATW	153375	LMI	156444	NOR	156507	FSR	158770	EMT
150284	ATW	153376	EMT	156445	FSR	156508	FSR	158773	EMT
150285	ATW	153377	FGW	156446	FSR	156509	FSR	158774	EMT
		153378	NOR	156447	FSR	156510	FSR	158777	EMT
153301	NOR	153379	EMT	156448	NOR	156511	FSR	158780	EMT
153302	EMT	153380	FGW	156449	FSR	156512	FSR	158782	FSR
153303	ATW	153381	EMT	156450	FSR	156513	FSR	158783	EMT
153304	NOR	153382	FGW	156451	NOR	156514	FSR	158784	NOR
153305	FGW	153383	EMT	156452	NOR			158785	EMT
153306	NXA	153384	EMT	156453	FSR	158701	FSR	158786	FSR
153307	NOR	153385	EMT	156454	NOR	158702	FSR	158787	NOR
153308	EMT			156455	NOR	158703	FSR	158788	EMT
153309	NXA	155341	NOR	156456	FSR	158704	FSR	158789	FSR
153310	EMT	155342	NOR	156457	FSR	158705	FSR	158790	NOR
153311	EMT	155343	NOR	156458	FSR	158706	FSR	158791	NOR
153312	ATW	155344	NOR	156459	NOR	158707	FSR	158792	NOR
153313	NOR	155345	NOR	156460	NOR	158708	FSR	158793	NOR
153314	NXA	155346	NOR	156461	NOR	158709	FSR	158794	NOR
153315	NOR	155347	NOR	156462	FSR	158710	FSR	158795	NOR
153316	NOR			156463	NOR	158711	FSR	158796	NOR
153317	NOR	156401	EMT	156464	NOR	158712	FSR	158797	NOR
153318	FGW	156402	NXA	156465	FSR	158713	FSR	158798	FGW
153319	EMT	156403	EMT	156466	NOR	158714	FSR	158799	EMT
153320	ATW	156404	EMT	156467	FSR	158715	FSR	158806	EMT
153321	EMT	156405	EMT	156468	NOR	158716	FSR	158810	EMT
153322	NXA	156406	EMT	156469	NOR	158717	FSR	158812	EMT
153323	ATW	156407	NXA	156470	NOR	158718	FSR	158813	EMT
153324	NOR	156408	EMT	156471	NOR	158719	FSR	158815	NOR
153325	LMI	156409	NXA	156472	NOR	158720	FSR	158816	NOR
153326	EMT	156410	EMT	156473	NOR	158721	FSR	158817	NOR
153327	ATW	156411	EMT	156474	FSR	158722	FSR	158818	ATW
153328	NOR	156412	NXA	156475	NOR	158723	FSR	158819	ATW
153329	FGW	156413	EMT	156476	FSR	158724	FSR	158820	ATW
153330	NOR	156414	EMT	156477	FSR	158725	FSR	158821	ATW
153331	NOR	156415	EMT	156478	NOR	158726	FSR	158822	ATW
153332	NOR	156416	NXA	156479	NOR	158727	FSR	158823	ATW
153333	LMI	156417	NXA	156480	NOR	158728	FSR	158824	ATW
153334	LMI	156418	NXA	156481	NOR	158729	FSR	158825	ATW

Number	Code		Number	Code		Number	Code		Number	Code		Number	Code
158826	ATW		158907	NOR		165018	CRW		166215	FGW		170308	FTP
158827	ATW		158908	NOR		165019	CRW		166216	FGW		170309	FTP
158828	ATW		158909	NOR		165020	CRW		166217	FGW		170393	FSR
158829	ATW		158910	NOR		165021	CRW		166218	FGW		170394	FSR
158830	ATW		158950	FGW		165022	CRW		166219	FGW		170395	FSR
158831	ATW		158951	FGW		165023	CRW		166220	FGW		170396	FSR
158832	ATW		158952	FGW		165024	CRW		166221	FGW		170397	AXC
158833	ATW		158953	FGW		165025	CRW					170398	AXC
158834	ATW		158954	FGW		165026	CRW		168001	CRW		170401	FSR
158835	ATW		158955	FGW		165027	CRW		168002	CRW		170402	FSR
158836	ATW		158956	FGW		165028	CRW		168003	CRW		170403	FSR
158837	ATW		158957	FGW		165029	CRW		168004	CRW		170404	FSR
158838	ATW		158958	FGW		165030	CRW		168005	CRW		170405	FSR
158839	ATW		158959	FGW		165031	CRW		168106	CRW		170406	FSR
158840	ATW					165032	CRW		168107	CRW		170407	FSR
158841	ATW		159001	SWT		165033	CRW		168108	CRW		170408	FSR
158843	NOR		159002	SWT		165034	CRW		168109	CRW		170409	FSR
158844	NOR		159003	SWT		165035	CRW		168110	CRW		170410	FSR
158845	NOR		159004	SWT		165036	CRW		168112	CRW		170411	FSR
158846	EMT		159005	SWT		165037	CRW		168113	CRW		170412	FSR
158847	EMT		159006	SWT		165038	CRW		168214	CRW		170413	FSR
158848	NOR		159007	SWT		165039	CRW		168215	CRW		170414	FSR
158849	NOR		159008	SWT		165101	FGW		168216	CRW		170415	FSR
158850	NOR		159009	SWT		165102	FGW		168217	CRW		170416	FSR
158851	NOR		159010	SWT		165103	FGW		168218	CRW		170417	FSR
158852	EMT		159011	SWT		165104	FGW		168219	CRW		170418	FSR
158853	NOR		159012	SWT		165105	FGW					170419	FSR
158854	EMT		159013	SWT		165106	FGW		170101	AXC		170420	FSR
158855	NOR		159014	SWT		165107	FGW		170102	AXC		170421	FSR
158856	EMT		159015	SWT		165108	FGW		170103	AXC		170422	FSR
158857	EMT		159016	SWT		165109	FGW		170104	AXC		170423	FSR
158858	EMT		159017	SWT		165110	FGW		170105	AXC		170424	FSR
158859	NOR		159018	SWT		165111	FGW		170106	AXC		170425	FSR
158860	NOR		159019	SWT		165112	FGW		170107	AXC		170426	FSR
158861	NOR		159020	SWT		165113	FGW		170108	AXC		170427	FSR
158862	EMT		159021	SWT		165114	FGW		170109	AXC		170428	FSR
158863	EMT		159022	SWT		165115	FGW		170110	AXC		170429	FSR
158864	EMT		159101	SWT		165116	FGW		170111	AXC		170430	FSR
158865	EMT		159102	SWT		165117	FGW		170112	AXC		170431	FSR
158866	EMT		159103	SWT		165118	FGW		170113	AXC		170432	FSR
158867	FSR		159104	SWT		165119	FGW		170114	AXC		170433	FSR
158868	FSR		159105	SWT		165120	FGW		170115	AXC		170434	FSR
158869	FSR		159106	SWT		165121	FGW		170116	AXC		170450	FSR
158870	FSR		159107	SWT		165122	FGW		170117	AXC		170451	FSR
158871	FSR		159108	SWT		165123	FGW		170201	NXA		170452	FSR
158872	NOR					165124	FGW		170202	NXA		170453	FSR
158880	SWT		165001	CRW		165125	FGW		170203	NXA		170454	FSR
158881	SWT		165002	CRW		165126	FGW		170204	NXA		170455	FSR
158882	SWT		165003	CRW					170205	NXA		170456	FSR
158883	SWT		165004	CRW		166201	FGW		170206	NXA		170457	FSR
158884	SWT		165005	CRW		166202	FGW		170207	NXA		170458	FSR
158885	SWT		165006	CRW		166203	FGW		170208	NXA		170459	FSR
158886	SWT		165007	CRW		166204	FGW		170270	NXA		170460	FTP
158887	SWT		165008	CRW		166205	FGW		170271	NXA		170461	FTP
158888	SWT		165009	CRW		166206	FGW		170272	NXA		170470	FSR
158889	SWT		165010	CRW		166207	FGW		170273	NXA		170471	FSR
158890	SWT		165011	CRW		166208	FGW		170301	FTP		170472	FSR
158901	NOR		165012	CRW		166209	FGW		170302	FTP		170473	FSR
158902	NOR		165013	CRW		166210	FGW		170303	FTP		170474	FSR
158903	NOR		165014	CRW		166211	FGW		170304	FTP		170475	FSR
158904	NOR		165015	CRW		166212	FGW		170305	FTP		170476	FSR
158905	NOR		165016	CRW		166213	FGW		170306	FTP		170477	FSR
158906	NOR		165017	CRW		166214	FGW		170307	FTP		170478	FSR

Number Cross-Link

❏ 170501	LMI	❏ 172211	LMI	❏ 180108	ICE	❏ 205009	PRE	❏ 221121	AXC
❏ 170502	LMI	❏ 172212	LMI	❏ 180109	FHT	❏ 205025	PRE	❏ 221122	AXC
❏ 170503	LMI	❏ 172213	LMI	❏ 180110	FHT	❏ 205028	PRE	❏ 221123	AXC
❏ 170504	LMI	❏ 172214	LMI	❏ 180111	FHT	❏ 205032	PRE	❏ 221124	AXC
❏ 170505	LMI	❏ 172215	LMI	❏ 180112	GTL	❏ 205033	PRE	❏ 221125	AXC
❏ 170506	LMI	❏ 172216	LMI	❏ 180113	FHT	❏ 205101	PRE	❏ 221126	AXC
❏ 170507	LMI	❏ 172217	LMI	❏ 180114	GTL	❏ 205205	PRE	❏ 221127	AXC
❏ 170508	LMI	❏ 172218	LMI					❏ 221128	AXC
❏ 170509	LMI	❏ 172219	LMI	❏ 185101	FTP	❏ 220001	AXC	❏ 221129	AXC
❏ 170510	LMI	❏ 172220	LMI	❏ 185102	FTP	❏ 220002	AXC	❏ 221130	AXC
❏ 170511	LMI	❏ 172221	LMI	❏ 185103	FTP	❏ 220003	AXC	❏ 221131	AXC
❏ 170512	LMI	❏ 172222	LMI	❏ 185104	FTP	❏ 220004	AXC	❏ 221132	AXC
❏ 170513	LMI	❏ 172331	LMI	❏ 185105	FTP	❏ 220005	AXC	❏ 221133	AXC
❏ 170514	LMI	❏ 172332	LMI	❏ 185106	FTP	❏ 220006	AXC	❏ 221134	AXC
❏ 170515	LMI	❏ 172333	LMI	❏ 185107	FTP	❏ 220007	AXC	❏ 221135	AXC
❏ 170516	LMI	❏ 172334	LMI	❏ 185108	FTP	❏ 220008	AXC	❏ 221136	AXC
❏ 170517	LMI	❏ 172335	LMI	❏ 185109	FTP	❏ 220009	AXC	❏ 221137	AXC
❏ 170518	AXC	❏ 172336	LMI	❏ 185110	FTP	❏ 220010	AXC	❏ 221138	AXC
❏ 170519	AXC	❏ 172337	LMI	❏ 185111	FTP	❏ 220011	AXC	❏ 221139	AXC
❏ 170520	AXC	❏ 172338	LMI	❏ 185112	FTP	❏ 220012	AXC	❏ 221140	AXC
❏ 170521	AXC	❏ 172339	LMI	❏ 185113	FTP	❏ 220013	AXC	❏ 221141	AXC
❏ 170522	AXC	❏ 172340	LMI	❏ 185114	FTP	❏ 220014	AXC	❏ 221142	VWC
❏ 170523	AXC	❏ 172341	LMI	❏ 185115	FTP	❏ 220015	AXC	❏ 221143	VWC
❏ 170630	LMI	❏ 172342	LMI	❏ 185116	FTP	❏ 220016	AXC		
❏ 170631	LMI	❏ 172343	LMI	❏ 185117	FTP	❏ 220017	AXC	❏ 222001	EMT
❏ 170632	LMI	❏ 172344	LMI	❏ 185118	FTP	❏ 220018	AXC	❏ 222002	EMT
❏ 170633	LMI	❏ 172345	LMI	❏ 185119	FTP	❏ 220019	AXC	❏ 222003	EMT
❏ 170634	LMI			❏ 185120	FTP	❏ 220020	AXC	❏ 222004	EMT
❏ 170635	LMI	❏ 175001	ATW	❏ 185121	FTP	❏ 220021	AXC	❏ 222005	EMT
❏ 170636	AXC	❏ 175002	ATW	❏ 185122	FTP	❏ 220022	AXC	❏ 222006	EMT
❏ 170637	AXC	❏ 175003	ATW	❏ 185123	FTP	❏ 220023	AXC	❏ 222007	EMT
❏ 170638	AXC	❏ 175004	ATW	❏ 185124	FTP	❏ 220024	AXC	❏ 222008	EMT
❏ 170639	AXC	❏ 175005	ATW	❏ 185125	FTP	❏ 220025	AXC	❏ 222009	EMT
		❏ 175006	ATW	❏ 185126	FTP	❏ 220026	AXC	❏ 222010	EMT
❏ 171721	SOU	❏ 175007	ATW	❏ 185127	FTP	❏ 220027	AXC	❏ 222011	EMT
❏ 171722	SOU	❏ 175008	ATW	❏ 185128	FTP	❏ 220028	AXC	❏ 222012	EMT
❏ 171723	SOU	❏ 175009	ATW	❏ 185129	FTP	❏ 220029	AXC	❏ 222013	EMT
❏ 171724	SOU	❏ 175010	ATW	❏ 185130	FTP	❏ 220030	AXC	❏ 222014	EMT
❏ 171725	SOU	❏ 175011	ATW	❏ 185131	FTP	❏ 220031	AXC	❏ 222015	EMT
❏ 171726	SOU	❏ 175101	ATW	❏ 185132	FTP	❏ 220032	AXC	❏ 222016	EMT
❏ 171727	SOU	❏ 175102	ATW	❏ 185133	FTP	❏ 220033	AXC	❏ 222017	EMT
❏ 171728	SOU	❏ 175103	ATW	❏ 185134	FTP	❏ 220034	AXC	❏ 222018	EMT
❏ 171729	SOU	❏ 175104	ATW	❏ 185135	FTP			❏ 222019	EMT
❏ 171730	SOU	❏ 175105	ATW	❏ 185136	FTP	❏ 221101	VWC	❏ 222020	EMT
❏ 171801	SOU	❏ 175106	ATW	❏ 185137	FTP	❏ 221102	VWC	❏ 222021	EMT
❏ 171802	SOU	❏ 175107	ATW	❏ 185138	FTP	❏ 221103	VWC	❏ 222022	EMT
❏ 171803	SOU	❏ 175108	ATW	❏ 185139	FTP	❏ 221104	VWC	❏ 222023	EMT
❏ 171804	SOU	❏ 175109	ATW	❏ 185140	FTP	❏ 221105	VWC	❏ 222101	EMT
❏ 171805	SOU	❏ 175110	ATW	❏ 185141	FTP	❏ 221106	VWC	❏ 222102	EMT
❏ 171806	SOU	❏ 175111	ATW	❏ 185142	FTP	❏ 221107	VWC	❏ 222103	EMT
		❏ 175112	ATW	❏ 185143	FTP	❏ 221108	VWC	❏ 222104	EMT
❏ 172001	LOG	❏ 175113	ATW	❏ 185144	FTP	❏ 221109	VWC		
❏ 172002	LOG	❏ 175114	ATW	❏ 185145	FTP	❏ 221110	VWC	**Electric Multiple**	
❏ 172003	LOG	❏ 175115	ATW	❏ 185146	FTP	❏ 221111	VWC	**Units**	
❏ 172004	LOG	❏ 175116	ATW	❏ 185147	FTP	❏ 221112	VWC	❏ 85	PRE
❏ 172005	LOG			❏ 185148	FTP	❏ 221113	VWC	❏ 87	PRE
❏ 172006	LOG	❏ 180101	GTL	❏ 185149	FTP	❏ 221114	VWC	❏ 91	PRE
❏ 172007	LOG	❏ 180102	ICE	❏ 185150	FTP	❏ 221115	VWC	❏ 2090	PRE
❏ 172008	LOG	❏ 180103	ICE	❏ 185151	FTP	❏ 221116	VWC	❏ 4732	PRE
❏ 172101	CRW	❏ 180104	ICE			❏ 221117	VWC	❏ 5176	PRE
❏ 172102	CRW	❏ 180105	GTL	❏ 201001	PRE	❏ 221118	VWC	❏ 5759	PRE
❏ 172103	CRW	❏ 180106	ICE			❏ 221119	AXC	❏ 5791	PRE
❏ 172104	CRW	❏ 180107	GTL	❏ 202202	PRE	❏ 221120	AXC	❏ 5793	PRE

Number	Code
6307	PRE
7105	PRE
8143	PRE
10096	PRE
11161	PRE
11179	PRE
11201	PRE
11825	PRE
13004	PRE
15345	PRE
28249	PRE
28361	PRE
28690	PRE
29298	PRE
29666	PRE
29670	PRE
29720	PRE
29896	PRE
61183	PRE
61275	PRE
61287	PRE
61742	PRE
61743	PRE
61798	PRE
61799	PRE
61804	PRE
61805	PRE
62351	PRE
62364	PRE
62384	PRE
62378	PRE
62887	PRE
65451	PRE
65302	PRE
65304	PRE
67300	PRE
68001	PRE
68002	PRE
68003	PRE
68004	PRE
68005	PRE
68008	PRE
68009	PRE
68500	PRE
68506	PRE
69304	PRE
69310	PRE
69318	PRE
69332	PRE
69333	PRE
69337	PRE
69339	PRE

Number	Code
70229	PRE
70257	PRE
70273	PRE
70284	PRE
70292	PRE
70296	PRE
70354	PRE
70527	PRE
70531	PRE
70539	PRE
70576	PRE
70607	PRE
71032	PRE
72501	PRE
72617	PRE
75033	PRE
75186	PRE
75250	PRE
75395	PRE
75407	PRE
76529	PRE
76712	PRE
76726	PRE
76740	PRE
76746	PRE
76797	PRE
76811	PRE
76812	PRE
76817	PRE
76875	PRE
77172	PRE
79998	PRE
79999	PRE
303032	PRE
306017	PRE
309616	PRE
309624	PRE
313018	FCC
313024	FCC
313025	FCC
313026	FCC
313027	FCC
313028	FCC
313029	FCC
313030	FCC
313031	FCC
313032	FCC
313033	FCC
313035	FCC
313036	FCC
313037	FCC
313038	FCC

Number	Code
313039	FCC
313040	FCC
313041	FCC
313042	FCC
313043	FCC
313044	FCC
313045	FCC
313046	FCC
313047	FCC
313048	FCC
313049	FCC
313050	FCC
313051	FCC
313052	FCC
313053	FCC
313054	FCC
313055	FCC
313056	FCC
313057	FCC
313058	FCC
313059	FCC
313060	FCC
313061	FCC
313062	FCC
313063	FCC
313064	FCC
313121	OLS
313122	FCC
313123	FCC
313134	FCC
313201	SOU
313202	SOU
313203	SOU
313204	SOU
313205	SOU
313206	SOU
313207	SOU
313208	SOU
313209	SOU
313210	SOU
313211	SOU
313212	SOU
313213	SOU
313214	SOU
313215	SOU
313216	SOU
313217	SOU
313219	SOU
313220	SOU
314201	FSR
314202	FSR
314203	FSR
314204	FSR
314205	FSR
314206	FSR
314207	FSR
314208	FSR
314209	FSR
314210	FSR
314211	FSR
314212	FSR
314213	FSR

Number	Code
314214	FSR
314215	FSR
314216	FSR
315801	NXA
315802	NXA
315803	NXA
315804	NXA
315805	NXA
315806	NXA
315807	NXA
315808	NXA
315809	NXA
315810	NXA
315811	NXA
315812	NXA
315813	NXA
315814	NXA
315815	NXA
315816	NXA
315817	NXA
315818	NXA
315819	NXA
315820	NXA
315821	NXA
315822	NXA
315823	NXA
315824	NXA
315825	NXA
315826	NXA
315827	NXA
315828	NXA
315829	NXA
315830	NXA
315831	NXA
315832	NXA
315833	NXA
315834	NXA
315835	NXA
315836	NXA
315837	NXA
315838	NXA
315839	NXA
315840	NXA
315841	NXA
315842	NXA
315843	NXA
315844	NXA
315845	NXA
315846	NXA
315847	NXA
315848	NXA
315849	NXA
315850	NXA
315851	NXA
315852	NXA
315853	NXA
315854	NXA
315855	NXA
315856	NXA
315857	NXA
315858	NXA
315859	NXA

Number	Code
315860	NXA
315861	NXA
316997	OLS
317337	FCC
317338	FCC
317339	FCC
317340	FCC
317341	FCC
317342	FCC
317343	FCC
317344	FCC
317345	FCC
317346	FCC
317347	FCC
317348	FCC
317501	NXA
317502	NXA
317503	NXA
317504	NXA
317505	NXA
317506	NXA
317507	NXA
317508	NXA
317509	NXA
317510	NXA
317511	NXA
317512	NXA
317513	NXA
317514	NXA
317515	NXA
317649	NXA
317650	NXA
317651	NXA
317652	NXA
317653	NXA
317654	NXA
317655	NXA
317656	NXA
317657	NXA
317658	NXA
317659	NXA
317660	NXA
317661	NXA
317662	NXA
317663	NXA
317664	NXA
317665	NXA
317666	NXA
317667	NXA
317668	NXA
317669	NXA
317670	NXA
317671	NXA
317672	NXA
317708	NXA
317709	NXA
317710	NXA
317711	NXA
317719	NXA
317722	NXA
317723	NXA

Data Tables

Number Cross-Link

❏ 317729	NXA	❏ 319365	FCC	❏ 320301	FSR	❏ 321341	NXA	❏ 321437	NXA
❏ 317732	NXA	❏ 319366	FCC	❏ 320302	FSR	❏ 321342	NXA	❏ 321438	NXA
❏ 317881	NXA	❏ 319367	FCC	❏ 320303	FSR	❏ 321343	NXA	❏ 321439	NXA
❏ 317882	NXA	❏ 319368	FCC	❏ 320304	FSR	❏ 321344	NXA	❏ 321440	NXA
❏ 317883	NXA	❏ 319369	FCC	❏ 320305	FSR	❏ 321345	NXA	❏ 321441	NXA
❏ 317884	NXA	❏ 319370	FCC	❏ 320306	FSR	❏ 321346	NXA	❏ 321442	NXA
❏ 317885	NXA	❏ 319371	FCC	❏ 320307	FSR	❏ 321347	NXA	❏ 321443	NXA
❏ 317886	NXA	❏ 319372	FCC	❏ 320308	FSR	❏ 321348	NXA	❏ 321444	NXA
❏ 317887	NXA	❏ 319373	FCC	❏ 320309	FSR	❏ 321349	NXA	❏ 321445	NXA
❏ 317888	NXA	❏ 319374	FCC	❏ 320310	FSR	❏ 321350	NXA	❏ 321446	NXA
❏ 317889	NXA	❏ 319375	FCC	❏ 320311	FSR	❏ 321351	NXA	❏ 321447	NXA
❏ 317890	NXA	❏ 319376	FCC	❏ 320312	FSR	❏ 321352	NXA	❏ 321448	NXA
❏ 317891	NXA	❏ 319377	FCC	❏ 320313	FSR	❏ 321353	NXA		
❏ 317892	NXA	❏ 319378	FCC	❏ 320314	FSR	❏ 321354	NXA	❏ 321901	NOR
		❏ 319379	FCC	❏ 320315	FSR	❏ 321355	NXA	❏ 321902	NOR
❏ 318250	FSR	❏ 319380	FCC	❏ 320316	FSR	❏ 321356	NXA	❏ 321903	NOR
❏ 318251	FSR	❏ 319381	FCC	❏ 320317	FSR	❏ 321357	NXA		
❏ 318252	FSR	❏ 319382	FCC	❏ 320318	FSR	❏ 321358	NXA	❏ 322481	FSR
❏ 318253	FSR	❏ 319383	FCC	❏ 320319	FSR	❏ 321359	NXA	❏ 322482	FSR
❏ 318254	FSR	❏ 319384	FCC	❏ 320320	FSR	❏ 321360	NXA	❏ 322483	FSR
❏ 318255	FSR	❏ 319385	FCC	❏ 320321	FSR	❏ 321361	NXA	❏ 322484	FSR
❏ 318256	FSR	❏ 319386	FCC	❏ 320322	FSR	❏ 321362	NXA	❏ 322485	FSR
❏ 318257	FSR					❏ 321363	NXA		
❏ 318258	FSR	❏ 319421	FCC	❏ 321301	NXA	❏ 321364	NXA	❏ 323201	LMI
❏ 318259	FSR	❏ 319422	FCC	❏ 321302	NXA	❏ 321365	NXA	❏ 323202	LMI
❏ 318260	FSR	❏ 319423	FCC	❏ 321303	NXA	❏ 321366	NXA	❏ 323203	LMI
❏ 318261	FSR	❏ 319424	FCC	❏ 321304	NXA			❏ 323204	LMI
❏ 318262	FSR	❏ 319425	FCC	❏ 321305	NXA	❏ 321401	FCC	❏ 323205	LMI
❏ 318263	FSR	❏ 319426	FCC	❏ 321306	NXA	❏ 321402	FCC	❏ 323206	LMI
❏ 318264	FSR	❏ 319427	FCC	❏ 321307	NXA	❏ 321403	FCC	❏ 323207	LMI
❏ 318265	FSR	❏ 319428	FCC	❏ 321308	NXA	❏ 321404	FCC	❏ 323208	LMI
❏ 318266	FSR	❏ 319429	FCC	❏ 321309	NXA	❏ 321405	FCC	❏ 323209	LMI
❏ 318267	FSR	❏ 319430	FCC	❏ 321310	NXA	❏ 321406	FCC	❏ 323210	LMI
❏ 318268	FSR	❏ 319431	FCC	❏ 321311	NXA	❏ 321407	FCC	❏ 323211	LMI
❏ 318269	FSR	❏ 319432	FCC	❏ 321312	NXA	❏ 321408	FCC	❏ 323212	LMI
❏ 318270	FSR	❏ 319433	FCC	❏ 321313	NXA	❏ 321409	FCC	❏ 323213	LMI
		❏ 319434	FCC	❏ 321314	NXA	❏ 321410	FCC	❏ 323214	LMI
❏ 319001	FCC	❏ 319435	FCC	❏ 321315	NXA	❏ 321411	LMI	❏ 323215	LMI
❏ 319002	FCC	❏ 319436	FCC	❏ 321316	NXA	❏ 321412	LMI	❏ 323216	LMI
❏ 319003	FCC	❏ 319437	FCC	❏ 321317	NXA	❏ 321413	LMI	❏ 323217	LMI
❏ 319004	FCC	❏ 319438	FCC	❏ 321318	NXA	❏ 321414	LMI	❏ 323218	LMI
❏ 319005	FCC	❏ 319439	FCC	❏ 321319	NXA	❏ 321415	LMI	❏ 323219	LMI
❏ 319006	FCC	❏ 319440	FCC	❏ 321320	NXA	❏ 321416	LMI	❏ 323220	LMI
❏ 319007	FCC	❏ 319441	FCC	❏ 321321	NXA	❏ 321417	LMI	❏ 323221	LMI
❏ 319008	FCC	❏ 319442	FCC	❏ 321322	NXA	❏ 321418	FCC	❏ 323222	LMI
❏ 319009	FCC	❏ 319443	FCC	❏ 321323	NXA	❏ 321419	FCC	❏ 323223	NOR
❏ 319010	FCC	❏ 319444	FCC	❏ 321324	NXA	❏ 321420	FCC	❏ 323224	NOR
❏ 319011	FCC	❏ 319445	FCC	❏ 321325	NXA	❏ 321421	NXA	❏ 323225	NOR
❏ 319012	FCC	❏ 319446	FCC	❏ 321326	NXA	❏ 321422	NXA	❏ 323226	NOR
❏ 319013	FCC	❏ 319447	FCC	❏ 321327	NXA	❏ 321423	NXA	❏ 323227	NOR
		❏ 319448	FCC	❏ 321328	NXA	❏ 321424	NXA	❏ 323228	NOR
❏ 319214	FCC	❏ 319449	FCC	❏ 321329	NXA	❏ 321425	NXA	❏ 323229	NOR
❏ 319215	FCC	❏ 319450	FCC	❏ 321330	NXA	❏ 321426	NXA	❏ 323230	NOR
❏ 319216	FCC	❏ 319451	FCC	❏ 321331	NXA	❏ 321427	NXA	❏ 323231	NOR
❏ 319217	FCC	❏ 319452	FCC	❏ 321332	NXA	❏ 321428	NXA	❏ 323232	NOR
❏ 319218	FCC	❏ 319453	FCC	❏ 321333	NXA	❏ 321429	NXA	❏ 323233	NOR
❏ 319219	FCC	❏ 319454	FCC	❏ 321334	NXA	❏ 321430	NXA	❏ 323234	NOR
❏ 319220	FCC	❏ 319455	FCC	❏ 321335	NXA	❏ 321431	NXA	❏ 323235	NOR
		❏ 319456	FCC	❏ 321336	NXA	❏ 321432	NXA	❏ 323236	NOR
❏ 319361	FCC	❏ 319457	FCC	❏ 321337	NXA	❏ 321433	NXA	❏ 323237	NOR
❏ 319362	FCC	❏ 319458	FCC	❏ 321338	NXA	❏ 321434	NXA	❏ 323238	NOR
❏ 319363	FCC	❏ 319459	FCC	❏ 321339	NXA	❏ 321435	NXA	❏ 323239	NOR
❏ 319364	FCC	❏ 319460	FCC	❏ 321340	NXA	❏ 321436	NXA	❏ 323240	LMI

Data Tables

323241	LMI	334011	FSR	350233	LMI	357028	C2C	360116	NXA
323242	LMI	334012	FSR	350234	LMI	357029	C2C	360117	NXA
323243	LMI	334013	FSR	350235	LMI	357030	C2C	360118	NXA
		334014	FSR	350236	LMI	357031	C2C	360119	NXA
325001	DBS	334015	FSR	350237	LMI	357032	C2C	360120	NXA
325002	DBS	334016	FSR	350238	LMI	357033	C2C	360121	NXA
325003	DBS	334017	FSR	350239	LMI	357034	C2C		
325004	DBS	334018	FSR	350240	LMI	357035	C2C	360201	HEC
325005	DBS	334019	FSR	350241	LMI	357036	C2C	360202	HEC
325006	DBS	334020	FSR	350242	LMI	357037	C2C	360203	HEC
325007	DBS	334021	FSR	350243	LMI	357038	C2C	360204	HEC
325008	DBS	334022	FSR	350244	LMI	357039	C2C	360205	HEC
325009	DBS	334023	FSR	350245	LMI	357040	C2C		
325010	DBS	334024	FSR	350246	LMI	357041	C2C	365501	FCC
325011	DBS	334025	FSR	350247	LMI	357042	C2C	365502	FCC
325012	DBS	334026	FSR	350248	LMI	357043	C2C	365503	FCC
325013	DBS	334027	FSR	350249	LMI	357044	C2C	365504	FCC
325014	DBS	334028	FSR	350250	LMI	357045	C2C	365505	FCC
325015	DBS	334029	FSR	350251	LMI	357046	C2C	365506	FCC
325016	DBS	334030	FSR	350252	LMI	357201	C2C	365507	FCC
		334031	FSR	350253	LMI	357202	C2C	365508	FCC
332001	HEX	334032	FSR	350254	LMI	357203	C2C	365509	FCC
332002	HEX	334033	FSR	350255	LMI	357204	C2C	365510	FCC
332003	HEX	334034	FSR	350256	LMI	357205	C2C	365511	FCC
332004	HEX	334035	FSR	350257	LMI	357206	C2C	365512	FCC
332005	HEX	334036	FSR	350258	LMI	357207	C2C	365513	FCC
332006	HEX	334037	FSR	350259	LMI	357208	C2C	365514	FCC
332007	HEX	334038	FSR	350260	LMI	357209	C2C	365515	FCC
332008	HEX	334039	FSR	350261	LMI	357210	C2C	365516	FCC
332009	HEX	334040	FSR	350262	LMI	357211	C2C	365517	FCC
332010	HEX			350263	LMI	357212	C2C	365518	FCC
332011	HEX	350101	LMI	350264	LMI	357213	C2C	365519	FCC
332012	HEX	350102	LMI	350265	LMI	357214	C2C	365520	FCC
332013	HEX	350103	LMI	350266	LMI	357215	C2C	365521	FCC
332014	HEX	350104	LMI	350267	LMI	357216	C2C	365522	FCC
		350105	LMI			357217	C2C	365523	FCC
333001	NOR	350106	LMI	357001	C2C	357218	C2C	365524	FCC
333002	NOR	350107	LMI	357002	C2C	357219	C2C	365525	FCC
333003	NOR	350108	LMI	357003	C2C	357220	C2C	365526	OLS
333004	NOR	350109	LMI	357004	C2C	357221	C2C	365527	FCC
333005	NOR	350110	LMI	357005	C2C	357222	C2C	365528	FCC
333006	NOR	350111	LMI	357006	C2C	357223	C2C	365529	FCC
333007	NOR	350112	LMI	357007	C2C	357224	C2C	365530	FCC
333008	NOR	350113	LMI	357008	C2C	357225	C2C	365531	FCC
333009	NOR	350114	LMI	357009	C2C	357226	C2C	365532	FCC
333010	NOR	350115	LMI	357010	C2C	357227	C2C	365533	FCC
333011	NOR	350116	LMI	357011	C2C	357228	C2C	365534	FCC
333012	NOR	350117	LMI	357012	C2C			365535	FCC
333013	NOR	350118	LMI	357013	C2C	360101	NXA	365536	FCC
333014	NOR	350119	LMI	357014	C2C	360102	NXA	365537	FCC
333015	NOR	350120	LMI	357015	C2C	360103	NXA	365538	FCC
333016	NOR	350121	LMI	357016	C2C	360104	NXA	365539	FCC
		350122	LMI	357017	C2C	360105	NXA	365540	FCC
334001	FSR	350123	LMI	357018	C2C	360106	NXA	365541	FCC
334002	FSR	350124	LMI	357019	C2C	360107	NXA		
334003	FSR	350125	LMI	357020	C2C	360108	NXA	373001	EUS
334004	FSR	350126	LMI	357021	C2C	360109	NXA	373002	EUS
334005	FSR	350127	LMI	357022	C2C	360110	NXA	373003	EUS
334006	FSR	350128	LMI	357023	C2C	360111	NXA	373004	EUS
334007	FSR	350129	LMI	357024	C2C	360112	NXA	373005	EUS
334008	FSR	350130	LMI	357025	C2C	360113	NXA	373006	EUS
334009	FSR	350231	LMI	357026	C2C	360114	NXA	373007	EUS
334010	FSR	350232	LMI	357027	C2C	360115	NXA	373008	EUS

Data Tables

❏ 373009	EUS	❏ 373310	EUS	❏ 375803	SET	❏ 376008	SET	❏ 377134	SOU
❏ 373010	EUS	❏ 373311	EUS	❏ 375804	SET	❏ 376009	SET	❏ 377135	SOU
❏ 373011	EUS	❏ 373312	EUS	❏ 375805	SET	❏ 376010	SET	❏ 377136	SOU
❏ 373012	EUS	❏ 373313	EUS	❏ 375806	SET	❏ 376011	SET	❏ 377137	SOU
❏ 373013	EUS	❏ 373314	EUS	❏ 375807	SET	❏ 376012	SET	❏ 377138	SOU
❏ 373014	EUS			❏ 375808	SET	❏ 376013	SET	❏ 377139	SOU
❏ 373015	EUS	❏ 375301	SET	❏ 375809	SET	❏ 376014	SET	❏ 377140	SOU
❏ 373016	EUS	❏ 375302	SET	❏ 375810	SET	❏ 376015	SET	❏ 377141	SOU
❏ 373017	EUS	❏ 375303	SET	❏ 375811	SET	❏ 376016	SET	❏ 377142	SOU
❏ 373018	EUS	❏ 375304	SET	❏ 375812	SET	❏ 376017	SET	❏ 377143	SOU
❏ 373019	EUS	❏ 375305	SET	❏ 375813	SET	❏ 376018	SET	❏ 377144	SOU
❏ 373020	EUS	❏ 375306	SET	❏ 375814	SET	❏ 376019	SET	❏ 377145	SOU
❏ 373021	EUS	❏ 375307	SET	❏ 375815	SET	❏ 376020	SET	❏ 377146	SOU
❏ 373022	EUS	❏ 375308	SET	❏ 375816	SET	❏ 376021	SET	❏ 377147	SOU
❏ 373101	EUS	❏ 375309	SET	❏ 375817	SET	❏ 376022	SET	❏ 377148	SOU
❏ 373102	EUS	❏ 375310	SET	❏ 375818	SET	❏ 376023	SET	❏ 377149	SOU
❏ 373103	EUS	❏ 375601	SET	❏ 375819	SET	❏ 376024	SET	❏ 377150	SOU
❏ 373104	EUS	❏ 375602	SET	❏ 375820	SET	❏ 376025	SET	❏ 377151	SOU
❏ 373105	EUS	❏ 375603	SET	❏ 375821	SET	❏ 376026	SET	❏ 377152	SOU
❏ 373106	EUS	❏ 375604	SET	❏ 375822	SET	❏ 376027	SET	❏ 377153	SOU
❏ 373107	EUS	❏ 375605	SET	❏ 375823	SET	❏ 376028	SET	❏ 377154	SOU
❏ 373108	EUS	❏ 375606	SET	❏ 375824	SET	❏ 376029	SET	❏ 377155	SOU
❏ 373201	EUS	❏ 375607	SET	❏ 375825	SET	❏ 376030	SET	❏ 377156	SOU
❏ 373202	EUS	❏ 375608	SET	❏ 375826	SET	❏ 376031	SET	❏ 377157	SOU
❏ 373203	EUS	❏ 375609	SET	❏ 375827	SET	❏ 376032	SET	❏ 377158	SOU
❏ 373204	EUS	❏ 375610	SET	❏ 375828	SET	❏ 376033	SET	❏ 377159	SOU
❏ 373205	EUS	❏ 375611	SET	❏ 375829	SET	❏ 376034	SET	❏ 377160	SOU
❏ 373206	EUS	❏ 375612	SET	❏ 375830	SET	❏ 376035	SET	❏ 377161	SOU
❏ 373207	EUS	❏ 375613	SET	❏ 375901	SET	❏ 376036	SET	❏ 377162	SOU
❏ 373208	EUS	❏ 375614	SET	❏ 375902	SET			❏ 377163	SOU
❏ 373209	EUS	❏ 375615	SET	❏ 375903	SET	❏ 377101	SOU	❏ 377164	SOU
❏ 373210	EUS	❏ 375616	SET	❏ 375904	SET	❏ 377102	SOU	❏ 377201	SOU
❏ 373211	EUS	❏ 375617	SET	❏ 375905	SET	❏ 377103	SOU	❏ 377202	SOU
❏ 373212	EUS	❏ 375618	SET	❏ 375906	SET	❏ 377104	SOU	❏ 377203	SOU
❏ 373213	EUS	❏ 375619	SET	❏ 375907	SET	❏ 377105	SOU	❏ 377204	SOU
❏ 373214	EUS	❏ 375620	SET	❏ 375908	SET	❏ 377106	SOU	❏ 377205	SOU
❏ 373215	EUS	❏ 375621	SET	❏ 375909	SET	❏ 377107	SOU	❏ 377206	SOU
❏ 373216	EUS	❏ 375622	SET	❏ 375910	SET	❏ 377108	SOU	❏ 377207	SOU
❏ 373217	EUS	❏ 375623	SET	❏ 375911	SET	❏ 377109	SOU	❏ 377208	SOU
❏ 373218	EUS	❏ 375624	SET	❏ 375912	SET	❏ 377110	SOU	❏ 377209	SOU
❏ 373219	EUS	❏ 375625	SET	❏ 375913	SET	❏ 377111	SOU	❏ 377210	SOU
❏ 373220	EUS	❏ 375626	SET	❏ 375914	SET	❏ 377112	SOU	❏ 377211	SOU
❏ 373221	EUS	❏ 375627	SET	❏ 375915	SET	❏ 377113	SOU	❏ 377212	SOU
❏ 373222	EUS	❏ 375628	SET	❏ 375916	SET	❏ 377114	SOU	❏ 377213	SOU
❏ 373223	EUS	❏ 375629	SET	❏ 375917	SET	❏ 377115	SOU	❏ 377214	SOU
❏ 373224	EUS	❏ 375630	SET	❏ 375918	SET	❏ 377116	SOU	❏ 377215	SOU
❏ 373225	EUS	❏ 375701	SET	❏ 375919	SET	❏ 377117	SOU	❏ 377301	SOU
❏ 373226	EUS	❏ 375702	SET	❏ 375920	SET	❏ 377118	SOU	❏ 377302	SOU
❏ 373227	EUS	❏ 375703	SET	❏ 375921	SET	❏ 377119	SOU	❏ 377303	SOU
❏ 373228	EUS	❏ 375704	SET	❏ 375922	SET	❏ 377120	SOU	❏ 377304	SOU
❏ 373229	EUS	❏ 375705	SET	❏ 375923	SET	❏ 377121	SOU	❏ 377305	SOU
❏ 373230	EUS	❏ 375706	SET	❏ 375924	SET	❏ 377122	SOU	❏ 377306	SOU
❏ 373231	EUS	❏ 375707	SET	❏ 375925	SET	❏ 377123	SOU	❏ 377307	SOU
❏ 373232	EUS	❏ 375708	SET	❏ 375926	SET	❏ 377124	SOU	❏ 377308	SOU
❏ 373301	EUS	❏ 375709	SET	❏ 375927	SET	❏ 377125	SOU	❏ 377309	SOU
❏ 373302	EUS	❏ 375710	SET			❏ 377126	SOU	❏ 377310	SOU
❏ 373303	EUS	❏ 375711	SET	❏ 376001	SET	❏ 377127	SOU	❏ 377311	SOU
❏ 373304	EUS	❏ 375712	SET	❏ 376002	SET	❏ 377128	SOU	❏ 377312	SOU
❏ 373305	EUS	❏ 375713	SET	❏ 376003	SET	❏ 377129	SOU	❏ 377313	SOU
❏ 373306	EUS	❏ 375714	SET	❏ 376004	SET	❏ 377130	SOU	❏ 377314	SOU
❏ 373307	EUS	❏ 375715	SET	❏ 376005	SET	❏ 377131	SOU	❏ 377315	SOU
❏ 373308	EUS	❏ 375801	SET	❏ 376006	SET	❏ 377132	SOU	❏ 377316	SOU
❏ 373309	EUS	❏ 375802	SET	❏ 376007	SET	❏ 377133	SOU	❏ 377317	SOU

Data Tables

377318	SOU	377453	SOU	378150	LOG	379019	NXA	390012	VWC
377319	SOU	377454	SOU	378151	LOG	379020	NXA	390013	VWC
377320	SOU	377455	SOU	378152	LOG	379021	NXA	390014	VWC
377321	SOU	377456	SOU	378153	LOG	379022	NXA	390015	VWC
377322	SOU	377457	SOU	378154	LOG	379023	NXA	390016	VWC
377323	SOU	377458	SOU	378201	LOG	379024	NXA	390017	VWC
377324	SOU	377459	SOU	378202	LOG	379025	NXA	390018	VWC
377325	SOU	377460	SOU	378203	LOG	379026	NXA	390019	VWC
377326	SOU	377461	SOU	378204	LOG	379027	NXA	390020	VWC
377327	SOU	377462	SOU	378205	LOG	379028	NXA	390021	VWC
377328	SOU	377463	SOU	378206	LOG	379029	NXA	390022	VWC
377401	SOU	377464	SOU	378207	LOG	379030	NXA	390023	VWC
377402	SOU	377465	SOU	378208	LOG			390024	VWC
377403	SOU	377466	SOU	378209	LOG	380001	FSR	390025	VWC
377404	SOU	377467	SOU	378210	LOG	380002	FSR	390026	VWC
377405	SOU	377468	SOU	378211	LOG	380003	FSR	390027	VWC
377406	SOU	377469	SOU	378212	LOG	380004	FSR	390028	VWC
377407	SOU	377470	SOU	378213	LOG	380005	FSR	390029	VWC
377408	SOU	377471	SOU	378214	LOG	380006	FSR	390030	VWC
377409	SOU	377472	SOU	378215	LOG	380007	FSR	390031	VWC
377410	SOU	377473	SOU	378216	LOG	380008	FSR	390032	VWC
377411	SOU	377474	SOU	378217	LOG	380009	FSR	390033	OLS
377412	SOU	377475	SOU	378218	LOG	380010	FSR	390034	VWC
377413	SOU	377501	FCC	378219	LOG	380011	FSR	390035	VWC
377414	SOU	377502	FCC	378220	LOG	380012	FSR	390036	VWC
377415	SOU	377503	FCC	378221	LOG	380013	FSR	390037	VWC
377416	SOU	377504	FCC	378222	LOG	380014	FSR	390038	VWC
377417	SOU	377505	FCC	378223	LOG	380015	FSR	390039	VWC
377418	SOU	377506	FCC	378224	LOG	380016	FSR	390040	VWC
377419	SOU	377507	FCC	378225	LOG	380017	FSR	390041	VWC
377420	SOU	377508	FCC	378226	LOG	380018	FSR	390042	VWC
377421	SOU	377509	FCC	378227	LOG	380019	FSR	390043	VWC
377422	SOU	377510	FCC	378228	LOG	380020	FSR	390044	VWC
377423	SOU	377511	FCC	378229	LOG	380021	FSR	390045	VWC
377424	SOU	377512	FCC	378230	LOG	380022	FSR	390046	VWC
377425	SOU	377513	FCC	378231	LOG	380101	FSR	390047	VWC
377426	SOU	377514	FCC	378232	LOG	380102	FSR	390048	VWC
377427	SOU	377515	FCC	378233	LOG	380103	FSR	390049	VWC
377428	SOU	377516	FCC	378234	LOG	380104	FSR	390050	VWC
377429	SOU	377517	FCC	378235	LOG	380105	FSR	390051	VWC
377430	SOU	377518	FCC	378236	LOG	380106	FSR	390052	VWC
377431	SOU	377519	FCC	378255	LOG	380107	FSR	390053	VWC
377432	SOU	377520	FCC	378256	LOG	380108	FSR	390054	VWC
377433	SOU	377521	FCC	378257	LOG	380109	FSR	390055	VWC
377434	SOU	377522	FCC			380110	FSR	390056	VWC
377435	SOU	377523	FCC	379001	NXA	380111	FSR	390057	VWC
377436	SOU			379002	NXA	380112	FSR		
377437	SOU	378135	LOG	379003	NXA	380113	FSR	395001	SET
377438	SOU	378135	LOG	379004	NXA	380114	FSR	395002	SET
377439	SOU	378136	LOG	379005	NXA	380115	FSR	395003	SET
377440	SOU	378137	LOG	379006	NXA	380116	FSR	395004	SET
377441	SOU	378138	LOG	379007	NXA			395005	SET
377442	SOU	378139	LOG	379008	NXA	390001	VWC	395006	SET
377443	SOU	378140	LOG	379009	NXA	390002	VWC	395007	SET
377444	SOU	378141	LOG	379010	NXA	390003	VWC	395008	SET
377445	SOU	378142	LOG	379011	NXA	390004	VWC	395009	SET
377446	SOU	378143	LOG	379012	NXA	390005	VWC	395010	SET
377447	SOU	378144	LOG	379013	NXA	390006	VWC	395011	SET
377448	SOU	378145	LOG	379014	NXA	390007	VWC	395012	SET
377449	SOU	378146	LOG	379015	NXA	390008	VWC	395013	SET
377450	SOU	378147	LOG	379016	NXA	390009	VWC	395014	SET
377451	SOU	378148	LOG	379017	NXA	390010	VWC	395015	SET
377452	SOU	378149	LOG	379018	NXA	390011	VWC	395016	SET

Data Tables

Data Tables

395017	SET	444011	SWT	450028	SWT	450119	SWT	455726	SWT
395018	SET	444012	SWT	450029	SWT	450120	SWT	455727	SWT
395019	SET	444013	SWT	450030	SWT	450121	SWT	455728	SWT
395020	SET	444014	SWT	450031	SWT	450122	SWT	455729	SWT
395021	SET	444015	SWT	450032	SWT	450123	SWT	455730	SWT
395022	SET	444016	SWT	450033	SWT	450124	SWT	455731	SWT
395023	SET	444017	SWT	450034	SWT	450125	SWT	455732	SWT
395024	SET	444018	SWT	450035	SWT	450126	SWT	455733	SWT
395025	SET	444019	SWT	450036	SWT	450127	SWT	455734	SWT
395026	SET	444020	SWT	450037	SWT	450543	SWT	455735	SWT
395027	SET	444021	SWT	450038	SWT	450544	SWT	455736	SWT
395028	SET	444022	SWT	450039	SWT	450545	SWT	455737	SWT
395029	SET	444023	SWT	450040	SWT	450546	SWT	455738	SWT
		444024	SWT	450041	SWT	450547	SWT	455739	SWT
411198	PRE	444025	SWT	450042	SWT	450548	SWT	455740	SWT
		444026	SWT	450071	SWT	450549	SWT	455741	SWT
421304	PRE	444027	SWT	450072	SWT	450550	SWT	455742	SWT
421399	PRE	444028	SWT	450073	SWT	450551	SWT	455750	SWT
421497	PRE	444029	SWT	450074	SWT	450552	SWT	455801	SOU
421498	PRE	444030	SWT	450075	SWT	450553	SWT	455802	SOU
421884	KRS	444031	SWT	450076	SWT	450554	SWT	455803	SOU
		444032	SWT	450077	SWT	450555	SWT	455804	SOU
423576	KRS	444033	SWT	450078	SWT	450556	SWT	455805	SOU
423905	BOM	444034	SWT	450079	SWT	450557	SWT	455806	SOU
423918	BOM	444035	SWT	450080	SWT	450558	SWT	455807	SOU
		444036	SWT	450081	SWT	450559	SWT	455808	SOU
424001	BOM	444037	SWT	450082	SWT	450560	SWT	455809	SOU
		444038	SWT	450083	SWT	450561	SWT	455810	SOU
442401	SOU	444039	SWT	450084	SWT	450562	SWT	455811	SOU
442402	SOU	444040	SWT	450085	SWT	450563	SWT	455812	SOU
442403	SOU	444041	SWT	450086	SWT	450564	SWT	455813	SOU
442404	SOU	444042	SWT	450087	SWT	450565	SWT	455814	SOU
442405	SOU	444043	SWT	450088	SWT	450566	SWT	455815	SOU
442406	SOU	444044	SWT	450089	SWT	450567	SWT	455816	SOU
442407	SOU	444045	SWT	450090	SWT	450568	SWT	455817	SOU
442408	SOU			450091	SWT	450569	SWT	455818	SOU
442409	SOU	450001	SWT	450092	SWT	450570	SWT	455819	SOU
442410	SOU	450002	SWT	450093	SWT			455820	SOU
442411	SOU	450003	SWT	450094	SWT	455701	SWT	455821	SOU
442412	SOU	450004	SWT	450095	SWT	455702	SWT	455822	SOU
442413	SOU	450005	SWT	450096	SWT	455703	SWT	455823	SOU
442414	SOU	450006	SWT	450097	SWT	455704	SWT	455824	SOU
442415	SOU	450007	SWT	450098	SWT	455705	SWT	455825	SOU
442416	SOU	450008	SWT	450099	SWT	455706	SWT	455826	SOU
442417	SOU	450009	SWT	450100	SWT	455707	SWT	455827	SOU
442418	SOU	450010	SWT	450101	SWT	455708	SWT	455828	SOU
442419	SOU	450011	SWT	450102	SWT	455709	SWT	455829	SOU
442420	SOU	450012	SWT	450103	SWT	455710	SWT	455830	SOU
442421	SOU	450013	SWT	450104	SWT	455711	SWT	455831	SOU
442422	SOU	450014	SWT	450105	SWT	455712	SWT	455832	SOU
442423	SOU	450015	SWT	450106	SWT	455713	SWT	455833	SOU
442424	SOU	450016	SWT	450107	SWT	455714	SWT	455834	SOU
		450017	SWT	450108	SWT	455715	SWT	455835	SOU
444001	SWT	450018	SWT	450109	SWT	455716	SWT	455836	SOU
444002	SWT	450019	SWT	450110	SWT	455717	SWT	455837	SOU
444003	SWT	450020	SWT	450111	SWT	455718	SWT	455838	SOU
444004	SWT	450021	SWT	450112	SWT	455719	SWT	455839	SOU
444005	SWT	450022	SWT	450113	SWT	455720	SWT	455840	SOU
444006	SWT	450023	SWT	450114	SWT	455721	SWT	455841	SOU
444007	SWT	450024	SWT	450115	SWT	455722	SWT	455842	SOU
444008	SWT	450025	SWT	450116	SWT	455723	SWT	455843	SOU
444009	SWT	450026	SWT	450117	SWT	455724	SWT	455844	SOU
444010	SWT	450027	SWT	450118	SWT	455725	SWT	455845	SOU

No.	Op	No.	Op	No.	Op	No.	Op	No.	Op
455846	SOU	456014	SOU	465012	SET	465175	SET	465925	SET
455847	SWT	456015	SOU	465013	SET	465176	SET	465926	SET
455848	SWT	456016	SOU	465014	SET	465177	SET	465927	SET
455849	SWT	456017	SOU	465015	SET	465178	SET	465928	SET
455850	SWT	456018	SOU	465016	SET	465179	SET	465929	SET
455851	SWT	456019	SOU	465017	SET	465180	SET	465930	SET
455852	SWT	456020	SOU	465018	SET	465181	SET	465931	SET
455853	SWT	456021	SOU	465019	SET	465182	SET	465932	SET
455854	SWT	456022	SOU	465020	SET	465183	SET	465933	SET
455855	SWT	456023	SOU	465021	SET	465184	SET	465934	SET
455856	SWT	456024	SOU	465022	SET	465185	SET		
455857	SWT			465023	SET	465186	SET	466001	SET
455858	SWT	458001	SWT	465024	SET	465187	SET	466002	SET
455859	SWT	458002	SWT	465025	SET	465188	SET	466003	SET
455860	SWT	458003	SWT	465026	SET	465189	SET	466004	SET
455861	SWT	458004	SWT	465027	SET	465190	SET	466005	SET
455862	SWT	458005	SWT	465028	SET	465191	SET	466006	SET
455863	SWT	458006	SWT	465029	SET	465192	SET	466007	SET
455864	SWT	458007	SWT	465030	SET	465193	SET	466008	SET
455865	SWT	458008	SWT	465031	SET	465194	SET	466009	SET
455866	SWT	458009	SWT	465032	SET	465195	SET	466010	SET
455867	SWT	458010	SWT	465033	SET	465196	SET	466011	SET
455868	SWT	458011	SWT	465034	SET	465197	SET	466012	SET
455869	SWT	458012	SWT	465035	SET	465235	SET	466013	SET
455870	SWT	458013	SWT	465036	SET	465236	SET	466014	SET
455871	SWT	458014	SWT	465037	SET	465237	SET	466015	SET
455872	SWT	458015	SWT	465038	SET	465238	SET	466016	SET
455873	SWT	458016	SWT	465039	SET	465239	SET	466017	SET
455874	SWT	458017	SWT	465040	SET	465240	SET	466018	SET
455901	SWT	458018	SWT	465041	SET	465241	SET	466019	SET
455902	SWT	458019	SWT	465042	SET	465242	SET	466020	SET
455903	SWT	458020	SWT	465043	SET	465243	SET	466021	SET
455904	SWT	458021	SWT	465044	SET	465244	SET	466022	SET
455905	SWT	458022	SWT	465045	SET	465245	SET	466023	SET
455906	SWT	458023	SWT	465046	SET	465246	SET	466024	SET
455907	SWT	458024	SWT	465047	SET	465247	SET	466025	SET
455908	SWT	458025	SWT	465048	SET	465248	SET	466026	SET
455909	SWT	458026	SWT	465049	SET	465249	SET	466027	SET
455910	SWT	458027	SWT	465050	SET	465250	SET	466028	SET
455911	SWT	458028	SWT	465151	SET	465901	SET	466029	SET
455912	SWT	458029	SWT	465152	SET	465902	SET	466030	SET
455913	SWT	458030	SWT	465153	SET	465903	SET	466031	SET
455914	SWT			465154	SET	465904	SET	466032	SET
455915	SWT	460001	SOU	465155	SET	465905	SET	466033	SET
455916	SWT	460002	SOU	465156	SET	465906	SET	466034	SET
455917	SWT	460003	SOU	465157	SET	465907	SET	466035	SET
455918	SWT	460004	SOU	465158	SET	465908	SET	466036	SET
455919	SWT	460005	SOU	465159	SET	465909	SET	466037	SET
455920	SWT	460006	SOU	465160	SET	465910	SET	466038	SET
		460007	SOU	465161	SET	465911	SET	466039	SET
456001	SOU	460008	SOU	465162	SET	465912	SET	466040	SET
456002	SOU			465163	SET	465913	SET	466041	SET
456003	SOU	465001	SET	465164	SET	465914	SET	466042	SET
456004	SOU	465002	SET	465165	SET	465915	SET	466043	SET
456005	SOU	465003	SET	465166	SET	465916	SET		
456006	SOU	465004	SET	465167	SET	465917	SET	483002	SIL
456007	SOU	465005	SET	465168	SET	465918	SET	483004	SIL
456008	SOU	465006	SET	465169	SET	465919	SET	483006	SIL
456009	SOU	465007	SET	465170	SET	465920	SET	483007	SIL
456010	SOU	465008	SET	465171	SET	465921	SET	483008	SIL
456011	SOU	465009	SET	465172	SET	465922	SET	483009	SIL
456012	SOU	465010	SET	465173	SET	465923	SET		
456013	SOU	465011	SET	465174	SET	465924	SET	489102	NRL

Data Tables

489105	NRL	508143	MER	504	WCR	1961	WCR	3229	OLS
489106	NRL	508201	OLS	506	WCR	1999	GSW	3231	RAF
489109	NRL	508202	OLS	546	WCR			3232	VSO
		508203	OLS	548	WCR	2127	WCR	3240	RIV
507001	MER	508204	OLS	549	WCR	2833	WCR	3241	CAD
507002	MER	508205	OLS	550	WCR	2834	RIV	3247	VSO
507003	MER	508206	OLS	551	WCR	2903	NRL	3255	DBS
507004	MER	508207	OLS	552	WCR	2904	NRL	3267	VSO
507005	MER	508208	OLS	553	WCR	2915	NRL	3269	DBS
507006	MER	508209	OLS	586	WCR	2916	NRL	3273	VSO
507007	MER	508210	OLS	807	WCR	2917	NRL	3275	VSO
507008	MER	508211	OLS			2918	NRL	3277	RIV
507009	MER	508212	OLS	1105	MHR	2919	NRL	3279	RIV
507010	MER	508301	OLS	1200	RIV	2920	NRL	3292	DBS
507011	MER	508302	OLS	1203	RIV	2921	NRL	3295	RIV
507012	MER	508303	OLS	1204	OLS	2922	NRL	3303	OLS
507013	MER			1205	NRL	2923	NRL	3304	RIV
507014	MER	901001	PRE	1207	VSO			3309	WCR
507015	MER			1209	OLS	3066	RIV	3313	WCR
507016	MER	**Coaching Stock**		1211	OLS	3068	RIV	3314	RIV
507017	MER	84	RAF	1212	RIV	3069	RIV	3318	DBS
507018	MER	159	WCR	1214	OLS	3093	WCR	3325	RIV
507019	MER	213	VSO	1219	OLS	3096	BOK	3326	WCR
507020	MER	239	VSO	1221	VSO	3097	RIV	3330	RIV
507021	MER	243	VSO	1250	RIV	3098	RIV	3331	DBS
507023	MER	245	VSO	1252	CAD	3105	WCR	3333	RIV
507024	MER	254	VSO	1253	OLS	3106	WCR	3334	RIV
507025	MER	255	VSO	1254	CAD	3107	RIV	3336	RIV
507026	MER	261	VSO	1256	NRL	3110	RIV	3338	DBS
507027	MER	264	VSO	1258	OLS	3112	RIV	3340	RIV
507028	MER	280	VSO	1375	BOK	3113	WCR	3344	RIV
507029	MER	281	VSO	1566	VSO	3114	RIV	3345	RIV
507030	MER	283	VSO	1644	WCR	3115	BOK	3348	RIV
507031	MER	284	VSO	1650	WCR	3117	WCR	3350	WCR
507032	MER	285	VSO	1651	RIV	3119	RIV	3351	OLS
507033	MER	286	VSO	1652	WCR	3120	RIV	3352	WCR
		288	VSO	1655	WCR	3121	RIV	3356	RIV
508103	MER	292	VSO	1657	CAD	3122	RIV	3358	DBS
508104	MER	293	VSO	1658	DBS	3123	RIV	3359	WCR
508108	MER	301	VSO	1659	RAF	3124	RIV	3360	WCR
508110	MER	302	VSO	1663	WCR	3125	JHS	3362	WCR
508111	MER	307	VSO	1670	WCR	3127	RIV	3364	RIV
508112	MER	308	VSO	1671	RIV	3128	WCR	3366	CAD
508114	MER	310	RAF	1679	DBS	3130	WCR	3368	DBS
508115	MER	313	GSW	1680	DBS	3131	RIV	3374	CAD
508117	MER	316	FSL	1683	RIV	3132	RIV	3375	DBS
508120	MER	317	GSW	1691	RIV	3133	RIV	3379	RIV
508122	MER	319	GSW	1692	RIV	3136	WCR	3384	RIV
508123	MER	321	FSL	1699	RIV	3140	RIV	3386	RIV
508124	MER	324	GSW	1730	WCR	3141	RIV	3388	DBS
508125	MER	325	VSO	1800	WCR	3143	WCR	3390	RIV
508126	MER	326	WCR	1813	RIV	3144	RIV	3392	WCR
508127	MER	329	GSW	1823	NYM	3146	RIV	3395	WCR
508128	MER	331	GSW	1832	RIV	3147	RIV	3397	RIV
508130	MER	335	VTN	1840	WCR	3148	JHS	3399	DBS
508131	MER	337	FSL	1842	RIV	3149	RIV	3400	DBS
508134	MER	348	WCR	1859	SRP	3150	BOK	3408	WCR
508136	MER	349	VTN	1860	WCR	3174	VSO	3414	DBS
508137	MER	350	WCR	1861	WCR	3181	RIV	3416	WCR
508138	MER	352	WCR	1862	WCR	3182	VSO	3417	RIV
508139	MER	353	VTN	1863	RIV	3186	DBS	3424	DBS
508140	MER	354	WCR	1882	WCR	3188	RAF	3426	RIV
508141	MER	464	BOK	1953	VSO	3223	RIV	3431	WCR

Data Tables

No.	Code	No.	Code	No.	Code	No.	Code	No.	Code
3434	OLS	5179	OLS	5876	CAD	6006	RIV	6179	OLS
3438	OLS	5183	OLS	5869	ATW	6008	CAD	6183	ATW
3766	WCR	5186	OLS	5881	OLS	6009	OLS	6310	RIV
3860	NYM	5193	OLS	5886	OLS	6012	OLS	6311	DBS
3872	NYM	5194	OLS	5888	OLS	6013	ATW	6312	WCR
3948	NYM	5200	WCR	5899	OLS	6014	WCR	6313	VSO
		5212	OLS	5900	OLS	6016	OLS	6320	RIV
4198	NYM	5216	WCR	5901	CAD	6021	OLS	6700	FSR
4252	NYM	5221	OLS	5903	OLS	6022	WCR	6701	FSR
4290	NYM	5222	WCR	5905	OLS	6024	RIV	6702	FSR
4455	NYM	5229	WCR	5906	CAD	6027	RIV	6703	FSR
4786	NYM	5236	WCR	5908	OLS	6028	OLS	6704	FSR
4817	NYM	5237	WCR	5910	RIV	6029	OLS	6705	FSR
4831	BOK	5239	WCR	5912	OLS	6031	OLS	6706	FSR
4832	BOK	5249	WCR	5913	ATW	6035	ATW	6707	FSR
4836	BOK	5276	RIV	5919	CAD	6036	DBS	6708	FSR
4856	BOK	5278	WCR	5921	RIV	6037	OLS	6720	RIV
4860	WCR	5292	RIV	5922	DBS	6041	WCR	6722	OLS
4902	RIV	5309	RIV	5924	DBS	6042	RIV	6723	CWR
4905	WCR	5322	RIV	5925	CAD	6045	CAD	6724	CWR
4912	WCR	5331	DBS	5928	VTN	6046	CAD		
4925	DBS	5341	RIV	5929	RIV	6049	OLS	9004	RAF
4927	RIV	5350	RIV	5930	OLS	6050	OLS	9104	WCR
4931	WCR	5365	RIV	5933	OLS	6051	RIV	9267	NYM
4932	WCR	5366	RIV	5936	OLS	6052	OLS	9274	NYM
4940	WCR	5376	RIV	5937	RIV	6053	OLS	9391	WCR
4946	RIV	5386	DBS	5940	OLS	6054	RIV	9392	WCR
4949	RIV	5419	WCR	5941	CAD	6055	OLS	9419	DRS
4951	WCR	5453	WCR	5943	OLS	6059	OLS	9428	DRS
4954	WCR	5463	WCR	5945	RIV	6061	OLS	9440	WCR
4956	DBS	5478	WCR	5946	RIV	6064	CAD	9448	WCR
4958	WCR	5482	DBS	5947	OLS	6067	RIV	9480	OLS
4959	RIV	5487	WCR	5948	OLS	6073	OLS	9481	NRL
4960	WCR	5491	WCR	5949	OLS	6101	OLS	9488	GCR
4973	WCR	5494	RIV	5950	RIV	6103	WCR	9490	OLS
4984	WCR	5520	RRS	5952	RIV	6107	RIV	9493	WCR
4986	RIV	5569	WCR	5954	DBS	6110	DBS	9494	DBS
4991	RIV	5631	DBS	5955	RIV	6115	WCR	9496	OLS
4994	WCR	5632	DBS	5957	OLS	6117	CAD	9497	CAD
4996	RIV	5636	OLS	5958	CAD	6119	ATW	9498	OLS
4997	WCR	5647	RIV	5959	DBS	6120	OLS	9500	OLS
4998	RIV	5657	DBS	5960	OLS	6121	OLS	9502	VSO
4999	RIV	5669	WCR	5961	RIV	6122	CAD	9503	ATW
		5679	OLS	5962	OLS	6134	CAD	9504	RIV
5000	NYM	5737	OLS	5964	RIV	6135	WCR	9505	OLS
5005	DBS	5739	RIV	5965	ATW	6136	OLS	9506	CAD
5007	RIV	5740	OLS	5969	OLS	6137	ATW	9507	RIV
5008	RIV	5745	OLS	5971	CAD	6139	DBS	9508	CAD
5009	RIV	5748	RIV	5976	ATW	6141	RIV	9509	ATW
5023	RIV	5750	OLS	5977	OLS	6150	OLS	9516	OLS
5027	RIV	5754	OLS	5978	OLS	6151	CAD	9520	RIV
5028	BOK	5756	WCR	5980	OLS	6152	DBS	9521	ATW
5029	NYM	5769	RIV	5981	NRL	6153	RIV	9522	DBS
5032	WCR	5787	CAD	5985	RIV	6158	RIV	9523	OLS
5033	WCR	5788	OLS	5983	OLS	6160	OLS	9524	ATW
5035	WCR	5789	DRS	5987	RIV	6162	ATW	9525	CAD
5037	DBS	5792	RIV	5991	OLS	6164	OLS	9526	RIV
5040	RIV	5793	OLS	5995	CAD	6168	CAD	9527	RIV
5044	WCR	5797	CAD	5997	RIV	6170	ATW	9529	DBS
5067	RAF	5810	CAD	5998	RIV	6173	CAD	9531	DBS
5125	WCR	5821	OLS			6175	OLS	9537	RIV
5148	OLS	5853	ATW	6000	WCR	6176	RIV	9538	OLS
5171	WCR	5866	CAD	6001	CAD	6177	RIV	9539	ATW

Data Tables

Number	Code	Number	Code	Number	Code	Number	Code	Number	Code
❑ 9701	NRL	❑ 10301	ICE	❑ 10556	VSO	❑ 11029	DBS	❑ 11282	ICE
❑ 9702	NRL	❑ 10302	ICE	❑ 10561	FSR	❑ 11030	DBS	❑ 11283	ICE
❑ 9703	NRL	❑ 10303	ICE	❑ 10562	FSR	❑ 11031	DBS	❑ 11284	ICE
❑ 9704	OLS	❑ 10304	ICE	❑ 10563	FGW	❑ 11033	DBS	❑ 11285	ICE
❑ 9705	OLS	❑ 10305	ICE	❑ 10565	FSR	❑ 11039	DBS	❑ 11286	ICE
❑ 9707	OLS	❑ 10306	ICE	❑ 10569	VSO	❑ 11040	DBS	❑ 11287	ICE
❑ 9708	NRL	❑ 10307	ICE	❑ 10580	FSR	❑ 11041	DBS	❑ 11288	ICE
❑ 9709	OLS	❑ 10308	ICE	❑ 10584	FGW	❑ 11044	DRS	❑ 11289	ICE
❑ 9710	OLS	❑ 10309	ICE	❑ 10588	CAD	❑ 11046	DBS	❑ 11290	ICE
❑ 9714	NRL	❑ 10310	ICE	❑ 10589	FGW	❑ 11048	VWC	❑ 11291	ICE
❑ 9801	FSR	❑ 10311	ICE	❑ 10590	FGW	❑ 11052	DBS	❑ 11292	ICE
❑ 9802	FSR	❑ 10312	ICE	❑ 10594	FGW	❑ 11054	DBS	❑ 11293	ICE
❑ 9803	FSR	❑ 10313	ICE	❑ 10596	OLS	❑ 11058	DBS	❑ 11294	ICE
❑ 9804	FSR	❑ 10314	ICE	❑ 10597	FSR	❑ 11064	CAD	❑ 11295	ICE
❑ 9805	FSR	❑ 10317	ICE	❑ 10598	FSR	❑ 11065	CAD	❑ 11298	ICE
❑ 9806	FSR	❑ 10318	ICE	❑ 10600	FSR	❑ 11066	NXA	❑ 11299	ICE
❑ 9807	FSR	❑ 10319	ICE	❑ 10601	FGW	❑ 11067	NXA	❑ 11301	ICE
❑ 9808	FSR	❑ 10320	ICE	❑ 10605	FSR	❑ 11068	NXA	❑ 11302	ICE
❑ 9809	FSR	❑ 10321	ICE	❑ 10607	FSR	❑ 11069	NXA	❑ 11303	ICE
❑ 9810	FSR	❑ 10323	ICE	❑ 10610	FSR	❑ 11070	NXA	❑ 11304	ICE
		❑ 10324	ICE	❑ 10612	FGW	❑ 11071	CAD	❑ 11305	ICE
❑ 10200	NXA	❑ 10325	ICE	❑ 10613	FSR	❑ 11072	NXA	❑ 11306	ICE
❑ 10202	CAD	❑ 10326	ICE	❑ 10614	FSR	❑ 11073	NXA	❑ 11307	ICE
❑ 10203	NXA	❑ 10328	ICE	❑ 10616	FGW	❑ 11074	NXA	❑ 11308	ICE
❑ 10204	3MP	❑ 10329	ICE	❑ 10617	FSR	❑ 11075	NXA	❑ 11309	ICE
❑ 10205	DBS	❑ 10330	ICE	❑ 10647	DBS	❑ 11076	NXA	❑ 11310	ICE
❑ 10206	NXA	❑ 10331	ICE	❑ 10648	FSR	❑ 11077	NXA	❑ 11311	ICE
❑ 10208	WSR	❑ 10332	ICE	❑ 10650	FSR	❑ 11078	NXA	❑ 11312	ICE
❑ 10211	DBS	❑ 10333	ICE	❑ 10666	FSR	❑ 11079	CAD	❑ 11313	ICE
❑ 10212	VWC	❑ 10401	NXA	❑ 10667	OLS	❑ 11080	NXA	❑ 11314	ICE
❑ 10213	PRE	❑ 10402	NXA	❑ 10675	FSR	❑ 11081	NXA	❑ 11315	ICE
❑ 10214	NXA	❑ 10403	NXA	❑ 10680	FSR	❑ 11082	NXA	❑ 11316	ICE
❑ 10215	DBS	❑ 10404	NXA	❑ 10682	OLS	❑ 11083	CAD	❑ 11317	ICE
❑ 10216	NXA	❑ 10405	NXA	❑ 10683	FSR	❑ 11084	CAD	❑ 11318	ICE
❑ 10217	VWC	❑ 10406	NXA	❑ 10688	FSR	❑ 11085	NXA	❑ 11319	ICE
❑ 10219	FGW	❑ 10501	FSR	❑ 10689	FSR	❑ 11086	CAD	❑ 11320	ICE
❑ 10223	NXA	❑ 10502	FSR	❑ 10690	FSR	❑ 11087	NXA	❑ 11321	ICE
❑ 10225	FGW	❑ 10504	FSR	❑ 10693	FSR	❑ 11088	NXA	❑ 11322	ICE
❑ 10226	DBS	❑ 10506	FSR	❑ 10698	OLS	❑ 11089	CAD	❑ 11323	ICE
❑ 10228	NXA	❑ 10507	FSR	❑ 10699	FSR	❑ 11090	NXA	❑ 11324	ICE
❑ 10229	NXA	❑ 10508	FSR	❑ 10703	FSR	❑ 11091	NXA	❑ 11325	ICE
❑ 10230	WSR	❑ 10513	FSR	❑ 10706	FSR	❑ 11092	NXA	❑ 11326	ICE
❑ 10231	OLS	❑ 10516	FSR	❑ 10710	DBS	❑ 11093	NXA	❑ 11327	ICE
❑ 10232	FGW	❑ 10519	FSR	❑ 10714	FSR	❑ 11094	NXA	❑ 11328	ICE
❑ 10233	DBS	❑ 10520	FSR	❑ 10718	FSR	❑ 11095	NXA	❑ 11329	ICE
❑ 10235	DBS	❑ 10522	FSR	❑ 10719	FSR	❑ 11096	NXA	❑ 11330	ICE
❑ 10236	WSR	❑ 10523	FSR	❑ 10722	FSR	❑ 11097	DBS	❑ 11401	ICE
❑ 10237	DBS	❑ 10526	FSR	❑ 10723	FSR	❑ 11098	NXA	❑ 11402	ICE
❑ 10240	OLS	❑ 10527	FSR	❑ 10729	VSO	❑ 11099	NXA	❑ 11403	ICE
❑ 10241	NXA	❑ 10529	FSR	❑ 10731	DBS	❑ 11100	NXA	❑ 11404	ICE
❑ 10242	CAD	❑ 10531	FSR	❑ 10733	OLS	❑ 11101	NXA	❑ 11405	ICE
❑ 10245	CAD	❑ 10532	FGW	❑ 10734	VSO	❑ 11201	ICE	❑ 11406	ICE
❑ 10246	CAD	❑ 10534	FGW			❑ 11219	ICE	❑ 11407	ICE
❑ 10247	NXA	❑ 10540	DBS	❑ 11005	DBS	❑ 11229	ICE	❑ 11408	ICE
❑ 10249	ATW	❑ 10541	VSO	❑ 11006	OLS	❑ 11237	ICE	❑ 11409	ICE
❑ 10250	DBS	❑ 10542	FSR	❑ 11007	VWC	❑ 11241	ICE	❑ 11410	ICE
❑ 10253	OLS	❑ 10543	FSR	❑ 11011	OLS	❑ 11244	ICE	❑ 11411	ICE
❑ 10255	WSR	❑ 10544	FSR	❑ 11013	DBS	❑ 11273	ICE	❑ 11412	ICE
❑ 10256	OLS	❑ 10546	DBS	❑ 11018	VWC	❑ 11277	ICE	❑ 11413	ICE
❑ 10257	DBS	❑ 10547	OLS	❑ 11019	DBS	❑ 11278	ICE	❑ 11414	ICE
❑ 10259	ATW	❑ 10548	FSR	❑ 11021	NXA	❑ 11279	ICE	❑ 11415	ICE
❑ 10260	OLS	❑ 10551	FSR	❑ 11026	OLS	❑ 11280	ICE	❑ 11416	ICE
❑ 10300	ICE	❑ 10553	FSR	❑ 11027	DBS	❑ 11281	ICE	❑ 11417	ICE

No.	Code	No.	Code	No.	Code	No.	Code	No.	Code
11418	ICE	12067	NXA	12156	OLS	12322	ICE	12461	ICE
11419	ICE	12069	WSR	12158	OLS	12323	ICE	12462	ICE
11420	ICE	12072	WSR	12159	NXA	12324	ICE	12463	ICE
11421	ICE	12073	NXA	12160	OLS	12325	ICE	12464	ICE
11422	ICE	12078	VWC	12161	FGW	12326	ICE	12465	ICE
11423	ICE	12079	NXA	12163	OLS	12327	ICE	12466	ICE
11424	ICE	12081	NXA	12164	NXA	12328	ICE	12467	ICE
11425	ICE	12082	NXA	12166	NXA	12329	ICE	12468	ICE
11426	ICE	12083	OLS	12167	NXA	12330	ICE	12469	ICE
11427	ICE	12084	NXA	12169	WSR	12331	ICE	12470	ICE
11428	ICE	12087	OLS	12170	NXA	12400	ICE	12471	ICE
11429	ICE	12089	NXA	12171	NXA	12401	ICE	12472	ICE
11430	ICE	12090	NXA	12173	WSR	12402	ICE	12473	ICE
11998	ICE	12091	NXA	12174	WSR	12403	ICE	12474	ICE
11999	ICE	12092	OLS	12175	WSR	12404	ICE	12476	ICE
		12093	NXA	12200	ICE	12405	ICE	12477	ICE
12005	NXA	12094	CAD	12201	ICE	12406	ICE	12478	ICE
12008	OLS	12095	OLS	12202	ICE	12407	ICE	12480	ICE
12009	NXA	12097	NXA	12203	ICE	12409	ICE	12481	ICE
12011	VWC	12098	NXA	12204	ICE	12410	ICE	12483	ICE
12012	NXA	12099	NXA	12205	ICE	12411	ICE	12484	ICE
12013	NXA	12100	FGW	12206	ICE	12414	ICE	12485	ICE
12014	WSR	12101	OLS	12207	ICE	12415	ICE	12486	ICE
12015	NXA	12103	NXA	12208	ICE	12417	ICE	12488	ICE
12016	NXA	12105	NXA	12209	ICE	12419	ICE	12489	ICE
12017	CAD	12107	NXA	12210	ICE	12420	ICE	12513	ICE
12019	NXA	12108	NXA	12211	ICE	12421	ICE	12514	ICE
12021	NXA	12109	NXA	12212	ICE	12422	ICE	12515	ICE
12022	OLS	12110	NXA	12213	ICE	12423	ICE	12518	ICE
12024	NXA	12111	NXA	12214	ICE	12424	ICE	12519	ICE
12026	NXA	12114	NXA	12217	ICE	12425	ICE	12520	ICE
12027	NXA	12115	NXA	12218	ICE	12426	ICE	12522	ICE
12029	OLS	12116	NXA	12219	ICE	12427	ICE	12526	ICE
12030	NXA	12117	WSR	12220	ICE	12428	ICE	12533	ICE
12031	NXA	12118	NXA	12223	ICE	12429	ICE	12534	ICE
12032	NXA	12119	CAD	12224	ICE	12430	ICE	12538	ICE
12034	NXA	12120	NXA	12225	ICE	12431	ICE		
12035	NXA	12122	VWC	12226	ICE	12432	ICE	13306	WCR
12036	OLS	12124	WSR	12228	ICE	12433	ICE	13320	WCR
12037	NXA	12125	NXA	12229	ICE	12434	ICE	13321	WCR
12038	CAD	12126	NXA	12230	ICE	12436	ICE	13229	BOK
12040	NXA	12127	WSR	12231	ICE	12437	ICE	13230	BOK
12041	NXA	12129	NXA	12232	ICE	12438	ICE	13440	WCR
12042	NXA	12130	NXA	12300	ICE	12439	ICE	13508	RAF
12043	CAD	12131	WSR	12301	ICE	12440	ICE	13581	RRS
12045	OLS	12132	NXA	12302	ICE	12441	ICE	13583	RRS
12046	NXA	12133	VWC	12303	ICE	12442	ICE		
12047	OLS	12134	OLS	12304	ICE	12443	ICE	14007	SUP
12048	WSR	12137	NXA	12305	ICE	12444	ICE	14099	SUP
12049	NXA	12138	VWC	12307	ICE	12445	ICE		
12051	NXA	12139	OLS	12308	ICE	12446	ICE	16156	NYM
12053	DBR	12141	NXA	12309	ICE	12447	ICE		
12054	WSR	12142	OLS	12310	ICE	12448	ICE	17013	SUP
12056	NXA	12143	NXA	12311	ICE	12449	ICE	17015	RIV
12057	NXA	12144	OLS	12312	ICE	12450	ICE	17018	VTN
12059	WSR	12145	WSR	12313	ICE	12452	ICE	17019	SUP
12060	NXA	12146	NXA	12315	ICE	12453	ICE	17025	SUP
12061	NXA	12147	NXA	12316	ICE	12454	ICE	17041	SUP
12062	NXA	12148	NXA	12317	ICE	12456	ICE	17056	RIV
12063	OLS	12150	NXA	12318	ICE	12457	ICE	17077	RIV
12064	NXA	12151	NXA	12319	ICE	12458	ICE	17080	RAF
12065	OLS	12153	NXA	12320	ICE	12459	ICE	17096	SUP
12066	NXA	12154	NXA	12321	ICE	12460	ICE	17102	WCR

Data Tables

No.	Code	No.	Code	No.	Code	No.	Code	No.	Code
17105	RIV	40106	FGW	40733	FGW	41028	FGW	41105	FGW
17159	DRS	40107	FGW	40734	FGW	41029	FGW	41106	FGW
17167	VSO	40108	FGW	40735	ICE	41030	FGW	41108	FGW
17168	WCR	40109	FGW	40736	FGW	41031	FGW	41109	FGW
17173	FGW	40110	FGW	40737	ICE	41032	FGW	41110	FGW
17174	FGW	40111	FGW	40738	FGW	41033	FGW	41111	EMT
17175	FGW	40112	FGW	40739	FGW	41034	FGW	41112	EMT
		40113	FGW	40740	ICE	41035	AXC	41113	EMT
18756	WCR	40114	FGW	40741	EMT	41037	FGW	41114	FGW
18767	WCR	40115	FGW	40742	ICE	41038	FGW	41115	ICE
18806	WCR	40116	FGW	40743	FGW	41039	ICE	41116	FGW
18808	WCR	40117	FGW	40744	FGW	41040	ICE	41117	EMT
18837	WCR	40118	FGW	40745	FGW	41041	EMT	41118	ICE
18862	WCR	40119	FGW	40746	EMT	41043	ICE	41119	FGW
18893	WCR	40204	FGW	40747	OLS	41044	ICE	41120	ICE
		40205	FGW	40748	ICE	41045	FGW	41121	FGW
19208	WCR	40207	FGW	40749	EMT	41046	EMT	41122	FGW
		40208	OLS	40750	ICE	41051	FGW	41123	FGW
21096	SUP	40209	OLS	40751	EMT	41052	FGW	41124	FGW
21224	RIV	40210	FGW	40752	FGW	41055	FGW	41125	FGW
21232	SUP	40221	FGW	40753	EMT	41056	FGW	41126	FGW
21236	SUP	40228	OLS	40754	EMT	41057	EMT	41127	FGW
21241	SRP	40231	FGW	40755	FGW	41058	ICE	41128	FGW
21245	RIV	40402	DBS	40756	EMT	41059	FGW	41129	FGW
21249	SUP	40403	DBS	40757	FGW	41061	EMT	41130	FGW
21252	MHR	40416	DBS	40801	FGW	41062	EMT	41131	FGW
21256	WCR	40417	OLS	40802	FGW	41063	EMT	41132	FGW
21266	WCR	40419	DBS	40803	FGW	41064	EMT	41133	FGW
21268	SUP	40424	GTL	40805	ICE	41065	FGW	41134	FGW
21269	RIV	40425	OLS	40806	FGW	41066	ICE	41135	FGW
21272	RIV	40426	GTL	40807	FGW	41067	EMT	41136	FGW
		40433	GTL	40808	FGW	41068	EMT	41137	FGW
34525	WCR	40434	DBS	40809	FGW	41069	EMT	41138	FGW
35089	NYM	40700	EMT	40810	FGW	41070	EMT	41139	FGW
35185	SRP	40701	ICE	40811	FGW	41071	EMT	41140	FGW
35290	DBS	40702	ICE	40900	FGW	41072	EMT	41141	FGW
35317	SUP	40703	FGW	40901	FGW	41075	EMT	41142	FGW
35322	SUP	40704	ICE	40902	FGW	41076	EMT	41143	FGW
35329	SUP	40705	ICE	40903	FGW	41077	EMT	41144	FGW
35333	SUP	40706	ICE	40904	FGW	41079	EMT	41145	FGW
35407	WCR	40707	FGW			41081	FGW	41146	FGW
35449	SUP	40708	ICE	41003	FGW	41083	ICE	41147	FGW
35457	SUP	40709	OLS	41004	FGW	41084	EMT	41148	FGW
35459	WCR	40710	FGW	41005	FGW	41085	FGW	41149	FGW
35461	SUP	40711	ICE	41006	FGW	41086	FGW	41150	ICE
35463	SUP	40712	OLS	41007	FGW	41087	ICE	41151	ICE
35464	SUP	40713	FGW	41008	FGW	41088	ICE	41152	ICE
35465	SUP	40714	OLS	41009	FGW	41089	FGW	41153	FGW
35466	VSO	40715	FGW	41010	FGW	41090	ICE	41154	EMT
35468	SUP	40716	FGW	41011	FGW	41091	ICE	41155	FGW
35469	RIV	40717	OLS	41012	FGW	41092	ICE	41156	EMT
35470	SUP	40718	FGW	41015	FGW	41093	FGW	41157	FGW
35476	SUP	40720	ICE	41016	FGW	41094	FGW	41158	FGW
35486	SUP	40721	FGW	41017	FGW	41095	ICE	41159	ICE
35508	SUP	40722	FGW	41018	FGW	41096	FGW	41160	FGW
35517	SUP	40724	FGW	41019	FGW	41097	ICE	41161	FGW
35518	SUP	40725	FGW	41020	FGW	41098	ICE	41162	FGW
		40726	FGW	41021	FGW	41099	ICE	41163	FGW
40101	FGW	40727	FGW	41022	FGW	41100	ICE	41164	ICE
40102	FGW	40728	EMT	41023	FGW	41101	FGW	41165	ICE
40103	FGW	40730	EMT	41024	FGW	41102	FGW	41166	FGW
40104	FGW	40731	OLS	41026	AXC	41103	FGW	41167	FGW
40105	FGW	40732	EMT	41027	FGW	41104	FGW	41168	FGW

Data Tables

41169	FGW	42045	FGW	42115	FGW	42182	ICE	42250	FGW
41170	ICE	42046	FGW	42116	ICE	42183	FGW	42251	FGW
41176	FGW	42047	FGW	42117	ICE	42184	FGW	42252	FGW
41179	FGW	42048	FGW	42118	FGW	42185	FGW	42253	FGW
41180	FGW	42049	FGW	42119	EMT	42186	ICE	42255	FGW
41181	FGW	42050	FGW	42120	EMT	42188	ICE	42256	FGW
41182	FGW	42051	AXC	42121	ICE	42189	ICE	42257	FGW
41183	FGW	42052	AXC	42123	EMT	42190	ICE	42258	FGW
41184	FGW	42053	AXC	42124	EMT	42191	ICE	42259	FGW
41185	ICE	42054	FGW	42125	EMT	42192	ICE	42260	FGW
41186	FGW	42055	FGW	42126	FGW	42193	ICE	42261	FGW
41187	FGW	42056	FGW	42127	ICE	42194	EMT	42263	FGW
41189	FGW	42057	ICE	42128	ICE	42195	FGW	42264	FGW
41190	ICE	42058	ICE	42129	FGW	42196	FGW	42265	FGW
41191	FGW	42059	ICE	42130	ICE	42197	FGW	42266	FGW
41192	FGW	42060	FGW	42131	EMT	42198	ICE	42267	FGW
41193	AXC	42061	FGW	42132	EMT	42199	ICE	42268	FGW
41194	AXC	42062	FGW	42133	EMT	42200	FGW	42269	FGW
41195	AXC	42063	ICE	42134	ICE	42201	FGW	42271	FGW
41201	GTL	42064	ICE	42135	EMT	42202	FGW	42272	FGW
41202	GTL	42065	ICE	42136	EMT	42203	FGW	42273	FGW
41203	GTL	42066	FGW	42137	EMT	42204	FGW	42275	FGW
41204	GTL	42067	FGW	42138	FGW	42205	EMT	42276	FGW
41205	GTL	42068	FGW	42139	EMT	42206	FGW	42277	FGW
41206	GTL	42069	FGW	42140	EMT	42207	FGW	42279	FGW
		42070	FGW	42141	EMT	42208	FGW	42280	FGW
42003	FGW	42071	FGW	42143	FGW	42209	FGW	42281	FGW
42004	FGW	42072	FGW	42144	FGW	42210	EMT	42283	FGW
42005	FGW	42073	FGW	42145	FGW	42211	FGW	42284	FGW
42006	FGW	42074	FGW	42146	ICE	42212	FGW	42285	FGW
42007	FGW	42075	FGW	42147	ICE	42213	FGW	42286	ICE
42008	FGW	42076	FGW	42148	EMT	42214	FGW	42287	FGW
42009	FGW	42077	FGW	42149	EMT	42215	ICE	42288	FGW
42010	FGW	42078	FGW	42150	ICE	42216	FGW	42289	FGW
42012	FGW	42079	FGW	42151	EMT	42217	FGW	42290	AXC
42013	FGW	42080	FGW	42152	EMT	42218	FGW	42291	FGW
42014	FGW	42081	FGW	42153	EMT	42219	ICE	42292	FGW
42015	FGW	42083	FGW	42154	ICE	42220	EMT	42293	FGW
42016	FGW	42085	FGW	42155	EMT	42221	FGW	42294	FGW
42019	FGW	42087	FGW	42156	EMT	42222	FGW	42295	FGW
42021	FGW	42089	FGW	42157	EMT	42224	FGW	42296	FGW
42023	FGW	42091	ICE	42158	ICE	42225	EMT	42297	FGW
42024	FGW	42092	FGW	42159	ICE	42226	ICE	42299	FGW
42025	FGW	42093	FGW	42160	ICE	42227	EMT	42300	FGW
42026	FGW	42094	FGW	42161	ICE	42228	ICE	42301	FGW
42027	FGW	42095	FGW	42163	ICE	42229	EMT	42302	FGW
42028	FGW	42096	FGW	42164	EMT	42230	EMT	42303	FGW
42029	FGW	42097	AXC	42165	EMT	42231	FGW	42304	FGW
42030	FGW	42098	FGW	42166	FGW	42232	FGW	42305	FGW
42031	FGW	42099	FGW	42167	FGW	42233	FGW	42306	ICE
42032	FGW	42100	EMT	42168	FGW	42234	AXC	42307	ICE
42033	FGW	42101	FGW	42169	FGW	42235	ICE	42308	FGW
42034	FGW	42102	FGW	42171	ICE	42236	FGW	42315	FGW
42035	FGW	42103	FGW	42172	ICE	42237	ICE	42317	FGW
42036	AXC	42105	FGW	42173	FGW	42238	ICE	42319	FGW
42037	AXC	42106	ICE	42174	FGW	42239	ICE	42321	FGW
42038	AXC	42107	FGW	42175	FGW	42240	ICE	42322	ICE
42039	FGW	42108	FGW	42176	FGW	42241	ICE	42323	ICE
42040	FGW	42109	ICE	42177	FGW	42242	ICE	42325	FGW
42041	FGW	42110	ICE	42178	FGW	42243	ICE	42326	ICE
42042	FGW	42111	EMT	42179	ICE	42244	ICE	42327	EMT
42043	FGW	42112	EMT	42180	ICE	42245	FGW	42328	EMT
42044	FGW	42113	EMT	42181	ICE	42247	FGW		

Data Tables

Number	Code	Number	Code	Number	Code	Number	Code	Number	Code
42329	EMT	44002	FGW	44068	FGW	99319	WCR	6322	SIE
42330	ICE	44003	FGW	44069	FGW	99326	WCR	6323	SIE
42331	EMT	44004	FGW	44070	EMT	99327	WCR	6324	SIE
42332	FGW	44005	FGW	44071	EMT	99328	WCR	6325	SIE
42333	FGW	44007	FGW	44072	AXC	99329	WCR	6330	FGW
42335	EMT	44008	FGW	44073	EMT	99348	WCR	6336	FGW
42337	EMT	44009	FGW	44074	FGW	99349	VTN	6338	FGW
42339	EMT	44010	FGW	44075	ICE	99350	WCR	6340	ICE
42340	ICE	44011	FGW	44076	FGW	99353	VTN	6344	ICE
42341	EMT	44012	AXC	44077	ICE	99354	WCR	6346	ICE
42342	AXC	44013	FGW	44078	FGW	99361	VTN	6348	FGW
42343	FGW	44014	FGW	44079	FGW	99371	WCR	6352	ICE
42344	FGW	44015	FGW	44080	ICE	99402	WCR	6353	ICE
42345	FGW	44016	FGW	44081	FGW	99405	SUP	6354	ICE
42346	FGW	44017	AXC	44083	FGW	99530	VSO	6355	ICE
42347	FGW	44018	FGW	44085	EMT	99531	VSO	6358	ICE
42348	FGW	44019	ICE	44086	FGW	99532	VSO	6359	ICE
42349	FGW	44020	FGW	44088	GTL	99534	VSO	6376	GBR
42350	FGW	44021	AXC	44089	GTL	99535	VSO	6377	GBR
42351	FGW	44022	FGW	44090	FGW	99536	VSO	6378	GBR
42352	ICE	44023	FGW	44091	FGW	99537	VSO	6379	GBR
42353	FGW	44024	FGW	44093	FGW	99539	VSO	6392	EMT
42354	ICE	44025	FGW	44094	ICE	99541	VSO	6395	EMT
42355	ICE	44026	FGW	44097	FGW	99543	VSO	6397	EMT
42356	FGW	44027	EMT	44098	ICE	99545	VSO	6398	EMT
42357	ICE	44028	FGW	44100	FGW	99546	VSO	6399	EMT
42360	FGW	44029	FGW	44101	FGW	99678	WCR		
42361	FGW	44030	FGW			99679	WCR	9393	ICE
42362	FGW	44031	ICE	45001	AXC	99670	WCR	9394	ICE
42363	ICE	44032	FGW	45002	AXC	99671	WCR	9701	NRL
42364	FGW	44033	FGW	45003	AXC	99672	WCR	9702	NRL
42365	FGW	44034	FGW	45004	AXC	99673	WCR	9703	NRL
42366	AXC	44035	FGW	45005	AXC	99674	WCR	9708	NRL
42367	AXC	44036	FGW			99675	WCR	9714	NRL
42368	AXC	44037	FGW	45018	WCR	99676	WCR		
42369	AXC	44038	FGW	45020	DBS	99677	WCR	72612	NRL
42370	AXC	44039	FGW	45026	WCR	99680	WCR	72616	NRL
42371	AXC	44040	FGW	45029	DBS	99706	WCR	72630	NRL
42372	AXC	44041	EMT			99710	WCR	72631	NRL
42373	AXC	44042	FGW	80041	RIV	99712	WCR	72639	NRL
42374	AXC	44043	FGW	80042	CAD	99713	WCR		
42375	AXC	44044	EMT			99717	WCR	80204	SUP
42376	AXC	44045	ICE	99035	SUP	99718	WCR	80211	NRL
42377	AXC	44046	EMT	99040	SUP	99721	WCR	80217	SUP
42378	AXC	44047	EMT	99041	SUP	99722	WCR	80220	SUP
42379	AXC	44048	EMT	99080	SUP	99723	WCR		
42380	AXC	44049	FGW	99108	VTN	99782	SUP	82101	VWC
42381	FGW	44050	ICE	99120	SUP	99792	SUP	82102	NXA
42382	FGW	44051	EMT	99121	WCR	99884	WCR	82103	NXA
42383	FGW	44052	AXC	99125	WCR	99953	SUP	82104	NXA
42384	EMT	44054	EMT	99127	WCR	99966	WCR	82105	NXA
42401	GTL	44055	FGW	99128	WCR	99968	VSO	82106	DBS
42402	GTL	44056	ICE	99132	WCR	99969	VSO	82107	NXA
42403	GTL	44057	ICE	99193	WCR	99991	SUP	82108	DBS
42404	GTL	44058	ICE	99194	WCR	99995	SUP	82109	OLS
42405	GTL	44059	FGW	99195	WCR			82110	DBS
42406	GTL	44060	FGW	99241	SUP	**NPCCS Stock**		82111	OLS
42407	GTL	44061	ICE	99304	WCR	6260	NRL	82112	NXA
42408	GTL	44063	ICE	99311	WCR	6261	NRL	82113	DBS
42409	GTL	44064	FGW	99312	SUP	6262	NRL	82114	NXA
		44065	GTL	99316	WCR	6263	NRL	82115	NRL
44000	FGW	44066	FGW	99317	WCR	6264	NRL	82116	DBS
44001	FGW	44067	FGW	99318	WCR	6321	SIE	82118	NXA

Number Cross-Link

Number	Code
82120	DBS
82121	NXA
82122	DBS
82124	OLS
82125	OLS
82126	VWC
82127	NXA
82128	OLS
82129	OLS
82131	DBS
82132	NXA
82133	NXA
82136	NXA
82137	DBS
82138	DBS
82139	NXA
82140	OLS
82141	DBS
82143	NXA
82144	DBS
82145	OLS
82146	DBS
82148	DBS
82149	OLS
82150	DBS
82152	NXA
82200	ICE
82201	ICE
82202	ICE
82203	ICE
82204	ICE
82205	ICE
82206	ICE
82207	ICE
82208	ICE
82209	ICE
82210	ICE
82211	ICE
82212	ICE
82213	ICE
82214	ICE
82215	ICE
82216	ICE
82217	ICE
82218	ICE
82219	ICE
82220	ICE
82222	ICE
82223	ICE
82224	ICE
82225	ICE
82226	ICE
82227	ICE
82228	ICE
82229	ICE
82230	ICE
82231	ICE
82301	WSR
82302	WSR
82303	WSR
82304	WSR
82305	WSR
92114	NRL
92159	OLS
92203	DBS
92901	OLS
92904	VSO
92931	OLS
92939	NRL
94103	DBS
94104	DBS
94106	DBS
94113	DBS
94116	DBS
94121	DBS
94137	DBS
94147	DBS
94150	DBS
94153	DBS
94155	DBS
94160	DBS
94166	DBS
94170	DBS
94176	DBS
94177	DBS
94191	DBS
94192	DBS
94195	DBS
94197	DBS
94203	DBS
94207	DBS
94208	DBS
94209	DBS
94213	DBS
94214	DBS
94217	DBS
94221	DBS
94222	DBS
94225	DBS
94227	DBS
94229	DBS
94302	DBS
94303	DBS
94304	DBS
94306	DBS
94307	DBS
94308	DBS
94310	DBS
94311	DBS
94313	DBS
94316	DBS
94317	DBS
94318	DBS
94322	DBS
94323	DBS
94326	DBS
94331	DBS
94332	DBS
94333	DBS
94334	DBS
94335	DBS
94336	DBS
94338	DBS
94340	DBS
94343	DBS
94344	DBS
94400	DBS
94406	DBS
94408	DBS
94410	DBS
94411	DBS
94412	DBS
94413	DBS
94416	DBS
94420	DBS
94422	DBS
94423	DBS
94427	DBS
94428	DBS
94429	DBS
94431	DBS
94432	DBS
94433	DBS
94434	DBS
94435	DBS
94438	DBS
94440	DBS
94445	DBS
94451	DBS
94458	DBS
94462	DBS
94463	DBS
94470	DBS
94479	DBS
94481	DBS
94482	DBS
94488	DBS
94490	DBS
94492	DBS
94495	DBS
94497	DBS
94498	DBS
94499	DBS
94501	DBS
94504	DBS
94512	DBS
94514	DBS
94515	DBS
94518	DBS
94519	DBS
94520	DBS
94521	DBS
94522	DBS
94525	DBS
94526	DBS
94527	DBS
94528	DBS
94529	DBS
94530	DBS
94531	DBS
94532	DBS
94534	DBS
94536	DBS
94538	DBS
94539	DBS
94540	DBS
94541	DBS
94542	DBS
94543	DBS
94544	DBS
94545	DBS
94546	DBS
94547	DBS
94548	DBS
95300	DBS
95301	DBS
95400	DBS
95410	DBS
95727	DBS
95754	DBS
95758	DBS
95761	DBS
95763	DBS
96100	OLS
96139	OLS
96175	WCR
96181	OLS
96371	DBS
96372	DBS
96373	DBS
96374	DBS
96375	DBS
96602	OLS
96603	CAD
96604	CAD
96605	OLS
96606	OLS
96607	OLS
96608	OLS
96609	OLS
99666	NRL

Service Stock

Number	Code
930010	EMT
950001	NRL
960010	CRW
960013	CRW
960014	CRW
960015	CRW
960021	CRW
960201	NRL
960202	NRL
960301	CRW
971001	NRL
971002	NRL
971003	NRL
971004	NRL
975025	NRL
975081	NRL
975091	NRL
975280	NRL
975464	NRL
975486	NRL
975494	NRL
975573	NRL
975574	NRL
975611	NRL
975612	NRL
975613	NRL
975814	NRL
975984	NRL
977337	NRL
977868	NRL
977869	NRL
977968	COL
977969	NRL
977974	NRL
977983	NRL
977984	NRL
977985	NRL
977986	NRL
977989	OLS
977990	NRL
977991	NRL
977993	NRL
977994	NRL
977995	NRL
977996	PRE
977997	NRL
999508	NRL
999550	NRL
999602	NRL
999605	NRL
999606	NRL

Data Tables

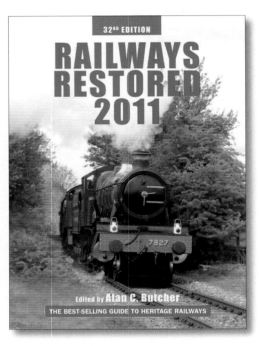 

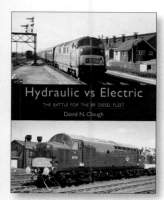
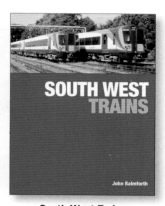

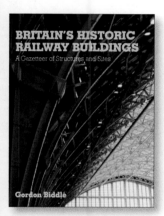
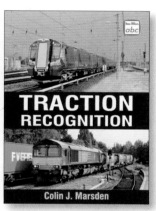
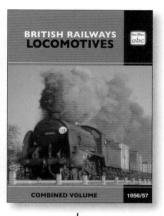 

218 mins (2 discs) • £24.95

The DVD of the Year!

100 mins • £19.95

Liverpool & Manchester

Driver's eye view

Narrated by Alan Hardwick

65 mins • DVD £16.95
Blu-ray £19.95

BIG FREIGHT 6

Train Crazy has once again teamed up with FREIGHTMASTER to bring you the biggest, heaviest and longest freight trains running in the UK today.

Filmed during 2010, Big Freight 6 looks at the freight scene from the year starting in the January snow and visiting various Hotspots from the FREIGHTMASTER books throughout the year.

Coal, steel, oil and cement. Intermodal, flasks, clay and logs. Ballast, mail, wagonload and water cannon trains to name just a few which are included on this DVD, hauled by everything from the Class 70 to the 37, 60 and 66 to pairs of 86s, 90s and 92s. At least two trains have five different locos on the front!

Filmed in 16:9 widescreen and running for two hours this programme is available on DVD and in high definition on Blu-ray - the first UK Freight DVD released on Blu-ray!

The Freight DVD of the Year!

120 mins • DVD £19.95
Blu-ray £22.95

Class 14 Diesel
High quality in small scale

Running number: 14029

Livery: BR Blue With Wasp Stripes

Finish: Pristine

Length: 71.5mm

372-952   Class 14 Diesel   ⑨

Running number: D9523

Livery: BR Green with Wasp Stripes

Finish: Weathered

Length: 71.5mm

372-951   Class 14 Diesel   ⑤

Running number: D9555

Livery: BR Green with Wasp Stripes

Finish: Pristine

Length: 71.5mm

372-950   Class 14 Diesel   ⑤

All products are designated an Era symbol using the Bachmann Product Period Key, as seen on our website.
Era ⑤ signifies locomotives suitable for period 1957 - 1966 British Railways Late Crest.
Era ⑨ signifies locomotives suitable for period 1995 onwards - Post Privatisation

N Scale   Bachmann Europe Plc. Moat Way, Barwell, Leicestershire, LE9 8EY